Donated To The Library by

Wendell and Shirley Olson
and
Gary and Arlene Snoeyenbos

in memory of

EUGENE KILLIAN

© DEMCO, INC. 1990 PRINTED IN U.S.A.

America's Youngest Warriors

Stories about
young men and women who served in the
armed forces of the United States of America
before attaining legal age

Compiled and edited by

Ray D. Jackson and Susan M. Jackson

Published by the

Veterans of Underage Military Service

ii

Library of Congress Catalog Card Number: 96-61959

ISBN 0-9656093-0-8

For more information or to order additional books, please write:

Veterans of Underage Military Service
VUMS Book Project
710 East La Jolla Drive
Tempe, AZ 85282

In Memory of
Jeremy Michael Boorda
1939 - 1996

Age 56	Age 16
Admiral	Seaman
Chief of Naval Operations	High School Dropout

"You don't have to be very old to grow up fast." — J. M. Boorda

iv

Printed in the United States of America by the

K. K. Stevens Publishing Company
P. O. Box 590
100 North Pearl Street
Astoria, Illinois 61501

Contents

Acknowledgements

The compilation of a book of this nature can be accomplished only with the help of many people. A mere acknowledgment cannot adequately express the gratitude and appreciation I feel for those who contributed their time, talents, and ideas.

Allan Stover deserves great credit for conceiving and promoting the original idea of publishing a book about underage veterans.

Members of the Veterans of Underage Military Service contributed not only their stories but also their time and patience in responding to my numerous phone calls and in reviewing several drafts of their stories. Discussions with Billie B. Boyd, Jr., Yank Sumpter, and Ron Smith were very useful. They provided a sounding board for ideas and offered valuable advice. In addition, Billie provided some material about underage veterans of the Revolutionary War and the Civil War;

Yank insisted that the book *look* like a book; Ron undertook research assignments that clarified several points. Evelyn and George Brouse offered suggestions and a great deal of moral support. Gene Hibbert reviewed an early draft and provided invaluable proofreading.

Jack Cannon not only contributed a story, but also provided an original water color painting for the book jacket.

Sue Booth, Mary Crass, Frances Gaddis, Mary L. Graham, Helen Olshefski, and Esther Zdanavage, wives of deceased members, worked with me to develop stories about their husbands, drawing from newspaper articles, books, and personal letters.

My wife, Susan Madrid Jackson, agreed initially to assist me on this project by fine-tuning the composition, editing, and proofreading. It soon became evident that the time and effort required on her part were greater than anticipated and that her involvement deserved more prominent recognition. I proudly share editorship with her.

My 13-year-old granddaughter, Amber Rae Olwell, read an early version of the book and made the perceptive suggestion about the order in which the stories should appear in the book, i.e., by date of enlistment.

Shirley Rish, a personal friend and colleague for many years, took on the crucial task of final review.

A heartfelt thanks!

Ray D. Jackson

A Note to the Reader

Shortly after organizing the Veterans of Underage Military Service (VUMS) in 1991, Allan Stover envisioned a book in which the experiences of its members would be collected. The book could serve as both a personal and historical account for these veterans to pass along to their families and other interested readers. By the time that the organization had grown enough to make his idea feasible, Allan was transferred overseas by his employer. In early September 1995, I assumed responsibility for the book and began compiling the few stories that had already been sent in. I solicited more contributions through a regular "Book Report" in the association's newsletter and received enough stories to complete a book much longer than I had originally contemplated.

As I received each story, I edited it for content and format, passed it on to my wife for further editing and proofreading, and returned the first draft to the contributor for review, revision, and approval. Some stories required several drafts, several mailings back and forth, and often, phone conversations, to make sure that the final version was satisfactory to both the contributor and to me.

I relied totally on the contributors for the content and the accuracy of each story submitted, making revisions needed only to enhance the format and language usage.

As the stories came in, I noticed that there were many common elements such as difficult circumstances in early life and long-lasting marriages later on. Thus came the idea of including "VUMS Notes," short notes throughout the book highlighting facts and interesting themes in the lives of this unique group of veterans, and adding bits of factual and historical information to help readers more fully appreciate the stories.

Ray D. Jackson

The
Background

*" ... I did nothing spectacular nor made any contribution
to my country or flag — except love the hell out of them
— still do after 50 years."*

This was part of the response of an underage veteran when asked if
he would allow his story to be published. His statement exemplifies
the attitude of the great majority of the men and women who chose to
serve their country before they had attained legal age. Most of them
play down their accomplishments, which in some cases are legendary,
but all of them express a strong love for the country which they so
proudly served.

The quote above was from a veteran of World War II who had first
joined the U. S. Army at age 14 and later served in the U. S. Navy.
During the World War II era, literally thousands of men and women
circumvented the age requirements in order to serve in the military.
Most completed their enlistments without ever being discovered to be
underage. Of those whose real age was revealed, some were allowed
to remain in the military, while others were given honorable
discharges and sent home. A few received bad-conduct discharges from
officers who were determined to "teach those kids a lesson."
Punishment seemed to depend more on who was interpreting the law
than on the law itself.

For years, most of these veterans talked little about their underage
exploits. Even five decades later, some were still afraid that the
government would punish them if their underage enlistments were to

be discovered. To this day, there are a few who will not reveal their underage service for fear of retribution.

In 1978, a small group of underage veterans started an association called the Underage Servicemen of America. While it was in its embryonic stage, the founder died and the association folded. It wasn't until 1991, when Allan Stover of Ellicott City, Maryland, began an association called the Veterans of Underage Military Service (VUMS), that men and women who had served underage began to receive recognition. Letters were obtained from all branches of the armed forces stating that no punitive action would be taken against those who served under the legal age limit. With these assurances, the association initiated an aggressive campaign to advise underage veterans that it was safe to "go public." Since its incorporation in 1991, the association has identified over 1000 underage veterans. Over 700 men and women are active members of the association at the time of this writing (December 1996). This is a small fraction of the estimated 100,000 underage veterans who served during World War II, the Korean War, and the war in Vietnam.[1]

One of the purposes for which the VUMS was formed, as stated in an early edition of the association newsletter, was "... to record for history the experiences of that unique group called underage veterans." This book is an attempt to record some of that history.

Before proceeding to the legacy of underage veterans and to their stories, some background information is needed to better understand the terminology and the sequence of certain events.

An underage veteran is generally considered to be one who served in the armed forces before reaching the age of 17. However, age requirements did not become uniform among the various branches of the military until 1948. Before then, the age requirements depended upon the branch of service and the gender of the applicant. The Navy, Marine Corps, and Coast Guard allowed enlistment at age 17 with parental consent and at age 18 without consent. Apparently, this has been the policy for most of this century.

During the early months of World War II, Army policy required enlistees to be 18 years old, with no option for 17-year-olds to join with

---

[1] Ray D. Jackson, "Rushing the Cadence — Serving Underage," *Leatherneck*, pp. 52-53, Dec. 1996.

parental consent. In fact, parental consent was required until the age of 21 if the choice was one of the more "hazardous" branches of the Army, e.g., the Air Forces or the paratroops. In 1948, all branches of the services adopted the policy of allowing enlistments at age 17 with parental consent and at age 18 without. This policy also applied to women.

Women have served in the armed forces of the United States since the Revolutionary War and in every war since that time. Many were doctors and nurses. Records of women serving underage during the early years of our country were either nonexistent or not readily accessible. During World War II, with the establishment of women's service branches, a number of women circumvented the system and served underage.

The Women's Auxiliary Army Corps was established on 15 May 1942. Women enrolled in the WAAC were technically not considered soldiers until 1 July 1943 when the Women's Army Corps (WAC) was established. The Women's Reserve of the U. S. Navy (WAVES) was established 30 July 1942, and the Marine Corps Women's Reserve was established on 13 February 1943.

Age requirements for women in all branches were age 20 with parental consent and age 21 without consent, until passage of the Women's Armed Services Integration Act on 12 June 1948.

In addition to the WAAC changing to the WAC, another name change has created some confusion. Throughout World War II, one of the most popular military songs included the words, "Nothing will stop the Army Air Corps." Later in the war, it became, "Nothing will stop the Army Air Force," with punsters adding, "except the weather." Actually, both names, "Corps" and "Force," were wrong. When airplanes were first used by the U. S. Army, they were assigned to the Signal Corps. Later, the U. S. Army Air Corps was formed, and that name was used until 20 June 1941. On that date, the Army Air Corps officially became the U. S. Army Air Forces, with an *s*. On 18 September 1947, the U. S. Air Force was formed as a separate service.

The
Legacy

Many young men and women who circumvented the system and entered military service underage during the World War II — Korean War era thought that they were the only ones, or one of a very few, who had ever done so. With the founding of the Veterans of Underage Military Service (VUMS) in 1991, most were surprised to find that hundreds of others had also served as youngsters. In fact, the legacy of underage service in the United States military goes back at least as far as the Revolutionary War.

During the American Revolution, Washington's army was comprised of volunteers who simply appeared on the scene and augmented the numbers of regular militia companies in which every man between the ages of 16 and 60 was expected to serve. Records of underage veterans of that war are scarce, but there is little doubt that boys younger than 16 served in Washington's army. Fortunately, the deeds of two youngsters who served as warriors and statesmen, and helped shape the nation, have been documented.

Jonathan Dayton joined the 3rd New Jersey Regiment in 1775 as an ensign at age 15. This was arranged by his father, the regimental commander. At 16, Jonathan was a lieutenant and took part in the heavy skirmishing between Washington's main army and British forces threatening Philadelphia. He also participated in the battles at

Brandywine Creek and Germantown and endured the cold and hunger at Valley Forge. By 1780, Jonathan was a captain. He transferred to the 2nd New Jersey Regiment, took his company to Virginia, and fought in the decisive Yorktown campaign.

After the war, Jonathan assumed responsibilities in the family's mercantile business and studied law. He entered politics and represented Elizabethtown in the legislature. When New Jersey selected delegates to the Constitutional Convention in 1787, Jonathan Dayton was appointed a delegate. He also had interests in the Ohio region. Later, a town in Ohio would be named for him.[2]

William Jackson was born in England in 1759. While he was a young boy, his parents died and neighbors arranged for his emigration to Charleston, South Carolina, to be reared by a family friend. His benefactor commanded the Charleston Battalion of Artillery. William attended many musters of the battalion and obtained an appointment as a cadet. The date of his entry into the 1st Carolina Regiment is not known, but it may well have been prior to his seventeenth birthday.

Jackson fought in a number of skirmishes during the war and was captured when the British took Charleston in 1780. He was exchanged and became a secretary to one of Washington's aides, and in 1782 served as Assistant Secretary at War. In 1787, he applied for the position of Secretary of the Constitutional Convention and edged out Benjamin Franklin's grandson for the post. After the convention, he was selected by George Washington to be his secretary, becoming one of the original civil servants in the executive branch.[3]

The patriotism and sense of adventure of youngsters who wanted to serve their cause during the Civil War is much better documented. By this time, record-keeping was more advanced and letters from the soldiers themselves have been preserved.

The Civil War may well have been called "The Boys' War." Authorities differ on the ages of soldiers in the Union armies, but it has been reported that of the 2,700,000 men in blue, about 800,000 were seventeen or under, about 200,000 were sixteen or under, about 100,000 were fifteen or under, about 300 were thirteen or under, and

---

[2] U. S. Army Center of Military History, Bicentennial Series Pub. 71-19.

[3] U. S. Army Center of Military History, Bicentennial Series Pub. 71-23.

about 25 were ten or under. Most of the young soldiers slipped in as musicians. There are many tales of buglers who were too small to climb into saddles without help, yet rode into pistol-and-saber battles with their regiments.[4]

> *Many an underage lad evaded enlistment rules by hiding the number 18 in his shoe, standing on it, and swearing he was "over 18."* [4]

Johnny Clem was a drummer boy at age 9.[5] At age 11, he was with the 22nd Michigan Regiment and became a mounted orderly on General George H. Thomas' staff, with the rank of lance sergeant.[3] Later, during peacetime, he became a major general.[4]

The First Minnesota Volunteers was a regiment formed in 1861 in response to President Lincoln's call for volunteers. One of the first applicants was Charley Goddard, a lanky and mischievous youth of 15 from Winona, Minnesota, who told everyone he was 18 and got away with it. Goddard's mother was opposed to his enlistment from the beginning. Apparently, she suggested in her letters to him that he should come home. His response was, "Jest think how I would be received by friends if I *deserted* and not only that but it would disgrace the name of Goddard." Charlie wrote to his mother often, and fortunately, his letters have been preserved.

During the Battle of Bull Run, his regiment was on the line, but Charlie was in a Washington hospital. His illness nearly ended his army career. "I was laying on the bed with my cloths on & there was a doctor come in one that did not belong to my ward," Charlie wrote his mother. "He asked me how old I was I suposed he only wanted to know to satisfy himself so I told him I was 17 years he did not say any thing but continued to make his rounds from room to room and the first thing I knew he handed me a discharge I took it and saw what

---

[4] Burke Davis, *The Civil War, Strange & Fascinating Facts*, The Fairfax Press, 1982. Originally published as *Our Incredible Civil War* by Holt, Rinehart and Winston, Inc.

[5] David Herbert Donald, *Living Through a Civil War*, in *We Americans*, a series by the National Geographic Society, 1975, 1988.

it was I said nothing but maid for the Regiment and told Capt H C Lester I did not want a discharge he told me I need not take it unless I wanted to this is the way the thing was arranged."

Charlie was wounded in the leg and shoulder on Cemetery Ridge during the Battle of Gettysburg, 2 July 1863. He was discharged at age 18 and returned to Winona to try to support his mother. He was increasingly plagued by his wounds and the illnesses that had followed him through the war. Nonetheless, he decided to seek public office and won the Republican nomination for county registrar of deeds. He also won the election, but a few weeks later he was dead at 23 years of age.[6]

The Confederate Army also had many underage soldiers, including:

George S. Lamkin of Winona, Mississippi, who enlisted when he was 11 and was severely wounded at Shiloh before his twelfth birthday.

E. G. Baxter, of Clark County, Kentucky, who is recorded as enlisting in the 7th Kentucky Cavalry when he was not quite 13, becoming a second lieutenant a year later.

John Bailey Tyler of the 1st Maryland Cavalry who was 12 when the war came. He fought with his regiment throughout the war without being wounded.

T. G. Bean of Pickensville, Alabama, who organized two companies of troops at the University of Alabama in 1861 at age 13. However, he did not serve until two years later, at age 15.

M. W. Jewett of Ivanhoe, Virginia, who is reported to have joined the 59th Virginia Regiment at age 13. He served at Charleston, South Carolina, in Florida, and at the siege of Petersburg.

W. D. Peak of Oliver Springs, Tennessee, who enlisted in the 26th Tennessee Regiment at age 14.

Matthew J. McDonald who served with the 1st Georgia Cavalry at age 14.

John T. Mason of Fairfax County, Virginia, who served with the 17th Virginia Regiment at the first battle of Manassas at age 14. Later, he was a midshipman on the *Shenandoah*, a Confederate Navy cruiser.

---

[6] Richard Moe, *The Last Full Measure - The Life and Death of the First Minnesota Volunteers*, Avon Books, New York, 1994.

Billings Steele, a grandson of Francis Scott Key, who crossed the Potomac to join Colonel John S. Mosby's Rangers at the age of 16.[3]

Six boys received the Congressional Medal of Honor for their exploits during the Civil War. These six are listed below, followed by their age *at time of deed*, not their age at time of enlistment.

Willie Johnston — 11 years and 11 months.
John Angling — 14 years and 2 months.
Oscar E. Peck — 14 years and 5 months.
Orion P. Howe — 14 years and 5½ months.
John Cook — 15 years and 1 month.
William H. Horsfell — 15 years and 2 months.[7]

It would be eighty years after the Civil War before another youngster under the age of 18 would be awarded the Medal of Honor. Six days after his seventeenth birthday, Jackyln Lucas, who had joined the U. S. Marine Corps at age 14, covered two Japanese hand grenades with his body, saving the lives of other Marines near him.[8]

During times of war, it is natural for youngsters to want to participate, as evidenced by the large number of young soldiers who participated in the Civil War. But between wars, the military was attractive as a means for young people to be on their own and satisfy their sense of adventure.

In 1897, 15-year-old Jones Morgan ran away from home and enlisted in the U. S. Army. He was assigned to the 9th Cavalry and became a Buffalo Soldier. He watched as Buffalo Soldier units joined Teddy Roosevelt's Rough Riders in their charge up Cuba's San Juan Hill on 1 July 1898. Men of the 9th Cavalry were the first to go over the top of the hill. His parents found him soon after that, and his military career ended. He had served two years. During a 1992 interview at his home in Richmond, Virginia, 109-year-old Jones Morgan recalled his days with the 9th Cavalry, "They used me for domestic stuff. Anything that needed fixing in the place, they sent

---

[7] Congressional Medal of Honor Society, West 46th Street and 12th Avenue, New York, New York.

[8] Edward F. Murphy, *Heros of WWII*, Ballantine Books, New York, 1991.

me." He died shortly after the monument to Buffalo Soldiers was dedicated in Fort Leavenworth, Kansas, 25 July 1992.[9]

Smedley D. Butler became a second lieutenant in the U. S. Marine Corps at age 16. He was born in West Chester, Pennsylvania, on 30 July 1881, the son of Thomas S. Butler, a 32-year veteran of the U. S. House of Representatives. After the USS *Maine* was blown up in Havana harbor in February 1898, Smedley tried to join the 6th Pennsylvania Volunteers, but was politely told to "run along home." He tried to join the Navy, but his father refused to give his consent. His father, who was then chairman of the House Naval Affairs Committee, returned to Philadelphia one evening and Smedley overheard him tell his wife, "Today Congress increased the Marine Corps by twenty-four second lieutenants and two thousand men for the period of the war." Later, Smedley told his mother that he was going to be a Marine, and if she didn't agree, he would run away and join a regiment where he wasn't known.

The next day, Smedley and his mother went to Marine Corps Headquarters in Washington. They spoke directly to Colonel Commandant Heywood. The Commandant said, "When I met your father the other day, he told me you were only sixteen." "No sir," Smedley lied, "That's my brother." The commandant asked, "How old are you then?" Smedley replied, "I'm eighteen, sir." He was accepted in the Marine Corps as a second lieutenant and retired in 1931 as a lieutenant general. He died in 1940.

Smedley Butler's thirty-three years in the Marine Corps is the source of many legends. The Marines called him "Old Gimlet Eye." He is one of very few men who have been awarded the Congressional Medal of Honor *twice*. The destroyer USS *Butler*, later a high-speed minesweeper, was named for him.[10]

Nathan E. Cook talked his sister into signing papers that allowed him to enlist in the U. S. Navy in 1901. Nathan, born in Hersey, Michigan, on 10 October 1885, was 15 years old. He saw action in the Boxer Rebellion in China, the Pancho Villa Mexican-border skirmish

---

[9] Adapted from an article in the *Columbus Ledger-Enquirer*, Columbus, Georgia, 21 July 1992.

[10] Lowell Thomas, *Old Gimlet Eye*, Farrer and Rinehart, New York, 1933.

in 1917, World War I, and World War II. During World War I, Nathan was in command of a subchaser. His ship sank two German submarines off the coast of Greece.

Nathan's most memorable experience occurred while serving aboard the USS *Kansas* in 1907. As the ship was leaving the port of Gibraltar, his appendix burst just as he picked up a hawser (heavy mooring line). The Navy doctor thought he was dead and notified his wife that they were sending his body home for burial. He was packed in ice, but he revived en route. Surgery was performed in Philadelphia, and he completely recovered.

Nathan Cook served forty-four years in the Navy. He died at the Veterans Medical Center in Phoenix, Arizona, on 10 September 1992, at the age of 106 years and 11 months. He is buried in the Arizona Veterans Cemetery, Cave Creek, Arizona.[11]

World War I again fired the minds of young people, and many manipulated the system to enlist.

Mike Mansfield left his Great Falls, Montana, home in 1917, and on 23 February 1918, at the age of 14, enlisted in the U. S. Navy for the duration of World War I. In 1919, while still 15 years old, he joined the U. S. Army for one year. In November 1920, he joined the U. S. Marine Corps and served for two years.

After his honorable discharge from the Marines, Mike returned to Montana and worked as a mucker and mining engineer until 1930. Although he had never completed grade school or high school, he was admitted to the Montana School of Mines in Butte, Montana, after completing a qualifying examination. He met and later married a Butte high school teacher, Maureen Hayes. With Maureen's academic, financial, and moral support, Mike transferred to the University of Montana at Missoula to continue his education. Later, he taught Latin American and Far Eastern history at Montana State University.

In 1942, Mike Mansfield was elected to the United States Congress and served five terms as Representative of Montana's 1st District. In 1952, he was elected to the United States Senate. In 1961, he was elected Majority Leader of the Senate and served in that position until

---

[11] Adapted from *The Stars and Stripes - The National Tribune*, 28 Sep. - 4 Oct. 1992.

his retirement in 1977 — longer than any majority leader in the history of the United States Senate.

Senator Mansfield served five presidents in a number of capacities. His final assignment was Ambassador to Japan, an office he held from 1977 until 1989. He and his wife currently reside in Washington, D.C.[12]

The Depression years between World War I and World War II provided incentive to a number of youngsters to enlist in the military. The onset of World War II ignited patriotic fervor throughout the nation and was an impetus for underage men and women to join the military in numbers not seen since the Civil War. One of these was a young man from Callicoon, New York.

Allen Clifton Heyn falsified his age and joined the U. S. Navy soon after the attack on Pearl Harbor. He was just 16 years old. He was soon one of 700 men aboard the USS *Juneau* heading for the South Pacific. Allen was the youngest crew member on the ship, and in the eyes of his shipmates, the least likely to survive a disaster at sea.

Two of Allen's friends were George and Al Sullivan. Along with their brothers Frank, Matt, and Red, the five Sullivan brothers had received special permission from the Navy to serve together aboard the *Juneau*. On the second day of the Battle of Guadalcanal, at 11:01 a.m, Friday, 13 November 1942, the *Juneau*, already suffering battle damage, was struck by a torpedo launched from a Japanese submarine, the *I-26*. A massive explosion rocked the ship and she quickly sank. Of the crew, 560 were killed in the explosion and 140 survived. Thinking that no one could survive such an explosion, and concerned that the submarine that launched the torpedo would soon strike again, the remaining ships were ordered to steam away and not search for survivors.

The survivors, clinging to rafts, had no food or fresh water. Sharks soon were circling and started taking their toll, attacking the men who were clinging to the rafts. Each day, fewer men were left. Of the 140 who survived the sinking, only ten are known to have reached safety. Allen Heyn, one of the ten, was with one of the largest groups of survivors, which included George and Al Sullivan. Allen, the sole

---

[12] Biographical sketch furnished by the office of Senator Mike Mansfield, 11 January 1996.

survivor of that group, was alone on a raft when he was finally rescued, eight days after the explosion that blew him off the ship.[13]

The preceding accounts are a very small sample of the legacy of underage veterans. Undoubtedly, the exploits and accomplishments of many more young warriors were just as compelling as these, but most were not recorded and have been lost to history. The remainder of this book is devoted to recording the histories of men and women who served before they could do so legally during the period from World War I through World War II, the Korean War, and the war in Vietnam. For the most part, the stories are written as told by the veterans themselves. Because of today's technology and improved record-keeping, which make it nearly impossible to enlist in the military underage, this group may represent the last of the legacy.

---

[13] Dan Kurzman, *Left to Die*, Pocket Books, New York, 1994; Edward E. Leslie, *Desperate Journeys, Abandoned Souls*, Houghton Mifflin Company, Boston, 1988.

The
Stories

The following pages contain 199 stories contributed by members of the Veterans of Underage Military Service, which represent more than one fourth of the current membership. The age and branch of military service at time of the enlistment is indicated under each name, for underage service only. Many contributors joined one branch of the military while underage, but reenlisted and served in other branches later on.

Because of the large number of contributors, and because of the long time span and the number of events covered, it would have been impractical to check all factual details. Therefore, we have relied completely on the contributors for the content and accuracy of their stories.

The sequence in which the stories appear is based on the date of first enlistment while underage. The first story is from a veteran who joined the Navy in 1917 during World War I, followed by the stories of those who served in the 1920s and 1930s. Most of the stories are from the era spanning World War II, the Korean War, and the Vietnam War. All but a few contributors furnished a picture with their story.

Merle M. Arthur

Age 16 – United States Navy

I was born in Washington, Iowa, just after the turn of the century, on 14 November 1901. When I was a boy, my father bought some farmland in Wisconsin from a lumber company after it had removed all the trees. The problem was that we had to remove

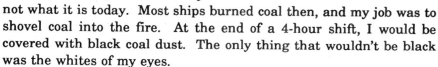

The ship's Marines came for me and I ended up paying a fine for that indiscretion.

the stumps before we could farm the land. We spent five years pulling up stumps without ever making a crop.

When I was 16, I left the farm and went to work in the Nash Auto Factory in Racine, Wisconsin. My job was to take inventory of the castings and put different castings in different bins. One day while I was visiting in Milwaukee, I saw a Navy recruiting sign that said "travel, adventure." It sounded good to me, so I went in, told them that I was 18, and signed up. I didn't have to prove my age, but I was nearly turned down because of a heart murmur. After three doctors checked my heart, they finally passed me.

I was sworn into the Navy on 17 June 1918 and sent to Bremerton, Washington, for training. The Navy notified my parents that I had joined and sent a flag to be placed in a window. My mother was very upset about my joining the Navy and wanted to get me out by sending proof that I was underage. My father prevailed, and they decided to let me serve.

After boot camp, I was assigned as a fireman on a ship. A fireman's job then was not what it is today. Most ships burned coal then, and my job was to shovel coal into the fire. At the end of a 4-hour shift, I would be covered with black coal dust. The only thing that wouldn't be black was the whites of my eyes.

After one 4-hour shift, from midnight to four in the morning, I showered and was in bed by five o'clock. I was awakened at six-thirty for muster at seven, but I just stayed in bed and went back to sleep. The ship's Marines came for me and I ended up paying a fine for that indiscretion.

One day, our ship broke its crankshaft in rough seas. We were adrift off the rocky northern California coast and would have been on the rocks in about an hour if another ship had not arrived to tow us to San Francisco. We spent Armistice Day, 11 November 1918, anchored in San Francisco Bay. The captain would not let us go ashore because he was expecting another ship to tow us to the Mare Island Naval Shipyard. We sat on that ship all evening across from Alcatraz and watched the rockets and fireworks going off in San Francisco and Oakland. We were right in the middle of it, but we couldn't leave the ship.

After taking the ship to Mare Island, I joined another ship, went through the Panama Canal, then made a number of trips taking supplies to Europe and bringing troops home. Many ships were required to bring the troops back, so the Navy took over some captured German ships, along with their crews. I was assigned to one, and when I went to the boiler room to shovel coal, the 200-pound German sailors just laughed at all 130 pounds of me. They really didn't think I could shovel the coal, but I did.

We were in the Mediterranean during one of the trips. This was shortly after the war and there was still a danger of mines. The captain would not allow the men to sleep in the bunks near the bow and told us to sleep on deck, but we would sneak back to our bunks, not afraid of the danger.

I wanted to be discharged at the Brooklyn Navy Yard so I could go to school in New York and study to become a marine engineer. But the Navy wanted to save the 10¢-a-mile travel pay back to the place of enlistment, so they gathered up all the midwesterners and sent us to the Great Lakes Naval Base. I had made a complete orbit and was back to my parents' house.

Merle Arthur went to work for the Baltimore and Ohio Railroad in Chicago, retiring as a signal maintenance worker some years later. He built and operated Art's Skating Rink in Chicago and later added a bowling alley. After being a "winter Texan" for a few seasons, he moved to McAllen, Texas, in 1972. He met his wife Pauline at a dance in McAllen. They married in 1982 and continued to dance, accumulating twenty-six trophies that are displayed in their home. During a cruise, Merle and Pauline went through the Panama Canal. Merle said that it hadn't changed in seventy years. Shortly after moving to McAllen, Merle joined the Rio Grande Valley Last Man's Club, composed of World War I veterans. Just before his 93rd birthday in 1994, Merle became the last man. A party was held on 11 November 1994 at the Elks Lodge in Weslaco, Texas. Merle received the champagne that he didn't get in 1918 while aboard ship in San Francisco Bay. Merle's daughter Darlene DeVos was an underage veteran during World War II, joining the WAC a year before she could legally do so (see page 365).

√ **VUMS Note ⇒ Our Admiral.** Both pictures of Admiral Mike Boorda on the dedication page were taken at the Great Lakes Naval Training Center, one at the start of his naval career, the other forty years later, near the end of his career. The photographs were furnished by the Office of the Chief of Naval Operations.

Howard V. Shebley

Age 16 – United States Marine Corps

When I was in high school, I took a course in civics that was taught by a very young teacher on her first teaching job. It was a totally new subject for the school. At the end of the term, thirty out of forty-two students flunked the course, and I was one of them. I was rather discouraged with high school.

> We were preparing to go to China, but ... we went to Nicaragua.

That summer I worked for the Pacific Gas & Electric for four dollars a day. When the time came for school to start in August 1927, I didn't sign up. I thought I was faced with a year and a half of high school. About that time, my father received a telegram informing him that I had been given an appointment as first alternate to attend the Naval Academy at Annapolis. The two boys who had received the appointments were very bright, and I was sure that they would both pass the entrance exams and enroll at Annapolis.

I had heard that if I joined the Navy I would have a chance to take the examination for Annapolis. In early October 1927, I went to Sacramento to the Navy recruiting office to enlist. The Navy recruiter was not in, but a Marine Corps recruiter was there. He informed me that I was right, that I could enlist in the Marine Corps and take the Naval Academy exam, but not at age 16. I filled out all the forms and returned home.

My date of birth was 21 January 1911. My parents would not sign the necessary papers unless I used my correct date of birth, so I had them put down 1911, and they signed it. The next day, on the way back to Sacramento, I made a 0 out of a 1 to make my birth year 1910, instead of 1911. I think the recruiter was wise to what I had done, but he went along with it.

I was sent to the San Diego Marine Barracks, was sworn in on 1 November 1927, and underwent three months of boot camp. My age was never questioned. I entered the Corps as a bugle boy, as I was considered to be in my seventeenth year. When I reached my birthday in January of 1928, I became 18 on the records and was designated a private.

I took the test for the Naval Academy while at the Marine Barracks in San Diego. I was told later that I had passed the exam, but it was too late to enter that year. I heard that the two bright boys for whom I was an alternate failed their exams.

When I was 17, I was assigned to Marine Corps Aviation. We were preparing to go to China, but our orders were changed and we went to Nicaragua. I participated in combat patrols as a crew member of a Curtiss Falcon. After a year on flight duty, I was assigned to the motor shop.

While in Nicaragua, I was interviewed by the Marine major in command of our unit concerning the possibility of attending the Naval Academy. He told me that an assignment to Annapolis from Nicaragua was doubtful and that I would be informed later if it was possible. I never heard any more about it. The Great Depression was on, and I just gave up on it.

I served four years in the Corps without a promotion and was discharged as a private on 31 October 1931. Although I had a third class specialist rating, the Depression had begun and there were very few promotions.

The Depression was at its worst after I got out of the Marine Corps. There were few jobs, but the price of gold was up and the old mines reopened. I worked in an underground gold mine in Grass Valley, California, for two years. There wasn't much future in the mines, so I quit.

In 1936, I went to work for the California Fish and Game Department as an assistant warden and was promoted to warden in 1938. I was in charge of a two-man patrol boat in Southern California waters. I operated the patrol boat until World War II began.

In 1942, shortly after the war started, I went to the Marine Corps to reenlist. They said that because I was married and was 33 years old, they would take me for Stateside duty only. Being restricted to Stateside duty was not for me, so in March 1942, I took a 3-day examination after which I was commissioned a lieutenant junior grade in the U. S. Coast Guard Reserve. I operated the first Coast Guard Beach Patrol on the beach between Arlight and Point Conception, California. In July or August 1942, I was assigned as officer-in-charge of a combination beach patrol training school and supply warehouse at the San Clemente State Park facility. I was promoted to full lieutenant in early 1943. I became aware of an Office of Strategic Services (OSS) group that was training across the highway at Camp Pendleton. I applied for assignment to the OSS, was accepted in April 1944, and served overseas with that group. I returned to the Coast Guard in May 1945.

I was assigned as prospective commanding officer of the USS *Westchester*, an AK (cargo) ship being built at the Leathan D. Smith Shipyard in Sturgeon Bay, Wisconsin. After it was completed and launched, I had the rare experience of sailing inland waters from Sturgeon Bay, Wisconsin, to Galveston, Texas, a total of 2054 miles. We crossed Lake Michigan to Chicago, went through the Chicago Canal locks to Saint Louis and on down the Mississippi. The ship was powered by two small tugs. At Saint Louis, we tied to a huge raft of grain barges and went down the river to New Orleans where we were detached from the raft of barges, and again powered by two small tugs, went through the intercoastal canal to Galveston.

At Galveston, I was assigned as commanding officer on the USS *Colquit*, another AK. The ship was commissioned by the Navy, and after its shakedown cruise and refueling, we proceeded to sea with the West Coast as our destination. When we were underway, our orders were changed and we took the ship to Curtis Bay, Maryland, the Coast Guard shipyard. Soon after that, I applied for and was granted release from active duty.

I returned to the California State Fish and Game department, and in June 1947, was promoted to patrol captain. On 1 January 1951, I went back to active duty in the Coast Guard and was assigned as executive officer of the Coast Guard West Coast Training Station at Alameda, California. I was released from active duty in 1952 and was assigned as commanding officer of the Coast Guard Reserve Training Unit. In 1956, I was transferred by the State Fish and Game Department to Monterey, California, where I supervised wardens along the coastal area counties from San Luis Obispo to Santa Cruz. At Monterey, I formed another Coast Guard Reserve Training Unit.

I retired from the Coast Guard as a captain, which is equivalent to a colonel in the Marine Corps.

Howard Shebley began working for the California Fish and Game Department in 1936. His service with the department was interrupted by World War II and the Korean War. He rose from an assistant warden to supervisory warden for the coastal area counties from San Luis Obispo to Santa Cruz. He retired from the department in June 1971. Howard and his wife Jeanne live in Oakdale, California. Their combined family includes four children (two deceased), four grandchildren, and eight great-grandchildren.

√ **VUMS Note** ⇒ *How young were they?* In the five years since it was founded, the VUMS association has located over 1000 men and women who served underage, but only 886 records are sufficiently detailed to analyze statistically. Three of the 886 enlisted during their 12th year, 20 during their 13th year, 99 during their 14th year, 283 during their 15th year, and 481 during their 16th year.

Archie W. Stewart, Jr.

Age 14 – Texas National Guard

In March 1936, at the age of 14, I lied about my age and joined the 36th Infantry Division, Texas National Guard, at Greenville, Texas. I joined the Guard because it paid one dollar

> *I joined the Guard because it paid one dollar per week, and I needed the dollar.*

per week, and I needed the dollar. I was born in Dallas, Texas, on 16 August 1921, grew up in Commerce, Texas, and went to Greenville once a week for drill. My father and stepmother moved from Commerce when I was 15, but I stayed. I had a room in a house that my father had rented to a young couple. I washed dishes and set the table at a nearby rooming house for my meals and worked for the *Dallas Morning News* and the *Dispatch Journal*. I was in charge of ten paper-delivery boys and their routes.

On 25 November 1940, the 36th Division, Texas National Guard, was mobilized. I was a corporal in Company M, 144th Infantry, at the time. We were sent to Camp Bowie, near Brownwood, Texas, for training. After war was declared, we were sent to the West Coast to guard sensitive areas. The northernmost place was Port Angeles, Washington. We went south to Portland, Oregon, and to Eureka and Jenner-by-the-Sea, California.

Our commanding officer wanted to send five of us to OCS (officer candidate school), but we had all failed the colorblind test. At each new post, he would send us individually to get physicals, and we would fail. When the company reached a new station near San Francisco, the captain sent all five of us to Hamilton Field for a physical. The medical technician thought that we were all trying to get out of something by intentionally failing the colorblind test, so he passed us.

After OCS, I was assigned to the 103rd Division and ended up training recruits at Camp Claiborne, Louisiana. Later I was assigned to the 65th Division to train troops at Camp Shelby, Mississippi, and was promoted to captain.

I was sent to England in the spring of 1944 pending assignment as a replacement to some unit that was going to be in the Normandy invasion. I arrived in Normandy on D+12, 18 June 1944, in command of 200 replacement troops. Within a short time, I was assigned as commander, Company H, 110th Infantry, 28th Division. The first day that I was with the 110th, I ran into an old friend from National Guard days in Greenville, Texas. Former Sergeant William C. Dobbs, now Captain Dobbs, was in command of Company E of the 110th Infantry.

Throughout July and August, we walked and fought through France and found ourselves in Paris in late August. The evening of 28 August, we slept in the rain, leaning against trees in the Bois de Boulogne and the next day, 29 August 1944, we marched twenty-four abreast down the Avenue Foch, by the Arc de Triomphe to the Place de L'Etoile, and down the Champs Elysees to the Place de la Concorde. The French ladies "rescued" about half of the troops by the end of the parade.

Our battalion spent the night in St. Denis, a suburb of Paris. I was assigned a room on the third floor of a hastily abandoned hotel, actually a house of ill repute. The room had a feather bed, a wash basin, a pitcher of water, and a "pop-up" type toilet in the hallway. When shoe heels were placed on the cover of the toilet, the lid opened, disclosing a sewer line. Some enemy resistance was encountered while we were leaving Paris. All rail lines had been bombed. I had a movie camera and took some pictures of the area.

At dusk on 2 September 1944, our regiment captured the city of St. Quentin. Afterwards, while moving through the city, we were suddenly engaged by a column of Germans in company strength. The Nazis, aided by several armored cars, attempted to break the regimental column. My jeep had stopped, and I was the first to fire on the enemy column. I shot one German and was aiming for the second one when my carbine jammed and he shot me. The bullet hit me in the cheek, split my jaw, and paralyzed one of my vocal cords. The Germans killed my runner, left me for dead, and drove away in my jeep. The 110th Infantry Regiment killed 125 Germans that day, but we had only fifteen casualties. My jeep was recovered, but my movie camera remained missing.

I was taken to the local hospital in St. Quentin, then to Paris, then to England. I was back in the States before Christmas and was hospitalized at the Brooke Army Medical Center in San Antonio for almost a year.

I was discharged from the Army with the rank of captain in October 1945.

Archie Stewart earned the Combat Infantryman Badge and the Bronze Star. He was awarded the Purple Heart for wounds received in action. After his release from the Army, he attended East Texas State College and received a B.B.A. degree in 1951. He was a supervisor and staff officer at Kelly Air Force Base from 1955 until he retired in 1980. In 1994, Archie returned to France to take part in commemoration of the 50th anniversary of the Normandy invasion. At St. Quentin, he was awarded the Medal of Honor of the City of St. Quentin. Archie and Mary Louise, his wife of fifty-one years, live in San Antonio, Texas. They have three children and three grandchildren.

Steward H. Kulp

Age 16 – United States Army

I was born in Bethlehem, Pennsylvania, on 20 September 1920 and graduated from Bethlehem's Liberty High School in June 1937. The Great Depression was fading away, but I was unable to find a job.

> *I was in Korea from five days before the initial invasion until nine months after the cessation of hostilities.*

Although the legal enlistment age was 18 and I was only 16, I decided to join the Army. I was unable to find a birth certificate, so my mother prepared a sworn statement showing my age to be 18. I enlisted in the Army at Allentown, Pennsylvania, and was sworn in on 19 June 1937 in Philadelphia. I was assigned to the 66th Infantry (light tanks) at Fort George G. Meade, Maryland.

In 1937, I attended the 66th Infantry Regimental Clerical School and took courses in typing, shorthand, and company administration. I went to Panama where I was the battery clerk for Battery C, 1st Coast Artillery, Harbor Defense, at Fort Sherman, on the Atlantic side of the canal.

As war clouds fluttered over Europe and Asia, the Panama Separate Coast Artillery Brigade came into being. Because of my clerical skills, I was transferred to brigade headquarters at Quarry Heights. I was secretary to the commanding general, Major General Sanderford Jarman, and I was in charge of the command-file section. In 1940, the chief of coast artillery gave a special sergeants major examination. I took the exam and qualified for staff sergeant.

I sailed from Panama on Easter Sunday morning, 1941. I was sent to the Antiaircraft Coast Artillery Training Center, Camp Davis, North Carolina. I was assigned to the 93rd Coast Artillery (antiaircraft, semimobile) where, on 28 June 1941, I was promoted to master sergeant. I was only 20 years old at the time. Among my souvenirs,

I have an old *Our Army* magazine which has an article stating that I was the youngest master sergeant serving as a sergeant major in the Army at that time.

In mid-1941, I took the Army warrant officer examination, and in February 1942, I was appointed as a warrant officer (junior grade) at Camp Haan, California. Subsequently, I was commissioned a second lieutenant in the Adjutant General's Department and was later promoted to captain. I served as classification and assignment officer of the Central Signal School at Camp Crowder, Missouri, and then as Chief of the Congressional Correspondence Section at the Army Records Branch in Saint Louis, Missouri.

About the time that hostilities ceased in the Pacific, I was assigned to General Headquarters, Far East Command. I was the casualty-assistance and service officer at General MacArthur's headquarters. General MacArthur signed a personal letter to the next of kin of each casualty in the Pacific theater. I was responsible for researching and preparing these letters.

I transferred to the Air Force as a master sergeant in 1947, at the time it became a separate service. In June 1950, while at the replacement depot at Fuchu, Japan, I was sent to the Fifth Air Force Advance in Korea to obtain some replacement data. The Fifth Air Force Rear was in Tokyo. Five days after I arrived, the North Koreans crossed the 38th Parallel. I was immediately assigned as the Wing Sergeant Major for the 18th Fighter-Bomber Wing. Our wing flew P-51 aircraft.

On Christmas Eve of 1951, the 18th Fighter Bomber Wing set up shop at K-55, Osan, Korea, about forty miles south of Seoul. We named the base "Dogpatch Air Base." Walt Disney sent us decals to put on our aircraft and buildings. We had Lil Abner, Mammy and Pappy, Daisy Mae, Earthquake McGoon, Mr. Joe Blifsk — the whole lot of Dogpatch characters.

I was assigned to the 58th Fighter-Bomber Wing at Taegu, Korea, on 9 September 1952. The 58th was a reinforced wing, flying F-84 aircraft. On the last day of the war, Colonel Arthur Agan, the wing commander, flew seventeen missions into North Korea. I met him after each mission and implored him to fly no more that day, but he continued until dark. Later, Colonel Agan wore four stars and became Commander of NORAD, the Air Force command center in the mountain at Colorado Springs, Colorado.

Before the war ended, I wanted my wife and children to come to Japan, so I put in for a transfer to Tachikawa, Japan. The Fifth Air Force erred and assigned me to Okinawa. I returned the assignment and remained in Korea while waiting for it to be corrected, which took nearly nine months. I was in Korea from five days before the initial invasion until nine months after the cessation of hostilities.

Finally, in 1954 my assignment was corrected, and I was transferred to the Far East Air Material Command at Tachikawa Air Base, Japan. I returned to the States in 1955 and was assigned to the Air Force Ballistic Missile Division, Inglewood, California. This was the location that the Air Force Space Program began under General Schriever. I was assigned to the security section, processing individual security clearances and doing other types of investigations.

I retired from the Air Force as a captain on 31 March 1961, after twenty-four years of service.

Steward Kulp went to work for the Defense Intelligence Agency immediately after retiring from the Air Force. Steward and Marie, his wife of fifty-five years, live in San Diego, California. They have four children, nine grandchildren, and one great-grandchild.

Harry W. Darrow, Sr.

Age 15 – United States Navy

I was born in Astoria, Long Island, New York, on 2 December 1921 and raised in Norwalk, Connecticut. When I was 15 years old, I was very disruptive in class, so the high school principal finally told me to go home and have

> ... the FBI had been looking for me for three years.

my mother sign papers that would permit me to get a job. My mother refused to sign the papers, and the principal wouldn't let me back in school. For almost a year I just went fishing and enjoyed myself.

When I wasn't fishing, I was trying to join the Navy. All through 1937, I constantly bugged the recruiting officers to let me enlist, but they kept telling me that I was too young. I was in the recruiting office so much that they called me their mascot. In addition to my being too young, Congress was cutting back on the military budget that year, so it was very hard to get in. Finally, the recruiters got

tired of my pestering them, so they accepted a baptismal certificate that my brother had forged for me. The certificate indicated that I was born on 2 December 1919. Now all I had to do was to get a letter of recommendation from both the high school principal and a leading citizen in the community and a letter from my mother giving her permission.

The Navy recruiters got in touch with the high school principal, and believe it or not, he gave me a great recommendation. I also received a recommendation from one of the community leaders, and my mother gave her consent. I was sworn into the Navy on 19 November 1937, thirteen days before my sixteenth birthday.

I was sent to Newport, Rhode Island, for boot camp. I had not been in boot camp very long when I suffered severe stomach pains and spent a couple of weeks in a naval hospital. The final diagnosis for the stomach pains was that I was eating too much food. My intestines were so small from not eating enough during the Depression years that I just couldn't take all that food.

In 1938, I helped put the light cruiser USS *Savannah* into commission and stayed aboard her for nearly two years. One time the *Savannah* was tied up alongside her sister ship, the USS *Brooklyn*, at the Philadelphia Navy Yard. I went ashore, had a few, and returned to the ship. I saluted the OD (officer of the deck), put my liberty card in the liberty-card box, and went below to my bunk. When I woke up the next morning, all I saw was strange faces. I soon learned that I was on the *Brooklyn*, not the *Savannah*. I went topside and told the OD what had happened. He chewed me out for being on the wrong ship and wouldn't give me my liberty card until one minute before 8:00 a.m. As soon as he gave me my card, I ran to the *Savannah* and made it just before colors.

I was a pointer on a 5-inch antiaircraft gun. During firing practice one day, the loader put a shell in, then put another one on top of it. When the shell rammed home, one shell went into the breach and the other went over my head and hit the steel scupper. By some miracle, it didn't explode. The chief gunner's mate pushed it over the side.

In 1938, we went to England and loaded all the available gold aboard the *Savannah* and brought it to the United States. It was expected that Hitler's troops would soon invade England, and they wanted the gold in a safe place.

I was discharged on 30 November 1940 and returned to Connecticut. I was supposed to sign up for the draft, but I didn't. After the attack on Pearl Harbor, I reenlisted in the Navy. I reported for duty on 26 December 1941 and was assigned to the Brooklyn Navy Yard. I served as master-at-arms for Captain H. V. McKittrick for three years.

I didn't know it at the time, but the FBI had been looking for me for three years. They thought that I was a draft dodger because I had never signed up for the draft. I found out about all of this when I was called into the commandant's office and was read the riot act for not registering.

On 1 March 1945, I applied for submarine school at New London, Connecticut, and was accepted, but I didn't stay long at the school. I was soon transferred to the West Coast and assigned to picket boats which were used to patrol submarine nets. Picket boats were about the size of PT boats. They carried 50-caliber machine guns and depth charges. At about this time, the Navy was rounding up sailors from all over the country, putting them in Marine fatigues, and training them with carbines in preparation for invading northern Japan. Shortly after Harry Truman authorized the use of the A-bomb, the war was over. I think dropping the bomb saved my life.

I was discharged from the Navy at Lido Beach, Long Island, New York, on 17 September 1945.

Harry Darrow drove an oil truck for a couple of years, then became interested in oil burners. He started cleaning oil burners for a company and worked up to the position of heating-system troubleshooter. He then opened his own oil and heating business and operated it for about ten years, then sold his company to a major oil company and went on their payroll. He was a plant manager at the time his company was sold, so in 1983, he took early retirement with a "golden handshake" and a pension. Harry and Nora, his wife of fifty-four years, live in Ashford, Connecticut. They have four children and three grandchildren. Harry is the Connecticut State Vice Commander of the Veterans of Underage Military Service.

Verne J. Wilkins

Age 15 – Washington National Guard

Home life for me during the 1930s was not very pleasant. I was born in Seattle, Washington, on 20 April 1923. My father was an abusive, domineering alcoholic who would take

> *I ... straightened a few of them out "in the Army way," behind the barracks.*

every cent that I earned and buy alcohol. I had to get away. The National Guard started expanding in 1938, so I added three years to my age and enlisted. A family friend who was already in the Guard vouched for me. When asked if I was 18, I vigorously nodded my head in assent.

My tour with the Washington National Guard began on 16 March 1938. I was assigned to Battery G, 205th Coast Artillery Regiment (Antiaircraft). We were nationalized on 3 February 1941, becoming the 205th Coast Artillery, U. S. Army, stationed at Fort Lewis, Washington.

I thought I was in paradise in the Army. I had trust and respect, something I had never had at home. It took me some time before I fully recovered from the violence to which I had been subjected.

It seemed like I was always the first man in the first squad of the first platoon during my time in the Army. I was 6'4" and weighed 200 pounds. I withstood a lot of hazing from the older noncommissioned officers because of my age. Finally, I got fed up with their hazing and straightened a few of them out "in the Army way," behind the barracks.

I was sent to Alaska and the Aleutian Islands in 1941 as a member of the 420th Coast Artillery Battalion. In 1944, I returned to the States and was stationed at the training center at Camp Bowie, Texas, for a short time. Then I was off to the European theater, where I served with an ordnance evacuation company in France and Germany.

When the war ended, I stayed on in the Army of Occupation and didn't return to the States until 1949. I was at Camp Kilmer, New Jersey, for about a year, then returned to Fort Lewis, Washington.

My stay at Fort Lewis was shortened because of the Korean War. In 1950, I went to the Far East and served in Japan and Korea. I returned to Fort Lewis in 1952, but my stay was short again. I was assigned to the Presidio in San Francisco, then became a member of the Army Military Assistance and Advisory Group at the U. S. Embassy in Chile. From Chile I went to the Canal Zone for about two years, serving at Fort Amador and later at Headquarters, Quarry Heights. I was at the Yuma, Arizona, test station for a short time, then finished my Army career at Fort Douglas, Utah, where I was the post personnel sergeant. During my last twelve years in the Army, I was a sergeant major. I retired from the Army 31 July 1961.

Verne Wilkins received the Army Commendation Medal and earned battle stars on his Asiatic-Pacific, European theater, and Korean Service ribbons. After his retirement from the Army, he completed his high school education and enrolled at the University of Washington, Seattle, where he obtained a bachelor's degree in engineering in 1966. He worked for the City of Seattle Engineering Department for two years, then was an engineer for sixteen years with the Seattle School District. After retiring from full-time work, he served as an advisor on the King County Metro Transit Elderly and Handicapped Transit Committee. His age caught up with him when the Army DEERS Office (Army medical care) said they were transferring him to Social Security and Medicare three years before he would be legally eligible. To prove his age, Verne obtained a copy of his birth certificate, but to his dismay, he found that it needed to be corrected. His first and middle names had been switched, apparently by the doctor who attended his birth. Changing that proved to be a difficult task. In addition to his birth certificate, he had to produce his passport, a notarized statement, and his Army discharge to get everything corrected on his records. Verne lives in Seattle, Washington.

Robert E. Weaver

Age 14 – West Virginia National Guard
Age 16 – United States Army

I was born in Weston, West Virginia, on 28 January 1923. My father, a veteran of World War I, felt strongly that all males should devote some time to serving their country. I can't remember for sure, but I

> On 7 December 1941, we were the first Army unit to go into action ...

think it was with his help that I enlisted in the National Guard at age 14. It was on 14 November 1938 that I joined the 201st Infantry, West Virginia National Guard. I remained in the Guard until I joined the regular Army on 10 January 1940.

I was sent to Fort Hayes, Ohio, where I was given a physical and inducted into the service. I was given three choices at Fort Hayes: infantry, field artillery, or combat engineers. I chose the engineers, and three days later, I was on my way to Fort Devens, Massachusetts, for basic training with the 18th Combat Engineers.

Our training was cut short, and we left Fort Devens in April 1940 with Fort Benning, Georgia, as our destination. Our transportation was dump trucks with covers over the beds and 2"x10" boards across the beds as seats. There were no back rests on the seats. This was our basic mode of transportation during all of 1940 and 1941. On our way to Fort Benning, we stopped at the West Point Military Academy and camped in the riding arena and in some of the vacant horse stalls. From there, we went to Fort Belvoir, Virginia, then on to Fort Knox, Kentucky, where we picked up additional equipment.

After completing the maneuvers in Georgia, we went to Dry Prong, Louisiana, to repair roads and bridges for the upcoming Red & Blue Maneuvers. During this time, we constructed a pontoon bridge across the Red River in record time. It was the longest bridge put up in the shortest time since the Civil War.

From Louisiana, we went to Fort Logan, Colorado, for a brief stay, then it was on to Camp McCoy, Wisconsin, for maneuvers with several National Guard units from different parts of the country. My old unit, the 201st Infantry, was involved. We returned to Fort Logan, Colorado, and remained there until the spring of 1941 when we went to Camp Hunter Leggett, California, for more maneuvers. From there we went to Vancouver Barracks in Washington. Our outfit received a citation for being the most traveled unit in the Army.

In July 1941, I was one of about thirty or forty men from our outfit who were sent to Oahu, Hawaii, to help establish a new unit called the 804th Engineers (aviation). Our duties were to construct and repair airstrips, build housing, etc., for the Army's Seventh Air Force. On 7 December 1941, we were the first Army unit to go into action at Hickam and Wheeler Air Fields, for which we received a citation.

After getting things back in order following the Japanese attack, we moved to the north end of Oahu and constructed an airfield and bunkers for aircraft. We used steel matting for the airstrip and put camouflage netting over the bunkers.

We went to Baker Island and Canton Island to build airstrips for refueling stations. Baker Island was just a hunk of coral sticking out of the ocean. It had no trees, no grass, just gooney birds. When the strips were completed, we went back to Oahu for new equipment, then were off to Makin Island to build another airstrip. When that job was completed, we returned again to Oahu for new equipment, then we were off again to Saipan to build two large airstrips for use by B-29s, other bombers, and fighter planes. Working with other engineer outfits, we put in three shifts to keep the construction going twenty-four hours a day.

In the last part of May 1945, I learned that I had enough points to go back to the States. I left Saipan, spent a few days on Oahu, then boarded a ship for the trip back to the mainland. I disembarked at Oakland, California, and four days later boarded a troop train for Fort Meade, Maryland, where I was scheduled to receive my discharge.

But I didn't get discharged. Instead, I was sent to an Air Force rest camp in Greensboro, North Carolina, for fourteen days. From there I was sent to Selma Air Force Base in Louisiana where I remained until 18 September, at which time I was told to report to the Indiantown

Gap Military Reservation in Pennsylvania. I finally received my discharge there on 22 September 1945.

I am proud to be an American, and I am proud that I had the opportunity to serve my country in her time of need.

Bob Weaver returned to Weston, West Virginia, and went to work as a house painter with his father. In August 1948, he moved to Baltimore, Maryland, and was employed by what is now the Department of Housing and Urban Development as a painter and later as a supervisor. He retired from HUD in 1988. Bob and his wife Joan live in Stevensville, Maryland. At the time he married Joan, she had a married son and a daughter who have provided Bob and Joan three grandchildren to enjoy.

√ **VUMS Note** ⇒ *Branch of service.* The 886 available records of underage men and women indicate that 298 chose the Army for their first enlistment, while 297 chose the Navy, 124 the Marine Corps, 80 the Army Air Forces and the Air Force, 59 the National Guard, 19 the Coast Guard, and 9 the Merchant Marine.

Dwight L. Adams

Age 16 – Tennessee National Guard

I enlisted in the 117th Infantry Regiment, 30th Infantry Division, Tennessee National Guard, on 3 December 1938, at the age of 16. I was living in Bristol, Virginia, at the time, and the Guard unit was in Bristol, Tennessee, just across Main Street, which was also the state line.

> *... one of my officers, two drivers, and I decided to go and meet the Russians unofficially.*

I graduated from the Bristol, Virginia, high school a few months after joining the Guard and went to Nashville, Tennessee, to live and work. I became a member of the Headquarters Detachment, 2nd Battalion, 117th Infantry, in Nashville. Following several short periods of active duty, we were mobilized into active federal service on 16 September 1940. The 30th Infantry Division was among the first units in the nation to be ordered to full-time active service. We were initially scheduled to serve one year, but with the war raging in Europe, we didn't know what to expect.

The division moved to Fort Jackson, South Carolina, where the 8th Infantry Division, a regular Army unit, was stationed. We cut down pine trees to clear an area, formed company streets, and pitched tents alongside the streets. We converted the tents into "hutments" by adding wooden floors and side walls with pyramidal tents stretched on top. Each "hutment" accommodated from six to eight soldiers.

In the early stages of the basic training cycle, our equipment and weapons were largely of World War I vintage, but with time, they were gradually replaced by newer, modern versions. For example, the M-1 Garand rifle replaced the 1903 Springfield and the British Enfield rifles.

Just before we were to be released from active duty on 15 September 1941, Congress enacted legislation that included extending our duty time indefinitely. The legislation passed by one vote, which was indicative of the different views about the role of the nation in the war raging in Europe. The voting took place three months before the Japanese attack on Pearl Harbor.

Following our entry into the war, the rapid expansion of the Army created a demand for new officers. By early 1942, when I was a staff sergeant in the battalion headquarters detachment, I decided to apply for OCS (officer candidate school). I was accepted and reported to the Infantry School at Fort Benning, Georgia, in April 1942. I received a temporary commission as a second lieutenant, Army of the United States, on 5 July 1942 at the real age of 19, although my records indicated that I was 21. As I recall, age 18 was the legal age for being commissioned.

After a short leave, I reported to the 83rd Infantry Division at Camp Atterbury, Indiana, and was assigned to Company D, 1st Battalion, 329th Infantry Regiment. This was an Army Reserve division, on paper, that was being activated for full-time service. Each company had one officer and ten to twelve noncommissioned officers as a cadre when we newly commissioned second lieutenants joined them. The officers were largely from the National Guard who had come from other active units, and the noncoms were fine, experienced "old soldiers" from the horse cavalry units that were being disbanded. We were very fortunate to learn soldiering from these men.

We received draftees to make up troop strength allotments, and began a lengthy process of basic, unit, and advanced training. After about a year and a half, we moved to Camp Breckenridge, Kentucky. The Army expanded during this time because it was training troops for the upcoming invasion in Europe and also fighting in North Africa and throughout the South Pacific.

In early 1944, we sailed for Great Britain to become part of the Allied forces preparing for the Normandy invasion. We shipped out of Plymouth, England, immediately after the invading forces had secured a beachhead at Normandy. Our task was to replace the 101st Airborne Division which had jumped into Normandy on the night before D-Day. A major storm in the English Channel damaged beaches and delayed the landing of elements of our division, but we went ashore, and the 1st Battalion, 329th Infantry, relieved elements of the 101st Airborne in the vicinity of Carentan. At this time, I was the senior first lieutenant of Company D and served as platoon leader of a machine-gun platoon.

Following the breakout from Normandy, we fought in the Brittany Peninsula at St. Malo and St. Servan. Then we moved across France and eventually into Luxembourg by early fall. I became company commander of Company D during the time we were fronting on the Siegfried line across the border in Germany. I was promoted to captain at age 22. I continued as company commander during our campaign in the Hurtgen Forest, the Battle of the Bulge, the crossing of the Rhine, and the drive across North Germany to the Elbe River.

Our battalion made an assault crossing of the Elbe in the vicinity of Barby-Zerbst and successfully held the bridgehead against counterattacking German forces. While we were waiting for the Russian troops to meet us, one of my officers, two drivers, and I decided to go and meet the Russians unofficially. We drove into Wittenberg, met the Russian units, had lunch, exchanged pistols, etc., and drove back to our bridgehead. Since this was not official, we didn't record this trip, so I do not remember the exact date. However, it was near the time that we crossed the Elbe River, which was the day after President Roosevelt died, 14 April 1945. We named the bridge that was erected across the river the "Truman Bridge." It is possible that our link-up was prior to the official meeting that took place late in April by units south of us, but we'll never know.

I returned to the States on leave in May 1945 and was subsequently released for reassignment. I joined the faculty at the Infantry School at Fort Benning, Georgia. The 83rd Division was slated to return to the States, then go on to the Pacific for the invasion of Japan.

In 1946, I received an appointment as a first lieutenant in the regular Army and went to northern Italy as a company commander in the 88th Division. From there I went to Vienna, Austria, and served with the 1st Battalion, 16th Infantry Regiment. I returned to Fort Benning for an advanced infantry officers' course, then remained for another tour as a faculty member of the Infantry School. I was promoted to major in 1951. I served as executive officer of the 88th Infantry's Heavy Mortar Battalion in Korea in 1953 and with Headquarters IX Corps in 1954. From Korea I went to Okinawa for two years, then back to the Infantry School at Fort Benning. I attended the General Staff College at Fort Leavenworth, Kansas, then returned to Fort Benning as deputy G-1 of the Infantry Center. From 1959 until 1962, I served with 7th Army Headquarters in Germany as a lieutenant colonel.

I was assigned to the position of Professor of Military Science, Army ROTC, at South Dakota State University, Brookings, in 1962. After five years there, I joined the 9th Infantry Division in Vietnam, initially as executive officer, and then as commanding officer of Task Force Funston and Dong Tam Base in the Mekong Delta region.

I returned to the States and again became Professor of Military Science at South Dakota State University. I retired from the Army on 1 November 1973 at the rank of colonel, with thirty-five years of service.

Dwight Adams earned the Combat Infantryman Badge in World War II, again in Korea, and also in Vietnam. He was awarded the British Military Cross, which is on the level of the Army's Distinguished Service Cross, the Silver Star with Oak Leaf Cluster, the Legion of Merit with Oak Leaf Cluster, the Bronze star with two "V" devices and four Oak Leaf Clusters, the Purple Heart, the Air Medal with an Oak Leaf Cluster, The Army Commendation Medal with Oak Leaf Cluster, the Republic of Vietnam Cross of Gallantry Medal, the Republic of Vietnam Legion of Honor Medal, and a number of service medals. He entered a second career in the field of political campaign management after his retirement from the Army. He was involved in the campaign of a retired Air Force officer and Medal of Honor winner who was seeking a U. S. Senate seat. He also took part in two congressional campaigns, three campaigns for governor of South Dakota, two presidential primary campaigns, and one general presidential campaign. The presidential campaigns have been with Senator Bob Dole, also a combat infantryman from World War II. Dwight served as State Chairman of the South Dakota Republican Party, and was a member of the Republican National Committee from 1989 to 1991. At the end of the presidential campaign in November 1996, he completed fifty-eight years of public service, and retired again. Dwight and Nevorah, his wife of fifty-one years, live in Brookings, South Dakota. They have three children, nine grandchildren, and three great-grandchildren.

Carl O. Gaddis[14]

Age 15 – United States Marine Corps

I enlisted in the Marine Corps in 1939 at age 15 and was in China before my sixteenth birthday. While I was there, I wasn't allowed to go into town with the

"I could put you in the brig in chains ..."

older Marines, so I stayed in camp and helped the Japanese cook with his work. In return, he taught me a good many Japanese words. After one year in China, I volunteered to be transferred to Guantanamo Bay, Cuba. A gunnery sergeant there "persuaded" me to continue my study of Japanese via correspondence with the University of Oklahoma, and to earn a high school diploma.

In mid-summer of 1941, I was stationed aboard the USS *Wasp* and thought I had been promoted to a seagoing Marine, or a "seagoing bell-hop," as the Navy called us. My position, however, was soon clarified by the following interview with the *Wasp*'s captain (a rank equal to colonel in the Marines or Army).

Captain: Gaddis, how old are you?

Gaddis: I'll be ......

Captain: I did not ask you what your age will be next month, or next year! How old are you now?

Gaddis: Seventeen, sir!

Captain: And you have already been an enlisted Marine for over two years? Did you lie when you joined? Did you forge your enlistment?

Gaddis: Yes, sir!

Captain: (after a stern look at me, giving me the feeling that I was the worst criminal he ever faced) Son, do you know what I could do to you? Don't even try to answer. I'm going to tell you. I could put you in the brig in chains until we return to Norfolk. But what I think I'll do is to restrict you to the confines of the ship. You're dismissed.

---

[14] Carl Gaddis sent this story and additional material to the VUMS before his death in 1993.

I saluted, did an about-face, and left his office. Halfway to my bunk I realized that everyone on board was "restricted." Heck, we were 300 miles from the coast!

When the ship docked in Norfolk, I was handed over to a brig sergeant at the Marine Base who informed me that I would have a room outside the brig, next to his own, and that I'd better be in that room, or inform him of where I would be, during my stay there. During the next ten days, I swept and swabbed decks, went to the PX, the movies, and ball games. There wasn't even a lock on my door.

During this time, I learned that most of the prisoners held there were being discharged with BCDs (bad-conduct discharges), DDs (dishonorable discharges), and furnished with cheap suits of civilian clothing to wear home. I dreaded the day of my release; I simply could not return home in disgrace.

That day came. My sergeant friend woke me before reveille and told me to go to the mess hall for chow, that I was going home at noon. Returning from the mess, I met the sergeant and got up the courage to ask him about my clothes. "On your bunk, Mac! I'm taking you to the back gate at noon, okay?"

What I found on my bunk was not a cheap suit from a pawn shop! It was my own set of "blues" a Marine friend on the *Wasp* had given me. At noon, my brig sergeant allowed me to dress in these handsome clothes, drove me to the back gate, gave me a $20 bill, and said, "Hit Highway 1 south, and hold your thumb up. Good luck, Mac!"

I was in Atlanta, Georgia, the next day. The rest is history. An ex-Marine hired me at a department store. I met some paratroopers from Fort Benning. The Japanese hit Pearl Harbor. I received an offer from the Marines to rejoin them and be a drill instructor at Parris Island. I chose the Army paratroops. I was injured on a night jump in Alabama, my nineteenth jump, and was taken off jump status because of a cracked hip bone. The Army then "learned" that I could read and write Japanese, so I was assigned to the Office of Strategic Services (OSS) in Hawaii to study advanced Japanese.

I took part in the battles at Leyte and Saipan, then went on to Japan. When I reenlisted in 1946, I moved from the OSS to G-2 Army intelligence and was sent to officers candidate school (OCS). I was a tech sergeant when I entered OCS and a captain when I came out and went back to what I was doing as a tech sergeant.

Later, I was on loan to the newly formed CIA and worked on civil-rights cases in the South. I was also stationed with the Third Army at Fort MacPherson and the Fourth Army at Fort Sam Houston.

All of this, plus a lot more, was my life in the military. From a high school dropout to a full bird (colonel) spy in twenty-five years. When you begin at 15, and wear the bird at 40, people believe you must have been in the Air Force. But no, I was an underage military bastard! But I made it, so God bless us all.

Carl Gaddis, while he was an Army captain, was ordered to apply for a position on the Atlanta Police Force. His tasks were to watch for subversive activities and civil-rights violations. In 1950, he was offered an appointment to the FBI and refused J. Edgar Hoover in person. For that, he was placed on Hoover's "Black List of Hell." After he retired from the Army, Carl became a golf pro and a stand-up comic. He referred to himself as "the clown prince of golf." Carl and his wife Frances lived in Ninety Six, South Carolina, where he died in 1993. He was the first South Carolina State Commander of the Veterans of Underage Military Service.

Walter F. Webber

Age 15 – Wisconsin National Guard
Age 16 – United States Army

I enlisted in the Wisconsin National Guard on 25 September 1939, not for patriotic reasons, but to help relieve my father's burden of feeding and clothing seven children. I felt that my drill pay would help pay for my school clothes and other needed incidentals.

> ..., I had the pleasure of sharing a couple of cans of beans with a cousin ...

Thirteen months later, on 15 October 1940, the entire 32nd "Red Arrow" Division, Wisconsin National Guard, was mobilized for federal service. I was 16½ years old. We were told that we would be on active duty for a period of one year. Little did we know that the year would stretch into five.

I was with the 120th Field Artillery of the 32nd Division when we left San Francisco, California, on 12 April 1942, destination unknown. We disembarked at Adelaide, South Australia, on 22 May 1942. Our first base was an abandoned military camp southeast of Adelaide in an area called Sandy Creek. Our first meal was served by Aussie cooks who forgot to remove the wool from the mutton before cooking it.

While I was at Sandy Creek, the infantry regiments were issued the M7 self-propelled gun carriers on which were mounted 105mm howitzers. Each artillery battalion had to transfer one gun crew to the infantry regiment they were supporting. As luck would have it, my section lost the coin toss, and I became an infantryman with the 128th Infantry Regiment.

In about the middle of June, the division was moved by truck and rail to a new base called Camp Cable, located seventy-five miles west of Brisbane, Queensland. At this time, we entered a very strenuous phase of jungle-warfare training. In mid-September, part of the 128th was moved to Townsville, Australia, and flown to Port Moresby, New

Guinea. The remainder of the regiment flew from Brisbane to Port Moresby a few days later, but all of our self-propelled howitzers remained at Camp Cable.

At Port Moresby, we were billeted in a makeshift staging area in preparation for movement over the Owen-Stanley Mountain Range to an abandoned airstrip in the vicinity of Wanigela Mission on Collingwood Bay, about sixty miles south of our objective, Buna, New Guinea. We were flown to Wanigela in Gooney Birds (C-47s), the workhorses of the Air Forces. We moved by foot from Wanigela to the objective area, arriving on 5 October 1942. Our life from then until the end of the Buna campaign was a living hell, not only because of the Japanese, but because of malaria, dysentery, and the lack of food and drinking water. For weeks I ran temperatures of 104° and 105°, but with no medicine available, there was not much we could do but carry on. After the Buna campaign was completed, the entire division returned to Australia for rest, regrouping, and retraining. Nearly 50% of the men in the division were replacements for casualties suffered during the Buna campaign.

On 2 January 1944, elements of our division made a beach landing at Saidor, New Guinea. The 128th Regiment was held in reserve and remained on Goodenough Island, about eighty sea-miles away. In February, the 128th was brought into the Saidor area to assist in a flanking movement that would force the Japanese into a pocket where they could be captured or annihilated.

On 22 April 1944, my regiment (the 128th) was one of two lead elements making an assault landing at Aitape, New Guinea. This campaign was as costly in human lives as was the Buna campaign, although the malaria, dysentery, and the water and food problems had been corrected. The campaign was completed in late July 1944, and the entire division was moved to Hollandia, New Guinea, for much needed R&R and refurbishing of clothing and equipment.

My unit was alerted for movement to Leyte in the Philippines in early November. We relieved units of the 24th Infantry Division at Limon, on the island of Leyte, around 20 November. Our objective was to recapture the Ormoc Highway and push the enemy off Corkscrew Ridge. On Thanksgiving Day of 1944, while passing through units of the 24th Division, I had the pleasure of sharing a couple of cans of beans with a cousin who was with the 24th. I hadn't seen him for ten years.

My career as an infantryman ended on 29 December 1944 at the conclusion of the Leyte campaign. My peacetime training was specifically in repairing and rebuilding the 75mm pack howitzer and the 105mm howitzer. Since the division ordnance company was short of qualified repairmen, I was tapped for the job. This was one Army job that I really loved.

The 32nd Division landed at Mabilao, Luzon, on 27 January 1945 and pushed east through San Manuel, San Nicolas, and Santa Maria toward the Caraballo Mountains. This "Villa Verde Trail" was to become the most difficult and the longest campaign in which the division was involved during World War II. My new unit, the 732nd Ordnance Company, trailed the division and worked around the clock to keep its weapons and vehicles running. The supply platoon of my unit was operating out of permanent buildings in the town of Santa Maria. On the evening of 26 May, a lone Japanese bomber slipped past our aircraft-warning system and bombed the supply platoon's buildings. Five men were killed and seventeen were wounded, two of which died later. The bombs completely destroyed the buildings and all of our repair parts and operating supplies. As a result of this action, the 732nd became the most decorated noncombat unit in World War II. The war ended for the 32nd Division on 2 September 1945 when the Japanese General Yamishita surrendered to the commanding general of the 32nd. I had survived 654 days of combat!

I went to Japan for a week, then was sent back to the States. I reported to Camp McCoy, Wisconsin, and was discharged on 22 October 1945, five years and seven days after I was inducted, supposedly for one year of training.

I returned to Chippewa Falls, Wisconsin, and lived with my parents while I tried to find suitable employment. I worked as a bricklayer's helper until I dropped a hod of brick while climbing a ladder. The bricks nearly hit the foreman, and he handed me a pink slip at the end of the day.

I started working for the federal government in the maintenance shops for Camp Williams and Camp Douglas, Wisconsin. The mission of the shop was to repair and maintain all of the equipment issued to units of the Wisconsin National Guard. I had to be a member of the Guard to hold this position, so I enlisted in the same unit that I served in during World War II, the 732nd Ordnance Company. The company was reorganized as a Guard unit in Tomah, Wisconsin.

In 1952, I attended officer candidate school at the Ordnance School, Aberdeen Proving Grounds, Maryland, and graduated as a second lieutenant. I returned to the Ordnance School and attended the Ordnance Officers Basic Course in 1955. I was promoted to captain on 1 April 1958 and assumed command of the 732nd Ordnance Company on 15 April 1958.

I was notified on 2 September 1961 that the 32nd Division, Wisconsin National Guard, was to be called to active duty due to the Berlin crisis and the Cuban missile crisis. We were activated on 15 October and shipped to Fort Lewis, Washington, for training. Twenty-one years before, when I was inducted into the Army, I was a lowly PFC with not a worry in the world. But this time, as a company commander with 210 officers and enlisted people to care for, I was a little nervous. The year went smoothly, and before we knew it, we were civilians again.

I received orders to report to the Ordnance School, Aberdeen Proving Grounds, Maryland, to attend the Ordnance Officers Career Course on 1 June 1964. This 6-month course was one of the highlights of my career. I was the only reserve officer in the class of sixty-three, most of whom were West Point graduates. I was promoted to Major in April 1966 and served in various staff positions. I was promoted to lieutenant colonel on 1 March 1970, and a month later, I assumed command of the 732nd Maintenance Battalion, Wisconsin National Guard. I served in several posts and then was assigned as State Maintenance Officer, a position I held until my retirement.

I retired from the Guard on 30 May 1979, and since my civilian job required that I be a member of the Guard, I also retired from that job.

Walt Webber was awarded the Bronze Star and the Soldier's Medal in addition to a number of campaign medals. He returned to Wisconsin after his release from the Army and worked in the state maintenance shop, Wisconsin National Guard. He combined his civilian work with his military duties until he retired from both jobs in 1979. Bored with retirement, Walt went to work as manager at a truck-refueling station for about three years, then retired for good. Walt and Mary, his wife of fifty years, live in Camp Douglas, Wisconsin. They have three daughters and five grandchildren. One daughter served in the Army.

Robert W. Leriche

Age 13 – United States Army Air Corps

I enlisted in the Army Air Corps on 18 October 1939 at Barksdale Field, Shreveport, Louisiana, eight days before my fourteenth birthday. I guess I joined for adventure. I don't remember what lies I

> *I don't remember what lies I told to get in, but I made it.*

told to get in, but I made it. It was hard keeping up with the grown men socially, but I was determined.

My first assignment was with Headquarters Squadron, 3rd Bomb Group, at Barksdale Field. Later, I went to Las Vegas, Nevada, for gunnery school. New groups were formed in 1940 and I was assigned to the 86th Squadron, 47th Bomb Group. The 3rd Bomb Group was

sent to the Pacific and the 47th to Europe, but I was sent to Manchester, New Hampshire, and assigned to the 8th Reconnaissance Squadron. We flew A-20s on coastal patrol. I was at the height of my glory.

In February 1944, I was finally sent to join my old outfit in Italy, the 86th Bomb Squadron of the 47th Bomb Group. We flew to Dakar, Africa, then to Casablanca and on to Naples, Italy. We were stationed at several locations in Italy, moved on to

Corsica, then to southern France. During my 25th mission, I caught some flak in my foot.

In February 1945, after completing sixty missions, I left for home and was sent to a convalescent hospital in Santa Ana, California. I had enough points, so I was discharged from the Army Air Forces. I reenlisted in 1946, served in Panama, and was discharged in 1949. I joined the reserves and was promoted later to master sergeant.

I was proud I served my country, proud then as well as now. I feel that my country owes me nothing. We didn't know why we were fighting when we were called upon to do so, but we did it anyway.

When the war was over, we simply took our mustering-out pay and our state bonus and said thanks. We didn't wait for someone to get us a job — we got our own. Though we lost many a man then, as men are lost in wars today, we didn't cuss our country out.

Bob Leriche was awarded the Air Medal with five Oak Leaf Clusters and the Purple Heart for wounds received in action. After his final discharge, he became an electrician. Bob did considerable research later and found that he was probably the youngest World War II veteran who was in the service before 1940. Bob and his wife Gladys had four children and two grandchildren. He lives in Campti, Louisiana.

√ **VUMS Note** ⇒ *C-rations and K-rations.* For readers with no military background who might be curious about the C-rations and K-rations mentioned often in these stories, here are some definitions taken from a dictionary of military terms:

C-rations were meals consisting of several prepared items, usually canned, issued when troops were out of range of field kitchens.

K-rations were emergency rations developed for U. S. forces in World War II to be used under combat conditions. Each ration contained three concentrated meals, separately packaged. The meals included bread or biscuits, canned meat, a powdered beverage, and a confection of some type.

More detailed, far more descriptive, and undoubtedly much more colorful definitions are available from the veterans who subsisted on them at times during their military service.

John B. Cramer

Age 15 – Colorado National Guard
Age 16 – United States Army

I was born in Ann Arbor, Michigan, on 6 December 1923. My father, who had been wounded in World War I while serving with the 32nd Division, was a student at the University of Michigan. We moved to Boulder, Colorado, in 1927

From then on I was known as the rookie who waved Maggie's drawers on the top kick.

after my father had accepted a position at the University of Colorado. As a student at Boulder High School, I was a little wild, but not mean and nasty, and was never in trouble with the authorities. My mother and father were excellent parents, and my childhood was rather uneventful.

In November 1939, with my parents' permission, I joined Company F, 157th Infantry, 45th Division of the Colorado National Guard. We encamped at Fort Logan, Colorado, during the Christmas season, and later we spent several weekends on the firing range at Camp George West. One weekend on the firing range, another young soldier and I were in the pits pulling targets. A request came over the field telephone for us to check the target we were working. We pulled the target, examined it, but didn't find a bullet hole. We raised the target and waved the red flag known as "Maggie's drawers," signifying a miss. Almost immediately we heard a voice barking over the phone, "This is Sergeant White (our first sergeant), check that target again." I replied over the phone, "I don't give a damn who it is, you missed." From then on I was known as the rookie who waved Maggie's drawers on the top kick.

As part of the general mobilization before World War II, the 45th Division was activated into federal service on 16 September 1940 for one year. During a discussion with my parents about whether I should request a discharge, my father said, "Well, if you want to listen to the music, you have to pay the band." I decided to stay with the outfit.

The day after we were activated, I was promoted to corporal. I didn't hold that rank very long. Looking back, I believe I was reduced in rank because of my immaturity.

We were sent to Fort Sill, Oklahoma. We participated in the Louisiana maneuvers, both in 1940 and in 1941. When Congress extended our active-duty period from one year to eighteen months, I decided that it was time to get out. I received an honorable "minority" discharge on 1 November 1941.

I returned to Boulder, Colorado, enrolled in high school, and graduated in August 1942. I enrolled in the University of Colorado for the fall quarter, was accepted in the NROTC program, and enlisted in the Naval Reserves. In January 1943, the war was in full swing. I was of legal age and just had to get back in the Army. Upon completion of the fall term, I withdrew from the University, was discharged from the Naval Reserves, and requested that the local Selective Service board draft me.

I was inducted in March 1943 and was assigned as a recruit to Company A, 310th Infantry Regiment, 78th Infantry Division, at Camp Butner, North Carolina. During basic training, an opening occurred and I was assigned as cadre; and on completion of basic, I was promoted to corporal. The mission of the 78th Division was to train recruits and transfers from other organizations in infantry drills and tactics. After thirteen weeks of basic and some advanced training, the recruits were sent overseas as replacements.

After maneuvers in Tennessee during January-February 1944, our division was sent to Camp Pickett, Virginia. During the spring, the division was brought up to strength and another round of training began. This time, the division was preparing for shipment to the European theater of operations. I had been promoted to staff sergeant by this time. We departed Camp Pickett on 14 October 1944 and arrived at Southhampton, England. We crossed the English Channel, debarking at Le Havre, France, on Thanksgiving Day, 1944.

The 78th Division was attached to the U. S. First Army and deployed in the Hurtgen Forest. We went into combat on 13 December and participated in the Battle of the Bulge from 16 December 1944 until 25 January 1945. I was wounded in a forest near Schmidt, Germany, on 6 February 1945. My good friend, Staff Sergeant Russell

B. McGirr, wrapped me up and took care of me until the regiment moved out. Russ often told me about his 6-year-old daughter and how he longed to see her again. I was picked up by litter bearers, evacuated from the front, operated on in a hospital in Liége, Belgium, transported to Paris, France, and then to a hospital in England.

I was discharged from the hospital and was on a 7-day leave in London on V-E Day. I returned to the 78th Division, which was then on occupation duty in Germany. It was there that I learned that my good friend Russ McGirr had been killed in action about three days after I had been wounded. I thought about his 6-year-old daughter and promised myself that I would contact her some day.

The 78th Division was scheduled to be redeployed to the Pacific. I was reclassified, sent to the 70th Division, then to the 3rd Division. The 3rd Division was composed of high-point men awaiting transport back to the States. I did not have enough points, so I was assigned to an outfit in Epernay, France. From there I went to a staging area, then home to Fort Logan, Colorado, where I was discharged on 5 December 1945.

John Cramer earned the Combat Infantryman Badge and was awarded the Purple Heart for wounds received in action. After his discharge from the Army, he returned to the University of Colorado where he finished his degree requirements in the School of Business in December 1948 and attended graduate school at the University of Chicago during the calendar year 1949. After working in a temporary position as a statistician for the U. S. Department of Labor for eight months, he accepted a permanent position with the Department of the Army at Fort Detrick, Maryland. In 1955, he accepted a position with Remington Rand, which merged with Sperry Gyroscope to become Sperry Rand, and later UNISYS. That job required a move to Minnesota. He returned to Maryland in 1959 and joined the Washington sales office of UNIVAC where he programmed applications for potential customers. In 1966, he resigned from UNIVAC and went into business for himself, writing computer programs on contract. After twelve years in his own business, he went to work for Metropolitan Area Transit Authority in Washington, D.C., then accepted a position as senior programmer with Bendix Field Engineering Corporation, Columbia, Maryland. He retired in

1988. John and Joyce, his wife of forty-three years, live in Davidsonville, Maryland. They have three daughters, a son, and six grandchildren. From time to time, John would remember his vow to contact the daughter of his friend Russ McGirr. In 1994, forty-nine years after his friend was killed, John and Joyce set out to locate the daughter. They found her in New England, had a very nice visit with her, and gave her pictures of her father's grave in Germany that they had taken during a trip to Europe in 1989.

√ **VUMS Note** ⇒ *No regrets!* Those two words express the feelings of so many underage veterans as they looked back at their experiences in the military. "I have never regretted..." and "I have no regrets..." and "I don't regret one moment..." were comments often found in their stories. They reflect an unwavering conviction that serving in the military so young was the right thing for them to do. Furthermore, answers to the question, "Would you do it over again?" confirm that conviction. "Hell, yes!" replied one; "Damn right, I would!" said another; and "Oh, yes, I would do it again — and again," wrote a third.

Donald J. Zitzelberger

Age 14 – United States Army

I have always been a lover of trains. My first real adventure with trains started in 1939 when I was 14 years old. Because of an unhappy home life, I packed my haversack,

grabbed all the coins in my dime bank ($8.00), threw on my only jacket with its broken zipper, and hopped a freight train in Cincinnati, Ohio. After spending several very cold nights in boxcars, I arrived in Sherman, Texas, on Sunday, 10 December 1939. It was my dream to join the CCC (Civilian Conservation Corps) located in a camp just outside of town.

I went to the police station where I believed that I could get a free bed for the night and perhaps even a free meal, but I didn't get either. Furthermore, the police officer informed me that I had to be a resident of Texas to join the CCC (which was false), but would I be interested in joining the Army? I was a tall 14-year-old, but with that statement I swear I grew right in front of that officer. He told me to go to the federal building the next morning and see the Army recruiting sergeant. I did as he said, and the first thing the recruiting sergeant did was to give me a meal ticket, which I immediately took to a restaurant for the best meal I'd had in ten days.

Although I was born on 10 January 1925 and would be 15 the next month, I told the recruiter that I was 17 in order to add some credibility to this deception. Then the real conspiracy started! The minimum age for joining the Army was 18, so the sergeant suggested that we move my birth date back to November, which would make me 18. He also suggested that I find someone to duplicate my father's signature. After all, it would take too much time to send mail to Cincinnati and wait for the response to return to his office. I told him that I was positive that my father would be very proud of my joining. He was 17 when he joined and served during World War I.

I arrived in Sherman, Texas, in a boxcar, but I left in style on an interurban train for Dallas, where I was sworn in on 12 December 1939. During the processing at Dallas, I had to correct another error. The recruiting sergeant had put down that I was a high school graduate, which qualified me for the Army Air Corps and the Signal Corps. I was very apprehensive because I knew that if I went into either of those branches, they would soon find out the truth that I only had a few months of first-year high school. I told the recruiters of the error and the mistake was corrected.

Another first-class train ride took me to Fort Benning, Georgia. I was assigned to Company B, 18th Infantry Regiment, 1st Infantry Division. We were on maneuvers for several months, preparing for the war that was coming. After six months with the 1st Division, I volunteered as a cadre to reactivate the 8th Division at Fort Jackson, South Carolina. I was promoted to corporal after being in the Army for seven months.

I was 16 years old by the time my father found me in early 1941. He was filled with pride, as I had predicted, when he learned from my company commander that I was being promoted to sergeant. He said, "You've got men under you my age — old enough to be your father."

I am nostalgic when I think of my train ride back to Cincinnati with my father on my first furlough. He asked me if I wanted to get out of the service, and I told him that I would probably make a career of "this man's Army."

We were sent to Hawaii shortly after the attack on Pearl Harbor. We were told that our original destination was the Philippines. I had been at Schofield Barracks about seven months when my father requested that I be discharged because of minority. His intent was to get me out of the infantry, but his request was denied because he had not signed my enlistment papers as Army regulations required at that time.

My outfit was scheduled to participate in the New Guinea campaign in 1943, but to my surprise, I was sent home with an honorable discharge, even though I was 18. After two months at home, I was inducted back into the Army and qualified for the Army Air Corps. (Actually it was the Army Air Forces, but I, like many others, didn't know the name had been changed until many years later.) I was accepted into the aviation cadet program and was sent to college for six months. My student squadron was on its way to preflight training when the Air Corps terminated the program and we reverted to enlisted status. However, I was accepted to infantry officers candidate school at age 19 and returned to Fort Benning via first-class train.

I was commissioned a second lieutenant and became a training officer at Camp Fannin, Texas. I did not make a career of "this man's Army," but was discharged in early October 1945.

Don Zitzelberger wanted to become a Catholic priest in a Trappist monastery. He persevered in the monastery for nine years, then left to marry and raise a family. He did not become a priest but became an ordained deacon as a married man. He worked as a pharmaceutical representative in California for twenty-eight years. He retired in 1989 after suffering a stroke. Don retired as a deacon but still finds fulfillment in reaching out to disadvantaged and at-risk children. Both Don and his wife Marsha volunteer at a domestic-crisis center in Sierra Vista, Arizona. They founded the Grandpa/Grandma Corps, a group of retirees who help in schools and spend time with children. Don and Marsha live in Sierra Vista. Don has four children and five grandchildren. He plans to take a first-class train ride on Amtrak in order to reminisce about his many train trips across this great country.

Curtis B. Goff

Age 16 – Florida National Guard
Age 16 – United States Army

My mother died twelve hours after I was born in McAlpin, Florida, on 21 January 1924. My aunt took care of me until my father remarried eighteen months later.

> *I was careful not to disclose that I had never seen a tank before.*

My father died when I was 14 years old, leaving my two sisters and me orphans. We were fortunate to have loving and caring uncles and aunts to take care of us. My dad's sister and her husband provided me a lovely home about four miles south of Lake City, Florida.

While attending the tenth grade at Columbia High School, I went to the National Guard Armory and enlisted in Company H, 124th Infantry. This was on 23 January 1940, two days after my sixteenth birthday. The company commander said to me, "Son, are you sure you are 18?" I replied truthfully, "My birthday was the day before yesterday." I was accepted with no further questions.

The National Guard met weekly for a couple of hours of drill and training. Our pay was $1.00 per week, and we were paid $1.00 per day during the two weeks of maneuvers during the summer. It was like an adventurous vacation with pay. There were rumors of war, but we all felt sure that France would stop any westward advance by Germany. History proved us wrong.

In the summer of 1940, we went by train to Louisiana for maneuvers, and in November 1940, our unit was inducted into the regular Army. The 124th Infantry was stationed at Camp Blanding, Florida, for more than a year before the attack on Pearl Harbor. I had been promoted to corporal and was the company clerk. After Pearl Harbor, the regiment was moved to Fort Benning, Georgia, and became part of the Infantry School for training officer candidates — "ninety-day wonders."[15]

The captain suggested that I attend the artillery school in Fort Sill, Oklahoma, and I could then be promoted to sergeant. I did that and I was promoted, but I lost my easy job of company clerk. The 124th Infantry was later moved to Fort Jackson, South Carolina, and continued training. In late 1943, we were shipped out in small groups as replacements to combat units in the Pacific and Europe. I felt fortunate to be sent to Europe. On my birthday, 21 January 1944, we left Newport News, Virginia, on a troopship, the USS *General Anderson*, for a 10-day trip to Oran, North Africa. From there we boarded a British ship for a cruise to Naples, Italy. We spent one night in tents in Naples, then boarded LCIs for a trip to the Anzio beachhead that had been established about ten days earlier. I was assigned to Cannon Company, 15th Infantry, 3rd Infantry Division. Our main weapons were M-8 light tanks. Being a replacement sergeant, I was designated tank commander of a crew that already had considerable combat experience in North Africa, Sicily, and southern Italy. As the youngest, least experienced, and a "greenhorn from the States," being tank commander was no easy task. I was careful not to disclose that I had never seen a tank before.

I learned fast, and battlefield experiences in which tanks were destroyed and our men killed and wounded provided a strong, unifying effect. Genuine, devoted, and abiding comradeship developed early in our unit and still exists more than a half century later.

On 5 June 1944, somewhere near Rome, we were engaged in a tank battle. When the action began, my tank crew consisted of three men, including me. Early on, the assistant gunner was hit and suffered a serious neck wound. After he was sent to an aid station, the assistant driver, William H. Smith, and I had the tank all to ourselves. Smith and I almost exhausted our full supply of ammunition within two hours. We lost Smith later in France.

After two weeks in Rome, we moved to the vineyards near Naples and prepared for the invasion of southern France on 15 August 1944.

---

[15] During World War II, graduates who completed a 3-month officer candidate school and were commissioned second lieutenants were frequently referred to as "ninety-day wonders."

We saw combat action in France and Germany and met the Russians in Salzburg, Austria. I declined a battlefield commission while I was in France. I had no desire for a military career.

I returned to the States and was discharged on 16 October 1945. At 22, I felt too old to return to high school for two years. Fortunately, Stetson University was accepting veterans under the GI Bill if they could pass the entrance examination.

My underage service in the Army was never mentioned while I was in college. After I finished school, I applied for a job with the federal government, using my true age. At the end of the 6-month probation period, I was asked to explain the discrepancy in my birth date. My discharge papers said I was born in 1922 and my birth certificate said 1924. I told the truth, and there was no problem. I really didn't lie in 1940, but I didn't tell the whole truth either. Now I know that I worried needlessly about being court-martialed. The statute of limitations has run out, and I have no regrets.

Curtis Goff and William Smith were each awarded a Silver Star for gallantry in action near Rome on 5 June 1944. Curtis attended Stetson University in Deland, Florida, receiving a B. S. in 1949 and a Jur.D. degree in 1950. He worked for the Internal Revenue Service at Orlando and Jacksonville for nearly five years, then opened his own law firm in Orlando, Florida. He continues to practice law in partnership with his daughter. Curtis and Hilda, his wife of forty-eight years, live in Winter Park, Florida. They have six children, all college graduates, and six grandchildren.

Wilson R. "Bill" Fischer

Age 14 – United States Naval Reserve
Age 15 – United States Marine Corps

I joined the U. S. Naval Reserve as a fireman striker in Newport News, Virginia, in February 1939, about a month before my fifteenth birthday. Later that year, we made a cruise on the USS *Texas* to the Caribbean, with a port of call in Boston, Massachusetts.

> *I was big for my age, and I guess I considered myself quite a big shot ...*

I was born in Ann Arbor, Michigan, on 23 March 1924. After my Naval Reserve experience, my parents sent me to a high school at the Gordon Military College in Barnsville, Georgia. On 15 March 1940, several of us cadets ran away and went to Macon, Georgia, to enlist in the Marine Corps. One other cadet and I were accepted, and we were sworn in on the same day. I don't recall what documents we presented, if any, and I assume that my mother signed for me. I was big for my age, and I guess I considered myself quite a big shot with the Naval Reserve and the military school experience behind me.

I was sent to Parris Island, South Carolina, for boot camp, then to the Marine Guard detachment at the Naval Gun Factory in Washington, D.C. From there I went to the guard detachment at the Naval Air Station, Anacostia, Maryland. In September 1940, I was assigned to the Marine detachment at the Naval Academy at Annapolis, Maryland. I served there until I was accepted for sea school in Portsmouth, Virginia, in November 1941.

After sea school, I was assigned to the Marine detachment on the USS *Idaho*. I spent Thanksgiving Day on a train to Boston to join naval personnel who were also assigned to the *Idaho*. We went to Newfoundland on a supply ship, but when we arrived, the *Idaho* wasn't there. Our group was split up and put on several destroyers that were scheduled to go to Iceland. Before sailing, we were pulled off the destroyers and put on a submarine tender that was returning to Rhode Island. We were en route on 7 December 1941. Upon landing in Rhode Island, we were immediately sent to Norfolk, Virginia, where the *Idaho* was in dock for repairs and refitting. We were right back where we had started three months before.

I stayed aboard the *Idaho* until late 1943, after the Aleutian Islands campaign. The *Idaho* was sent to Bremerton, Washington. I was in a small group that was transferred to San Diego. Some of the group went right back overseas, but I was lucky and was transferred to a field medical-training battalion at Camp Pendleton, California, and stayed there until I was discharged on 24 October 1945.

During the last five to six months that I was at Camp Pendleton, while off duty, I was able to work part time for the old Railway Express Agency in Santa Monica, California, as a deliveryman. After I was discharged I went to work for the Railway Express full-time.

Bill Fischer worked his way up from driver to division supervisor in charge of all Railway Express operations in Southern California, Arizona, and New Mexico (230 offices). He left Railway Express in 1959, moved to San Diego, and worked for Mission Van & Storage until 1980, at which time he became executive vice-president. He was vice-president of marketing for United Van Lines until 1988 when he planned to retire and move to Tokyo so his wife could take care of her aging mother. The United Van Lines agent in Tokyo found out he was there and talked him into working for the company as director of foreign services. In 1992, Wilson and his wife Kazumi returned to the United States, lived in San Jose, California, for a time, then moved to Desert Hot Springs, California, where they make their home.

Calvin W. Mason

Age 16 – Texas National Guard

I was born in Waldron, Arkansas, on 23 September 1923. My family moved to west Texas when I was about 4 years old, and in 1935 we moved to Mineral Wells, Texas. My father died in 1939, and

> *I thought that being a soldier was the greatest thing in the world.*

things went from bad to worse. I sold papers, mowed lawns, and did anything else I could do to help my mother make us a living.

I tried to get into the CCC (Civilian Conservation Corps), but they had a waiting list. However, F Troop, 124th Cavalry Regiment of the 56 Cavalry Brigade, Texas National Guard, was based in Mineral Wells. I talked my mother into signing a paper stating that I was 17 years old, and I enlisted in F Troop on 1 April 1940.

F Troop drilled on Sunday morning, once a month. We got paid every three months. I thought that being a soldier was the greatest thing in the world. In June 1940, we went to Louisiana for three weeks of maneuvers with the Army. That was the first time I had been away from home, and it sure seemed like a long time.

On 18 November 1940, President Roosevelt called all National Guard and Reserve units for a year of active duty. I had been in the Guard for seven and a half months and was promoted to PFC just before we were federalized. My pay was $36.00 per month. I never drew the $21.00 per month that many of the guys did during World War II.

Since we had a lot of new men who had enlisted to get their year in, we were sent to Fort Bliss, Texas, for basic training. The entire brigade lived in tents in the sand outside of Fort Bliss proper. The 1st Cavalry Division, minus its 5th and 12th Regiments, was stationed at Fort Bliss. The 5th Regiment was at Fort Clark, Texas, and the 12th Regiment was at Fort Ringgold, Rio Grande City, Texas, and at Fort

Brown, Brownsville, Texas. The brigade headquarters was at Fort McIntosh, Laredo, Texas. The 124th Regimental Headquarters and the 1st Squadron went to Fort Brown, Brownsville, Texas and the 2nd Squadron went to Fort Ringgold. Our sister regiment, the 112th, went to Fort Clark. Men in the 5th and 12th Regiments were not happy because they had been in one place for many years. Many of the men had married local women, and the forts on the border were their homes. We spent almost the whole war on the Mexican border. I finally wound up in the 63rd Infantry Division and went to France and Germany. I was introduced to combat at the ripe old age of 21.

I reenlisted in June 1946 and went to Italy where I was assigned to the 351st Infantry Regiment of the Trust Brigade. We manned the Morgan Line after the 88th Infantry Division was sent home. We were the only reason the Yugoslavs didn't take over the city and state of Trieste, Italy.

December 1947 found me at Fort Bragg, North Carolina, with the 82nd Airborne Infantry Division. In June 1950, I was sent to Fort Campbell, Kentucky, and assigned to the 11th Airborne Division to help fill the 187th Airborne Regimental Combat Team (ARCT) which was preparing for duty in Korea.

I made two combat jumps with the 187th ARCT in Korea. I returned to the States in 1951 and was assigned to the 503rd Regiment of the 11th Airborne Division at Fort Campbell. In 1955, I went back to Japan for a year, serving with the 508th Regimental Combat Team at Camp Wood. I returned to Fort Campbell in 1956 and joined the 101st Airborne Division. From 1961 to 1962 I was assigned to the 505th Airborne Battle Group in Germany.

Upon my return from Germany, I was again assigned to the 187th ARCT and served with them for a year. My last assignment was with the 501st Airborne Regiment, 101st Airborne Division, at Fort Campbell.

I retired from the Army at Fort Campbell in November 1965, after serving twenty-five years. I wouldn't take anything for my time in the service, but I don't think I would want to do it again.

Calvin Mason earned the Combat Infantryman Badge during World War II and received his second Badge for service in Korea. He was awarded the Bronze Star for valor and two Purple Hearts for wounds received in action. After his retirement from the

Army, he went to work for American Enka Corporation (a rayon, nylon, and polyester plant) in Morristown, Tennessee. He retired on Social Security in 1985. He now travels, attends military reunions, and visits relatives in a number of states. Calvin and his wife Launa live in Morristown, Tennessee. They have a combined family of six children.

√ VUMS Note ⇒ By hook or crook. Although a few veterans who enlisted underage managed to do so completely on their own, most had to have help from others, including family members, recruiters, and friends. Sometimes strangers were paid to stand in as "fathers."

A simple lie about age did the trick sometimes, but more often, the lie had to be verified by parents and documentation, or both. The tactics used to convince parents to sign the necessary papers varied from gentle persuasion to outright threats of running away forever. Faced by a highly determined youngster, a parent would finally give in — most with misgivings, but some with a sigh of relief. One mother altered the birth certificate of her 15-year-old recalcitrant son herself, and firmly suggested that he join the Navy.

The methods used to deal with the required documentation reveal great determination and ingenuity. Birth certificates and baptismal certificates were cleverly altered, the required signatures were artfully duplicated, and well-meaning adults were conned into helping out. Recruiters helped mostly by not asking too many questions and by conveniently "looking the other way." At times they suggested ways to fool the system, like telling underweight applicants to eat a lot of bananas so they could meet weight requirements of the physical exam. For the most part, it was a combination of tactics that enabled youngsters to circumvent the age regulations. One veteran summed it up nicely when he was asked how he managed to enlist underage: "By hook or crook!"

Donald W. Hansen

Age 15 – Washington National Guard
Age 16 – United States Army

In September 1939, a few months before my sixteenth birthday, I was watching a National Guard drill in my hometown of Everett, Washington. A

"You sure look old enough, so why not join?"

first lieutenant standing nearby came over to me and asked if I would like to join. I told him that I was not old enough. He said, "You sure look old enough, so why not join?" So we went to the company clerk, I filled out the papers, and signed up right there and then. At no time did anyone ask my age.

Drills were on Monday night and payday was every three months. On my first payday I received $21.00. I took $20.00 and bought my first pair of eyeglasses. Our unit was the 161st Infantry of the 41st Infantry Division, Washington National Guard. We went to camp during the summer of 1940 and participated in maneuvers.

On 16 September 1940, exactly two months before my seventeenth birthday, the 41st Division was activated, and I was now in the Army. We went to Camp Murray, Washington, where we lived in squad tents. The winter of 1940-41 was very miserable. Ninety percent of our unit caught the flu. It wasn't until the spring of 1941 that we moved into barracks and had better living conditions.

I considered applying for a minority discharge, but I had six months in before I obtained proof of my age. Since I had completed half of the required year of service, I decided to stay in, get my year over with, then go back to school. The 41st Division was scheduled to go to the Philippines in the fall of 1941, but my year was up and I was discharged on 17 September 1941.

In February 1943, I went back in the Army and was assigned to the 69th Infantry Division, which was then forming at Camp Adair, Oregon. In April 1943, we spent six days on a troop train traveling to Camp Shelby, Mississippi. We were called the BBB (Bolte's Bivouacking Bastards).

In the fall of 1944, we departed for England, landing at Southhampton. We went to Winchester a short time later, then across the English Channel where we participated in the Battle of the Bulge. I was standing in a chow line in Remis, France, after that battle, when a classmate from home spotted me. We spent a couple of days together visiting and reminiscing.

After the war was over, we were stationed in Heidelberg, Germany. A buddy had relatives in Germany, so he and I arranged for some time off, obtained a jeep, and went looking for them. We found his grandmother and some of his aunts in Coblenz. He had a nice visit with them and was brought up to date on all the family news that was known at the time.

I returned to the States in late 1945 and was discharged in February 1946.

Don Hansen was a fireman for the city of Everett, Washington, for twenty-six years and owned and operated a tavern for eighteen years. After retiring, Don and Lucille, his wife of 49 years, built a home on Whidbey Island, Washington. They have five children, fifteen grandchildren and eight great-grandchildren, with three more on the way.

Carl E. Goodman, Sr.

Age 16 – United States Army

I was born in Groveton, Texas, on 25 January 1924. My parents divorced when I was 3 years of age. My mother remarried when I was 5 to a wonderful man whom I came to know and respect

> **We were not allowed to associate with the regular troops in any way.**

as my father. My formative years were spent in the oil fields of Texas, Oklahoma, and New Mexico. During this time I was not in the same school for an entire term because we followed my stepfather's work. When I was 15, my stepfather, a driller, was severely injured and was no longer able to work in the oil fields, so we moved from New Mexico to Texas to pursue farming and ranching.

I was in high school by this time and had to walk three miles to catch a bus for a 19-mile ride each way, every day. I was very interested in sports, but I couldn't participate because of the travel distances and time which didn't allow for practice. At the beginning of my junior year in September 1940, I was very bored with rural life, and the Army seemed to be the place for me. It required a tremendous amount of persuasion, but my mother finally agreed to sign the consent form for my enlistment. Now that I am a parent, I can readily understand her reluctance to sign, since it was evident the United States would be at war soon.

I was sworn into the Army on 23 September 1940 at the 23rd Infantry Quadrangle, Fort Sam Houston, Texas. After the swearing-in ceremony was over, I was transported to Dodd Army Airfield, which had just been converted to the U. S. Army Recruit Reception Center, for four weeks of basic training. I was assigned to D Company, which only existed on paper at that time. The recruits were required to erect 8-man tents for housing and to perform all the tasks necessary to organize the unit. This was accomplished while we were still in civilian clothes.

The first night brought a typical Texas thunderstorm with heavy rain and high winds. By morning, not a tent was left standing, and we were forced to start all over again. Four weeks later, on 24 October 1940, we graduated from basic training. Eight of us spent another four weeks with the 12th Field Artillery Battalion, 2nd Infantry Division, Fort Sam Houston, to get us ready for full duty. During those four weeks, we were quartered in 8-man tents, four men to a tent, on the parade ground across the street from the regular barracks. We were not allowed to associate with the regular troops in any way. We ate at a separate table, used the latrine at a scheduled time, and could not enter the permanent buildings at any time unescorted, or even talk to anyone outside of our group. This caste system would not be lifted until we were ready for regular duty.

The next several months were spent with routine training, but I was able to attain the rank of private first class with a fifth class specialist rating, and I received the equivalent of corporals' pay, $42.00 per month. This was prior to the onset of World War II. I did not know it at the time, and didn't learn about it until after the war, but the Army knew that I was underage and had written to my mother. They told her that they would discharge me if she wanted them to, but I could stay in if it was all right with her. I remember her asking me many times, "How do you like the Army?" I loved it, of course, and told her so. She never tried to get me out.

On 7 December 1941, I was with my unit on temporary duty at Fort Sill, Oklahoma, supporting the Artillery School Gunnery Department. We were immediately alerted for return to our home station to await further orders. Training was intensified, and cadres were being formed to activate reserve divisions. I was assigned to help form the 102nd Infantry Division at Camp Maxey, Texas, in September 1942. My unit was Headquarters Battery, 381st Field Artillery Battalion, which had been commanded by Captain (later President) Harry S. Truman during World War I. I served in combat in Germany with this unit.

I returned home after V-E Day and was discharged from the Army, but I was unable to find adequate employment. I reenlisted in the Army with plans for making it a career. The next seventeen years were very active and rewarding. I was fortunate to see service in the military police, the signal corps, ordnance, and the armored infantry. I served two combat tours in Korea, the first time with the 512th Military Police Company in Pusan and the second time with the 51st Criminal Investigation Detachment based in Seoul. I was overseas for a total of thirty-one months.

I was serving as a recruiter at the time I retired from the Army on 1 July 1962. I finished high school while I was in the Army, attended college, and completed many highly technical courses. Would I do it again? You better believe it!

Carl Goodman earned the Combat Infantryman Badge and was awarded the Bronze Star for valor while in combat in Germany. After his retirement from the Army, he worked at McClellan Air Force Base, Sacramento, California, and at Travis Air Force Base, Fairfield, California, as a refrigeration and air-conditioning engineer, and later in the mechanical-engineering section. He retired from the civil service in 1979 and returned to Texas in 1994. Carl and his wife Glenda live in Mesquite, Texas. They have a combined family of three children and five grandchildren.

Spencer B. Jackson

Age 15 – United States Army

I always wanted to join the Army. My grandfather was in the Spanish American War, and my father was in World War I. As a civilian, I trained with the National Guard in my hometown of Beckley, West Virginia, where I was born on 28 October 1925. By

... they informed me that I had captured a German general and his staff.

the time I was 15 years old, I was ready to enlist. I told the recruiters that I was 18 and convinced my parents to sign for me. I joined the Army on 13 December 1940 and left that night for Fort Thomas, Kentucky, with a group of ninety-three men. I was sworn into the Army the next day, 14 December 1940, one month and eighteen days after my fifteenth birthday. My dream had come true; I was now a soldier in the U. S. Army.

We were given GI haircuts and we drew our clothing. Of course, the clothing didn't fit very well. We traded items with each other until we finally had uniforms that fit reasonably well, but we sure looked like a bunch of sad sacks. We had been issued a $2.00 canteen book, so we went to the PX. Everybody ordered a beer, but I ordered a coke. I had never drunk very much liquor – well, maybe a little of my father's home brew or a sip or two of my grandfather's

moonshine. Anyway, at the PX the men with me said, "You drink beer with us, or you are not one of us." I thought I would show them, so I drank two 20-ounce glasses of beer. They almost had to carry me back to the barracks. I was given the nickname "Two Beer Jackson." That name followed me throughout my Army career. In combat, my code name was "Two Beer."

I was sent to Fort Benjamin Harrison, Indiana, where I was assigned to Company D, 11th Infantry Regiment. From there we went to Fort Custer, Michigan, for six weeks of recruit drill. That was before basic training as we know it today was started. Our sergeants were World War I veterans, and they were hell on us. They quickly made soldiers out of us.

I spent about eight and one-half months in the States, training and participating in maneuvers in Illinois, Wisconsin, and Tennessee. In August 1941, we were told that we were going overseas and that draftees couldn't go, so all regular Army men were transferred to the 10th Infantry Regiment, and all men who were drafted were assigned to the 11th Infantry Regiment. One day while we were standing inspection, the regimental commander, Colonel Robert Bell, and the executive officer, Lieutenant Colonel Breckenridge, stopped in front of me. Colonel Bell gave me a hard, stern look and said, "How old are you, soldier?" I replied, "Eighteen years of age, sir." He said, "What year were you born?" I replied, "1922, sir." He looked at me again, turned to Colonel Breckenridge and said, "Check this man's age." It was hot and I was sweating and nervous because I was only 15 years old. Colonel Breckenridge took out his notebook, asked my name, rank, serial number, home address, and my mother's and father's names. Then he showed me his notebook and asked me if everything was correct. He had written, "Don't worry, no investigation."

I met Colonel Breckenridge on the company street the next day. He asked me why I wanted to stay in the Army when I could have gotten out. I told him that I wanted to be the first in our family to go overseas. He looked at me with a grin and said, "I have had a lot of men lie like hell to me to get out of the Army, but you are the first one to lie like hell to stay in. I admire any young man with your courage." He saluted me and walked away. The colonel later became commander of our regiment. He retired in 1962 as a major general.

We boarded ship and sailed on 5 September 1941. We guessed that our destination was Iceland, and we were right. We spent twenty-three months in Iceland, training, working dock details, and building roads. After 7 December 1941, German planes flying from Norway would frequently pay us a visit. They would drop a few bombs and strafe some of the roads with 20mm cannon and machine-gun fire. We would shoot at them with our machine guns, M-1s, and Model 1903 rifles.

We sailed for England in August 1943, stayed there for three months, then went to northern Ireland. We trained for the Normandy invasion for eight months, and on D-Day, 6 June 1944, we landed on

Utah Beach. We took Hill 183 with only light casualties. When Operation Cobra started, we were assigned to the Third Army under General George S. Patton. After we broke out of Normandy, we went wild. We had the Germans on the run. We took Ardvorrhis, a town that cut off the Cherbourg and Brest Peninsulas, and trapped a lot of Germans.

The Germans made two heavy counterattacks. The artillery, tanks, infantry, and the Air Forces stopped them. The German losses were so great that what was left of their forces took off running with Patton's Third Army on their tails. We were headed straight for Paris, but the high command held us back so that the Free French could take the city. We crossed the Seine River at Fontainbleau, bypassed the city, and took a number of small towns in the outskirts of Paris.

We were moving up a street in a small town when several shells hit, and I ducked into a basement for cover. I started looking around to see if anyone else was in there, and to see if I could find a bottle of booze. I saw some light at the far end of the basement and thought that French civilians might be taking cover there. I eased the door open with my rifle, and to my surprise, there were seven German soldiers sitting around a table looking at maps and papers. When they looked up, they saw that I had my M-1 rifle pointed right at them. One who could speak English said, "How did you get in here?" I ignored the question, told them to stand up and drop their pistol belts, and to put their hands over their heads. I marched them out in the street and turned them over to some other guys who were taking prisoners to the rear.

I went back in the room where I had captured the Germans to get some of the booze they left behind. I was about half loaded when two majors and a captain walked in. They were Army intelligence officers, and as they went over the papers and maps, they informed me that I had captured a German general and his staff. I didn't think much more about it; all I had on my mind was staying alive, women, and booze. Two days later, the CO called me in to his command post and informed me that he had put me in for the Silver Star.

We were held up from September to November because we were short of supplies. In the meantime, several of my buddies and I captured a German payroll, so we decided to go back to Paris for a 72-hour R&R. Four of us went over the back fence, dressed in fatigues, carrying our M-1 rifles and belts full of ammo. We proceeded to get drunk and tried to go into the Red Cross club. The man at the door said that we couldn't come in unless we were dressed in ODs with khaki ties. We told him that we were going to buy the place and fire him. Like fools, we flashed a lot of French money. When the man asked for our passes, we told him that we didn't need passes, that our rifles and our money were our passes. We left the place with French girls on each arm. Soon, it seemed that they were holding an MP convention, there were so many of them looking for us. They caught us, loaded us on a truck, and sent us back to the 10th Infantry. We thought that we would be court-martialed and lose our stripes, but we got off with a warning that one more foul-up and we would spend the next ten years in Leavenworth, Kansas. You know, there is one medal I got that I really didn't deserve — the Good Conduct Medal!

After we were replenished with gas, ammunition, food, and new boots, we took off again. We captured Verdun, where one of the big battles of World War I took place, and moved on to Metz, France. Metz was one of the most fortified cities in Europe. We suffered 30% casualties while taking that city. I was wounded by shrapnel from a "bouncing Betty," an antipersonnel mine. After Metz, we took Sauerbrecken, Germany. On 14 December 1944, the Germans counterattacked in what soon was known as the Battle of the Bulge. Patton pivoted most of the Third Army and moved toward Bastogne. After that setback, we pushed through the Siegfried Line and crossed the Rhine River. When I say "we," I am referring to the 10th Infantry Regiment, 5th Infantry Division, Third Army. We moved through Austria and into Czechoslovakia.

In early May 1945, I took a twelve-man patrol along with an artillery spotter and dug in on the top of a mountain. We could see for miles. On the morning of 8 May 1945, we saw a large German force moving into a big field. The artillery spotter called back for fire, requesting five rounds from all guns. As he was talking on the phone, a surprised look came over his face and he dropped the phone and said, "The war is over — the Germans have surrendered." We shouted with joy, but we still couldn't believe it. We went down to the German camp, still leery. A German officer told us we could have anything we wanted, that everything belonged to the victors. I took several pistols that I brought home to my father.

I spent a couple of months on occupation duty, then returned to the States. I had been overseas for three years, nine months, and twenty-three days. I was discharged from the Army on 6 July 1945 and went back to my hometown, Beckley, West Virginia. The only jobs that paid good money were in the coal mines. I had been to hell and beyond on top of the ground, so I didn't want to do it again underground. After about three weeks, I knew that I couldn't hack civilian life, so I reenlisted in the Army and stayed in until I retired on 14 December 1970 at the rank of master sergeant.

I am very proud to be an underage veteran, part of a unique group, a vanishing breed. We went into the military when we were too young to shave, drink, or vote, willing to fight and die for our great country. There is only one thing I regret: I gave more of my time to the Army and work than I did to my wife and children.

Spencer Jackson was awarded the Silver Star for capturing a German general and his staff. He earned the Combat Infantryman Badge and the Bronze Star with Oak Leaf Cluster, and received the Purple Heart for wounds received in action. He went to work for the Baltimore Gas and Electric Company, Baltimore, Maryland, after his retirement from the Army. He was involved in a near-fatal accident ten years later and was told by doctors that he couldn't work any more. But they didn't tell him that he couldn't do volunteer work. He has been a volunteer at the Baltimore Veterans Administration Hospital for nearly fourteen years and at the hospital-based Home Care Program where he has been honorary staff-assistant for nearly thirteen years. At this writing he has completed 30,962 hours (and counting) of volunteer work. He has received more than fifty awards in recognition of his outstanding record, including the Secretary's Volunteer Service Award from the Secretary of Veterans Affairs, and a Governor's Citation from the governor of the state of Maryland. He was also Nationwide Volunteer of the Year for the Department of Veterans Affairs in 1990-91. Spencer lives in Baltimore, Maryland. He has five children, eleven grandchildren, and five great-grandchildren. His wife is deceased.

James W. Potter

Age 15 – United States Army

I was born in Goshen, Virginia, on 3 June 1925, but we were living in Staunton, Virginia, when three underage country boys, including me, thought they were grown men and decided to join the Army. I was 15 years old, so I changed my birth date to 3 January 1923, and my two friends also changed their birth dates. My father signed my enlistment papers. The recruiter told me that when I brought my enlistment papers back to the office, I should eat a lot of bananas along the way because I was underweight.

> *... one of the men saw the rising-sun logo on an aircraft.*

The three of us were sworn in on 5 April 1941. At that time, we had a choice of where we could be assigned. We chose the Army Engineers at Schofield Barracks, Oahu, Hawaii. Most of the barracks at Schofield were referred to as "Quadrangle Square," and were located next to Wheeler Field, a fighter airfield.

On the morning of 7 December 1941, breakfast was just about over. I was 16 years old and on KP. Just as I walked out of the mess hall to holler out, "Last call for breakfast," there was an explosion at Wheeler Field, and black, oily smoke arose from that direction. I looked toward Wheeler Field and thought that we would be going on a training exercise. But it couldn't be that, because we used flour to simulate explosions in training, and this didn't look like flour. I ran back into the kitchen and shouted, "There's black smoke, aircraft flying, debris flying, something's wrong!" All of us went back outside and one of the men saw the rising-sun logo on an aircraft. We realized then that it was a real attack by Japanese planes.

The strafing started about that time. The planes would drop their bombs first and then return to strafe. They would pass right over our barracks on their way to Wheeler Field. We had to wait for the arms officer to arrive with the key before we could get our weapons. As the Japanese planes came in to strafe, we would run to the other side of the barracks. Wheeler Field was a big ball of black, oily smoke coming from the damaged aircraft and the bombed fuel-storage areas. We looked off to the right a little, and we could see a big cloud of black smoke in the Pearl Harbor area and at Hickam Field where the bombers were based.

On 1 October 1941 the 24th and 25th Infantry Divisions were activated from the Hawaii Department at Schofield Barracks. I was assigned to the 24th Division. We participated in the Dutch New Guinea campaign, capturing the airfield at Hollandia in April 1944. Our division landed at San Pedro Bay, Leyte, Philippine Islands, on 20 October 1944. A short time after we had secured the beach, General Douglas MacArthur made his well-publicized return to the Philippines by wading to the shore.

I left my unit in the Philippines in January 1945 but it was March before I arrived in the States. I was discharged on 26 September 1945 at the Army Medical Center in Washington, D.C. I attended business school for a time, then reenlisted in the Army and was sent to Germany. I was discharged for the second time in 1955.

Jim Potter attended Dunsmore Business College, Staunton, Virginia, after his discharge in 1945. After his second tour in the Army, he became an agent with National Airlines in Newport News, Virginia, and later transferred to Orlando, Florida. Jim and Mary, his wife of thirty-five years, live in Orlando, Florida. They have one daughter and one grandson.

Richard H. Johnson

Age 12 – New Hampshire National Guard
Age 14 – United States Navy

I was born in Claremont, New Hampshire, on 13 December 1928 and joined the New Hampshire National Guard at age 12. In 1941, the government had a requirement that a minimum number of men be on the rolls in a National Guard unit in order to keep the

I went from a 16-year-old juvenile to a man in a matter of seconds.

armories open. Recruits of legal age were hard to come by, so many of the units did not check the ages of enlistees very carefully. Taking advantage of this situation, I joined the Guard in June 1941. It was fun playing cowboys and Indians with real rifles and blank

ammunition. When the Guard was federalized just before the war, they wouldn't let the younger ones go. I guess they thought that we were old enough to be on the rolls in peacetime, but we were not old enough to go to war.

I didn't look at it that way. After the Guard left, I stayed in school for awhile, but I wanted to go to war! In 1943, I changed the date on my birth certificate to read 1925 instead of 1928 and proceeded to try to enlist. I tried both the Army and the Marines, but they both told me, "Go on home and grow up." Finally, I tried the Navy. I showed the recruiter my altered birth certificate. He took it and checked something on the papers he was filling out, then said, "You should destroy this, it could get you in trouble." I asked, "Won't I need it again?" He said, "No. I have already checked off that you had it." He showed me where he had checked on the papers, and as soon as I left his office, I destroyed the certificate.

I was sworn into the Navy on 8 November 1943 and sent to the Naval Training Center at Newport, Rhode Island, for boot training. During training, a member of my company who was from my hometown told the authorities that I was only 14. I was told to report to the OD (officer of the day). He told me that I would be court-martialed because I was underage and had used a forged birth certificate to get in. My attorney, a commander, told me that I would not be allowed to remain in the Navy, but when I appeared before the court-martial board, I was to say that I loved the Navy and wanted to stay in. He also said that I would be returned to active duty in the Navy the day before my eighteenth birthday and serve until one day before my twenty-first birthday, a so-called minority enlistment.

I appeared before the court-martial board and was told that upon completion of boot camp, I was to take my seabag to the brig where I would be issued civilian clothing and released from the Navy.

After graduating from boot camp, I reported to the brig as I had been ordered to do. I told them my name, but they couldn't find it on their list. They told me to report to the outgoing unit and maybe they could help me. I went to that office and found that they did not know what to do with me either. They told me to hang around and they would find out what was going on.

A few days later, they told me that someone from the Office of the Secretary of the Navy had contacted my parents and discussed a transcript of my court-martial hearing with them. It had been decided that I would be allowed to remain in the Navy and would be sent to Navy schools, but would not be allowed to go overseas until one day before my eighteenth birthday. I was given orders to report to the Norfolk Naval Hospital for training in the hospital corpsman school in Portsmouth, Virginia. From Portsmouth I went to the Naval Land Forces Equipment Depot in Norfolk, Virginia.

I requested sea duty, but they just laughed at me. On a weekend pass I went home to Claremont, New Hampshire, and stayed AWOL for ten days. When I returned to the base, I was given another hearing and sentenced to ten days in the brig on bread and water in solitary confinement. On the ninth day I was taken to see my commanding officer. He told me that I was just a kid and was headed for trouble. He wanted to know what he could do to help me. I told him I wanted to be on a ship and in combat. He gave me the names of three ships that he was to transfer personnel to, and asked me which one I wanted. I picked a brand new fleet oiler, the USS *Taluga* (AO-62).

The next day when I reported aboard the *Taluga*, I was the happiest teenager in the world. I was assigned to the deck force. My watch and battle station was a 40mm gun.

In August 1944, we left Norfolk and headed for the South Pacific. While we were still off the east coast of the United States, we were chased by German submarines. We went through the Panama Canal, stopped at Pearl Harbor and the Marshall Islands, then went on to Ulithi. On the way we listened to Tokyo Rose. One day she specifically mentioned the *Taluga*, telling us that we were all going to die. We all laughed about that, but we did wonder how she knew the ship's name.

When we reached Ulithi, I was made coxswain of a 50-foot motor launch, which was the liberty launch for the ship. I was in charge of three crew members and was just 15 years old! We left Ulithi with the Third fleet for a time, then returned to the anchorage. The ship anchored alongside us, the USS *Mississinewa* (AO-59), was sunk by a manned torpedo. Two manned suicide torpedoes had been launched from a Japanese submarine. One had been sunk by a destroyer-escort, but the other managed to get into the anchorage and hit the *Mississinewa*. I watched the crew swimming in the burning oil until they were all gone. Later, while we were at sea, a tanker alongside us exploded. I was on watch when it happened and could see a hole in the ship large enough to drive a train through.

In early 1945, we were beside the USS *Hancock* in Ulithi when she was hit by a kamikaze. Another ship in our group was also hit by a kamikaze. During the invasion of Okinawa, we were subjected to numerous raids by kamikazes, some in groups as large as one hundred aircraft. Suicide boats were always trying to ram us.

Our turn came on 16 April 1945. We were steaming off the coast of Okinawa carrying 5,000,000 gallons of fuel and a large supply of ammunition when a kamikaze slammed into the *Taluga*'s forward gas tanks. This caused a massive explosion. I was at my battle station twenty feet from where the plane first hit. I went from a 16-year-old juvenile to a man in a matter of seconds. The general-quarters alarm was sounded, and shortly thereafter, the order to abandon ship was given. I just didn't go. I stayed aboard to help fight the fires and man the guns in the event of another attack. I preferred to stay on board and take my chances rather than to jump in the water. We were able to extinguish the fires, and the ship stayed afloat. We went back to

Ulithi and tied up alongside the USS *Jason* while our ship was repaired. We returned to the fleet and took part in the attacks on the home islands of Japan.

After the war we went to China, Korea, and Russia, then back to the States. I was assigned to the USS *Statler* after I returned from leave. I had tears in my eyes when I left the *Taluga*. She fought in twenty major battles in World War II, the Korean War, and in the war in Vietnam. She was decommissioned in 1989. I had asked for the *Taluga* and for combat; I learned to love both the ship and the Navy. I had gone aboard the *Taluga* as an underage sailor and came off as a man with the knowledge of what hell war could be.

I was discharged, but I soon returned to the Navy. I served on a seaplane tender, the USS *Timbalier* (AVP-54), and a barracks ship, the USS *Colleton* (APB-36). During the Korean War, I was on the destroyer-escort USS *Heyliger* (DE-510). We patrolled the waters between China and Taiwan.

I stayed in the Navy until 1954. By this time I had four children and just couldn't make it on Navy pay. I was discharged in November 1954 at the same base where I had reported for boot camp, Newport, Rhode Island.

Dick Johnson was awarded the Navy Commendation Medal with a "V"-device for valor for his actions during the invasion of Okinawa. He entered law enforcement after his discharge from the Navy. In 1956, at the age of 27, he became police chief of Hampden, Maine. At that time he was the youngest police chief in the state of Maine. Later he served as police chief in Thomaston, Maine, then joined the Maine Department of Public Safety from which he retired in 1985. In 1988, Dick formed the USS Taluga *Association and initiated the tradition of yearly reunions. Barbara, Dick's wife of forty-two years, died on 16 April 1993. They had six children and six grandchildren. Dick lives in Rockland, Maine. He is the Maine State Commander of the Veterans of Underage Military Service.*

William S. Trero

Age 13 – United States Marine Corps

A Marine recruiting poster hung on the wall of my dad's barber shop in Birmingham, Alabama. I saw that poster every day. It said, "Uncle Sam Needs You!" The recruiting office was

By the time we hit Tarawa in November 1943, I was 15 years old.

right down the street, so I went in one day and said that I wanted to join the Marines. The officer handed me some papers and told me to get my parents' signatures. I looked over the papers, entered my birth date as 28 April 1924 instead of 28 April 1928, and forged my parents' signatures.

I was sworn into the Marine Corps on 15 September 1941 at the age of 13 years, 4 months and 17 days. I reported to San Diego, California, for boot camp and was assigned to Platoon 137. After boot camp, I went to Camp Elliott, California, and joined B Company, 1st Battalion, 6th Marines, 2nd Marine Division. The 6th Marines had just returned from Iceland when I joined the regiment.

A couple of months after the attack on Pearl Harbor, when I had been in the Corps about six months, I was ordered to report to my commanding officer. He told me to sit down. I could see that he had a letter from my mother, and I thought that I would be going back to Alabama. Instead of asking me about my age, the CO asked me, "What would you do, if, while firing your machine gun, all of your buddies lay dead around you?" I said, "I would continue firing my machine gun." The CO ordered, "Get back to your company!"

In November 1942, we were sent to New Zealand, and on 4 January 1943, we arrived on Guadalcanal for the last phase of that campaign. By this time I was 14 years old. I was setting up a tent one day when I unwittingly picked up a bangalore torpedo to use as a tent peg. A captain nearby almost became hysterical when he saw what I was going to do, but he reacted in time to save me from disaster.

While on patrol one day, I spotted some Japanese entrenched nearby. I hurried to Gunny Buffkin and excitedly reported what I had seen. The gunny told me to just go and kill them, so I did. Later, I think it was about 26 January, we were in an intense fire fight when we noticed an aerial battle between American and Japanese planes going on above us. The dog-fight was so bizarre that those of us on the ground stopped shooting at each other and just watched what was going on in the air. While we were watching the dog-fights, several Japanese bombers came in at low altitude and bombed our area.

While I was on Guadalcanal, I was wounded in the leg by shrapnel from a mortar. I doctored the wounds myself because I was afraid they would send me back home if I said anything. We left Guadalcanal on 19 February 1943, a little more than six weeks after we arrived. We returned to Wellington, New Zealand, to recuperate and prepare for the next operation. We didn't know it at the time, but we were destined for Tarawa.

By the time we hit Tarawa in November 1943, I was 15 years old. Those three days were rough. During a banzai attack, the water jacket on my machine gun was pierced by enemy fire and hot water spewed about. My second gunner and good friend, George Chimenti, felt the hot liquid on his body and thought for sure that he had been wounded.

After Tarawa was secured, we set up our machine guns on the beach because we expected the Japanese to try to recapture the island. Meanwhile, five or six of us were scrounging around and found a rubber boat. We had not had food other than C-rations since we had left the troopship days ago. We saw a merchant ship out in the harbor, so we decided to take the rubber boat and row to the ship, hoping to trade for some food. We loaded the rubber boat with Japanese rifles, flags, and anything else we could pawn off as a souvenir, and we started rowing towards the ship.

The more we rowed, the farther away the ship seemed to be. We finally got there and were welcomed aboard. We distributed our load of souvenirs to the crew, paying special attention to the cook and the captain. I gave the captain a Japanese pistol and he gave me three bottles of booze. (Believe it or not, I didn't drink.) The cook asked me what kind of pie I liked. I replied, "Blackberry," and he not only gave me a pie, but also half a crate of eggs, slabs of bacon, bread, and other goodies.

We stayed on the ship longer than we had planned, and it was starting to get dark before we reached the beach. As we approached in the dark, we were challenged by the sentries who thought that we might be the enemy. We started shouting our name, rank, and serial number as loudly as we could to convince them we were Marines. The next morning, we had a feast with all the food we had brought back from the ship. We sure had a lot of friends that morning! I swear that everyone on the island joined us for breakfast.

After Tarawa we went to Hawaii to a camp on the Big Island, appropriately named Camp Tarawa. Here we recuperated and trained for the next invasion. We hit Saipan on 15 July 1944. By now I was an "old man," 16 years of age. On the first day of the invasion, we had moved inland a little ways when the Japanese counterattacked. I was hit by machine-gun fire in the left leg. I was lying in a rice paddy when some Japanese soldiers passed close by. Fortunately, they were concentrating on pressing their attack and didn't pay much attention to me. By morning the Marines had prevailed, and two tank drivers found me, carried me back to the beach, and dumped me in a giant shell hole with other wounded. Man, I was hurting! I was lying next to a colonel who was also wounded. He passed me a bottle' of brandy. That helped. A lot of men in that hole didn't make it.

I was evacuated to the hospital ship USS *Samaritan* and later shipped to the naval hospital in Hawaii for medical treatment. From there I went to a hospital in Livermore, California, then to a hospital in New Orleans to await discharge.

I was discharged on 7 April 1945, twenty-one days before my seventeenth birthday — twenty-one days before I could legally enlist, with parental consent.

Billy Trero received the Purple Heart for wounds received in action. After his discharge from the Marines, he went to Bakersfield, California, and worked as a roughneck in the oil fields. He returned to Alabama in 1949 to box in amateur fights. He won the state Golden Gloves middleweight title and other amateur titles. In 1950, he moved to Houston, Texas, and boxed in ten amateur fights, winning nine by KO, and won a Junior Olympics title. He turned professional and fought for nine years.

While he was still boxing, he became involved with ironworking and later started Trero's Re-bar — Foundation Company. He contracted for work on bridges, drill shafts, wharves, anything that required foundations. In February 1996, he retired from his contracting business but remained very active in veterans organizations. In June 1996, Billy became Commander, Texas District 17, Veterans of Foreign Wars. Billy and Louise, his wife of forty-one years, live in Trinity, Texas. They have four daughters and seven grandchildren.

√ **VUMS Note** ⇒ *The name game.* Some veterans managed to enlist underage by changing their given names. Most, but not all, reverted to using their given names later on. Several adopted their older brothers' names and used their birth certificates to circumvent the age requirement. One dropped his last name and used his middle name in its place. One changed his last name to that of his stepfather, added an "e", and goes by that name to this day. Another used the full name of his older brother and maintains that name today, which, in his words, "confuses the hell out of the Social Security Administration."

Gordon Zane

Age 16 – United States Navy

It was 1941, I was 16 years old, an avid sports fan, and that year was one of the most eventful in major-league baseball history. Joe Dimaggio hit safely in fifty-six consecutive games, a record still standing. Ted Williams hit over .400, the

> *I had been at sea almost two years when, ... the captain ... said, "You can start shaving, son!"*

last player to do so. And in the World Series, catcher Mickey Owen of the Brooklyn Dodgers missed the final strike-three of the game, enabling the New York Yankees to win the game and the World Series. These were some of the last memorable sports events to occur as the country moved closer to war. I followed the games closely from my hometown of Woodbury, New Jersey, where I was born on 3 June 1925. Simultaneously, I was watching the war approach.

In September 1941, President Roosevelt ordered the U. S. Navy to fire at any German naval vessels encountered in the Atlantic, the so-called "undeclared war" of the fall of 1941. I wanted to be involved, so, armed with an affidavit asserting I was 17 years of age, I joined the Navy on 17 September 1941. Within days I found myself at the San Diego Naval Training Station, marching with a rifle.

On 6 December 1941, I arrived at the Naval Hospital in Balboa Park, San Diego, to commence training at the Hospital Corps School. Just before dinner, we mustered outside the building and were welcomed by the commander of the school. He assured us that half of us would be given five days' leave at Christmas and the other half would get five days' leave at New Year's. He summed up by saying, "And that's final!"

The next morning, we were called to muster again, told of the Japanese attack on Pearl Harbor, and told to forget the leaves mentioned the previous day. San Diego was blacked out for fear of possible Japanese air raids. Immediately after Pearl Harbor, the Navy appropriated the El Prado area of Balboa Park and transferred the Hospital Corps School there. Although I was a medical student, I was issued a rifle and assigned guard duty, my post being at the entrance to the museum area. I had the midnight to 4 a.m. watch. It was dark and very quiet as I patrolled the area. All of a sudden I heard the roar of a lion! I was a bit more than startled. No one had bothered to tell me that we were close to the San Diego Zoo. A month later, we were transferred to the main part of the park where certain museum buildings had been converted to barracks, classrooms, and a mess hall. We mustered around the famous lily pond.

After two months, I graduated and was sent to work on hospital wards at Puget Sound Naval Hospital, Washington. Just after the Doolittle raid on Tokyo, thirty of us were shipped by submarine tender to San Francisco and then to the old Naval Hospital at the entrance to Pearl Harbor. There we worked on a ward with 120 sick sailors, from 8 a.m. to 8 p.m, six days a week. On the seventh day, we were granted liberty from 10 a.m to 6 p.m. We were required to carry gas masks over our shoulders while in Honolulu, and the Islands were blacked out every night.

I watched the Yorktown sail out of the harbor on its way to the Battle of Midway, where it was sunk. Just prior to the battle, I escorted Admiral Nimitz up to Admiral Halsey's hospital room. I learned later that they had conferred and decided on Halsey's successor to command the fleet, Admiral Spruance. A week before the battle, I missed being assigned as a hospital corpsman to the Marines at Midway by virtue of a line being drawn under the name "Wright," the name just before mine!

I volunteered for sea duty, and in July 1942, I was assigned to the USS *Lassen*, an ammunition ship. I spent the next three years on the *Lassen*, clocking over 100,000 miles at sea. On one memorable occasion I assisted at an appendectomy performed at sea at midnight when we were located on the equator. During a stop at New Caledonia in 1943, I was briefly reunited with my brother. He and a cousin, both Marines, were stationed there. They had no idea I was there, so you can imagine their surprise when I walked into their tent and interrupted their poker game. I had been at sea almost two years when, one day at inspection, the captain stopped and came back to me and said, "You can start shaving, son!" On a trip back to the States, we missed the ammunition depot explosion at Port Chicago, California, by the skin of our teeth. We pulled into the harbor just one day after it happened.

Before we pulled into the harbor, there was an incident that was straight out of the Caine Mutiny, a la Captain Queeg. We had a refrigerator in the sick bay for certain medical supplies, which occupied only one shelf. In the hot South Pacific, we medics sometimes put candy bars on one of the vacant shelves. The ship's medical officer, for some reason, didn't approve of this and told us to refrain from putting candy bars in there. Unfortunately, a day before arriving back in San Francisco, during our final inspection, the captain opened the refrigerator. There, along with the pharmaceuticals, was a lone Hershey bar on an otherwise vacant shelf. The captain went on with his inspection as the medical officer turned purple. Afterwards he demanded to know who was responsible. There was no response to his demand, so he announced that none of us would be permitted to leave the ship in San Francisco. We hadn't seen civilization for a year! We met and discussed possible courses of action. Should we write letters to Congressmen, or letters to the editor of *The San Francisco Chronicle*? Should we form a committee to petition the captain for relief? Fortunately for all, the doctor came to his senses and grudgingly reversed his decision. I never did find out who put that candy bar in the refrigerator.

I suppose, like most servicemen, I experienced the arrogance and pettiness of some aspects of the military life. On one occasion, after a year in the western Pacific, my shipmates and I went ashore in San Francisco on liberty. We were stopped by shore patrolmen and given citations for wearing our hats on the back of our heads instead of over our eyebrows. Our captain subsequently admonished us to "look like man o'warsmen!" I guess it was more important to look like one than to be one.

Back in the Pacific, we sailed continuously off the coast of Okinawa from March to July 1945, transferring ammunition at sea to the fighting ships. On one occasion, I watched as two kamikaze planes struck a carrier on our starboard bow. We endured a horrendous typhoon in June 1945 that so badly damaged the ship that we put in for repairs at Leyte Gulf in the Philippines.

At Leyte, I left the ship to return to the States for a 30-day leave, during which time the war ended. I was discharged on 20 October 1945.

Gordon Zane completed high school by correspondence while aboard ship in the Pacific. After his discharge, he attended the University of California at Berkeley under the GI Bill, graduating with a degree in economics and accounting in 1950. He was an accountant and later, a business officer at the University of California for seventeen years. Meanwhile, he worked his way through law school. After obtaining his law degree, he enjoyed a career as a deputy attorney general for the state of California, retiring from that position in 1985. Gordon and Joan, his wife of forty-two years, moved to Sun City West, Arizona. In 1995 they took a South Pacific cruise and revisited some of the islands Gordon had first seen over fifty years before. He reported that the harbor at New Caledonia was devoid of ships now, compared to the many Navy ships that were there during the war. Gordon and Joan have three sons and two grandchildren.

88

Harry B. Thomas

Age 15 — United States Marine Corps

I was born in Crossett, a small lumber town in southeast Arkansas, on 3 November 1925. During the Great Depression we moved to Louisiana to live with my mother's

> *... as I lay there, blood from the guy in the bunk over me started dripping down on me.*

sister for a time, then went to Little Rock, Arkansas, where the eight of us moved in with five of my father's relatives. After a year or so, we moved to our own small house where we had a milk cow and some chickens. Circumstances forced us to move at least five more times. I believe I went to every school in Little Rock. By the time I was 15, I felt like I was grown up.

Every time I saw the Navy recruiting poster that said, "Join the Navy and See the World," I got the idea that maybe I could join the Navy and go to China. I had read a lot about the Chinese and desperately wanted to go there. The first chance I got, I went to the Navy recruiting station and took the test and the physical. The chief said, "You'll hear from us in a week or ten days." I dropped out of the ninth grade, and I rode my bike to and from home for ten days as if I were going to school. But there was no word from the Navy. I went back to the station and the chief said, "Son, come back in a couple of years and we'll talk to you again." I thought, "Oh Lord, what am I going to do?"

When I walked out of the federal building in Little Rock that day, I thought I would die. I met two boys on the street who were leaving for the Marines that evening. I found out that one was 16 and the other 17. I ran about five blocks to the Marine recruiting station and talked to a captain about the Marine Corps for awhile. I told him that I was born on 3 November 1923. I took my physical and went back to talk with the captain some more. My papers were brought to the captain, he checked them, looked me straight in the eye and said, "I think you will make a Marine, but I need these papers signed by your parents within an hour in order to get you on the train that leaves for San Diego at 6:30 this evening." He got the papers back in about thirty minutes because I went down the stairs and around the corner to a cafe, bought a coke (I had one quarter to my name), sat there and drank the coke, then signed the papers myself. I took the papers back to the captain. When he swore me in, I was the happiest boy in Little Rock, Arkansas.

The captain came to the train station that evening to see us off. It was 14 October 1941, and we were on our way to San Diego for boot camp. It didn't take long in boot camp for me to wonder what I had got myself into. I grew up during the Great Depression when things were tough, working at three jobs to help my family when I was eight years old, but that was easy compared to boot camp.

I was assigned to Platoon 159. We had been in boot camp about seven weeks when the war with Japan started. After boot camp, I was in a group of volunteers who were to be sent to different schools. When they asked for volunteers for cooks and bakers school, I stepped forward, but the commanding officer came up and told me that I would be going to sea school. I was thrilled to hear this, and I loved sea school.

After sea school, I was sent to Pearl Harbor where I joined the Marine Detachment aboard the USS *Astoria*. We were attacked by torpedo planes during the battle of Midway. We fired sixty rounds from my antiaircraft gun without stopping. I saw the aircraft carrier USS *Yorktown* get hit and sink during this battle.

After the Battle of Midway, we returned to Pearl Harbor and went into dry dock for repairs. On 7 August 1942, we participated in the Battle of Guadalcanal. We fought for two days, then on the night of 9 August, during the Battle of Savo Island, the *Astoria* was sunk. This was a bad night for us. We lost the *Astoria*, the *Quincy*, the *Vincennes*, and the Australian ship *Canberra*, all heavy cruisers.

I was wounded in the face, hand, hip, leg, and ankle during the battle. Rickman, the first loader on my gun, carried me out of the way of the men fighting the fires. After things cooled off a little, the wounded who couldn't walk were placed up forward near the bow as the ship was sinking to the stern. The ship's captain, "Wild Bill"

Greenman, was the best. I was told he stayed with the ship until the last minute, even though he had shrapnel wounds all over his body.

A destroyer, the USS *Bagley*, appeared out of the dark amidst all the explosions and shell fire. She came alongside the *Astoria*, took off all the wounded, then ran like hell. When I was taken aboard the *Bagley*, I was handed down through a bow hatch to a compartment crammed with bunks full of wounded. There were even some pads on the deck. It looked more like sleeping quarters than a sick bay. I was put in a bunk, and as I lay there, blood from the guy in the bunk over me started dripping down on me. It nearly drove me nuts. Finally, they gave me morphine and I conked out.

When I came to, we were being transferred to one of the old steamship liners that had been converted to a troopship. I think it was the *Wharton* or the *Coolidge*. We went to New Caledonia, where the critically wounded were taken off and put in an Army hospital. I watched as a sailor that I knew, Leo S. McKenna from San Francisco, left the ship. He had a serious head injury and was barely walking, but he was alive.

We were given Army clothes because we didn't have anything to wear. We went to the New Hebrides where we were transferred to another ship and set sail for Pearl Harbor. In Hawaii, we were at the hospital on "Red Hill" for a short while, then we were sent on our way back to the States. I was sent to the Oak Knoll Naval Hospital, Oakland, California.

While at Oak Knoll, I found the phone number of Leo McKenna's parents and called them. They told me that Leo had been listed as dead. I told them that I had seen him get off the ship at New Caledonia. They came straight to the hospital to see me, and while they were there, they got the commanding officer of the hospital to check on their son. They found out that he was still alive and still in New Caledonia. He made it home.

After about six months, I was transferred to the Seattle Naval Hospital, where I spent another nine months. I spent most of my time in Seattle giving talks about the war and helping to sell war bonds.

I was given a medical discharge at the Marine Barracks, Naval Air Station, Seattle, Washington, on 27 November 1943. I loved the Marine Corps, and I always will.

Harry Thomas was awarded the Purple Heart for wounds received in action. After he attended the University of Arkansas in Fayetteville for a year, he moved about and worked at several jobs for a time. He worked for International Paper Company, then he went into electrical and refrigeration work. He worked for the Singer Sewing Machine Company in Norfolk, Virginia, for three years, then returned to Arkansas to farm for a year. Houston, Texas, was his next stop, then it was on to Galveston, Texas, where he operated a fishing camp and a shrimp boat. Harry loved that business, but a freak storm destroyed it. In 1969 he was selected by the Battleship Texas Commission to be caretaker and acting captain of the USS Texas, which was berthed in the Houston ship channel near the San Jacinto Battleground. He lived on the ship for three years by himself and conducted tours for hundreds of people each day. In 1970, when the 4th Marine Division held its reunion on the ship, he fired the 14-inch guns four times. Harry lives in Hot Springs, Arkansas. He has two sons and three grandchildren.

Omega Gene Hibbert

Age 14 – United States Army

I was born in Oklahoma City, Oklahoma, on 12 January 1927 and grew up during the Great Depression. We were dirt poor during those times. As a youth, my hero was a man that I had never seen, my Uncle Philip. He was killed in action during

> *... within two weeks, I had trouble recalling what my "true love" looked like.*

World War I while he was serving with the infantry in France. He died three days before the armistice was signed. From the time I was old enough to understand the story about Uncle Philip, I wanted to be an infantry soldier.

In 1941, I began bugging my mother to sign for me to join the Army. My mother and father had divorced and my mother was remarried. When she refused to sign for me, I ran away from home several times. During those sojourns I hitchhiked, rode freight trains, and walked a

lot, which would later serve me in good stead. I was hungry most of the time. What little money I made went for food. I tried picking cotton for $1.00 per 100 pounds but found it easier, and more profitable, to steal pecans and sell them for 10¢ a pound. When I returned, skinny and under-nourished from my last escapade, my mother shook her head and said, "I guess the Army would be a safer place for you."

The minimum age for joining the Army at that time was 18. My mother accompanied me to the recruiting office and lied for me. I was 14 and may have looked to be 16, but no more. The Army was in the midst of the big prewar mobilization, and I guess the recruiters were under the usual pressure to make their quotas. Anyway, I was soon on a bus to Fort Riley, Kansas, where, still in civilian clothes, I was immediately put on KP duty. I was sworn into the Army a few days later, on 10

November 1941, and was shipped to Camp Wolters, Texas, for thirteen weeks of infantry basic training.

Twenty-seven days after I was sworn in, the Japanese bombed Pearl Harbor and we were at war! I called my mother, and she said that she was going to get me out of the Army. I told her that if she did, she would never see me again. I guess she knew I meant it. We didn't know it then, but we would not meet again until 1945.

We went on a 7-day training schedule, with time off only on Sunday for chapel services. After the ninth week of training, about half of us were shipped to Fort Ord, California, and joined a division. We went on a 25-mile hike with full field packs shortly after arriving. Welcome to the infantry!

We departed San Francisco in March 1942 and landed on the island of Hawaii where we were assigned to beach defense. When the threat of a Japanese invasion subsided, we moved to Oahu, Hawaii, where I signed up for immediate action. I became a member of Company I, 161st Infantry, 25th "Tropic Lightning" Infantry Division. In December 1942, we landed on Guadalcanal in the Solomon Islands and saw light combat there. I turned 16 during that operation. I revealed my true age after leaving the States, but my age was never a problem.

From the 'Canal we went to New Georgia and fought for three months, after which the infantry regiments were considerably below strength because of battle casualties and sickness. We all got malaria and dysentery, over and over again. The medics just treated us in the units. No way could the hospitals handle so many patients.

After a year in the Solomons, we went to New Zealand for rest and recuperation. That was the bright spot of the entire war for most of us. The New Zealanders treated us very well. I fell madly in love with the daughter of a Scottish dairy farmer. I didn't see how I could possibly leave that girl. I actually toyed with the idea of missing the boat when we got ready to ship out for New Caledonia. But I did my duty, and within two weeks, I had trouble recalling what my "true love" looked like.

We received replacements and were reequipped in New Caledonia. We trained continuously and became the best-trained and best-conditioned unit I ever served with during a twenty-nine year career, including the Korean War and the war in Vietnam.

We shipped out from New Caledonia and landed on Luzon, Philippine Islands, where we encountered the hardest fighting that we had so far experienced. My rifle company had forty-two men killed and more than one hundred wounded during that campaign. Toward the end of the campaign, when we had secured our last primary objective, there were only five men left from my original platoon. Four of the five had been wounded at least once during the operation and had returned to duty.

I turned 18 years old on the island of Luzon. I had been overseas more than three years. The Army announced a system of awarding points for battle stars, decorations, months overseas, and dependent children. Men with eighty-five points or more would be eligible to return to the U. S. and subsequently be discharged. I was scheduled to go home at the time the A-bomb was dropped on Hiroshima. My unit was training for the invasion of the Japanese homeland. There would have been many casualties had it not been for the A-bomb.

I arrived in the U. S. on 21 September 1945. Dinah Shore welcomed us from a blimp flying over the harbor at San Pedro, California. It was a poignant moment when I heard of her death last year (1995). I had served three years, five months, and twenty-two days overseas. I was discharged on 5 October 1945 with 107 points.

After leaving the Army, I drifted aimlessly for several years. I finally realized that I actually missed military life. In 1949, I reenlisted as a private in the 2nd (Indian Head) Infantry Division. When the Korean War broke out, we were at Fort Lewis, Washington. Within a short time I was on my way to Korea as a member of Company C, 38th Infantry, 2nd Division. I was later wounded and evacuated to the States. As it turned out, I went from private first class to sergeant first class in five months. So, the Korean War was, in a way, fortuitous for me.

In 1967, I volunteered for service in Vietnam and was assigned to Company A, 1st Battalion (Airborne), 327th Infantry, 101st Airborne Division.

I retired from the Army at Fort Riley, Kansas, on 1 May 1974 after serving for over twenty-nine years.

I was awarded a few medals during those years but am most proud of my three awards of the Combat Infantryman Badge, for World War II, for Korea, and for Vietnam. Only 230 soldiers have been awarded the CIB three times. The Army recognized us by enshrining our names on plaques in the Infantry Museum at Fort Benning, Georgia, in 1984. I am especially proud that all my CIBs were for service in rifle platoons. This may not mean much to a non-infantryman, but grunts know what I mean. I went from being the youngest in my unit during World War II to the oldest as a 40-year-old rifle platoon sergeant with the 101st Airborne Division in Vietnam. I truly feel privileged to have been granted the opportunity to serve over such a span of years.

After all the years as a grunt, I still get up and run three miles every day, trying to stay alive a little longer. Sometimes I chase my wife around the house, but after I catch her I often forget what I was chasing her for. But all in all, life is good!

Gene Hibbert, in addition to earning three Combat Infantryman Badges, received a Bronze Star and was awarded a Purple Heart for wounds received in action, both during World War II. He was wounded again in Korea and received his second Purple Heart. He earned another Bronze Star in Vietnam. After he retired from the Army, he started driving a school bus for the Northeast Independent School District in San Antonio, Texas. Before retiring from the school district in 1992, he was a driver trainer/evaluator and a field-trip scheduler. Gene and Kim, his wife of twenty-seven years, live in San Antonio, Texas.

James R. Malloch

Age 14 – United States Marine Corps

I was a 14-year-old juvenile delinquent who had quit school, run away from home, and was surely headed for trouble. I was born in Charlotte, North Carolina, on 28 February 1927. My parents later divorced, and my mother worked hard trying to support four children.

After well over a year in the South Pacific, malaria got the best of me.

The country was slowly recovering from the Depression that had lasted for more than ten years. Times were rough, especially in the South. I had no guidance at home, and my school grades were so bad that the school principal was going to expel me if they didn't improve. I often relied on a boyhood friend's father for advice. He would take us camping, fishing, and hunting – trips that I really enjoyed.

I had always admired the U. S. Marines. I had read about their activities in France during World War I, and I was determined to enlist in the Corps, so at age 14, I decided it was time to try. I left home and hitchhiked to Savannah, Georgia, with my life savings, $6.00, in my pocket. I slept in the lobby of the YMCA and ate my meals in a small cafe where breakfast was 25¢ and lunch was 50¢. The next morning, I went to the U. S. Marine Corps Recruiting Station, scared stiff! The first thing the recruiting sergeant asked me was, "How old are you?" I told him, "Seventeen, sir!" He explained to me that I had to have my parent's notarized signature on my papers. I took the forms and immediately returned home to Charlotte.

I gave the papers to my mother, but she refused to sign anything that said I was 17. I begged her to sign. My mother's friends advised her that it would be better for me to be in the Marines than in reform school. Finally, she reluctantly signed the papers stating that I was 17 and had her signature notarized.

I returned to the recruiting station in Savannah, Georgia, this time by bus, and handed the papers to the recruiting sergeant. Everything was in order, and I was sworn into the U. S. Marine Corps on 26 November 1941 for a 4-year enlistment. The sergeant treated me to lunch, then put me on a bus to the Marine Corps Recruit Depot, Parris Island, South Carolina.

While I was in boot camp, the Japanese bombed Pearl Harbor and the United States was at war. After graduation from boot camp, I was assigned to the 5th Defense Battalion, an antiaircraft, barrage-balloon, artillery unit. The battalion had just returned from duty in Iceland with the 6th Marine Regiment and was reorganizing at Parris Island.

We left Parris Island for Norfolk, Virginia, where we boarded a ship headed for the South Pacific. We went through the Panama Canal and arrived in Wellington, New Zealand, in June 1942. Our unit was attached to the 1st Marine Division, and we participated in the Guadalcanal/Tulagi campaign. On 4 November 1942, we made an amphibious landing at Aola Bay on Guadalcanal along with the 2nd Marine Raider Battalion and the U. S. Army's 147th Infantry Regiment. I was 15 years old.

The purpose of the landing at Aola Bay was to secure the area and build an additional airfield on Guadalcanal. The Navy Seabees and Marine engineers had tried to tell the Navy brass that the Aola Bay area was too swampy for an airfield. It was a former coconut plantation. Finally, Admiral "Bull" Halsey, who had recently taken command of the South Pacific Forces, canceled the Aola Bay operation.

In December 1942, all units were moved back to the Henderson Field area where they were needed to support the 1st Marine Division, which was in a life and death struggle with the Japanese. My unit was sent to Tulagi to defend that island.

In 1943, the Marine Corps formed the 11th Defense Battalion on Florida Island, just across the bay from Tulagi. I was one of a large number of personnel who transferred from the 5th Defense Battalion to the 11th Defense Battalion. The 11th Defense Battalion participated in the New Georgia Island campaign. We helped capture and set up the defense around the airfield at Munda in August 1943. I was 16 years old.

Meanwhile, my father had contacted a U. S. Senator from North Carolina to try to have me sent home. The senator contacted Marine Corps Headquarters, and a request to have me transferred back to the

States was sent to my unit. My battalion adjutant, a really old salt, had the request on his desk when he called me in. He said to me, "Son, if you don't want to go home and want to remain with your unit, I'll arrange it. I will not answer this letter until you are 17 years of age." I was about 16½ at the time. I never heard another word about it. In my letters I told my father that I wanted to stay with my outfit. He was *very* unhappy.

After well over a year in the South Pacific, malaria got the best of me. In December 1943, I was evacuated to a naval hospital in Auckland, New Zealand, weighing 97 pounds when I checked in. By March 1944, when I was evacuated back to the United States, I weighed 120 pounds.

I was discharged from the hospital in May 1944 and was assigned to the 5th Marine Division at Camp Pendleton, California. After a series of malaria attacks, I was admitted to the naval hospital at Camp Pendleton. The Navy doctors said that only a cooler climate would help me, so in September 1944, I was transferred to the Marine Corps Supply Depot, San Francisco, California. Meanwhile, in February 1945, my old outfit, the 5th Marine Division, landed on Iwo Jima. Had I not received a medical transfer, I would have been a participant in that invasion! I never had an attack of malaria again.

I remained at the Marine Corps Supply Depot until after the war had ended. I was discharged on 1 December 1945, after completing my 4-year enlistment. I was 18 years old.

On the anniversary of the Marine Corps birthday, 10 November 1948, I reenlisted and was assigned to the base message center at the Marine Corps Base at San Diego, California. In 1950, I was transferred to the Signal Battalion, 1st Marine Division, at Camp Pendleton, California. I was with the 1st Marine Division when we made the assault landing at Inchon, Korea, on 15 September 1950. We captured Seoul within a few weeks. A short time later, we returned to Inchon, boarded ships, and headed for Wonsan on the east coast of North Korea. By the time we reached Wonsan harbor, on 19 October 1950, South Korean forces had arrived there by land. The harbor was full of mines, so we waited aboard ship until 26 October when the mines were cleared and we could land. Meanwhile, Bob Hope had flown into Wonsan and was giving a performance for the troops there while we sat out in the harbor.

Once ashore, we started moving toward the Chosin Reservoir. Our unit was set up at Koto-ri when the lead infantry units at Yudam-ni and Hagaru started back under intense pressure from the Chinese. The Chinese were all around us at Koto-ri. When he had a little spare time, our commanding officer, a real shooting enthusiast, would take a rifle, rest it on the hood of our communications van, and shoot at the Chinese in the surrounding hills.

During our trek out of the mountains to Hamhung, the Chinese were attacking and ambushing our convoys almost continuously. At times, all hands were returning fire with rifles, machine guns, mortars, and artillery. All available personnel were basic infantrymen, including cooks, company clerks, and communicators. As a communicator, I had as my weapon a 0.30 caliber carbine (M-2). The weapon froze up more than once from the cold. It was bitterly cold; temperatures were 30° to 40° below zero at times. We had many cases of frostbite.

In my opinion, discipline and leadership were the reason the 1st Marine Division was able to return to the port city of Hungnam as a unit, bringing out our wounded, our dead, and our equipment. After pulling out of Hungnam in December 1950, we returned to South Korea, regrouped at Masan, and were soon moving north again.

After returning from Korea in December 1951, I was assigned to Base Communications, Recruit Depot, San Diego, California. In 1955, I was assigned to the U. S. State Department as part of a security guard detachment during the United Nations' tenth anniversary meeting in San Francisco.

Other tours of duty during my Marine Corps career included drill instructor, Marine Corps Base (Recruit Depot), San Diego; student and instructor in a number of Marine Corps/Navy communications schools; and service with the 3rd Marine Division on Okinawa, the 1st Marine Air Wing in Japan, and the 1st Marine Division at Camp Pendleton, California. I was NCO in charge of communications during the closing down of the U. S. Marine Corps "Department of the Pacific" at 100 Harrison Street, San Francisco, in 1960.

I was message center chief of FMFPAC (Fleet Marine Force, Pacific) in Hawaii at the time of my retirement on 1 March 1967. I served more than twenty-two years on active duty and retired as a gunnery sergeant (E-7).

Jim Malloch retired from the Marine Corps in Hawaii and was immediately employed by a civilian contractor doing work for the Air Force and NASA. His company maintained communications for the Air Force Missile Test Site at Vandenberg Air Force Base, California, Kwajalein Island, Canton Island, radar-tracking ships, and the NASA space program. Jim was involved in maintaining communications links with the radar-tracking sites in the Pacific area during the Apollo program, including the moon landings. In 1974, Jim and his family returned to his hometown of Charlotte, North Carolina, where he was employed in the security department of the Federal Reserve Bank of Richmond, Charlotte Branch. He retired in 1989. Jim and June, his wife of fifty years, live in Sunset Beach, North Carolina. They have four children and three grandchildren.

√ **VUMS Note** ⇒ *Words of rejection.* A phrase used frequently in rejecting youngsters when they tried to enlist underage began, "Son, come back ..." Some variations of these words of rejection were:

"Son, come back in a couple of years and
    we'll talk to you again."
"Come back when you grow up." ·
"Come back when you are *really* 17."
"Get the hell out of here, and come back
    when you are 18!"

Norman J. Swanson

Age 16 – United States Navy

It was not by design that I became an underage veteran. I never enlisted, nor was I drafted into the armed forces. I fought with the U. S. Marine Corps, but was never a Marine. I wore Navy clothing for only a

> *Our food ration was one cup of cooked barley twice a day ...*

few weeks, yet I have documentation stating that I was a member of the naval service of the United States for over four years. Confused? Let me explain.

I was born in Chicago, Illinois, but I spent much of my early life in Grand Coulee, Washington, where I completed high school in 1941 at the age of 16. My brother, who had gone to Wake Island to work on the construction of a naval base there, wrote to me and suggested that I join him on Wake. He said that I could earn enough in one year to get a good start at the university.

Within a week, I had contacted the Morrison-Knudsen Company in Boise, Idaho, the general contractor on Wake. I signed on with them and soon departed from San Francisco on the Matson luxury liner, the *Matsonia*, bound for Honolulu. After a medical checkup, I boarded a Navy supply ship, the USS *Regulus*, bound for Wake Island. I was a very naive 16-year-old.

Wake Island was a Navy communications station and a refueling stop for the Pan American Airways "China Clipper." Commander Winfield Cunningham, who had enrolled in the U. S. Naval Academy at age 16, was in charge of sixty-eight Navy personnel there, and Major James Devereux commanded 388 Marines. Six U. S. Army personnel manned the main radio transmitter. Pan American employed about seventy people to service the Clippers and staff the local hotel. There were 1200 civilian employees of Morrison-Knudsen Company under the direction of Dan Teters.

We lived much like the military, slept in a barracks, ate in a mess hall, and rode to the work sites in company vehicles. Everything was going well until about noon on Monday, 8 December 1941 (Sunday, 7 December in the United States). On that day I was working on a building at the end of a new airfield. We were getting into our vehicles to go to the mess hall at lunch time when we noticed a large flight of airplanes approaching. We first thought they were U. S. Navy aircraft but soon observed that they were twin-engine, land-based bombers, and our Navy did not have land-based bombers.

The first indication that they were hostile aircraft was the explosion of bombs at the central edge of the new runway where the Marine pilots of VMF-211 parked their F4F Wildcat fighters. At the time, eight of their twelve planes were parked there while the pilots were eating lunch in a nearby tent. Four aircraft were flying patrol. The first bombs destroyed all of the parked aircraft, the tent with the pilots, and a large fuel storage tank. More than twenty Marines were killed while having lunch.

By the time I heard the first bombs explode, we were being strafed. The civilian camp was damaged considerably. As soon as the noise of the Japanese aircraft engines had waned, all of the civilians met to find out what had happened. We were informed of the attack on Pearl Harbor earlier in the day and told that we could probably expect help, but in the meantime, we should all pitch in and help the military personnel with whatever needed to be done. Essentially, we all "joined the Marines" and became active service personnel without the benefit of boot camp.

I joined Marine Gunner (Warrant Officer) Clarence McKinstry's troops at Peacock Point. My job was to assist in supplying ammunition for a 3-inch antiaircraft gun battery. I was also trained in the operation of 30- and 50-caliber machine guns. Many civilians helped man the 5-inch shore batteries. In the early morning of 11 December, after four days of bombing, about thirteen Japanese ships appeared on the horizon. The Japanese planned to take the island with a small landing force, but the Marine 5-inch shore batteries opened fire and sank at least two ships. The four remaining F4F Wildcats of VMF-211 caused considerable damage to the retreating Japanese fleet and sank a destroyer.

For the next eleven days, we were bombed constantly, which resulted in many casualties. We were all awaiting the relief forces, but they didn't come. On the morning of 23 December 1941, a fleet of more than twenty-five Japanese ships approached the island. At the break of dawn, the bombardment began, lasting for about an hour. When it ceased, we could see landing craft with hundreds, if not thousands, of enemy troops approaching the coral beach. I thought, "This is it!" We didn't have a chance. We were given orders to surrender.

When the Japanese troops arrived, we were ordered to remove all of our clothing, marched to the center of the airport runway, and herded into a circle surrounded by Japanese sailors with tripod-mounted machine guns. We were ordered to lie down and not speak to anyone or we would be shot. We remained naked on the airstrip for two days and nights. We were given a small amount of bread and some water from barrels that had previously contained gasoline. Military and civilian personnel were treated the same, since none of us wore clothing and no questions were asked. Finally, on Christmas Day we were marched to the civilian camp area where we were given a short-sleeved khaki shirt and khaki shorts and were permitted to wear shoes. We were forced to clean up the bombed area and repair the roads and airport.

On 12 January 1942, all military and all but one hundred of the civilians were ordered aboard a former Japanese luxury liner, the *Nita Maru*. The one hundred remaining at Wake were to run specialized equipment such as the desalinization plant. I learned later that two escaped and were never heard from again. The remaining ninety-eight were executed by the Japanese on 7 October 1943.

As we boarded, the Japanese sailors took all of our belongings. We were placed in steel holds of about one hundred feet square. Sanitary facilities were square five-gallon cans normally used to ship soap. The cans were not secured, so they would slide across the deck and frequently spill. We were not permitted to talk or even to whisper. The punishment for disobeying the rules was death, as some of the prisoners found out. We were frequently beaten, and the bread and water provided twice each day was just enough for survival.

We disembarked at Shanghai, China, on 24 January 1942 and marched to the Woo Sung POW camp. We were dressed for summer, but the weather was cold and damp, like Seattle in winter. We were each issued one wet cotton blanket and ordered to sleep on straw mats on raised platforms in the barracks. My brother and I teamed together to take advantage of two blankets and our combined body warmth.

Our first work assignment was to dig a canal ten feet deep and thirty to forty feet wide, using hand shovels. The site was near where a major battle had occurred between the Chinese and the Japanese. Frequently, we would dig up bodies. After about three months, we were marched to another camp called Kiang Wan. The project was to build a huge model of Mount Fujiyama on the flat Shanghai plain. We used hand shovels to fill small rail cars, push the cars to the dumping area, and return for more. We excavated a lake while we were building a mountain. Our food ration was one cup of cooked barley twice a day with a bit of dikon (radish) soup occasionally.

After a year or so at Kiang Wan, some of us were taken to Osaka, Japan, where we were forced to work in a shipyard. One day, ten of us were ordered to carry a ship plate from one part of the shipyard to another. The plate was so heavy and awkward that we dropped it and my fingers were smashed. The next day the pain was unbearable. In an attempt to ease the pain I lit a cigarette, which was against the rules. A Japanese guard caught me smoking, and as punishment he beat my sore fingers with his walking stick and ordered me not to complain or the beating would be repeated. This was typical of the treatment we received daily throughout the war.

In late winter of 1944-45, American B-29s dropped clusters of fire bombs on Osaka, causing great destruction. Some hit our camp, injuring several prisoners of war. Because of the bombing, the Japanese moved us to the small town of Naoetsu, near the city of Niigata, where we were to work in a steel mill. This was the worst of all places because the work was harder and the food poorer, and there was less of it. The body insects were more plentiful, and the place was very dirty from the steelworks. We were told at the camp that if any American soldiers set foot on the Japanese mainland, we would be killed immediately. One day I saw a Japanese newspaper with the headline "Atom Bomb," but there was no description of the weapon or of the destruction caused by it. None of us had any idea what "Atom Bomb" meant.

On the day that Japan surrendered we didn't know what happened, but the Japanese camp guards disappeared. Soon, U. S. Navy fighter planes flew over and dropped duffel bags without parachutes. The bags were filled with candy bars, cigarettes, and chewing gum. The only thing that survived was the chewing gum. I was so hungry that I walked out of camp to a nearby farm to find something to eat. I traded an old pair of shoes to a farmer for a chicken, took the chicken to camp, made a little campfire and cooked it. It was so tough that my brother and I agreed that I should have cooked the shoes instead.

A day or so later, a flight of B-29s dropped barrels containing food, clothing, shoes, and soap by parachute. We now had plenty of food, cigarettes, and other luxurious things such as good toilet paper, something we hadn't seen for nearly four years.

We were told that we would have to stay in camp until transportation could be arranged, and that we should stay near the camp because it was not known how the Japanese civilians and ex-soldiers would react to our presence. We were especially cautioned not to go to Niigata. The next day most of the ex-prisoners were either in Niigata or traveling around the countryside. My first desire was to get a shave, a haircut, and a super massage, which I obtained in the village of Naoetsu for the price of two packs of Lucky Strike cigarettes.

About three weeks later, a train took us from Naoetsu to Yokohama, where we were fumigated to destroy body insects, given new Navy clothing, and then directed to a place where there were newspaper reporters. My brother Jim and I sought out a reporter for the *Oregon Journal*. The reporter got word to our relatives that we were alive. They had not had word from us for about three years.

We pulled into San Francisco on 3 October 1945, more than four years after departing from the same terminal for Wake Island. We were met by a large crowd, including wives and parents. My brother's wife came running to meet us. When she reached us, she asked which one was her husband. We were so thin that she couldn't tell us apart.

In 1981, forty years after World War II began, the U. S. Government conferred on the civilian personnel at Wake Island the status of military veterans because they had taken part in the defense of the island and were treated as prisoners of war. I was issued a DD-214 indicating that I was on military status while on Wake Island and while I was a prisoner. Shortly thereafter, I was issued a DD-215 itemizing the medals to which I was entitled as a veteran of World War II.

So in 1981, I became a veteran for service rendered from 1941 to 1945, part of which was underage. In 1995, I became a life member of the Veterans of Underage Military Service.

Norman Swanson had gone to Wake Island for the purpose of earning enough money to enter a university. In 1946, he enrolled at the University of Washington with about $2000 in savings from his work on Wake. Later, the government granted the ex-prisoners captivity pay, and Norman received $5000 each year for three years, enough to complete his bachelor's degree in chemical engineering. He worked as a civil engineer at Grand Coulee Dam for a time, then accepted a position at the Hanford Nuclear Works, where he worked for about six years. He then worked for Atomics International developing new atomic power systems. Later, he went to the Argonne National Laboratory where he worked on the development of safe fuel materials for use in large power reactors. He retired in 1983, but to avoid boredom, he worked for Southern California Edison in their power reactor program for about a year. He then retired for medical reasons. Norman and his wife Karen live on a small farm in Ridgefield, Washington. They reared seven children and have eleven grandchildren.

Frank A. DiNapoli

Age 15 – United States Navy

A few days after the attack on Pearl Harbor, I was at a post office in my hometown of Boston, Massachusetts, and noticed some blank birth certificates lying on the counter. I picked one up, went home, filled it out, putting my day

... one torpedo crossed our bow and the other one caught us just aft of midship and exploded.

of birth at 3 July 1924 instead of 3 July 1926, and my parents signed it. With my new birth certificate, I went to the Navy recruiting office and had no problem enlisting. I was sworn into the Navy on 18 December 1941, at the age of 15.

I was sent to Newport, Rhode Island, for three weeks of boot camp. I left Newport one morning and by that afternoon I was aboard a destroyer, the USS *Gwin* (DD-433), at the Boston Navy Yard. We stayed in the harbor overnight, and the next morning we were at sea, headed towards Iceland. We were on submarine patrol and convoy duty, escorting ships to England. We ran into a few subs, dropped some depth charges, and got credit for sinking one. We picked up an emergency call from the Coast Guard Cutter

Hamilton. She had been torpedoed and was sinking. We caught up with her before she sank and rescued some survivors.

The North Atlantic was a hell of a place. We were there during January and February, and it was cold! I got seasick. I was sick for five or six days, and I mean sick! I didn't care whether I lived or died. I just lay on the deck as the sea water washed all over me. Many a time I thought about going to the skipper to tell him how old I was so that I could get my ass out of there, but I stuck it out. It's funny, I never got seasick again, and we went through some awful storms.

In March 1942, we received orders to go to the West Coast. We went through the Panama Canal, pulled into San Diego for a day, then went on to San Francisco. When we left Frisco in early April, we didn't know where we were going. After we joined up with a task force that included the carrier USS *Hornet*, we learned we would be escorting the *Hornet* to a spot near Japan where sixteen Army bombers would take off to bomb Tokyo. This was the famous raid on 18 April 1942 led by Colonel James Doolittle. We returned to Pearl Harbor for a few days, then sailed for the South Pacific. Our first real action was the Battle of the Coral Sea during which the USS *Lexington* was sunk on 8 May 1942. We picked up some survivors from the *Lexington*. Japanese planes were really raising hell, and we shot down quite a few.

Our next engagement was the Battle of Midway. The USS *Yorktown* was hit during the battle. She was listing, so we went alongside her trying to try to take off personnel and to salvage any gear that we could. We received word that there were enemy subs in the area, so we pulled away and started patrolling. We finally got word that everything was secure, but this time we didn't go alongside the *Yorktown*. The destroyer USS *Hammann* went alongside and tied up to the *Yorktown*, doing the same thing we were doing before the report about submarines. I don't know exactly what happened, but the *Yorktown* and the *Hammann* blew up at the same time. Boy, you talk about an explosion! We heard later that a Japanese sub had snuck in and fired a couple of torpedoes.

The *Hammann* sank fast. When she reached a certain depth, her depth charges went off. There were a lot of survivors in the water, and when her depth charges went off – oh, my God, what a mess! You wouldn't believe the condition of some of the guys we pulled from the water. Some were bloated so badly they looked pregnant. The concussion and pressure blew water up their rectums, literally blew their bellies right out. We picked up quite a few survivors.

We went back to routine patrolling after Midway, hedgehopping among the islands. Once in a while, we would be raided by Japanese planes. In August 1942, we assisted in the invasion of Guadalcanal by the 1st Marine Division. We were bombarding the beach while Japanese planes and shore batteries were firing at us. A shell hit us right on the deck. It didn't do too much damage, but three men were killed by shrapnel. The next day we held funeral services for the three men who were killed. That was my first experience with men being buried at sea. It just ripped the heart out of this 16-year-old.

We patrolled back and forth up the Slot where Japanese ships would come bringing reinforcements to Guadalcanal. We called the Japanese task force that kept coming down the Slot the Tokyo Express. We skirmished with them a few times. During the nights of 13 and 14 November 1942, we were up there along with two battleships, the USS *South Dakota* and the USS *Washington*, and four other destroyers. We ran into the Tokyo Express, and boy, all hell broke loose! Three of our destroyers were sunk right away. The *South Dakota* was hit quite a few times, and we were hit twice. We were burning and out of action, but we could see all the action that was going on around us, the blasts of gunfire and the ships getting hit. We finally got the fires out and found that we could get underway.

We followed the *South Dakota* and the *Washington* out of the Slot and went to New Caledonia for repairs. They could only do so much there, so we went to Pearl Harbor, then back to the States. We pulled into San Francisco and went from there to the Mare Island Navy Yard, where they patched us up. We were there about a month, then headed for the South Pacific and the same old bullshit, patrolling, convoy duty, and escort duty.

We joined another task force, getting ready for the invasion of the New Georgia Islands and Bougainville. This was the early part of July 1943. We were going up the Slot just about every night. Things were really rough. We would go up there as soon as the sun set and stay there all night. We would shell the beach and engage any Japanese ships trying to land reinforcements. As soon as the sun would come out, we would haul ass back to our base, load up with more ammunition and a few stores, and get ready to go out again at sunset. We did this for about a week and a half. Some of the men were saying that our luck was going to run out after a while, but most of us said, "No, not the mighty *Gwin*, nothing will happen to the mighty *Gwin*."

One night the cruiser USS *Helena* and the destroyer USS *Strong* were leading our force. They both got hit and were sunk. The next morning we were looking for survivors. We were patrolling close to the shoreline when we saw a group of people on the beach waving. A lot of them were covered with oil so we couldn't tell whether they were natives or Americans. We got as close as we could, lowered our boats, went to the beach, and picked up about one hundred survivors of the *Helena*. Boy, were they glad to see us! We got them aboard and hauled ass out of there.

The following night we had to go back up to the same area again. This time we went with three cruisers and ten destroyers. We ran into the Tokyo Express again, and this time we really caught hell. We fired torpedoes at a Japanese cruiser and sank her. After the battle was over, we got word that three Japanese destroyers were leaving the area. The *Gwin* and two other destroyers started out after them. While we were chasing them, they made a sharp right turn and fired a spread of torpedoes. We spotted the torpedoes, but it was too late. They were headed right towards us. We could see them streaking through the water. Our skipper yelled, "Hard starboard!" Just as we turned, one torpedo crossed our bow and the other one caught us just aft of midship and exploded. The ship just about jumped out of the water. Fires broke out, and everybody was yelling and screaming while trying to get things under control. The 20mm magazine caught fire, and the shells were exploding, throwing shrapnel every which way. The aft part of the ship was sinking and water was on the decks. We still had power, but the rudder was stuck at hard right, so we just kept going around in circles. The two 5-inch aft gun mounts were blown off and the gun crews killed. Eighty to ninety men were killed.

We finally got the fires under control. In the meantime, all the other ships had gone. As I remember, we could send on our radio but we couldn't receive. We were sending out SOS signals. We picked up the sound of a ship coming up on our stern. We didn't know whether it was American or Japanese. We thought it probably was the enemy coming in to finish us off. We maneuvered our ship so she was facing in the direction of the oncoming ship. Our two forward guns were still operable, so we were all set to open fire. We figured that if we were to go down, we would go down fighting.

Fortunately, the ship turned out to be an American destroyer, the USS *Ralph Talbot*, which came back to help us out. She pulled along- side of us to salvage important equipment. It was starting to get light by this time. We were near a lot of enemy-held islands. We were spotted by Japanese planes and were soon being strafed and bombed. Soon our planes came and fought them off.

The *Talbot* decided to take our ship in tow, but our stern was way below water and we were sinking fast. Towing was out, so we all abandoned ship and were picked up by the *Talbot*. As we pulled away, we could see that the *Gwin* was going down little by little, so the *Talbot* fired a couple of torpedoes to finish the job. Boy, that was an awful feeling. Seeing her go down was just like losing your home. She was a nice little ship. We had gone through hell on her and everybody loved her. She sank on 13 July 1943, ten days after my seventeenth birthday.

We went back to New Caledonia, and were there for about two weeks. We were told that the men who were aboard ship the longest would soon be going back to the States. I happened to be one of the fortunate ones. They took us, survivors from other ships, Marines, Army, Air Corps, all survivors of battles, and put us aboard an Army transport, the USS *Seawitch*. I think it was on old luxury liner that the Army had taken over during the war and converted to a troopship. We came back to the States in luxury. We couldn't believe the food they served us. We had movies every night. It was great!

At the receiving station in San Francisco, I found out that I had to go to the hospital. I was sent to a hospital in Santa Cruz, California, that used to be an old summer resort. Boy, what a beautiful spot that was — right on the beach. We were treated like kings, with liberty every day. The only time we had to be there was for 0800 sick call.

After about three weeks in the hospital, I was scheduled for assignment to another destroyer. However, they determined that I wasn't fit for sea duty. I was to be assigned to shore duty, to a non-combatant ship, or be given a medical discharge. I didn't want to serve on a noncombatant ship, and I didn't want a medical discharge because I wanted to join the regular Navy and make it my career. My orders came through for shore duty. I was assigned to a recruiting station in Albany, New York. I couldn't believe it! I was to be stationed just a stone's throw from my hometown, Boston, Massachusetts.

I reported to the recruiting station in Albany and remained there until the war was over. I was going to reenlist, but I met a girl who talked me into getting out. I was discharged on 12 November 1945.

Frank DiNapoli earned five battle stars on his Asiatic-Pacific ribbon. After his discharge from the Navy, he started out as a laborer in construction and joined the union. Later he joined the Mason's Union and worked as a bricklayer and cement finisher for over forty years. He retired in 1988 at the age of 62. He has kept in touch with old shipmates on the Gwin. Frank and his wife Marie live in Niverville, New York. They have a combined family of eleven children and twenty-four grandchildren.

Joseph A. Moynihan

Age 16 – United States Navy

When Pearl Harbor was attacked, I was a 16-year-old senior in a Lawrence, Massachusetts, High School. Seized with patriotic fervor, I enlisted and within two weeks I was at the Naval Training Station, Newport, Rhode Island, one of many hundreds of

> *After a total of three weeks of boot camp we were marched to a waiting troop train.*

enlistees. We were originally housed in brick barracks that had been there in the Revolutionary War era (circa 1775). After a couple of days, my company and others were loaded into open motor launches with our seabags and hammocks and taken to Quonset Point Naval Air Station. The distance might not have been that long, but it seemed like an eternity, with the waves breaking over the bow soaking us and the cold December weather causing the water to freeze on us.

At Quonset Point, we learned how to march, how to follow orders, how to tie knots, etc. We were also exposed to how the United States Marines handled prisoners who were under their control. It was enough to make any sensible sailor vow never to get in enough trouble to be put under the "guidance" of Marine guards.

Before long, we were back at N.T.S. Newport, R.I. After a total of three weeks of boot camp, we were marched to a waiting troop train. I can still recall a little old lady standing on a hillside along our line of march waving to us, and no doubt, wishing us God-speed. On that day, 10 January 1942, the train took us to Boston, Massachusetts, where we were assigned to the USS *San Diego* (CL-53), a brand new antiaircraft light cruiser that had just been put in commission that morning. You can imagine how those "plank owners" (those who were aboard when the ship was commissioned) must have been shaking their heads in dismay as they watched hundreds of "boots" come aboard. After all, they had to train us.

After shakedown cruises to Annapolis, Maryland, and Casco Bay in Maine, we left Boston and headed for our Pacific assignment. This was in May 1942. On the first night at sea, the lookouts spotted a surfaced German U-boat off our port quarter some distance away just below the horizon. The crew was already at general quarters because the time was just before dusk. That sighting must have given our captain some pause. Here he was with a brand new ship, an inexperienced crew, and the ship's first contact with the enemy. What to do? It would be pretty embarrassing to have his new command sunk practically within sight of the East Coast. Quickly, he made the prudent decision to continue steaming on as before and out of harm's way.

The next adventure was going through the Panama Canal. Here was something I had been reading about in school just a few weeks before, and now I was there. Amazing! Our next port of call was our namesake city, San Diego, California. A new city, new things, new places to see, more adventures. Heady stuff!

On my seventeenth birthday, 1 June 1942, we departed San Diego headed toward the Pacific and Pearl Harbor, Hawaii. The carnage that took place on 7 December 1941 was still evident. From there the *San Diego* went on an odyssey unmatched by any other light cruiser in our Navy. She earned fifteen battle stars, survived a typhoon at sea, travelled over 300,000 miles in the war zone, never lost a man, and was only slightly damaged. She was the first man-of-war to enter Tokyo harbor, a reward no doubt, for her exemplary war record.

I was transferred from the *San Diego* in December 1943, having served nearly two years aboard. After a leave, I reported to the Fargo Barracks in Boston, Massachusetts, where I languished for weeks. When I asked for something to do, they assigned me as a brig guard. Finally, I began to volunteer for everything that came up. I put in for sea duty, submarines, the V-12 program, anything that would get me out of the receiving station. I received orders to report to the destroyer USS *Forrest*, and wouldn't you know it, at the same time I was accepted into the V-12 program. The V-12 program took precedence, and the Navy sent me to Bates College in Lewiston, Maine. I found out later that I was there at the same time as Bobby Kennedy.

My next assignment was to the USS *LST 872*. Many momentous things happened while I was serving on that ship. President Franklin Roosevelt died and was succeeded by Harry Truman; I extended my enlistment for two years; the two atomic bombs were dropped on Japan; and the war came to an end. I was in San Francisco on V-J Day. What a night that was!

The peacetime Navy wasn't too hard to take. I served on the USS *William R. Rush* (DD-714) and visited many ports in the Caribbean and along the Gulf Coast. Our ship took part in the 8th Fleet's visit to New York City. We went on liberty in "The Big Apple," and it was fate that led a group of us swabbies to visit the famed Roseland Ballroom where I had the good fortune to ask a girl to dance, little knowing that she would become my wife.

I was discharged in March of 1947, joined the inactive reserves, and went to work in the telephone industry. I was recalled to active duty for a short time during the Korean War.

Joe Moynihan earned eight battle stars on his Asiatic-Pacific theater ribbon. After his discharge, he worked at Bell Telephone Laboratories and later transferred to the New York Telephone Company. He was transferred to New England Telephone in 1957, retiring from that company in 1985. While living in New Hampshire, Joe and his wife Jean raised three daughters and four sons, and now have nine grandchildren. After retiring, Joe and Jean moved to Largo, Florida, where they enjoy living in spite of minor inconveniences such as hurricanes and being residents of the lightning capital of the nation. Joe tired of having so much time on his hands, so he accepted a job as a driver for the Aristocrat Limousine Company. He thoroughly enjoys touring Florida in his limo.

Mike Singer

Age 15 – United States Marine Corps

Those listening to the radio on 7 December 1941 were shocked to hear the announcement that the Japanese had bombed American naval bases in the Hawaiian Islands and that thousands of American servicemen had been

I didn't realize at the time how brave these men were.

killed. Two of my older brothers were already in the Army. The following week I went to the Marine recruiting office and enlisted. I told them that I was 18 and they believed me, but in reality, I wouldn't even be 16 until 25 January 1942.

After boot camp at San Diego, we went to Camp Elliott, California, where I was assigned to the 3rd Battalion, 1st Marine Regiment, 1st Marine Division. During my time with the 3rd Battalion, I served with both Item Company and King Company.

The stay at Camp Elliott was short, and we were soon on our way to the South Pacific. In August 1942, we landed on Guadalcanal. We went to Australia in late 1942 to rest and regroup, then we went on to eastern New Guinea. We landed at Cape Gloucester, New Britain, just after Christmas 1943. After that campaign, we went to Pavuvu in the Russell Islands to regroup and train for the invasion of Peleliu.

We landed on Peleliu on 15 September 1944. Colonel Lewis B. "Chesty" Puller was our regimental commander. It is an understatement to say that it was rough on Peleliu – it was pure hell. It was there that I received my most serious wound. About 6:30 one morning, we were advancing behind a Sherman tank when a machine gun in a pillbox opened up on us. I was shot in the legs, and my left leg was broken. I lay there all day with bullets flying all around me. I drank two canteens of water that day. It was almost nightfall before the stretcher-bearers could get to me and get me out. It wasn't until 1996 when I read an article in *The Old Breed News*[16] that I realized who had come for me.

At that time, all the military services were segregated. African-American Marines were not allowed in the line companies but were relegated to service battalions and worked as stevedores and ammo carriers. On Peleliu, there were so many casualties on the line that replacements and even stretcher-bearers were not available. After their jobs on the beach were completed, service battalion Marines were released to volunteer wherever they were needed. Many volunteered to fight on the line as infantrymen and serve as stretcher-bearers. They were the ones who came to my rescue and brought me back to the aid station. I didn't realize at the time how brave these men were.

I was taken back to an aid station where corpsmen patched me up. I give them a lot of credit for doing a great job. I was evacuated later to a hospital ship and was brought back to the States. I spent nearly a year in several different hospitals. In early 1945, I learned that one of my brothers had been killed in the Battle of the Bulge.

After I was released from the hospital, I was ordered to go overseas again. I was still limping and dragging my left leg as I was going up the gangplank of a troopship. When I was partway up the gangplank, I heard the announcement that the war was over. Needless to say, I was greatly relieved. I was discharged in September 1945.

Mike Singer was awarded the Silver Star, the Bronze Star, three Purple Hearts, three Presidential Unit Citations, and several other medals. After the war, he owned and operated a large truck stop and service center in the Chicago, Illinois, area. From the time he left the service, he has been very active in veterans organizations and has volunteered many hours in nursing homes and hospitals. He has held a number of state and national offices in the Jewish War Veterans Association. Mike and Jean, his wife of forty-nine years, live in Flossmoor, Illinois. They have two daughters and five grandchildren. Mike is the Illinois State Commander of the Veterans of Underage Military Service.

---

[16] Edward Andrusko, "Black Angels on Peleliu," *The Old Breed News* Vol. XLVI, August 1996. *The Old Breed News* is the official publication of the 1st Marine Division Association.

Blase F. Wagenbrenner, Jr.

Age 15 – United States Navy

Attending the 1939 New York World's Fair was a memorable experience for a 13-year-old boy, but the thrill and excitement of seeing the many exhibits was tempered by sadness when the lights were turned off at the Czechoslovakian Pavilion and at the Polish Pavilion.

> *Dad was so angry with me for dropping out of school that he not only said, "No," but "Hell no! Send him out to sea!"*

Hitler had already seized the Rhineland and Austria, my mother's birthplace, and was now moving east with his blitzkrieg. The sight of the darkened pavilions brought tears to my eyes.

In June 1941, the Battle for Britain was raging and I wanted to help. I was 15 years old at the time and entertained the thought of going to Canada and volunteering for the Royal Canadian Air Force. My father, who was on active duty with the U. S. Navy at the time, talked me into staying in school. He promised me that if the United States went to war he would help me enlist.

On that fateful Sunday, 7 December 1941, my father and I were at my Aunt Rose's house when I heard the radio announcement that Pearl Harbor had been bombed. Dad immediately donned his uniform and returned to his ship. I wrote to him that night and reminded him of his promise to help me get into the service if we went to war. He tried twice to keep me in school, but he finally realized that I was serious about going to Canada if he didn't keep his promise. In February, he asked me what branch of service I wanted. My first choice was the U. S. Marine Corps. We went to the Marine recruiting office, but the recruiter would have nothing to do with us when we told him I was only 15 years old.

At our next stop, the U. S. Navy recruiting station, we found a receptive recruiter. His concerns were that the family might object and blow the whistle on me and dad. When he understood that my mother had passed away when I was seventeen months old and that my sister had no objections to my enlisting, he processed the papers. I had a hand-written baptismal certificate that showed my birth date as 24 June 1926. The six was looped through and the recruiter said that it could be a four. He asked Dad if he would swear that I was 17. He did, and I suddenly aged two years. The recruiter also asked my father if he wanted me to serve on his ship. Dad was so angry with me for dropping out of school that he not only said, "No," but "Hell no! Send him out to sea!" On 30 March 1942, I proudly took the oath of enlistment in the U. S. Navy as Fred Wagenbrenner, although my full name was Blase Ferdinand Wagenbrenner, Jr.

I was on my way to boot camp at Newport, Rhode Island, that night. On 4 May 1942, we donned our dress blues for the first time, fixed bayonets for the first time, and marched out to what was our graduation review. On 5 May 1942, I reported aboard the USS *Livermore* (DD-429) at Boston, Massachusetts, and within the week, we headed out into the North Atlantic as a convoy escort. My great adventure was underway!

We went to Londonderry, Ireland, and to Greenock, Scotland. While I was in Scotland, a shipmate and I were befriended by a Scottish family. We found out that the "wee ones" (children) didn't know what oranges were. On our next liberty, we left our gas masks on board and filled our gas-mask bags with apples and oranges. The joyous smiles of the "wee ones" upon receiving these gifts were heartwarming.

We participated in Operation Torch, the Allied landings in North Africa, in November 1942. Later, we went to the South Atlantic on anti raider patrol. From July 1943 until May 1944, I was a student, and later on, an instructor in the Naval Mine Warfare School, Yorktown and Little Creek, Virginia. I then attended the Submarine School at New London, Connecticut. After a short tour in a relief crew at Mare Island, California, I joined the USS *Crevalle* (SS-291) and participated in her sixth and seventh war patrols.

We participated in the Iwo Jima and the Okinawa campaigns and went through the mine fields at Japan's Tsushima Straits with Hydeman's Hellcats, commanded by Commander Earl Twining Hydeman. The Hellcats consisted of nine submarines: the *Bonefish*, *Spadefish*, *Sea Dog*, *Crevalle*, *Skate*, *Tunny*, *Tinosa*, *Flyingfish*, and *Bowfin*. During this raid, the Japanese lost twenty-eight steel-hulled ships, each totaling more than 500 tons, and forty-seven lesser craft. The USS *Bonefish* was lost with all hands.

My enlistment expired while we were in the Sea of Japan. The captain told me that he would put me ashore if I desired because, technically, I would be a civilian at midnight. I really didn't want to be put ashore in Japan in June 1945, so I declined the captain's generous offer and extended my enlistment for two years.

After the war, I served on a number of ships, including the *Flyingfish*, *Billfish*, *Bang*, *Greenfish*, *Bennington*, *Duxbury Bay*, *Pompon*, *Trout*, *Dogfish*, *Saratoga*, *Proteus*, *Darter*, and *Chivo*.

When I turned 21 for the second time in June 1947, I decided it was time to set the record straight. I told the captain of the *Greenfish* that I wanted to correct my service record. He asked me what was wrong, and I told him my given name was Blase Ferdinand Wagenbrenner, Jr., not Fred Wagenbrenner. He said that was no problem. Then I dropped the other shoe and informed the captain that my birth date was not correct. He asked, "Did they have the wrong day?" I replied, "No, sir." Then he asked, "Is it the wrong month?" Again I replied, "No, sir." Finally, he asked, "Is it the wrong year?" This time I replied, "No, sir, it is two years!"

By this time I was an electrician's mate first class, qualified in submarines. The captain said that he would reenlist me, keep me aboard, and would report the facts to the Chief of Naval Personnel for a final decision. I was greatly relieved when the captain's action was approved and my Navy career was no longer in jeopardy.

In April 1959, I received orders to attend Admiral Rickover's Basic Nuclear Power School at New London, Connecticut. I would be the senior chief petty officer in the class. Although I had dropped out of high school seventeen years before, I accepted the challenge of this accelerated course and graduated with distinction, fourteenth in a class of 227. I attribute this achievement to the solid basics I received in my three years as a student at Brooklyn Technical High School.

I was commissioned an ensign in January 1960, and after a tour at Commander Mine Force Atlantic, I reported to the USS *Saratoga* as the electrical officer. In March 1963, I was assigned to the USS *Darter* (SS-576) and earned my "gold dolphins," the submarine officer qualification insignia.

I served on the Sub Board of the Navy's Board of Inspection and Survey at Charleston, South Carolina, from January 1966 until

February 1968. From there I went to the staff of the Naval Missile Center, Point Mugu, California, as ballistic missile officer. My duties were those of director of Polaris and Poseidon operations. I attended the SSBN Weapons Course at Dam Neck, Virginia, finishing fourth in a class of nine. Not bad for a high school dropout, considering that my classmates were all college graduates.

It was a tremendous thrill, an exciting experience, and a real challenge to conduct missile operations from Johnston Island and to shoot missiles downrange from Hawaii to Kwajalein. But things got even better. In June 1969, I was assigned to the Commander, Submarine Division 71, as division engineer. The division, called the "Wise Tigers," consisted of nuclear attack submarines manned by some of America's best. The ballistic missile submarines had their "blue" and "gold" crews. Our nuclear attack submarines had but one crew, at times referred to as the "black and blue" crew.

In June 1970, I was assigned to the USS *Chivo* (SS-341), at Charleston, South Carolina, as engineering officer. This was my twilight cruise prior to my retirement. I was surprised by the *Chivo's* excellent engineering performance, as she was twenty-seven years old. On 1 July 1971, I retired from her decks, and she was transferred to the Argentine Navy. Seeing her go down the channel was like saying goodbye to an old flame. I was a lieutenant when I retired.

Blase Wagenbrenner received the Submarine Combat Insignia with one gold star and later the New York State Conspicuous Service Cross in recognition of combat service in submarines. He spent a few years as an unhappy civilian after his 1971 retirement from the Navy, then returned to sea with the U. S. Merchant Marine and retired from that duty in 1985. Forced to be a civilian, Blase put his energies into the Boy Scouts of America and the American Legion. He was a scouting-camp commissioner and camp-program director at Camp Krietenstein, Indiana, in 1990 and 1991. His wife Alice, also a good scout, was arts and crafts director for a week at the camp. Their scouting activities had to be put aside in 1991 when Alice underwent quadruple heart by-pass surgery. Not to be outdone, Blase had a triple by-pass operation in 1992. Blase and Alice live in Charleston, South Carolina. They have eight children, thirteen grandchildren, and two great grandchildren.

Robert C. Bartholow

Age 16 – United States Marine Corps

I was born in Pittsburgh, Pennsylvania, on 3 October 1925 and raised on a farm near Benton Harbor, Michigan. I ran away from home four times before I was 15 years old.

I had 131 attacks of malaria – a memento of Guadalcanal.

The last time, I went to Pittsburgh to be with my grandmother. I always got up early, a trait I had learned by necessity on the farm. I sold newspapers on busses and street cars on the north side of Pittsburgh.

I started the tenth grade in Pittsburgh. In one class, when the teacher had to leave the classroom, she would assign a student to be in charge during her absence. After school had been in session for about a month, the teacher put me in charge and left the room. Well, I was pursuing romantically a certain young lady and enticed her into the closet with me. About the time I had her partially undressed, the teacher returned. I was scolded and sent to the principal's office. I

thought that I would be expelled and that this would embarrass my grandmother, so I left the building.

I took the streetcar downtown, using my badge from the newspaper which allowed me to ride free. I hoped to enlist in the Navy and become a submariner. At the Navy recruiting office, I was asked how old I was. I told them I was 17, but the recruiter said that the Navy was taking only 18-year-olds at the time. Feeling badly rejected, I went to the Army recruiter and told him I was 18.

He said, "Son, you are not 18, come back in a couple of years." So rejected again, I started walking out of the courthouse. As I passed a Marine officer, he asked me, "Are you ready to enlist?" I replied, "Yes, sir!" They processed me that day and told me to take my papers home and have them signed and notarized.

I went back to the high school at the end of the school day to find out what had been said about the classroom incident. I ran into a friend of mine who also sold newspapers. I told him about enlisting in the Marines but that I didn't know how to get the papers notarized. My friend told me to sign the papers and *he* would notarize them. I signed my grandmother's name and handed the papers to him. He put down a silver dollar, set the papers on it, put another silver dollar directly over the first one, then took off his shoe and hit the dollars very hard with the heel, making a "seal" like that of a notary.

Instead of going to school the next morning, I went straight downtown to the Marine recruiting office. I was sworn in at 8:00 a.m. on 5 May 1942 and left the same day for Parris Island, South Carolina. I called my grandmother at one of the stops, and told her what I had done. She didn't approve, but reluctantly gave her consent.

After boot camp, I was sent to Quantico, Virginia, for a short time, then went overseas with the 21st replacement draft. When I landed on Guadalcanal, the island was ours but was not secure. I was assigned to Charlie Company, 3rd Amphibious Amtrack Battalion and was with the 3rd when we landed on Emiru and later on Guam.

En route to Guam, a fellow Marine borrowed $20.00 from me to get into a card game. After the landing, when the beach was secure, he climbed aboard my amtrack, paid me my $20.00, and thanked me. He said he had been quite lucky the last night aboard ship. After paying me, he jumped off the amtrack, landed on a mine, and was killed.

Later, during the Guam campaign, a group of twenty-five Japanese soldiers came out of the hills one night and engaged us in a fire fight. We wiped them out! The next day some Seabees came to dig a large ditch and bury the enemy dead. What a surprise! The chief petty officer in charge of the Seabees was Sherwood Brown, my dad's closest friend. I had been raised calling this man "Uncle Brownie." Chief Brown was in charge of building a headquarters for Admiral Nimitz.

Brownie was very glad to see me. He told me that when he could, he would let my father know where I was. Then he asked if there was anything I needed. After I talked to the sergeant and the captain, they told me to ask Brownie if we could get some lumber for tent sides and floors. Brownie told us to bring a truck that night and he would leave the compound gate open. We went to the compound with two trucks and a few men. We loaded all the lumber and power tools we needed and headed back to our company area.

The next day, Brownie came by and said that he was worried. He had reported that some Japanese had come out of the hills and taken lumber and power tools from the compound. The officer to whom he had reported the loss asked him how they would be able to run the power tools. I told Brownie not to worry and to be sure to leave the gate open again. That night we returned and took the generators. Everything was OK the next day — the Japanese had returned!

Being a radio operator, I was transferred again, this time to the 12th Marine Regiment to train as a forward observer. I was attached to Charlie Company, 1st Battalion, 9th Marines, for the landing on Iwo Jima. Our company was the first to cross the third airstrip and reach the beach across the island from where we had landed. The officer to whom I was assigned as a radioman asked for the microphone and informed headquarters that we had reached the beach. The commanding general came on the radio and said that he didn't believe it. To prove it we were to bring back a canteen of salt water. We did!

War was hell, and I was scared as hell during combat, but I was young enough to not let the bad memories haunt me. I had 131 attacks of malaria — a memento of Guadalcanal.

I was discharged in late 1945 and returned to Bridgman, Michigan. For a while after my discharge, I drew a pension, but I wouldn't go to the VA hospital, so they discontinued the pension.

Bob Bartholow drove truck for a time, then became a heavy-equipment mechanic. He was a service engineer for the Harris, Press & Shear Company, Cordele, Georgia, until 1970 when he moved to Orlando, Florida. He opened his own industrial-hydraulics shop in Orlando the same month that Disney World opened in 1971. He sold his business in 1978, bought a boat, planning to be gone six only weeks. He ended up traveling throughout the Caribbean and South America, returning three and a half years later. Shortly after his discharge from the Marines, Bob served as an usher at a friend's wedding. He met the maid of honor, and nine days later they were married. Bob and Clara, his wife of fifty years, live in Avon Park, Florida. They have two sons, two grandchildren, and two great-grand-children. Both sons served in the Navy. Bob became a ham radio operator shortly after the war. His call sign is K4GND, with the "GND" meaning "good-natured devil," according to his wife Clara.

Orville E. "Yank" Sumpter

Age 15 – United States Marine Corps

I was weighing cotton in a field near Bakersfield, California, on 7 December 1941. The next day, during the high school gym class, we were told to listen to our president on the radio. President Roosevelt asked Congress for a declaration of war. At noon, my buddy and I went to the recruiting office

> ... *some cans of ammunition shifted and knocked me off the truck, all of me except my leg, ...*

to enlist. He was 17 but I wouldn't be 15 until the next day, 9 December 1941. My buddy enlisted in the Navy, and I stopped at the Marine recruiting office. Maybe I stopped there because of the dress blues, first to fight, Semper Fi, and all that. The recruiting sergeant asked my age, and I told him that I was only 15. He said, "You are big enough, but not old enough. Get permission from your mother or dad." He told me that if I could get a birth certificate or a sworn statement certifying that I was 17, I could enlist. He said that a telegram would suffice.

My father had died in 1934, my mother was in the Midwest, and I was living with an uncle in California. It took a few months, but finally my mother sent a telegram to the recruiting sergeant. It merely said that I was 17 and gave her permission for me to enlist. The telegram was stapled inside of my record book. I was sworn into the regular Marine Corps on 15 May 1942 in Los Angeles, California. One of the men with whom I was sworn in had figured out that I was underage, but he never told anyone, as far as I knew. My high school coach, the dean of boys, and my mechanical-drawing teacher also knew that I was underage, but they wished me well.

As I said, the recruiter knew that I was only 15, but I believe that anyone who could walk and talk could enlist at that time. I met a number of men (boys) whom I knew were underage. You could tell by their faces — most of them had only peach fuzz or a few whiskers. At least I was shaving!

I was sent to the Marine Corps Base, San Diego, California, for boot camp. Boot camp was a piece of cake because the time I had spent on the farm had made me tough and strong. We were issued the old "stove pipe" packs, and our green uniforms were of World War I vintage — high collar with brass belt hanger — typical USMC, scraping the bottom of the barrel. Before going overseas, we were issued the new two-piece packs and new greens and khakis, although we kept our Springfield model 1903 rifles. The Springfield was a fine piece of equipment.

We left San Diego in July 1942 aboard the SS *Day Star*, which was a fugitive from the scrap yard. I'm sure that the Japanese would have bought her for scrap before the war if they had known where to look. There were four salt-water showers below and the heads were on the deck. We were rationed one and a half meals per day. Some of us did some "moonlight requisitioning" of raw onions and raw potatoes from crates lashed topside. Tasted good!

We docked at Pearl Harbor and went to Camp Catlin for a few days, then went on to Midway Island to beef up the outfit there. We were formed into a special-weapons group and were quickly taught how to operate the 40, 37, and 20mm cannons and the 0.30 and 0.50 caliber machine guns. We made our own land mines in anticipation of beach landings by the Japanese.

There was a large number of old China Marines in our outfit. Some had been aboard ship on their way to Wake Island and the Philippines when they were turned back after those places had been overrun by the Japanese. They were old salts, seagoing Marines, horse Marines, China Marines, many with a lifetime of service. They were an interesting bunch of people for this 15-year-old to be around.

One day in June 1943, we were replenishing ammunition to the gun positions. I was standing next to the tailgate on a 6x6 truck when some cans of ammunition shifted and knocked me off the truck, all of me except my leg, which was caught and crushed between some cans of ammunition. I was taken to sick bay and patched up somewhat. That night was the last time the Japanese shelled the island, as far as I know. I was doped up fairly heavily and can barely remember the sound of the guns. A corpsman rolled me out of my bunk and covered me with a mattress to protect me if a shell landed nearby.

The cast that was put on my leg became soaked with blood, so the corpsman put another cast over the first one, since I was still bleeding quite a bit. He knew that I would be going back to Pearl Harbor the next day on a PB4Y2 aircraft. At Pearl Harbor, I was taken to the naval hospital at Aiea.

The question at the hospital was whether to remove the lower portion of my leg or to try to fix it using a new-fangled contraption developed by a veterinarian for race horses. The contraption was a splint consisting of four pins, two adjustable blocks, and a turnbuckle. I woke up to find a corpsman drilling holes in my leg with a shoulder-type brace and bit. That was a bit startling. Anyway, the splint was installed, and every few weeks it was adjusted as the bone knitted. After a time, my leg became infected, and I was shipped to the Mare Island Naval Hospital in California. An operation and treatment for osteomyelitis followed, along with more waiting. After eleven months I returned to duty in San Diego.

By this time, our old Major General Commandant Holcomb had retired, and A. A. Vandegrift, who had commanded the 1st Marine Division on Guadalcanal, became Commandant of the Marine Corps. General Vandegrift put out the word, "All hands who have not been overseas will go, and all those who have been, will go again." I went again.

My leg gave me all kinds of trouble. I had been in Hawaii for about a week when I was hospitalized for three weeks. Then it was off to Saipan for a few days but back to Pearl Harbor for four to five weeks of hospital time. Seems like every time I turned around my damn leg would start to leak and bone would work its way out. I must have had five gallons of penicillin shot into me. The last time, I received 144 shots, one every two hours. If you don't think your poor old heinie won't get sore with that many shots, try it!

When the A-bombs were dropped and the war was over, our division became part of the occupation forces. We were stationed near Nagasaki, on Kyushu. I spent the last five months of my overseas duty in Japan. I had served a little more than three years overseas. Because I was a regular, "points" did not count towards my time for discharge. I served my four years and was discharged on 18 May 1946.

Yank Sumpter went to work in the oil fields two days after being discharged from the Marine Corps. He started at the bottom and worked his way up to become a directional-drilling engineer and drilling consultant. He worked for several corporations and had his own business for a time, but his work always related to the oil fields. He retired after forty years in the industry. After thirteen moves, Yank and Phyllis, his wife of forty-eight years whom he had first met in the fourth grade, finally settled in Ingram, in the hill country of Texas. They have four sons and thirteen grandchildren.

√ *VUMS Note* ⇒ *Two can play the same game.* At age 18, an underage vet who had altered his birth certificate and enlisted at 16 met a beautiful young lady, and after a short courtship, they decided to marry. At the marriage license office, she produced a driver's license showing that she was also 18. After the ceremony and some champagne, they retired to the bridal suite of a local hotel. He was awakened the next morning by an insistent pounding on the door. When he opened the door, he looked into the face of a very large deputy sheriff who informed him that the girl's mother was looking for her 13-year-old daughter! The girl told the sheriff to get lost and that she was going to Fort Bragg with her paratrooper husband. That was the end of it.

Billie B. Boyd, Jr.

Age 16 – United States Army Air Forces

When World War II began, I was a high school senior in McCool, Mississippi. I graduated on 20 April 1942 and had decided that I wanted to be a flight engineer and gunner on a bomber. One problem: to get into

> *Man, you talk about "cutting a rusty," I cut one, ...*

the Army Air Forces, I had to be at least 18 years old, and I was only 16. My dad, a World War I Navy veteran, thought that I should wait awhile, and my birth certificate mysteriously disappeared from the house – perhaps so it couldn't be used prematurely in a fit of patriotic fervor.

I talked my mother and my high school principal into accompanying me to the recruiting office ninety miles away, without my father's knowledge. On 12 May 1942, I was accepted into the Air Forces after my mother and the principal "declared" that I was 18 years old in lieu of a birth certificate, and that my father was unavailable to come along. From that time on, the family joke was that I was born before my mother was married.

I was sent to Camp Shelby, Mississippi, and sworn in on 18 May 1942. Six months and twelve days later, after graduating from aircraft and engine-mechanics school and flexible-gunnery school, I was promoted from private to staff sergeant and assigned to the 386th Bomb Group, which had just been activated. I was the flight engineer and gunner on a Martin B-26, one of a crew of six. The pilot was Staff Sergeant D. E. Casey, one of several sergeant-pilots assigned to the 554th Squadron.

After training in Florida and Louisiana, we were assigned to the European theater, flying out of England against German-occupied France, Belgium, and Holland. I flew my first combat mission on 30 July 1943.

On 26 March 1944, I completed my forty-ninth combat mission with the 386th Bomb Group. The day after this mission, I was advised that I had been selected to return to the States to attend flexible-gunnery instructors school, and that orders would filter down in approximately two weeks. I was grounded from further combat duty. I will never forget the feeling that I just might make it back home alive and in one piece!

My crew, with whom I had trained and flown forty-seven missions in our aircraft, *The Bad Penny*, wished me well and left for a 21-day R&R leave in Scotland. By this time, former Staff Sergeant Casey was Captain Casey, having been commissioned and promoted several times. He was a cool, quiet-mannered, super quick-minded pilot. I will never forget returning from a mission late one afternoon to find our base in England heavily fogged in. The planes were circling the field trying to find the end of the runway, all low on fuel. Suddenly a flare was fired from the end of the runway. We were already even with the runway, but perpendicular to it, and we couldn't back up. Casey immediately chopped the throttles, called for full flaps, unbuckled his seat belt and stood up with his left foot jamming the rudder to full left, and nosed her down on the runway while the aircraft was still in forward-right momentum. Captain Casey was second to none in my book.

I had flown one mission as a waist gunner with another crew and a mission as tail gunner with a different crew, substituting for a tail gunner who had been wounded on a previous mission. I didn't like the tail-gun position; it was just too bouncy. I didn't *ever* want the top-turret position because it meant that my chest-pack parachute had to be located on the floor, too far away for comfort. When the group was formed in December 1942, Staff Sergeant Casey had given me a choice of gun positions. I chose the waist guns for two reasons: I preferred the hand-controlled, swivel-mounted gun, and in the event of having to bail out, I was closest to the exit aft of the bomb bay. On the average, only about fifty percent of the crew managed to bail out of a damaged B-26.

While waiting impatiently for my Stateside orders which were due any day, I realized that if I were to draw flight pay for April, I had better catch a noncombat flight and log at least four hours' time. I finally managed to get on a flight scheduled for 12 April. The flight was to go to Slapton Sands, England, where ground troops were practicing for the landings in Normandy.

The night before the scheduled noncombat flight to Slapton Sands, the crew with which I was to fly was ordered into the combat schedule for 12 April. I was not aware of this. Lo and behold, I was awakened at 0530 hours and told to report to the combat briefing room. Man, you talk about "cutting a rusty," I cut one, but to no avail. The squadron commander was in London on pass, and no one else would assume the authority to excuse me from the mission.

I began to sweat and brood after the briefing. First, the bombardier was sick. The engineer-turret gunner was shifted to the bombardier's nose position, and I was assigned to the turret, the position I disliked the most. As fate would have it, the mission was delayed for several hours because of cloud cover over the target area in Belgium. After noon, we were ordered back to the waiting aircraft and we took off at 1310 hours. With luck, we would return in four hours.

After forming at 12,000 feet into six flights of six bombers each and one flight of four, we headed for the English Channel and our rendezvous with our fighter escort, the 11th Fighter Group, Royal Air Force, flying Spitfires. Each bomber was carrying sixteen 250-pound general purpose bombs. There were three things we could count on without fail: good coverage by our escort, fighter opposition, and accurate antiaircraft fire.

During the 90 to 120 seconds it takes to make a bomb run, the aircraft cannot take evasive action. However, it takes only seventeen seconds for a 35-pound 105mm flak shell to reach 12,000 feet, and when they come up in bunches, it do make a difference!

A few seconds before the bombs were released, the bomber shook like a wet dog drying off. If we had gone just another eye blink in distance before the 105mm shell exploded, it would have been directly underneath the center of the bomber, and we would have been vaporized history. As it turned out, a good-sized hunk of the hot steel fragments impacted into the very steel-bottomed turret seat upon which I was sitting, shorting out the azimuth control and causing the turret to rotate uncontrollably. Other fragments penetrated hither and yonder, severing the hydraulic main pressure line, making holes in the wings and belly of the aircraft, over one hundred holes in all. In addition, a red-hot piece embedded itself in my upper lip. This went unnoticed by me until the radioman/waist gunner pointed to my bleeding face as I was disconnecting the turret-power umbilical cord. I extracted the fragment, and in a couple of minutes, the gunner had the bleeding stopped by using a compress. At that point, I was actually afraid to drop my flying clothes and examine my rear end because I was of the opinion that the hunk of steel that had hit the bottom of the turret seat had made instant meat loaf out of an 18-year-old prime rump. It was numb, numb, numb!

After I had advised the copilot that the turret was useless and major damage was done to the hydraulic system, he ordered me to the cockpit where I finally took a look at my posterior. It was red, but there was no sign of forced entry.

When we arrived at home base, the pilot advised the control tower that we would be landing with no brakes and that there were wounded aboard. At that moment, I protested to him, "I'll be all right. We don't need an ambulance. I'll be all right." I cranked the flaps down, and shortly after touchdown, the pilot pulled the emergency air bottle for the brakes. This blew the tires (as expected), and for what seemed like an eternity, we skidded along on wheels that were flat on the bottom and fast wearing down. We stopped at the very end of the runway.

Under protest, I was ordered into the waiting ambulance. The more I protested to the ambulance crew, "I'll be all right — I don't need to go," the more they were convinced that I was in shock. They finally grabbed me, tied me down onto a litter, and away we went to the squadron dispensary. "Doc" Mikita asked me, "What's up, Billie?" I responded, "Nothing. I'll be all right." He put me on a seat, cleaned, probed, swabbed, salved, and bandaged my lip after giving me a shot of whiskey. He asked me how I felt. I said, "OK. How about another shot?" He said, "Get out of here! You'll be all right!" I said, "That's what I've been telling everybody!"

When I arrived back at the squadron area, my Stateside orders were there. Fifteen hours later, I was on a train heading for Scotland to catch the Dutch liner *Nieuw Amsterdam*. My Purple Heart caught up with me on 31 January 1990.

I returned to the States and became a gunnery instructor at the age of 18. While in that post, I met my future wife Juanita, who was in the WAC.

I was a flight engineer on C-54s out of Frankfurt during the Berlin Airlift in 1948-49. I flew two missions to Berlin on Christmas Day 1948. We took off in very dense fog on the second mission. We could barely see the runway lights. The fog remained heavy during the 1-hour 55-minute flight. Berlin was socked in, and we had to make a ground control approach (GCA) between a row of bombed-out buildings and over a cemetery. The only thing we could see was the red approach lights over the cemetery. The GCA operator said, "Hold your glide, power off, and if you will pull back on the control column, you will feel the wheels touch." After stopping on the runway, we had to be towed to the unloading area because we could not see to taxi. I *still* think of that one! Ironically, it was a former staff sergeant who was the pilot at the controls during that flight.

On 15 August 1950, I was commissioned a reserve second lieutenant and remained on active duty. I was promoted to captain in the regular Air Force in 1957 while on duty in France as an aircraft maintenance officer and to major in 1963 while serving as an Atlas-F missile maintenance supervisor. I retired from the U. S. Air Force on 1 March 1965 at the age of 39.

Billie Boyd was awarded the Distinguished Flying Cross with Oak Leaf Cluster, the Air Medal with seven Oak Leaf Clusters, the Purple Heart for wounds received in action, the Air Force Commendation Medal, and was credited with shooting down two enemy aircraft. After leaving the Air Force, Billie worked for seven years as plant manager/chief engineer for a large hospital and six years as a juvenile-court probation officer. He fully retired in 1982 to live the good life in the hills of eastern Tennessee. Billie and Juanita, his wife of forty-nine years, live in Rutledge, Tennessee. They have two children and five grand-children.

Charles E. Brown

Age 14 – United States Navy

On 7 December 1941, I was lying on the living room couch reading comic books and listening to Lowell Thomas on the radio. His program was interrupted by an announcement that elements of the Imperial Japanese Navy were bombing Pearl Harbor.

> *I had served over three years in two war zones and was not yet 18 years old.*

I was just 14 years old, but as I listened to this announcement, the hairs stood up on the back of my neck and I became very angry. I thought that I had to do something to help defend my country. Needless to say, my mother was against my enlisting because of my age. I nagged her until she finally gave in and agreed to sign the papers. Of course, I had to tell a little white lie about my age to the recruiters. Nevertheless, I enlisted in the United States Navy on 25 May 1942.

I left Williamson, West Virginia, my hometown, and went to the naval base at Norfolk, Virginia, where I began twenty-eight days of boot training. On the twenty-eighth day at approximately 1400 in the afternoon, we completed our training and by 1600 we were marched to the theater where I received my first sea-duty assignment, the USS *Kennebec* (AO-36). The *Kennebec* was making preparations to get underway at the time. We sailed to Baytown, Texas, picked up a load of aviation gasoline, transported it to Newfoundland, and returned to Texas. After three trips to Newfoundland, I was transferred to what I call the infamous Pier 92 Receiving Station in New York. While I was there, I was assigned to duty as a seaman guard, and I stood watches on the SS *Normandie* after she had been sabotaged and burned at dockside.

I was then transferred to Bayonne, New Jersey, and assigned to the USS *Elizabeth C. Stanton* (APA-69). I was immediately sent to Little

Creek, Virginia, for amphibious training in preparation for the invasion of North Africa. Shortly after I returned to the *Stanton*, we loaded troops and sailed for North Africa.

Our convoy landed troops at Fédala, North Africa, right above Casablanca. I was an LCV boat coxswain and brought the third boatload of troops to the beach. We lowered the ramp on the beach and the troops went ashore. Just as we were raising the ramp, a large wave pushed the boat farther up the beach and left us stranded. Once the water receded, there was no way we could get the boat back in the water. The Germans were strafing and dive-bombing the beach, so we couldn't stay there. We took the two 30-caliber machine guns from the front end of the boat and what ammo was available and ran across the beach into a wooded area. We laid the barrels of the machine guns in forks of trees and shot all the ammunition we had at the enemy aircraft. I doubt very seriously that we hit anything, but we returned fire.

After we ran out of ammunition, we realized that we were in an exposed area, so we went deeper into the woods. About ten minutes later we came to a dirt road. We walked out on the road and didn't see anything coming one way or the other. However, we couldn't see very far up to our left because of a bend in the road. After a few minutes, we heard a vehicle coming, so we went back in the woods and hid. We finally spotted an American jeep. When it was close, we jumped out on the road and almost got ourselves shot because we startled the sergeant who was driving the jeep. He wanted to know what the devil the Navy was doing up on that back road. We explained to him about getting our boat stranded high and dry on the beach. He was with an artillery division that was stationed up on the hills above Casablanca. We went with him to his position and stayed there for five days. Finally, the lieutenant in charge of the battery said that we had to go back to the beach and try to get back to our ship. He said that we had probably been reported missing in action, and furthermore, they didn't have food for us.

We got back to the ship without too much trouble. After the fighting receded around Casablanca, our ship went into the harbor to unload our supplies of food and ammunition. The ship's captain let us get four hours' rest before we started unloading. However, his orders were to unload immediately upon arriving dockside. Because he gave us four hours' rest, he was relieved of his command. This made all of us angry, and we worked like devils to get that ship unloaded. When we left the port, we had a new captain.

I was assigned to a special group of boat handlers and sent to Oran, North Africa, and from there to Arzew, North Africa, to help unload supplies. From there I went to Algiers. I ran a small boat to and from the beach carrying armed guard gunnery crews and merchant seamen from the merchant ships that were in the harbor unloading supplies. We also stood watches at the Hotel St. George, which was then the armed forces headquarters. In the daytime, we stood watches at the St. George and at night at the admiral's villa. One night, an Arab tried to get over the fence into the admiral's villa. He wouldn't stop when I shouted at him, so I shot him. They immediately fined me $50.00 for the bullet, gave me a carton of cigarettes, and transferred me to Bizerte.

At Bizerte, I boarded the sub chaser SC-534 and started doing convoy duty. We had a smoke generator on the stern of the ship, and during an air raid, we would go round and round the convoy laying a smoke screen. During the invasion of Sicily, we went in at Salerno. Later, we went to Naples and patrolled the beach up to Anzio. We were shelled several times because we had Army observers aboard who were sending information about the German positions to our troops on the beach.

I left the SC-534 after the invasion of southern France. I was sent home after serving twenty-eight months in Europe. I reported in at Norfolk, Virginia, after a home leave and was assigned to the USS Vulcan (AR-5), an auxiliary repair ship. We left Norfolk, Virginia, passed through the Panama Canal and out to New Caledonia, our first stop in the Pacific. From there we went to Guadalcanal, then to the Ulithi Islands. We arrived at Guam shortly after the fighting was over. We were in the typhoon of 1945 during which two destroyers were lost with all hands aboard.

We were anchored in Leyte Gulf in the Philippines the night the Japanese surrendered. We got underway soon after and were in the first contingent of ships to go into a seaport near Hiroshima. From there I boarded an old four-stacker tin can, the USS Stewart (DD-224), for a trip back to Guam where I was assigned to a hospital relief ship and came back to the States. I had served over three years in two war zones and was not yet 18 years old.

After a home leave I decided to stay in the Navy. I attended Aviation Boatswain's Mate School in Philadelphia, Pennsylvania, and served on several aircraft carriers, including the USS *Block Island* and the USS *Saratoga*. My final duty station was the Naval Air Station, Whiting Field, Milton, Florida, where I retired in May of 1964.

I was proud to serve my country then, and I am still proud to this day.

Charles Brown earned four battle stars on his European theater ribbon. After retiring from the Navy, he operated his own automotive service station. He is now on total disability from a service-connected injury to his back that has required three surgeries. He underwent triple by-pass surgery in 1979. Charles and his wife Juanell live in Hazlehurst, Georgia. They have five children and 13 grandchildren.

√ **VUMS Note** ⇒ *Pearl Harbor survivors.* Two contributors to this book were at Schofield Barracks, Oahu, Hawaii, on 7 December 1941 and vividly remember the Japanese attack. James Potter was 16 years old at the time (see page 73) and Robert Weaver was 17 (see page 32). Both remained in the Pacific theater throughout the war years, returning to the States in 1945.

Otis M. Long

Age 15 – United States Navy

When I was about 13 years old and living in Richmond, Virginia, like a lot of kids, I got involved with the wrong bunch, three older boys. It started as a joke. We would steal

Shortly after my seventeenth birthday ... our ship was hit by three torpedoes ...

reflectors from bicycles and sell them. Next, we began stealing bikes and hub caps from cars. I saw the handwriting on the wall and started making excuses why I couldn't go along with them. I was afraid that we would get arrested.

By this time I was 15, and just after Pearl Harbor was bombed, I asked my mother if I could join the Navy. Of course, just like any mother, she wouldn't hear of it. My father had passed away in 1937, and my mother was trying to raise three kids by herself, which was

very hard. I talked to her for about two weeks, explaining to her the mess I was in with the older boys and assuring her that if she would let me join, I would send her an allotment home each month to help her with expenses. She finally consented, and on my first try, I was turned down for having too much sugar in my urine. I was told to lay off sweets, drink a lot of water, and come back in eight weeks.

I had turned 15 in May, and in June of 1942, I enlisted in the regular Navy for a 4-year hitch. I was sent to Norfolk, Virginia, for boot camp and then to Corpus Christi, Texas, for assignment to an aircraft squadron. I went to gunnery school in Corpus Christi and became a tail gunner in a squadron of PBMs (flying boats). In early 1943, I went to the Aviation Ordnance School in Pensacola, Florida, and from there to Key West, Florida, where I was with another aircraft squadron (VP 202). We flew antisubmarine patrols off the coast of Florida.

Late in 1943, I was transferred to an aircraft carrier, the USS *Block Island*, at Norfolk, Virginia. My first combat occurred during our first trip out in the Atlantic. Our group sank two German submarines. I was 16 years old at the time. I can't remember how many subs our group sank, but I think it was about nine in the two trips I was on. We took some German prisoners aboard our ship. I remember remarking to one of my shipmates that the German sailors looked so young, and I was about the same age.

Shortly after my seventeenth birthday, 29 May 1944, our ship was hit by three torpedoes and sank later. Just before I jumped off the flight deck, I put on my Mae West life jacket (Navy men know what that is). When I punctured the gas bottle to blow up the life jacket, it didn't work. From all my previous training about abandoning ship, the one thing that stuck in my mind was to get away from the ship fast once I was in the water to avoid being pulled under by suction as the ship went down. I felt the life jacket would have slowed me down anyway, so I looked no further for one. Being a strong swimmer, I felt I could do all right without one, so I jumped.

After swimming a safe distance from the ship, I noticed that one of my shipmates had gone under the surface just ahead of me. I managed to pull him back to the surface and tow him a few hundred feet to an officer's raft where he was pulled to safety. After I swam for a couple of hours, I noticed a shipmate towing another man to safety, so I helped him. To make a long story short, our destroyer-escorts sank the sub during the time we were in the water. The other ships in our convoy picked up all the survivors within a few hours.

I was big for my age, and I don't recall anyone suspecting me of being underage other than a few shipmates who said that I looked a young 17. I also have no regrets that I served my country in combat while I was underage. My own feelings tell me that it made a better man of me.

In 1951, I joined the active Navy Reserve and was called to sea duty on a seaplane tender in the Pacific. It was at this time that I changed my records and corrected my date of birth.

The three guys that I was hanging around with in my early teens are now hardened criminals. One is serving 20 to 40 years for armed robbery, another is serving a life sentence for murder, and the third one was shot and killed after he jumped through a window at the courthouse when he was sentenced to 20 to 30 years. But for the grace of God and my foresight, I could have been right with them.

Otis Long joined the Maryland State Police in 1952 and served with that organization for twenty-five years. Three times during his career, he faced death from a gun in the hands of a criminal. After the third time, when a gun pressed against his head failed to fire, he decided that he had stretched his luck far enough, so he retired. Otis enjoys a lot of time on the golf course. He is editor of the U.S.S. Block Island Association Newsletter through which he keeps in touch with his shipmates of fifty years ago. Otis and his wife Charlotte live in Linthicum, Maryland. They have a son, a daughter, and two grandsons.

√ **VUMS Note** ⇒ *Captain's mast.* Several underage veterans who served in the Navy tell about being called to a captain's mast. This is a disciplinary hearing for minor infractions, conducted by a commanding officer who also decides on the appropriate punishment. The term, "captain's mast," carries over from the time of sailing ships when this kind of hearing was conducted, literally, at the mainmast.

Freddie C. Chase

Age 16 – United States Navy

I was born in Newburyport, Massachusetts, on 22 August 1925. Newburyport, a small coastal city, is the smallest incorporated city in the country and is purportedly the birthplace of the U. S. Coast Guard. Several of my classmates were involved in the fishing business. At the age of 9, I took my first cruise on one of their boats,

After that operation, I decided that I didn't like being a sitting duck, ...

a 45-foot tuna boat. I would help pull and rebait traps on lobster boats. My first jobs were small tasks such as cutting chum, learning how to bait hooks, and cleaning the boats. I loved it! I was given my first opportunity to learn how to run a boat at age 12. By the time I was 15, I was doing so well that I was charting courses and running (with expert assistance) a 36-foot charter boat.

After the war started, newspapers carried an article describing the recruitment of residents of the state to form a detachment of "USS *Massachusetts* Native Sons" for duty aboard the *Massachusetts*. I wanted to enlist in January 1942 along with several classmates from the local high school. Four of us decided to find a way to change the birth dates on our birth certificates. One of the parents learned about our efforts, so all of our parents got together and decided that we should wait until the four of us had finished our first two years of high school. Then, if we still wanted to continue our efforts to join the military, they would sign our papers.

In the interim, the four of us continued to experiment with ways to change the date on our birth certificates. We dampened one number, in my case a "5," with several light, erasing strokes, blowing away the debris after each stroke until the number had disappeared. One of my friends, who was fairly adept at drawing, found the right ink and was able to change the numbers to show each of us as having been born a year earlier.

It was a successful project. The recruiters, after close scrutiny of our appearance and ages, decided that we were authentic, and we were accepted. We were sworn in on 21 June 1942 and sent to Newport, Rhode Island, for six weeks of boot training. My three friends were assigned to the USS *Massachusetts*, but I was sent to signalman school at Newport. I graduated as a signalman third class and was assigned to the MTB (motor torpedo boat, or PT boat) school at Melville, Rhode Island. After six weeks, I was on my way to the Amphibious Training Command at Little Creek, Virginia. The reason for this last transfer was that I had been putting in too many requests for transfer to the USS *Massachusetts*, the ship to which I was scheduled to be assigned originally.

Upon completion of amphibious training, I was assigned to the USS *Betelguese* (AKA-11) as a landing-craft signalman. During our first amphibious operation at Fédala Beach near Casablanca, North Africa, on 8 November 1942, I was the signalman for the boat group officer. After that operation, I decided that I didn't like being a sitting duck, standing alone on the engine cowling of an LCVP with a set of semaphore flags, while everyone else was hiding in the well of the boat during the landing.

When I returned to the ship, I requested permission to cross-rate, that is, change my specialty from signalman to coxswain. My request was granted, and after some training, I became an amphibious-boat coxswain. We made two more amphibious landings, one at Oran-Bizerte (Tunisia) and the other at Licata, Sicily. During the Sicilian operation I picked up a little shrapnel in my side, shoulder, and leg, but nothing serious.

I served thirteen months in the European theater, then was detached from the *Betelguese* and sent to Newport, Rhode Island, to join a precommissioning crew of the USS *Tuscana* (AKA-3). We put the *Tuscana* into commission at Baltimore in March 1944 and went through the Panama Canal and into the Pacific theater of operations where we spent twenty-three months.

While aboard the *Tuscana*, I participated in operations at Kwajalein, Eniwetok, and Ulithi. I was really in the thick of it during the invasions of Saipan, Tinian, Iwo Jima, and Okinawa. I picked up more shrapnel during the landing on Okinawa, but the wounds were not too serious.

On 30 April 1945, off the coast of Okinawa, the ship's radar screen picked up a low-flying bogey (enemy aircraft). The signal appeared for a moment, then disappeared on the seaward side of the surrounding hills. The next morning, while we were engaged in fighting off a Japanese air attack on the ships anchored in the harbor in Nagagusaki Bay, our port lookout spotted a low-flying Japanese float plane that was coming directly at us. The plane hit our ship on the port side of the wheelhouse and flying bridge, then glanced off and crashed on the port side of a troopship anchored just astern of us. We suffered some casualties, but not as many as the other ship. The early arrival of the bogey the next morning, and the fact that it was a "float" type of aircraft, led us to believe that it was the plane that we had briefly spotted the night before. Apparently, the plane landed unseen, and at the appropriate time the next morning, took off, came over the hills, and headed straight for the closest ships. As a result of the damage suffered in that action, we were ordered back to Pearl Harbor, then dispatched to San Francisco for repairs.

Our ship was undergoing repairs at the time that V-J Day was announced. After celebrating the war's end, we loaded troops destined for the occupation of Japan and returned to the Pacific.

I was discharged from the Navy on 22 January 1946. I joined the Naval Reserve in 1947 and taught seamanship courses at several Naval Reserve Centers. I was recalled to active duty in March 1950 and went aboard the USS *Wyandot* (AKA-92) for duty in Korea. I was assigned to the USS *Robert H. McCard* (DD-822) during my time in Korean waters. Later, I served aboard the USS *H. R. Dickson* (DD-708), the USS *DeHaven* (DD-727), and the USS *Paul Revere* (APA-228). During the war in Vietnam, I served aboard the USS *Marsh* (DE-699), the USS *Tulare* (LKA-112), and the USS *Mauna Kea* (AE-22). My shore duty assignments were in the San Francisco Bay area, in San Diego, and in Long Beach, California.

A voluntary program was instituted in January 1980 to develop enlisted men as surface-warfare specialists. The program included learning the functions and responsibilities of every department aboard ship or other command. After I had been in the program ten months, I qualified as a surface-warfare specialist and became the first chief petty officer on my command to be awarded the ESWS (enlisted surface-warfare specialist) device.

When I retired as a master chief boatswain's mate on 30 September 1983, I was credited with forty-one years, three months, and six days of Naval service. Twenty-three years, eleven months, and four days of that time was on active duty. I never did see the USS *Massachusetts*!

Fred Chase was awarded two Purple Hearts for wounds received in action. He also received the Navy Commendation Medal with combat "V," and the Naval Reserve Meritorious Award, along with a number of service medals. His civilian career was mostly in law enforcement, including more than eleven years as a deputy sheriff for Los Angeles County, California. After retiring from the Navy, he worked briefly for the U. S. Postal Service, then from 1984 until 1989, he worked as a rigger for a federal government agency in California. Fred and Katherine, his wife of twenty-six years, live in Mount Pleasant, South Carolina. Fred had two sons and two grandsons. His older son Freddie went to Vietnam at age 19 as an Army helicopter pilot. He volunteered to fly tree-top level missions in a small scout helicopter to draw enemy fire, then call in Cobra gunships. He flew forty-seven missions in five and a half weeks before he was killed in action.

Norbert S. Olshefski[17]

Age 15 – United States Army Air Forces

Norbert Olshefski was born in Nanticoke, Pennsylvania, and attended grammar and high school in the region. Norb and his high school buddy were very anxious to

> *Over a target inside Germany, the plane was hit by flak in the number one engine ...*

go into the service. He convinced his widowed mother to alter the date on his birth certificate, and on 25 June 1942, at the age of 15, he joined the Army Air Forces. After basic training and radio and gunnery school, he was posted to the 94th Bomb Group of the 8th Air Force in England. He was a radio operator and a ball-turret gunner in a B-17 Flying Fortress.

It was 26 July 1943 when Norbert's B-17, the *Cherokee*, took off on its fifth mission. Over a target inside Germany, the plane was hit by flak in the number one engine, and the right wing was badly damaged. As they fell behind the other aircraft and headed for the North Sea, they were attacked by a flight of ME-109 German fighter planes. Norbert was shot through the arm, so he left the ball turret and climbed into the fuselage of the aircraft. Shortly after the German fighters turned back, the propeller on number one engine separated from the engine, crashed into number two engine, went under the wing and ruptured the fuel tanks, then knocked the ball turret loose. Had Norbert been in the turret, he would have lost his life.

The *Cherokee* was forced to ditch in the North Sea. A British aircraft spotted the downed fliers in their rafts and radioed for a British rescue boat to pick them up. Norbert was taken to a hospital

---

[17] This account was compiled from the following sources: conversations and correspondence with Helen Olshefski; The *Washington Times*, 4 September 1992.

in England. It was there that the military found out how old he was
and discharged him for being underage.

Norbert returned home, completed his last two years of high school,
then attended Wilkes College in Wilkes-Barre, Pennsylvania.

From 1948 to 1952 he served in the Army as a public information
specialist and reporter with the *Pacific Stars and Stripes* in Japan. He
was also a war correspondent for the *Stars and Stripes* in Korea. He
served in the Army again from 1954 to 1957. While serving in
Bremerhaven, Germany, in 1955, he saw an officer in the PX who
looked familiar. The officer was the navigator on the *Cherokee* on the
flight when Norb was wounded.

Norbert received the Purple Heart, the Air Medal and a
Distinguished Unit Citation, in addition to a number of service medals.

After his discharge from the Army, he worked as a reporter, rewrite
man, and photographer for the Associated Press in Little Rock,
Arkansas. In later years, he worked on publications in Bremerhaven,
Germany, and Syracuse, New York. For a time he was a copy editor
on the *Allentown Morning Call* in Pennsylvania. He joined the
Washington Star as a copy editor in 1966 and was assistant photo-
editor when the paper closed down in August 1981. He then joined the
Washington Times where he was deputy copy-desk chief until his
retirement in 1991.

Norbert became very active in the Boy Scouts of America when his
son became a scout. Norb stayed involved for over twenty years and
held almost all of the scout positions in the Bowie, Maryland, area and
received many scouting awards.

Norbert Olshefski died on 3 September 1992 in Lanham, Maryland.
He and his wife Helen had three daughters and a son. Their son died
in an auto accident in 1978. Norbert and Helen lived in Bowie,
Maryland.

Bill J. McGehee

Age 16 – United States Marine Corps

I was born in Oklahoma City, Oklahoma, on 27 December 1925. Shortly after my family moved to Houston, Texas, in July 1941, I left home and went on my own. I

"Colonel, a guy could get killed doing this!"

quit high school in my senior year in order to join the military. The Navy promised to put me in the Navy Band in Washington, D.C., if I would enlist for six years. I didn't think the war would last for six years. Besides, I had designs to join the FBI. I thought that if I joined the Marine Corps, I would learn about weapons and would get to fight the Japanese.

At the age of 16, I coerced my parents into signing a paper stating that I was 18 years old and proceeded to join the Marine Corps. I was sworn in on 16 July 1942 in the Federal Building in San Antonio, Texas. I went to San Diego, California, for basic training, and it was almost a year later when I went overseas. I joined Charlie Company, 1st Battalion, 5th Marine Regiment, 1st Marine Division, in Melbourne, Australia, in July 1943. After the New Britain campaign, I was transferred to battalion headquarters as a runner and driver for the battalion commander, Lieutenant Colonel Robert A. Boyd. I was also his bodyguard in combat.

We were in the first wave of landing craft to hit the beach at Peleliu on 15 September 1944. I followed Colonel Boyd through the hell of that battle for a month. He was a hands-on leader in combat. He would establish his command post, leave his executive officer in charge, and set up an observation post on the front lines, where he preferred to be. My duties included running messages from the observation post to the command post. One day I said, "Colonel, a guy could get killed doing this!" He nodded and smiled. We both understood; it was kill or be killed. After Peleliu, Colonel Boyd was promoted and reassigned.

We landed on Okinawa in April 1945. Our new battalion commander was Lieutenant Colonel Charles W. Shelburne. The first few days after the landing were relatively easy, but things became rough as we moved south. When we finished taking the hills on the south end, we were moved to the north end to await further orders. Most of us felt that the next island we would hit would be in Japan.

I do not recall hearing about the atomic bomb being dropped, but I do recall the night I learned the war was over. We were playing poker that evening, using a cot as a table. While we were playing, we heard the sound of big guns being fired. It had been some time since any of us had heard that sound. The five of us playing poker casually raised our heads and looked at one another. Someone went to the tent entrance and called out, "What's going on?" The word was relayed — the war was over. One player said, "Oh!" Another said, "OK, I'll see that and raise five dollars." We continued to play. The war was over, the game was not.

After the war, the 1st Division was sent to China, but I returned to the States. I got my first furlough after two and a half years overseas and spent Christmas of 1945 with my parents in Houston. I returned to California and was stationed at the Naval Amphibian Base at Coronado until I was discharged on 16 July 1946.

I consider it an honor to have served under the command of Lieutenant Colonel Robert A. Boyd on Peleliu and Lieutenant Colonel Charles W. Shelburne on Okinawa. The 1st Battalion, 5th Marines, was very fortunate to have them as commanders.

On 16 July 1996, fifty years to the day after I was discharged, I visited Brigadier General Shelburne at the Veterans Administration Hospital in Kerrville, Texas. I was also a patient and a volunteer at the hospital. A nurse took me to a room and pointed him out to me. She said, "That is Mr. Shelburne sitting there, the one in the brown shirt." I thought, "Mister?" I was not prepared for so common a title, certainly not for a retired Marine Corps General. This did not sit well with my mental image of that giant of a man. When I approached him, he was staring dead ahead with his eyes seemingly focused on the space immediately in front of him. His face was bland. There was no hint of expression. I wondered, "What is he thinking? Or is he thinking?" I had been told that he was suffering from Alzheimer's disease. As I stood directly in front of him, I sensed he was not really seeing me. His gaze did not extend even that short distance. I said, "Hello, General, my name is Bill McGehee. I knew you in the Marine Corps when you were a colonel," and extended my right hand. He raised his face slightly until his eyes were in line with mine. His only comment was, "Brigadier General." Then he turned his gaze straight ahead again.

Seeing the colonel was a very emotional experience. I saw a man who had been stripped of mind and body. No longer a thinker and doer, a man of no rank, only a "mister." I felt a cold chill of appreciation and thanked God for leaders like Colonel Shelburne. I suppose that if he were God himself, I would still call him "colonel."

Bill McGehee finished high school and then attended the University of Houston under the GI Bill. After receiving a B.A., he attended the South Texas Law School in Houston, graduated with a degree in law, and practiced as a trial lawyer for thirty years. He was forced to retire after suffering several strokes. Currently, he receives a 100% service-connected disability pension from the Veterans Administration. Bill lives in Kerrville, Texas. He has one child and seven grandchildren.

Alvie M. "Al" Brandon

Age 15 – United States Navy

My parents were sharecropping a farm downriver from Chattanooga, Tennessee, when I was born on 18 August 1926. By the time I was 12 years old, I was self-supporting. I worked at odd jobs on the farm, sold newspapers, did janitorial work

> **Many of my shipmates ... have paid the price for their exposure to radiation.**

after school, and was involved with the NYA (National Youth Administration) during the summers.

In 1942, at the age of 15, I joined the CCC (Civilian Conservation Corps). I did this by giving myself another birth day and birth year, making me 18 years old. Two weeks after I joined, the CCC was disbanded. By now, I was determined to join the military. I figured that if I could change my age and get into the CCC, I could do the same thing to get into the military.

My first attempt to enlist was at the Marine Corps recruiting station in Chattanooga. I took the tests, passed the physical exam, and was waiting for the sergeant to give me my papers. However, the officer-in-charge must have been suspicious because he told the sergeant to mail the papers to my dad for his signature. I knew Dad wouldn't sign, so I went to the Navy recruiting office in Huntsville, Alabama. I passed everything, and the chief gave me the forms to take to my dad for his signature. That worked. Dad never did know how I managed to get into the Navy.

I was sworn into the Navy on 17 July 1942 and was sent to the Naval Training Station, San Diego, for boot camp. After boot camp, I volunteered for submarine duty but was assigned to the Naval Air Station, Norman, Oklahoma. I was sent to England and assigned to Fleet Air Wing Seven. I was a crewman on a PB4Y-1, the Navy version of the B-24 Liberator bomber. Our mission was to patrol the Atlantic for submarines. During our first patrol, a reward of $100 was offered to the first crew to spot a periscope.

Joe Kennedy, Jr., the oldest brother of future president Jack Kennedy, was a member of our group. His aircraft exploded over England, killing him and another officer. After the war, a movie was made documenting his life.

When the war was over in 1945, I was transferred to the surface Navy and assigned to the USS *Conserver* (ARS-39). In July 1946, we participated in Operation Crossroads, the first atomic test after the atomic bombs were dropped on Japan. The test took place at Bikini Atoll. Two bombs were exploded during the tests, one in the air and the other one under the sea. Over 40,000 people and 200 ships were involved. Our ship was the first into Bikini and the last out. My job was to help assure that all the vessels were seaworthy for the test and to do whatever salvage work was needed. After the tests, I helped check for radiation. I used a Geiger counter to measure how "hot" the ships were and recorded the information. Many of my shipmates and their offspring have paid the price for their exposure to radiation. To this day, I have spots on my skin that came from radiation.

I returned to the States and in July 1947, I was discharged from the Navy. I immediately joined the Navy Reserves and was assigned to be a basic training instructor in Birmingham, Alabama. Meanwhile, I finished high school and started college.

While I was in the Navy Reserves, I was offered a commission in the Army National Guard, but there was a problem. I had been using my Navy age from the time that I first enlisted, and according to the records, I was 30 years old. The age of eligibility for a National Guard commission was 28, my true age. I wrote my congressman and explained the situation. I also obtained a birth certificate, which I had never done before. It must have been an act of providence, but everything worked out, and in 1953 I was commissioned a second lieutenant.

At the time that I was commissioned, I was a narcotics agent in Phenix City, Alabama, leaving there after martial law was lifted in 1954. I transferred to the Army Reserves, reverted to the rank of warrant officer, and began instructing classes for Army Reserve personnel at Fort Rucker, Alabama. I taught courses until 1980 when

I became training officer for two reserve units in Clarksdale, Mississippi.

After serving forty years, I retired from the military on 28 September 1982. As I look back to the time I entered the Navy in 1942, I can't recall ever worrying about being underage or being reprimanded or released from the service. I had a great military career.

Al Brandon utilized the GI Bill and earned a degree in general science from Troy State University, Fort Rucker Campus, in 1978. Since his retirement from the military in 1982, he has enjoyed traveling. Al and his wife Jo live in Pensacola, Florida. They have a combined family of seven children, thirteen grandchildren, and one great-grandchild. While on their honeymoon cruise, Al and Jo won a prize for newlyweds with the most grandchildren.

√ **VUMS Note** ⇒ *The CCC.* The Civilian Conservation Corps (CCC), mentioned in a number of stories, was established in 1933 and lasted for seven years. It proved to be one of the most successful programs of the New Deal in its effort to counteract the Great Depression. The CCC had a twofold purpose: to give unemployed young men jobs, and to conserve the country's natural resources. Two and a half million young men served in the CCC nationwide in numerous conservation projects which included improving parks and recreational areas, erecting fire towers in forested areas, building small dams, and planting trees. An amazing number of trees, 200,000,000, were planted in the Great Plains area to reduce the chances of another dust bowl such as the one of the 1930s.

Ray L. and Roy M. Crass

Age 15 – United States Navy

Roy Crass — Ray and I were identical twins, born on 24 May 1927. There were twelve boys and five girls in our family. Five of us served during World War II and three during Korea and Vietnam.

> *... with daylight, I saw my twin brother sitting in the opposite side of the hole. He also had his rifle cocked and waiting.*

Ray and I joined the Navy on 27 July 1942, at the age of 15 years and 64 days. We were sent to the Naval Training Center at Farragut, Idaho, for boot training. During a physical examination, it was discovered that we were both colorblind. We were told that we couldn't serve as members of a ship's company because we were colorblind, but that we would be assigned to a Seabee battalion. I thought they meant colorblind battalion.

After a 30-day leave, we reported to Waterbury, Virginia, where we were assigned to training with the Seabees. We then were shipped to Hawaii where we served with the 3rd Naval Construction Regiment, which was assigned the task of cleaning up Pearl Harbor.

Roy   Ray

After that, we were assigned to the 50th Naval Construction Battalion and shipped to Midway Island where we helped build a submarine base. We were assigned next to an underwater demolition team, UDT 1038, for the 17 February 1944 invasion of Eniwetok in the Marshall Islands. At that time, members of underwater demolition teams were called "frogmen." After Eniwetok, we returned to the 50th NCB in Hawaii.

We were assigned again to UDT 1038 to assist in the invasion of Saipan, Mariana Islands, on 15 June 1944. Ray and I went ashore a week before the landing to scout the beach area and again on the night before the invasion. That same night, four frogmen from another team took along a large piece of plywood. They headed for a beach near the little town of Agat, which was to be one of the main landing areas for the Marines the following morning. They pulled the plywood through the shallow water and carefully propped it up on the beach facing the sea. The next morning when the Marines stormed ashore, they found a 5' x 2' sign that read;

> Welcome Marines
> Agat USO two blocks
> Courtesy of UDT-4

Ray and I made it back to our ship in time to return to the beach, but this time with the Marines. Ray went in with the first wave of troops, and I went in with the fourth wave.

The fighting on Saipan ended on 9 July 1944, and after two weeks' rest, we took part in the invasion of Tinian Island on 24 July 1944. Several days after the landing, Ray and I decided to make an unscheduled patrol. We got into a fire fight with some enemy soldiers near a cane field. Ray saw them throw a grenade at us, so he knocked me down, covered me, and took the full brunt of the explosion. He saved my life, but he carried shrapnel in his body for the rest of his.

The fighting on Tinian ended on 1 August, and we were again assigned to the 50th NCB, which was now based on Tinian. We helped build an air base for the B-29 bombers. That base is where the *Enola Gay* took off to drop the atomic bomb on Hiroshima on 6 August 1945. On 9 August, another B-29, *Bock's Car*, dropped the second atomic bomb on Nagasaki. In the fall of 1945, we were shipped back to the good old USA for discharge. We, Ray and Roy, were called the "Tool Totin' Twins" while we were in the Seabees.

Ray Crass — During the invasion of Tinian, Roy and I were attached to the First Marine Division. I was with the first wave of troops going into combat, and Roy was in the fourth wave. It was 3:30 in the morning, still dark as hell, and after landing and going about halfway across the island, we noticed a number of pillboxes nearby, so we dug in. I cleaned out a shell crater to make a big foxhole. Just as I jumped in, someone came from behind me and jumped into the opposite side of the hole. I had no idea if he was Japanese or American. I really couldn't shoot and then ask, so I just made sure that the safety was off my rifle and got ready to shoot as soon as it was light enough to see. Meanwhile, I prayed like hell that it wasn't the enemy.

To my surprise, with daylight, I saw my twin brother sitting in the opposite corner of the hole. He also had his rifle cocked and waiting. He told me he really thought many times about shooting, but just couldn't have lived with it if he had shot one of his own men instead of an enemy. So, I guess God was with us in many more ways than we think.

Roy Crass, a master plumber, worked in construction in Wisconsin. He retired in 1989. He loves to hunt deer in the woods near his home in Slinger, Wisconsin, where he lives with his wife, Frances. Roy and Frances have two children, ten grandchildren, and three great-grandchildren.

Ray Crass was the chief maintenance man for West Bend Corporation for a number of years, then went into the fast-food business. After retiring from that, he moved to Florida and worked in real estate. He was reminded of the escapade on Tinian each time he went through security at airports. The security alarm would go off because of the grenade fragments still in his body. Ray wrote his story before his death on 23 August 1994. His wife, Marinette "Mary" Crass, lives in Sebring, Florida. Ray and Mary had one son, four grandchildren, and three great-grandchildren.

Donald F. Moore

Age 15 – United States Marine Corps

I was born in Johnson City, Tennessee, on 9 August 1926, but all my earliest recollections stem from life on a Texas farm. Somewhere between this farm and the start of my formal education, we

> *... the eleven of us hit the hole, and there was room for eleven more!*

moved to San Antonio, Texas. In my early teens, I worked at a gas station and a grocery store, delivered milk to homes, and finally, worked at Western Union.

By this time, my mother had remarried, and I believe I was a little jealous of her new husband. When war erupted a few months later, I wanted to enlist, but mother wouldn't hear of it. Finally, in July 1942, I blackmailed her by threatening to run away from home if she refused to sign the papers so that I could join the military. I wanted to join the Navy because a favorite uncle had been a sailor. I didn't pass the physical because of flat feet and a double-mastoid operation I had as an infant. After failing the Navy physical, I told my mother I was going to try the Marines. She thought she would placate me and agreed to it. I didn't know it at the time, but the Navy doctors had told her that I would never get into any branch of the service because of my flat feet and mastoid operation. Two days later, much to her chagrin, I was on my way to San Diego, California. I became a Marine on 3 August 1942.

After a 7-week boot camp at San Diego, I was assigned to Battery A, 2nd Special Weapons Battalion, 2nd Marine Division. Three weeks later, we boarded a ship from the Dutch East Indies, the D.E.I. *Brastigi*, and set sail for the South Pacific. We were fed one meal per day and were allowed a canteen full of water (one quart) each day. That 17-day trip to New Zealand was not a pleasure cruise.

Our stay in New Zealand was very short. We sailed for Guadalcanal on Christmas Eve, arriving there on 3 January 1943. Our outfit was assigned to the 6th Marine Regiment whose duty was to perform mop-up operations. Although the beaches were secure, old battle-hardened Marines told us that our first duty was to dig foxholes.

Our eleven-man squad decided to dig a community foxhole. We dug and dug, but there was no way that all eleven of us could fit into the hole. When we tried it out for size, arms and legs would be sticking out all over, but when Japanese aircraft started dropping bombs that night, the eleven of us hit the hole, and there was room for eleven more!

The next day, we moved to the front lines and had our machine guns set up in a defensive position by evening. Our squad leader had gone to find material to conceal the gun. When he returned in the late evening, the gunner saw him coming and apparently thought he was the enemy. Without requesting an identity sign, the gunner opened up and killed the squad leader.

That night, a bomb, claimed to be the largest the Japanese had, was dropped in our midst. All of our foxholes were nearly filled with cascading dirt. The bombing was a nightly affair. When we returned to New Zealand, we were so mindful of the sound of a siren, it took us a long time to realize it was no longer Japanese aircraft bombing or strafing us.

I developed a serious case of malaria and was hospitalized numerous times. We boarded ship for our journey to Tarawa in October. After that island was secured, we traveled to the big island of Hawaii. Our new home was on the Parker Ranch, about sixty miles from Hilo. Fate took a hand shortly after our arrival, and our platoon of about sixty men was sent back to the States to organize a new defense battalion. We returned to the Pacific for the push on Okinawa.

I can't say that we did anything spectacular the entire time that I was in the Marines, but I guess that even peeling potatoes in the galley contributed to the Japanese downfall. I was on Okinawa when the A-bombs were dropped on Japan. I firmly believe that millions of lives were ultimately saved by this action. I was very happy when we finally secured transportation back to the States. I was discharged on 25 November 1945.

Don Moore returned to Texas and became a plumber after his discharge from the Marines. In 1956, he began his own contracting business in which he is still actively involved. Don and Louise, his wife of fifty years, live in Natalia, Texas. They have five children and seven grandchildren.

Thomas C. Hise

Age 15 – United States Navy

I was born in Bluefield, West Virginia, on 26 May 1927, the youngest of six children, four boys and two girls. My father was killed in a railroad accident when I was 9 years old. On 7 December 1941, when Pearl Harbor was

> *I participated in four invasions in the European theater, all before I was 18 years old ...*

bombed, I was only 14 years old, but I was ready to enlist the next morning. I asked my mother to let me join the Navy, but she refused. One brother was already in the Navy, another would soon join him, and a third would join the Army. It took eight months of pleading before my mother would let me lie about my age and enlist.

I was sworn into the Navy on 5 August 1942 and was sent to the Great Lakes Naval Training Center for three weeks of boot camp. After one week's leave, I reported to a destroyer, the USS *Cowie* (DD-632) in Casco Bay, Portland, Maine. We participated in the invasion of North Africa in November 1942 by providing fire support for the troops who were landing at Safi, near Casablanca.

We participated in the invasion of Sicily in 1943. The *Cowie* provided fire support for the troops at Gela on 11 July. With an Army spotter plane providing target information, the *Cowie* and the USS *Laub* destroyed a number of tanks of the Herman Goering Panzer Division. All of Sicily was in control of Allied forces thirty-eight days after the initial landings.

Early in 1944, I was transferred to the USS *Murphy* (DD-603). The *Murphy* had a unique history. While forming a convoy just out of New York harbor in 1943, she was rammed by a U. S. tanker and cut in half. The bow sank with thirty-eight members of the crew still aboard. The stern was towed to the Brooklyn Navy Yard and fitted with a new bow. I was a member of her first crew after she was rebuilt. Aboard the *Murphy,* we participated in the Normandy invasion of June 1944 in which our primary duty was to screen the battleship USS *Texas* while she was shelling the beach. The battleship was not assigned to any one beach as were the Army units, but roamed to where she was needed along Utah, Omaha, Gold, Juno, and Sword Beaches. The last three beaches were where the British forces landed.

We left Normandy and went to the island of Malta in the Mediterranean to prepare for the invasion of southern France, called Operation Dragoon, that took place on 15 August 1944. Our initial assault was at Toulon, and once again we screened the USS *Texas* as well as the USS *Nevada.* We rescued two American fighter pilots and captured three Germans who were trying to escape in a small boat.

I participated in four invasions in the European theater, all before I was 18 years old, which was the minimum legal age for one to be in combat. A 17-year-old could join the military with parental consent but was not allowed in combat until the age of 18.

In January 1945, the *Murphy* was assigned to escort the cruiser, USS *Quincy,* which was carrying President Roosevelt to the Yalta Conference. After the conference, we were ordered to proceed to Jidda, Saudi Arabia, to pick up King Ibn Saud and bring him to the Great Bitter Lake in Egypt for a conference with President Roosevelt. The USS *Murphy* was the first U. S. warship ever to enter the Port of Jidda, Saudi Arabia, the first warship to transport a king, and the first to enter the Suez Canal since World War I.

The king and his party were aboard our ship for six days. It was a challenge for us to provide enough living, dining, and praying space for more than 100 people on a destroyer. We erected a huge canvas tent on the forecastle of the ship to house the king, then laid carpets to cover the steel deck. Included in the king's party was a group of 7-foot-tall Nubian guards armed with scimitars, and ten live goats. We built a goat corral on the fantail and rigged a flagstaff for the slaughtering and dressing of the goats for the king's meals. The king's religious beliefs forbade the cleansing of the goats' blood from the ship's decks. We observed the protocol and endured the fierce stench that rose from the stern during the cruise. In accordance with Arab custom, the king presented gifts to the *Murphy's* skipper and her 200-man crew. The ship's officers received inscribed gold watches, jeweled swords, and ceremonial Arab clothing and headdress. The chief petty officers were given the equivalent of $75.00 in cash, and the lower ranks each received the equivalent of $65.00. That was more than a month's pay!

After the cruise to Saudi Arabia, I was transferred to the precommissioning detachment for the USS *Little Rock* (CL-92) in Newport, Rhode Island. I was a plank owner and made the cruise to South America on the *Little Rock*. In May 1946, my enlistment was up, the *Little Rock* was preparing for a world cruise, and I already had four years of sea duty. I chose to go ashore in Philadelphia to reenlist and secure a shore-duty billet.

In the early 1950s, I was transferred from shore duty to the recommissioning crew of a World War II light carrier, the USS *Tripoli*. The *Tripoli* was to transport American fighter planes to NATO and SEATO countries. This duty took us to fifteen different NATO-country ports to discharge aircraft and also to Korea and Japan. After more than two years on the *Tripoli*, I served another tour of shore duty, this time in Port Lyautey, French Morocco. In 1957, I was assigned to the USS *Yellowstone* whose tasks were to service and repair destroyers.

I retired from the Navy in 1962 as a ship's serviceman first class.

Tom Hise went to work as a civilian for the Navy Resale Program after retiring from active duty. His work took him to numerous naval facilities: the Amphibious Base, Little Creek, Virginia; Pearl Harbor, Hawaii; Taipei, Taiwan; Naval Air Station, Oceana, Virginia; Naval Base, Subic Bay, Republic of the Philippines; Naval Base, Charleston, South Carolina; HSA Naples, Italy; and the Naval Submarine Base, New London, Connecticut. He retired from that program in 1982. Tom was recently honored by being selected to help lay a wreath at the Lone Sailor Statue at the Navy Memorial in Washington, D.C., in commemoration of the fiftieth anniversary of the invasion of southern France. Tom and Ruth, his wife of nearly fifty years, operated a uniform-tailor shop in Virginia Beach, Virginia, for five years. After closing the shop, Tom opened a military museum, which has 30,000 artifacts. Tom and Ruth live in Virginia Beach. They have four children, five grandchildren, and two great-grandchildren.

Calvin L. Graham[18]

Age 12 – United States Navy

Calvin Graham was probably the youngest member of the armed forces of the United States to see combat in World War II and perhaps the youngest since the Civil War. His story was told in a 1988 TV film, "Too Young the Hero."

> *He was immediately thrown in the brig and stripped of his medals.*

Calvin was born in a cotton field near Canton, Texas, on 3 April 1930. His parents were sharecroppers, and the entire family was working in the fields at the time of his birth. His father died when Calvin was young, and his mother later remarried. After a fight with his stepfather, Calvin and his older brother Frank were told to move out of the house. They stayed at a cheap hotel in Houston until Frank

was able to join the Navy at age 14 by forging his mother's signature and using the hotel manager's notary stamp. After Frank left, Calvin went to live with a married sister. Imbued with patriotism, wanting to follow in Frank's footsteps, and feeling that he was a burden to his sister, Calvin made up his mind to join the Navy. On 14 August 1942 he went to the Navy recruiting office where he met a 15-year-old who was also standing in line waiting to enlist.

The two boys began the enlistment process by filling out papers and taking various tests. At the end of the day, the applicants without birth certificates were given papers to take home for a parent to sign, verifying that they were 17 years old. The recruiter emphasized that the signature had to be notarized. The

---

[18] This account was compiled from the following sources: conversations and correspondence with Mary L. Graham; *Fort Worth Star Telegram*, November 1992; *The Dallas Morning News*, 10 November 1992; News release, Congressman Martin Frost, 24th District, Texas, 21 June 1994.

two boys knew that their parents would not sign their forms, so their signatures would have to be forged. Calvin remembered how Frank had obtained a notary seal. The two boys went to the hotel where Calvin had stayed. His friend went across the street and waited until Calvin was talking with the manager, then called the hotel and told the manager that smoke was coming from a window on the fourth floor. As Calvin had planned, the manager asked him to watch the desk while he checked on the fire. Calvin agreed, and as soon as the manager was out of sight, he went to the desk, found the seal, and stamped both his and his friend's forms. The boys then exchanged the forms and signed the names of each other's parent. They returned to the recruiting office the following day, 15 August 1942, and were sworn into the Navy. Calvin was 12 years, 4 months and 12 days old.

During a dental examination at the Naval Training Center, San Diego, California, a dentist noted that Calvin's 12-year molars weren't in yet. The doctor told Calvin that he was too young to be in the Navy and to take his file to the medical officer to be discharged. Calvin waited until the doctor's back was turned, then placed his file with all the others and remained in boot camp.

After boot camp, Calvin went to Pearl Harbor where he was assigned to the USS *South Dakota*. They were soon in the South Pacific. During their first battle, Calvin's gun crew accounted for seven of the twenty-six enemy aircraft that the ship shot down. Later, the ship's captain called Calvin to his office. He had received a message from the Navy Department that his mother had told them that he was only 12 years old. He confessed his age to the captain but asked to remain aboard instead of being put ashore at New Caledonia to wait for transportation back to the States.

A short time later, in November 1942, during the Battle of Guadalcanal, the *South Dakota* was hit forty-seven times by enemy fire. One explosion threw Calvin down three decks of stairs. He was seriously injured by shrapnel that tore through his jaw and mouth. In spite of his injuries, he helped pull fellow sailors from danger. He was awarded the Bronze Star, the Purple Heart, and the Navy Unit Commendation Medal.

After the battle, the *South Dakota* returned to the Brooklyn Navy Yard for repairs. The ship's captain told Calvin that if he could get his mother's permission, he would see what he could do about keeping him in the Navy. Calvin received his mother's permission while on leave.

A few days before the *South Dakota* was to sail, Calvin received notice that his grandmother had died. He requested to see the captain to ask for emergency leave. Because of wounds he had received, the captain had been transferred from the ship to a hospital and the executive officer was acting as captain. He refused Calvin's request for emergency leave, but gave him a 4-day pass. Four days' time was not long enough for him to get to Houston and back before the ship sailed. The acting captain, aware of this, told him to report in to the nearest recruiting office, tell them how old he was, and they would take care of him. He said he didn't want a 12-year-old aboard his ship.

Calvin went to his grandmother's funeral, then turned himself in as he had been told to do. He was immediately thrown into the brig and stripped of his medals. He was in the brig for three months until he was able to smuggle out word to his sister about his incarceration. After his sister threatened to call the newspapers to report that the Navy was holding a 12-year-old in the brig, the Navy relented. In April 1943, shortly after his thirteenth birthday, he was kicked out of the Navy without an honorable discharge and without veterans benefits. He did not receive discharge papers at the time. Later, in the course of treatment at a Veterans Administration hospital, his wife Mary noticed a paper in his VA folder that stated that Calvin was released under honorable conditions.

In 1947, at the age of 17, Calvin joined the U. S. Marine Corps. After he had been in the Corps about three years, he fell from a pier while on duty and broke his back, ending his military career and leaving him in a wheelchair.

He wrote to congressmen and presidents and finally, in 1978, the Navy reinstated all of his medals with the exception of the Purple Heart. He was awarded $337 in back pay but denied health benefits except for disability status for one lost tooth. Calvin maintained that it wasn't the money but his pride and self-respect that he wanted restored.

In 1988, President Reagan signed legislation that granted Calvin full disability benefits, increased his back pay to $4,917, and allowed $18,000 for past medical bills, contingent upon Calvin furnishing receipts for the medical services. By this time, some of the doctors who had treated him were deceased and many receipts were lost. Calvin received only $2,100 of the possible $18,000.

Money for the rights to his story for the TV movie, "Too Young The Hero," amounted to $50,000, but 50% went to two agents, and 20% went to a writer of an unpublished book about Calvin. Calvin and his wife Mary received $15,000, before taxes.

Calvin Graham died at his home in Fort Worth, Texas, on 6 November 1992 at the age of 62. Eighteen months later, on 21 June 1994, his Purple Heart was presented to his widow Mary by Secretary of the Navy John Dalton at a ceremony in Arlington, Texas.

√ **VUMS Note** ⇒ *Patriotism.* Numerous moving expressions of patriotism pervade these stories. "Love for my country," was the answer from an underage veteran when he was asked why he had enlisted at such a young age. Patriotism, according to another, "...was a feeling shared by almost everyone throughout the nation during World War II." A third veteran observed how united the country was, and how its citizens were "... so giving and helpful to one another."

Americans were strongly influenced by the patriotism of the day. Some youngsters had the experience of "being seized with patriotic fervor" and enlisting. Having family members in the service and seeing military role models in the movies also inspired patriotic feelings. There was usually a strong sense of duty accompanying these feelings of patriotism.

One particularly poignant expression of patriotism comes from a grandfather who had been looking over his war medals with his little grandson. He said to his grandson, "... those medals and ribbons were souvenirs of a misspent youth who loved his country and flag very much and had gone off to a faraway country to do a job that his country had asked him to do...."

Paul Z. "Pablo" Martinez
Age 16 – United States Army

At age 15 I was working for the NYA (National Youth Administration) in San Antonio, Texas, where I was born on 13 March 1926. Some of the kids from our neighborhood and I worked as bus boys in the mess hall at Kelly Air Force Base. After I had turned 16, some of us decided to join the Army. I lied about my age, using the birth date of my older brother, 22 March 1924. Within two weeks, I was at Camp Toccoa, Georgia, then known as Camp Tooms, for thirteen weeks of basic training.

... within twenty-four hours, we were surrounded in Bastogne.

Our training was unique, to say the least. As we were the 2nd Battalion of the 506th Parachute Infantry Regiment, one of the first Parachute Infantry Regiments formed, we were trained in all classes of weapons, demolitions, survival tactics, and hand-to-hand combat; and we received tough physical training. We were the elite of our time. We made a forced march from Toccoa to Atlanta, Georgia, 120 miles in 72 hours, boarded a train, and went to Fort Benning for parachute training. The 2nd battalion of the 506th PIR graduated, and we received our parachute wings on 25 December 1942. I'll never forget that day.

From Fort Benning we went to Camp McCall, North Carolina. Then we went on maneuvers in Tennessee during August of 1943 and joined up with the 101st Airborne Division. In September 1943, we sailed for England where we trained hard for the invasion of Normandy.

Our unit was among the first to cross the channel. We parachuted into France at 1:00 a.m., 6 June 1944, five hours before the sea landings. I was wounded on 10 June near Carentan, France, and was shipped back to England to recuperate. After spending three weeks in a hospital, I went back to my outfit, and on 17 September 1944, we went into combat again, this time into Holland. We fought our way to Eindhoven and other towns up and down what is now known as "Hell's Highway." It is on the record that we were on the front lines for either 65 or 67 days.

We were pulled out of Holland in the last days of November and sent to Mourmelon, France. We all thought, "Boy, some rest and maybe a trip to Paris." But the Nazis had other ideas. At 2:00 a.m. on 18 December, we were roused from our beds. We picked up our combat gear, loaded on trucks, and within twenty-four hours, we were surrounded in Bastogne. This was one of our most memorable battles. We thought Normandy and Holland were bad, but it was here in Bastogne and in nearby towns that we were not only fighting the Germans but also the elements.

Our next campaign took us all the way to Berchtesgaden, Germany, Hitler's hideout. The day we arrived there, the war was over. From Berchtesgaden we went to Zell am Zee for a few months until the 101st was deactivated, and then we were sent home. I was honorably discharged on 10 December 1945, at the age of 19.

I rejoined the Army on 15 May 1947 and was sent to the 511th Parachute Infantry Regiment of the 11th Airborne Division in Japan. We returned to the United States in February 1949 and reopened Fort Campbell, Kentucky. I served with the 11th Airborne until I got out of the Army in August of 1952. I was a drill instructor during the Korean war. I left the Army because I fractured a femur during a jump at Campbell, and the doctor told me I couldn't jump anymore.

Paul Martinez made two parachute jumps in combat. He earned the Combat Infantryman Badge and was awarded the Bronze Star with Oak Leaf Cluster for heroism and the Purple Heart for wounds received in action. His unit also received awards from the governments of France, Belgium, and Holland. Since leaving the service, he has worked in several trades which, in his words, were "nothing to brag about," but he made a good living and raised five children. Paul and Juanita, his wife of forty-seven years, had five children, fifteen grandchildren, and one great-grandchild. Paul lives in Los Angeles, California. Juanita died on 12 July 1996. A son was an instructor with an Airborne unit at Fort Benning during the Vietnam War, and another served in the Air Force.

Earl W. Stevens, Jr.

Age 16 – United States Navy

I was born in Collins, Iowa, on 28 April 1926, the youngest of three boys. We moved to Colorado six months after I was born. In August 1942, my oldest brother Max was 19

I just knew that I was in big trouble.

years old and was about to be drafted, so he decided to join the Navy. My parents, my other brother Charles, and I went to Denver to see Max enlist. At the recruiting office, we listened to the recruiters talk about the Navy. The more they talked, the more I wanted to join. When Charles, who was 17, decided to enlist, I *really* wanted to go with him and Max. I asked my dad to sign for me. He asked me if I could handle it. Of course, I said yes! I think the recruiters knew that I wasn't old enough, but Dad signed papers stating that I was 17, and there was a war on. My dad had joined the U. S. Army while underage during World War I.

On 23 August 1942, the three of us were sworn into the Navy and sent to boot camp in San Diego. In boot camp, a few fellows started figuring out our ages, but our big brother Max and a few friends who knew our secret hushed them up. During the first few days of boot training, Max became ill and was sent to the hospital for an operation. He did not finish boot camp with Charles and me, but did finish later.

After we had been in training for about ten days, Charles and I were called out of drill formation and sent to the office. I just knew that I was in *big* trouble. I told Charles that he was old enough, but that I would probably be put in the brig. When we got to the office, they didn't say anything about ages but took us to the main gate. There in the reception room was my mother. We were told to visit with her while they got our brother Max. Would you believe, my *father* had joined the Navy and just arrived at boot camp? That made four of us in boot camp at the same time! The Navy wanted a picture session with the four of us. I was really surprised at what was going on and greatly relieved that I wasn't being sent to the brig for being underage.

The remaining time in boot camp was routine, with the exception of a few more picture sessions. Charles and I didn't get a leave after boot camp but were sent directly overseas and assigned to the USS *New Mexico* (BB-40). We were together until after the Aleutian campaign. After the loss of the five Sullivan brothers, the Navy didn't want brothers on the same ship. Our brother Max served on a destroyer. On 18 December 1944, his ship, the USS *Spence* (DD-512), sank in a typhoon off the Philippines. Max went down with his ship. My father served on a sub-chaser on the East Coast of the United States. Mother tried to join the Navy (WAVES), but they wouldn't allow an entire family to serve in the same branch of the military. She worked in an aircraft factory during the war.

I was discharged on 28 April 1946 as an electrician's mate first class. I joined the Naval Reserve on 1 August 1946 and was recalled to active duty on 1 October 1949. I served on the USS *Forest Royal* (DD-872) in Korean waters, after which I was discharged for the second time in 1950.

Earl Stevens participated in ten naval battles in the Asiatic-Pacific and Philippine theaters. After leaving the Navy, he went into the construction trade and became a journeyman lineman. He has worked on the construction of high-voltage transmission lines for many years. He has held numerous offices in the International Brotherhood of Electrical Workers Union, Local 769. Earl and Linda, his wife of fifty years, live in Phoenix, Arizona. They have six children, eleven grandchildren, and three great-grandchildren. Earl was the first Arizona State Commander and is currently the Southwestern District Commander of the Veterans of Underage Military Service.

Robert H. Cline

Age 14 – United States Navy

My parents moved from Iowa and Pennsylvania to Washington State by immigrant train in the late 1800s. They homesteaded in northern Washington, which was the poorest part of the state. There was no electricity, no radio, and no newspapers. We hauled our

> **This was off Tassafaronga, and what a hell of a battle that was!**

drinking water from a well to our house by stoneboat.[19] I was born near Brewster, Washington, on 2 October 1927. I attended school up to the fifth grade. It was a 5-mile horseback trip down the mountain to school.

By the time I was 12 years old, I'd had enough of the rough life, so a cousin and I took off for "the good life." We wanted to see where that railroad track went. We worked at every available job. We worked for the Japanese farmers around Puyallup and Auburn. I thought they were great people. We rode with Japanese section gangs on the railroad. We picked hops, pears, oranges, lettuce, cherries, and potatoes. We worked in a wrecking yard, hoed beets, pitched hay, and set pins in bowling alleys throughout Washington, Oregon, California, and Idaho – God knows what else we did! We went where the rails went, but we never got to ride the Wabash line. My favorite song was Roy Acuff's "Wabash Cannonball." I got to see him in Nashville a few years before he passed on.

I came back through Wenatchee in July 1942 in my Erskine car – no more rails for me. I worked in the wheat harvest and thinned apples. One day I went to town and parked my car in front of the post

---

[19] A stoneboat is a sled, usually pulled by horses or mules, which was used to haul stones from a farm field. The low bed allowed stones to be rolled or pried up onto the sled.

office. A sailor on a recruiting poster beckoned me in. I got the scoop and the necessary papers to join the Navy and proceeded to Brewster to get my parents to sign the papers verifying that I was 17. I manipulated my parents into signing by telling them about the military insurance policy and promising them an allotment check.

On 24 August 1942, just shy of my fifteenth birthday, I was sworn into the Navy. I was on my way to San Diego "via the cushions and a porter to serve us" (inside a railroad car for a change). At the Naval Training Center, I was assigned to Company 42-507, and after a short boot camp, I was sent to Pearl Harbor aboard the USS *Lurline*. At Pearl, I went aboard the USS *Minneapolis* (CA-36) and went on to Guadalcanal via Samoa and Espíritu Santo.

On 30 November 1942, I was at my battle station, starboard sky forward, when we intercepted a Japanese fleet. This was off Tassafaronga, and what a hell of a battle that was! We lost our bow and three fire rooms and took two torpedoes, one forward and one amidship. We jettisoned everything possible and headed for a safe beach. We pulled into Tulagi and ran the *Minneapolis* aground. Then we camouflaged the ship with netting and palm boughs and made a temporary bow out of coconut trees. What seemed like a lifetime later, the *Minnie*, with a skeleton crew of about ninety men aboard, limped into Espíritu Santo where we obtained boiler tubes and a temporary bow, then headed for Pearl Harbor. It was a long way home. We were in enemy submarine territory and were forced to travel at a very slow speed.

We arrived in Pearl dirty and half-starved. I hadn't had a fresh-water shower in about three months. We were taken to the Royal Hawaiian Hotel where they fed us the best. My hotel room had a plaque on the wall that said President Roosevelt had stayed in that room during his last visit to Honolulu. I thought, "How plush can it get? I'm really coming up in the world!"

With a new bow and the fire-room hole patched, we left for Bremerton, Washington. We gave the number one 8-inch gun turret to the USS *New Orleans*, which also had her bow blown off, and the *Minnie* was sent to Mare Island, California, where she would get a complete overhaul. At Bremerton, I was given a 30-day leave with an extra ten days if I wanted it.

I made the mistake of going home. Every time I said anything about the war and the action I had been in, I was humiliated by people who didn't believe that a 15-year-old could have been in the war. I left home and went back to my ship at Mare Island, back to "the good life." We were getting ready for a shakedown cruise when the ship's new commander got a letter from my mother. People at home were putting the pressure on her to get that "lying little bastard" out of the Navy. They drummed me off the ship with a $12.00 zoot suit and an "ineptitude" discharge. I thought, "How shitty can it get?" My division boatswain's mate just couldn't believe it. I had held my end up all the way and then some!

The county auditor and a smart lawyer told me that I'd really blown it. They said that I would never hold a government job, vote, or anything else! I went back to Wenatchee, found my cousin, and headed for Canada. We had heard that we could join the French Foreign Legion there. My granddad lived in Oliver, British Columbia, so we spent a few days trying to get contacts in Penticton and Kelowna. We had a run-in with a radical group of Doukhobors[20] who didn't appreciate our patriotism. They told us not to let the sun go down on us in Canada. It was getting late, about two hours to sundown, and we had over a hundred miles to go to the border. The old '29 Chevy with a rumble seat fired up on the first crank and never missed a beat. The six cars loaded with Doukhobors never had a chance to catch us!

On my seventeenth birthday, 2 October 1944, I went back to the Naval recruiter in Wenatchee, told him of my predicament and asked if I could reenlist. He told me he would see what he could do. He called me back in a few days. I went in and they *really* gave me an I.Q. test, which I passed with flying colors.

I went back to Brewster to get permission to join because I was still underage, and to get married. A one-armed judge conducted the wedding. I heard him remark afterward, "This marriage won't last until sunup!"

In November 1944, I was on my way to "the good life" at the Naval Training Station, Farragut, Idaho. After going through boot camp for the second time, I was sent to Portland, Oregon. Ten of us were

---

[20] Doukhobors were members of an independent religious sect originating in Russia in the 18th century. They expressed opposition to civil authority by refusing to pay taxes, do military service, etc.

assigned to a flat-bottomed barracks barge, the APL-43. APLs don't have engines; they have to be towed. We rode the barge down the Columbia River to Astoria, over the bar, and on to Pearl Harbor. From Pearl, an Army tug towed us to Eniwetok. For three days during rough storms that were close to a typhoon, we never saw the tug. They had almost cut us loose because they thought we had sunk.

I wanted to get back to the fleet, but I was stuck on this dastardly island with no fresh water and no vegetation. Hell, I had left that kind of life at home years before, and now with the war over, I was stuck in this God-forsaken place as a coxswain supplying small vessels from the supply ships. Our unit started getting "ninety-day-wonders" (ensigns fresh out of officer candidate school) who were regulation-crazy, and I started getting in trouble. I decided that if I couldn't get into the fleet, I would try to get out while I was still ahead. Just before Christmas in 1945, I caught the USS *Nashville* back to Pearl. I would have loved to stay aboard, but it wasn't in the cards. After Pearl, I went to Treasure Island and received an honorable discharge at Shumaker, California, on 11 January 1946, at the age of 18.

Several years later when they tested the H-bomb at Eniwetok Atoll, I was grinning from ear to ear. My feeling was, "Blow it to hell — who needs it?"

Bob Cline went to work at Grand Coulee Dam after his discharge from the Navy, running a tugboat there for about a year. He then joined a carpenters union and worked in heavy construction, which included building bridges, commercial buildings, and dams. After being general foreman on three dam projects in Alaska, he called it quits and retired after forty-five years on the job. Bob's marriage to Hertha Vess lasted far past the judge's prediction of sunup the next morning. Hertha, Bob's wife and buddy for forty-nine years, died in 1994. They had four daughters and seven grandchildren. All four daughters attended college. Bob lives in Wenatchee, Washington.

Eddie H. Payne

Age 16 – United States Navy

I was born in Gilbertown, Alabama, on 26 April 1926. I wasn't doing very well in school, and I had always wanted to be a sailor. So I added a year to my age, and with my parents' permission, enlisted in the

We could actually see the 16-inch shells flying over us ...

Navy on a "kiddy cruise," which meant that I would serve until my phony twenty-first birthday.

I was sworn into the Navy on 3 September 1942 at Birmingham, Alabama, and sent to boot camp at Camp Green Bay, Illinois. After completing boot training, I was assigned to the destroyer USS *Cowie* (DD-632). We made eleven Atlantic crossings escorting convoys during my two years on the *Cowie*. One of our officers, Ensign Isaac C. Kidd, Jr., was just out of the Naval Academy. Ensign Kidd was the son of Rear Admiral I. C. Kidd, Sr., Commander, Battleship Division One, who was killed aboard the USS *Arizona* during the attack on Pearl Harbor. Ensign Kidd was a fine officer, and I would have the privilege of meeting him again during my career.

I got my first taste of combat at Casablanca, North Africa, New Year's Eve of 1942. Later, during the invasion of Sicily in 1943, we were escorting a cruiser near Sicily and were at relaxed general quarters. I had gone below decks to the head. As I came back on deck, I saw a German aircraft fly directly over us at an altitude of about 200 to 300 feet. Apparently we were both surprised, because no shots were fired by him or by us. He climbed out of firing range, then came back and dropped a bomb. Our ship was zigging and zagging at full speed, trying to miss the bomb. I was with the midship repair party at the base of the bridge. We stood there and watched the bomb falling directly at us, and it seemed like it took forever for it to reach us. The bomb hit on the port side, about 200 feet from the ship. We were lucky!

We were returning from a convoy trip from England and were only three days out of New York when we hit the worst storm I have *ever* been in. It lasted from the time of the evening meal until about 9:00 a.m. the next day. Our ship took impossible rolls. Our boats were shattered, life rafts torn loose, small-gun armor flattened, and much more damage was done to the ship. The engines were running at full speed, but we lost about ten miles overnight.

Being regular Navy, I was a little gung ho, so I asked for a transfer. I ended up at the Little Creek Amphibian Base, Virginia. I was there a very short time when it became evident that I did not want to have any thing to do with amphibians. One morning they asked for volunteers, and about 500 men put their hands up. After a few days of screening, physical exams, and a little swimming-pool checkout, they accepted about 300 of us. At this point, we still did not know, or care, what we were getting ourselves into. All we were concerned about was getting away from Little Creek.

We ended up at Fort Pierce, Florida. Fort Pierce was a NCDU (Navy combat demolition unit) training base. NCDU teams were the forerunner of the Navy UDT (underwater demolition teams) and the SEALS (sea air and land team). We underwent about six weeks of the most physical, mind-boggling, explosive training I had ever dreamed of. The Seabees would build concrete beach obstacles, and we would blow them up as fast as they could construct them. From the 300 who started this program, only around 150 finished. About the time we completed training, our name was changed from NCDU to UDT. I was assigned to UDT-21. Each team consisted of about 100 men, four operating platoons, and one headquarters platoon.

In the fall of 1944, about a dozen men, all veterans of the Normandy invasion, joined our team. We left Fort Pierce by troop train for San Pedro, California. Everything was hush-hush. We arrived in San Pedro on Thanksgiving Day 1944, and we were immediately put aboard a troopship and were underway by midnight. We learned eventually that we were going to Maui, Hawaii, where the Navy had an advanced-training base for UDTs. Most of our training was in the water, which included reconnaissance, blasting coral heads, etc.

After more training, at least *twelve* shots for this and that, and hand-loading about forty tons of explosives on the ship, we were on our way west. We ended up in the Philippines where we underwent a few days of training and had to contend with a few raids by Japanese planes. We were soon off for Okinawa, the biggest operation ever in the Pacific in terms of casualties for all the services and the number of ships lost.

About ten UDTs (about 1000 men) made reconnaissance missions on 29 March 1945. As we swam to shore, the ships supporting us were bombing and strafing the beaches. During our reconnaissance, we didn't find any mines or coral heads, but we found rows of wooden posts driven into the coral at the water line. The next day, we went in with explosives and destroyed the posts. We had support fire from the various ships as we had the day before. Our biggest concern on both days was the fear that some of our own ships' big shells would fall short and land on us. We could actually see the 16-inch shells flying over us from the battleships. We spotted a couple of Japanese machine-gun nests, but they didn't fire on us.

We worked the Okinawa area, performing recons and blasting on different islands for over three months. We blasted channels for LSTs to land supplies at Ie Shima. We were working there on 21 April 1945, the day that the famous news correspondent Ernie Pyle was killed. He was about 200 to 300 yards inland from us at the time of his death. He had been scheduled to interview us that evening.

As anyone who was there knows, the Navy suffered heavy losses at Okinawa. One or two ships were sunk every night. Our ship was credited with sinking two suicide boats. We were close to the USS *Dickerson* (APD-21) when she was hit by a kamikaze and a moment later by a 500-pound bomb. We pulled alongside her and started fighting fires and getting the wounded off. We got all the personnel off that we could, put boats in the water to pick up survivors, and backed clear of her, fearing that she might blow up. While alongside the *Dickerson*, it was decided that we would put a rubber boat in the water. I jumped and landed in the boat, but my partner, who had the paddles, jumped and landed in the water. The wind and rough water sent the rubber boat around the stern of the *Dickerson*. I didn't have paddles, but I finally got clear of the ship by swimming and pulling the rubber boat with me. I was picked up about thirty minutes later.

We returned to the amphibian base at Camp Pendleton, California, on 21 July 1945 and received a few days' leave. I returned from leave on the 12th or the 13th. On the morning of 14 August, we were told to pack our bags, and we were taken by bus to the San Diego airport. San Diego was wall-to-wall people celebrating V-J Day. During the three hours we were waiting for an airplane, I ran into three guys that I knew from the USS *Cowie*.

We flew to Guam where we boarded the USS *Begor* (APD-127) and headed for Japan. We entered Tokyo Bay on 28 August 1945, USA time. After a short reconnaissance, we landed at Futtsu Saki Island Army Fort at the entrance to Tokyo Bay. We touched shore five days before the official surrender on 2 September 1945. We were the first seagoing personnel ashore on Japan at the war's end. In Tokyo Bay, we boarded Japanese ships, went into gun emplacements, cleaned out the pier at Yokosuka Navy Base, and helped tie up the cruiser USS *San Diego*. For several months after the peace treaty was signed, we worked down the coast, destroying suicide boats and two-man submarines. We returned to the amphibian base at Coronado, California, in November 1945, loaded with souvenirs. We had obtained a Japanese rifle for all enlisted men. We had pistols and shotguns for officers and chiefs. This included the crew of the ship that brought us to California. A number of people had Japanese swords.

During the next few years, I served on a number of ships and at shore stations. In 1960, I was promoted to chief and went to the PX at the Submarine Base at Pearl Harbor looking for a chief's hat. I met I. C. Kidd, Jr., who had just been promoted to captain and was looking for a captain's hat. I was watching television in New York City in 1976 when Admiral I. C. Kidd, Jr., Commander-in-Chief, U. S. Atlantic Fleet, appeared on the program. I sent him a copy of the USS *Cowie*'s 1942 Christmas menu, and I received a very nice reply.

While in Hawaii in 1960, I was with the EODU-1 (Explosive Ordnance Disposal Unit) at Pearl Harbor when the nuclear submarine *Sargo* tied up at the submarine base there. A fire developed while it was taking on oxygen. The man at the controls was killed, and the aft torpedo room was flooded. EODU-1 was called in but there was not much we could do that evening. As water was being pumped out the next morning, several of us went down and found a mess. Using battle lanterns for illumination, we searched for the body. We found that one torpedo in a rack had undergone a low-order detonation. Had it gone high-order — who knows? The reactor area of the sub was not far away. I'm sure that a lot of heads rolled, and news coverage was kept to a minimum.

We found the body and also found a torpedo stuck in the port tube. I went into the tube from the outside using a shallow-water diving rig. With a battle lantern and a wrench, I worked for thirty to forty minutes to remove the nose plate so that a device could be attached and the torpedo pulled out. This near disaster, I'm sure, caused a lot of changes in command at the sub base.

The following month, a scuba diver found a two-man Japanese submarine in about seventy feet of water. The sub had been there since the raid on Pearl Harbor. Another diver and I went down to inspect it. The crew had obviously escaped. A Navy salvage ship picked it up and brought it to land where our EODU-1 gave it a going over. We removed two torpedoes and a scuttling charge that had failed to explode. A souvenir or two were taken from the sub.

I retired from the Navy on 15 March 1962 at the age of 35, just a little over a month before I turned 36.

Eddie Payne became a rigger on an operation at San Clemente, California, after retiring from the Navy. He went next to Kwajalein for the Kentron Corporation for eighteen months, where he received and issued explosives and missiles. After that, he went to Eniwetok as a rigger/diver, then to Washington State for a time, and then back to Hawaii where he operated a Chevron service station until 1971. After a few small jobs, he returned to Alabama where he had bought seventy-five acres a few years before. He always wanted to jump out of a perfectly good airplane, so he made a tandem jump on his sixty-fifth birthday and another one his seventieth. He plans to travel more and work on family and UDT/SEAL history.

Stanley B. Szczepanski

Age 16 – United States Army

I was born in Philadelphia, Pennsylvania, on 11 April 1926 and grew up on a farm in southern New Jersey. I remember listening to the radio on Sunday, 7 December 1941, and hearing the news that the Japanese had bombed Pearl

> *... one month after my seventeenth birthday, I was commissioned a second lieutenant ...*

Harbor. Right after the announcement, a low-flying plane suddenly passed over our home, and my mother, who had once been involved in a revolution in Poland, thought that it was an enemy plane.

My older sister joined the Army Nurse Corps in the spring of 1942. A few months later, my mother died, and I decided to enlist. Although I was only 16 years old, I "modified" a baptismal certificate that convinced the recruiter that I was 18, and I was sworn into the Army on 8 September 1942.

After basic training at Fort Bragg, North Carolina, I was selected for officer candidate school at Fort Sill, Oklahoma. On 20 May 1943, one month after my seventeenth birthday, I was commissioned a second lieutenant in the field artillery. I spent many a restless night wondering when someone would discover my true age, but my age was never questioned. I learned later that I was one of the youngest, if not *the* youngest, person to be commissioned an officer during World War II.

After training in the States for a year, I volunteered for overseas service and was assigned to the European theater. In September 1944, during a delay en route to the port of embarkation, I married my high school sweetheart. I arrived in England a few weeks later.

I joined the 690th Field Artillery Battalion in Aachen, Germany, in December 1944. Our primary duties were to establish military governments in occupied cities and camps for displaced persons from other countries.

One time during all of this activity, I found myself in the front seat of a jeep with two pregnant women in the back seat and a baby carriage hung over the front of the jeep. One of the women was due to give birth in about three days, but the other was due that same day. I was really sweating it out because I had never played the part of a midwife before and didn't want to try it then. I drove around on bumpy roads for over an hour and a half, looking for a hospital that would take them in. With every bump, I had visions of my having to try to imitate Dr. Kildare with only my jeep for a hospital. They had never taught me how to do that in gunnery school. Fortunately, I found a hospital in time!

After V-E Day, part of our mission was the exchange of displaced persons between the United States and the Russian Occupied Zones. Most of the displaced persons that we returned to the Russians had been brought to Germany as forced laborers. You can imagine their reaction when they learned they would be returning to their homes again.

We would take convoys of Russians into the Russian Zone and bring back convoys of French, Belgian, and Dutch to the American Zone. Each time we took a convoy across, we had to stop on the Russian side while a band played them a welcome and threw flowers at them. While everyone appeared very happy during those occasions, it was interesting to note that the farther we went into the Russian Occupied Zone, the more subdued the Russian displaced persons became. On the return trip, however, it was just the opposite — the further we got into the American Zone, the more the French, Belgians, and Dutch seemed to celebrate. There were a number of Germans in the Russian Zone who tried every trick imaginable to have us take them back with us to the American Zone.

Later, I served as an instructor at the newly formed Constabulary School in Sonthofen, Germany. After nineteen months overseas, I returned to the States and was released from active duty on 17 June 1946 with the rank of first lieutenant.

In December 1948, I volunteered for active duty and was assigned to occupation duty at Atsugi Air Force Base, Japan. I was transferred later to Kyushu, Japan, and assigned to the 24th Infantry Division. Our daughter Patricia was born in Japan and contracted polio there.

In the spring of 1950, I requested to be released from active duty so that I could bring my family back to the States and obtain treatment for my daughter. My request was granted, and I was released from active duty on 21 June 1950. We were aboard ship heading home just days before the Korean War started.

I have always been proud of my Polish ancestry and my World War II service. I appreciate the fact that those of us who told white lies in order to enlist no longer have to continue that deception.

Stan Szczepanski worked for the Department of the Army in the military procurement field for twenty-five years. He began his civil-service career in Philadelphia, Pennsylvania, and was later transferred to the U. S. Army Missile Command, Huntsville, Alabama, where he became chief of the Procurement and Production Division, Lance Project Office. At his retirement in 1976, Stan received a Department of the Army Decoration for Meritorious Civilian Service. Stan and Sara, his wife of fifty-two years, live in Decatur, Alabama. They have nine children, eight grandchildren and one great-grandchild. One son recently retired from the U. S. Air Force.

David Morris

Age 16 – United States Navy

I was 15 years old at the time World War II began, and I figured that the draft would catch up with me by the time I was 18, but an older buddy who had gotten his girl friend pregnant wanted me to run off with him and join the Navy. At that time,

> *After two weeks of boot camp and one week of mess-cook duty, I went off to war.*

we were living in Wilmington, Delaware, where I was born on 17 September 1926. To overcome the age problem, I forged my birth certificate, convinced my mother to sign my enlistment papers, and on my sixteenth birthday, 17 September 1942, I was sworn into the U. S. Navy.

I was sent to boot camp at the U. S. Naval Training Station, Great Lakes, Illinois. After getting up at 5:00 a.m. and drilling all day, I thought that perhaps I had made a mistake, so I informed the

barracks chief petty officer that I was underage. The chief's comment to me was, "We have a birth certificate on file, plus a letter from your mom stating that you are 17. Not only that, but you are in the *regular Navy* for the next four years." At that point, I remembered that I hadn't wanted to join the reserves because I thought they were just weekend warriors.

After two weeks of boot camp and one week of mess-cook duty, I went off to war. Within six weeks after my sixteenth birthday, I was at sea on the destroyer-tender USS *Hamul* (AD-20). After a short cruise from Mobile, Alabama, to Casco Bay, Maine, I transferred to the destroyer USS *Niblack* (DD-424) as a member of a 40mm-gun crew.

We escorted the first support convoy to Casablanca after the Allied landings on the Moroccan Coast. We performed escort duties and screened the mine-laying operation near Gela during the invasion of

Sicily and participated in the first Navy bombardment of the Italian mainland near Palmi, Italy. During the invasion of Salerno, our ship celebrated my seventeenth birthday by bombarding seventeen different targets.

After the invasion at Anzio, I returned to the States. My R&R leave was cut short by an assignment to another tin can (destroyer), the USS *McCook* (DD-496). We sailed for England and began preparing for the invasion of Normandy. The *McCook* was bombed and disabled by German planes that caught her in the English channel. We thought that we would miss the big one (D-Day), but by cannibalizing parts from other ships that were out of action, our ship was put back into service in time to be a lead destroyer during the invasion at Omaha Beach, Normandy.

By 0616 of D-Day, 6 June 1944, the *McCook* had neutralized all her assigned targets: three pillboxes, thirteen machine-gun nests, and three shore guns. We then turned to targets of opportunity. By the end of the first day, we had neutralized an additional seven pillboxes, eight gun emplacements, and ten stone houses in which enemy machine guns and snipers had been located. The *McCook*, after taking on ammunition and fuel, provided support in the invasion area until 14 July.

In mid-July, we left the Normandy area and proceeded to the Mediterranean for Operation Anvil, the invasion of southern France. Most of our time was spent screening larger ships and trying to help knock out the big 14-inch harbor guns in the port of Toulon. I stayed in the assault area until my eighteenth birthday. I was now old enough to be drafted!

In the later part of 1944, I returned to the States once more. Bigger and better things were to come. The *bigger* was that I was transferred to a new heavy cruiser, the USS *Fall River* (CA-131), and the *better* was that we were to sail to the Marshall Islands in the Pacific. We participated in Operation Crossroads, the nuclear bomb tests at Bikini Atoll in 1946.

I returned to the States on the USS *St. Croix* (APA-130) with a load of radiated materials from the bombed experimental areas. I arrived home on terminal leave just days before my twentieth birthday — my twenty-first, according to my forged birth certificate.

I was discharged at the Philadelphia Navy Yard in December 1946 at the ripe old age of 20 years and 3 months.

Dave Morris earned eleven battle stars on his campaign ribbons, eight in the European theater, two in the Atlantic, and one in the Pacific. He took the GED tests to earn his high school diploma, entered business college, then completed several refrigeration-engineering and electrical-engineering courses. He became a district executive with the Boy Scouts of America in Baltimore, Maryland, and later, the Council Scout Executive of Middletown, New York, and Council Scout Executive of Reading, Pennsylvania. After nineteen years with the Boy Scouts, he served as Executive Director of the Jewish Federation of Reading-Berks County. Dave suffered a massive heart attack in 1975 and had open-heart surgery. After his surgery, he was semiretired, but that didn't last long. After nine months, he became part-time Director of the Cerebral Palsy Association of Reading and later went full-time as Associate Campaign Director for the United Jewish Appeal, working out of the Northeast Regional Office in River Edge, New Jersey, with campaigns in four states. He has worked as a volunteer with many humanitarian groups. Currently, he is the historian for the USS Niblack and President of the USS Fall River Association. Dave and Rhoda, his wife of 47 years, live in Lauderhill, Florida. They have a son, a daughter, and three grandchildren. Prior to moving to Florida in November of 1996, Dave was the Pennsylvania State Vice-Commander of the Veterans of Underage Military Service.

Reginald D. Stewart

Age 14 – United States Navy

I was a juvenile misfit of World War II. The timing of my birth, 12 January 1928, in Worcester, Massachusetts, was such that I was too young to serve in the military, but too old to stay at home. I was in trouble up to my

> *... a torpedo from a German submarine hit our ship ...*

neck all of the time. We lived in an industrial area where most people worked shifts in plants that operated twenty-four hours a day. I would skip school and work setting pins in bowling alleys that featured tournaments day and night. I made almost as much money as my divorced mother made working as a waitress. But I ran around with a group of tough kids and was always in trouble.

A Worcester city policeman who happened to be one of my mother's customers picked me up for running away from home. He told me in no uncertain terms where I was heading and that he would help put me there. He also told me about a kid who had lied about his age and enlisted in the Army. After giving this a lot of thought, I contacted a guy who was being drafted and obtained a copy of his papers.

On 21 September 1942, I went to Springfield, Massachusetts, and using the borrowed papers, enlisted in the U. S. Navy as Raymond Sampson Hutchinson. I was immediately sent to the Great Lakes Naval Training Station for boot camp. In January 1943, nine of us were sent to Sampson, New York, to work with civilians and other Navy personnel to set up a new boot camp. After many requests for transfer, in September 1943 I was sent to the Armed Guard Center in Brooklyn, New York. From there I went to the Armed Guard Gunnery School at Shelton, Virginia. I reported back to the Armed Guard Center in Brooklyn in December 1943.

I reported aboard the SS *Margaret Lykes* on 3 January 1944. Soon after, we sailed for Nova Scotia to rendezvous with a convoy heading for Murmansk, Russia. The harbor at Murmansk was a frequent target of German aircraft. Ironically, more than twenty years after I was in Murmansk, I became good friends with a German immigrant who had settled in the Oregon town where I lived. During the war, my friend had served with the German Air Force and had flown the Messerschmitt ME-109. He bombed and strafed the ships in Murmansk harbor many times, including the very day that I was there!

On the way back from Russia, we stopped in England, picked up a load of British supplies, and took them to a Royal Air Force depot located about twenty miles east of Oran, North Africa. We then returned to New York, reloaded, and went to the Caribbean where we loaded and unloaded cargo at several Caribbean ports. On the way from Cuba to New Orleans, a torpedo from a German submarine hit our ship in the #1 hold near the bow. We limped into New Orleans where I was temporarily assigned to the Armed Guard Center there. The *Margaret Lykes* was taken to a shipyard in Texas to get a new bow.

On 6 July 1944, I reported aboard a Liberty ship, the SS *William D. Pender*. We went through the Panama Canal and on to Eniwetok and Kwajalein in the South Pacific. We returned to the States, reloaded, and went to Dutch Harbor in the Aleutian Islands. At Dutch Harbor, we turned the ship over to the Russians and caught a ride to Seattle on a destroyer-escort.

I was assigned to the SS *Texmar* on 20 October 1944. The *Texmar* was one of the C-type Liberty ships commonly known as "Kaiser's coffins." The stern gun on the *Texmar* was a 4.51-inch monster that had been taken off the old battleship *Texas*. To fire the gun, one had to load an 80-pound projectile, then forty pounds of powder, and then put a primer in the breach and pull a lanyard. What a prize that was!

We went to Tocapila, Chile, for a load of sulphur. On our way north, off the coast of Mexico, a fire broke out in #3 hold. The fire was still burning when we reached San Pedro, California. A Navy tugboat and a seagoing barge came alongside and put out the fire.

I was reassigned to Dam Neck, Virginia, for a gunnery refresher course on 25 January 1945. Less than a month later, on 16 February 1945, I was assigned to the USS *Bunker Hill*. We went through the

Panama Canal to Iwo Jima and back to Seattle. On 29 April 1945, I was assigned to the USAT *Cherikof* for duty transporting Army supplies and troops between Seattle and the Aleutians in preparation for the invasion of Japan.

Just before being assigned to the *Texmar* in October 1944, I was charged with assaulting an officer. I received a captain's mast (disciplinary hearing) but was cleared of the charges. I admitted my fraudulent enlistment at that time and told them my name was not Hutchinson. Commander William Coakley helped me get my records straightened out and made it possible for me to stay in the Navy under my true name. I owe Commander Coakley and the police officer in Worcester, Massachusetts, whose name I cannot remember, more than I could ever pay. May God bless them for what they did for me. Many of the boys that I ran around with during my younger days in Worcester have spent time in prison, and some of them are still there.

I was discharged from the Navy on 20 December 1945 at Bremerton, Washington.

Reggie Stewart worked in a timber mill near Tacoma, Washington, for a few months and then went to Worcester, Massachusetts, to enroll in a printer's apprentice program under the GI Bill. He returned to Washington in 1947 where he worked for the S.P.& S. Railroad in Vancouver. In 1949, he moved to Ilwaco, Washington, where he worked for the Ilwaco Telephone Company, becoming manager after several years. Later he transferred to a larger company in the Willamette Valley in Oregon where he stayed until he retired in 1988. Reggie and Barbara, his wife of more than fifty years, live in Lebanon, Oregon, during the summer and at Casa Grande, Arizona, during the winter months. Reggie and Barbara have a daughter, a son, six grandchildren, and three great-grandchildren.

Gordon W. Frank

Age 16 – United States Navy

I was 16 years old, school was a drag, and I didn't care to drive horses all my life, so I went to Madison, Wisconsin, to work for the Coca Cola Company. Madison was thirty miles from Beaver Dam, Wisconsin, where I was born on 15 January 1926.

> *I'm quite sure that I was the bombardier that sank the last enemy ship during World War II.*

I was living in the YMCA at Madison, scrubbing floors to pay for my room. When I saw a Navy recruiting poster, bells went off in my mind. I hitchhiked back to Juneau, the county seat, went to the courthouse and obtained a copy of my birth certificate. I took the certificate back to the YMCA in Madison and a religious counselor erased the year 1926 and wrote in 1925. Two days later, I was in Milwaukee, Wisconsin, ready to join the Navy. The recruiting office was so crowded that I had to wait until 5 October 1942 to be sworn in.

I was sent to the Great Lakes Naval Training Center for boot training. We had to sleep in hammocks laced to jackstays. It was really hard to get into the hammocks and even harder to stay in them. After one of the most painful series of shots in the arm, I fell out of my hammock and landed on my arm on the hardwood floor. Ouch! During boot camp, our company won the "Rooster" honor (a flag awarded each week to the boot company excelling in drill and neatness) four weeks in a row and got to keep it. That just proves how mean our chief was.

After boot camp, I was sent to the Naval Section Base in the town of Port Townsend, Washington. It was quite an experience for a recent boot to mix with the old salts. Somehow I got to Bremerton, Washington, for submarine training. That lasted only as long as it took me to find a way out of there. I was then sent to the Oak Harbor Seaplane Base on Whidbey Island, Washington.

I was in the beach crew for a short while. Our job was to go into the sea and put wheels on seaplanes so they could be pulled on shore. We would put on rubber suits, pump them up with air, then go into the water. One time I was tipped over in the water after being hit by the tail of a PBY5, and all the air went to my feet. I was bobbing around with my feet in the air and my head in the water until someone pulled me out.

When there was an opening, I went to work in the ordnance shop and started striking for a rate (studying for a rating in a specialty). While I was working there, a squadron of PBYs was being assembled for duty in the Aleutian Islands. I wanted to go with them, so I signed up for bombardier school and was accepted.

We left Oak Harbor on 26 November 1943 and .went to Annette Island, Yakutat, Kodiak, Dutch Harbor, Adak, and Amchitka, in Alaska. We flew patrols every other day. On 24 December 1943, we sighted an unidentified aircraft, but it flew away. On 15 January 1944, we flew close to Paramashiru in the Kurile Islands. Around 1 February 1944, we tried taking off and landing with fog dispensers, trenches filled with burning fuel on each side of the runway, but the idea was given up after the trial.

In August 1944, our crew was nominated to fly as escort cover for a cruiser carrying President Franklin D. Roosevelt. We escorted the President's ship from near Midway Island to the States, landing at Adak, Dutch Harbor, Kodiak, Juneau, Annette, and Yakutat. I watched all the President's parades and listened to his speeches along the way. It was very interesting.

During our stay in Juneau, we didn't have any money with us, so we couldn't even have our laundry done. We asked the Red Cross for a loan, but we were refused. A Catholic priest gave us some money, which we later repaid. After delivering the President to the States, we retraced our flight path and returned to Amchitka.

Our squadron, VP-62, returned to the States in late November 1944. After a 36-day leave, I reported to the naval station at Hutchinson, Kansas, where I stayed for about a month, then it was on to Jacksonville, Florida, for another month. In March 1945, I went to Miami, Florida, and joined VPB-104, a squadron that flew PB4Y1 bombers (the Navy version of the B-24 Liberator). I qualified as a master bombardier over Cuban waters.

We left for Clark Field, Luzon, in the Philippine Islands in May 1945, stopping at many islands along the way. On 6 July and again on 9 July, we made bombing runs over Formosa, encountering heavy antiaircraft fire. On 12 July, we bombed two junks, after which an American submarine surfaced and took two survivors as prisoners. On 15 July, we bombed a river steamer at Hong Kong.

On 30 July, I injured my head when the top hatch on a PB4Y2 blew off. The pilot landed, and I was taken to a hospital tent and stitched up. For a pain killer, the doctor handed me his quart bottle of "Old Fitzgerald" of which I took a good, large medical dose. He asked me for my name and serial number because he was going to give me a Purple Heart. I talked him out of it because I was afraid they might find out that I lied about my age to enlist, and I would have to suffer the consequences.

On 5 August, we had a very hot time over Amoy, China, where they shot at us with the so-called "star shells." We sank a river boat three days later. On 14 August, we sank a "Sugar Dog," our code for a Japanese transport. When we landed after a flight of just over nine hours, we learned that the war was over. I'm quite sure that I was the bombardier that sank the last enemy ship during World War II.

Three months later, we flew back to the States, landing at Floyd Bennett Field, New York, on 22 November 1945. I was discharged at Great Lakes, Illinois, on 26 February 1946. I still retain my "blood chit," bombardier patch, and a Chinese $1,000 bill from the Central Bank of China.

Gordon Frank was a member of VPB-104, the only naval unit to receive two Presidential Unit Citations during World War II. After his discharge from the Navy, he worked for his father as a bartender for several years, then worked for Kraft Foods for twenty-eight years, retiring in 1985. He was an Olympic boxing coach for Wisconsin for twelve years. His hobby is constructing and flying radio-controlled model airplanes. Gordon and Kathryn, his wife of forty-eight years, live in Beaver Dam, Wisconsin, during the summers and spend their winters in Texas and other warm climes. They have four children and five grandchildren.

Donald J. Hunt

Age 15 – United States Navy

I was born in Brooklyn, New York, on 15 November 1926. Both of my parents died when I was very young, and I was raised by my stepfather. In the early 1930s, he traveled west seeking work. We lived in Denver, Colorado, for a short period, then

> The ME-109 dropped a 500-pound bomb directly on the tank deck of our LST.

moved to Boulder City, Nevada, where my stepfather found work at Boulder Dam (now Hoover Dam). We came back east in 1934, and I grew up in the area around Brooklyn and Port Jervis, New York.

In June 1942, about six months after Pearl Harbor, I had to quit school and was sent to Newark, New Jersey, to work on high roofs. I decided that if I was old enough to work, I was old enough to join the Navy. I doctored up my birth certificate, and on 6 October 1942, I enlisted in the Navy.

I went to boot camp at Great Lakes, Illinois. After boot camp, I was selected to attend primary diesel school at the Navy Pier, Chicago, Illinois, and advanced diesel school at Cleveland, Ohio. From there I went to Little Creek, Virginia, for small boat training in 36-foot LCVPs. After serving on several LSTs, I was transferred to shore duty at Bizerte, North Africa. We were bombed and strafed by German aircraft almost every night. On the day that the city of Tunis in Tunisia fell to the Allies, we were transported overland through the desert to the Port of La Goulette, near Tunis. As we entered Tunis, we passed tanks and trucks that were still burning and smoking.

Shortly after I arrived at La Goulette, I was assigned to the USS *LST-313*, and we started preparing for the invasion of Sicily. We were to land troops at Diamond Beach, near Gela, Sicily. Early on the morning of 10 July 1943, our LCVP was launched from the *LST-313*.

Our orders were to escort five Army DUKWs (amphibious trucks, pronounced "ducks") to the beach. Each DUKW carried a 105mm howitzer, ammunition, and a crew of ten. The soldiers were from the 33rd Field Artillery Battalion, 26th Infantry Regiment, 1st Infantry Division (the Big Red One).

The seas were extremely heavy, causing us difficulty in launching our LCVP. As the DUKWs waddled off the ship through the bow doors, the waves would lift them and slap them against the side walls of the ramp opening. Finally, at 2:00 a.m., the DUKWs were in the water. In total darkness, we headed for the beach, fifteen miles away. The only confirmation of direction we had was when large naval shells passed over us heading for the beach. The light from the hot shells lit up the ocean, creating a beacon for us to follow.

As a passing shell lit up the water, we could see that one of the DUKWs was sinking. It took us several hours to rescue the ten men because of the rough seas. Just as we had them in our boat and were again headed toward the beach, another DUKW sank. Miraculously, we rescued all the men and again proceeded toward the beach. Two more DUKWs sank, and we went through the same rescue procedure. We had fifty-three men in a Higgins boat whose rated capacity was thirty-six men. We finally made it to the beach at dawn, one DUKW and one overloaded LCVP.

After we landed and the soldiers left the LCVP, the heavy surf caused the boat to broach and roll over onto the beach. The *LST-313* was still several miles at sea, so we spent the balance of the day on the beach unloading supplies and running for cover as the German ME-109 aircraft kept up a constant strafing of the beach and the incoming landing-craft. Late in the afternoon, we saw that the *LST-313* was proceeding to the beach with her pontoon causeway fastened to her bow. When the causeway hit the beach, we jumped on it and started toward the ship. We were about halfway there when we saw an ME-109 coming in to strafe and bomb the area. We ran back to the beach just as the plane approached. The ME-109 dropped a 500-pound bomb directly on the tank deck of our LST. Had we run to the ship instead of to the beach we would have reached her just as the bomb hit. The ship burned for two days and was totally destroyed. Many Army personnel were casualties.

We hitched a ride back to Africa and made several supply runs to Sicily on other LSTs. Our ship's crew was finally assembled and shipped back to the States. After a survivor leave, we picked up a new ship, the USS *LST-286*, at the America Bridge Company in Pittsburgh, Pennsylvania. We sailed down the Ohio and Mississippi Rivers to New Orleans where the ship was outfitted and commissioned. Then we sailed for England via Halifax, Nova Scotia.

We participated in the invasion of Normandy at Omaha Beach, making several runs back and forth across the channel before our screw was fouled during a big storm that hit the beach about two weeks after D-Day. We went into dry dock at Plymouth, England, for repairs, then headed to the Mediterranean to take part in the invasion of southern France.

After a few trips hauling prisoners between Africa and southern France, I was transferred back to Little Creek, Virginia, for training on LSM rocket ships. I didn't particularly like that duty, so I volunteered for UDT (underwater demolition team) training at Fort Pierce, Florida. I was disqualified for UDT training because of severe sinus problems. I was then transferred to the fleet inspector's office in New York City, to inspect LCT units that had been brought back from Europe, reconditioned, and were being prepared for shipment to the Pacific.

After the New York duty, I was assigned to the USS *Midway* (CVB-41) and was aboard for her commissioning and for trial runs to Cuba. I was assigned as senior petty officer in the forward emergency diesel-generator room. We were preparing for deployment to the Pacific when the war ended.

I received an honorable discharge at Shelton, Virginia, on 7 February 1946 after serving three years and four months in the Navy. It is somewhat ironic that I never learned to swim, and to this day I can't swim.

Don Hunt began working as a mason's helper shortly after his discharge from the Navy. Later he became a plumber's helper and a licensed electrician. Within a few years, he owned and operated his own general-contracting business. He sold his businesses in 1987 but refused to be idle. He currently owns and operates Eagle Country Land & Homes, a real-estate brokerage firm in Sparrowbush, New York, where he resides. Don has seven children, fifteen grandchildren, and three great-grandchildren.

Norman R. Shaw

Age 15 – United States Navy

I was born in Logan, Ohio, on 25 June 1927. Being the youngest of four children meant that I was the recipient of all the hand-me-downs, including patched underwear. My father worked for the Post Office, and as I found out many years later, made $40.00 per week during the worst of the Depression years.

"Hey, that's my baby brother's name, but it can't be him, he's only 15 years old!"

My mother and father were divorced in 1936. Sometime in the early spring, my mother went away, but I was not informed until school closed in June that she wasn't coming back. Our next-door neighbors, Dora and Charles Mock, were like a family to me. I called them Aunt Dora and Uncle Charlie. Dora's twin sister Nora was married to Charles Kreider, who owned a farm near Gibisonville, Ohio. His son lived there and worked the farm. I moved to the farm in early summer. My father paid $10.00 a month for my keep, but I started earning my keep from day one.

I started by gathering eggs every morning, feeding the chickens, carrying water from the springhouse to the kitchen, and doing almost any job that needed doing. I was soon milking a cow, and when I became adept at that, I was assigned two cows to milk. I was glad that there were only three cows because I was soon milking them all. When school began that fall, I would be awakened at 5:00 a.m. to milk the cows, feed the chickens and horses, carry water to the kitchen, have breakfast, change clothes, grab my books, and catch the bus to school. Chores were waiting for me when I returned from school. I lived on the farm for two years, and although the work was hard, I have only fond memories of that life and the many people in it. After six weeks in the fourth grade at the country school in Gibisonville, I was moved to the fifth grade.

I returned to Logan, Ohio, in time to start the seventh grade in September 1939 at age 12. My sister was married, and my brothers were in high school. My father and I had a very close relationship during the years 1939 and 1940, but late in 1940, he remarried. His new wife was an old-maid schoolteacher, and from that time on, my life was pure hell. We moved to a large house where I had a very large bedroom to myself, but the injustices heaped upon me by my stepmother are too numerous to mention. For example, she counted the slices of bread left in a loaf after it had been opened, and if she found that I had used two slices of bread for a peanut butter sandwich, she gave me Hail Columbia! Imagine coming home after football practice at school and being harangued for hours over two slices of bread!

We had settled down for our noon meal on 7 December 1941 when we heard the news about Pearl Harbor. My brother Todd was in the Navy, stationed at Kanehoe Bay, Hawaii, at the time. Another brother, Bill, had joined the Navy in 1940. When school ended in late May I was at loose ends. I turned 15 in June, and just after the Fourth of July, a friend and I ran away from home. We hitchhiked to Indianapolis, hopped a freight train to East St. Louis, and walked from the rail yards to the western fringes of St. Louis, Missouri.

My friend returned to Ohio, but I hitchhiked to Corpus Christi, Texas, where my brother Bill was stationed at the Naval Air Station near there. I located my brother and moved into a boarding house. I registered as a junior in high school and got a part-time job at an IGA food store. My mother arrived a week later from Newark, Ohio, and we moved into Naval housing.

By October 1942, I was heading for real trouble. I was running with a bunch of Navy brats who got in trouble and were caught by the deputy sheriff. I was involved, and if one of them told on me, I would be in trouble too. I pleaded with my mother to let me join the Navy — to make my getaway, as it were. She did, and I did. I went to the Navy recruiting office and obtained the necessary papers. I wrote on the papers that I was born in St. Louis, Missouri, on 25 June 1925. My mother signed the papers as my legal guardian, although my father was actually my legal guardian.

I was sworn into the Navy in Houston, Texas, on 20 October 1942 and left that evening for boot camp in San Diego, California. After five weeks in boot camp, I attended the West Coast Sound School at the destroyer base at San Diego for six weeks and was promoted to soundman third class on 19 January 1943. A soundman is now known as a sonarman.

I was assigned to a destroyer, the USS *Abner Read* (DD-526). On 5 February 1943, the crew of the *Abner Read* was at Treasure Island waiting for transportation to Pier 54 in San Francisco to board and proceed with commissioning ceremonies. While I was waiting, I happened to walk into a large room of the barracks where the draft lists for the various ships were posted. I saw two sailors looking at the draft list for the *Abner Read*'s commissioning detail. I was standing behind them as they scanned the list. One of them said, "Hey, that's my baby brother's name, but it can't be him, he's only 15 years old!" I walked over to him, tapped him on the shoulder, and as he turned around, I saw that it was my oldest brother Todd. Talk about one chance in a million — that was one! Todd, a Pearl Harbor survivor, was on his way to Athens, Georgia, for training as an enlisted aviation pilot.

In March 1943, I was transferred to the USS *Caldwell* (DD-605). Although I was 5' 11" tall, soon after I boarded the *Caldwell,* a sailor named Sivo started calling me "Baby Shaw." The name was soon picked up by the entire crew, but it was one that I didn't appreciate.

By May 1943, we were in the Aleutians participating in the retaking of Attu on 15 and 16 May. From the Aleutians we steamed south to Pearl Harbor and joined a task force headed for Tarawa in the Gilbert Islands. After Tarawa, we participated in the invasions of Kwajalein, Eniwetok, and Wotje in the Marshall Islands, followed by Saipan, Tinian, Guam, Truk, Hollandia, Manus, Wewak, Halmahera, Ulithi, Peleliu, Samar, Surigao Strait, and Ormoc Bay.

We hit Ormoc Bay on 7 December 1944. On 11 December, we took two kamikaze hits on our starboard side under the pilothouse. We returned to the States for repairs and were back in the Pacific in time for the invasion of Borneo.

I was discharged in January 1946, returned to Corpus Christi, Texas, and immediately enrolled in high school as a junior. I graduated in January 1947, then reenlisted in the Navy. I served two years on the USS *Linnet* (AMS-24), followed by a tour on the USS *Soley* (DD-707). In 1950, I was a member of the recommissioning crew of the USS *Braine* (DD-630). We participated in the landing at Inchon on 15 September 1950. As the war progressed, we made numerous sorties as a fire-support vessel and sank or damaged many North Korean patrol craft. We assisted in the evacuation of Army and Marine units from Hungnam in December 1950.

In 1961, I served aboard the USS *Independence* (CVA-62). The *Independence* was the flagship of a large naval task force in international waters close to Cuba during the Bay of Pigs operation. My billet came under the command of the Armed Forces Special Weapons Program. I was considered to be an expert in the use of electrical/electronic fuzing and firing devices. During the early stages of the operation, three other specialists and I left the *Independence* by helicopter and were inserted into Cuba. We were there for about four hours, then picked up and returned to the ship. The carrier's aircraft were fueled and armed, ready to assist as necessary. However, at the most crucial moments of the exercise, orders came for the task force to stand down and return to the East Coast. The entire crew was somewhat disappointed at this sad state of affairs.

I returned to Yorktown, Virginia, in January 1962 and spent nearly two and a half years there. I went to Thurso, Scotland, in 1964 as the electronics maintenance officer. That was the best tour of duty I ever had.

I was ordered to Vietnam in 1966 to be executive officer, public-works officer, and electronics officer at the U. S. Naval Communications Station, Cam Ranh Bay. Before shipping out for Vietnam, I attended language school, small-arms school and survival training at the Coronado Naval Base and the Camp Pendleton Marine Base. When I arrived at Cam Ranh Bay, there was nothing but sand, sea, and jungle. When I departed in October 1967, we had put together the second largest communications complex in the world.

I was with a group of thirty Marines at a partially completed communications building on Monkey Mountain near Danang when we got into a fire fight with the Viet Cong. Later, I was on a swift boat (PCF) when we ran into a Viet Cong landing party off Chou Lai.

I will never forget my first trip from Saigon to Cam Ranh Bay. There were seven on the flight in a Navy DC-3. The flight was uneventful, but the fireworks started after we landed. We were unloading our gear from the aircraft and setting it on the parking apron when a jeep drove up with an Air Force bird colonel as a passenger. The colonel dismounted, put his hand on his sidearm, and ordered us to get our gear off his parking apron. He let us know that he was the officer commanding the U. S. Air Force Base, Cam Ranh Bay, and we were to get our asses off his property. At that instant, a jeep driven by a Navy lieutenant, my new skipper, arrived. The lieutenant didn't say a word, just started loading me and my gear in the jeep and away we went. I never found out what happened to the other six men. Welcome to Vietnam!

I retired on 1 September 1969 as a CWO-4 (chief warrant officer) after twenty-six years of service. During those twenty-six years, no one questioned my age, and I didn't change the records to reflect my true birth date until about fifteen years ago.

Norman Shaw earned nine battle stars on his World War II Asiatic-Pacific ribbon, three on his Korean Service ribbon, and two on his Vietnam Service ribbon, for a total of fourteen stars. He was awarded a Navy Expeditionary Medal for his service during the Bay of Pigs, but because of the secrecy surrounding the operation, the medal was not officially identified with his actions there. After he retired from the Navy, Norman was a journeyman industrial-electrician for the Menasha Corporation, North Bend, Oregon, and a computer technician, Oregon Farm Bureau Federation. In 1984, Norm and Jeanne, his wife of forty-six years, moved to Corpus Christi, Texas, to be near family. For ten years, they volunteered two days a week at the Corpus Christi International Seamen Center.

Fred L. White

Age 15 – United States Navy

I was born on 8 January 1927 in Bristol, Virginia, a small town on the Virginia-Tennessee border where Main Street forms the state line. After the

> *We spent five days within six miles of ground zero.*

attack on Pearl Harbor, I couldn't wait to enter the service and help defend my country. In October 1942, I went to the Navy recruiting office and told them that I was born in 1925. I took the papers home and talked my father into signing them. I was sworn into the Navy later that month, on 28 October 1942.

I was sent to the Great Lakes Naval Training Center in Illinois for six weeks of boot training. From there we went to Norfolk, Virginia, where we put in at a dockside warehouse. The building was bare, so we tied our hammocks between steel posts and spent the night. The next morning, we were loaded aboard a troopship, the USS *Harris*. Late that same day, we left Norfolk with a large number of ships in convoy. The convoy was attacked by German submarines the next day, and two ships were hit. We learned later that they sank.

We passed through the Panama Canal and stopped at a small island called Tobago, located in the Pacific twenty-six miles off the Panamanian coast. I left the *Harris* at Tobago and joined a torpedo-boat squadron. The torpedo boats patrolled the shipping lanes and provided security for the Panama Canal.

In early 1944, I received orders to return to the States for reassignment with a 30-day delay en route. I tried for three weeks to get transportation back to the States. Finally, I hitched a ride on a British aircraft carrier that was going to Norfolk, Virginia, to pick up a load of new lend-lease aircraft. The ship was very dirty and smelly. I slept on the flight deck because of the smell below. The day before docking at Norfolk, all the old British aircraft were pushed over the side. I never could understand that.

After my leave, which was the only time I was home during the war, I reported aboard the USS *Ottawa* (AKA-101), a new ship that was placed in commission at Charleston, South Carolina. After our shakedown cruise, we went back through the Panama Canal to Pearl Harbor. We transported troops and equipment all over the Pacific. We went to many places: Manila, Lingayen Gulf, Subic Bay, Luzon, Saipan, Guam, Tinian, Ulithi, Espíritu Santo, Eniwetok, New Guinea, Okinawa, and to Nagasaki and Nagoya in Japan.

While we were unloading at Saipan, a Japanese plane from one of the small islands nearby came over and dropped a bomb. The concussion overturned a stack of hatch covers and one struck me in the back, fracturing a vertebra and bruising a kidney. I was paralyzed for five days and wore a brace for months. That was the most frightening experience in my life. I lost the bruised kidney to cancer in 1995.

We endured kamikaze attacks at Okinawa. The Japanese planes would come in just above the water. They missed us, but some ships were not so lucky. We could hear the planes coming, but it seemed like an eternity for them to reach us.

We were getting ready to invade Japan when the A-bomb was dropped. After the peace treaty was signed, we entered the harbor at Nagasaki to unload troops and equipment. We tied the ship to a concrete pier, the only thing left standing after the city was leveled by the A-bomb. We spent five days within six miles of ground zero. I often wonder about the troops we put on shore, whether they were affected by the radiation.

We were caught in a typhoon off the coast of Okinawa in 1945. The waves looked like mountains, and our ship received a lot of damage. We were sent back to Pearl Harbor for repairs. I returned to the States shortly after that, and I was discharged from the Navy at Nashville, Tennessee, on 31 December 1945.

Fred White began a career in trucking shortly after his discharge from the Navy. He was a long-haul truck driver for thirty-six years, retiring in 1984. Fred and Betty, his wife of twenty-five years, live in Morristown, Tennessee. Fred has five children and eleven grandchildren.

Chester C. "Chuck" Sutor

Age 15 – United States Coast Guard

I was born in Chicago, Illinois, on 31 July 1927, the seventh in a family of eight children. I was raised in Chicago's southwest side in a neighborhood of mostly Eastern European immigrants. I can't remember anyone who spoke with prejudice against others.

> *Since I had used my brother's birth certificate, I had to use his name.*

Neighbors helped neighbors, as we had to do in order to survive the Depression.

On 7 December 1941, I was 14 years old and a sophomore in high school. Although I maintained passing grades, I was not doing well in school. Like most teenagers of that time, I spent my free time hanging around the park or on street corners. The guys in my neighborhood usually went to work after school. Because of the war in Europe, businesses were getting orders and were hiring again.

After Pearl Harbor, most of the 18-year-olds that I hung around with joined the armed forces, and many of the 17-year-olds left school and enlisted. All of a sudden, only a few of my friends were around, and the neighborhood seemed empty. At age 14, although I was younger than most of the group, I did the same things that the older ones did (played cards, dice, baseball, basketball, etc.) and felt that I could do as well as they could in the service.

My older brother turned 17 on 2 June 1942, but instead of enlisting, he decided to finish his last year of high school before entering the service. At that time one of my buddies turned 17 and planned to enlist. I went with my friend to the old post office building in Chicago with my brother's birth certificate in hand. We went to the Marine recruiting office to enlist. My friend was accepted, but I was not. I was 5'4" and weighed 120 pounds – not big enough for the Marines.

The doctor who examined me also gave physicals to U. S. Coast Guard recruits. He told me that they were waiving the height and weight requirements, and he thought I could pass the test. I simply went down two floors in the old post office building, applied to join the Coast Guard, took the test, and passed.

Since I had used my brother's birth certificate, I had to use his name. The Coast Guard checked with the school and found that Casimir (Casey) Sutor was a straight-A student. In July, I received a letter from the Coast Guard stating that I had been accepted and would be called in the next thirty to ninety days. The letter was addressed to Casey, but he knew what I had done, and he passed it on to me. It was OK with him.

With the letter was a form for my parents to sign, giving their permission for me to enlist. Both of my parents were immigrants and neither had attended school. My father worked in a factory while my mother raised eight children. I convinced my parents that it was legal for me to join the Coast Guard, so my father signed the form even though he couldn't believe that they would take such a kid.

I turned 15 on 31 July 1942 and was called to report to the receiving station in Chicago in early October. I was sworn into the U. S. Coast Guard on 12 November 1942. A group of us were put on a train and sent to Manhattan Beach, New York, for boot camp. The boatswain's mates in charge of us taught us some discipline, but there was neither personnel nor materials available for training. I waited there about two weeks, then was sent to the Brooklyn Navy Yard. I was assigned to the USS *Manhasset* as a seaman second class. I had never been on a ship before and thought it was huge. Actually, it was only 240 feet long and carried a crew of 180.

The *Manhasset* was in dry dock at the time. It was a converted freighter that had been fitted with 5-inch guns fore and aft, six 20mm antiaircraft guns, and a lot of roll-off and blast-off depth charges. It had "mousetraps" at the bow. These were rockets used for shallow depth-charge explosions. It also carried freight. The purpose of this type of ship was to deceive the enemy into thinking it was a simple freighter, but in fact, it was armed to do battle with submarines. The ship would stay on the outside perimeter of a convoy and act as a decoy. Since she looked like a regular freighter, the subs would come in close, and we would pick them up on our sound gear and alert the rest of the escort ships.

We left New York and went north, picking up more ships at Boston as well as some Canadian ships and escorts. Then we sailed the regular North Atlantic convoy routes, which went from Newfoundland to Greenland, on to Iceland, and finally to England. I was involved with dozens of depth-charge attacks on submarines, but I saw only one German sub. It surfaced about fifty yards from us but sank seconds later with all of its crew.

I spent most of the war on convoy duty in the North and South Atlantic patrols. One day we were with a convoy in the phosphorus-laden Gulf Stream waters of the Caribbean Sea. I was on watch on the flying bridge. All of a sudden, I saw two phosphorescent wakes side by side, coming directly toward our ship. My partner saw them also. We were both too surprised and scared to react. We could only watch as the two torpedoes came at full speed to within three feet of the ship, then turned and started jumping in front of the ship's bow. They were porpoises, not torpedoes! At least six others on watch that night had the same experience. It might seem funny now, but I was so shook up that I stuttered for a couple of weeks.

In May 1944, I transferred to the USS *Mojave*, a 280-foot cutter, and continued with convoy duty. Sometimes we would go south to the Panama Canal Zone or to Guantanamo, Cuba, then to the Azores, and into the Mediterranean to North Africa. Most of the time, we stayed in the North Atlantic because it was busier.

During these voyages, I got rather lucky at gambling and won several thousand dollars, a fortune at that time. I had been in for one and a half years and thought that I would like to return home a rich man, so I wrote to my brother Casey and asked him to write to the skipper of my ship and tell him that I was underage and that I should be home with my mother. Casey did as I asked and wrote me that he had done it, but I was not called for captain's mast until we had left Boston harbor with another convoy. The captain asked me if I wanted out, and I said yes. He said he'd put me off the ship the first port we came to and have me flown back to the States for discharge.

We stopped at Greenland, and I was taken to a large Army air base to await transportation home. I waited there for two months for transportation that never materialized. Finally, my ship pulled into the harbor and I got back on. By the time we got to Boston I was 17. I was told that I was now of age and would be kept in the Coast

Guard. I was happy with the outcome because I really liked the Coast Guard, and besides, I had spent all the money that I had won.

My name was changed from Casimir to Chester on the records, but my age was not changed. Not another word was ever mentioned about it. I stayed on the *Mojave* until October 1945, then transferred to the USS *Reading*, a patrol frigate, also on Atlantic patrols. Four months later, I left the ship at the Norfolk Navy Yard. I was discharged there in March 1946. About four months after that, I received a draft notice. I took my discharge papers to the draft board, and I never heard any more about the matter.

I have never regretted serving while I was underage, and I am very proud of what I did. I would do it again in a second! What I experienced during those times made me a better man — and later, a better parent.

When my brother Casey finished high school, he joined the Navy and served as a pharmacist's mate on a hospital ship in the Pacific. No one ever raised the question of two Casimir Sutors in the service at the same time. Also, my two older brothers were in the Army, and my sister joined the WAVES in 1944. My immigrant parents were very proud that five of their eight children were serving their country. They just thought that it was their duty as Americans to send their children when their country called.

Chuck Sutor returned to Chicago after his discharge from the Navy. He worked as a carpenter until 1957 when he became manager of the construction-loan payout department of a large savings and loan association in Chicago. From 1961 until he retired, he was a construction superintendent and project manager for a number of construction projects in the Chicago area. Loretta, Chuck's wife of forty-nine years, spent the World War II years entertaining wounded veterans in military hospitals. She and two classmates developed an act pantomiming the Andrews sisters. Chuck and Loretta's experiences during the war years contributed greatly to the rearing of their four daughters, especially in their education. They are very proud of the fact that all four graduated from college and pursued advanced degrees. Chuck and Loretta live in Sun Lakes, Arizona, but spend their summers in Idaho. They have five grandchildren and two great-grandchildren.

J. Ronald Lansinger

Age 15 – Maryland State Guard
Age 16 – United States Marine Corps

I was born in the Remington section of Baltimore, Maryland, on 25 May 1927, my mother's fifth and last child. My father disappeared three months before I was born. Some people said that he deserted his family, but

> I had to endure the hell of boot camp again!

no one knows for sure. My boyhood was unpleasantly poor. We all worked hard to help my grandmother and my working mother. My first job was dressing fresh chickens on Saturdays. For a 12- to 15-hour day I was paid 50¢, plus a chicken. The chicken was our Sunday meal. I had that job from age 7 until I was 12. During the week, I would earn tips for transporting groceries, selling newspapers and magazines, baby sitting, cleaning furnaces, and other chores. I made enough at these jobs to bring my weekly earnings up to about $5.00, all of which went to my mother.

We lived in a very patriotic era, and we were well aware that war was on its way. The day after Pearl Harbor, I altered a birth certificate and a baptismal certificate and unsuccessfully tried to enlist in the Marines. The recruiter discovered that my papers were bogus, ending my hopes of enlistment. I tried all the other branches of the service with the same result. In October 1942, I forged a letter supposedly written by my mother giving me consent to join the

Maryland State Guard. I was accepted in the Guard and served until May 1943. At that time my bogus age was 18, so I went to the draft board, registered, and requested immediate induction into the Marine Corps. I was in boot camp at Parris Island, South Carolina, when my mother received a copy of my discharge from the Maryland State Guard. She immediately started the process of getting me discharged from the Marines.

Meanwhile, I was assigned to the 3rd Marine Aircraft Wing and was sent to the University of Oklahoma at Norman to train as an airframe and engine mechanic. In late June 1944, we were in Corvallis, Oregon, waiting to be shipped to Ewa, Hawaii, when my mother's action caught up with me. I was given my second World War II discharge with newspaper fanfare, but I was devastated. I was a 6'1", 180-pound Marine who had been trying to serve his country for almost three years, and I was being sent home like a little boy because of my mother's dependency and persistence. My brother was in the Army Air Forces, my sister was in school, my grandmother had died, and my mother was in poor health.

By the time I was 18, my sister was working, my mother's health had improved, and my brother was home after receiving his honorable discharge. On my eighteenth birthday, I once again signed up at the draft board and asked for immediate induction into the Marines. I had to endure the hell of boot camp again! I tried to get them to assign me to a squadron, but no, they sent me to boot camp the second time, even though I was a highly skilled mechanic.

Shortly after I completed boot camp, the A-bomb was dropped and the war was over. I received my *third* and *final* World War II discharge on 15 November 1945 at the age of *18½*. I had served a little over two years but not one day in combat, which had been my desire for over three years.

Ron Lansinger resumed his education after his final discharge from the Marine Corps. He completed a GED, then attended the University of Maryland and the University of Baltimore. He majored in accounting, business administration, and business law. His wartime service with the 3rd Marine Aircraft Wing had given him the "flying bug," so he learned to fly. Then he started selling cars and advanced rather quickly. He obtained his own dealership and sold it in 1976, allowing him to retire at age 49. Retirement lasted three weeks, and he became a real-estate investor specializing in the food and beverage sector of commercial properties. He retired for good in 1990. Since then, he has done some volunteer work with the Veterans Administration and some local charities. Ron and Bettie, his wife of more than forty-two years, live in Timonium, Maryland. They have two children and one granddaughter.

Jerome A. "Jerry" Moore

Age 14 – United States Army
Age 15 – United States Navy

The year 1940 was the turning point of my life. I was raised in a somewhat abusive and non-loving home on a five-acre strawberry farm between Seattle and Tacoma, Washington. I was born in Spokane, Washington, on 12

> *A priest had come and given me last rites.*

December 1927. Life was rough for all of us during the Great Depression, and in 1940, my parents went through a bitter divorce. After the divorce, my father just disappeared.

I had two brothers and a sister. A short time after the divorce, my 13-year-old sister and I were taken away from my mother and placed in foster homes. A foster home did not work out for me, and I was put into a boys' home, which was essentially an orphanage for unwanted boys.

After I had been in the boys' home for about a year, another boy and I ran away. We split up after a couple of days of going hungry. I started hitchhiking east, hoping to reach North Dakota where my grandparents on my dad's side lived. I worked on farms and construction jobs along the way just to get by. I had made it as far east as Laurel, Montana, by the time I was 14 years old. I lied about my age and got a job with the Northern Pacific Railroad doing track-repair work in the switchyard. I didn't have a Social Security card, so they issued me a railroad social security number and card. By November 1942, it was bitterly cold in Montana, and I thought that there must be something better to do.

After talking with some soldiers who were riding on freight trains as guards, I decided that the Army was for me. I registered for the draft and asked for immediate induction. Within two weeks, I was on my way to Fort Douglas, Utah, where I was sworn into the Army on

23 November 1942. I was sent to Camp Seibert, Gadsden, Alabama for basic training. I was put in charge of a group of recruits headed to Alabama. I took care of our orders, our train tickets, and our meal tickets.

I was just finishing up the sixth week of basic training when I became sick. We were learning how to use a gas mask, and at first I thought that I was sick from the gas. I didn't go to lunch, but I laid myself down on my bunk and went into a coma. I woke up three or four days later while a doctor was tapping my spine. I had spinal meningitis. A priest had come in and given me last rites. Later, the priest told me that when he saw me in the hospital he thought I was an officer's kid.

The doctors thought I was going to die, so they contacted my grandmother. She told them that I was only 15 years old. After six weeks of recuperating in the hospital, I was given an honorable discharge from the Army and put on a train back to Laurel, Montana.

This time I made it to my grandmother's home north of Williston, North Dakota, where it was 30° below zero and there was no running water or electricity. When spring came, she gave me a train ticket back to Seattle. I didn't have a home in Seattle anymore, and I certainly wasn't going back to an orphanage. There were many jobs available during the war, and I worked in construction for a time. In June 1943, I signed on with a salmon-fishing boat headed for Alaska. After four months at sea, I decided the Navy was for me. Almost a year to the day after I had joined the Army, I was in the Navy. My mother made me list her as beneficiary on my military life-insurance policy as the price for signing my enlistment papers.

After boot camp at Farragut, Idaho, I went to diesel-engine school at San Diego, California. I became interested in submarines while I was in diesel-engine school. I had read that submariners received 50% more pay plus 20% more sea pay, which sounded good to me. In May 1944, I went by train to New London, Connecticut. By the time I finished submarine school and advanced diesel-engine school, it was January 1945.

I was assigned to a submarine that was still under construction. After six weeks of waiting, I was reassigned to the USS *Blackfish*. We headed to the North Sea area but were called back to the States before we reached Portsmouth, England.

Shortly after I returned to New London, the war in Europe ended. I was transferred to Bremerton, Washington, and assigned to the USS *Duluth*, which was in dry dock for repairs. In about three weeks, we headed for the South Pacific to join the 7th Fleet as part of Task Force 38. We were riding out a typhoon off the island of Guam when the war ended. The typhoon was the scariest thing that I ever experienced.

I stayed on the *Duluth* until the end of my enlistment. We made a goodwill tour to Australia and participated in the Philippine Independence Day celebration at Manila Bay on 4 July 1946.

While I was in the Navy, I finished my high school education through the Armed Forces Institute. I was a motor machinist's mate second class at the time of my discharge in March 1947.

Jerry Moore worked in construction as a heavy-equipment operator and later did commercial salmon fishing in Alaska after leaving the Navy. He worked for a large water-utility district in the San Francisco Bay area for thirty-four years and was assistant superintendent of construction and maintenance at the time of his retirement in June 1989. Jerry and Viola, his wife of forty-four years, live in Grants Pass, Oregon. They have three children and six grandchildren.

Willie C. Manson, Jr.

Age 13 – United States Navy

I came from a broken home. My mother left me with a cousin when I was two, and I saw her only on holidays. When her cousin died, I went to stay with an uncle. I was never close to my mother. Although I loved her very much, I had a

> *I spent three years in the Pacific during World War II, all before my seventeenth birthday.*

hard time calling her "mother." I was not comfortable with that, so I called her by her first name. We grew very close prior to her death at 89. I never knew my father until about ten years ago. I met him one time and had dinner with him two years before he died.

My oldest brother was in the Seabees. He had come home and had told me stories about the Navy. The uniform was especially appealing to me. When he left, I begged my mother to let me join the Navy, but she said, "No, you are too young." But I cried so long that she relented. When I went to the Navy recruiting office to enlist, they asked how old I was and I said, "Seventeen." They did not believe me, but they gave me the go-ahead anyway.

I enlisted in the Navy Seabees on 1 December 1942. My thirteenth birthday had been on 21 November 1942. From boot camp I went to Port Hueneme, California, and soon after that, I left on a special troopship for Espíritu Santo in the New Hebrides Islands. Japanese aircraft would attack our base between one and two o'clock each morning. I was not afraid during the attacks. The island was very beautiful, and I would like to return for a visit some day.

From Espíritu Santo, we went to Okinawa where we remained until after V-J Day. Then I returned to the U. S. and was discharged. I spent three years in the Pacific during World War II, all before my seventeenth birthday.

I had not finished elementary school, so I went back to school after I got out of the Navy in 1945. After finishing the ninth grade, I reenlisted in the Navy. Shortly after I went aboard ship, I took the GED tests. I never studied for the tests, but I took all five tests in one day and passed them all. I attended many military schools such as damage control school, class-B electrician school, minesweeping electrician school, and others. I had the opportunity to attend nuclear power school but declined because I was recently married and didn't want to be away for a long time.

During my twenty years in the Navy, I served aboard many ships: USS *Laning* (APD-55), USS *Grackle* (AMS-13), USS *Goldfinch* (AMS-12), USS *Egret* (AMS-46), USS *Newport News* (CA-148), USS *Intrepid* (CV-11), USS *Sperry* (AS-12), and USS *Fremont* (APA-44).

I was promoted to electrician's mate first class, was reduced to second class after a captain's mast, and later was again promoted to first class. I passed the exam for chief electrician's mate, but did not make the quota. I retired from the Navy as an electrician's mate first class in 1964.

After I retired, I immediately went to work for the Virginia Transit Company. I would put in twelve or more hours each day, then work another four hours in the shipyard as an electrician.

Willie Manson was a bus driver for the Virginia Transit Company for twenty-seven years, from which he received a number of safe-driving awards. He has been a member of the Kempsville Presbyterian Church in Virginia Beach, Virginia, for nearly ten years. Willie heads up a ministry for his church called "The Good Samaritan Team," which helps needy and destitute people in Virginia Beach and surrounding communities. They repair autos, roof houses, care for lawns, pay bills, and do whatever is needed. Their work is financed by donations from various sources. Willie and Annie, his wife of 45 years, live in Virginia Beach. They have six children and four grandchildren.

Clifford R. "Dick" Jenke

Age 15 – United States Navy

In the fall of 1942, when I was 15 years old, I decided to join the Navy. My good friend Bobby Lee Pettit wanted to join also, but he was only 13 years old, almost two years younger than I was.

> *... Richard, you have made your bed, and now you have to sleep in it.*

I went to the Navy recruiting office in Houston, Texas, to enlist on 7 December 1942. The recruiter, a chief boatswain's mate, didn't believe that I was 17. He questioned me for about two hours, trying to trick me into admitting that I was underage, but I stuck to my story. Finally, I told him that the Army Air Corps recruiter had been trying to talk me into joining, and if the Navy didn't want me, I'd go in the Air Corps. That did it. He gave me the papers and told me to have my parents sign them. That proved to be another problem.

I got home about six o'clock that night. My mother asked me why I had skipped school that day. I told her that I was out looking for a job. I asked my dad to sign the papers so that I could go into the Navy, and he said he would if my mother would. Of course, she wouldn't hear of it. We went around and around until about 11:00 p.m. that night. Finally I said, "Momma, if you don't sign my papers, I'll walk out that door and you'll never see me again." At that statement she capitulated and agreed to sign. I really felt cocky. I had won the battle. At 11:15 p.m. the three of us got in the car and went to a notary that we knew, woke him up, and got his signature. My mother was very quiet on the way home, but when we got there she said in a very firm voice, "Richard, you have made your bed, and now you have to sleep in it. When you get into training and things get tough and you want out, I won't help you. If you tell them that you are underage and they call me to confirm it,

I'll tell them that you are not underage, and you know who they will believe." That took all the cockiness out of me and made me wonder what I had gotten myself into.

I processed the paper work the next day, and on 9 December 1942 I was sworn into the Navy and sent to San Diego, California, for five weeks of boot camp. I had been in camp about two weeks when my friend Bobby Lee Pettit showed up. Somehow, he had talked his mother into signing for him. I don't know how he did it because he wouldn't be 14 for another week or so.

After boot camp, I was sent by ship to the Alameda Naval Air Station, Alameda, California, then to Sydney, Australia. From Sydney I went to Brisbane, Australia, where I volunteered for submarine duty with Squadron Eight, Task Force 72, U. S. Seventh Fleet, which was headquartered in Brisbane. I was assigned to the USS *Scamp* (SS-277) and served aboard her for almost a year. On my sixteenth birthday, two and one-half months after joining the Navy, I was on my first war patrol.

The *Scamp*'s patrol areas were the Solomon Islands and the Mariana Islands. Within a year's time, our ship sank a Japanese cruiser, a large transport, and several merchant ships.

In early March 1944, I was transferred to Squadron Nine, based in Perth, Australia, and assigned to the USS *Dace* (SS-247). We and our sister ship, the USS *Darter*, made war patrols in areas near the Celebes, Malaysia, Borneo, and the Philippine Islands. In the Gulf of Leyte, we destroyed a new Japanese cruiser and damaged another cruiser and an aircraft carrier. This occurred just before the invasion of the Philippines. The Japanese cruiser that we destroyed, the *Maya*, was with her sister ship, the *Atago*. We sank the *Maya*, and our sister ship, the *Darter*, sank the *Atago*. It was a first, sister ships sinking sister ships. The *Atago* carried the Japanese admiral and his staff who commanded the task force that was heading toward Leyte to intercept the American landings there. We received a message from Admiral Nimitz after the encounter, congratulating us for firing the first shot in the battle for the liberation of the Philippines.

Because I dropped out of high school, I knew very little about mathematics and physics. However, a petty officer first class that I worked with had graduated from the Massachusetts Institute of Technology with a master's degree in electrical engineering. With his tutoring, and with a lot of hard work and many hours of studying, I was promoted to electrician's mate second class while still 16 years old. I was very fortunate.

After I had been overseas for thirty months, my ship came back to the States, and I received a 30-day leave. After my leave, I returned to the *Dace* and served aboard her until the end of the war. On 9 November 1944, my first ship, the USS *Scamp* went down in the Sea of Japan with all of her crew aboard.

I was discharged on 22 November 1945 but soon reenlisted and served through the Korean War. I left the Navy in September 1954.

Dick Jenke earned the Submarine Combat Award, the Philippine Liberation Medal with one star, and a number of other service medals. He was on nine war patrols during World War II. After leaving the Navy, he worked for thirty-nine years in electronic sales, distribution, and management. For a year or so prior to his retirement in August 1996, he was an expediter for an automobile-auction company. Dick and his wife Irma live in Houston, Texas. They have a combined family of six children and seven grandchildren. Dick's two sons served on guided-missile ships while on duty with the Navy.

Bobby L. Pettit

Age 13 – United States Navy

I was born in Houston, Texas, on 31 December 1928, the last day of the year. When I was 9 years old, one of my uncles, a Navy veteran of World War I, took me to the Houston Ship Channel where the USS *Houston* was berthed. We were given a tour of the ship, and I was completely

> *He cursed me, took my uniforms, and handed me a piece of paper that stated ... my enlistment was void!*

captivated. I knew then that I would be in the Navy some day.

Three weeks before my thirteenth birthday, the Japanese attacked Pearl Harbor. This sealed my fate. I knew it would be just a matter of time before I would enlist. A few months after I started the eighth grade in the fall of 1942, my friend Dick Jenke joined the Navy. Dick was a couple of years older than I was, but he was still only 15. I figured that if Dick could join, I could join. I went to the Navy recruiting station in Houston, the same station where Calvin Graham had enlisted at age 12 four months before, and Dick Jenke had enlisted at age 15 only two weeks earlier.

At the recruiting office, I told the recruiter that I was 17, took all the tests, and passed the physical examination. I was not required to present a birth certificate, but I had to get my mother's signature. My father had died when I was nine months old. It took much convincing before my mother would sign. She consulted with my uncles, and they told her to let me go, so she reluctantly signed the papers. She never felt right about doing that and would not accept the government allotment.

I was sworn into the Navy on 22 December 1942 and left for boot camp in San Diego, California, during the first week of 1943. I was there only a short time when I met my old friend Dick Jenke. Boy, were we glad to see each other! I would see him again at Pearl Harbor.

After boot camp, I went to Terminal Island in San Pedro, California, and then I went aboard the USS *Tallulah* (AO-50), a fleet oiler. We immediately left for the South Pacific. As soon as we left the breakwater in San Pedro, we were in some mighty rough water. I was so seasick I wanted to die. I made five runs to the South Pacific carrying fuel oil, aviation gas, and fighter aircraft to that area. I recall places like Samoa, Fiji, New Caledonia, Funafuti, New Hebrides, Majuro, Kwajalein, and Manus, but I have forgotten many places. We sailed in a zigzag course, unescorted and without the benefit of radar. We were a prime target for Japanese submarines, but fortunately, we didn't encounter any. In November of 1943, we participated in the invasion of Tarawa. We had radar and heavier armament by this time. I have never seen so many ships as there were in our task force. In January 1944, we participated in the invasion of Kwajalein in the Marshall Islands.

All the while, I was pestering my superiors for a transfer to destroyer duty. I even volunteered for submarine duty, but my request was denied. Finally, when we arrived back at Pearl Harbor following the Marshall Islands operation, I was transferred ashore to await further transfer to the receiving station at Balboa Park, San Diego. I was an electrician's mate third class at that time. While at the receiving station, I tried to transfer to the Marines but was unsuccessful.

After a short time at the receiving station, I was transferred to the newly constructed USS *LCI(L)-750* (landing craft, infantry). This was not a destroyer, and I was not happy with the assignment. We trained around San Diego and then set sail for the South Pacific with other LCIs in our group. An LCI is rather small to be crossing the Pacific, only 159 feet long, but we made it. We participated in landings along the eastern coast of New Guinea, then along the northern coast.

While operating out of Hollandia, we formed up with a task force for the invasion of Morotai on 15 September 1944, the first step toward the Philippines. We returned to Hollandia and then headed towards Leyte in the Philippines. We made numerous landings in the Philippines, including Ormoc, Mindoro, Nasugbu, Calapan, Palawan, Romblon, and Marinduque. At Nasugbu, we landed troops of the 11th Airborne Division, and on 1 March 1945, we landed troops of the 24th Infantry division at Lubang. Notes taken from the ship's log read: "Beitz received flash burns; Gardner goes to hospital; enemy aircraft overhead; Christmas Day 1994 in Leyte harbor; General Quarters; December 26 temperature 115 degrees; took on troops of 11th Airborne Division; took on Jap prisoners; retrieved bodies for transport to Mindoro; troops ashore."

My LCI was the flagship of our group for a period of time. We were the only ship in our group with radar. As the only electrician's mate aboard, I was responsible for operating and maintaining the radar. I had three days of schooling in Pearl Harbor to prepare me for this task. This was insufficient, to say the least. My ship rated an electrician's mate first class, and I was only a third class when I came aboard. I searched the Pacific for a ship or station that had the Navy training manuals to prepare me for second class and for first class. I found the manuals, and my engineering officer, Lieutenant (jg) Charles Bradley, taught me a lot of mathematics. I passed the second class, then the first class tests to become, as far as I know, the youngest electrician's mate first class in the fleet, at the age of 16.

In July 1945, our flotilla was ordered back to the States for conversion and upgrade in preparation for the landings on the mainland of Japan. I was in Pearl Harbor en route from the Philippines to San Pedro, California, on 6 August 1945 when the first A-bomb was dropped. Between Hawaii and San Pedro we heard rumors that the war had ended, then we finally received the official notification. It was over! We celebrated and lighted the ship.

We arrived in San Pedro with no fanfare, and I went home to Houston on leave. We departed for San Francisco upon returning. With the war over, I saw no need for me to be sitting in San Francisco Bay. I wanted to return home and go to school. I asked my mother to send me a copy of my birth certificate that would show that I was only 16 and not old enough to be in the Navy. We had a new captain by then. I showed him my birth certificate and told him I needed to be discharged so I could return to school, having left during the eighth grade. Very quickly, I was aboard a troop train headed for the separation center at Camp Wallace, Texas, near Houston.

I was certain that I would be processed out the same as all my comrades, but luck would not have that. I was summoned to the office of the lieutenant in charge. He questioned me about falsifying my age in order to enter the Navy. He cursed me, took my uniforms, and handed me a piece of paper that stated I had served in the Navy since 1942 under false conditions and that my enlistment was void!

I soon learned that without a discharge, I had a problem. I had no veterans benefits and no GI Bill of Rights. I sought a job with Western Electric and was told that they would like to hire me, but I could not prove that I had served nor that I had been discharged. At the advice of my uncle, who was a Navy veteran, I brought my problem to the attention of Jesse Caveness, the head of the Veterans Service Center in Houston. Mr. Caveness was outraged at the way the Navy had treated me. He called the newspapers and Congressman Albert Thomas of Houston. With nationwide news coverage, I began receiving letters of support from across the country. Two Texas oil men called me to their office and told me not to worry about college. If the government wouldn't help me, they would.

My case was brought to the attention of the Secretary of the Navy, James V. Forrestal. I soon received an honorable discharge signed by the Chief of Naval Personnel, dated 7 November 1945. I now had veterans benefits.

Bob Pettit earned five battle stars on his Asiatic-Pacific ribbon and one star on his Philippine Liberation Medal by the time he was 16 years old. Back in Houston, he attended Sam Houston High School at night, worked as an electrician during the day, and graduated from high school in three years. Bob enrolled at the Agricultural and Mechanical College of Texas (now Texas A&M University) under the GI Bill in 1948 and received a B.S. in electrical engineering in 1952. He was employed by Western Electric as a field engineer, assisting with installation, maintenance, and operation of complex radar gunfire-control systems for the Navy. Bob worked at shipyards in the U. S. and with the Sixth Fleet in the Mediterranean. His entire professional career as an electronics engineer was dedicated to working with the military and space organizations of the U. S. Government. He was President of the National Space Club during 1970-71. Most of his career was with Texas Instruments Incorporated. in Washington, D.C. Bob lives in Leesburg, Virginia. He has four children and five grandchildren. Bob was the first Virginia State Commander of the Veterans of Underage Military Service.

Oliver J. Butler, Jr.

Age 15 – United States Navy (Fleet Marine Force)

I was born in Memphis, Tennessee, on 13 June 1927. After the attack on Pearl Harbor, I wanted to be in the military and I especially wanted to be a Marine. I tried unsuccessfully to join the Marines, but I

"... hang in there, and keep your eyes open and your ass down."

failed for two reasons: the recruiters knew I was underage, and my mother was adamantly opposed to my being a Marine. I then tried to join the Army and again failed.

Finally, in the fall of 1942, I convinced my father to let me lie about my age and to give his official consent to my enlistment in the Navy. I was sworn into the Navy on 23 December 1942 and sent to boot camp at the Naval Training Center, San Diego, California. While in boot camp, I learned that I could be transferred from the Navy to the Marine Corps by volunteering to be a hospital corpsman. I promptly volunteered and was promptly accepted. I went from boot camp to the Navy Hospital Corps School at Balboa Naval Hospital and from there to the Fleet Marine Force Medical Field Service School at Camp Elliott, California.

After the completion of my training, I shipped overseas and joined the 1st Marine Division in Australia. I was platoon corpsman for the 1st Platoon, Easy Company, 2nd Battalion, 1st Marine Regiment. The division had recently returned from Guadalcanal and was preparing for the Cape Gloucester campaign. We thought we would be returning to Australia after Cape Gloucester, but instead we were sent to Pavuvu in the Russell Islands where we set up camp and started training for the invasion of Peleliu. While I was at Pavuvu, Colonel Lewis B. "Chesty" Puller took command of the 1st Marines. Chesty was a legend by then, and we were all proud that he was our new commander.

We landed on Peleliu on 15 September 1944. By that time I had achieved the ripe old age of 17. On the second day, my platoon had dug in for the night along a dirt road. We were to attack Bloody Nose Ridge the following morning. We were literally on the front line with no one in front of us except Japanese. I looked up from my foxhole and saw Chesty Puller approaching from my left. He was casually strolling along the front of the line, oblivious of the occasional "ping" of sniper fire in his direction. To my surprise, he stopped in front of my foxhole and said, "How are things going, Butler?" To this day, I can't think of how he knew my name, but he did. I responded, "I'm doing fine Chesty, but we've sure lost a lot of men, and I hope we get some replacements up here tomorrow." He replied, "I know son, but hang in there, and keep your eyes open and your ass down."

I was wounded the following day and evacuated to a Navy hospital ship where I underwent surgery. I was transported to Los Negros in the Admiralty Islands, then flown to Guadalcanal, which by that time was completely a rear-echelon area, and hospitalized for further treatment. I was in Navy Mobile Hospital Number 8, or MOB-8, as we called it. The Navy medical officer in charge of my case took it upon himself to issue orders transferring me from the Fleet Marine Force. I guess he thought he was doing me a favor. I did not share his misplaced concern for my welfare, so I went AWOL from MOB-8. Still bandaged, I caught a mail boat to Pavuvu. The 1st Marine Division had left Pavuvu for Peleliu, and I knew it would return there after the campaign was over.

I rejoined my unit without relating to anyone the circumstances of my return. Several weeks later, I received a summons to report to the battalion commander, Lieutenant Colonel Russell Honsowetz. When I reported to the colonel, he looked up at me from his seated position and asked, "Butler, what is this crap about you being AWOL from MOB-8 on Guadalcanal?" I truthfully explained the circumstances to him. He looked at me with a half-smile on his face and said, "OK, you're excused. I think I can take care of this." I never again heard anything about my being AWOL.

Sometime after that incident, an honors formation was convened for the 2nd Battalion. A number of officers and enlisted men were to receive awards for their service during the Peleliu campaign, and I was privileged to be one of those receiving recognition. Colonel Puller, accompanied by Colonel Honsowetz, made the presentations. As Puller presented me with the Navy and Marine Corps Medal and the Purple Heart, Colonel Honsowetz winked at me.

I returned to the States in February 1945 and was assigned to the Marine Detachment of the Naval Ammunition Depot, Crane, Indiana, and was later stationed with the Marine Detachment at the Great Lakes Naval Station, Illinois. I was discharged from the Navy at the Lambert Field Naval Air Station, St. Louis, Missouri, on 12 June 1946, one day before my nineteenth birthday.

In 1950, while attending law school in Arkansas, I enlisted in the Army Reserves, the only reserve unit in that area. In May 1951, I received a commission as a first lieutenant in the Army and served on active duty for two years during the Korean War.

The 1st Marine Division Association held a convention in August 1952 at the Mayflower Hotel in Washington, D.C. I was stationed at the Pentagon at the time. I decided to attend the convention although I would be wearing the "wrong" uniform, my Army uniform, but with the 1st Marine Division patch on my right shoulder. I did not wear a name tag. I walked into the meeting room at the Mayflower where the bar was set up and immediately heard Chesty Puller's voice coming from the vicinity of the bar. I walked over to the bar to say hello to Chesty, who was then a major general. Before I could say a word, Chesty looked at me and said, "Butler, what are doing in that fucking uniform?" I was amazed. I had not seen him nor talked to him since 1944. Yet, he not only remembered me, but he also remembered my name. I stammered something to the effect, "Chesty, it sure is good to see you again, and for the record, I'm still trying to keep my eyes open and my ass down." He laughed and turned to the bartender and said, "You can give this dogface lieutenant a drink. It's all right, he's really a jarhead. He's just in the wrong fucking uniform."

I was released from active duty in 1953, but I remained in the reserves. I retired from the Army in 1978 with the rank of Colonel of Infantry.

I truly believe that the personal success which I have enjoyed during my life can be attributed in large part to the role models I had as a youth while serving as an enlisted man with the 1st Marine Division during World War II.

Oliver Butler received the Legion of Merit, the Navy and Marine Corps Medal, the Bronze Star, the Purple Heart, the Army

Commendation Medal, the Navy Commendation Medal, the Presidential Unit Citation, and several other awards for his military service. He received a B.A. in English from Arkansas State College in 1949 and a Juris Doctor from the University of Arkansas in 1951. In 1971, he graduated from the U. S. Army Command and General Staff College, and in 1974, from the U. S. Army War College. He was a trial attorney for the U. S. Department of Justice in Washington, D.C., from 1953 to 1957 and was an assistant regional attorney for the National Labor Relations Board in Washington, D.C., and New Orleans, Louisiana, from 1957 to 1959. From 1959 until 1982, he held several positions, including assistant general counsel and head of litigation for Texaco, Inc., in Houston, Texas. From 1982 to 1995, he practiced law and was an arbitrator in Brownsville, Texas. In 1995, he moved to Houston, Texas, and currently serves as an arbitrator. Oliver and his wife Betty live in Houston. Their combined family includes Oliver's two children, Betty's four children, and a total of eleven grandchildren. Oliver's son, while serving with the Army in Vietnam, was wounded and decorated for heroism.

Daniel W. Kriss

Age 14 – United States Navy

I joined the U. S. Navy in December of 1942. I was very patriotic, but that was not my only motivation for enlisting. Two of my teenage friends who were older than I had joined the Navy and

> *Persuading my father to sign for me was the most difficult part of my plan.*

were killed when the light cruiser USS *Juneau* was sunk by a Japanese submarine during the battle of Guadalcanal, November 1942.

I developed a rather ingenious plan for enlisting in the Navy at age 14. Instead of enlisting in my hometown in New Jersey, I decided to take a train to New York City where I would blend in with a large group of applicants and not draw attention to my youthful appearance. Next, I had to alter my birth certificate. It wasn't easy, but I did it. Persuading my father to sign for me was the most difficult part of my plan. He finally agreed. I believe that his missing out on overseas duty with the U. S. Army in 1916 had something to do with it. I also had to withdraw from junior high school, so I went to the principal's

office with a made-up story that our family was going to move to another state. I asked if I had to take my records with me to my new school. They told me that the school I was to attend would request them later. After getting some dental work done to satisfy the Navy, I still had to get three personal character references as required by the Navy for all enlistees in 1942. Having succeeded in every phase of my plan, I was finally accepted by the Navy, four and one-half weeks after first applying.

I was sworn in on 31 December 1942 and was immediately placed on inactive duty. On 5 February 1943, I was ordered to active duty and sent to the Sampson Naval Training Station in upstate New York for boot training. I turned 15 on 9 February 1943.

My first ship assignment was a new Fletcher Class destroyer, the USS *Chauncey* (DD-667), which was docked at the Brooklyn Navy Yard awaiting commissioning and her crew. The *Chauncey* was commissioned on 31 May 1943, and I began my seagoing service as a "plank owner," the Navy term for a member of the ship's original crew. Following the shakedown exercises, the *Chauncey* left the East Coast and headed for the Pacific theater of war via the Panama Canal. After a brief stop at San Diego, we arrived at Pearl Harbor on 19 September 1943 and within days left on our first combat patrol.

We were part of the destroyer screen for the air strikes on Wake Island on 5-6 October 1943. We then steamed on to Espíritu Santo in the New Hebrides Islands to become part of the Navy's combat forces in the south and southwestern Pacific.

My battle station was in the ammunition-handling room of a 5-inch gun. It was my job to push powder cases up into the gun mount. I was at this battle station when our ship escorted the aircraft carriers *Essex*, *Bunker Hill*, and *Independence* in a daring strike on Japanese ships in Simpson Harbor, Rabaul, New Britain, on 11 November 1943. It was a daring raid because no heavy and light cruisers were available, and only destroyers accompanied the carriers. The Japanese retaliation was swift. We were attacked by more than eighty-five dive bombers and torpedo planes. It was our first real combat action, and our ship shot down three enemy planes.

En route to Rabaul, our ship passed over the exact spot off Guadalcanal where the USS *Juneau*, with my friends aboard, went down one year earlier, almost to the day. I have always had a feeling of close friendship with them because of this experience.

The *Chauncey* remained with Task Group 50.3 during the invasion of Tarawa in the Gilbert Islands and of the Marshall Islands. In April 1944, we were part of the destroyer screen for escort carriers in the invasion of Aitape and Hollandia in New Guinea.

By the time we arrived in the Mariana Islands for the invasion of Saipan, Tinian, and Guam, my battle station was changed. I was now part of a 20mm-gun crew. After the Marianas were secured, we moved on to the Palau Islands and then to the Philippines where my ship was part of the destroyer screen for the transport ships that took the Army troops in for the landings on Leyte in October 1944.

We returned to the States for overhaul and repairs in late December 1944. By mid-February, we were on our way back to the combat areas.

We participated in the invasion and the battle for Okinawa as part of Admiral Spruance's Task Force 58 and Admiral Halsey's Task Force 38. In addition to supporting and protecting the large aircraft carriers, battleships, and heavy cruisers that bombarded Okinawa, we escorted these battle forces to the home islands of Japan (Kyushu, Shikoku, and Honshu) to bombard and conduct air strikes on military targets, the first surface ships of the U. S. fleet to do so.

The worst part of this combat period was that my ship was among numerous destroyers assigned as radar pickets. We were stationed forty to fifty miles north of the task force to give early warning of approaching Japanese aircraft. This often placed us within visual distance of the home islands of Japan. The Japanese kamikazes were very difficult to defend against and very effective in damaging and sinking ships. More than twenty destroyers were sunk by kamikazes. Their frequent attacks forced us to remain continuously at battle stations for days at a time.

As with most combat veterans, I have many memories of my service in the Pacific during the war. These include the almost daily air attacks on our ships, the many torpedoes we had to dodge, and the nightmare of radar picket duty off Okinawa and Japan. My most memorable experience occurred in the closing months of the war. During one kamikaze attack, a Japanese twin-engine "Frances" bomber attempted to crash-dive into our ship. It appeared that the pilot would succeed, but only seconds before he would have hit our ship, we "splashed" (shot down) the aircraft. Had he succeeded in crashing into us, the point of impact would have been very close to my battle station. Most certainly my shipmates and I would have been killed.

Another memorable experience was not a combat-related event but weather-related. My ship was one of a few destroyers assigned to patrol the area between Okinawa and Kyushu during late August 1945. After the Japanese surrender, American troops were air-lifted by Army transport planes to Japan for occupation duty. Our mission was to rescue them in case one was forced down. While we were on this duty, our ship was caught in a raging typhoon. For several hours we were in danger of capsizing. We survived with no personnel casualties, but the topside of the ship was severely damaged.

The *Chauncey* remained with Task Force 58 and patrolled the sea off Japan during the months of September and October. In mid-

November, after several trips to China, we headed back to the States, arriving on 3 December 1945.

I served aboard the *Chauncey* from the time of her commissioning in May 1943 until January 1946, when I left her at San Pedro, California. I served for three years in the Navy, with all but about five months of that time in the Pacific. On 20 January 1946, at the age of 17 years and 11 months, I was discharged. I didn't tell anyone my true age while I was in the Navy, not even my best friend. When I arrived home, I went to register for the draft as I had been told to do when I was discharged. This time I told them my true age. The clerk just laughed and told me to come back when I was 18.

I am very proud of my wartime service in the U. S. Navy. I am especially proud of being one of the youngest Navy combat veterans of World War II and of being a member of a unique and distinctive organization, the Veterans of Underage Military Service.

Dan Kriss and his shipmates earned nine battle stars on their Asiatic-Pacific theater ribbon. He went to school under the GI Bill of Rights after he returned home. Shortly after turning 21 years of age, Dan became a police officer and earned a college degree during his 30-year career in law enforcement. He retired from the Fairfax County Police Force with the rank of captain but went on to serve as Chief of the Dulles International Airport and the National Airport Police until 1980. While with the Fairfax County Police, Dan played a key role in establishing a regional police academy (the first in Virginia) and later participated as an instructor in police training programs throughout the state. In 1968, he was assigned by his chief to a neighboring county to conduct a study of needs to establish a county police force separate from the sheriff's department. The new department was established in 1970. The Fairfax County Board of Supervisors, on three separate occasions, commended Dan for his outstanding work in resolving several problems that existed in the communities in his police jurisdiction. Business associations as well commended him for his effective direction of his officers in greatly reducing law violations in shopping centers. Dan is now fully retired. He and his wife Julia live in Herndon, Virginia. They have a daughter, a son, and four grandchildren.

Robert H. McDannold

Age 16 – United States Navy

My older brother was in the Navy, and his ship, the USS *Detroit*, was in port at Pearl Harbor on 7 December 1941. I had turned 15 just five days before. I was in my first year of high school, but my thoughts were not of school. All that I could think about was getting into the

> ... so it is possible that I was the youngest member of the U. S. armed forces to witness the Japanese surrender.

Navy and going to war. I had to do my duty just like my brother and other red-blooded Americans like John Wayne, John Garfield, and Clark Gable.

In early 1942, I was standing in the hall with several of my buddies before classes started at school. I said to them, "Hey, we can go over to Long Beach and join the Merchant Marine. I heard that you can join the Merchant Marine even if you are only 14, and the Merchant Marine pays more than the Navy." So three other guys and I hitchhiked from Phoenix to Long Beach. We slept under a bridge near Sedona, Arizona, the first night. We had a total of $1.75 among the four of us. We arrived in Long Beach and went to the Merchant Marine headquarters to sign up. They told us we couldn't sign up at 14 but had to be at least 16, then we would have to go to training school and couldn't go to sea until we were 17. Since none of us were 16 and we didn't have any credentials with us anyway, we gave up on the Merchant Marine.

We found a hotel with an outside veranda and went to sleep in the bench swings. My three friends woke up earlier than I did the next morning, so they went to the Long Beach Amusement Park, leaving me asleep on a bench. They were picked up by the police for vagrancy because they didn't have any money. When I couldn't find them, I checked with the police, and they were in jail. My mother sent me some money to get them out, and we returned to Phoenix.

In November 1942, several days before my sixteenth birthday, I went to the Navy recruiting office, told them I would be 17 on 2 December, and filled out the enlistment papers. My dad went along with my lie, told the recruiters that my birth certificate had been destroyed in a fire, and signed the papers.

I was sworn into the Navy on 2 January 1943 and immediately sent to the Naval Training Center at San Diego for boot training. I graduated from boot camp on 1 March 1943 and went with forty-five other men to Mare Island, California, where we were assigned to a heavy cruiser, the USS *Portland* (CA-33). The *Portland* was at Mare Island being repaired after suffering torpedo hits during the battle of Guadalcanal in November 1942.

As soon as I was aboard the *Portland*, I tried to get into the radio gang, but I was assigned to the 5th Division. As were most boots, I was put on mess-cook duty. I kept trying to get into the radio gang, and I guess I pissed someone off because I was transferred to the 1st Division and again assigned to mess-cook duty. I kept trying to get into the radio gang and even passed the test for third class radioman. Finally, I received the news that there was an opening in the radio gang, and I was selected. I was overjoyed. Upon reporting to the radio gang, I was assigned to — yes, you guessed it — another tour of mess-cook duty!

I finally got settled in the radio gang and began copying and delivering messages. My general quarters station was in the CIC (Combat Information Center). I was happy with my job and with all the swell guys I was privileged to work with. I also took over the job as editor-in-chief of the ship's paper, *The Port Beam*.

As soon as repairs to the *Portland* were completed at Mare Island, we departed for the Aleutian Islands, and I experienced combat for the first time in the Kiska/Attu area during June and July 1943. By November, we were in the Gilbert Islands for the invasion of Tarawa, and the following month we went to the Marshalls. January 1944 found us providing support for the occupation of Kwajalein and Majuro Atolls and for Eniwetok Atoll the following month. During March, we bombarded Palau, Yap, Ulithi and Woleai, and in April, Truk, Satawan and Ponape. We participated in the Hollandia operations, then in September, we went back to the Southern Palau Islands to support the

Marines at Peleliu. In October, we supported the landings at Leyte in the Philippines and later that month participated in the famous battle for Leyte Gulf, which included the battle of Surigao Strait.

In November, we supported the carrier force that attacked Luzon and participated in the Visayas attacks. In December, we were involved with the landings on Mindoro and the following month supported the landings at Lingayen Gulf. In February, we were off Corregidor and Bataan, supporting the landings there. From March through June, we were in Okinawan waters in support of the invasion. During this period, we were at sea for over five months. We were refueled and resupplied at sea.

Life aboard the *Portland* was anything but routine for a 16-year-old seaman. When we were not in a major battle, we were off some Japanese-held island bombarding them with our big guns. We were frequently under air attack. At my GQ station in the CIC, I was in voice contact with all the U. S. planes in the air. I would tell them where the Japanese aircraft were, how far out, how high, how many, and their heading. I listened to the pilots shouting to each other and could hear the sound of their machine guns. We were credited with shooting down twenty-two Japanese aircraft and assisting in downing eleven others. We sank two enemy destroyers, assisted in sinking two battleships and two other destroyers, and damaged others.

We were in Buckner Bay, Okinawa, when we received word of the Japanese surrender. We were ordered to go to Pearl Harbor, pick up Vice Admiral George D. Murray and his staff, and proceed to Truk. The USS *Portland* was designated to receive the Japanese envoy who would formally surrender all of the Japanese troops and civilians on the bypassed islands. The USS *Missouri* was designated as the place of the main Japanese surrender ceremony in Tokyo Bay. The two ceremonies took place at the same time on 2 September 1945.

I was the youngest member of the crew of the *Portland*, and I am not aware of another underage veteran on the *Missouri*, so it is possible that I was the youngest member of the U. S. forces to witness the Japanese surrender.

After the Japanese surrender, the *Portland* and the *Missouri* left for Pearl Harbor where they joined with eight other ships to form Task Force 11. Under the command of Vice Admiral Forest P. Sherman aboard the USS *Enterprise*, the ten-ship force soon became known as the "Victory Fleet." We went through the Panama Canal and on to

New York for the big Navy Day celebration. We couldn't believe the welcome we received as we entered New York harbor. Boats in the harbor were tooting and honking and pumping streams of water into the air. When we tied up, civilians came aboard and hugged and kissed the sailors. What a welcome! Later, we had a ticker-tape parade, and President Harry S. Truman dedicated the newly renamed "Avenue of the Americas."

I was to go to San Pedro, California, for discharge, but before I left the ship, I went to the lost-and-found room to see if I could find my missing peacoat (a sailor's short coat of thick wool.) The master-at-arms there said, "If you can't find yours, just grab any one." I took a peacoat with the name J. R. O'Rear stencilled with white paint inside the coat.

I was discharged at San Pedro on 22 January 1946 and returned to Phoenix. I wore the peacoat while hunting, fishing, and working in the yard during cold weather. I saw the name J. R. O'Rear every time I put it on. It finally wore out and I gave it to a clothing drive. Now — fast-forward eighteen years.

In 1963, I applied for a job teaching in the bush country of Alaska and was accepted at a four-teacher school in Aniak. The teacher who had been there the longest was designated head teacher. At our school, it was a burly Texan named Ray who was the most senior. He had taught in the bush country for seven years. One day, Ray and I were playing gin rummy in my apartment and somehow the subject of "crabs" (not the kind you eat) came up. I happened to mention that we had a lot of them aboard my ship. Ray said that they were aboard his ship also, and they just couldn't seem to get rid of them. Ray then asked me what ship I had served on. When I replied, "The USS *Portland*," he gave a slight chuckle and said, "Mary (Ray's wife) told you to say that!" When I assured him that she hadn't, he looked at me disbelievingly and said, "OK, what was her number?" When I said, "CA-33," he almost fell out of his chair. Ray had been on the same train from boot camp to Mare Island as I had been. He was one of the forty-five boots who went aboard the *Portland* in March 1943! His assignment was down below in the engine room and mine was topside.

We dug out old pictures and yes, we did remember each other. We hugged each other like long-lost brothers. Can you imagine the odds of the two of us meeting eighteen years later in a small Alaskan bush village some 400+ miles from Anchorage?

Now here comes a billion-to-one shot. Ray's full name was Jewel Ray O'Rear, the same J. R. O'Rear whose peacoat I had taken from the ship and literally worn out. When I told Ray about the peacoat, he looked at me strangely and said, "I always wondered what happened to it!"

I traded three years of high school for nearly three years of war. I am very glad that I had the privilege of serving my country.

Bob McDannold earned nine battle stars on his Asiatic-Pacific theater ribbon and two stars on his Philippine Liberation ribbon. Although he had not finished high school, upon returning to Phoenix, he took a college-entrance exam and enrolled at Phoenix Junior College where he played varsity football in the fall and tennis in the spring. Later, he enrolled at Arizona State University in Tempe and received a B.A. in education in 1961. While he was a student at ASU, he lettered in tennis at the age of 36 and is on record as being the oldest student to letter in sports at that university. While pursuing an M.A. in education, he met and married Carolyn, another student. Soon after that, they decided they wanted to teach in the bush country of Alaska. He was accepted at a four-teacher school in Aniak, Alaska. During the summers, Bob was a commercial pilot for "a bush airline operation." After more than eight years in Alaska, Bob returned to Arizona and started his own construction company, building tennis courts and running tracks. He retired in 1989. Bob and Carolyn now live in Scottsdale, Arizona. They have two children.

George O. DeWitz

Age 15 – United States Navy

I was born in Spokane, Washington, on 15 May 1927 and grew up in Portland, Oregon, where I attended Commerce High School. After the attack on Pearl Harbor, it was difficult for me to

> *Torpedoes and periscope sightings were a daily and nightly nightmare.*

concentrate on anything but the war. Nothing else had any interest or meaning for me. In 1942, when I was 15 years old, I was 6-foot tall and weighed 170 pounds.

In December 1942, I went to the Navy recruiting office in Portland to enlist. I didn't use a birth certificate but obtained consent papers that my legal guardian was to sign, and I signed them myself. I was sworn into the Navy on 15 January 1943. I left one snowy evening by train for the Farragut Naval Training Center, Farragut, Idaho. After boot camp, I stayed at Farragut for gunnery school. I volunteered for armed guard duty in the Pacific after graduation. I became a gunner on an oil tanker, the SS *York*.

Sailing from Fremantle, Australia, through the Indian Ocean to Bahrain in the Persian Gulf was a constantly terrorizing experience. It took forty days to make it to the Gulf and back. I made four trips through those Japanese submarine-infested waters. The Japanese submarines, operating out of the Dutch East Indies, Java, and Sumatra, were always lurking in wait for a tanker loaded with oil, gas, or high-octane aviation fuel aboard. Tankers were blowing up all around us. Torpedoes and periscope sightings were a daily and nightly nightmare. In a 1-hour period, eight ships were sunk within a few hours' sailing time from us, but we were never hit. We were at general quarters for ten days without relief. That comes out to 240 hours in a damp, cold, gun tub with only "horsecock" sandwiches to eat.

When a tanker ship was hit by a torpedo, it didn't sink, it blew up. There was a standard joke among the Navy Armed Guard crew. When we talked to American submarine sailors, we told them that tanker sailors were issued parachutes, not life jackets. If we were torpedoed, we were going up, not down. There were lots of jokes and bravado but also much silent introspection and fear.

On one run out of Fremantle, we were only a short distance from land when we entered an oil slick formed from the sinking of a tanker. The slick could be seen from horizon to horizon. It took three days to sail through it. There were no clean-up crews then — Mother Nature did the job.

We were making about twenty knots one afternoon while I was standing the 4:00 to 8:00 watch on the fantail. All of a sudden, I saw the wake of three torpedoes streaking through the water off the port stern. I kicked in the alarm, gave the position of the torpedoes, dropped my sound-powered headset, and started to run to my gun station in the bow of the *York*. As I was running, my knees turned to lead. I felt like I was running in a dream. Finally, I reached my battle station 325 feet away and waited for those torpedoes to strike home. They didn't, thank God! The moonlit ocean was like a searchlight that night. The sub was still hounding us, and we were silhouetted against a gigantic moon. Suddenly there was a noise like something in the ship snapped. A boiler blew sixty tubes, and our speed dropped from twenty knots to six. We were given orders to head for Bombay, India. The entire crew was assigned watch. For forty-nine hours we waited in our gun stations, expecting to be blown out of the water at any time. The sub couldn't miss us at the speed we were traveling. But we were lucky and were not attacked. Apparently, the sub was out of torpedoes and didn't want to surface and fight with us.

We limped into Bombay and anchored in the bay called the "Gateway to India." The next morning when I went on deck, I saw vultures perched all over the ship. I couldn't believe this ugly sight. It gave everyone an eerie feeling. As a child, I was afraid of birds. But vultures, God! I thought that we were condemned to Dante's Inferno.

Everyday the bumboats[21] would come out to our anchored ship, supposedly to repair the boiler tubes. They argued, they haggled, they got angry, they shouted, and left. They couldn't agree on who was to be boss. After two weeks of that screwy action, they decided on someone and went to work. It took almost three weeks to complete a job that could have been done in six hours in any American port.

The crew, including myself, took liberty in that foul and horrible port. Sick, starving bodies were crawling in the streets. When they died, vultures would eat the bodies. The stink of rot was beyond imagination. There was nothing to do but get drunk and forget what you saw. Some of the crew went to cat houses. There were cages filled with 9-year-old prostitutes on the street. The cages were barred enclosures covered with old rugs or blankets. It made me sick, especially when I thought of my 9-year-old sister. I was 16 and wondered how in hell this could go on. It was a moral sickness.

When our ship was fixed and we made ready for sea, we were stopped by the port director. The officials came aboard and were met by our captain. Apparently, some sailors had "escaped" without paying their whorehouse bills. No one confessed to this, but here we were, with a war going on, and we had to pay a whorehouse bill before we could leave the harbor. After three hours of haggling, the captain came to some financial agreement with the officials and they left.

We set watch and sailed out to sea. The radio operator told me that ten ships had been sunk while we lay idle in Bombay. We were back in harm's way again and our brains accepted the fact that we were seconds from becoming a fireball in the water.

In early 1945, I was transferred to the regular Navy for destroyer duty and assigned to the USS *Norris* (DD-859). We were on picket duty for the carrier USS *Shangri-la*. We pulled many Navy pilots out of the water. We almost capsized during a typhoon in the China Sea. Two destroyers went down, and as they sank, water was sucked into their smokestacks, causing them to blow up. I saw five Chinese junks capsize, leaving families clinging to the hulls. We couldn't stop. If we had, we would have slipped into a trough, and we would have gone belly-up, too.

---

[21] Bumboats were small craft that brought supplies to ships anchored in the harbor. We called them bum boats because their crews were always begging.

We were involved in war at times, but the shooting never lasted more than thirty minutes. It wasn't like the Indian Ocean. Ships were sunk, but strangely enough, with all those Navy juggernaughts around, somehow we felt safe. We were never alone. Alone at sea is when you get scared. When you are alone, you lose confidence in your safety. But that philosophy holds true in civilian life as well as in the service. You feel safe only when you belong, when you have others around you to depend on. But we never had that in the Indian Ocean. We sailed alone.

After the war, we patrolled the seas in the Orient for awhile, trying to stop boats and other craft from landing Communists on the coastline. It was a wild, screwed-up mission, going back and forth from China, to Korea, to Japan, and Hongkong. I was later transferred to the shore patrol and found myself on permanent duty in Shanghai and in other Chinese cities.

I was discharged at the Alameda Naval Air Station, California, on 27 October 1947. I had enlisted for a 6-year regular Navy hitch, but I was a right arm rate, a gunner's mate first class, and they didn't need us any more. So I signed out – just as I had signed in.

I don't regret one moment of that youthful experience. Would I lie about my age, sign those Navy documents myself that my parents should have signed? Yes, I would do it again! For me, it was the best of times and the worst of times. Never will I, nor will anyone else, see this USA that I love so much be so united and so giving and helpful to one another.

George DeWitz attended a high school program at Reed College in Portland after his discharge from the Navy. He owned and operated two radio stations in Washington and Oregon for fourteen years. He sold his stations and attended Mount Hood Community College for a time, then to stay interested, he went into the advertising business. Currently, he owns and operates the DeWitz, DeWitz, and Rouzee Advertising Agency in Portland, Oregon. George and Marilyn, his wife of forty-two years, live in Boring, Oregon. They have six children and nine grandchildren.

George R. Brouse

Age 15 – United States Army

I was born George R. Stumpf in Philadelphia, Pennsylvania, on 10 October 1927. I felt a strong sense of duty to my country and wanted to get into the war. I was not successful in altering my birth certificate,

> *I not only changed my birth month and year, I changed my name.*

so I could not enlist because of my age. In 1942, when I was 15 years old, I ran away from home with the intention of joining the Royal Canadian Air Force. I got as far as the Canadian border where I was turned back because my name, Stumpf, was "too German."

I happened to pass by a draft board that had signs saying that 18-year-olds must register for the draft, so I went in and registered, giving my birth date as 10 December 1924. Had I used October as my birth month, I could have been cited for being late in registering. I not only changed my birth month and year, I changed my name. I used my stepfather's last name, Brous, and added an "e" to it. My name has been Brouse since that time.

After registering for the draft, I volunteered for induction and reported to the Schuylkill Arsenal, going from there to Indiantown Gap, Pennsylvania. I volunteered for the paratroopers and was sent to Toccoa, Georgia, and to the 511 Parachute Infantry Regiment. After basic training, I went to Fort Benning for jump training and graduated on 10 April 1943.

On my seventh jump at Fort Benning, I landed very hard on a blacktop highway, and I lay in a ditch at the side of the road for seven hours before the medics found me. At the base hospital, they found that my legs and back were fractured.

After I recovered enough to go back on duty, I was transferred to Greensburg, Pennsylvania, then to Camp Patrick Henry, and from there to Newport News, Virginia, where we boarded the SS *America* for shipment overseas. I found out later that we were going to North Africa.

In North Africa, I was assigned to Easy Company, 39th Infantry, 9th Infantry Division. We fought at El Guettar, Hill 609, and in the Bizerte area. While we were in a staging area near Bizerte, the area was attacked by German Stuka dive bombers. I was in a 5-foot-deep foxhole, but, unfortunately, it was very close to an ammunition dump. A German bomb hit the ammo dump, and I found myself about twenty feet away from my foxhole, dazed and with a total loss of hearing and speech that lasted for some time.

We were told that the 9th Infantry Division was slated to spearhead the invasion of Sicily. We were loaded on LCIs (landing craft, infantry) in Bizerte harbor and stayed floating in the harbor for days, only to learn that another unit had spearheaded the invasion and casualties were very heavy. While with the 9th Division, I was offered a battlefield commission, but I was afraid to accept it because of the chance that it would be discovered that I was underage. I was also recommended for a Silver Star twice, but nothing came of it.

Later, I was assigned as a chauffeur to Allied Force Headquarters of the Quartermaster General, then to Allied Force Headquarters in Casserta, Italy, where I met and chauffeured VIPs coming and going to Capodiccina Airport. After a disagreement with the officer-in-charge, I was sent to the 8th Replacement Depot. I joined Able Company, 87th Mountain Infantry, 10th Mountain Division, near Florence, Italy, and was in combat with that unit through the Apennines, the Po Valley, and the Udine Area.

In July 1945, I was sent back to the States with an advanced detail of the 10th Mountain Division in preparation for the Division to move to the Pacific theater. The 10th was scheduled to invade Japan near Fujiyama. When we arrived in New York, I was given a 30-day furlough which was extended another fifteen days. While I was on furlough, the war ended and I reported to Camp Chaffee, Arkansas, for discharge.

I joined the inactive Army Reserves when the Korean War started. I was called to active duty on 1 April 1951, again reporting to the Schuylkill Arsenal. I showed the examining doctor medical papers detailing my leg and back problems. He asked what my military occupational specialty was. When I told him light and heavy machine guns, he took the papers, threw them in a waste can, and yelled,

"Next!" I was assigned to the 359th Engineer Aviation Supply Company as a buck private. I was transferred later to Headquarters Company, Engineering Aviation Brigade, where I finished my tour. I was released from active duty as a sergeant first class in January 1953.

George Brouse earned the Combat Infantryman Badge and was awarded the Bronze Star for heroism during the Po Valley campaign. After the war, he became a plumber and was a contractor and building inspector in Philadelphia for many years. He is now retired and on permanent disability. George was a member of the Coast Guard Auxiliary sixteen years, attaining the rank of District Officer. George and Evelyn, his wife of 48 years, live in Philadelphia, Pennsylvania. They have a daughter and three grandchildren. They also have three dogs and about 200 birds. George is the National Commander of the Veterans of Underage Military Service.

√ VUMS Note ⇒ *All in the family.* Some underage veterans didn't have a problem with their fathers about enlisting underage because their fathers had done the very same thing themselves during World War I. Others followed in the steps of older brothers or other relatives who had enlisted underage. The membership roll of the Veterans of Underage Military Service show one father-daughter and one father-son pair, as well as eight pairs of brothers, including two sets of twins.

Ted R. Puskarcik

Age 15 – United States Navy

In late 1942, I thought that the war would be over before I could get into the military. The Marines were on Guadalcanal, the Japanese had been defeated at Midway, and the invasion of North Africa was underway. I took my birth certificate, which showed

> *If I had given the true direction, the torpedo would have hit us broadside.*

that I was born on 27 May 1927, and folded it across the date a number of times, then changed 1927 to read 1925. I went to the U. S. Navy recruiting office in Youngstown, Ohio, and enlisted, using the altered birth certificate and an affidavit, but I still had to get parental consent. My brother was already in the Army Air Forces. My dad worked hard in the steel mills and was very patriotic. Dad was reluctant to sign my enlistment papers (six sheets in all), but I gave him a very convincing, peaceful, and friendly argument. I reminded him that jobs were scarce in our area and that the Navy would train me for a job. That argument worked, and he signed my papers.

During the physical examination, it was determined by the Navy that I should get some dental work done before I could be accepted. This posed a problem of how to pay for it. My mother died when I was 13 years old, and the following year, my father gave me a bicycle to help distract me from our loss. I sold that bike and used the money to get the dental work done that the Navy required. I was sworn into the U. S. Navy on 3 February 1943 at Cleveland, Ohio, and was immediately sent to boot camp at Great Lakes, Illinois. I was in Company 169, Camp Moffitt.

After thirteen weeks of boot camp, I was assigned to the Armed Guards, given two weeks of gunnery school on the shores of Lake Michigan, then was assigned to Armed Guard School at Gulfport, Mississippi, for six more weeks of gunnery school. Without the supportive gun crew I was with, I may not have made it through the school. One had to be proficient at all stations of the gun. I weighed less than 130 pounds, and when working as first loader, I had difficulty in placing the 65-pound training projectile into the breech of the 4.5-inch gun. Because of my size, I was unable to slam it home hard enough for the breech mechanism to close. Two older crew members took me to the gun docks one evening and helped me work out the problems I was having. They never questioned my age.

On completion of the training, we were in formation waiting to board a train to our next assignment. The master-at-arms, a big, round, first class boatswain's mate with 30-years' service, called out a few names, including mine, and told us to fall out. As the rest of our group boarded the train, they kept looking back to see if I was coming. The boatswain's mate said, "Forget it, you're not going!" As the train left I had to put on my sunglasses so no one would see the tears running down my cheeks.

I was told to appear before the commandant at a specified time. I did, and he confronted me about my age. I was 16 by then. He scolded me for what I had done, reminded me of the money the government spent on my training and expenses, then asked, "Do you want to go home or remain in the Navy?" I told him I wanted to stay in the Navy. He made me sign some papers and adjusted my insurance to 16 years of age. I thanked him, saluted, and left. I was never told how they found out about my age.

I was assigned to duty in the officers' mess hall. It was great! I got to eat fine food, had my choice of cereal in the morning, and had all the ice cream that I wanted. My work wasn't difficult, and I gained at least fifteen pounds. I was later transferred to the general mess which fed regular ships' company, gun crew trainees, and transients. That was duty that I didn't care for.

One day while I was serving on the chow line, two fellows from my hometown of Campbell, Ohio, came through. One didn't recognize me, but the other one did. He asked me what I was doing there. I put my finger to my lips and told him I'd see him later and explain. When I met them and told them my secret, they were astounded, but agreed not to tell. I started to hang out with them, hoping that I could get on their gun crew so that I could ship out.

While serving at the officers' mess I had gotten to know the commandant well enough to request a favor from him. I told him that two of my hometown friends were shipping out and I wanted to go with them. He didn't like the idea of my getting in a combat situation at my age, but he reluctantly granted my request. Unfortunately, my friends went to Virginia, and I went to New Orleans, Louisiana.

From the Armed Guard Center in New Orleans, I was assigned to a Liberty ship, the SS *William Byrd*, which was under construction at Jacksonville, Florida. The superstructure was still on the dock when we saw the ship for the first time. We took the ship out for its shakedown cruise off the coast of Florida. We test fired the 4.5-inch stern gun on this cruise. The first time we fired the gun at a very low angle, the blast hit the gun tub, which was improperly placed, and blew back toward us. I couldn't hear for two weeks after that and still have a hearing loss to this day. After this incident, the gun mount and tub were rearranged so that the gun barrel always overlapped the tub.

Our first voyage, in November 1943, was to Antillia, Cuba, where we picked up a load of sugar destined for Liverpool, England, via New York. With all five holds full of sugar, the ship rode very low in the water. The crossings, to and from, were anything but uneventful. We were rammed three times, and we passed very close to three mines.

Our second voyage on the *Byrd* was from Boston to Swansea, Wales, with a load of ammunition. On other crossings, I watched as nearby ships were torpedoed. Ships carrying fuel and ammunition would virtually vaporize when hit. I saw this happen several times. Sometimes I would feel better knowing that our cargo was highly volatile because I knew that if we took a fatal shot, I would never know what hit me.

Another trip destined for Khromshah, Iran, was full of adventure. We went through the Sargasso Sea, a sea that I didn't know existed before. When we entered the Mediterranean Sea, we went on immediate alert. We were standing general quarters watches almost the entire trip from Gibraltar to Port Said. We went through the Suez Canal, travelled the length of the Red Sea, and sailed into the Indian Ocean for our terminus in the Persian Gulf. One night I was standing bow-watch when the sea suddenly lit up with hundreds of fluorescent cartwheel-shaped circles about twenty feet in diameter, intermingled as far as I could see. A few days later, we encountered a sand storm at sea. White sand almost as fine as talcum powder covered everything in sight, similar to snow in a windstorm. Those of us on watch had to put on goggles and cover our mouths and nostrils to keep the sand out.

On the return trip, when we were just a few days from Gibraltar and were at general quarters, an English ship on our starboard side and a Scandinavian tanker astern were both hit by torpedoes. While looking through the telescope sights of our stern gun, I saw a British cruiser bring a submarine to the surface with depth charges, shine its searchlights on it, and destroy it with a barrage of cannon and machine-gun fire.

A torpedo incident happened while I was on the midnight bow-watch with a friend, Tom Van Poortfliet. My viewing area was from 0° to 45°. Van's area was from 315° to 360°. We were talking, and we thought that it would be better if we exchanged our viewing quarter so we would be partially facing each other. Van was revealing to me that he had joined the Navy at age 16 but wanted me to keep it a secret. I did not tell him that I was only 16. In fact, I never revealed my true age to anyone except the commandant back at Gulfport.

Our watch routine was to use binoculars for two hours and then switch to headphones for two hours. Just as I was switching to headphones, I spotted a torpedo coming at us from the port side at about 340° to 345°. I reported the torpedo sighting to the helmsman, but I told him that it was coming from the starboard quarter at about 15° to 20°, the angle that I had memorized when I came on watch before exchanging viewing quarters with Van. This error saved the ship and the entire crew. The helmsman turned the ship into the wake of the torpedo, foreshortening the travel, and the torpedo whizzed by us. If I had given the true direction, the torpedo would have hit us broadside. Van and I shared more than one secret that night.

The second Liberty ship that I served on was the SS *William H. Crawford*. Our first voyage took us to Omaha Beach, Normandy, France, in July 1944. A shipmate and I were fortunate to be able to go ashore on a field trip, mix with the GIs, and explore the devastation. Upon leaving France for England and ultimately back to the States, we encountered a storm in the North Atlantic. The ship buckled in the heavy seas, causing a 1½-inch gap from starboard to port just in front of the main superstructure. Winds were 60 to 70 knots, waves were 50 to 60 feet high. During the five days of the storm, we didn't travel more than five miles. Our hydraulic steering gear broke down three times and we had to go to direct hands-on steering. We were almost rammed several times. It seems hard to believe, but a sea gull followed us across the Atlantic until we were within two days of New York harbor.

During December 1944 and January 1945, the *Crawford* was anchored in the port of Antwerp. One day a German fighter flew so low over us that we could see the pilot's face. Apparently, he was surveying targets in the harbor. This was during the Battle of the Bulge, and the Germans had hoped to cut off large sections of the Allied front by capturing Antwerp. They fired V1 and V2 rockets at the harbor almost hourly every day. Axis Sally stated on the radio that blood would flow in the streets of Antwerp on New Year's Day, but that was the day we had the fewest incidents.

During my service in the Armed Guards, I made over twenty voyages from the East Coast of the United States to Europe and back, but my last trip was to the Philippines. From there I returned to San Francisco, California, where I was discharged from the Navy on 11 February 1946.

I returned to my hometown of Campbell, Ohio, and found that my training as a gunner's mate in the Navy didn't help much in finding a job, and I had no previous occupation.

Ted Puskarcik studied art for a short time at Youngstown University, then worked at odd jobs until getting employment with the General Outdoor Advertising Company as a sign painter. His main job was painting roadside bulletin board and wall signs. He was fortunate to work with a journeyman painter who helped him develop his talent as an artist. After five years of painting signs, he worked as a draftsman for the Store Engineering Company, designing cabinets and hardware for stores. This led to layout work, floor plans, and merchandizing. He moved to another company, the Youngstown Cabinet Works, Inc., where he was a senior designer. Next came work for a shopping-center developer where he designed shopping centers, malls, motels and hotels. He worked as an industrial designer for several engineering firms and steel companies before retiring in May 1989. Ted now devotes his talents to woodcarving. He carves statuettes, figurines, and novelties. Ted and his wife Tillie live in Campbell, Ohio. They have five children (one deceased) and eight grandchildren.

John W. "Jack" Rice

Age 16 – United States Navy

I was born in Greenwood, South Carolina, on 12 December 1926. I had strong feelings of patriotism and was anxious to get into the service. I convinced my parents to sign my enlistment papers and was sworn into the Navy on 4 February 1943.

> *I have never regretted my decision to tell a lie about my age.*

I was sent to Bainbridge, Maryland, for boot camp and remained at Bainbridge to attend a hospital corps school. My first assignment was at the U. S. Naval Hospital, Norman, Oklahoma, where I remained until February 1944. While packing to leave, I was having trouble getting everything into my seabag. My loud griping about the situation was overheard by two chief petty officers, both having service stripes from their wrists to their elbows. One chief politely interrupted my ranting with this question: "Pardon me, son. Is this your first war?" It was a perfect squelch.

I saw my first Navy ship after a full year as a sailor. This was the USS *LST-230* docked in Boston harbor. I got my first glance at the ship as we pulled along the dock in a troop train. We boarded the *LST-230* and slowly made our way across the Atlantic to Plymouth, England, with a port of call at Halifax, Nova Scotia, along the way.

I was among a large number of hospital corpsmen who were assigned to LSTs in preparation for the invasion of France. Our purpose was to assist in the treatment of wounded who were evacuated from the beaches. I was aboard the USS *LST-315* on D-Day, 6 June 1944. On 9 June, our flotilla of five LSTs came under attack by German E-Boats in the English Channel. Two LSTs were lost, along with a large portion of General Patton's troops and equipment.

In August 1944, I returned to the States, and along with 443 other corpsmen, was assigned to the Medical Field Service School at Camp Lejeune, North Carolina. We were all assigned to duty with the U. S. Marine Corps upon completion of training. I was sent to Camp Pendleton, California, for a short time, then I was assigned to a field hospital unit of the 6th Marine Division on Okinawa. At the time of the Japanese surrender, I was with the 29th Marine Regiment on Guam. I remained with the Marines during occupation duty in China, serving both in Tsingtao and Tientsin.

I completed high school while I was in China by taking the GED tests. I returned to the States in late 1946 and was discharged at the Mare Island Naval Shipyard, Vallejo, California, on 3 January 1947, with a rating of pharmacist's mate first class.

I have always felt that I was particularly privileged to serve in three areas of the United States — the East, Midwest and West — as well as in Europe and the Far East. The Navy was not kidding when it advertised "Join the Navy and See the World." Military service provided me with untold opportunities, benefits, and experiences for which I will be eternally grateful. I have never regretted my decision to tell a lie about my age. It changed my life. To this day, I maintain relationships with those with whom I served over fifty years ago.

Jack Rice attended Newberry College, South Carolina, after his discharge from the Navy. He graduated in 1950 and spent the next forty-three years in the insurance industry. He retired in 1994 as an underwriting executive. In 1989, Jack was elected president of the Institute of Home Office Underwriters, a national organization of insurance executives. Jack and Ray, his wife of forty-four years, live in Jacksonville, Florida. They have two daughters and four grandchildren.

Gerald J. "Jerry" Beno

Age 16 – United States Marine Corps

I was born in Green Bay, Wisconsin, on 6 August 1926. I attended Catholic schools until the tenth grade, then transferred to a public school. I was not very fond of school, so after a few months of my junior year, I quit school and joined the Marines.

... "I haven't been anywhere yet and I'm a goner already."

I got out my dad's old typewriter, found an eraser, and changed all the 1926s on my birth certificate to read 1925. It looked real good. I enlisted in the Marines in December 1942, but it was on 16 February 1943 that I was sworn in. I went to San Diego, California, for boot camp. What a different life I had gotten myself into! After a 6-week boot camp, I was sent to Bremerton, Washington, for a couple of months. From there I was sent directly to Adak in the Aleutian Islands.

We had quite an experience traveling from Seattle to Adak in mid-winter aboard an old tanker. The North Pacific is said to have the roughest weather in the world. During a period of rough seas, the ship developed a small crack in the hull. When I heard about the crack I said to myself, "I haven't been anywhere yet and I'm a goner already." But the ship didn't sink, and we arrived at our destination.

After several months at Adak, I was transferred to the Marine detachment aboard the USS *Charleston* (PG-51). The *Charleston* was a patrolling gunboat, one of only two *Erie*-class gunboats that were built. Her sister ship, the *Erie*, was sunk by the Germans in 1942. The Marines aboard the *Charleston* were antiaircraft gunners and formed boarding parties when necessary. My original job was a loader on a 1.1-inch antiaircraft gun, a fairly old model that was troublesome and jammed a lot, but we kept it firing.

In 1944, my job was changed to operator of the Mark-14 sight that was mounted above the 1.1-inch gun.

The *Charleston*'s job was mostly patrolling and convoying supply ships. The weather was our worst enemy. We listed 60° during one storm, which is almost lying sideways. In early 1945, the *Charleston* was sent alone into the fog-shrouded waters north of Japan. Our mission was to travel back and forth, sending out phony radio signals to make the Japanese think there was a large fleet in the area. This caused the Japanese to keep some of their fleet in the area instead of sending them to the central Pacific where they were needed. We also convoyed landing craft to Russia. They were to be used in the eventual invasion of Japan from the north.

I left the *Charleston* in June 1945 and was assigned to the Naval Proving Grounds at Dahlgren, Virginia. Rumor had it that we were to go back to the West Coast to train for the invasion of Japan, but the A-bomb stopped that. I was discharged on 25 November 1945 after serving almost three years. I was still only 19 years old.

I still have that altered birth certificate in a frame on a wall in my den, along with my ribbons and the expert-rifle and bayonet medals I earned. On that same wall is a commemorative M-1 Garand rifle, the same as the one I carried for three years in the Marines. People still ask me today if I thought I did the right thing. All that I can tell them is, if I hadn't done it when I did, but had waited to be drafted, I might not be here today. I learned in the Marine Corps that you don't get something for nothing, that you have to work for it, a lesson that has served me well throughout the years.

Jerry Beno returned to Green Bay, Wisconsin, after his discharge from the Marines and started in the plumbing business with his father. After his father died in 1960, Jerry took over the business at age 35. He is still operating it successfully at age 70. Jerry and Pat, his wife of forty-nine years, live in Green Bay. They have seven children and seventeen grandchildren.

Herbert "Bud" Kloppenburg

Age 16 – United States Marine Corps

I was so patriotic that I tried to enlist in the Marines when I was only 15, but my mother said, "No way." I was doing very well in school and she insisted that I complete high school, which I did when I was 16½. I joined the

> *I almost told him he was nuts, but I didn't ...*

Marines on <u>23</u> February 1943. My birthday was <u>23</u> July 1926. It seems that all my big deals as a Marine happened on the same day of the month, the <u>23</u>rd.

I had been in the Corps only about three months when I was sent to Guadalcanal on a mop-up detail. The battle was over, but there were still a few Japanese around. I went from the Solomons to New Zealand with the 6th Marines, 2nd Marine Division. We left New Zealand after a few months, and on 20 November 1943, we invaded Tarawa. They "got me good" there, shot me in both legs, the left leg below the knee, the right leg straight through the knee. That put me out of combat for awhile. I was wounded on <u>23</u> November 1943.

I was sent to a hospital at Pearl Harbor, then, on 17 December 1943, I was put on a hospital ship. At that time, I was in a body cast. Admiral C. W. Nimitz and his staff came aboard and awarded me the Bronze Star and the Purple Heart. I still have the papers he signed that came with the medals. After he awarded me the medals, he said, "Get well soon, son, we need men back in the Pacific." I almost told him he was nuts, but I didn't, of course. I had turned 17 in July.

Soon after Admiral Nimitz left the ship, we sailed for San Diego, arriving there on <u>23</u> December 1943. By the middle of July 1944, I was walking fairly well. I was sent back to Pearl Harbor, and after about a month, went to Maui and joined the 24th Marines, 4th Marine Division. We started on our way to Iwo Jima in January 1945. By this time, at age 18, I was a corporal and an old salt. I made the complete Iwo Jima campaign without receiving wounds that a band-aid wouldn't cover. After Iwo, we returned to Pearl Harbor for a "big beer party," then we went back to our main camp at Maui.

Shortly after my 19th birthday in July 1945, the A-bomb was dropped. I said, "Thank God," then, and I still feel that way. We were within weeks of invading the Japanese mainland. I am sure that would have taken many lives on both sides. Some time in October 1945, I came back to the States and received an honorable discharge on 23 November 1945.

I always seemed to get a good job at our base camps, both in the 2nd Marine Division and the 4th Marine Division. I enjoyed many, many good times in the Marine Corps. I was young, wild, and single. So much for that.

Bud Kloppenburg received the Bronze Star for heroism on Tarawa, and a Purple Heart for wounds received there. On 18 August 1947, he went to work for the Standard Oil Company (now Chevron) and remained with them for forty years, mostly in California and Alaska. He completed nine years of college and earned three A.A. degrees during this time. One day while he was working on an offshore oil platform, an explosion occurred. He was blown against the rails, but a co-worker was blown into the water. Bud rescued his co-worker from the water and applied first aid to a leg so severely injured that the kneecap was torn loose. Bud put the kneecap in his pocket and commandeered a boat to rush the injured man to a hospital in Santa Barbara. He gave the doctor the kneecap, which was expertly replaced. The injured man recovered so well that now he's able to play golf. Bud received an outstanding employee award from Chevron for saving his co-worker's life. His last assignment for Chevron was as area foreman for field operations in the state of Alaska. He retired on 31 October 1986. Bud and his wife "Tina" (Mary Ruth) live in Cherry Valley, California. They have six children, eleven grandchildren, and one great-granddaughter.

H. Sherry Heldman

Age 16 – United States Marine Corps

I was the youngest of seven children, all of whom were either in the military or were civilian defense workers in 1942-43 at the height of World War II. A 20-year-old friend suggested that we join the Women Marines together. After

> *... it was my OCS application that did me in.*

figuring out how to alter a copy of my birth certificate to read 1920 instead of 1926 as the date of birth, we rushed to the Marine recruiting office. A few days later, we were given an entrance exam. My friend didn't qualify, but I did. I passed all the mental and physical aptitude tests at age 16 while pretending to be 22 years old.

I was assigned to the original 6th Regiment of Women Marines and sent to Hunter College, New York, for basic training. We underwent a grueling 6-week course that transformed us from young girls to serious adults. We also had our lighter moments, like standing regimental review for Madame Chiang Kai-shek. Upon completing boot camp, I was transferred to Camp Lejeune, North Carolina, and assigned to the motor pool.

Before leaving New York, I applied for OCS to become an instructor in motor mechanics. By the time I got to Camp Lejeune, my true age of 16 had already been discovered. I was never told how they found out, but I deduced it was my OCS application that did me in. The transcript of grades from my high school revealed that I was still a student at the time I was sworn into the Marines. I must say, the big brass at Camp Lejeune treated me with admiration and did everything in their power to get a special dispensation so that I could stay in, but to no avail. I was given an honorable discharge "for the convenience of the government" on 2 August 1943, two days before my seventeenth birthday.

I've always regretted not having a military career of my own, but I did get twenty years of military experience because my husband was a career Navy man, most of which was spent attached to ships. The Marines taught me teamwork, self-discipline, and how to be neat and efficient, with a place for everything and everything in its place. On the other hand, the Navy taught me to cope with a nomadic lifestyle while juggling the responsibilities of running a household, raising a family, and furthering my education. You couldn't raise a family on a sailor's income, so I had to work to help make ends meet. This required having to change jobs with each transfer. I became very proficient at packing household goods. There was no room for sentimentality, especially if an item was bulky, valuable, or fragile.

My husband Richard taught me everything I know about cooking, but I cringed whenever he went near our kitchen at home because he couldn't cook for fewer than fifty people. We always had plenty of leftovers in the fridge. We had a modern marriage long before equality was considered politically correct. On the rare occasions when Richard had shore duty, he didn't hesitate to take on any chores that needed doing or to baby-sit while I was at work or at school, and I never had to pick up after him because he had plenty of experience living in cramped quarters on board ship.

All in all, my entire military experience has served me well. Although my memory is not what it used to be, ever so often something will occur and I will say to myself, "I learned that in the Marines – or in San Francisco – or in New York – or in Panama – or in Gitmo – or in Key West – or in Newport, Rhode Island – or in Philadelphia – or in Connecticut." So most of what I have accomplished is the direct result of the military experiences I had in my formative years.

I'm a firm believer that all education, both academic and technical, from high school on, should be provided in a military-like setting so children can learn to *focus* on being self-reliant and on their life's work without unnecessary distractions.

Sherry Heldman's husband Richard died in October 1971, seven years after retiring from the Navy. The Survivor's Benefit Plan that allowed a surviving spouse to receive a portion of the deceased's retirement pay was not passed until September 1972. Ten years later it was made retroactive for spouses of civilian retirees, but not for military retirees. Attempts to redress this situation have been made in the Congress, so far without success. Sherry lives in Boca Raton, Florida. She has a daughter and two grandchildren living in the Bronx, New York.

√ **VUMS Note** ⇒ **The GI Bill.** Having interrupted their schooling in order to enlist, a large majority of underage veterans took advantage of the opportunities provided by the GI Bill to go back to school after their discharges. The types of schooling which they selected under the GI Bill ranged widely, from completing high school to earning the highest academic degrees. They enrolled in a broad range of educational institutions as well as in programs far too varied and too numerous to list. They included business, engineering, flying, law, education, science, and fine arts, to name only a few.

Concerned about the impact of the returning GIs on the nation's economy, Congress passed the GI Bill (Public Law 344) in 1944, which is still in existence today in modified form. The GI Bill not only provided educational benefits (mainly tuition, books, and subsistence allowances), it also provided for home mortgage and business loans. Rough estimates of the number of veterans who have taken advantage of the GI Bill since its inception over fifty years ago run as high as 20 million.

Jack A. Theoldore

Age 12 – United States Navy

We moved to San Diego, California, in 1935 from Tulsa, Oklahoma, where I was born on 18 March 1930. I was 5 years old when I started working at the Westgate Fish Cannery in San Diego. I put the cans in which the women packed the fish on the

> **She asked the Navy why a boy who was not even 15 years old was missing in action.**

conveyor belt. I was paid 3¢ per package of 200 cans. At 6 years of age, I worked with my dad as a night watchman at the Embarcadero. That included lighting the landing lights at Lindberg Field. We also picked up brass casings at a nearby Marine Corps base. That's when I started thinking about joining the military.

I watched every film on the military that I could, including "Hell Divers," "All Quiet on the Western Front," "Dawn Patrol," "The Fighting 69th," and anything else that had Army, Navy, or Marines in it.

We moved to Point Richmond, California, in 1939, about the time that the Army's 417th field artillery set up coastal defense guns on the Point. I was at the Army base more than I was at school. At that time I had a paper route in the mornings and was a pin-setter at a bowling alley in the evenings.

On 7 December 1941, I was in a movie theater when the lights came on and it was announced that the Japanese had bombed Pearl Harbor! Hell, I never even knew where that was. The announcer told all military personnel to report back to their bases. I got up and left with the soldiers. It was then that I knew I had to get into the service. I was 11, going on 12, and was afraid that the war would be over before I could get in.

Early in 1943, I found my birth certificate and took it with me to school. I worked on it until my birth date read 1925 instead of 1930.

This made me very nearly 18. On 16 March 1943, I took the bus to San Francisco. I went to the Marine recruiter but was told to try the Army. I guess they turned me down because of my size, 5'6" and 145 pounds. Instead of trying the Army, I went to the Navy recruiting office, which was just down the way. I told them that I would be 18 in a few days and didn't want to go into the Army. Somehow they bought my story and accepted my birth certificate. I took my physical and did the paperwork that day. About six o'clock that evening, they gave me a consent form, told me to have my mother sign it, and to return in the morning. I knew I couldn't go home, so I walked the streets and catnapped in doorways. The next morning, I signed my mother's name to the form and reported to the recruiting office. The yeoman was mad as hell with me because I didn't get the papers notarized, but the chief said, "The hell with it, he is already on orders to boot camp." So they took several of us into a large room and swore us into the Navy.

That night I was on my way to boot camp in Camp King, Naval Training Station, Farragut, Idaho. I kept up with everyone in boot camp in spite of my age. I shot expert on the rifle range and made record runs in physical training. During the last week of boot camp, a notice was posted on the bulkhead that said "strong swimmers" were needed in San Diego. I asked what they needed strong swimmers for and was told that it was for life-guard duty. "Oh boy," I said, "I used to do the rough-water swim in San Diego — this will be a piece of cake!" Two weeks later I was standing in front of Building 3, right behind the PX, on the U. S. Marine Corps Base, San Diego, California. I didn't know the details at the time, but I was part of an interservice transfer, and I would be essentially a Marine, with both a Marine and a Navy serial number. I soon found out that "strong swimmer" meant underwater demolition and expertise in Marine raider and reconnaissance techniques. At the time, I didn't realize that I would be going through Marine boot camp.

I was in my Navy blues when I reported to the Marine Corps Base, so you can guess how much hell I went through among the Marines. I was finally issued a Marine uniform, and it was then that I found out what boot camp was all about. I told myself that I was going to get out of this, but then I would see some of the guys that couldn't take it, and I told myself that they would have to kill me to get me to quit. After five good fights, I guess I proved myself to the DI (drill instructor), and he made me the platoon guidon. I have a lot of stories about Marine boot camp at age 13!

When we went to the rifle range at Camp Matthews, I shot expert with all weapons that I fired. They sent me next to Balboa Park for special work in raider techniques and exploring. Then I went over to Coronado and worked with underwater demolition teams (UDT) 11 and 13, the "strong swimmers." Next, I went to Camp Gillespie for parachute training. At that time, we were led by Marine master and gunnery sergeants. No officers were assigned to our unit.

After a big show of issuing us cold-weather gear and snow suits at the Marine base, they put us on a train and we left San Diego. We were on the train for two days. On the last night, we disembarked at B Street pier, San Diego. I don't know whether they confused the enemy or not, but they sure confused us.

We went on board a troopship, and it took us eighteen days to get to Pearl Harbor, again trying to confuse the enemy. I had finally made it to the war! Or so I thought. I was sent to Kauai. For a few weeks, we tried to land a jeep and a 75mm artillery piece on the shore in a 15-foot surf. No way! They put us back on troopships and we sailed south.

We went ashore on Tarawa on 20 November. I was TDY (temporarily attached) to the 2nd Battalion, 8th Marines, 2nd Marine Division, and was in the advance scout party that was scheduled to land at Red Beach 3. On the way in, our Higgins boat was hit and George "Big Red" Reid and I were thrown into the water. By the time we waded to the shore, we found ourselves on Red Beach 2, near the pier. When we got there, I felt a pain in my left leg. I looked down and my knee looked like hamburger. I couldn't stay where I was, so I just kept moving, although I had to drag my leg. Standing on the pier was Bill Hawkins who, I soon found out, commanded the 2nd Scout & Sniper platoon. Lieutenant Hawkins yelled at us to pick up some ammo and follow him. That Hawkins was one hell of a Marine. He kept yelling at us, "Come on, those bastards can't hit anything!" We went over the sea wall, and Big Red and I formed a team and started knocking out gun emplacements with hand grenades and satchel charges. We knocked out six machine-gun bunkers. Lieutenant Hawkins was killed the next day. He was awarded the Congressional Medal of Honor posthumously.

After Tarawa, we went south to an island called Apamama, fifteen miles from the equator. There was no resistance, and it turned out to be sort of a vacation, but I was one giant heat rash all the time we were there. We then went back to Pearl where I was put in the hospital to get the coral and metal out of my knee.

In May 1944, we went to the Mariana Islands for the 15 June invasion of Saipan. My knee was still bothering me. Running, swimming, and jumping were difficult, so it was decided that I would ride this time. I was attached to the 4th Tank Battalion, 4th Marine Division, and I became a tank gunner. Our job on Saipan was to cut the island in half and to take Aslito airfield. My tank was shot up during the operation and I was wounded twice. On 25 July, we went to Tinian in a new tank. When that operation was completed, we went back to Hawaii.

When my tank was put out of action on Saipan, I was sent back to get help. I ran into a mortar squad that was short-handed, and I was told to join them for an operation. I guess the reports on my whereabouts got mixed up because a telegram was sent to my mother with the message "... regret to inform you that your son Corporal Jack Theoldore was reported missing in action." My mother came unglued. All this time she thought that I was with my dad and stepmother in Sacramento. She asked the Navy why a boy who was not even 15 years old was missing in action. I was in the hospital at Schofield Barracks, Oahu, Hawaii, when a Navy lieutenant came in and said to me, "You were born in 1930, not 1925. You are going back to the Navy, and we will hold you here until you come of age."

Major Rip Collins, who commanded the 4th Tank Battalion on Saipan, stopped by the hospital to check on his wounded men. I told him my problem, and I asked him if he could arrange for me to stay with his outfit. He told me that there was nothing he could do. So I was sent to the amphibious base at Pearl Harbor as a coxswain, taking people from Ford Island to the fleet landing. The instantaneous transformation from Marine corporal to Navy coxswain was a bit of a shock.

When I found out that the USS *Belleau Wood* was going back to the States, I walked on board with a work party and just stayed on board until we got to the Alameda Naval Air Station in San Francisco Bay. I left the ship there and went to see my mother in San Diego, then went back to San Francisco and turned myself in. They sent me to

Treasure Island to await discharge. They couldn't decide on the type of discharge to give me, dishonorable for coming home without orders, minority, or what? In the great wisdom of the Navy, they wrote out a "cancellation of enlistment," a type of discharge not used since the Civil War. I was released on 22 March 1945, four days after my 15th birthday. By this time I was 6-feet tall and weighed 200 pounds.

I went back to school for about three months, but I ended up punching out the gym teacher. The Veterans Administration in San Diego somehow sorted out the fact that I had both a Navy and a Marine serial number and got my records in order. I took the GED test and was told that my score was equivalent to a person with one and one-half years of college and that I could enroll in any school I wanted under the GI Bill, so I took up flying. I thought to myself that if I ever got into another war I didn't want to be on some beach pushing up the sand in front of me to stop the bullets as I had to do on Tarawa and Saipan.

I took flying lessons at Speer's Flying Service, El Cajon, California, and was a licensed pilot at age 16. However, nobody, not even the Veterans Administration, told me that I couldn't get a job flying until I was 25 because I couldn't get insurance until then.

When I was 17, I joined the Army, was sent to Fort Ord, California, and served for three and one-half years. I went through leadership school, which was equivalent to another boot camp, then was assigned to the military police and the Criminal Investigation Detachment (CID). In 1950, I was discharged from the Army and went back to school in San Diego.

When the Korean war broke out, the Marines offered to make me a tank commander, but by then I had 2000 hours flying time, so in mid-1950, I joined the Air Force. After serving as a pilot-observer on a B-36 for a time, I volunteered to fly single-engine aircraft in Korea. I arrived in Korea in November 1951. My first assignment was as a forward-observer with a Republic of Korea infantry regiment directing close air support strikes. We were supposed to learn what was going on, on the ground, before flying support missions. I was wounded while on this assignment. After I was assigned to a P-51 squadron, I flew close support missions and also went looking for tanks and trains in North Korea. My P-51 was damaged by enemy fire on one flight, and I had to ditch in the Sea of Japan. I lost another aircraft because of equipment malfunction. I was wounded twice while on flying status.

I returned from Korea in 1953 and was released from active duty as a captain. I stayed in the active reserves until 1956, then reverted to inactive status and later retired as a major.

Jack Theoldore was awarded a Silver Star for heroism on Tarawa when he was 13 years old and a Bronze Star for heroism on Saipan when he was 14 years old. He was wounded once on Tarawa, twice on Saipan, and received three Purple Hearts. When he was with the Air Force in Korea, he was awarded a Distinguished Flying Cross, an Air Medal, and three more Purple Hearts. After his release from the Air Force in 1953, he managed an automotive service station at the Marine Corps Base, San Diego, for three years. Later, he was executive vice-president of Don Davis Enterprises on the Navajo Reservation in Arizona. He set up the first automobile dealership on the reservation and was instrumental in locating a five-acre mall at Tuba City, Arizona. In 1980, he returned to San Diego where he worked for the Electronics Division of General Dynamics, building test equipment for the F-16 fighter. He retired in 1991. Jack and his wife Margaret live in Spring Valley, California. They have four sons, thirteen grandchildren, and one great-grandson.

Elsie Sexton

Age 16 – Women's Auxiliary Army Corps
Age 16 – United States Army (WAC)

I don't remember what motivated me to join the Women's Auxiliary Army Corps (WAAC) at age 16, but I clearly remember going to the Army recruiting office in Portland, Oregon, and having papers thrust at me and being told, "Sign here." The WAAC had been formed less than a year before, and they were looking for bodies. I told them I was 22 years old, and they never questioned me about it.

> *Bob Hope came to entertain the troops. ... I was selected to dance with Bob – what a thrill!*

I was sworn into the WAAC in April 1943 and was sent to Fort Oglethorpe, Georgia, for basic training. The Women's Army Corps was formed on 1 July 1943, allowing us to become members of the regular Army. General Eisenhower came to Fort Oglethorpe, told us we were doing a great job, and asked everyone to "go regular Army." Of course, I did.

I remained at Fort Oglethorpe for a time. I was promoted to corporal and assigned to train new recruits. In June 1944, I was transferred to Camp Carson, Colorado.

Bob Hope came to entertain the troops while I was at Camp Carson. There were two of us female soldiers in the theater. I was selected to dance with Bob – what a thrill!

There were 200 female soldiers at Carson at that time, along with three infantry divisions of males, plus a pack-mule outfit and limited-service personnel. Our mess sergeant dated the military police mess sergeant, so we got a lot of their food. We could have one guest a week for food, so there was always a long list of males wanting to eat with us.

I worked in supply and was in charge of warehouses for officers' field equipment, footwear, and weapons. I had the rank of specialist, the same grade as buck sergeant. We had German POWs working for us, but they were not allowed in the weapons warehouse.

When a unit was to be transferred, it was always a big secret, and we were busy before and after. Before, we were busy issuing items, and afterward, we had to remain at our job site so we would not give any hint that there had been a transfer.

My company commander at Fort Carson knew that I was underage. She told me that she wouldn't say anything if I didn't cause any trouble. My mother also knew that I had enlisted underage, but she didn't say anything because she thought I was safe as long as I was in the States. When I received orders to go to Europe, she immediately took steps to have me brought home. My brother had been severely injured in Europe during the war, and she was not going to let me leave the States.

I was discharged at Camp Beale, California, in December 1945 at age 19.

I had dropped out of high school to enlist, but I was able to complete my studies by going to school at night. The Army encouraged us to do so. I never had any trouble about my age while I was in the Army, and I would not trade my military service for anything. It was a great education for a country kid. I still "live military," but now it is more with the Air Force than with the Army since in Anchorage, the Air Force base is much larger than the Army base.

Elsie Sexton married a professional soldier, and as most military families do, they moved frequently. Their longest stay at one location was twenty-one months at Fort Riley, Kansas. After serving more than twenty years in the Army, her husband was killed while on duty in Alaska. Elsie decided to make Alaska her home and has lived in Anchorage since that time. She works with the homeless, dabbles in politics, bowls, belongs to a singles club, and manages her own business. She has six children, five grandchildren, and two great-grandchildren. Elsie is the Alaska State Commander of the Veterans of Underage Military Service.

John E. Peck

Age 16 – United States Army

In 1942, at the age of 15, I wanted to serve my country so badly that I doctored my birth certificate to show that I was 17. I proceeded to a Navy recruiting

I still did not know what I had volunteered for.

office, but when the recruiter saw what a lousy job I had done trying to alter the certificate, he just laughed and told me to come back when I was really 17.

In the meantime, I went to work in a glass factory in my hometown of Arnold, Pennsylvania. The man working next to me mentioned that he had turned 18 and had to sign up for the draft. That night a light bulb lit up in my head. I simply assumed the status of being born on 18 December 1924 instead of my real birth date of 18 December 1926. Shortly after my birthday, I went to the local draft board and told them I had to sign up for the draft because I was 18 years old. No questions were asked, nor was proof of age required, so I became an 18-year-old.

I waited until February 1943, then I went to the draft board and told them that I wanted to go with the first group of 18-year-olds. Again, no questions were asked, and no proof of age was required. In March 1943, I took my physical and was classified 1A.

I started my Army career on 23 April 1943. I was sent to Fort Meade, Maryland, for a week and from there to Camp Wheeler, Georgia, for infantry basic training. The rifles we were issued were 1903 bolt-action Springfields. Since I was left-handed, I had trouble with the bolt action, so they transferred me to a heavy machine-gun battalion. After basic, I was sent to Fort Meade, Maryland, as a truck driver for an MP company, a job I disliked very much. One day I noticed a bulletin asking for volunteers for a dangerous mission. I immediately signed up, was reassigned, and was sent to Newport

News, Virginia, for shipment overseas. I still did not know what I had volunteered for.

We left Newport News and went around the Horn of Africa headed towards India. Only a few Army personnel went around the Horn during the war. We were scheduled to go through the Suez Canal, but we were rerouted around the Horn because a troopship that left the States just ahead of us had been sunk in the Mediterranean Sea. At least, that is what we were told. We stopped in Cape Town, South Africa, for fuel and supplies.

We arrived in Bombay on 1 May 1944, went by train to Ramgarh, then flew to an airstrip near Myitkyina, Burma. I was assigned as a heavy machine gunner with the 2nd Battalion of Merrill's Marauders. This was the first clue that I had about what I had signed up for. I didn't know it at the time, but the Allies' objective was to open the Burma Road so that supplies could be sent to China by land.

A few days after arriving in Burma, I found out why you don't swim in ponds there. I jumped in a pond and swam for awhile. When I got out, I noticed that I had about a dozen leeches on me. Needless to say, I went swimming only in fast-moving rivers after that.

During my first combat encounter, we were hit by a Japanese 150mm cannon shell. I wasn't wounded, but I was completely deaf for several days, and I am hard-of-hearing to this day. In the last days before Myitkyina fell, we were set up on the north road leading into the town. We came under sniper fire. My first gunner was hit in the head, and I was hit in the hand and legs. My wounds were not serious enough for me to be evacuated, so I stayed with my gun until we captured Myitkyina on 3 August 1944.

I was evacuated to the 44th Field Hospital to have the wounds in my hand and legs cared for. It had been so long since I had been wounded that I was diagnosed as having jungle rot. Consequently, I never received the Purple Heart that I thought I deserved.

I remained in the hospital about thirty days and then returned to my company in time to start our next mission, which was south to Bhamo. After Bhamo, we moved on to Tonkwa and finally to the Mong Wi Valley. We covered nearly 600 miles, walking and fighting all the way.

After we took Mong Wi, the Burma Road was secured and our mission was completed. We were sent to Kunming, China, for reassignment. Since there was no American infantry in China, we were assigned to a transportation outfit and took supplies to Chinese troops in the interior.

When the war ended, I had enough points to be rotated home. I went to Calcutta, India, then to Seattle, Washington, ending up at Camp Atterbury, Indiana, where I was discharged from the Army on 22 December 1945. After nearly two years without seeing my family, I arrived home on 25 December 1945. I believe that was the best Christmas present my mother ever received.

John Peck earned the Combat Infantryman Badge, the Bronze Star, and a Presidential Unit Citation (PUC) during combat in Burma. The Bronze Star and PUC were awarded to all of Merrill's Marauders for service above and beyond the call of duty. He was wounded in action, but never received a Purple Heart. After his discharge from the Army, John returned to Arnold, Pennsylvania, where he drove busses and 18-wheel tractor-trailers. In 1964, he moved to Texas and worked for International Harvester Company for several years, then worked as a rigger for the Army Overhaul Depot, also called the Army Helicopter Depot, which was located at the Naval Air Station, Corpus Christi, Texas. He received a medical retirement in 1976. John's wife died in 1982. He has four children and eight living grandchildren and one deceased. John lives in Bastrop, Texas.

Thomas T. Lowery

Age 15 – United States Navy

I was born at Atmore, Alabama, on leap-year day, 29 February 1928, the third youngest of four boys. My father, a veteran of World War I, died in 1940. Two of my brothers joined the Navy shortly after World War II started. I

> ... at age 16, I was in charge of men much older than I was. One man was older than my father!

wasn't doing very well in school, and I wanted to join the Navy also. The recruiter knew that I was underage, but he never questioned me when I told him I was 17. I think my mother had talked to him and asked him to let me enlist. She thought that I would be better off in the Navy with three meals a day and a place to sleep, which was better than the life I was leading.

I was sworn into the Navy on 12 May 1943 at Birmingham, Alabama. I was sent to Building 25, Naval Air Station, Pensacola, Florida for a haircut and a Navy uniform. From there it was to boot camp at "Bloody" Barin Field, Foley, Alabama. After graduating from boot camp, I went to NAS Pensacola and was assigned to PBY Squadron 8-A, Hangar 632. Then I was sent to Patrol Plane Mechanics School, NAS Pensacola, after I had spent some time with the beach crew and the tractor crew. Upon my completion of that school, I was promoted to aviation machinist's mate third class and assigned to a PBY flight crew as flight engineer and plane captain. As a plane captain at age 16, I was in charge of men much older than I was. One man was older than my father!

Squadron 8-A had dual missions: training PBY pilots, both American and foreign, and patrolling the Gulf of Mexico and the Caribbean Sea for German submarines. Our patrol planes were loaded for bear with depth charges, bombs, two 50-caliber machine guns in the blisters, twin 30-caliber guns in the nose, and one 30-caliber gun in the tail hatch. We would rendezvous with ship convoys, refuel at a seaplane base, and rendezvous again with the convoy on the way back to Pensacola. I racked up many training and patrol flight hours during those years, in good, bad, and ugly weather. I survived two plane crashes at sea. One was a dead-stick landing, and in the other, the plane dove into the ocean from 200 feet and sheared the wings off. Fortunately, the entire crew survived both crashes. I flew with some of the best and some of the worst pilots in the world.

I was an aviation machinist's mate second class at the time I was discharged from the Navy on 16 May 1946 at Lake Pontchartrain Navy Base, New Orleans, Louisiana. I returned to Atmore, Alabama, and joined Battery D, 711th Antiaircraft Artillery Battalion, Alabama National Guard. We were activated for duty with the 3rd Army on 4 September 1950. We were sent to an area near Detroit, Michigan, where we set up our antiaircraft battery. I was a sergeant with the radar unit for the guns. We were the backup for the DEW (distant early warning) line across Canada.

I was sent to a school at Fort Bliss, Texas, to learn to operate a new radar unit for missile guidance. We used 90mm antiaircraft guns instead of missiles at that time. When I returned to the Detroit area, I spent a lot of time teaching others about the new systems. I was discharged from the Army on 31 August 1952 at Fort Rucker, Alabama.

Tom Lowery returned to high school after his discharge from the Navy. He played high school football until the season was over, then took the GED tests and enrolled at the University of Auburn for a year on the GI Bill. He later went to electronics school and also completed many technical courses. He was employed by the Department of Defense as an aircraft electronics-systems instructor at the Naval Air Rework Facility, NAS Pensacola. His work area at the time he retired on 31 June 1973 was Hangar 632, the same hangar used by his squadron while he was in the Navy. After leaving the civil service, Tom was involved with a number of enterprises. He was a carpenter, a real-estate agent, and a charter-boat operator. He was the special-effects captain during the filming of the movie "Jaws II" in Pensacola. He had bit parts in two movies filmed in California, a diver in one and a tugboat captain in the other. Tom lives in Pensacola Beach, Florida. He has four sons, seven grandchildren, and two great-grandchildren.

Bob Stump

Age 16 – United States Navy

I was born in the Tolleson area west of Phoenix, Arizona, on 4 April 1927. Most of the guys that I ran around with during my sophomore year in high school were seniors. The seniors who

> *... I didn't want to spend the war in the dispensary at Ford Island.*

were older than 18 were deferred until they graduated, and then most were drafted. I decided to go with them. I boosted my age a year, talked my dad into signing the enlistment papers, and was sworn into the Navy on 14 June 1943.

After boot camp at the Navy Training Center, San Diego, California, I was assigned to the dispensary at the U. S. Naval Air Station, Ford Island, Pearl Harbor, Hawaii, and became a pharmacist's mate striker (apprentice). I tried to get transferred to sea duty because I didn't want to spend the war in the dispensary at Ford Island.

My first attempt at a transfer was to the escort-carrier USS *Ommanney Bay*, but it was unsuccessful. My second attempt, aided by Dr. Robert B. Blomberg, was successful. I was assigned to the USS *Tulagi* (CVE-72) as a pharmacist's mate in November 1944. The USS *Tulagi* was involved in the invasions of Luzon in the Philippines, Iwo Jima, and Okinawa. During the invasion of Luzon, I watched from the *Tulagi* as the *Ommanney Bay* sank after being hit by a Japanese suicide plane.

We returned to San Diego in July 1945, and I was transferred to the Los Alamitos Naval Air Station, Long Beach, California. I joined the crew of the USS *Lunga Point* (CVE-94) on 30 November 1945. While I was on the *Lunga Point*, we made two trips to the Pacific to help bring our troops home. In February 1946, we took the *Lunga Point* to Tacoma, Washington, for decommissioning.

I was discharged from the Navy in March 1946. My Navy service was among the most important experiences in my life.

Bob Stump completed his high school education after his discharge from the Navy and attended Arizona State University, graduating in 1951 with a degree in agriculture. A lifelong cotton farmer, Bob devoted all his time to farming until 1956 when he was elected to the Arizona State Legislature where he served for eighteen years. Bob was elected to the U. S. House of Representatives in November 1975. In January 1976, he was sworn in as a Congressman from Arizona's Third Congressional District, and has served in that office continuously since then. In 1994, Bob became Chairman of the House Veterans Affairs Committee and the Vice-Chairman of the House Armed Services Committee. He resides in Tolleson, Arizona, and in Washington, D.C., when Congress is in session. Bob has three children and five grandchildren.

Cornelius F. "Neal" Murray

Age 16 – United States Navy

I was born in Cresskill, New Jersey, on 9 June 1927, the youngest of three boys. We were blessed with a sister, Jane, in 1933. She and our mother were our spiritual anchors during World War II. Dad worked at the Brooklyn Navy Yard. My oldest brother Harold was a flight engineer and gunner on a B-24 bomber. In August 1943, he was forced to bail out of his aircraft after bombing the Ploesti oil fields in Romania and became a prisoner of war. My next oldest brother, Vincent, was a career Navy aviation machinist's mate and served aboard several aircraft carriers.

> ... "Neal, BuPers ... informs me that they don't make mistakes. Get used to being MoMM 2/c."

I didn't want to be left out of the war, nor did my buddy, Joe Decker. Joe and I had been to the Navy recruiting offices at 90 Church Street, New York City, and to one in Paterson, New Jersey, so many times that we were banned from them. We kept returning to the offices hoping we would find a crew on duty different from the one that had refused us the previous time. We could not find a fool-proof method of doctoring our birth certificates, but the challenge to outwit the bureaucracy was still on. Joe opted to use his older brother's name and identification papers, successfully enlisted, and went on to serve on a battleship. I decided to get drafted.

My given name, Cornelius, was reduced to "Neal" early on, mainly to avoid the nickname "Corny." On 8 March 1943, three months before my sixteenth birthday, I went to the draft board and registered as Neal F. Murray. I had hoped not to call attention to myself in order not to be noticed as being too young, but when I was asked my birth date and I replied, "Today," the elderly matron registering me called out to everyone in the hall, "Imagine, he came in on his birthday!" Everyone applauded, then went about their business, thank God.

My parents saw the draft card come in the mail, and later, the notice to report for a physical. But since they were of the "let nature take its course" persuasion, they said not a word, at least not to me!

I reported for my physical, and everything went well until the final step, an interview with a psychologist. Somehow, he seemed to know that "Neal" really meant "Cornelius," my school transcript was on the desk in front of him, and that I was trying to get in underage. However, he could see that I was very anxious to get into the military, so he didn't make an issue of it.

Dozens of draftees were lined up in three rows in a large room as the final process began. At the head of each line was a desk. At one desk sat a Navy recruiter, at the next one a Marine, and at the third one an Army sergeant. As I moved forward in line, I could hear them call out the branch of service each draftee was assigned. As I got closer, I could tell that the recruiters would just look at the person in front of them and assign that person to whatever branch they thought he would best fit. Being in the line in front of the Navy recruiter didn't guarantee that you were going to be assigned to the Navy. I started to count how many were sent to each branch, but I couldn't figure out if there was a system. I hopped from one line to the other, hoping to end up being chosen for the Navy. I ended up in front of the Marine — but I didn't want to be a Marine! He looked at my 6-foot, 150-pound chicken-chested frame, smiled and said, "Step up, sailor, you're in the Navy."

I was sworn into the Navy on 1 July 1943 and was in Boot Company 414, U. S. Naval Training Center, Newport, Rhode Island, the following week. In September, I attended the U. S. Navy Diesel School in Richmond, Virginia, and graduated from the course with the rating of fireman second class, three red stripes on the cuff. I was assigned to the training staff, LCT-5 (landing craft, tanks), Flotilla #1, at the Amphibious Training Base, Solomons, Maryland.

While I was on the training staff, I was encouraged to take the exam for MoMM 3/c (motor machinist's mate third class), a new rating that superseded fireman first class. I took the exam with a group of several dozen sailors. While filling out the fact sheet for the exam, I came upon a space marked "Rating for which this exam is being taken." I entered MoMM 2/c, one grade higher than I was supposed to.

After taking the exam, I was assigned to monitor an "engine breakdown" cruise on an LCT into Chesapeake Bay. Several days later, when I returned to base, it was payday. I checked for my name on the pay list and discovered my rating was now MoMM 2/c. I was paid at the new rate, but I waited a week or so before reporting the error. Several weeks later, my engineering officer sent for me. He said, "Neal, BuPers (Bureau of Personnel) in D.C. informs me that they don't make mistakes. Get used to being MoMM 2/c. Congratulations, and study hard to catch up." Skipping a stripe was only the forerunner of dozens of events to come that appeared purely serendipitous to me.

Duty with the training staff was as slow and methodical as high school had been. I had dropped out of high school because of that, and now I was not the young warrior that I wanted to be when I enlisted. I was ready to drop out again, so I wrote a panic note to my parents saying, "Get me out of here!" The note was ignored because "nature was taking its course!"

Against the advice of well-meaning officers, I asked for a transfer to an LCT crew. I was assigned to the Amphibious Training Base, Camp Bradford, Naval Operating Base, Norfolk, Virginia. For a very short time, I trained with the crew of the USS *LCT-505*, making ship-to-shore transits and landings at Virginia Beach. The Amphibious Training Command of the U. S. Atlantic Fleet had one mission: to hit the beaches with the men and materials needed to assure victory.

In December 1943, our crew of twelve left Norfolk by train for Vallejo, California. Our skipper, Ensign Donald E. Georger, was in my opinion, the best damned LCT skipper in the world. After a brief stay at the Navy Yard, Mare Island, we became plank owners of the USS *LCT-962*, which we commissioned at Oakland, California. Our skipper berthed the ship close to the Ferry Slip at the foot of Market Street, San Francisco. He began a practice of keeping us isolated from any other Navy authority. Liberty was free for the asking as the ship was being made ready by specialists. When the *LCT-962* was ready to be put into service, it was separated into three pieces and loaded onto a Liberty merchant ship. We off-loaded at Pearl Harbor, put all the pieces together, berthed in West Loch (a water arm of Pearl Harbor), and waited to form up in convoy.

While waiting at Pearl, we experienced the horrors of war before actually entering a war theater. Six LSTs (landing ship, tank) tied up side by side were being loaded with ammunition. A tremendous explosion ensued and all six were sunk with the loss of many lives. Our skipper's caution in keeping us isolated paid off and saved us from damage.

The USS *LCT-962* was finally loaded onto the open deck of an LST that became one of a convoy of 600 Fifth Fleet ships labelled "Operation Forager." It included 127,000 assault troops, 30,000 garrison troops, more that 1000 carrier-based and U. S. 7th Air Force aircraft.

Normandy was not the only invasion that took place in June of 1944. About 14,000 miles from Normandy at 215° West longitude, lie the Mariana Islands, where another invasion took place that month. Task Force 58, commanded by Admiral Marc A. Mitscher, began shelling Saipan and its sister island, Tinian, on 12 June 1944. On 15 June when air supremacy was attained and the invasion beaches were softened-up by battleship and cruiser bombardment, the assault landings began. Our LCT was launched from the LST off the Saipan coast early in the morning of 15 June. Along with many other landing craft, we took troops, tanks, artillery, and all manner of rolling stock and supplies to the beaches in support of the assault Marines.

Task Force 58 was protecting our western flank. Four days after the landings on Saipan began, fifteen U. S. carriers, seven battleships, twenty-one cruisers, and sixty-nine destroyers faced a Japanese task force composed of nine carriers, five battleships, and more cruisers than the U. S. fleet had. In the ensuing battle, over 390 Japanese aircraft were destroyed, three carriers were sunk, and four others damaged. U. S. submarines accounted for three of the carriers. The battle became known as the "Great Marianas Turkey Shoot."

D-day on Guam was 20 July 1944. We landed troops and supplies, then headed back to Saipan to participate in the Tinian landings on 24 July. We continued to supply the island forces for over a year and were at Tinian in 1945 to watch the *Enola Gay* take off with the first A-bomb.

Meanwhile, Navy Seabees and Army engineers built deep-water piers that permitted ocean-going cargo ships to unload directly, without the need for LCTs. During a lull in our activity, we asked our skipper to beach the ship when we saw several dozen women and children on a Guam hillside. He complied, and we distributed civilian clothing we had all chipped in to buy on our liberties in Honolulu over a year before. It took some persuasion to overcome their fear. The women were delighted with the gifts, and the kids couldn't stop giggling!

One by one, each of the crew was replaced and sent Stateside. I was finally sent to an outgoing unit camp on a Saipan hill. There I was told to look for my name and the name of a ship that would take me home on a list that was posted daily on a tree. Two weeks of fruitless looking had me thinking I would be there forever. Below in the harbor I saw a big, beautiful aircraft carrier. Scuttlebutt said she was the *Bon Homme Richard* and she was part of the so-called Magic Carpet Fleet that was carrying troops home to their loved ones. I took my seabag and joined others going to the carrier. A water taxi took us to a cargo net hung from the hangar deck, so we climbed, seabag and all, up the net. An officer with a clipboard couldn't find my name on his list, so he simply wrote in my name, rate, and serial number at the end, muttering to himself about administrative inefficiency. The *Bon Homme Richard* hosted my first really grand Thanksgiving dinner. We had much to be thankful for.

I was discharged from the Navy at Lido Beach, Long Island, New York, on 3 March 1946. I was handed my DD-214 and told to look it over to see if everything was correct. All the service ribbons and other data were correct, but it had not been noted that I rated the newly created Amphibious insignia. I asked to have it added, but I was brushed off.  Several other sailors in the group rated the insignia also, so we went on a sit-down strike. We were not going to leave the office until the clerks made the corrections. They did.

Neal Murray returned to Cresskill, New Jersey, and worked in a grocery store for a time. Later he went to work for the U. S. Postal Service and remained with that agency for thirty-six years. Neal and his wife Grace live in Bergenfield, New Jersey. They have nine children and twenty-one grandchildren.

Beaufort Hartley

Age 16 – United States Navy

It all started when the principal of the all-male school I attended decided that I needed a few whacks on my backside to gain my undivided attention. So I made a hasty decision to forego the spanking and leave school. The school was Lanier High in Macon, Georgia, where ROTC was not elective, but mandatory.

I would bring this dastardly war to an end in short order – if I were only allowed to enlist.

I enjoyed the military atmosphere of ROTC, so at 5'1" tall and 100 pounds, I thought I would put my talents to work in the U. S. Navy. I changed the date on my birth certificate, ate what must have been 100 pounds of bananas, and presented my manly frame to the recruiter. I had just turned 15 years old and had no pubic hair. Unlike the recruiters where Calvin Graham enlisted, the recruiter in Macon was very nice to me, and I might say, sympathetic to my patriotic urge. However, he was emphatic in denying my enlistment.

Then I presented my fake birth certificate to the National Youth Administration, where they promptly sent me to a welding school in Augusta, Georgia, and paid me $10.00 per month, plus room and board and the promise of a job. After completing the school and passing a welding test, I was employed at the Southeastern Shipyards in Savannah, Georgia, earning 99¢ an hour. I had never heard of such money! I worked there until I reached age 16.

Remembering my botched attempt at changing the date on my birth certificate, I tried again. I will never believe that I fooled the recruiter. I still didn't have pubic hair, but apparently I was the only new recruit with ROTC training and therefore knew my right foot from my left. I had won — they accepted me with the proviso that my father sign for me. Now, my father was a macho veteran of service on the Mexican border in 1916 and of service in France during World War I. He was a Siberian[22] during the Russian Revolution and a recently discharged B-17 tail gunner during World War II. I knew gaining his approval would be no easy task.

I used reverse psychology. I began by bragging how tough I would be — if only I were in the service. I would bring this dastardly war to an end in short order — if I were only allowed to enlist. I would probably outshine his exploits in the war — if only I could enlist. Finally, his ego bruised by this little upstart, he exclaimed, "If they would take you — ha, ha, I would surely give it my blessing." I had my enlistment papers in my pocket and immediately whipped them out and handed them to him. With a very unforgettable, blank expression on his face, he signed. I had beat the old master sergeant!

I was sworn into the Navy on 14 July 1943 and was sent to the Naval Air Station, Pensacola, Florida, where I was assigned to Company 17 for three weeks of boot training. I thought, "No sweat, no fear — three weeks and I'm outta here." My first duty station was at the Naval Auxiliary Air Station, Whiting Field, Milton, Florida. While I was there I flew with the plane carrying the yard mail to Saufley, Barin, Cory, Ellison, Bronson, and several other Naval air stations. I was accepted for Class-A aviation radioman school and left for the Naval Aviation Technical Training Center, Jacksonville, Florida.

After just five days of radio school, I was told that my voice was too wheezy to understand on the radio. Actually, I think my voice was just changing. I was reassigned to a "new construction," a newly commissioned ship, the USS *Shaula* (AK-118). We pulled into Portsmouth, Virginia, on our first cruise, and tied up behind the USS *Card* (CVE-11), which had just been awarded the Presidential Unit Citation for antisubmarine warfare. My brother was on board the *Card*, and we were able to visit. It was the last time I would see him until well after the war was over. He was, and still is, the apple of my eye.

We went through the Panama Canal. After a wild liberty in Colon, Panama — mercy, did I grow up fast! Then it was on to Hawaii, Eniwetok, Manus in the Admiralties, Leyte, Guam, Ulithi, Okinawa,

---

[22] During the Russian Revolution, U. S. forces were stationed in Vladivostok to guard Bolshevik prisoners. The troops were called "Siberians."

and finally, the occupation of Japan. By this time I was a 40-year-old man in an 18-year-old body. But, I was a proud old man! I was discharged on 3 March 1946.

Looking back, I think the reason my brother and I joined the Navy instead of the Army was that, when we were boys, our father would threaten us by saying, "I will be your commanding officer some day!" He was a master sergeant, but we thought that he was a general, and we didn't want him as our commanding officer.

Would I do it again? Damn right, I would! God bless the United States of America and all those who served.

Beau Hartley earned three battle stars on his Asiatic Pacific ribbon and received both the German Occupation Medal and the Japanese Occupation Medal. Fifteen years after his discharge from the Navy, he graduated from Sheffield High School, Sheffield, Alabama. He continued his education with correspondence courses in industrial management. Beau began working on construction of nuclear power plants soon after leaving the Navy. He was injured while he was working as head foreman at the Brown's Ferry Nuclear Power Plant, Athens, Alabama, which caused him to retire in 1977. After he recovered, he worked as a security guard at a bank, mostly to keep busy. During a holdup of the bank, Beau was involved in a shoot-out with the robber and was wounded in the foot. He finally retired for good in 1988. He was a forty-five year member of Local 760 of the Steamfitters Union and served as its president for a term. Gail, Beau's wife of thirty-nine years, died in June 1996. Beau lives in Killen, Alabama.

Robert N. Quinn

Age 15 – California State Guard
Age 16 – United States Navy

Ordinarily, on a January morning in 1942, I would be sitting in a classroom at Byrd High School in Shreveport, Louisiana. Instead, I was sitting in a boxcar, huddled with my arms around my legs trying to keep warm.

> *So there I was, sitting in an empty boxcar, cold and hungry.*

Just a week before, I had gone to the Marine recruiting office in Shreveport to enlist. I told the recruiters that I was 17 and filled out all the application papers. When I presented the papers to my parents for their signatures, they refused to sign. I threatened to run away, but they were adamant. The next morning on the way to school, I forged my father's signature on the papers and asked a girl on the school bus to forge my mother's name. I took the papers to the recruiting office and they told me they would check them over and call me. After a week the Marines hadn't called, so I ran away from home.

So there I was, sitting in an empty boxcar, cold and hungry. It was too late to change my mind. I got off the train in Port Arthur, Texas, where I set pins in a bowling alley to get money for food. After a short stay in Port Arthur, I hitchhiked to Los Angeles, California. Again, pin-setting at the Sunset Bowling Alley on Sunset Boulevard provided money for food. I had to do more than set pins, so I joined the California State Guard. They accepted my statement that I was 17 without bothering to check. I was assigned as a guard at the water reservoirs near Los Angeles. Later, I was transferred to San Francisco where I served as a guard on the San Francisco Bay Bridge.

I left the Guard in November 1942 and hitchhiked to New York where I worked for a short time as a busboy in Joe's Italian Restaurant, a popular eatery in Brooklyn. I had been gone more than a year when I returned home. They told me that just after I had left the year before, the Marines had called and told them that I was accepted and I was to report in. By this time I didn't want to be a Marine, I wanted to be in the Navy. My parents were as adamant as ever when I told them that I wanted to join the Navy. When they refused to sign my enlistment papers again, I packed my suitcase and prepared to leave. Reluctantly, they signed the necessary papers attesting that I was 17. By letting me join, they would at least know where I was. I was sworn into the Navy on 23 July 1943.

After boot camp at the San Diego Naval Training Station, I was assigned to Landing Craft Unit #32 and trained as a coxswain on amphibious landing craft at San Diego's Silver Strand. At the completion of our training, our unit left for the South Pacific. We went to Espíritu Santo in the New Hebrides Islands and then to Guadalcanal in the Solomon Islands.

In late spring of 1944, our unit boarded the USS *George Clymer* (APA-27) at Guadalcanal and sailed to Kwajalein in the Marshall Islands to prepare for the invasion of Saipan. On 14 June 1944, we were off the west coast of Saipan in the Mariana Islands. The next morning, under heavy fire, we transported Marines to the beach. Four days later, the Japanese fleet was sighted heading for Saipan, causing our force of transports to depart for Eniwetok in the Marshall Islands where we remained until sailing again for the Marianas in July. Saipan had been secured, and the fleet had destroyed three Japanese aircraft carriers and shot down nearly 500 Japanese aircraft in what has been dubbed as the "Great Marianas Turkey Shoot."

We landed troops on the beaches of Guam on 21 July 1944, and the island was secured three weeks later. After the Guam operation, I transferred to the aircraft carrier USS *Salamaua* (CVE-96). In January 1945, the *Salamaua* took part in the Battle of Lingayen Gulf where she was hit by a kamikaze. We limped back to Guam for repairs.

We returned to Guam for repairs again in June 1945, a result of the typhoon that hit Okinawa on 5 June. After being repaired, the carrier was assigned hunter/killer duty in the China Sea between the west coast of the Philippine Islands and Formosa. We remained on this duty until getting word of the Japanese surrender after the atomic bombs were dropped on Hiroshima on 6 August and on Nagasaki on 9 August 1945.

We met the U. S. Army's Eighth Occupation Force near Manila and escorted them into Tokyo Bay on the morning of 1 September 1945. The next morning, we witnessed the signing of Japan's unconditional surrender aboard the USS *Missouri*.

I left the Navy on 28 March 1946, obtained a high school equivalency diploma by passing the GED tests, and went to work for Western Electric as an installer. In 1948, I reenlisted in the Navy for four years, serving three years at Guantanamo Bay, Cuba, and one year on Vice Admiral Badger's staff at 90 Church Street, New York City. I was discharged for the second time in June 1952.

Bob Quinn used knowledge gained from his work at Western Electric to install a rhombic antenna, switchboards, and teletypes at a remote location in Cuba. He received a commendation from the Navy for his expertise. After leaving the Navy for the second time in 1952, Bob joined a fledgling company by the name of International Business Machines (IBM). He didn't realize at the time that IBM really stood for "I've Been Moved." Bob started as a customer engineer in the Office Products Division of IBM in Shreveport, Louisiana, and was subsequently transferred to Houston, Texas. In 1958 he was promoted to branch manager of the Galveston office and later to the Beaumont office. In 1967 he was named branch manager of the downtown Los Angeles office. From LA he went to the New York office where he was manager of the Field Support Services. After that he managed the Miami, Florida, office until he requested to be transferred to the Fort Worth, Texas, office in 1973. While in Fort Worth, Bob was named his division's "Manager of the Year" in 1979 and 1980. He retired in Fort Worth after thirty-one years with IBM. He and his wife Joanne now live in a resort area named April Sound on the banks of Lake Conroe in Montgomery, Texas. Bob and Joanne have three children and three grandchildren.

Harold B. Johnson

Age 16 – United States Navy

My sixteenth birthday was 19 March 1943, and four months later I joined the Navy at Elizabeth City, North Carolina. I was sworn in at Raleigh, North Carolina, on 28 July 1943. Although I was only 16, my father signed my enlistment papers

> *... a German V-1 flying bomb hit both ships, killing a large number of officers and crew.*

certifying that I was 17. My mother was mad at him from that day until I was discharged three years later.

My Navy career really got off to a flying start. The first night after I was sworn in at Raleigh, as I was getting ready for bed, I put my wallet under my pillow, as my mother had instructed me to do before I left home. I went to the train station the next morning heading for boot camp, but my wallet stayed behind under the pillow where I had forgotten it. During boot camp at Bainbridge, Maryland, I had no money, no Social Security card, nothing. My drill instructor at boot camp was named Tom Mix, but he wasn't the cowboy movie star.

After boot camp, I was sent to Solomons, Maryland, for naval amphibious training. From there we went to Evansville, Indiana, to pick up the amphibious landing ship USS *LST 493*. Our ship was commissioned in December 1943, and we sailed down the Mississippi River to New Orleans, where guns and armaments were installed on it. After loading supplies aboard, we sailed for a shakedown cruise in the Caribbean Sea. We then sailed up the East Coast and docked in New York where we loaded an LCT, a smaller landing craft, on the main deck and stored various war materials on the tank deck. In February 1944, we sailed into the North Atlantic headed for Great Britain.

It took our convoy about sixteen days to make the trip to Great Britain. The North Atlantic is a rough place during the winter. We unloaded the LCT in the Clyde River and proceeded up-river to Glasgow, Scotland, where we unloaded the other material. We then traveled down the Irish Sea to the southern English port of Falmouth where we conducted training and beaching maneuvers with the Army for the upcoming invasion of France.

On 4 June 1944, we loaded Army trucks and tanks and prepared for the invasion scheduled for 5 June. The invasion was rescheduled for 6 June because of bad weather. On the morning of the 6th, the Normandy coast of France was a mass of ships and boats of every size and description. The battleships, cruisers, and destroyers were firing at targets on the beach as well as inland as the assault troops headed for the beach. Sunken ships and equipment littered the water, and the beach was a place of chaos and death. While unloading troops on the beach, several of our sister ships (LSTs) were hit by German coastal artillery guns. Other LSTs were sunk by mines and by German E boats (motor torpedo boats.) Our ship made it through that day without damage or casualties. It was later that our luck ran out.

On 28 June 1944, while beaching on the coast of France with a load of Army troops and tanks, our ship hit a submerged object that ripped a gash in the bottom of the ship. Both engine rooms were flooded, causing the ship to sink. Since we were near the shoreline, the ship was not submerged. A British salvage crew came aboard and secured a temporary patch over the hole in a few days,. The *LST 425* towed the *LST 493* back to a London dry dock for repairs and engine overhauls.

In London we were tied up at the dock next to the *LST 312* and the *LST 384*. On the night of 8 July 1944, a German V-1 flying bomb hit both ships, killing a large number of officers and crew. The blast caused a tremendous concussion on our ship and started fires all over the place. Again, we were lucky and our ship was not seriously damaged.

Later, on a trip from England to France, Army tank drivers did not show up as scheduled to unload the tanks from our ship at Le Havre. In place of the soldiers, sailors crawled into the machines, pushed buttons and pulled levers, and presently the tanks were roaring ashore, each with a white-hatted sailor's head bobbing happily out of the cockpit as they exited the ship's bow doors.

Other trips were made up the Seine River to Rouen, France, with Army trucks and tanks. During the Army siege of the Brest

Peninsula, we went through the Bay of Biscay, passed the Channel Islands, and on to St. Michel En Greves in Brittany with a load of heavy artillery ammunition for the Army.

About this time, my mother made up for her suggestion of putting my wallet under my pillow. She put a bottle of Coca Cola in the middle of a cake and mailed it to me. This was a "no-no" because glass containers were not supposed to be mailed. It was the first coke I had in over a year and it was really good, even if it was hot!

In the early morning hours of 12 April 1945, we lost our ship. I was the helmsman on duty in the wheelhouse as we approached the outer harbor at Plymouth, England. It was stormy and the seas were rough. A long breakwater stretched across the entrance to the outer harbor with only a small area for ships to pass through. The breakwater was about five miles from our intended anchorage in the inner harbor. Shortly before we reached the small passage through the breakwater, our radar stopped working. Because of a navigational error, we rammed into the big rocks on the seaward side of the breakwater at 4:41 a.m. The navigation officer tried to back the ship off the rocks, but with very rough seas and a punctured hull, it proved to be impossible. The ship broached and started to pound violently against the rocks. As the waves began washing over the main deck it became impossible to stand up without holding on to a life line or some part of the ship's superstructure. The tank deck was flooded as was the auxiliary steering room, the crew's quarters, and the engine rooms. The ballast, fuel oil, and water tanks were punctured and flooded. The ship had to be abandoned and was salvaged later. Although no lives were lost, it was a frightening experience.

Some of the crew, including me, stayed at Shapters Field, a U. S. Navy Amphibious Supply Base at Plymouth, England, for about two months while a court of inquiry was held. On the same day that we lost our ship, President Roosevelt died.

In June 1945, after the war in Europe was over, we were flown to Bremen, Germany, by the 8th U. S. Air Force. We stayed at a German submarine training school barracks for about two weeks, then we were taken to Bremerhaven, Germany, to be part of the crew on the recently captured German luxury liner *Europa*. At that time, the *Europa* was the third largest ship in the world next to England's *Queen Mary* and *Queen Elizabeth*. It was the largest naval prize of the war ever taken by the United States.

We stayed at a German shipyard in Bremerhaven during the summer of 1945 while the ship was being converted to the U. S. Navy Troop Transport *Europa*. At first, there were only about one hundred U. S. Navy personnel on the ship, along with all of the ship's original German crew. Their crew's quarters were located in the bow section of the ship, while our quarters were in the stern section. The German crew stayed aboard throughout the summer of 1945.

While on the ship in Bremerhaven, I became acquainted with a member of the original German crew who spoke English. I went on liberty with him a number of times. We went to his parents' home and toured different parts of the city. Most of the city was in ruins because of the massive bombing it had received. In September, we were scheduled to sail for Southhampton, England. Most of the German crew was to stay in Germany. Just before the ship departed from Bremerhaven, my friend who was leaving the ship handed me several letters written by his mother and sisters addressed to his brother in Seacaucus, New Jersey. No mail had been allowed to leave Germany for the United States since 1939. I agreed to take the letters to his brother, but I didn't tell anyone about it because it was probably illegal at the time for me to take them. His brother and his family were overjoyed to get the letters. They told me that they didn't know if any family members in Germany had survived the war.

By the time we sailed for Southhampton, the Navy crew numbered over 1000. We loaded Army troops at Southhampton and departed for New York, arriving there five days later. A few of the original German crew, including the captain and the engineering officers, made the first voyage with us to show our crew how to operate the machinery, engines, etc. All operating instructions were in German. After the initial voyage, the USS *Europa* made many trips across the Atlantic, bringing back to New York up to 10,000 troops on each trip. I was a crew member on the *Europa* until my discharge at Camp Shelton, Norfolk, Virginia, in March 1946.

Harold Johnson started a long-distance trucking business after his discharge from the Navy. He operated a small fleet of 18-wheel tractor-trailers that went from coast to coast and to Mexico and Canada. A few years ago, Harold was hit by lightning as he was about to get into one of his trucks. The lightning bolt traveled down his left side, leaving a split under his left arm and exiting through his left foot. A section of the cement curbing that he was standing on was blown away leaving only pebbles, dust, and a big hole in the ground. Harold was thrown about twenty-five feet and knocked unconscious. When he came to in the hospital he couldn't move and had no feeling in his body. The doctors told him he would be totally paralyzed in his left side for the rest of his life and that his teeth would probably become brittle and fall out. None of these predictions came true. His feeling returned in about two weeks, and after the burns healed, he continued with his life. He retired in 1994 after forty-eight years in the trucking business. Harold's wife Rosa died of cancer in September 1980 at the age of fifty, and his youngest daughter Kimberly, age 18, died four months later. Harold has one living daughter and five grandchildren. He lives in Elizabeth City, North Carolina. Harold is the North Carolina State Vice-Commander of the Veterans of Underage Military Service.

√ **VUMS Note** ⇒ *"Great Marianas Turkey Shoot."* In their stories, three underage veterans recalled their part in the Battle of the Philippine Sea of 19 June 1944. A few days after the invasion of Saipan, a large Japanese fleet sailed from the Philippines in a northeasterly direction towards the Marianas in a desperate "do or die" attempt to save the Japanese bastion of Saipan that had been invaded by U. S. troops a few days before. The U. S. Navy's Task Force 58 was waiting, and in the ensuing battle, four of the nine Japanese aircraft carriers were sunk. The enemy lost more than ten aircraft for each one lost by the Americans, well over 300 in all. The battle was soon dubbed the "Great Marianas Turkey Shoot" by the Americans.

Jack Ware

Age 14 – United States Navy

The summer after I finished the seventh grade I decided to join the Navy. I was only 14 years old but was 5'8" and weighed 170 pounds. Four of my brothers were in the service, three in the Navy and one in the Marines. Two of my brothers had talked my

> *The ship's executive officer called me to the bridge and asked me how old I was.*

mother into letting them join the Navy at age 16. I convinced my mother to sign the form attesting that I was 17 by telling her that I was going to go in the service one way or another, so she might as well help me. She agreed and signed my papers at the recruiting office in Clinton, Oklahoma. During the bus ride from Clinton to Oklahoma City, I began to wonder what I had gotten myself into.

I was taken to the old Federal Building in Oklahoma City and was sworn in on 17 August 1943. A group of new recruits was put on a train for San Diego, California, and the Naval Training Center there. We arrived late at night, and the first thing I heard when I got off the train was, "You'll be sorry."

After six weeks of boot camp, I was sent to the San Diego Destroyer Base for six weeks of amphibious landing-craft school, then to San Francisco to board a ship bound for Pearl Harbor. We left San Francisco on a destroyer, and before we had passed under the Golden Gate Bridge, I began to get sick, I mean *sick*. It took five days to get to Pearl Harbor, and I was sick all the way, but I was never again seasick.

I will never forget the sight of the USS *Arizona* when we entered Pearl Harbor. As we sailed by, we were given a command to salute, a tribute that was made every time we passed by her.

About a week before Christmas 1943, the ship to which I was to be assigned returned from Tarawa in the Gilbert Islands, the site of one of the fiercest battles the Marines fought during World War II. The ship, the USS *Monrovia* (APA-31), had a crew of 500 and could carry about 2000 troops.

My first combat experience was in February 1944 at Kwajalein in the Marshall Islands. The *Monrovia* had brought part of the 7th Infantry Division from Hawaii for the landings. When the warships began the bombardment, I could not believe what I was seeing. This was also my first time to experience the results of battle, the dead who were brought back from the beach and then buried at sea with full military honors.

We picked up part of the 4th Marine Division at Hilo, Hawaii, and transported them to the Mariana Islands for the invasion of Saipan in June 1944. The next month, we took part of the 77th Infantry Division to Guam for the invasion there. My last combat experience was the invasion of Leyte in the Philippine Islands. We brought part of the 1st Calvary Division there.

Leyte is also the place where my age caught up with me. The Japanese had just started their kamikaze attacks, and my mother became very worried about me. She wrote the Navy Department and confessed that she had signed for me when I was 14. The ship's executive officer called me to the bridge and asked me how old I was. I told him, "Fifteen." He told me to pack my seabag, I was going home. I was discharged at Treasure Island, San Francisco, on 17 January 1945.

When I returned to Arapaho, Oklahoma, I started back to school. I was in the seventh grade when I left, but they put me in the ninth grade with the kids I had gone to school with in 1943. I moved to Cordell, Oklahoma, and graduated from high school there in 1949. I went to Southwestern State College in Weatherford, Oklahoma, for nearly two years, then enlisted in the U. S. Air Force. This was in April 1951, during the Korean War. My time in the Air Force was spent entirely in the United States. I was discharged in 1953 and returned to school at Southwestern.

People have asked me why I did such a thing back in 1943 at that age. My answer is: love for my country. I was devoted to doing the best job I could.

Jack Ware completed his education at Southwestern State College in 1955 and began his teaching career in Sugar City, Colorado.

In 1956, he accepted a teaching and coaching job in Watonga, Oklahoma. In Watonga, he was principal of the junior high school for four years, then transferred to Watonga High School where he retired as principal in 1986. He and his wife Doris have three daughters, ten grandchildren, and seven great-grandchildren. Jack and Doris live in Watonga, Oklahoma.

√ **VUMS Note** ⇒ *The Youngest Men-of-War.* An exhibit of the Navy Memorial Foundation at the Naval Heritage Center in Washington, D.C., titled "The Youngest Men-of-War," features photographs and short biographies of twenty-five veterans who enlisted underage. It was first displayed from 1 September 1995 through 13 October 1995, and proved to be so popular that it was repeated the following spring. Jackson Hoffler, an underage veteran, compiled the photographs and biographies. The Naval Heritage Center constructed the display which consisted of ten 32" x 40" panels, with two or three photographs and biographies on each. Four or five new panels are to be added in April 1997.

The Navy Memorial Foundation has made the panels available as a traveling exhibit, which was first displayed at the annual reunion of the VUMS in Springfield, Missouri, in March 1996. It was displayed in the Northwest later that year, and was scheduled to be shown in Kalamazoo, Michigan, in mid-summer 1997. Members of the VUMS who have seen the display have expressed great appreciation for the Navy Memorial Foundation's recognition of underage veterans through this exhibit.

Jackson Hoffler

Age 14 – United States Navy

In August 1943 I made several trips to the Naval Recruiting Station in Elizabeth City, North Carolina, trying to join the Navy. My father was dead, and all of my brothers were in the service. I was still in school, but I kept getting into trouble for fighting.

> *"Boy, don't lie to me because you don't even have your twelve-year molars."*

The Navy recruiter finally agreed to let me enlist in the Navy if I could get parental consent. Although I was only 14, he put 17 on my application and went with me to get my mother's signature. My mother didn't mind my going into the service because I was driving her bananas, but she would not lie about my age. Every time the recruiting officer said, "Mrs. Hoffler, all I want is your name on this paper," she would say no. Finally, my brother-in-law said, "If that's all you want, give me those papers." He went down the street for about half an hour, and when he returned, my mother's name was on the papers. I found out later that my sister had signed them.

I went to Raleigh, North Carolina, for my physical, during which I was informed that I was six pounds underweight. Someone told me to eat five pounds of bananas, drink a gallon of water, and come back in the morning. That is what I did, and the next morning I passed the physical.

I was sworn into the Navy on 23 August 1943 and was immediately sent to Bainbridge, Maryland, for basic training. I had to have a dental exam shortly after arriving at Bainbridge, and during the exam I had an experience very similar to what Calvin Graham had undergone. The dentist looked at my teeth, then asked me how old I was. I told him I was 17. He said, "Boy, don't lie to me because you don't even have your twelve-year molars." He handed me my papers and told me to report somewhere, I don't remember where. I went out one door, then came back in another. I watched, and when the dentist wasn't looking, I put my papers on the pile with all the others and walked out.

During basic training we were exposed to mustard gas. I didn't know what was going on, but I was sprayed in the ear with the gas, resulting in a partial loss of hearing in my right ear.

After basic training, I went to Little Creek, Virginia, and later to Fort Pierce, Florida, where I was trained as a small-boat crewman. I was assigned to the USS *LST-512*, and in January 1944 we crossed the North Atlantic in convoy. When we were about 300 miles out of Scotland, our ship broke down. It took three and one-half days to get underway again. During this time, the weather was very bad, and of course, German submarines were known to be in the area. We finally reached Glasgow, Scotland, and began preparations for the invasion of Normandy.

We took part in several training exercises, including Exercise Tiger. During this exercise, we were to land troops at Slapton Sands, England. As we approached the area, German E-Boats came out of the fog and attacked the flotilla. Two LSTs were sunk and three were damaged, but our LST was not hit. I could see the E-Boats speeding through the fog during the attack, passing very close to our ship. About 1000 men lost their lives during the attack.

On 6 June 1944, we landed troops at Omaha Beach. I was a gunner on an LCVP that ferried troops, ammunition, and supplies to the beach and brought back wounded men. This went on all day. An LCVP was supposed to have a crew of five, but there were only two of us, Curtis Hatley and I, manning this one.

The morning of 7 June found us making our rounds to the beach and back throughout the day. In the evening, we were taking a load of small arms ammunition to the beach when we hit an underwater obstruction that had a small field mine attached to it. The mine blew our ramp away and the boat sank. We were about a quarter of a mile from the beach. Curtis and I swam to the beach and made our way to the base of the hill just as it got dark. We dug in for the night. Meanwhile, the *LST-512* went back to England, leaving us on the beach.

We had been told to report to the beachmaster if we were stranded on the beach. On the morning of 8 June, we reported to the beachmaster of the 6th Naval Beach Battalion. He immediately put us to work. I was hit in the throat and the temple by a piece of tin on 12 June. They sewed up my throat wound, and I spent about four days recuperating before returning to work for the beachmaster. On the evening of 4 July 1944, I was on my way back from Cherbourg, France, where I had delivered a load of ammunition, rations, and medical supplies. I camped with the 129th Combat Engineers, U. S. Army at dark. About midnight, I left the trench we were in to go to a temporary latrine. On the way back, we came under heavy bombardment. I broke into a run, and just as I tripped on a tent rope, a shell exploded and blew me back into the latrine. I was pinned under a truck for about an hour, and my left wrist and left leg were damaged. I managed to return to Omaha Beach with the truck and trailer and reported to the Army medical unit on the beach.

I stayed with the medical unit until 13 July when I was returned to the *LST-512*. I was carried on board on a stretcher because of the shrapnel in my knee. I reported to the officer of the day (OD), but he didn't know anything about me. Curtis Hatley and I were not even missed! I heard later that Hatley was killed by shrapnel from a mortar about two days after I was hit.

I was immediately taken to the sick bay for treatment. Within the hour, the OD came to the sick bay, told me that they had found my records, and that I had been listed as AWOL from 9 June until that day. I was told that I was to be given a court-martial for being AWOL. The ship's records show that I was given a court-martial, sentenced to twenty days in the brig on bread and water, and fined $36.50. I never attended a court-martial, never went to the brig, but they did fine me $36.50 by taking it out of my pay.

When we reached England, I was taken from the ship to a hotel that was being used as a field hospital. I stayed there several weeks, then I was sent to the U. S. Naval Hospital #12 in Nutley, England. An Army doctor was scheduled to perform surgery on my knee. The doctor was drunk when he walked into the operating room, and I refused to allow him to operate on me.

I returned to the U. S. on the USS *West Point*, the former SS *America*, and received treatment at the naval hospital in Chelsea, Massachusetts. I was there about two months, then was given a convalescence leave, after which I reported to the naval hospital in Norfolk, Virginia. At Norfolk they found me fit for duty and sent me to Little Creek, Virginia, as a crewman on a PT boat that was getting ready to go to the Pacific. The captain of the PT boat saw that I was not physically fit, so he sent me back to the naval hospital at Portsmouth, Virginia.

I was a patient at Portsmouth until I received a medical discharge in August 1945. While I was there, they found out that I was only 15 years old. I was awarded ten percent disability benefits because of nerve damage to my left hand. Four other men and I were scheduled to receive Purple Hearts from a Navy captain who was the chief of surgery. Two days before I was to be discharged, the captain had a stroke and was taken to the Bethesda Naval Hospital for treatment. I never received my Purple Heart.

Jack Hoffler returned to the sea after leaving the Navy. He served with the Merchant Marine for four years, then became a charterboat skipper out of North Carolina and Florida. Currently, he is retired. Jack didn't think much about not receiving a Purple Heart when he left the Portsmouth Naval Hospital at age 16. Years later, when he inquired about it, he was told that his medical records did not confirm that he rated the medal. He obtained his medical records which clearly showed that, while on the beach at Normandy, he received a concussion from an exploding shell and was wounded on his neck, chin, and left wrist. He has waged an unsuccessful battle with the Navy Department for the past five years attempting to get his medal and vows to continue the fight. Jack returned to Slapton Sands in 1994 and was the official bugler during the ceremonies commemorating the 50th anniversary of Exercise Tiger. On 7 June 1994, he played taps at the ceremony commemorating the 50th anniversary of the liberation of Normandy at the Brittany American Cemetery, St. James, France. Jack is the Commander of the Veterans of Underage Military Service for North Carolina and the District of Columbia, and a Trustee of the Navy Memorial Foundation. Jack and his wife Sandra live in Hertford, North Carolina. They have a daughter and three grandsons.

Theodore Webb, Jr.

Age 13 – United States Navy

I was interested in military service from the time I was old enough to know what the words meant. My grandfather fought in the Civil War at the age of 14 with Steed's Battalion of the Mississippi Cavalry, and my father joined the Army

> *I did not see the prison camp, but I watched as the prisoners limped to the ship.*

at age 14, served on the Mexican Border, and later fought in France. To keep me out of trouble, my father enrolled me in a military school while he worked on a military reservation in North Carolina. So beginning in the sixth grade, I attended the Gulf Coast Military Academy in Gulfport, Mississippi. The first year at the school I was a private first class, and the second year I was second lieutenant in charge of the second platoon. At the school, I learned that I could take an order and I also could give one.

While I was home during the summer of 1943, a friend and I decided to join the Navy. I was not yet 13, but my friend and I were large for our age. At the Navy recruiting station, I told them that my birth date was 8 August 1926 instead of the true date of 8 August 1930. I wasn't required to show a birth certificate, but I had to have the signature of a parent to confirm that my age was 17. I took the papers and signed my name, but I put "Sr." after it instead of "Jr." I was sworn into the Navy on 23 August 1943, two weeks after my thirteenth birthday.

Instead of returning for the third year of military school, I was off to boot camp. After six weeks of boot training at Bainbridge, Maryland, I went to Norfolk, Virginia, to train for duty on a new destroyer-escort, the USS *Kretchmer* (DE-329), which had just been completed and was awaiting her crew at Orange, Texas.

While I was in Norfolk, I found out that the Navy had sent a letter to my father asking if I was underage, but he had never replied. The executive officer asked me if I was 17 and I told him I would be in January. I missed at least two weeks of training because of a high fever. The doctor said that I had "cat fever." When we were scheduled to go to Orange, Texas, to board the *Kretchmer*, I was still sick. The executive officer asked me if I wanted to stay in Norfolk until I was well, then be assigned to another ship. I told him I wanted to go with my shipmates. I did everything I could to lower my fever enough to be discharged from sick bay, and I made the trip to Texas.

In December 1943, I boarded the *Kretchmer*, which would be my home for the next two and one-half years. As a member of the deck force, my duties included helmsman, bowman, after-steering helmsman, and whaleboat operator.

I was assigned to man the after-steering apparatus one day while the ship was going through a narrow channel in the Sabine River towards the Gulf of Mexico. The ship's bridge lost steering control, so they switched control to me in after-steering. This was the part of my training I missed while I was in the hospital at Norfolk. So here I was with zero training in after-steering, and the bridge passed the main steering to me! I was told by phone what to do to keep from running into the river bank. I must have impressed someone because later I was asked to be the main helmsman while we refueled from tankers at sea.

On our shakedown cruise, we went between Guantanamo Bay, Cuba, and Trinidad. We would stop ships to check whether they were refueling enemy submarines. For much of 1944 we patrolled in the Atlantic, making thirteen crossings in convoy. Several times our ship was ordered to locate and destroy submarines that were detected near our convoys. The weather was so severe at times that a destroyer sank, and some sailors on other ships were washed overboard. While near a harbor in England, we were credited with helping to sink a German submarine. We were ordered to the Pacific in early 1945, originally destined for radar picket duty off the coast of Japan. Fortunately for us, the war ended before we actually went on picket duty.

In the spring of 1945, we were anchored near the marina at Saipan. There were several LCVPs on the shore that were left behind after the invasion a few months before. The ship's captain obtained one of the

LCVPs from the depot on the beach and ordered that several of us whaleboat operators be trained as LCVP operators. Whaleboats are steered with a tiller, and LCVPs have gears and a steering wheel. After three hours of training on the operation of an LCVP, I was ordered to take the captain to the flagship, the aircraft carrier USS *Santee*. Everything went fine until we pulled alongside the carrier. I came in too close and hooked the Jacob ladder, breaking one side of it. The captain turned to me and said, "Webb, you are supposed to drive this thing just like a car." I had never driven a car, but it would be forty-two years later at a reunion before I admitted that to the captain.

When we were anchored off Eniwetok Island, we were allowed to go swimming. Someone suggested that the catwalk on the mast would be a good place to dive from. Only one other fool besides myself tried the dive. Some time later, our convoy duties took on the responsibility of watching for airplanes that ended up in the sea after attempting to land on the carrier. Because of our fearless diving from the catwalk, the other seaman and I were assigned as official swimmers who would dive into the sea and help pilots get out of their planes before they sank. During this time, only one aircraft missed the carrier and crashed. Fortunately for me, the other diver, a 6-foot tall ex-football player, was called to handle the situation. He dove in and released the stunned pilot's harness and pulled him from the cockpit before the aircraft sank. With my small frame and 132-pound weight, I probably couldn't have pulled the pilot out. For rescuing the pilot, the aircraft carrier rewarded our crew with ice cream.

My most memorable experience in the Navy was when we sailed into a harbor in Formosa (now Taiwan) to rescue prisoners of war. It was on 6 September 1945 when the *Kretchmer* led several ships through a narrow inlet into a harbor. The waters were mined, and aircraft from the *Santee* flew bombing and strafing sorties to blow a path through the mine field. I didn't realize how dangerous this was until it was all over.

A group of Marines went ashore and disarmed the battalion of Japanese soldiers who were guarding the camp. I did not see the prison camp, but I watched as the prisoners limped to the ship. We loaded most of them in whaleboats and took them to the *Santee* offshore. We kept fifty-eight aboard the *Kretchmer* and took them to Manila.

The bodies of the newly freed prisoners were like those you see today on TV reports of the atrocities in Bosnia. They had been deprived of food and some were just bones. Some were survivors of the infamous death march of Bataan in 1942. We helped rescue about 1200 American, British, Australian, Dutch, and Chinese prisoners.

A few years ago, I read an account of the rescue of the prisoners written by a sailor who was on the *Santee*. The final two paragraphs in that account stick in my mind. As we pulled into Manila harbor, a *Santee* sailor said to a British soldier, "Well, I guess this rescue is about the greatest thrill of your life." The soldier, replied, "No, the greatest thrill came when the B-29s started bombing Formosa. We knew then that the Yanks were on their way."

In the spring of 1946, the *Kretchmer* made a goodwill tour around the world. We stopped in many ports and went through the Panama and Suez Canals. I rode a camel in Egypt and saw many sights that most 15-year-olds only hear about.

I was discharged from the Navy on 5 June 1946, two months before my sixteenth birthday. I had served two years, nine months, and twelve days, of which about thirty months were at sea. I still was not old enough to obtain a driver's license, and it would be over two years before I would be required to register for the draft!

Ted Webb returned to work for his father, a contractor in Wilmington, North Carolina, after his discharge from the Navy. His father urged him to continue his education, so he finished middle school, high school, and one year of college in a three-year period. He then transferred to Elon College near Burlington, North Carolina, where he majored in health and physical education, graduating in 1953. While he was at Elon, he played on the football team and met the girl who would become his wife. He worked with the Wilmington YMCA for two years, then was a manager with a life insurance company for eight years. In 1964, he gave in to a long-held desire and began teaching in the public schools. His teaching duties included coaching football in a junior high school and tennis in the local high school. He retired in 1992 after twenty-eight years of teaching. He married Aleane Gentry Webb in 1953 on national television, the CBS "Bride and Groom Show." Ted and Aleane live in Timberlake, North Carolina. They have two sons.

Frank Durbin III

Age 15 – United States Navy

I was born in Salem, Oregon, on 31 July 1928. Around my first birthday, we moved to Pittsburg, California, where I was raised. I was very patriotic and imbued with love of country. My father knew how badly I wanted to join the Navy

> *At the same time, my wife, now fully awake, asked me, "That is the damned Navy, isn't it?"*

at age 15, so he reluctantly agreed to assist me. He had enlisted in the Army underage during World War I and was severely wounded during the fighting in France.

I went to the Navy recruiting office in Martinez, California, took the tests, passed the physical, etc., and brought the papers home that my father needed to sign. He had access to a notary public at the Shell Chemical Company where he worked, so he had my papers notarized along with other documents. I was sworn into the Navy at the Federal Building in San Francisco on 3 September 1943 at the age of 15.

For boot camp, I was sent to the Naval Training Center in San Diego, after which I went to the Naval Aviation Technical Training Center, Memphis, Tennessee. There I attended and graduated from the aviation radioman and RADAR schools. I then attended the Naval Aviation Gunnery School at Yellow Water, Florida. From Yellow Water, I went to the Naval Air Station, Deland, Florida, for training as a radioman/gunner in the SBD Dauntless aircraft; then in August 1944, I transitioned to the SB2C Helldiver aircraft. I was assigned to the USS *Attu* (CVE-102) in December 1944 and was soon in the Central Pacific theater. We flew numerous patrols over islands in the Marianas that had been bypassed and were still occupied by Japanese.

In March 1945, the *Attu* was ordered to join Task Force 58.2 and participate in the invasion of Okinawa scheduled for 1 April 1945. We joined the task force during the night of 31 March. At dawn on 1 April, we were thrilled by the sight of hundreds of ships surrounding us. There were ships as far as the eye could see. The thrill of that sight has never left me.

After the Battle of Okinawa, I was based in the Marianas, first at the Naval Air Station, Marpi's Point, Saipan, and later at the Naval Air Station, Orote, Guam.

After the war, I returned to the States and was discharged at Camp Shoemaker, California, on 10 April 1946. I joined the Naval Air Reserve in January 1947 at the Naval Air Station, Oakland, California, where I served as a radio operator in squadrons that flew SB2C Helldivers, PBY Catalinas, and PV2 Venturas.

At about this time, my mother noticed an article in a newspaper stating that a general amnesty had been granted to underage veterans. She suggested that I get my age corrected on the Navy records, so I did.

I was with VPML-57 in 1951 when the squadron was recalled to active duty for the Korean War. I vividly recall that day. Normally, at the end of the drill weekend at the Naval Air Station at Alameda, paychecks would be given out on the grinder (drill field) while we were still in formation. On this weekend, we were told to go to the chow hall for our checks and that the CO would have a few words to say to us. When we were all inside the hall, the doors were quietly locked and Marines with rifles quietly surrounded the hall. I turned to the guy next to me and said, "This don't look so good to me." It wasn't — we were informed that we were recalled to active duty.

Our squadron was redesignated VP-871, transitioned to PB4Y-2 Privateer aircraft, and sent to the Naval Air Station, Sand Point, Washington. I was assigned as first radioman and right waist gunner on a PB4Y-2. Our crew and one other were suddenly dispatched to the Naval Air Station, Atsugi, Japan, where we joined Detachment Able of VP-28. We were sent to K1, an airfield near Pusan, Korea, and later to K14, an airfield near Seoul. We flew thirty combat missions during "Operation Lamplighter" from these two fields. These missions were in conjunction with VMF(n)-513 (Marine Night Fighter Squadron-513). Our job was to illuminate the North Korean targets for the Marine F7Fs and F4U Corsairs. On one mission, our crew attacked an enemy convoy, created a roadblock by destroying the first truck, then proceeded to destroy the remaining twenty-four trucks and damaged a train. Thirty secondary explosions occurred during the attack. The thirty secondary explosions, the number of trucks destroyed, and the amount of additional damage, set a record for a single fire fight.

I came back from Korea in February 1952, was released from active duty, and returned to the University of California, Berkeley, where I was an engineering student. I reenlisted in the Naval Reserve in 1958, again at the Naval Air Station in Oakland. I served in F2H Banshee, S2F Tracker, helicopter, and C-118 transport squadrons. When the Cuban missile crisis and the Berlin crisis arose in quick succession, I returned to active duty with the Navy and served as a recruiter at the Naval Air Station, Alameda, and at the branch recruiting station at Daly City, California, from 1961 until 1963. I was promoted to chief petty officer at this time.

During the summer of 1965, the eighteen nationwide Naval Reserve Commands each sponsored an 85-day boot camp for new reserve enlisted men. Our command's boot camp was at Alameda, and I served as training chief. My unit came out first in all facets of the training, and all who were involved received promotions. Later that year, I flew as a crewman on a C-118 transporting priority cargo to Vietnam. I was promoted to warrant officer in 1965.

One day in January 1968, the telephone rang at 4:00 a.m. My wife answered it from her side of the bed. With quite a bit of unprintable language, she slammed the phone back on its cradle. I asked her who it was. She replied, "A bunch of your Navy buddies at an all-night party." I asked, "What did they say?" She said, "It was the Bureau of Navy Personnel and they wanted to talk to Warrant Officer Durbin." This worried me somewhat because I wasn't so sure that it was a bunch of inebriated bluejackets.

The phone rang again, so this time I answered it. It was a lieutenant commander from the Bureau, all right. I asked him, "Why did you call me at four a.m.?" He told me that it was 7:00 a.m. in Washington, D.C. I asked him what he wanted. He said that they were doing a computer search for an AvWEPS officer (avionics weapons officer) and found me. They needed an AvWEPS officer to report immediately aboard an aircraft carrier in San Francisco Bay that was departing for Vietnam. I hemmed and hawed and finally asked if this was an involuntary recall and he said no, but that they would continue to search through the list for volunteers, and that they reserved the right to recall whomever they finally decided upon.

By this time, my wife was waking up and listening to my end of the conversation. The officer on the phone said, "Look, I don't have time to talk all day. If we send you the orders, will you report immediately to the USS *Hancock* and depart for Vietnam?" At the same time, my wife, now fully awake, asked me, "That is the damned Navy, isn't it?" I looked at her and said, "Yes." Hearing that reply, and assuming it was the answer to his question, the officer in the Pentagon said, "That's fine, we'll get the orders right out," and hung up immediately. I returned home four years and one month later, after two full tours of duty in Vietnam.

During my tours in Vietnam, I served as avionics/weapons officer of the USS *Hancock* (CVA-19). We took part in "Operation Rolling Thunder," the bombardment of North Vietnam, Laos, and Cambodia. The DECM (defensive electronic countermeasures) shop was under my supervision. During both of my deployments, no aircraft from the *Hancock* was downed by SAM missiles.

After I returned from Vietnam, I was a team leader at the NAESU (Naval Aviation Engineering Service Unit), at Barbers Point Naval Air Station, Hawaii, for a year. I returned to the San Francisco area and was released from active duty in February 1972. I joined a reserve squadron, VP-91, flying P3B Orion aircraft. I was the avionics/weapons officer with this squadron for eleven years. During this period, I served 106 days in the Western Pacific, thirty-five days in the Aleutians, and sixteen days in Spain.

In 1983, I was assigned as training officer in MMV-0280 (Mobile Vans Unit-0280) and later went to Diego Garcia, a British Island in the South Indian Ocean, where I served in the maintenance department.

I retired on my sixtieth birthday, 31 July 1988, at the rank of CWO-4. My naval service, both active and reserve, spanned forty-five years. I had the honor of being the last nonflag rank (less than admiral or general) World War II veteran on the active rolls. I was the only reservist called to active duty five times and was one of very few men who fought in World War II, the Korean War, and the war in Vietnam.

Frank Durbin earned two battle stars on his Asiatic-Pacific ribbon during World War II, three stars on his Korean Service ribbon, and four stars on his Vietnam Service ribbon. He was awarded the Navy Achievement Medal, the Air Medal with one star, Combat Crew Wings with three combat stars, and numerous other medals. He also received the Rear Admiral Richard D. Fowler Outstanding Reservist Award. In between his tours of active duty with the Navy, Frank graduated from the University of California, Berkeley, in 1954 with a degree in petroleum engineering. He worked for Schlumberger Electronics Oil Well Surveying Corporation in the San Joaquin Valley of California from 1954 until 1956. He worked at the Lawrence Radiation Laboratory, Berkeley, California, in 1957 and taught at Tracy High School, Tracy, California, from 1958 to 1961. From 1962 until 1968, he taught science and mathematics at Polytechnic High School in San Francisco, and from 1972 until 1988, he taught at Mission High School in San Francisco. He retired from teaching in 1988, the same year he retired from the Naval service. Frank and his wife Marion (also ex-Navy) live in Daly City, California. He has one daughter.

Roland J. Stoupa

Age 15 – United States Army

I was born in Cleveland, Ohio, on 9 May 1928. As a child I had otitis media, and shortly after my fourteenth birthday, a doctor punctured my right eardrum as a treatment for this condition. I was so ill

> *I was one month past my sixteenth birthday when I went into combat ...*

at the time that I was given last rites by a priest. Having a punctured eardrum was a sure-fire way to avoid military service as far as the selective service was concerned. I had my "million dollar wound" at age 14. However, I was determined to serve my country.

When I was 15 years and 4 months old I went to the draft board and registered as an 18-year-old. I was over 5'9" inches tall and weighed 150 pounds. I knew that there might be a problem about my ear during the physical, so when the doctor started to examine my

right ear, I told him that I had a bad earache. He passed me right then. I guess he thought that I was trying to B.S. him, but I knew that if he examined me closely, I would fail the exam. I asked to be inducted the same day that I took my physical, 7 September 1943. I took the oath and was off to camp by 3:00 p.m. that afternoon.

I trained at Camp Gruber, Oklahoma, where I was assigned to G Company, 222nd Infantry, 42nd Infantry Division, as an assistant gunner on a 60mm mortar. In February 1944, I was transferred to Camp Phillips, Kansas, where I was with K Company, 313th Infantry, 79th Infantry Division.

We left Boston, Massachusetts, aboard the HMS *Strathmore*, an English troopship, on 7 April 1944. Upon arrival in England, we were based at Ashton in Makersfield, Lancashire. Several days during May I had ear problems and was sick in my quarters or on light duty.

I was one month past my sixteenth birthday when I went into combat as an infantry rifleman. Our regiment landed in France on D+8, 14 June 1944, at Utah Beach. We fought at Sebeville, Picanville, Ravan, Colomby, Hau-De Haut, and Hau-Gringor, France. I was wounded at Hau-Gringor, near Cherbourg. Our company had 186 men when we landed at Utah Beach. Only 130 were left after Cherbourg was captured.

I was sent to the 304th Medical Battalion on 24 June 1944 and three days later was transferred to the 622nd Clearing Company. From there I went to the 96th U. S. Hospital in England and returned to the United States on 26 August 1944. I was hospitalized at the Crile General Hospital, Cleveland, Ohio. I was honorably discharged from the Army at Camp Atterbury, Indiana, on 12 December 1944, at the age of 16 years and 7 months. I was awarded 50% service-connected disability pension.

After my discharge from the Army, I had many problems, including the fact that I was a 16-year-old alcoholic. I could not adjust to civilian life. I felt that the people at home just didn't understand! I guess they couldn't be expected to understand what I and many other veterans had experienced. When you are an infantryman in combat, you try to become immune to the constant crises of life and death in order to survive. The cries of wounded, deaths of close buddies — memories remain forever in the depths of your heart and mind.

I tried to reenlist in the Army when I was 17 but was turned down. The recruiting sergeant suggested that I try the Marine Corps. During my physical, the doctor bent the rules and passed me as fit for service. When he examined my right ear, he commented, "What the hell is wrong with you? With that ear, do you know what you are getting into and the condition you are in? You have already served in the war, and that should be enough!" I will always be indebted to that doctor for bending the rules and allowing me to join the Marines because this changed the course of my life for the better. As a civilian, I couldn't explain my problems. I had no one to talk to or confide in. I was still suffering from otitis media of the right ear and from shell shock and concussion resulting from combat. I enlisted in the Marine Corps to be with people with whom I was compatible.

I was sworn into the Marine Corps on 23 July 1945 and was sent to boot camp at the Marine Barracks, Parris Island, South Carolina. In order to join, I had to waive any right to the 50% disability compensation that I was receiving. I was 17 years and 2 months old at the time.

While in Marine boot camp, I had flashbacks of my Army combat experiences and was disturbing others in the platoon. A sergeant asked me if I wanted to see a doctor about my problem and informed me that the Marines had copies of my Army medical records. I refused to see a doctor because I knew that if I were examined closely, I would be discharged from the Marines. The sergeant made arrangements for me to sleep in the back of the hut away from the squad area so I would not disturb others during the night when I had a flashback. I stayed in the Marines until 17 June 1946. On 31 August 1946, my 50% disability compensation was reinstated. I received $69.00 per month.

I had the privilege of serving with the best, the U. S. Army and the U. S. Marine Corps, during World War II. I can understand the readjustment problems veterans have. *Semper Fidelis.*

Roland Stoupa was awarded the Bronze Star for meritorious achievement, the Purple Heart for wounds received in action, the Combat Infantryman Badge, and the French Fourragère. After leaving the military, Roland became a carpenter and worked on projects ranging from family homes to nuclear power plants. In 1984, he retired with a 100% service-connected disability pension. Roland and Marie, his wife of fifty years, live in Prince George, Virginia. They have three sons and four grandchildren. One son is a veteran of the Vietnam War, and a grandson is currently on active duty with an Air National Guard squadron.

T. Steve Jolly

Age 14 – United States Merchant Marine
Age 15 – United States Marine Corps

I was born in Lewiston, Idaho, on 31 May 1928, but we moved to Oregon within a year. My mother died at age 39, and my father became a hunter, trapper, and hermit. I had lived in fifteen

> We had a beautiful view of Mount Suribachi off to our left.

different foster homes by the time I was 14 years old. I needed a place to go, and the Merchant Marine sounded good to me. I went to the Merchant Marine recruiting office in Portland, Oregon, and told them that I was 16 years old and that I was born in Hobbs, New Mexico. I had heard that birth certificates were not issued in Hobbs at that time, so there would be no way for them to check.

I was sworn into the Merchant Marine on 12 September 1943 at the age of 14 and was sent to Catalina, California, for boot training. We were on a training cruise a week before graduation when I was ordered to report to the captain's office. He asked me, "How old are you?" I could see myself headed for the brig, so I told him the truth. It was time for chow, so the captain asked if I would eat with him because he wanted to talk to me. He asked me why I wanted to be in the Merchant Marine. I told him that it was because of patriotism, that I loved my country and wanted to do my share. He told me that he understood, but that I was still too young. He then asked me, "What would you do if you were in my place?" I gave him a response typical of a 14-year-old, "I don't know."

The captain said that he understood how I felt and told me that he felt the same way when he enlisted at age 14. He then made me an offer, saying to me, "If you will agree to stay aboard my ship as an instructor in the fire room, I will not make a report of this." He added, "Don't give me your answer now, but get back to me." A week later,

I graduated from boot training, received my seaman papers, and was on my way. I never saw the captain of the training ship again.

I went aboard my first ship as a merchant seaman in Stockton, California. We sailed for Santos, Brazil. On this trip, I became friends with an old-timer who took me under his wing. One day, as waves were breaking over the ship during a heavy storm, he said to me, "Son, back in the days when I was a boy, when men were men and the ships were made of wood, you could stand watch in the crow's-nest, and when the ship rolled one way you would heave, and when it rolled the other way you would wash your mouth out."

When we reached Santos, Brazil, another young sailor and I went ashore. Somehow, we missed getting back aboard ship and it sailed without us. We must have drunk some bad water to be in such a condition because we were too young to drink anything else. We went to the American Legation in São Paulo and told them of our plight. They put us on another ship as crew members, supposedly headed back to the States via the East Coast. The ship was an old rust-bucket with coal-fired boilers, and since I was a fireman, I shoveled coal. The ship flew the Panamanian flag and usually made trips only along the coast. The captain was German, the first mate was Russian, and the crew were all Hindu, except for the two of us. Strangely enough, the food always tasted of curry.

Off the coast of Cuba, we met a bunker ship that loaded our bunkers with coal. After loading, we headed north again, but not to the U. S. as planned. We met a convoy and were on our way to the North Atlantic. Five days out, we happened to find a stray torpedo to run into. Only ten of us made it off the ship before it went down.

After a stay in a hospital, I decided to join something that was not as wet, and a lot safer. So I joined the Marines. Although I was only 15, I had no problem enlisting. I showed the recruiters my fancy seaman papers and certificates, which were sufficient proof of age. I was sworn into the Marines on 15 June 1944.

I went to beautiful, sunny California, and after boot camp at the Marine Corps Base, San Diego, I went to Camp Gillespie for parachute training. At the Marine jump school, we were told that we were the world's best fighting machine but that they were going to teach us how to be even better. We were going to learn how to jump out of a plane at 350 feet without a parachute. If we had to jump from a greater height, we would then be issued parachutes so as to not hurt ourselves.

After jump school, I shipped overseas and was assigned to Baker Company, 2nd Marine Raider Battalion, under the command of Colonel Evans F. Carlson. When the battalion was first formed in 1942, it was Colonel Carlson who introduced the Chinese term "gung ho" and proposed it as a motto for the battalion. The term can be loosely translated as "work together," but it soon came to mean an aggressive fighting attitude and has since became a commonly used term, implying working together with great enthusiasm and dedication.

In mid-1944, the 2nd Battalion was deactivated and became part of the newly formed 4th Marine Division under the command of Colonel Shapely. We walked and crawled the sunny beaches, climbed the cliffs, and strolled through the green valleys of Saipan, which was, in truth, a living hell.

On 19 February 1945, the 4th Division visited the black sands at the south end of Iwo Jima. We had a beautiful view of Mount Suribachi off to our left. After thirty days and casualties of almost 17,400 (of which 5,900 were killed), we returned to Guam and from there to New Zealand for R&R. In late 1945, we went to the romantic land of North China where we helped Japanese troops pack up and go home.

While in North China, three other members of my original rifle team and I volunteered for permanent railroad patrol. We guarded the trains from the coast to Tientsin and on to Peking. At that time, the Communists were harassing the trains by firing at us and blowing up the tracks. One fire fight lasted for two days, until a relief column came to help us out.

I returned to the States and was discharged from the Marine Corps on 10 December 1948, and shortly after, I joined a Marine reserve unit in Eugene, Oregon. Our unit was activated a very short time after the Korean War started. After a brief stay at Camp Pendleton, we were off to Korea with the 1st Provisional Marine Brigade. I was with the brigade in the Pusan Perimeter only a short time before I was assigned courier duty. I traveled all over the Far East as a courier.

In writing this, I am in no way trying to portray these years as being all fun and games – God knows, they weren't. But I do believe that we, the ones who have gone through these conflicts and wars, would much rather remember some of the good times we had, the friends we made, and the camaraderie we enjoyed, rather than remember the wounded, dead, and dying, along with the destruction that we saw.

I remained in the Corps for twenty years and retired as a gunnery sergeant on 28 November 1965. When my children were little, I would tell them of "the black sands of Iwo Jima" and about the miles of tunnels and caverns, and of the underground hospital and living areas. Two of my three sons became career Marines. A few years ago, I received a phone call from number three son, who was still in the Marine Corps at that time. As we do each year, he called on 10 November, the Marine Corps birthday. He said, "Dad, I hope you appreciate what I have done for you; it has taken a year to set it up." I asked him what he meant. He told me that he had gone through channels to the Commandant of the Marine Corps and received his permission, and the permission of the Japanese government, to take a contingent of the 27th Marines back to Iwo Jima in my honor.

A videotape was made and many pictures were taken as we walked along Green Beach and Red Beach. With the video camera running, my son said, "Dad, listen to the crunch of the sand — just like you told me when I was a kid." The photos and videotape, along with written reports, were placed in the Marine Archives. This was a fantastic way for a son to honor a dad. I am mighty proud!

Steve Jolly received a Meritorious Service Award and two Presidential Unit Citations. After retiring from the Marines, he returned to Oregon and became a state employee. He worked as a corrections officer for several years, then worked in rehabilitation for the remaining time of his seventeen years with the state of Oregon. His rehabilitation work was at the Fairview Hospital and Training Center in Salem. Steve received five awards for saving the lives of five handicapped people. Steve and Barbara, his wife of forty-nine years, live in Keizer, Oregon. They have five children, seven grandchildren, and three great-grandchildren. Two of their sons retired from the Marine Corps. Steve is the Oregon State Vice-Commander of the Veterans of Underage Military Service.

Edgar C. "E.C." Adams

Age 15 – United States Navy

In August 1943, Joe Stastny, a friend of mine who was in the Navy, came home on leave. The girls just flipped over him in his sailor uniform. I knew then that I was going to be a sailor. My friend was 17 years old, but he told me that he knew

> *"... I would appreciate it if you would put your toe on the scale and read it again."*

some guys that were younger than 17 who were in basic training with him. I had turned 15 on 30 July 1943, and the news that guys under 17 had joined was all that I needed to begin looking for ways to join the Navy. I went to the Navy recruiting office in my hometown, Anderson, South Carolina, told them that I was 17, passed the test, and was given papers that had to be signed by a parent and notarized.

My mother died when I was 12, and I was living with my stepfather who had raised me. I knew that Dad would not sign my papers, so I signed his name and took the papers to a notary, hoping to get him to put his seal on them. Of course, the notary, who knew my dad, asked why he wasn't there. I told him that Dad was too busy and just couldn't make it to his office. It took about three weeks and a lot of little white lies, but finally the notary put his seal on the documents.

As soon as the notary handed me the papers, I headed for the post office building where the Navy recruiters were. I met my uncle, Guy Philyaw on the way. Uncle Guy noticed the words "U. S. Navy" on the papers I had in my hand and knew immediately what I was trying to do. He told me that I was too young to join the Navy and that he was going to the recruiters' office and tell them so. I said to him, "Uncle Guy, I'll run away from home, and you will never see me again if you do!" He knew that I meant it, so he didn't expose me.

I went on to the recruiting office and completed the paperwork. The next day, I was sent to Camp Croft, an Army camp in South Carolina, for a physical. I passed everything until I stood on a scale. A medic said, "You just don't weigh enough to get in." I said to him, "Look, I have gone through hell trying to get into the Navy. I would appreciate it if you would put your toe on the scale and read it again. If I pass this, I'm in." He did as I asked, and I was sworn into the Navy on 16 September 1943.

I went to Bainbridge, Maryland, for basic training. When I came home on boot leave, I found the girls still flipping over the sailor uniform. I went to Norfolk, Virginia, for training as a crewman on destroyer-escorts, then left for California for more training. On 12 May 1944, our crew was assembled in San Francisco and we put the USS *William C. Cole* (DE-641) into commission.

We left for San Diego on our shakedown cruise on 31 May 1944. On 24 September 1944, we crossed the equator for the first time. I found out what it's like to become a "shellback" (one who has crossed the equator by ship) after being a "polliwog" (one who hasn't). Believe me, being initiated as a shellback is something you never forget!

After escorting many battleships, carriers, and transport ships in and out of many islands in the South Pacific, we left the island of Ulithi with the Seventh and Tenth Fleets for the big one — Okinawa.

On 31 March 1945, we sighted Okinawa, and the next day, 1 April, we invaded. That's one April Fools' Day and Easter Sunday I will never forget. At first we had only near encounters with suicide planes, but on 25 May 1945, we had quite a battle with them. We were attacked by three planes. I was the pointer on a 1.1-inch gun that was credited with one of the two planes shot down by our ship. Another ship shot down the third plane.

After some duty at Iwo Jima and Luzon, we returned to Saipan and rode out the typhoon that hit there. We then headed for the States and docked at Bremerton, Washington. After a 40-day leave, I was transferred to Charleston, South Carolina, where I was discharged on 19 March 1946.

I didn't like what I saw on the outside, so I reenlisted in August 1946. I was stationed at Corpus Christi, Texas, and Pensacola, Florida, and served aboard the USS *Wallace L. Lynn* (DD-703), home-based in New Orleans, Louisiana. I received my second discharge in August 1948.

I returned to South Carolina, joined the Naval Reserve, and trained to be a plumber under the GI Bill. In August 1950, two months after the start of the Korean War, I reenlisted in the regular Navy for the third time. I was aboard the USS *Renshaw* (DDE-499) at sea off the coast of Hawaii when mail was delivered and I received a large brown envelope. In it was my discharge from the Naval Reserve. I said to my friends who were standing around, "Look, I just received my discharge. Tell the captain to turn this ship around. I want to go home." We all had a good laugh.

I injured my leg in an accident while I was on the *Renshaw*. The injury was serious enough that I was sent to the Tripler General Hospital in Honolulu, then to the U. S. Naval Hospital, Vallejo, California, and on to Chelsea Naval Hospital, Chelsea, Massachusetts. I did temporary duty aboard the USS *Tarawa* (CV-40) out of Charleston, Massachusetts, for a short time. I was medically discharged on 5 December 1952, my fourth and final discharge from the Navy.

E.C. Adams returned to South Carolina after his final discharge from the Navy, finished his apprenticeship as a plumber, and went to work in construction. He was a senior field mechanical engineer with a major construction company when he retired on 1 February 1989. E.C.'s first wife Barbara, whom he met while on his second Navy cruise, died in 1981. They had three children and two grandchildren. E.C. and his soon-to-be wife, Louise Cobb, reside in Anderson, South Carolina.

A. W. "Sam" Mahony

Age 16 – United States Navy

I was a 15-year-old klutz determined to enlist in the U. S. Navy while still two birthdays shy of the minimum enlistment age of 17. My scheme was to go to the Cook County Board of Vital Statistics in downtown Chicago, obtain a birth certif-icate, ever-so-expertly erase my correct

> ... I was legally old enough to "join the Navy and see the world" when the stuff hit the fan at Peleliu.

birth date, and type in another date that would make me 17. I would then execute this fraud and fool the U. S. Navy. I went to the Board of Vital Statistics, requested a copy of my birth certificate, and guess what? The clerk couldn't find a record of my birth! She came back twice to check the spelling of my name and my birth date, and after each search she came up empty-handed. She explained that my records had been lost, handed me a blank, legal-sized affidavit, and said to me, "Fill this out and bring it back to us, and it will serve as your official birth record." This was like giving a thief a license to steal. I walked out of there with a lively gait, humming "Anchors Aweigh" because I knew that I was well on my way!

It was early March 1943, and I knew that I looked pretty damned young, so I selected 13 March 1926 as my phony date of birth so it would look like I had just turned 17. I was actually born on 13 September 1927. After I forged my parents' signatures as witnesses to my birth, I had to get the affidavit notarized, and this posed an almost insurmountable problem. Every one of the many notaries I went to insisted that they witness my parents' signing of the document. So out of desperation, I took the affidavit back to the Vital Statistics Office without getting it notarized, hoping to get it accepted anyway. The clerk directed me to a staffer, a notary public who promptly notarized it, no questions asked. Now I had papers proving I was 17. Whoopee!

The next stop was the Navy enlistment center where I failed the physical because of excess albumin in my urine. Every few weeks, I would go back and pee in the bottle and cross my fingers, but it was always the same result: no go.

One time, for the hell of it, I tried to enlist in the Coast Guard. During the physical, I got dizzy when they stuck the needle in for the blood test. It was obvious to them that I was a kid. They said I was rejected because of excess albumin, but to my surprise, they sent a letter to my house giving the reasons for my rejection. They listed albumin and a bunch of nonexistent problems and tacked on the end of this lengthy paragraph of ailments "... and insufficient chest measurement." My mother opened the letter when it arrived and got a big laugh out of it.

Undaunted, I went on a water-drinking binge because health studies had taught me to drink a lot of water to flush out the human body. With only a bit of exaggeration, I spent half my time drinking water and the other half searching for a place to relieve my bladder. After doing this for the entire month of July, I went to the recruiting office to fill the bottle for Uncle Sam. Usually, a low-ranking sailor would be at the check-in desk, but this time a crusty old chief petty officer wearing several hashmarks was sitting there. I had just had a crew cut, so my hair was very short, accenting my youthful appearance. The chief took one look at me and snapped in a loud, booming voice, "What the hell are you doing here, kid?" I replied, "I'm here to join the Navy." He boomed again, "You what?" After I told him I already had my physical, he stared at me at close range for several seconds in a state of utter disbelief, but said nothing more. I peed in the bottle, and for the first time, I checked out albumin-free. So once again, I thought I was on my way.

I was told that my enlistment papers would be sent to my father's address because the Navy required that he sign them. My parents were separated, and my father lived in a rooming house not far from the family. So my buddy and I waited in front of Pop's place in order to sneak a look through the daily mail. After a few days, the papers arrived. Wow — one step closer!

My buddy forged my father's signature, but I was faced again with the same problem: I couldn't find a notary who would put his seal on the enlistment papers without witnessing the signature. As a last resort, I went back to the Vital Statistics Office and to the same guy who notarized my phony birth certificate several months earlier, and he affixed his seal with no questions asked.

After my papers were turned in, a post card was supposed to come telling me when to report for duty. I was about as anxious to get that post card as a kid waiting for Santa Claus on Christmas Eve. Although I waited down the street for the mail every day, somehow I missed intercepting its delivery. My mother received it and said nothing to me about it until a week or ten days later. Then, during one of our arguments, she threw the post card at me and said something like, "Go join the Navy!" This ended my six-months' effort to go off to war.

I reported for duty on 23 September 1943, ten days after my sixteenth birthday. After eleven weeks of boot camp, followed by four months of signalman school at the Great Lakes Naval Training Center, I was sent to the boat basin at Camp Pendleton Marine Corps Base, Oceanside, California. I was assigned there to what was called an XAP team. After further signal training, the XAPs were to be based in Hawaii, and from there, assigned to be the signalmen on merchant ships. It was considered easy duty, a cream-puff deal, to just receive and send messages, but it wasn't for me.

At this time, the Marines' 4th JASCO (joint assault signal company) was being formed at the boat basin. I asked my commanding officer for a transfer to JASCO. No action was taken for more than ten days, so I asked my CO again for a transfer. His reply was, "Are you *crazy?*" He then went on to describe in bloody detail what Marines face in combat and what a rough life it would be. It was not a pretty picture. When he finished, I repeated my transfer request. In three days I was in JASCO, a unit composed of 400 Marines and 100 sailors. The unit directed air strikes and naval gunfire and provided ship-to-shore communications.

After about six weeks of amphibious training, we boarded the *Poelau Laut,* a Dutch merchant ship used as a troopship during the war. Thirty days later, we disembarked on Pavuvu in the Russell Islands (near Guadalcanal) and became part of the 1st Marine Division, with my platoon serving in support of the 1st Battalion, 7th Marine Regiment. We boarded ships about a month later and sailed to the Palau Islands for the invasion of Peleliu. D-Day was at 8:00

a.m. on 15 September 1944, Western Pacific time. But back in Chicago, my birth place, it was about 4:00 p.m. on 14 September, just one day past my seventeenth birthday. At last, I was legally old enough to "join the Navy and see the world" when the stuff hit the fan at Peleliu.

Our platoon descended the cargo nets about 7:00 a.m. and boarded a wooden Higgins boat, which would carry us closer to shore where we would transfer to an armored amphibious tractor for the trip to the beach. We were scheduled to hit the beach at 10:30 a.m., in the eighteenth wave. However, the Japanese artillery, mortars, and land mines had knocked out so many landing vehicles that none were available to take us ashore until 3:00 p.m. or later. We rode around in the Higgins boat all day in a "box seat," viewing a war. The landing area appeared to be a wall of smoke, punctuated with intermittent flashes of exploding shells. Navy ships moved in to give close gunfire support, some with pinpoint accuracy, while dive bombers made numerous sorties overhead.

When our ride to the beach finally came, it was in an Army DUKW, an amphibious vehicle that is essentially a combination truck and boat. I was one of the first to board the DUKW and I sat up front, right behind the driver. About a half mile from shore and above a coral reef, I could see a huge boulder under the water directly ahead of us. I thought that if I could see it, then both of the Army guys in the driver's seat would see it, and since they made no effort to go around it, I assumed that they knew it was OK to go straight ahead. Wrong! The DUKW hit the boulder and stopped dead in the water. We were stuck! After a half hour, we hailed a passing Marine amphibious tractor, and about forty-five minutes later, the tractor returned with another one. We were on the beach within a few minutes. That night, I shared a foxhole with two other Navy signalmen. It was scary because of a lengthy Japanese mortar-barrage that had shells exploding all around us much of the night.

After two months on Peleliu, we shipped back to Pavuvu and regrouped for our next combat assignment, which turned out to be Okinawa. My platoon was scheduled to hit the beach three days after D-Day, but I wanted to go in with the assault troops, so I asked to be assigned to a naval gunfire-liaison team. I was accepted into one of the teams and landed in the third wave of assault troops as part of the 1st Battalion, 7th Marine Regiment, 1st Marine Division.

D-Day on Okinawa fell on April Fools' Day, 1 April 1945, which was also Easter Sunday. I was also promoted to seaman first class on that day. The landing forces in our sector encountered little resistance, and in a matter of three days, we had crossed the island with only a few casualties; while to the south, one of the biggest land battles of the Pacific war was beginning to develop. After a few weeks, naval personnel were ordered back from the front-line assignments to company headquarters, where I remained for the rest of the campaign.

After the island was secured, we started preparing for the invasion of Japan, which never came to be, thanks to the A-bomb, for which my progeny and I are most grateful. Otherwise, I could very well have been among the million or so casualties that experts predicted would result from the invasion.

I had been warned about what the life of a Marine would be like. On Peleliu, the cemetery was adjacent to our bivouac area. I saw bodies stacked up daily, waiting for burial, and smelled the ever-present stench of death. When I was briefly hospitalized on Okinawa with an ankle sprain, I caught a glimpse of many amputees and other severely wounded men. Indeed, I was most fortunate that I didn't have to slug it out with the enemy at close quarters as the Marine infantry had to do on the front lines. I was lucky enough to be *just close enough* to have a "box seat" to view the war and then have the A-bomb come along and save my life. How lucky can you get!

Sam Mahony eventually got into sales after his release from the Navy. For the past twenty years, he has published an entertainment paper for part of the central Illinois area, mainly covering the night-life scene. Sam is the father of seven children and has thirteen grandchildren. He lives in rural East Peoria, Illinois.

Calvin H. Lyle

Age 15 – United States Navy

In the spring of 1943, I was a high school student in St. George, Utah. My first afternoon class was gym, followed by algebra. I left my algebra book in gym class one day, and the algebra teacher sent me back to look for it. Meanwhile, someone had found it and turned it in to the office. It took me more time to locate my book than the teacher thought it should. He met me in the hall, and instead of accepting my reasons for taking so long, he swatted me alongside the head a couple of times. I turned and left the building, vowing never to go back to school.

I consider joining the Navy at age 15 the most significant event of my life.

I left St. George and went to work as a laborer for the Bureau of Reclamation at Boulder Dam (now Hoover Dam), near Las Vegas, Nevada. I was only 15, but I adjusted my age to 17 to get the job. It didn't take long to find out that this was work and that it wasn't as exciting as I had thought it might be.

On a Friday afternoon in mid-September 1943, I went to Las Vegas and enlisted in the Navy, giving my age as 17. My mother's signature was required on the papers, but it was too late in the day to travel 135 miles to St. George to get it. Instead, the recruiting officer sent a telegram to obtain her authorization. I went to St. George that weekend and coaxed her to sign the telegram. She finally relented and signed, thinking that when I got to Salt Lake City

to be sworn in, they would check my birth certificate and send me home. They didn't check my records in Salt Lake City, and I was sworn in on 23 September 1943. I left immediately for the Naval Training Center at Farragut, Idaho, for boot training. I was a member of boot company 832-43, Regiment 5.

After returning from leave and recovering from a bad case of double pneumonia, I was ordered to Memphis, Tennessee, to attend Aviation Radioman School. From there I went to the Naval Air Gunnery School at Hollywood, Florida. I graduated from gunnery school in the top 10% of my class and was promoted to aviation radioman third class within a year after joining the Navy. Next, I went to the Naval Air Station at Opa Locka, Florida, where I became part of a TBM-3 crew. When we completed operational training in October 1944, we were assigned to Torpedo Squadron 10 (VC-10). VC-10 was in the process of absorbing replacements and re-forming. The squadron had been aboard the USS *Gambier Bay* (CVE-73) when she was sunk during the battle of Leyte Gulf.

After a short period of training, we deployed from San Diego in the early spring of 1945. We went to Guam and met our ship, the USS *Fanshaw Bay* (CVE-70) after a stop at Kaneohe Bay. We met other CVEs at Eniwetok atoll, then joined Task Force 44 at Adak, Alaska. We were part of Vice Admiral Jack Fletcher's North Pacific Force. By this time, the war was over and we were sent to Matsu Bay, Northern Honshu, Japan, as part of the occupation force. Our squadron, VC-10, was decommissioned at the Naval Air Station, Alameda, California, in October 1945.

From 1946 to 1950, I was stationed at a number of locations, including NATTC Memphis; Naval Air Gunners School, Yellow Water, Florida; the Naval Air Station at Banana River, Florida; Naval Air Station, San Juan, Puerto Rico; Naval Air Station, Quonset Point, Rhode Island; back to San Juan; then to Naval Air Station, San Diego, for shore duty. I was assigned to the Commander Air Force Pacific Communications Center and was on duty when word came that the North Koreans had invaded South Korea in June 1950.

After two years of shore duty, I was transferred to VC-35, Naval Air Station, San Diego, where I was assigned as an electronic maintenance technician on the USS *Boxer* (CV-21). I was promoted to Aviation Radioman Chief while on the *Boxer*. Later, I trained as an air crew member, and in January 1956, went aboard the USS *Shangri-La* (CVA-38). During this deployment, I was selected to be a LDO (limited duty officer) and was transferred to the Naval Training Center, Newport, Rhode Island, where I was commissioned an ensign in June 1956.

After completing officers training school, I went back to the Naval Aviation Technical Training Center, Memphis, Tennessee, as a student in aviation electronic officers school. After graduating in 1957, I was assigned to Electronic Countermeasures Squadron Two, Naval Air Station, Port Lyautey, Morocco, as an airborne ECM evaluator, ECM training officer, and avionics officer. In July 1961, I was assigned to the Electronic Warfare Division, Naval Missile Center, Point Mugu, California. I retired from the U. S. Navy on 1 February 1967 as a 39-year-old lieutenant after serving twenty-three years, four months, and five days on active duty.

While on shore duty in San Diego, I had to obtain a security clearance, and I knew the background check would uncover my correct age. I went to the personnel officer and told him my story. After I provided him with a certified birth certificate, and after consulting with the Bureau of Personnel, he corrected the record to reflect my true birth date.

I consider joining the Navy at age 15 the most significant event in my life. It provided me with the very things that were missing in my childhood, namely, discipline, direct supervision, and motivation. Although I had vowed never to return to school, I started taking classes shortly after enlisting in the Navy. I was able to obtain my high school diploma through the GED program. In fact, because I had passed the GED tests, the high school that I had walked out of in 1943 issued me a regular diploma with the class of 1946. I feel that I have been in school for the past forty-seven years because my entire career has been one great learning experience.

Calvin Lyle received a letter of commendation from the Chief of Naval Operations, Admiral Arliegh Burke, for classified work performed in Turkey and Pakistan during the period 1958-61. In March 1967, he went to work as a field service engineer with the AAI Corporation, Hunt Valley, Maryland. For eighteen years his job with AAI was to visit various Air Defense Command locations and teach a 360-hour maintenance training course to fire-control technicians. He retired from AAI on 31 July 1991 after twenty-four years and five months of service. Calvin and his wife Wanda live in Fairfield, California. They have five children from previous marriages, thirteen grandchildren, and one great-granddaughter.

Daniel S. Hennessey, Sr.

Age 15 – United States Navy

"Ladies and gentlemen, we interrupt this program with the following news bulletin: the Imperial Japanese Air Force is attacking the United States military installation at Pearl Harbor in the Hawaiian Islands. The U. S. Navy is reported to have suffered

> *When I reached the foot/arch test, I did my little ballet and sailed right through.*

heavy damage from the bombing raid. Further bulletins will be broadcast as they are received. We now return you to the regular broadcast." I was 13 years of age when I heard that broadcast, but the die had been cast, and I was going to join the Navy as quickly as possible.

I lived in Plainfield, New Jersey, in a two-family house with my mother and a younger brother who was five years my junior. I was born in Albany, New York, on 14 July 1928. My mother was employed full-time as a professional office supervisor and commuted daily to New

York City. My father was an alcoholic and was usually separated from my mother. I was more or less the man in charge of the family – my brother and myself.

The first step in my quest to become a sailor was to establish that I was older than I actually was. In 1942, as I was approaching my fourteenth birthday, I retrieved my original official birth certificate from the family's papers. It was a printed document, but the vital statistics were written in black ink. I very carefully applied one small drop of household bleach with the end of a glass iodine applicator to the top half of the "8" in the date 1928. Presto! With a little touching up, 1928 became 1926, and I was now within a year of the minimum age for enlistment in the Navy.

The next step was to establish a background for my 1926 birth date. I registered for a Social Security card, which was issued without question, then I applied to the high school for working papers. New Jersey law allowed 16-year-old students to work part-time after school if they had a Social Security card and permission from the school they attended. I received my working papers and worked at several afternoon/evening jobs in a book bindery and a defense plant.

It seemed like forever, but finally the calendar said 14 July 1943, and I could now enlist in the Navy. Another part of my strategy was to go to a major recruiting station. I figured that with the pressures of the war, they might not be prone to check the details as much. I was wrong. I chose the Navy recruiting station in New York City, a little over an hour away from my home by rail. On the way to the station, I ate from seven to ten pounds of bananas, being careful to time it so it wouldn't require a premature trip to the bathroom. This little trick was so that I would be sure to pass the minimum weight requirement.

Everything went well for awhile. The paperwork went fine, no questions asked. Then came the physical exam. A line of naked males snaked down a long corridor from one checkpoint to another. Again, everything was going just fine until I stepped over a door sill into a large pan of water. A corpsman told me to step out of the pan onto a blotter paper on the floor. He looked at the blotter and said to me. "OK, you can get dressed and go home." I asked, "What do you mean?" He replied, "You've failed the physical. You have about the flattest feet I have ever seen." I looked at the pattern of my footprints on the blotter. It looked almost like someone had made imprints of two building bricks side by side, flat as hell.

Well, this was a fine pickle! After all my background work, I am rejected because of a couple of flat feet that I have had all my life. I said to the corpsman, "Doc, if you can spot flat feet that way, how do you tell the ones that are OK?" I guess he took pity on me because he said, "Wait a minute kid." He put another blotter down and the next man stepped in the water, then on the blotter. The corpsman looked and said to him, "OK, keep moving." He pointed to the wet pattern and said, "Its pretty obvious." I looked and saw a nice round pad where the heel should be. There was a narrow shank print that ran along where the side of the foot should be, up to the ball of the foot. Where the arch should be was a big, dry space. The corpsman said, "So long," and I got dressed and went home.

I was down, but not out. I got an old bed pan and a good supply of old newspaper. In my bathroom at home I practiced daily — step into the water, step onto the paper, check the print. Within ten days I had it down fairly pat. Step in the water, step onto the paper and throw all of my weight to the outside of my feet, moving fast and — presto, a passing footprint. I was ready to try again.

I told my friend Joe that I had the solution to the flat-feet problem down pat and that I was going to New York City and join the Navy. He decided to go with me, so we were off to the recruiting station. The paperwork was no problem, and we were ordered into the physical exam line. When I reached the foot/arch test, I did my little ballet and sailed right through. Both Joe and I were accepted. We were told to come back on Friday with a change of underwear and a toothbrush and that we would be sworn in and sent on our way.

On Friday, we arrived at the recruiting station at 0800. There was a line of men passing through a gate monitored by two recruiters. At the gate, the men would call out their names, and the recruiters would check a list and give them instructions. Joe's name was checked off, and he went through the gate. I gave my name, the recruiter thumbed through the list, found my name and said, "You go home and come back in a couple of years when you are old enough." I said, "What?" He said, "Next!" Way up the hall I saw Joe looking back with a wide-eyed stare. I gave him a wave of the hand, turned, and walked away. It would be a long time before Joe found out what happened to me.

It was now into September 1943 and I had been 17 for a month and a half and still had not been successful in my efforts to join the Navy. Not to be thwarted, I devised a new plan. I had some experience in cross-country hitchhiking and riding the rails, and I had an aunt and uncle in Los Angeles, California. I didn't tell my aunt and uncle that I was coming, but I told my mother and asked her, "If you get a permission letter from the Navy, please sign it and send it back. If I don't make it into the Navy, I don't know what my next step will be." When the time came, the letter was duly signed and returned.

I hitchhiked, rode the rails, slept in culverts, and finally arrived at my aunt and uncle's house. I slept on the couch that night, and the next morning began hunting for a Navy recruiting station. It took me three days before I spotted one in a small town south of Los Angeles. I went in, went through all the preliminaries, and I was told to report to the Los Angeles City Hall on 29 September 1943, to be sworn in.

You can bet your bottom dollar that I was there — I was first in line. I was sworn in, and left immediately for the Naval Training Station, San Diego, California, for five weeks of boot training. After boot camp, I was assigned to a radar operators school at Point Loma, California. Radar was new to the Navy, and radar school was considered a plum assignment.

In December 1943, I was assigned to, and became a plank owner of the USS *Proteus* (AS-19), the newest and most modern submarine tender to be built at that time. At the time, the *Proteus* was the largest ship ever built on the West Coast. It cost $25,000,000. We loaded and cleaned the ship and took it on a shakedown cruise along the coast of Mexico and back to San Francisco. The ship was commissioned on 31 January 1944, and after a short stay in San Francisco, we sailed west in the Pacific. Our first stop was at the submarine base, Pearl Harbor, Hawaii.

Our job was to overhaul, refit, and replenish submarines. We left Pearl Harbor and were located at the submarine base at Midway Island from 3 May 1944 until 30 November 1944. Just before my sixteenth birthday, 14 July, I received my most prized "birthday present" from the U. S. Navy. I was promoted to petty officer third class, specifically, a radar operator's mate third class. This was the highest rate that I held while I was in the Navy.

We were at Guam in the Mariana Islands from 16 February until 16 August 1945. Then, on 16 August 1945, we received orders to join the Third Fleet, commanded by Admiral William F. Halsey, and steam into Tokyo Bay to prepare for the final acceptance of the Japanese surrender. On Sunday, 2 September 1945, the *Proteus* was present in Tokyo Bay when the surrender ceremonies took place on the USS *Missouri*. I was thrilled to be a part of this historic event. I had turned 17 less than two months before.

We left Tokyo Bay in November 1945 and returned to the States via Guam, Hawaii, the Panama Canal, New London, Connecticut, and the Navy base at Portsmouth, New Hampshire. I was transferred to the Naval Separation Center at Lido Beach, Long Island, New York, in early April 1946 and received an honorable discharge on 11 April 1946. Three months after my discharge, I turned 18 and registered for the draft.

Except for registering for the draft, I entered civilian life with my adopted birth date of 14 July 1926. On 16 March 1949, I joined the

Plainfield, New Jersey, Police Department as a probationary patrolman. I never really paid attention, but by my true age, I was not yet 21 years old, the minimum age for a police officer. My career went smoothly, and I was promoted to detective in 1953. In 1958, I was first on the promotion list for sergeant. This was the time that "the chickens came home to roost." An anonymous letter to the city government, obviously from another man on the promotion list, accused me of fraudulent enlistment in the police department. I was summoned before the Union County Grand Jury. After hearing my case, the jury refused to return formal charges against me and stated that it was an interdepartmental disciplinary matter.

Two state assemblymen introduced a bill (#716, dated 16 November 1959) in the New Jersey State Assembly that amended the New Jersey State Law to forgive my underage police enlistment, based on my underage U. S. Navy enlistment and my honorable discharge. On 7 December 1959, I received notice from the office of the Governor of the state of New Jersey that Assembly Bill 716 had been signed and was now law.

Dan Hennessey remained with the police department of Plainfield, New Jersey, until he retired as Captain of Police on 31 December 1974. On 2 January 1975, he assumed duties as Superintendent and Chief of Police of Marple Township, Delaware County, Pennsylvania, a post that he still holds. In January 1994, Dan was inducted into the Hall of Fame of Pennsylvania Region 13, International Police Association. Dan holds a B.A. from Neumann College and an M.A. from St. Joseph's University. He is a senior instructor under the Municipal Police Officers Education and Training Commission and instructs at the Delaware County and Philadelphia City Police Training Academies. Dan and Emma, his wife of forty-eight years, live in Broomall, Pennsylvania. They have five children and seven grandchildren.

Nicholas Poma

Age 15 – United States Navy

I was born in Detroit, Michigan, on 23 October 1927. In 1928, when I was only a few months old, my mother slipped and hit her head on a sidewalk. She completely lost her memory and couldn't remember any of us kids, nor how to care

> *... we saw the massive wave cover our ship, right where we had been standing.*

for us. We were placed in foster homes by the state. I was 12 years old before I found out I had a family of my own. That was in 1940 when my father came to see me. My four brothers and my sister visited me later.

During the winter of 1942, my brother John came to our one-room school and asked the teacher if he could take me to town to buy me things for Christmas. As we were walking through the snow to the car, John asked me, "How would you like to go home?" I said, "Oh yes, please!" As we left for home I think my heart was going faster than the car!

Before we went to my parents' house, I was told about our mother's memory loss and warned that she might tell me to get out. When I met her for the first time, she didn't know me from Adam. I felt bad about this, but being home with my family made up for everything.

After about a week, my mother and I were getting along, but not as mother and son. I hung around with my brother John whenever I could. I was with him when he went to the draft board and told them he was 18 years old, although he was only 17. He got away with it and was drafted into the Army.

After John was gone, I started hanging around with the wrong bunch and was heading for trouble. I knew I had to do something fast, so I went to the draft board, as my brother had done, and registered as an 18-year-old. I was drafted into the Navy in 30 September 1943 at the age of 15.

While I was in boot camp, I was worried that I wouldn't be able to keep up with the older men and that the Navy would find out I was underage and send me home. But on graduation day, there I was, out on the drill field carrying the colors for my company. I don't think my feet touched the ground once that day. I wished that my family could have seen me.

After boot camp and a 30-leave, I was sent to Norman, Oklahoma, for training, after which I was put on a train to go to Norfolk, Virginia. We had a 3-hour layover in St. Louis, Missouri, so a friend and I got off the train to look around. It didn't take us long to meet some girls who took us to a bar where they didn't ask how old we were. We missed the train. I was picked up two weeks later, taken to Great Lakes, Illinois, and put in the brig for two months, on bread and water for the first two weeks.

After serving my time, I was sent to Houston, Texas, to report aboard the USS *Lawrence C. Taylor* (DE-415). My train arrived in Houston at 5:00 p.m. I didn't have to report aboard ship until 8:00 the next morning, so I looked around and met a very beautiful redhead who was nice enough to show me her city. The only thing was, I was so tired from the train ride that I couldn't keep my eyes open. She took me to her home where I met her mother. Before I knew it, I was asleep on the couch.

I hadn't told them what time I had to be on the ship, so they didn't wake me. It was 11:00 a.m. when I woke up. They drove me to the shipyard to find the *Taylor*. Need I tell you, the first place I got to see on the ship was the brig. My sentence was two weeks of bread and water in the brig and one and a half months' restriction to the ship. I never saw Houston again.

We went to Bermuda on a shakedown cruise, then to Boston, Massachusetts, and on to Norfolk, Virginia. Yep, I made it back to the ship on time! From Norfolk we went to Guantanamo Bay, Cuba, then through the Panama Canal, and on to Pearl Harbor, where our ship was put in dry dock for repairs. The several weeks that the ship was in dry dock gave us time to meet the beautiful girls of Pearl. Yes, I made it back on time.

After leaving Pearl, we joined with four other destroyer-escorts and a small carrier to form Escort Division-72. Our division, known as "hunter-killers," was specially trained to hunt submarines. On 18 November 1944, while conducting antisubmarine patrols around the ships taking part in the invasion of Leyte, we made contact with a sub. It took us fourteen hours and eight attacks to sink that submarine. We learned later that it was the I-26, the same Japanese submarine that torpedoed one of our cruisers, the USS *Juneau* (CL-52), in 1942, killing the five Sullivan brothers and 685 of their shipmates.

We were caught in the great typhoon off Luzon on 18 and 19 December 1944. During the typhoon, our fleet lost three ships, 790 men, and 200 planes. Twenty-eight ships were damaged, three of them from our Escort Division-72. During the typhoon, it felt like the ship was tearing herself apart. My buddy suggested that we go topside in case the ship were to sink. When no one was looking, we unlatched the weather-tight door to the weather deck. As we stepped out, we saw a towering wave overtaking the ship. We rushed to get off the lower deck and up to the torpedo deck. As we reached the torpedo deck and looked back, we saw the massive wave cover our ship, right where we had been standing.

We worked our way up to a gun mount and climbed in. From where we were, we could see everyone on the bridge, so we kept the gun between us. The wind was so loud that we had to put our hands and mouth to each others' ears to be heard. All at once, we saw a giant wave push our ship's bow straight up like it was pointing to the sky. As I watched her fight to pull herself up this mountainous wave, I remembered how big she had looked when I first saw her, but seeing her fight to climb that wave, she looked so small.

When the ship's bow went over the top of the wave and started down, the twin screws in the stern came out of the water. The vibration was so bad the ship just shuddered. We next found ourselves racing down a tremendous incline. It was just like being on a giant roller coaster — one minute we would be looking straight up for the top of the wave, and the next minute we would be looking straight down into a valley. At no time did we see any other ships. Finally, my friend and I made our way below deck. No one even knew we had been gone.

One day in January 1945, during the invasion of Luzon, I was told to report to the captain's cabin. As I stood at attention in front of him, he said, "At ease Nick, I want to talk with you, and I want you to tell me the truth. How old are you, Nick?" I replied, "Nineteen, sir!" The captain said, "Come on, Nick, you can tell me your real age." I replied again, "Nineteen, sir!" The captain picked up a sheet of paper off his desk and said, "Nick, I just received a message from the Navy Department. Do you want me to read it? It's about you." I said, "Yes, sir." The captain read, "You have a minor on board by the name of Nicholas Poma. His family has been looking for him. He would be of age by the time he reached the States, so we will leave it up to you whether to send him home or keep him aboard."

The captain then asked me how I got into the Navy and why. I told him and he said, "Nick, if you went back home, you would be a hero, and they would roll out the red carpet for you." I told him that I would like to stay as long as the crew was not told my real age. He said OK, and he kept his promise. I think a few people may have thought that I was underage, but they didn't know for sure.

In February 1945, we joined an escort carrier force of five baby flattops and seven destroyer-escorts and headed for Iwo Jima. During the invasion, the USS *Bismarck Sea* was mortally damaged by two kamikazes. One dropped into the elevator shaft and turned her into a sweltering inferno. She was just a few hundred yards from our port bow. As the crew jumped from the ship, it looked to us like they were jumping into the fire. Our new captain, Lieutenant Commander James Robert Grey, USN, swung the ship hard left and slowed until we drifted slowly in among the bobbing little lights. Each life jacket had a small flashlight tied to it, which made it look like there was a myriad of blinking candles in the black, murky water. The small lights, intended as a rescue aid, proved otherwise. A Japanese plane spotted them and came in low to strafe the survivors in the water, killing many of them. We worked all night dragging 121 burned and half-drowned men from the rough sea. No one slept that night.

After seventy-six days of ASW (antisubmarine warfare) sweeps around Okinawa during the battle there, we again joined the Third Fleet while they bombarded Honshu, Japan.

On 16 July 1945, our ship and another destroyer-escort investigated a report that a large Japanese submarine had been sighted on the surface sixty-seven miles from our task group. We arrived in the area and made sonar contact right away. We fired a full pattern of twenty-four Mark II projectiles and started to move away at full speed. Before the change of speed could take effect, we felt a violent explosion. A minute later another violent explosion rocked our ship. It was obvious that the sub was breaking apart.

Our whaleboat was lowered to recover debris. Among the many items we picked up was a pamphlet that contained a map of the United States showing in detail all of our oil-producing centers. Lines on the map indicated the approximate position of the Big-Inch Pipeline. Twin engine bombers were also noted to be approaching the United States from both the Atlantic and the Pacific.

After the war, we learned that the submarine was the I-13. It was one of two AM-class Japanese submarines that carried three aircraft, the other being the I-14. In May 1945, the I-13 and I-14, in conjunction with the I-400 and I-401, were gearing up for an attack on the Panama Canal. The four submarines carried a total of ten aircraft. Repeated delays and shortages of fuel caused the target to be changed from the Panama Canal to Ulithi, a major U. S. Navy anchorage south of Guam. Our ship sank the I-13 on her way to Truk, but the others arrived there safely and planned the raid for 17 August 1945. On 15 August 1945, Emperor Hirohito broadcast the order for the immediate surrender of all Japanese forces, and the plan was scrapped.

We were scheduled to accompany the Third Fleet into Tokyo Bay for the official surrender ceremonies, but we had been forty days at sea without replenishment of supplies and were forced to head for Guam. Throughout all of the time we spent in the Pacific, the *Taylor* was the only ship in our group that completed every operation undertaken without anything happening to cause it to return to base for repairs.

On 11 September 1945, we took elements of the 1st Marine Division to Jinsen, Korea, and a few weeks later, we took elements of the 6th Marine Division to Tsingtao, China. On 27 October 1945, we pulled into Hulutao harbor, Manchuria. As a whaleboat from our ship approached the pier, Chinese Communist soldiers fired on it. We learned later that they suspected that the American ships were bringing Chinese Nationalist troops ashore.

On 22 December 1945, our ship, the USS *Taylor*, was ordered to return to the United States. We arrived in San Francisco on 15 January 1946, and I was discharged on 22 April 1946 at age 18, after two and one-half years of service.

Nick Poma earned seven battle stars on his Asiatic-Pacific ribbon. When he returned home, his mother still did not remember him.

He owned a poolroom in Detroit, Michigan, for a time, then owned a card room in Redmond, Washington. He worked for Boeing Aircraft in Seattle and for a military ordnance depot at Port Chicago, California. In 1961, he was told he had emphysema, and in 1962, he came down with Buerger's disease, which resulted in the amputation of his right leg. Nick was married for a time, but it didn't work out. He had a son and two granddaughters by this marriage. His son died in 1990 at the age of 41. In 1970, Nick married Shirley Steadman, who had three daughters from a previous marriage. Shirley died of lung cancer in 1988. Nick now lives in Brush Prairie, Washington.

√ **VUMS Note** ⇒ *A letter of thanks from a grandmother.* Fifty-one years after the sinking of the USS *Bismarck Sea* off Iwo Jima, Nick Poma received a letter from the wife of a naval officer rescued by the crew of his ship. It reads in part:

When the *Bismarck Sea* was kamikazed off Iwo Jima and you were on the destroyer that rescued so many, did they say to you, "Oh, no, you must throw me back, I must have a seaman of legal age rescue me, not one who lied to get in the Navy!" I know how grateful Warren and I are to the men on the destroyer who stood by and saved them. So thank you all again — here I am, fifty years later and with ten grandchildren who wouldn't be here if it weren't for people like you!

With love — Dodie (age 74)
a. k. a. — Lt(jg) Dorothy Stanley, USNR (1943-1946)
a. k. a. — Mrs. Warren C. Thompson (1948-1996+)
a. k. a. — grandmother to ten because Warren was saved from the ship's sinking by underage *and* legal age sailors!

Wilma P. "Penny" Lawson

Age 15 – United States Army (WAC)

As far back as I can remember I have had a love for the military. When I was a child, my grandfather would take me to Chickamauga Battlefield to recite the history of the Civil War. He

> *... I remember our company commander ... saying ... "Take care of our baby."*

would point out where each battle was fought, how many casualties were inflicted, and so forth.

Military uniforms were, and still are, more appealing to me than the high fashions of any year. To me, a uniform stands for commitment, valor, and discipline. These are some of the thoughts I had during my formative years that helped make me determined to enter the Army. To be perfectly candid, another reason for enlisting was that I needed a home. I was homeless before it became socially acceptable to be homeless.

On 8 November 1942, at the age of 14, I married a young soldier who was stationed at Fort Oglethorpe, Georgia. He had applied for Airborne school prior to our marriage, and shortly after, he was transferred to Fort Benning, Georgia, for Airborne training. We never had the opportunity to live together, even for a short time. In April 1943, he was sent to Africa to join the 82nd Airborne Division, with which he served until he was wounded in Holland.

Meanwhile, I secured a fraudulent document stating that I was 21 years old. I talked to a recruiter, enlisted, and was sent to Nashville, Tennessee, for testing and a physical examination. Girls were being rejected at an alarming rate. I lived in mortal fear that I would not be accepted; obviously, I was. I took the oath and was sworn into the Army on 5 October 1943 at age 15, five years before I could legally do so — even with parental consent.

I was sent to Daytona Beach, Florida, for basic training. Each day we had drill, physical training, guard duty, and classes. I never asked for, nor received, any favors. I maintained the pace that was expected of every recruit. My company was my family. We shared our joys and our tears. We learned discipline, respect, and order. I still remember our Sergeant Nash after all these years. She taught us many skills, with patience. Once, while instructing us, she commented, "There is the right way and the Army way." Needless to say, we did it correctly. She had an endearing way of making you want to do your assignment to the best of your ability.

We had both ends of the spectrum in our company. I was a youth of 15, and there was a woman of undetermined age who had false teeth. Each night, she would place her teeth in a clean glass of water for all to see.

After completing basic training, many in our company, including Sergeant Nash, were shipped to Camp Hood (now Fort Hood), Texas. On our departure, I remember our company commander looking at me, and in a never-heard-before compassionate manner, saying to Sergeant Nash, "Take care of our baby." I wondered if she knew.

In Texas, I was assigned to the 1848 WAC Detachment. I requested and was assigned to, the motor pool. I truly enjoyed that job. Each hour and each day provided a new challenge. I drove heavy trucks, ambulances, and staff cars, transporting officers to their destinations. I also transported German prisoners of war, under guard, of course.

Every few months, a notice would be posted on the bulletin board for volunteers to go overseas. I always signed the notice, thinking that I could do more "over there," but I never got the chance to go.

During my last year in the Army, I served as a librarian in the station hospital. I gave brief book reviews on the intercom for the patients. I assisted in checking out books and in all the things necessary to keep the library in order.

We had jitterbug contests at the field house frequently. How we did enjoy those dances! My partner and I won the contest one night and were presented with a large cake, which we shared with everyone present.

I really think that even in the lighter moments, we all were cognizant of the terrible price being paid on the battlefield by our young men. After all, for the most part, that was the reason we chose to serve, to do what we could on the home front.

At long last my husband came home from the war. He left as a young boy and came home a man. He has many scars, longer-lasting than his leg wound, that will go to his grave with him.

After my husband was discharged, I was discharged too, on 4 November 1945. One lesson I learned in the Army is that you stay with an assignment until the task is completed. I think that discipline has helped me to persevere through the hard times. I truly loved the Army and would recommend it to anyone if it were the same as yesteryear.

Penny Lawson attended school for two years under the GI Bill. She and her husband Doyle eventually moved to Chattanooga, Tennessee, where Doyle worked for the post office. He is now on dialysis, but shows the same strength of character that helped him through the war. Penny and Doyle recently celebrated their fifty-third wedding anniversary, and their "tour of duty" is not over yet! They have three children and two grandchildren. One grandson is a Navy petty officer aboard the USS Monterey *off the coast of Bosnia.*

James A. Popplewell

Age 14 – United States Navy

I started plotting to join the Navy when I was 13 years old. My classmates had always been two or three years older than I because I had started school at age 4. My friends and I were very patriotic, having played at killing Nazis since the middle

> *My folks would never give their permission, so I would have to run away.*

thirties, and later the Japanese after Pearl Harbor. In 1943, a lot of my friends and acquaintances began to join the military. The Navy was a popular choice and one that appealed to me. I had to find a way to join. I would need a real birth certificate, an altered one would not do.

A neighbor boy with whom I played, and whom I knew as well as my own brother, was 17 years of age. I knew enough about him and his family to obtain an official duplicate of his birth certificate for 50¢. I did that by filling out and filing an application at city hall. I was 13 and the piece of paper necessary to enlist was in my pocket, but no one knew anything about it. My folks would never give their permission, so I would have to run away. I was ready to enlist, but I was not ready to run away.

On my fourteenth birthday, my folks gave me an expensive fountain pen. After school a couple of days later, I was showing the pen to a friend in the bathroom when one of the school toughs grabbed it and threw it in a toilet. Without thinking, I dumped the tough in the toilet after the pen and left the school grounds. I knew I was in trouble, and I decided the time was ripe to enlist.

I knew that if I enlisted in Kansas City the chances of getting caught were great, so I hitched a ride to St. Joseph, a large town about fifty miles away. I joined the Navy the next day. What I didn't realize was that the recruiting office in St. Joseph was a substation of the Kansas City office and that the paperwork that had been completed was sent to Kansas City for processing. This was my undoing.

My father questioned all my friends, but no one knew anything. Later, one of them told Dad that I was always talking about joining the Navy. Dad went to the recruiting office and asked them to search the records for my name. They didn't find it, but my neighborhood friend's name was there, and Dad had just seen him earlier that day. Dad knew what I had done, but the Navy wasn't convinced. It took awhile, but he proved that it was I who was in the Navy, not my neighbor. During the last week of boot training, I was sent to the chaplain's office and told I had been discovered as being underage. Instead of going to sea school, I was transferred to a casual company. My folks had the option of giving their consent for me to remain in the Navy, but my mother refused. The name I had used was changed back to my real one, and I received an honorable discharge. I drew mustering-out pay and GI Bill benefits. My only regret is that I had to run away to join. I was never able to go back to school, and it would be many years before I could admit, or be, my true age.

In 1945, at the age of 15, I joined the Kansas City, Missouri, Fire Department. They were hiring 17-year-olds at that time because of wartime shortages. Even here, I would later learn, there were others who had also sneaked in underage. It was an exciting experience. I was assigned to companies that were kept busy with fires. We worked twenty-four hours on and twenty-four hours off, averaging a 72-hour week. We often worked double shifts and sometimes two or three weeks or more without a day off. Not much time to think about being a kid!

In November 1946, at the age of 17, I joined the Marines for three years. I was assigned to Marine Barracks, Yokosuka, Japan, for two years, but while I was there, I was put on detached duty to the Commander, Naval Forces Far East, and served in Tokyo for fourteen months. I was discharged in November 1949, but I was recalled in 1950 because of the Korean War. I was not sent to Korea. While I was in the Marines, I was on military leave from the fire department, and I returned to the department after being discharged.

I joined the Kansas Army National Guard later. I was called to active duty in March 1968 as a warrant officer and was sent to flight school. I was 39 years old when I graduated from flight school, possibly the oldest candidate to complete the course. I was a CWO-2 and assigned as command and control pilot for B troop, 7th Armored Squadron, 1st Air Cavalry, at Vinh Long, Vietnam, from June 1969 until November 1969.

In July 1976, while on a routine flight, the tail rotor on my helicopter failed. I received injuries to my spinal cord and was retired disabled as a CWO-3 in May 1977. I had retired as a fire captain in the Kansas City Fire Department the previous year.

I gives me considerable satisfaction to know that I served in three branches of our country's military services: the Navy, the Marine Corps, and the Army. I was in the Navy and the Marine Corps during wartime while very young, but did not serve in a war zone. I was much older before I had that experience. Vietnam was my war.

Jim Popplewell received the Bronze Star for leadership and initiative in combat and the Air Medal with a "V" for the destruction of a number of automatic weapons and enemy troops. He was awarded the wings of a Senior Army Aviator. Jim made up for missing high school by attending Park College, Parkville, Missouri, where he received a B.A. in 1975, and an M.A. from Central Michigan University in 1979. He received an elementary teaching credential in 1987 and a supplemental credential (single subject) in computer concepts and applications from the University of California, Riverside, in 1989. He was an elementary teacher for the California Department of Corrections for five years, using computers to teach remedial education. Jim and his wife Ernestine (Erne) live in Moreno Valley, California. They have two sons, a daughter, and one grandson. Jim is the California State Commander of the Veterans of Underage Military Service.

Betty J. (Kelly) Adams

Age 16 – United States Navy (WAVES)

It was more or less a lark when I joined the Navy at age 16. I convinced my mother to sign a notarized statement

I truly loved the Navy ...

stating that I was 20, and a Navy recruiter did the rest. To this day, I do not know how the recruiter got me in. Just as the WAVE officer was to swear me in, she asked if I could produce a birth certificate. I said yes. She swore me in, but never asked to see the certificate. This was on 24 October 1943. I enjoyed my three years of service very much. It was the smartest thing I ever did.

I reported to boot camp on 2 December 1943 at Hunter College, Bronx, New York, after which I was stationed at an area that is now part of Arlington Cemetery. After a couple of years there, working as

a master-at-arms and on a maintenance crew, I was transferred to the Patuxent River Naval Air Station. I'm sure all my commanding officers knew I was underage, but after talking to me, they would drop the subject and never bring it up again.

During my years in the Washington, D.C., area, I met and fell in love with a Navy man with whom I was stationed. After we planned to be married, I decided to tell my commanding officer at Patuxent my true age. I was discharged on 9 December 1946.

At that time, they didn't station military couples together, and we were afraid of being separated.

I have wonderful memories of men and women I met and with whom I was stationed, and places that I visited. I wish I could find some of my old friends, but I'm sure that would be impossible. I have many fond memories, and that means a lot. I truly loved the Navy and kept in close contact with my best Navy friend until 1988, when she became ill and sold her home in Wisconsin.

Betty Adams worked as an electronics assembler in Altamonte Springs, Florida, for thirty-seven years. She retired in 1996 and now resides in McGregor, Texas.

√ **VUMS Note** ⇒ *The Medal of Honor.* Two members of the VUMS, Jim Logan and Jack Lucas, won the Medal of Honor during World War II.

James M. Logan joined the Texas National Guard at age 15 in 1936. A native of Luling, Texas, Jim was with the 141st Regimental Combat Team of the 36th "Texas" Division when they hit the beaches at Salerno, Italy, on 9 September 1943. He charged 200 yards through intense fire to silence an enemy machine gun, then went on and took out several other machine-gun nests. His Medal of Honor citation states that Jim "... aided materially in ensuring the success of the beachhead at Salerno."

Jacklyn H. Lucas enlisted in the Marine Corps in August 1942 when he was 14½ years old. His age was discovered and he was relegated to a rear echelon unit in Hawaii. In January 1945, Jack stowed away on a ship bound for Iwo Jima. After nearly a month at sea, he turned himself in and was assigned to Charlie Company, 1st Battalion, 26th Marines, 5th Marine Division. On 20 February 1945, six days after his seventeenth birthday, Jack and three other Marines came under Japanese fire. When a grenade landed among them, Jack jumped on it just as a second one landed near him. He pulled both grenades under him, absorbing the blast and saving the lives of his buddies. Jack survived the blast, although he was severely wounded. He was awarded the Medal of Honor by President Truman on 5 October 1945. At the age of 17, Jack was the youngest Medal of Honor recipient since the Civil War.

Harold M. Brinson, Sr.

Age 14 – United States Navy

I was born in Charleston, South Carolina, on 20 July 1929. In 1943, I wanted to join the Navy but I was only 14 years old. We had a very large family Bible in which the birth dates of all family members were entered. My sister and I altered it so that my birth date became 5 December 1926.

At 15, I was having the best time of my life!

Armed with the family Bible to establish my age, I went to the recruiting office and enlisted in the Navy. I was sworn in on 6 January 1944 at Fort Jackson, South Carolina, and was sent to Jacksonville, Florida, for boot camp. After boot camp I was stationed at the Naval Air Base, Beaufort, South Carolina, for nine months. Next, I went to Fort Pierce, Florida, for amphibious training, followed by more training at the Amphibious Training Base, Solomons, Maryland. After the amphibious training was completed, I was transferred to the Navy receiving barracks at Portland, Oregon, to await completion and commissioning of the USS *LCS(L)-93*.

I was at the receiving station for about two months. There was no discipline at the station. Everyone seemed to be on his own and could come and go as he pleased. At 15, I was having the best time of my life! I enjoyed all the free benefits available, such as wine, women and song. I hated for it to end, and this is where I goofed up.

My ship left for San Diego, and I missed it. My buddy and I stayed in Portland for seven days, thinking that we could hitchhike to San Diego and meet the ship there. We started hitchhiking and were resting by the side of a road in Eugene, Oregon, when we were picked up. We were brought back to Portland, then sent to Bremerton, Washington. We were charged with missing our ship and sentenced to ninety days in the brig. My record had been spotless until that time. My mother found out that I was in trouble and notified the Navy of my true age.

I was sent to a retraining center at Farragut, Idaho, for about a month and a half, then was given an honorable discharge on 5 May 1945, at the age of 15. If I had been older and more experienced, I'm sure that I would have handled the situation differently.

Harold Brinson went to work for the Raybestos-Manhattan Company in North Charleston, South Carolina, as a rubber-cover specialist. In 1975, after twenty-five years with that company, he resigned to go into business for himself. Harold and Jeanne, his wife of forty-six years, operated the Sand Bar Seafood Restaurant on Folly Beach, South Carolina, for five years. The restaurant was very successful, but Harold retired in 1980 because of heart problems. He has had two open-heart surgeries since retiring but is still going strong. Harold and Jeanne live in Charleston, South Carolina. They have four children, ten grandchildren and one great-grandchild.

Jacob F. "Jake" Aman

Age 16 – United States Navy

I grew up in Dayton, Ohio, where I was born on 29 July 1927. In 1943, when I was 15 years old, I went to the draft board and registered, telling them that I was 18. In the meantime, I ran away from home and went to Florida where I worked as a bellhop for awhile, then went to New Orleans. From

That was my first experience with the shore patrol, and I learned never to ask, "Why?"

New Orleans, I was hitchhiking my way west when I was involved in a terrible accident, so I returned to Ohio.

When I arrived home, I found that the draft board had been looking for me. My father told them that I was only 15, so they stopped looking. I wanted to go into the service, so I went to the draft board again, registered, and told them that I wasn't working. I was streetwise and knew that they would draft me if I wasn't working and would probably not take the time to check me out. I wanted to be a paratrooper, but someone told me that I would have to go into the

Army, then volunteer for the Airborne, and that I might not be accepted. I didn't want to be in the regular Army, so when I was drafted and given the choice of the Army, Navy, or Marines, I chose the Navy.

Three weeks later, on 10 January 1944, I was sworn into the Navy and was on my way to boot camp at Great Lakes, Illinois. After boot camp, we were given a few days leave, so I took the train home. I ordered a beer in the dining car and while I was drinking it, a sailor wearing a shore patrol

arm band (military police) said to me, "Make that your last one, mate." I asked, "Why?" That was my first experience with the shore patrol, and I learned to never ask, "Why?"

I was sent to the New Hebrides Islands in the South Pacific where, in May 1944, I was assigned to the aircraft carrier USS *Corregidor*

(CVE-58). We returned to Pearl Harbor to join a convoy of ships preparing for action in the Mariana Islands. It took three days to get the convoy together. In every direction, as far as you could see, there were American ships. It gave me a good feeling to see all that naval power.

On 17 and 18 June 1944, we took part in the Battle of the Philippine Sea that American sailors dubbed the "Great Marianas Turkey Shoot." The battle cost the Japanese three aircraft carriers and nearly all of their trained pilots.

We were caught in a typhoon on 20 April 1945. The ship cracked in four places, but luckily, we made it back to Pearl where repairs were made to the hull, then went on to the States where the ship was in dry dock during May and June 1945. We returned to the South Pacific and spent most of our time hunting submarines until the war ended.

We left the Pacific in January 1946, stopped in San Diego for a few days, then went through the Panama Canal to Norfolk, Virginia. I was discharged at Norfolk on 21 April 1946.

I was working for the National Cash Register Company in Dayton, Ohio, when the Korean War started. A friend was in the Navy Reserves, so I asked him how soon he could get me in. He told me about thirty days. I went on active duty in September 1950 and served aboard the USS *Hamul* (AD-20). I was released from active duty in January 1952.

Jake Aman earned four battle stars on his Asiatic-Pacific ribbon. He went to work for Southern Pacific Railways on 1 July 1952 and retired from that company in 1982. He was a locomotive engineer for twenty-one of the thirty years he was with the railroad. Jake lives in Calistoga, California. He has three children, seven grandchildren, and two great-grandchildren.

Seth T. Wilson, Jr.

Age 16 – United States Navy

My father joined the Army at age 16 and served for thirty years. I was born in the Canal Zone on 29 December 1927. I was an "Army brat," but I was a brat in more ways than one. We were stationed at Fort

> **We were off Formosa ... when we were hit twice by kamikaze.**

Monroe, Virginia, when I quit high school and became a juvenile delinquent. I finally wised up and talked my parents into letting me join the Navy. They signed a notarized statement saying that my birth certificate had been lost and my birth date was 29 December 1926.

On 14 January 1944, I enlisted in the Navy. After boot camp at the Naval Training Center, Bainbridge, Maryland, I was a member of the commissioning crew (a plank owner) of the USS *Ticonderoga* (CV-14). I started out as a plane pusher on the flight deck. We were off

Formosa on 21 January 1945 when we were hit twice by kamikaze. As a result of the attack, 345 of our crew were either killed, wounded or missing.

After the war, my rating was changed from seaman to fireman. In 1946, I was transferred to the USS *Guadalupe* (AO-32) and served as an engineering petty officer. While the *Guadalupe* was in Tsingtao, China, I received my first honorable discharge, but I immediately reenlisted and was assigned as engineering petty officer on

the USS *Macomb* (DMS-23) out of Charleston, South Carolina. I was next assigned to shore duty at Newport News, Virginia, from September 1948 until May 1950.

In May 1950, I reported aboard the USS *Wisconsin* (BB-64) as a member of her first crew after being recommissioned for the Korean War. In 1951, we were off the coast of Korea providing gunfire support to the troops. We were hit by shore fire on one occasion. I stayed on the *Wisconsin* until April 1954, at which time I was assigned to the

USS *Taconic* (AGC-17), again as an engineering petty officer. After two years on the *Taconic*, I was sent to the Great Lakes Naval Training Center to attend electronics school. A year later, I reported aboard the USS *Sierra* (AD-18) as an electronics chief petty officer in the repair department. Six months later, I was assigned to the USS *Cone* (DD-866). Less than a year later, I was ordered to the U. S. Naval Communications Station, Port Lyautey, Morocco, where I served as the electronics maintenance chief for two and one-half years.

I was commissioned an ensign on 2 June 1960 and returned to the Naval Training Station at Newport, Rhode Island, for three months of officers school. I was then ordered to attend the electronics officers school at the Great Lakes Naval Training Center for one year.

I served for two years on Guam as the electronics maintenance officer at the Naval Communications Station. I then served as the electronics maintenance officer with Commander Destroyer Squadron-36 on the USS *John Paul Jones* (DD-932) out of Norfolk, Virginia. For the next two years, I served on the staff of Commander Services Forces Atlantic Fleet at Norfolk, Virginia. From Norfolk, I was sent to Vietnam as the naval communications officer for all naval detachments in the I-Corps out of Danang. After returning to the U. S., I was assigned to the Destroyer/Submarine Antisubmarine Warfare School at the Norfolk Naval Base.

As a result of my age, time in service, and time in grade, I could not expect to be promoted to lieutenant commander. Therefore, I resigned my commission of thirteen years and transferred to the fleet reserve as a master chief petty officer and retired at that rank on 30 June 1973. I retired from the naval service as a lieutenant with thirty years of service on 1 November 1973.

Seth Wilson received the Navy Commendation Medal with combat "V." During more than thirty years in the Navy, he earned five battle stars on his Asiatic-Pacific ribbon, two stars on his Philippine Liberation Medal, one star on his Korean Service ribbon, and three stars on his Vietnam Service ribbon. After his retirement from the Navy, he worked as a ship surveyor for the U. S. Army for sixteen years, retiring as a GS-11. Seth and his wife Evelyn live in Hampton, Virginia. They have two children and three grandchildren. Seth is the Virginia State Commander of the Veterans of Underage Military Service.

Lewis A. Mason

Age 15 – United States Navy

I ran away from home at the ripe old age of 15 and enlisted in the U. S. Navy V-6 Reserves. I was born in Ardmore, Oklahoma, on 20 November 1928, the son of a Depression-era sharecropper. Growing up during the Depression years

> When I joined the Navy, I dropped my last name and concocted a whole new life history.

was not easy. My only diversion from hard work was my membership in the Boy Scouts of America.

At birth I was christened Lewis Alexander Mason. When I joined the Navy, I dropped my last name and concocted a whole new life history. The recruiter needed numbers, so he took me to a local judge who appointed his secretary to be my legal guardian. I was sworn into the Navy as Lewis Alexander on 29 January 1944 at Oklahoma City, Oklahoma.

I was shipped to the Naval Training Station at San Diego and became part of Boot Company 44-79. We completed training on 15 March 1944, and on 11 April 1944, I was assigned to the ships' company of *LCI(L) 407*. I had the good fortune to be selected to attend gunnery school by the captain of the *407*. After gunnery school, I became a gunner's mate striker in the gunnery division aboard ship. While the *407* was in San Diego, its conversion from an

infantry landing craft to a gunboat was started. The bow 20mm and the two 20mms on the forward gun deck were replaced with 40mms. Brackets were mounted on the outboard side of both ramps, on which rocket launchers were hung.

When we arrived at Pearl Harbor, we passed a little too close to an aircraft carrier, and our mast hit the flag bag of the carrier and broke. Our skipper was immediately relieved of his command, and the executive officer was elevated to skipper. While we were in Pearl, the

407 had both ramps removed, and fifty Mark IV rocket launchers were installed. On each side of the well deck, just aft of the rocket launchers, 20mm guns were installed, completing the conversion to a gunboat. While all of this was going on, I had the good fortune of being trained as a diver. I have a love of the underwater world to this day.

We left Pearl Harbor and participated in the first wave of the invasions of Leyte, Los Negros, Pegun, Brass and Fernaldo Islands, Nassugbu, and Okinawa. I was injured during the invasion of Leyte and again when a kamikaze plane hit the *407* at Okinawa.

I was transferred to the USS *War Hawk* (AP-168) on 14 October 1945. We went to Taku, Tientsin, Peking and Shanghai, China, with a load of American-educated Chinese nationals. We put them ashore secretly at various places along the China coast.

In Shanghai, I was injured again in a head-on collision between a LCVP and a LCM on the Whangpoo River. It was dark, and a heavy fog obscured all vision. I was standing on the well deck with my back against the door of the LCVP. When the collision occurred, not only was my back injured, but both of my legs were driven through the deck plates of the LCVP. To this day, I have trouble with my legs and back.

On 5 February 1946, I was transferred to the *LSM 125* but spent most of my time in the Balboa Park Naval Hospital, San Diego. While I was there, I attended photography school in the occupational therapy department of the hospital.

I was discharged from the Navy on 19 April 1946 at Norman, Oklahoma, at the age of 17, after serving two years and four months on active duty. At this time, I went through the very tedious and time-consuming task of getting my name and personal history straightened out.

Lewis Alexander Mason resumed his full name after leaving the Navy. He attended Southern Nazarene University in Bethany, Oklahoma, and studied to be a minister of music with a minor in public school administration. After graduation, he went with churches that could not afford to pay a minister and worked at whatever jobs were available in the community to provide income. In Corpus Christi, Texas, he was a field accountant for a construction company building a gasoline plant. In Edmond, Oklahoma, he worked for the public schools. In Madill,

Oklahoma, he was manager of production control for Ardmore Air Force Base. In Oklahoma City, he was the manager of the motion picture department of the Federal Aeronautics Administration's Aeronautical Center, spending eleven years in that job. In Lake Havasu City, Arizona, he set up and managed the sub-assembly plant for the manufacture of the McCullough J-2 Gyroplane. He retired in 1974 because of ill health but has operated a scuba-diving school in his spare time. He is currently on 100% disability retirement because of injuries received while in the Navy. He has continued working with the Boy Scouts and is the recipient of the Silver Beaver. Lewis and Yvonne live in Fort Worth, Texas. Lewis has three children from his first marriage, and he and Yvonne have a daughter. They have six grandchildren and three great-grandchildren.

√ **VUMS Note** ⇒ *Troubled homes.* Many underage veterans had to deal with the trauma of a broken home, usually caused by the separation, illness, or death of their parents. There were instances of abandonment and of abuse as well. Some spent part of their childhood in orphanages or foster homes. One veteran had lived in fifteen different foster homes by the time he was 14 years old. These childhood experiences were often an influence in the decision to enlist underage. "To be perfectly frank," admitted one in her story, "another reason for enlisting was that I needed a home." Indeed, over time, several came to regard the military as their "home" and those around them as their "family."

Dorothy Hinson Brandt

Age 16 – United States Army (WAC)

In February 1944, when the Army recruiting officer in Charlotte, North Carolina, arrived to open his office, he found me fast asleep against the entry door. I had stopped by to enlist after finishing an 8-hour graveyard shift at the local

> *"It is so easy to remember and so hard to forget."*

defense plant, where I inspected tracer bullets. That was the beginning of an adventure that would continue throughout my life.

I had two brothers in the Navy, one in the Army, and one in the Army Air Forces. At the time, enlisting seemed the only patriotic thing for me to do. Patriotism was a feeling shared by almost everyone throughout the nation during World War II.

My parents naturally objected to my enlisting for two reasons: I was much too young, and I was their only daughter. Women in the military were still pioneers, and no one knew exactly what to expect. Although I was only 16, I convinced my neighbor to sign an affidavit stating that I was 20 years old. He reluctantly agreed after I persuaded him that, since he was too old to enlist, I would go and do the job in his place. I broke the news to my parents as gently as possible. They were sure I would soon become homesick. They would then tell the Army my true age, and I would be returned. That, however, never entered my mind! Sadness at our separation was compensated by a feeling of pride in the service that was shared by all.

On 15 February 1944, I became a brand new soldier at Fort Bragg, North Carolina. After a brief orientation, I left for Fort Oglethorpe, Georgia, where I joined recruits from all over the nation and began basic training. The recruits represented a wide range of age groups and occupations. We'll never know how many were underage. Bunk mates around me included a Powers model from New York, a woman logger from Oregon, a minister's daughter, a show girl from Las Vegas, a set of twins, and a mother-daughter combo from Virginia. The friendships that were formed among this diverse group of individuals provided very special experiences. Together, we struggled to learn Army regulations, pulled KP and guard duty, marched in formation, and griped a lot. Many tear-stained faces glistened in the morning sun when our training was over and we departed for our Army careers.

I was very disappointed when I was assigned to the base post office, but within a few months I received new orders to be an acting training-sergeant. It was quite an experience for me to be telling people twice my age what to do and when! As a surprise, on Mother's Day, a group of recruits bought me a beautiful corsage and took me to a fancy restaurant for dinner. That was a Mother's Day I shall never forget. They did not know it, but I was young enough to be the granddaughter of some of them.

Whenever the opportunity arose, I requested overseas duty. When the orders finally came, I reported to Fort Des Moines, Iowa, for overseas training. When we finished that phase, I was assigned to General Mark Clark's 15th Army Group in Verona, Italy. My first glimpse of the destruction of war was when we arrived by ship at Le Havre, France. Since the French were our allies, we could not understand the hostility shown towards us. We learned very quickly that they held us responsible for the bombing of their town, which had been occupied by the Germans.

In Verona, we saw hungry children everywhere digging in garbage cans for food. After that, I never ate the chocolate bars from my rations but passed them on to someone who needed them much more than I. It was also in Verona where we got acquainted with our first foreign troops. A British detachment was nearby, and they invited us to tea every afternoon.

I was in Verona only a short time before I was transferred to Vienna, Austria. Vienna was a city struggling to survive after a long, hard war. The four powers, American, British, French, and Russian, each controlled a section of the city. We were free to travel in all parts of the city except the Russian sector. That was absolutely forbidden. The cold war had already begun, but at the time we had no idea what these words meant.

I had a memorable encounter with a young Russian when I tried to take a picture of the only bridge left standing over the river. He ran towards me with his gun drawn and yelled, "Forbidden, forbidden!" Under the circumstances, I was quite frightened and with a big smile told him that I really had only wanted a picture of him, not the bridge. He smiled in return, and we both stood in front of the bridge for a photograph. Maybe he was only 17 also.

While I was stationed in Vienna, I made friends with an Austrian lady who did work for us such as washing and ironing. She thought her son was still in an Allied prisoner of war camp, but there had been no word since the war ended. One day, she came running to me with a big smile across her tear-stained face, shouting that her son was coming home. She wanted me to join her for the occasion. Her husband had been killed early in the war, and she had no other family near. I scrounged some C-rations to add to the boiled potatoes, and we ended up with what we considered a real feast. Her son arrived, pale and thin. None of that mattered now that he was home! It was an evening etched in my memory as we celebrated his safe return. He and I were both just 18.

Once, I flew on a military aircraft to Paris where my brother was stationed and spent a fabulous short leave with him. After Paris, I visited a few days in London. While I was there, I was one of the fortunate few who were selected by the USO to have tea in a garden at Buckingham Palace while the king and queen were present. I thought nothing could top that for a farm girl from North Carolina!

While I was in London, I visited with an English family whose only daughter had married an Austrian years before. I brought them word from their daughter in Vienna and pictures of their grandchild whom they had never seen. After the war, with so many sad messages being delivered daily throughout Europe, I felt it a real honor to bring them some good news.

By now, I had been overseas long enough to have accumulated twenty-one seniority points, enough for me to be sent home. It was then that I made the decision to inform my company commander of my correct age so that my records would be in proper order. She advised me against it because she was afraid I might possibly receive a dishonorable discharge since I was underage. It turned out to be good advice, which I wisely accepted.

It had been two years since I was sworn in at Fort Bragg, and it was there that I was returned to receive my honorable discharge. On

21 March 1946, I proudly returned home with discharge in hand and an education worth its weight in gold.

On 16 April 1946, after a wonderful reunion with family and friends, I was approached by an Army recruiting sergeant. The Army was recruiting a company of ex-WACs for a 1-year assignment to Heidelberg, Germany. This sounded challenging, so I reenlisted for one year. All they had to do for us ex-WACs was issue orders and uniforms and we were on our way. I was assigned to the records section of the Adjutant General's office, Third U. S. Army of Occupation. Heidelberg was to set the stage for the rest of my life.

I made friends with a young German girl, just my age, who had been a German soldier. She had enlisted after her brother had lost both legs in the war. She was bitter in defeat because she had believed in her country and thought she knew what they were fighting for. We spent a lot of time discussing war, how it happened, and why. We agreed war is hell, whether you win or lose. When I left Heidelberg, she gave me a picture of her and her brother posing proudly in their uniforms and on the back she had written, "It is so easy to remember and so hard to forget."

It was in Heidelberg that I met another American soldier, who was to become my partner for life. We spent romantic evenings walking along the Neckar River and watching sunsets from the Heidelberg Castle, high above the city. Romantic dreams sometimes do come true.

In April 1947, I left Heidelberg and was discharged at Fort Dix, New Jersey. After serving three and one-half years, with two of them overseas, I was still not old enough to legally enlist. My partner and I were married in July 1947. Sharing the Army experience as teenagers gave our lives more compatibility than most people are fortunate enough to have. Marrying your Army buddy can raise eyebrows at times, but I highly recommend it.

Dorothy Brandt and her husband John worked on the Navajo Indian Reservation in New Mexico and Arizona. Later, they worked with the Ute, Apache, and Sioux. Dorothy continued her education after John was recalled to active duty during the Korean War. In the late 1950s, they went to Truk Atoll in the South Pacific, where they worked for three years. They spent eight years in Thailand where Dorothy, as a representative of the American Field Service, organized a high school exchange program that brought young people from many countries together for a year. A book of Dorothy's poems, Ranch Memories at Thirty Below, *was recently published. Dorothy and John live on a cattle ranch near Alamosa, Colorado, where they raise registered Texas longhorn cattle and Arabian horses. They have one daughter and two grandchildren. Their granddaughter graduated from West Point in 1990, served in Saudi Arabia during Desert Storm, and is currently stationed in Korea. She is a career officer carrying on the family's military tradition.*

√ **VUMS Note** ⇒ *Memories of the Great Depression.* About sixty years have passed since the Great Depression, yet many underage veterans remember it well. They describe life in those times with words such as "rough," "bad," "not easy," and "dirt poor." There were very few jobs available. Many families were on relief, left with very little on which to live, sometimes forced to sell the little they owned in order to survive. One contributor recalls, "As a child, I lived with a fear about survival, something no child needs." Another relates an experience in Navy boot camp which was brought about by deprivation during the Great Depression. He was suffering severe stomach pains and had to spend two weeks in a naval hospital. The final diagnosis was that his intestines were so small from not eating enough in earlier years, that he just couldn't take all that food.

William L. "Bill" Davies

Age 15 – Oregon State Guard
Age 16 – United States Navy

My father served with the 20th Engineers, U. S. Army, from 1916 to 1918. He was on the only American transport flagship that was sunk by the Germans during World War I. Most of the survivors were from the Pacific Northwest, and after the war they held annual meetings, one of which I

> *... I did not want to join the Army because I had developed a strong aversion to the word "foxhole."*

attended. Needless to say, I grew up hearing many war stories and seeing many photos that my dad had taken, including many taken in France. Having come from a patriotic family, when World War II came along, I wanted to join the military, but I did *not* want to join the Army because I had developed an aversion to the word "foxhole."

I turned 15 on 10 December 1942, and by hook or crook, I joined the Oregon State Guard, which had replaced the National Guard that had been called to active duty. There I learned the basics of drill and the use of weapons. I spent many weekends standing guard at bridges in the state of Oregon. I was a corporal when I was discharged from the Oregon State Guard just before I joined the Navy.

After my sixteenth birthday, my dad assisted me in forging a birth certificate indicating that I was 18. Armed with this document, I enlisted in the U. S. Navy and was sworn in on 18 February 1944.

During boot camp at Farragut, Idaho, I went through the usual tests to determine what, if any, skills I might possess. Unfortunately, for those two and one-half days, I had the "runs," which kept me running to the head. Consequently, I could not finish any of the tests. But when it came to the Morse code testing, I sat and squeezed my cheeks as they never had been squeezed before, and I did finish that one test. I passed the test, and a short time later, I was sent to Aviation Radioman School in Millerton, Tennessee, near Memphis. I had a strong desire to be involved with aviation all during my youth, and now my dream would be realized.

I was assigned to Patrol Bomber Squadron VP-2 in Corpus Christi, Texas. We flew patrols over the Caribbean Sea. Later, I was transferred to VP-98. We flew out of San Diego, California, patrolling the west coasts of the United States and Mexico. After the war, VP-98 was disbanded, and I ended up at the Naval Air Station, Wilmington, California, working as a telephone switchboard operator using the old style plug-in connectors.

I had flown thousands of miles over water and had survived two forced landings in the Gulf of Mexico, but the pool at the Long Beach Naval Base almost did me in. The day before I was to be discharged, I went swimming in the base pool. I got a leg cramp and had gone under for the second time before someone pulled me out. Fortunately, I was OK and was discharged on schedule the next day, 17 June 1946.

While I was in the Navy, I took a number of correspondence courses and completed the requirements for my high school diploma. The courses were accepted by my high school, so I went home on leave in February 1946 and graduated at mid-term with my original class. I was the only one in uniform.

In the fall of 1946, I enrolled at Lewis and Clark College, Portland, Oregon. I needed additional money while I was in college, so I joined a Naval Reserve submarine unit in Portland. The company that I was working for in 1948 transferred me to Medford, Oregon. The Navy did not have a reserve unit in Medford, so I was transferred to inactive reserve status.

When the Korean War broke out, the Navy panicked and called all of their aviation-rated people in the active and inactive reserves back to duty. I was given seven days to report for duty in Seattle, Washington, in uniform. I was assigned to VU-3 in Miramar, California. The squadron flew target-guided missiles and drones. When someone from the Navy Department in Washington, D.C., found out we were flying unmanned aircraft over the San Diego area to the Pacific Ocean, we were moved from Miramar to the Naval Air Station at Ream Field, Imperial Beach, California, which was right on the beach. I was an electronics instructor in a course that used target-guided missiles to train gunnery crews that would later operate from cruisers. Actually, I was detached from the squadron and assigned the Border Field, a very small base located on the southwest corner of the United States/Mexican border.

I was released from active duty on 15 December 1951. Today, I have three military discharges, many fond memories, and very few regrets.

Bill Davies returned to work for the Retail Credit Company in Eugene, Oregon. In 1958, he moved to Sacramento and began working for Index Research Services. He started at the bottom and worked up to be general operations manager of the company's Loss Control Engineering Department, a position he still holds. He has been with the company longer than any other employee. In addition to his work, he has been very active in Optimist International and the Boy Scouts of America. In 1972, he received a Silver Beaver Award from the Golden Empire Council, BSA. Bill and his wife Pennie live in Sacramento, California. They have three children, six grandchildren, and two great-grandchildren.

Stanley E. King

Age 15 – United States Army
Age 16 – United States Army
Age 16 – United States Army Air Forces

When I was born in Ranger, West Virginia, on 7 January 1929, I was delivered by a midwife who never recorded my birth date. My parents separated, and home life for me can best be described as

> *"... Get the hell out of here, and come back when you are 18!"*

abusive. In February 1944, one month after my fifteenth birthday, I joined the U. S. Army. My uncle was aware of my home life, so I took the papers certifying that I was 17 to him, and he signed as my father.

I was sent to Fort Custer, Michigan, where, after serving for four months, I volunteered for the Airborne Division. I wasn't sure what the Airborne was, but since everyone seemed to make a big deal out of it, I signed up. To get into the Airborne, we had to take a special

physical. After the doctor examined my ankles, hips, and knees, he asked me how old I was. I replied, "Eighteen, sir!" He said, "You are lying. I can tell by your bone structure that you are not that age. Get the hell out of here, and come back when you are 18!" That ended my military career as a 15-year-old.

The next year, 1945, I went to live with my grandparents in Ohio. I became friends with three boys who were my age, and the four of us decided to join the Army. One of the older boys came up with the idea of registering for the draft and listing our ages as 18. We went to the draft board, told them we were 18, and that we were registering late because we didn't want to go into the service. The strategy worked. They told us we could be charged with draft evasion, but instead of charging us, they drafted us immediately. The irony is that the boy who thought up this scheme was declared 4-F.

I was inducted at Fort Hays, Ohio, and sent to Fort McClellan, Alabama, for infantry training. After two months of basic training, the company commander, Captain Darby, called me into his office. He said that he had been watching me and that he knew that I was not 18 years of age. I told him the truth, that I was only 16. He said that by military regulations he was supposed to send me home immediately. He then asked me why I wanted to be in the military so badly. I told him that I had come from a very abusive home and had been taken away from my mother at the age of six weeks. He then told me that he had enlisted for about the same reason but that he had been of legal age. After a few minutes he said to me, "King, I am going to forget about this talk and let you finish basic training. But if you foul up one time, I am going to send you home."

During the last two weeks of training, they asked for volunteers to train as aerial photographers in the Army Air Forces. I decided that aerial photography was better than being in the infantry, so I was one of three volunteers. You should have heard the kidding we went through for the next three weeks.

World War II was winding down. We were sent to England and then to France and Germany. I was assigned to the 357th Fighter Group, which was stationed at a German air base a short distance from Munich. Our group flew P-51 Mustangs. One of our pilots was a captain by the name of Chuck Yeager. Captain Yeager, an ace fighter pilot, later became a well-known test pilot and a brigadier general in the Air Force. I served in Germany for twenty-seven months. While I was there, on 18 September 1947, the U. S. Army Air Forces became the U. S. Air Force. In 1948, our C-46 and C-47 transports participated in the Berlin Airlift.

I was discharged from the Air Force in 1948. When Air Force Active Reserves units were formed in 1951, I joined the 459th Troop Wing at Andrews Air Force Base and served for six years. I was a first sergeant of a communications squadron. During this time, I was recalled to active Air Force duty for eight months. We were assigned to carry troops from the 101st and the 82nd Airborne Divisions. The Airborne let us make parachute jumps with them, all illegally. I made eleven jumps. We were returning from Fort Bragg, North Carolina, in a C-119 one weekend when we had to make a crash landing. We all walked away from the crash. My wife was watching as the aircraft hit the ground. She asked me if that was part of our training, not realizing what really happened.

I had another close call in Vietnam. We were just taking off in a helicopter when it was hit by enemy fire. We were not very far off the ground, so we received only a few bruises and scratches. This was during 1959 and 1960, when I was serving as an advisor with Operation Phoenix, a civilian advisory group set up to assist operations in Cambodia, Laos, Thailand, and Vietnam. It was supposed to be a hush-hush operation, but it was merely planning and gathering information for a future operation. It is somewhat ironic that, after all my years on active military duty, my combat encounter was as a civilian.

Stan King returned from Southeast Asia and worked for a telephone company in Washington, D.C., for eleven years. The company serviced a number of federal agencies that required him to obtain a top-secret security clearance. Since his birth was never recorded, his earlier misstatement of his age was never brought up, although, in his words, "Whenever an official-looking person came up to me, I shook in my boots." Later, he owned security companies in Arizona, California, and Tennessee. In 1985, he moved to the Rio Grande Valley in Texas where he worked as a sales representative for an electronics firm. He met his wife-to-be Amalia there. Stan, a trained physical therapist, and Amalia, a speech therapist, combined their talents and started providing private home care for patients suffering from strokes, Alzheimer's disease, and Parkinson's disease for six months each year. Stan was married several times before he met Amalia. He has seven children, raised eight stepchildren, and has four grandchildren. Amalia has five children, ten grandchildren and two great-grandchildren. Stan was the first appointed state commander of the newly organized Veterans of Underage Military Service and was the first Texas State Commander. Amalia was the first commander of the association's Auxiliary. Stan and Amalia live in San Antonio, Texas.

Warren G. Bates

Age 14 – United States Navy

I enlisted in the Navy in March 1944 at New Orleans, Louisiana, at the age of 14 by forging my mother's name to the enlistment papers. I went through boot camp in San Diego, and trained for a month at Camp Elliott, near San Diego.

> *I was blown over the side, and more than 800 shipmates died or were wounded.*

In June 1944, I was on my way to the Pacific on the USS *Franklin* (CV-13). We were in combat in the Mariana Islands, Palau Islands, Philippine Islands, and Okinawa. We were hit by bombs and kamikaze planes. I was injured in October 1944 in the Philippines and was sent to Aiea Hospital in Hawaii. I was lucky, since about 150 of my shipmates died. After two weeks, I was sent back to duty. On 19 March 1945, we were off the coast of Japan when our ship was hit by two 500-pound bombs. I was blown over the side, and more than 800 shipmates died or were wounded.

Later, I was transferred to Ford Island at Pearl Harbor. On 1 June 1945, I received orders to report to the commanding officer. The yeoman at his office told me that they had received a letter from my mother saying that I was underage (15). They asked me if I wanted to get out. I asked if I could have leave, but they said no. I would have stayed in the Navy if they had said yes, but there was no doubt in my mind what to do when they said no. That same day, I was on an attack cargo ship heading for the naval base at Treasure Island in San Francisco Bay. Three days after arriving at Treasure Island, I received an honorable discharge from the U. S. Navy. There were about 200 underage boys waiting to be discharged while I was there. On the train going home, I met an underage Marine from Alabama who was 16 years old. He had been wounded twice on Iwo Jima.

Warren Bates was awarded the Bronze Star for heroism and the Purple Heart for wounds received in action. After leaving the Navy in 1945, he became an electrical contractor. He was the electrical inspector for the city of Cranston, Rhode Island, at the time of his retirement in 1991. Warren and his wife Theresa have one daughter and one granddaughter. They live in Cranston, Rhode Island. Warren is the Rhode Island State Commander of the Veterans of Underage Military Service.

√ ***VUMS Note*** ⇒ *Two presidents and a king.*
Three underage veterans recalled in their stories memorable experiences which involved two American presidents and a Saudi king. In 1944, one was a member of a Navy air crew that flew escort cover for the cruiser taking President Roosevelt from Midway Island back to the States, with stops in Alaska. He watched the President's parades and listened to his speeches at stops along the way.

Another was a crew member of the destroyer that escorted the cruiser carrying President Roosevelt to the Yalta Conference in February 1945. After the conference, the destroyer picked up King Ibn Saud in Saudi Arabia and took him to a conference with FDR in Egypt.

In 1947, At Camp Shangri-la (now Camp David), President Truman invited a Marine who was serving as his personal guard to spend the evening with him and his family, and to bring his two Marine buddies along. The three Marines, the President, his wife Bess, his daughter Margaret, and an admiral and his wife shared a quiet evening watching movies.

William S. Miller

Age 16 – United States Army

During World War II, my buddy Carl Hale and I wanted to do our part in the war. We couldn't wait to be of age. When we were 15 years old, we changed our birth dates in our old Bible records,

> *A lady at the draft board probably realized that we were faking it.*

took them with us to the draft board in Kingsport, Tennessee, and registered as 18-year-olds. A lady at the draft board probably realized that we were faking it. She told us that she hoped we realized what we were getting ourselves into.

We were called in for an examination, which I passed, but Carl was turned down. It really disturbed us that we couldn't go in together as we had planned. I had second thoughts about going in alone, but I felt it was too late to change my mind.

However, I soon discovered what I was getting myself into. I was sworn in on 26 April 1944, a month after my sixteenth birthday, and was sent to Camp Shelby, Mississippi. About six weeks later, I was sent to Company D, 21st Infantry, at Fort McClellan, Alabama, for basic training. I served six months and four days in the Army before they caught up with me. My mother became concerned about me, so she sent a copy of my birth certificate to the officials and enlisted the help of Congressman Carl Reece of Tennessee to get me discharged.

On 1 February 1946, I enlisted in the U. S. Army Air Forces and served three and one-half years. I was sent to the 43rd Air Base Group, 9th Air Force, in Erding, Germany. On 2 September 1947, I was seriously injured in an accident on the base. I recovered from my injuries and went on to serve out my enlistment. I was discharged from the Air Force on 31 June 1949.

Bill Miller took up carpentry, spent five years working for a housing contractor, then worked on the assembly line in a fiber drum factory. He retired on a disability pension in 1987. Bill and Alice, his wife of forty-five years, live in Jonesborough, Tennessee. They have six children and seven grandchildren.

358

Walter Holy

Age 16 – United States Army

My thoughts about military life began in the ninth grade when my teacher made a snide remark about Colin Kelly, Jr., who was our first publicized hero during World War II. At first, it was believed (erroneously) that Kelly had crashed his damaged bomber into a Japanese battleship near the Philippine

> *... I got lost on the Autobahn, was almost run over by French tanks, and ended up behind German lines.*

Islands. The teacher said that the only reason Kelly had crashed into the battleship was to become a hero, that sinking the ship was secondary. I was not this teacher's favorite student after I strongly disputed her version.

In 1944, at the ripe old age of 16, a friend and I decided to join the Navy. Not having birth certificates that showed us to be old enough to enlist, we decided on another path. We boldly proceeded to the draft office, signed up for the draft, and filled out an immediate-induction request. Shortly after, on 4 May 1944, we were ordered to report for

induction. What I did not know at the time was that my older brother had volunteered for the Marine Corps. It was a bit breathtaking for my brother and me to report to the same station at the same time and my age not be discovered. My "adjusted" birth date effectively made us twins, born 24 days apart.

During the time I was in basic training at Camp Roberts, California, the Allies invaded Normandy. There was an immediate call for volunteers for the parachute service, since the D-Day landing did not go well for the paratroopers. I was anxious to volunteer, but was concerned about the colorblind test. Much to my delight, the nurse asked me to pick a green cotton ball. Like a dummy I asked, "What shade of green?" With that fool question, I didn't even have to pick one.

Then it was off to Fort Benning, Georgia, by slow troop train. I peeled potatoes for the four days it took to cross Texas. Training at Fort Benning was really rough, but since I wasn't old enough to have good sense, I really enjoyed it. After one week of fitness training, then four weeks of jump training, we were fully qualified paratroopers.

A few days after becoming a paratrooper, I was falsely accused of disrespect to an officer, of being drunk on duty, and of insubordination. Conviction on these charges would have given me free room and board at the military prison at Leavenworth, Kansas. The seriousness of the situation caused me to admit my true age. After I was cleared of the charges, the commander asked me where I wanted to go, implying that I could get out of the Army because of my age. My reply was, "Overseas, of course." The commander approved of my response.

Getting overseas proved to be a task in itself. Our ship was in the last large convoy to sail for Europe, I believe. On our fourth day at sea we had a rude awakening at 4:20 in the morning. The bow of our ship was cut off during a collision with an old battleship that had been converted into an aircraft carrier. The ship's crew immediately closed and padlocked all watertight doors in order to save the ship. This was done in spite of the fact that a number of troops were still in the damaged bow. We could hear them screaming as the waves washed them out of the ship. Only one small life ring was thrown overboard to about 100 men in the water. It was impossible to launch the ship's life rafts because they had been painted so many times they had become an integral part of the ship's structure. We were all told to report on deck. One person arrived with neither an overcoat nor a life jacket. An officer gave the man his coat and life jacket. The man put them on, jumped overboard, and was never seen again.

I learned later that it was five hours before either ship reported that there were casualties and that men were in the water. Destroyer-escorts began searching for survivors immediately after receiving the word, but found very few men still alive.

Under the watchful eye of a destroyer-escort, we made our way to the Azores. We should have been interned there because the island was a neutral country. This was circumvented by declaring the 2400 troops as merchant seamen. From the Azores, we were transferred by destroyer-escorts to an English ship with civilian passengers that was on its way to Liverpool from New Zealand. The food served was mutton and boiled potatoes, both totally unfit for human consumption.

Our sympathy went to the civilian passengers who had had to endure such fare since leaving New Zealand.

We left Liverpool by train for Southhampton, where we boarded another ship destined for Le Havre, France. We were to sail at 11:00 p.m., so I decided to get some rest. In the morning, I commented to one of the English sailors that Le Havre didn't look any different than England. He laughed and said that we were still in England. The ship had departed on schedule, but in the middle of the English Channel, the engine blew up and the ship was towed back to the same pier from which it left the night before.

We were transferred to the Polish ship *Sobieski*. Since I was of Czech descent, I knew good Polish food when I smelled it. I was in hog heaven. A number of battle casualties who had been hospitalized in England were scheduled to join us on board the *Sobieski*. When they heard that this was the fifth ship our group had been on just to get to the continent, they rebelled and refused to board. They were not about to go back to the combat zone with such an unlucky group. The authorities did not force them to board with us but allowed them to catch another ship the next day.

I joined the 101st Airborne Division during the campaign in central Europe. I had two experiences during this time that I will always remember. One was the sight of a concentration camp. It was difficult to believe the conditions under which human beings struggled and died. The second was while I was driving a German Opel car, taking our company records to another location. Along the way, I was directed to take a wounded man back to an aid station. Well, I got lost on the Autobahn, was almost run over by French tanks, and ended up behind German lines. I saw a German soldier alongside the road with two bottles showing from his pack. I stopped, hoping to get a bottle from him. Somehow, I understood him when he told me that I was in the wrong area and I must get out. He did give me a bottle, which turned out to be a very poor wine. I must have gotten away with this dumb action because I was driving a German car and was not wearing my helmet. Just as I left that area, I noticed an American armored vehicle a moment before it was demolished by an artillery shell. That convinced me to get out of there fast!

We reached Berchtesgaden, Germany, on the last day of the war in Europe. We stayed on occupation duty for a few months, then went to

Joigny, France. While we were regrouping and preparing to depart for the Pacific theater, the Japanese surrendered.

I was sent to the 508th Parachute Regiment at Frankfurt, Germany, where we served as honor guards at SHAEF (Supreme Headquarters, Allied Expeditionary Forces) headquarters. I returned to the States in July 1946 and was assigned to the 82nd Airborne at Fort Bragg, North Carolina. When they threatened to make us glider troops, I wanted out, so I volunteered to return to Germany. However, I was sent to Trieste, Italy, where we sparred with the Yugoslavs.

I was discharged from the Army on 20 December 1948 after serving four years, seven months, and sixteen days. I celebrated my twenty-first birthday twenty days later.

I went to work for the Crown Zellerbach Paper Company in West Linn, Oregon, and after a couple of years, I joined the Oregon Air National Guard. In November 1956, I entered active duty with the U. S. Air Force at Lowry Air Force Base, Denver, Colorado. After two weeks at Lowry, I was sent to Amarillo Air Force Base, Texas, where I remained for ten years. For five years, I was an instructor on B-47 aircraft at the resident school. I then moved to the Field Training Squadron, where I instructed Belgian and Dutch Air Force personnel on the F-104 Starfighter. In August 1962, our detachment went to the Netherlands for six months to assist in training on the F-104. We spent thirty days in Germany and then went to Norway for three months, again to train their people on the F-104.

Upon returning to Amarillo, I was immediately sent to Edwards Air Force Base, California, to train personnel on the J-79 engine. From Edwards, I went to Field Training Headquarters, Wichita Falls, Texas.

In June 1967, I was assigned to duty in the Republic of China, Taiwan, for a period of two years. Officially, our unit was attached to the U. S. Embassy, but we worked directly with the First Wing of the Chinese Air Force. I returned to the States in July 1969 and was assigned to Malmstrom Air Force Base, Montana, where I worked in support of the Minuteman missile program.

I received orders to go to Vietnam in September 1970. As a senior master sergeant, I was second in command of the jet-engine repair facility. I found the facility in total shambles. Morale was at rock bottom, and an entire squadron of aircraft was grounded because engines were lacking. At my request, the squadron commander court-martialed twelve men. We started ordering the correct parts and soon had all the grounded aircraft in flying condition. This did not come about without cost. My life was threatened, as was the life of my supervisor. During this time, a hand grenade was thrown into a patio area where forty APs (air policemen) were having a barbecue. Eighteen were badly injured.

I left Vietnam in 1971 and was again assigned to Malmstrom AFB, Montana, with basically the same duties as I had before. In April 1973, I was transferred to Davis-Monthan AFB, Tucson, Arizona. We worked with the U-2 aircraft, drones (pilotless aircraft), T-33s, C-130s, and CH3 helicopters. In 1974, I did a short tour in Thailand as superintendent of maintenance for the drone program. In April 1975, I was assigned chief of the propulsion branch at Griffiss AFB, New York. The following year, I was reassigned to Zweibrucken, Germany, as wing maintenance superintendent.

I was approaching my thirtieth year of service and had been informed that I would not be permitted to serve beyond thirty years, so I started looking forward to retirement. My squadron commander called me to his office and asked if I would be willing to serve an additional year beyond thirty. I said, "Yes, if it would be at McChord AFB, Washington." We returned to Washington for the one year extension, which was extended for a second year. On 1 June 1984, after thirty-two years of active duty, I retired with the rank of chief master sergeant.

Walt Holy earned the Combat Infantryman Badge about the time of his seventeenth birthday. During his career, he received four Air Force Commendation Medals and two Air Force Meritorious Service Medals. Since retiring in 1984, Walt has devoted his time to traveling and enjoying leisure time at home. He reports that retirement time goes by at warp speed, whereas duty time went by at half speed. Walt and Frances, his wife of forty-six years, live in Vancouver, Washington. They have two children and one grandchild.

Eugene W. Tabaka

Age 16 – United States Navy

I quit high school in my sophomore year. I was only 16 years of age at that time. Because of the war effort, you were allowed to work at that age, with parental consent. I went to work in the Oregon Shipyard at Swan Island in Portland, Oregon. We built Victory ships. Towards Christmas of 1943, another

> *I ... worked in the engine room where the temperature would sometimes reach 130 degrees.*

fellow and I went to the Portland Navy Recruiting Station to join the Navy. I presented a falsified birth certificate, took my physical, was sworn in, given a date to return, and was sent home to get my parents' consent.

When I returned, the Navy told me that I wasn't old enough. Although I was sworn into the Navy, I had to wait until I was 17 before I could go on active duty. Apparently, they had checked with the Oregon Shipyard through my Social Security number. On my birthday, in June 1944, they called me to active duty and sent me to Farragut, Idaho, for boot training.

After boot camp, I went to Camp Elliott near San Diego, California. Shortly before Christmas of 1944, I was assigned to the USS *Pinola* (ATO-33), a Navy seagoing fleet tug. We towed barges from California to Pearl Harbor, Hawaii. At Pearl Harbor, we towed targets and did standby duty off the coast and worked within the harbor itself.

I was a fireman second class and worked in the engine room where the temperature would sometimes reach 130 degrees. The tug was powered by a three-cylinder steam reciprocating engine. While we worked out of Pearl Harbor, our watches were two hours on and four hours off because of the heat.

Shortly after the death of President Franklin D. Roosevelt in 1945, we were reassigned to the Navy Command at Dutch Harbor, Alaska. There we picked up a motorless tug and towed her to Bremerton, Washington.

The USS *Pinola* was decommissioned at Bremerton on the last day of January 1946 and a few weeks later sank at dockside. She was built at Bremerton in 1919 and died at Bremerton in February 1946.

I was reassigned to the USS *Dixie* (AD-14) and went to Portland, Oregon, to go aboard. I found out that the *Dixie* was leaving to go overseas again for the A-bomb tests. The war was over and I didn't want to go back overseas, so I talked to the chaplain and was transferred back to Bremerton where I was discharged in June 1946.

Eugene Tabaka joined the Naval Surface Reserve and a short time later transferred to the U. S. Naval Air Reserve at Sandpoint Naval Air Station, Seattle, Washington. He worked for Boeing Aircraft Company for a time, then worked for Ford Motor Company for thirty-four and a half years. For thirty consecutive years, he was involved with the longest ongoing conservation work party in the state of Washington. He has worked with sportsmen's clubs for more than twenty-three years and served as president for eight of the twenty-three years. In 1983, he was named "Outstanding Sportsman of the Year," and in 1994, he was named "Outstanding Old Timer Sportsman of the Year." Eugene and Ruth, his wife of forty-six years, live in Seattle, Washington. They have three children and six grandchildren. He is the Washington State Commander of the Veterans of Underage Military Service.

Darlene E. (Arthur) DeVos

Age 19 – United States Army (WAC)

As a young girl, I was fascinated by men in military uniforms and saw them as special people who probably performed all sorts of heroic deeds. (I didn't know about KP and latrine

> *Imagine my embarrassment when I returned to work – after the big sendoff...*

duty.) So in 1941, when the young men in my hometown began joining the services, I was envious and wished fervently that I could join too. It just didn't seem fair; after all, I wanted to serve my country just as much as they did, especially after Pearl Harbor. When the WAAC was formed in 1942, I thought my wish had come true – only to learn I'd have to wait three long years to join. Seemed like an eternity!

After I finished high school, I started work in a defense plant and met someone there who could get me a false birth certificate. At last, a solution! I enlisted in the WAC at age 19, one year underage, and after enjoying my farewell party and with gifts from my co-workers, I set off on my great adventure – happy and proud but a little scared.

On 5 July 1944, I was sent to Fort Oglethorpe, Georgia, for basic training. When word that I was in the Army reached my (then) husband in Germany, he contacted my CO and told her I was underage. Crying and pleading didn't get me anywhere, and I was sent to Fort Sheridan, Illinois, and discharged on 15 August 1944. Imagine my embarrassment when I returned to work – after the big send-off they had given me. I took a lot of friendly teasing and was the talk of the plant for awhile.

Eleven months later, I enlisted again – legally. On 5 July 1945, I was sent to Fort Des Moines, Iowa, for more basic training and then to Fort Lawton in Seattle, Washington. I was assigned to post headquarters as a message center runner, and a few months later was made section chief. It was a case of being in the right place at the right time. I was promoted to sergeant and later, to staff sergeant. As section chief, I was sometimes assigned soldiers returning from overseas, men awaiting discharge orders and assigned to the message center to keep them occupied. As I was obviously a little in awe of these veterans, and worse yet, a woman, I didn't think they'd take me too seriously. But they were just happy the war was over and that they were finally on their way home, so they were willing to tolerate one more pesky sergeant.

Although I loved my job and Army life, when my best friend married and requested discharge, I decided it was time for me to go home, too. I received my second honorable discharge on 10 September 1946.

My Army career was brief, but I shall always remember those fifteen months as the best of times. I believe I was right as a young girl — service men and women truly *are* special people. I'm proud that I was one of them.

Darlene DeVos worked for fourteen years in a roller-skating rink her parents built and as an executive secretary for the Standard Oil Company (Amoco) in Chicago, Illinois, for twenty-two years. She retired in 1985 and moved to Florida. She is the mother of two sons and has five grandchildren. Darlene's father, Merle M. Arthur, also an underage veteran, served in the Navy during World War I (see page 15).

George Eordekian

Age 15 – United States Coast Guard

I remember 7 December 1941 as if it were yesterday. My parents, brother, two sisters, and I were in the kitchen having breakfast when we received news on the radio of the attack on Pearl Harbor. Our thoughts

> *I was determined to leave that ship and steward duty.*

immediately turned to my other brother who was on the aircraft carrier USS *Lexington*. We didn't know until the next day when we read it in the papers that all the carriers had gone out to sea on the day before the Japanese attack.

My brother had joined the Navy in 1940, and in my mind, I wanted to follow him. Now, after the Japanese attack, that was it! I was determined to go into the service as soon as possible. I had turned 13 just two weeks before the attack. But I wasn't dumb – I planned my goal with all the wiles of a fox. I wasn't about to march down to the recruiting station. Not yet, anyway. I reasoned that I would be risking discovery and would be blackballed. I could just see my name and picture on posters at all four branch recruiting stations in our area warning: "WATCH OUT FOR THIS KID – DON'T LET HIM JOIN UP." I knew that I had to be smarter than they were.

I immediately bought a shaving kit. I had heard that if you started shaving with nothing to shave, hair would start to grow. I still don't know whether this is true. But in any event, my face became rough from the soap and razor, and eventually there was some hair to shave. The second phase of my plan was to age as rapidly as possible. I stayed up late at night and got as little sleep as I could manage. I noticed that my eyes and face began to look tired, and they were. After about a year of this preparation, I felt ready at the age of 14. My first choice was to be a naval fighter pilot. But fearing that I would be blackballed because you had to be

18 and a high-school graduate to be a pilot, I canceled that idea. So I didn't shave for a week, and I tried to stay up all night just before I went to a Navy recruiting station to enlist. I told the recruiters that I was 17, filled out the papers, and took the physical. I was rejected because I had a deviated septum. I went home and told my folks that I wanted my nose fixed so I could breathe better. It was fixed.

I let some more months go by because I thought that as the war progressed, the military services would be short of men and would be more apt to overlook some things. I was right. This time I went to the Coast Guard because I had heard that they were advertising more aggressively. I was now 15 years old. I passed my physical and was told to bring in my birth certificate. I said that I didn't have one, which was the one time I told the truth. I sent to Boston for a copy of my birth certificate, hoping my parents were wrong about the year I was born. All of this time, my parents didn't know what I was up to. After a few weeks, I went back to the recruiters and told them my birth certificate hadn't come yet. I was told, "We can't wait. Get your folks down here to sign, and be ready to be sworn in."

I had told my parents that I was going to leave home and go to Wyoming and be a cowboy, or a telegrapher in Vermont, or join the Canadian Merchant Marine if they didn't let me join the Coast Guard. My father trembled as he signed the papers. I was sworn in on 13 July 1944. I was one of the happiest Huckleberry Finns imaginable when I got on that military train a couple of days later, headed for boot camp on Government Island in the Bay area.

I had a short boot camp, and in October 1944, I was assigned to the USS *Eberle* (AP-123), a newly commissioned Coast Guard troopship. On our maiden voyage from San Francisco to Los Angeles, I was constantly seasick. I visited my family in Los Angeles and was two hours late coming back from liberty. I had my first captain's mast and received three days' extra duty. I was taken off the ship because of chronic seasickness and told I would be sent overseas to some island. The scuttlebutt was that some of us would be going to New Guinea or to the Philippines.

Around this time, I began feeling bad about my life and feeling guilty. I was afraid to die, and I had no faith. I went to the chaplain, who was a Roman Catholic, and he asked what he could do for me. I was tongue-tied and didn't know what to say, so I said, "Could you loan me two dollars?" He did, and I paid him back the next day.

The Coast Guard hymn, "Eternal Father, Strong to Save," made a deep impression on me. It was always played or sung at chapel services. One night I was invited by a buddy to go to his aunt's house across the bay for a home-cooked meal. After the meal, my buddy said that he had a date and left. I was surprised and angry. His aunt told me that she was going to a revival that evening and that I could go if I wanted. I said that I would go, thinking that I should respect her hospitality. Walt Disney's cousin gave an illustrated talk about the gospel. After hearing other speakers, singing, and praying, I prayed by myself, and that night I found peace. I was no longer, nor was I ever again, afraid of death. I sent a telegram to my mother and told her what had happened. Five days later, I was on my way overseas.

We arrived at Leyte at the end of April 1945, having heard about the death of President Roosevelt on the way over. I was assigned to a stationary oil tanker, the USS *Aberenda* (IX-131). This ship had been commissioned in 1903 and had been in service during World War I. It had one 3-inch gun aft. Our job was to supply oil to U. S. ships in Leyte Gulf, ships that ranged in size from destroyer-escorts to battleships. We were also preparing for the invasion of Japan.

My particular job was officer's steward. After a number of weeks in this assignment, mainly in the galley, the chief steward became tyrannical with me with what I perceived to be evil intent. After my regular 8-hour shift, he would tell me to do extra work, scrubbing down the walls, for example. One morning I didn't report for duty but stayed in my bunk instead. After about an hour, one of my buddies warned me that I'd better report for duty. After another hour, the OD, an ensign, ordered me to the captain's cabin.

After I entered his cabin and saluted, the captain sternly told me to sit down. He looked straight at me and asked how old I was. I said, "Eighteen." I felt that he was looking through me as he began telling a little of his early life, adding that he was 16 when he joined the Merchant Marine some twenty years before. He spoke as a father (and captain), and inquired if I knew the wartime penalty for refusing to obey orders. I said, "No, sir." He said, "The penalty is to be shot by a firing squad, and the least penalty is a summary court-martial and ten years of hard labor." He then asked if I understood what he would have to do if I refused to obey the orders of my superior. I said, "Yes, sir." He then told me to go to the chief steward and say, "I'm ready to take all orders." I did what he told me to do. But this isn't the end of the story. I was determined to leave that ship and steward duty. I kept going over and over in my mind how I could accomplish that.

My luck finally arrived in the form of a dysentery epidemic. With a thousand or so ships in the gulf, the waters were fetid. Diseases were brought on board when wet ropes were pulled from the water. When I heard about the epidemic, I saw my chance. That night I threw the garbage pail over the side, as was part of my duty. I shook the pail to gather some sea water, brought it up, and drank some. Sure enough, in a few days, I was laid low with dysentery. They took me off the ship on a stretcher with my duffel bag, and an inward smile. I was put on a hospital ship, the USS *Relief*, for nine days. The nurses were nice; at times they asked me if I wanted ice cream.

After my hospital stay, I was sent to the island of Leyte to await assignment to another ship. I learned that I would be aboard a seagoing tug. The war ended about that time. We heard that the Air Force had dropped a couple of big bombs, called A-bombs, and that the Japanese surrendered. That night was as light as day with all the ships around us celebrating with flares and rockets.

Now that the war was over, men were being sent home. Those who entered the military the earliest were going back the soonest. Between August and November I waited my turn, but nothing happened. I was told I'd be one of the last ones to be sent home. I was getting anxious and I wanted my records straightened out, so I told the chief petty officer at headquarters what my real age was and that I wanted to get back to the States so I could go back to school. He said, "Come back tomorrow, and I'll let you know what we can do for you." I went back the next day, and I was told that I would be sent back to the States and be given an honorable discharge because I had stuck it out.

I was discharged on 2 January 1946. I didn't have much going for me when I entered the service, but I got a big lift forward in life from the experience.

George Eordekian returned to high school immediately after his discharge from the Coast Guard. He enrolled as a junior and was given one and a half years of credit for "experience." He used the GI Bill while finishing high school, attending a trade school, and going to college. He eventually became a railroad telegrapher, a teacher, and an engineer, among other things. George lives in Tujunga, California.

Charles T. King

Age 14 – United States Navy

One day during World War II, I cut school and went to the draft board to register. I was 14 years old, but I told them that I had just turned 18. I signed up for immediate induction, which gave me my choice of service, the U. S. Navy. When I received my notice to go in for a physical,

> *... I took some lard from a can and plastered my hair down.*

I was concerned that I looked too young, so I took some lard from a can and plastered my hair down. I passed the physical and was sworn in on 20 August 1944 and left that very night by train for the Great Lakes Naval Training Center. The train was so hot that the lard I had put on my hair that morning started to melt and run down my face. What a mess!

My parents never knew where I was until I called. My mother wanted me home, but I talked her into letting me stay and not giving my age away. I went to gunner's mate school in Bremerton, Washington, and soon after was sent to Hawaii on the USS *General H. W. Butner*. At Pearl Harbor, I was assigned to the USS *Saratoga* (CV-60) and for short periods of time, to the LST-685. I was wounded by shrapnel during the Iwo Jima campaign.

I was later assigned to the USS *Chikaskia* (AO-54) and served on her longer than any other ship. We were in Task Force 38 under the command of Admiral "Bull" Halsey. Our ship was caught in the typhoon at Okinawa and was there during the kamikaze attacks in May 1945. At this time I was 15 years old.

Immediately after the Japanese surrendered, we went Sasebo, Japan. While we were there, some of us were taken by train to Nagasaki to view the destruction caused by the atomic bomb. We left Sasebo and sailed for Australia, stopping at Guadalcanal along the way. We were one of the first ships to stop in Sydney, Australia, after the war for ten days of R&R (rest and recreation) leave. It was great! We went through the Suez Canal on our way back to the States.

I reenlisted on 18 December 1945 and was sent to submarine school in Pearl Harbor and was assigned to the USS *Carp* (SS-338). After two weeks on the *Carp*, I decided I didn't like submarines. In 1946, I participated in two atom bomb tests at Bikini Atoll in the Marshall Islands.

I was discharged on 13 November 1947 with the rank of gunner's mate second class. No one ever found out my age. I had the record corrected a few years after I was discharged. If I had it to do over again, I wouldn't hesitate one moment!

Charlie King was awarded the Purple Heart for wounds received in action. After leaving the Navy, he worked in construction for many years. Now retired, Charles and Barbara, his wife of twenty-five years, love to travel and have attended several Navy reunions and have become reacquainted with several old shipmates. Charles and Barbara had both been married previously. Their combined family includes eleven children, nine grandchildren, and three great-grandchildren. They live in Louisville, Kentucky.

James A. Boone

Age 15 – United States Navy

I was born in Little Rock, Arkansas, on 19 March 1929 and was adopted shortly after. When I was 15, my adoptive parents agreed to let me join the Navy. Dad was 66 and Mom was 60. We had two farms but no help to work

> ... we had to sleep outside at 58½° below zero!

them. Dad was too old and I was too young. By joining the Navy, I would have a job and I could send them money. I changed the dates on school records and took them with me in place of a birth certificate when I enlisted. I was sworn into the U. S. Navy Reserves on 8 September 1944 and left for boot camp in San Diego in October 1944. I was in Company 44-435.

After boot camp, I went to Camp Elliott for a short time, then was assigned to the USS *Breton* (CVE-23), a small aircraft carrier. My first combat was at Ulithi. A kamikaze hit the flight deck of the USS *Saratoga*, which was about 1500 yards from us at the time. This occurred three weeks before my sixteenth birthday.

During the Okinawa campaign, our orders got fouled up. We had a group of Marine F4U Corsairs aboard that were to take off and land at a recently captured airfield on Okinawa. The four CVEs in our group carried about 250 aircraft. We were supposed to be 200 miles off Okinawa, but because of some foul-up we were only thirty miles from the island. The kamikazes found us on the third day. The ground troops had not completely secured the airfield, but the Corsairs took off anyway. They took out every Japanese plane around, then went on into the airfield. None of our eight ships was hit, although one Japanese plane got within 100 yards of us before an F4U took him out. The Marine planes had no choice but to go to the airfield because only about half of them could have landed on our small carriers.

After the war, on 10 November 1945, I enlisted in the regular Navy for two years. I was still only 16 years old. Upon reenlisting, I was allowed to choose three types of ships that I would like to serve on. Since I had served on carriers during my first cruise, I was tired of big ships. It seemed that every place that I had to go from my duty station on the bridge was across the hangar deck or the flight deck. It seemed like all ladders would have "officers' country" signs on them, so I would have to detour to where an enlisted man could go. Therefore, I put in for small ships.

I got what I asked for. I was assigned to an LCI(R) on the West Coast. We were to take her through the Panama Canal, through the Florida Keys, and on to the Charleston Navy Yard. It took us two months at seven to eight knots to make the trip. After the ship was decommissioned, I was sent back to the West Coast. This time, when I was asked what kind of ship I wanted, I put down aircraft carriers, battleships, and heavy cruisers. The Navy had made its point.

When my enlistment was up, I decided to join the Army. By this time, I was 19 years old and married with two children. I thought that I could spend more time at home with my family if I were in the Army rather than in the Navy.

I enlisted in the Army in January 1948. I spent some time in Germany, then was assigned to train troops at Camp Chaffee, Arkansas. When Camp Chaffee was closed, I asked for and was granted an assignment to one of the best, if not *the* best, divisions in the Army, the 2nd Armored Division at Fort Hood, Texas. The division was first organized by then Colonel George S. Patton.

When the war in Korea started, troops that had been on garrison duty in Japan were rushed to Korea. These troops were not well trained. My outfit, the 92nd Armored Field Artillery Battalion, 2nd Armored Division, was among the first units to be sent from the States.

From 16 September 1950 until November 1951, I served in both the Ninth (IX) and Tenth (X) Corps Artillery. I was a forward observer NCO. During that time we were in six campaigns and were attached to several different organizations. We had the honor of working with the best damned division in Korea, the 1st Marine Division. We were attached to the Marines about five or six times . They knew how to move fast! In fact, they were the only division that we worked with that could keep up with our self-propelled, 155mm howitzers (SPs).

They were always glad to see us arrive with those eighteen SPs. The shells for those monsters were about the size of an 8-inch naval gun and weighed about 100 pounds.

We were not attached to the 1st Marine Division at Chosin. We were shooting for everybody. The Marines and the 92nd AFA proved what well-organized attacks by trained troops can do against large numbers of poorly trained, badly equipped troops.

I came back to the States in October 1951 and was sent to Fort Polk, Louisiana, to help train the 37th National Guard Division. Hell, Korea was easy compared to working with those weekend warriors!

I pulled a few strings and was sent to Fort Bliss, Texas, as a G-2 sergeant on the staff of Brigadier General Walters. General Walters was the son-in-law of General Patton. After about a year and a half at Fort Bliss, I was sent to Fairbanks, Alaska, to be first sergeant for the Army troops at Eielson Air Force Base. I was lucky enough to go on one field problem when we had to sleep outside at 58½° below zero!

I returned to Texas and was assigned to recruiting duty. For two and a half years, I averaged 222% of my recruiting quota. But I had help. My territory was West Texas where the young men wanted to see more of the world than West Texas. I just helped them out.

After fifteen years and seven campaigns in the military, my health had deteriorated. In 1958, I was medically retired with a pension based on twenty years of service. Over the years, it has been increased to 100% service-connected disability. Would I do the same thing over? Hell yes!

Jim Boone, after retiring from the military on a medical disability, worked as a supervisor for Foremost Dairies, was a route salesman for Sunbeam Bread, then owned four 18-wheel tractor-trailer rigs that hauled freight cross-country. The so-called gas war of 1974 put him out of the trucking business, so he enrolled in Texas Wesleyan College to study transportation law, graduating in 1978. Jim and Gladys, his wife of fifty years, live in McAllen, Texas. They have five children. In 1987 Jim and Gladys adopted two of their granddaughters, ages 5 months and 23 months at the time. They have twelve other grandchildren and seven great-grandchildren.

Maxine V. Gordon

Age 16 – United States Marine Corps

Whitehall, New York, is home to me. I was born there on 17 April 1928 and lived there all my life except when I was in the service. My mother died when I was six, leaving a family of one girl and eight boys. Seven of us boys were in the service, six of us at the same time.

> **Twenty-five days after I was recalled, I was in Korea.**

In early November 1944, I went to an evening movie with a buddy. After the movie, we stopped at a soda fountain on Main Street. While we were talking, my buddy told me he had signed up for the Marine Corps and would be leaving for Albany, New York, the next day. I told him that I would join the Marines with him. The next morning, we went to the recruiting station where I saw a stack of papers on a table. The recruiting sergeant told me to take some if I wanted. I took the papers home and filled them out, but wrote in 1927 as my birth year instead of 1928. I also changed my baptismal papers to read 1927.

I enlisted in the Marine Corps in Albany, New York, on 9 November 1944. Somehow, during the process of enlisting, my first name, which was Maxim, showed up on my service records as "Maxine." Correcting it would have been difficult, so I didn't try, and I have gone by the name Maxine since that time.

I was sent to boot camp at Parris Island, South Carolina. After boot camp, I was still only 16, but I couldn't quit because I had older brothers in the Army and the Navy, and I didn't want them to think I couldn't make it. After a week's leave, I was sent to Camp Pendleton, California, then on to Guam as a replacement in the 12 Marine Regiment, 3rd Marine Division. We were training for the invasion of Japan when the A-bomb was dropped and the war ended. I was sent to China where I stayed for about a year. I returned to the States in late 1946 and was discharged on

29 October 1946. When I returned home, I learned that my 15-year-old brother Gene had joined the Navy.

I enlisted in the Marine Reserves and went about adapting to civilian life. In the fall of 1950, I was recalled to active duty and sent to Camp Lejeune, North Carolina. Twenty-five days after I was recalled, I was in Korea. We landed at Pusan and moved up to Andong, where I joined the 1st Marine Division. I was assigned to the 11th Marines, which was the artillery regiment of the 1st Marine Division. We moved around quite a bit. One time we came to a road crossing and General Douglas MacArthur was standing there, but without his corn cob pipe.

My brother Gene had joined the Army shortly after his discharge from the Navy and was stationed in Japan. While I was on the front lines in Korea, he wrote to me and asked me what I needed. I told him that I definitely did *not* need cigarettes and candy. So he sent me a box filled with cigarettes and candy!

I rotated back to the States in 1952 after a year of combat duty in Korea and was released from active duty. I have never been sorry for the time I served in the Marine Corps.

Max Gordon has been self-employed for most of his civilian life. He currently owns and operates a bar and restaurant in Whitehall, New York. Max and Marilyn, his wife of forty-four years, live in Whitehall. They have three children, six grandchildren, and one great-grandchild.

Harry A. Belanger

Age 16 – United States Marine Corps

In early 1943, help was hard to come by, so a family friend asked me to work on the Puget Sound tug boats. At that time, I was barely 15 years old, having been born in Seattle, Washington, on 26 February 1928, and raised there.

> *I knew that my number was up, but I didn't even know what my number was.*

The job on the tug boats lasted about four months – until they discovered that I was grossly underage. After that tour of inland "sea duty," I signed on with the Army Corps of Engineers as a deck hand on a medium-sized former pleasure yacht that we used to transport Army Air Forces personnel throughout the Aleutian Islands. This job lasted until I was discovered to be definitely underage.

Because of my experience at sea, I obtained seaman's papers and a seaman's passport and joined the Merchant Marine. I traveled all over the South Pacific, including Australia, on merchant ships. With blackouts, air raids, and other alerts, it was a memorable period in my life.

In December 1944, I decided there was a better way to serve my country. The Marine Corps was my choice. Enlisting presented a problem because I was still only 16 years old. My first encounter with a Marine recruiting sergeant was disastrous. He threw me out of his office. I retreated to a coffee shop and watched as he left for lunch. "Lunch" was a saloon, and I knew he wouldn't return for at least two hours.

I went back to the recruiting office and said to the woman Marine who was left in charge, "The sergeant told me that you would complete the papers for me to enlist in the Corps." Within an hour and a half, I was processed and officially enlisted in the Marine Corps. Fortunately, the sergeant didn't return from "lunch" until after I had left.

I was sworn in on 18 December 1944 and was sent to the Marine Corps Base, San Diego, California, for boot camp. Having spent some time at sea in combat zones, I had observed our fighting men from the various services. Therefore, I was not surprised at the vigorous and complete training we received at boot camp, but there is one incident that is etched in my memory. We were learning to march, and I got out of step, fouling up everyone behind me. The sergeant halted the platoon, commanded me front and center, and hit me on the front of my helmet, driving the screw of the Marine Corps emblem into my forehead. I started to bleed. The sergeant said, "What's the matter with you, private?" I replied, "Nothing, sir!" He said, "You're lying, you're bleeding!" I replied, "Yes, sir!" His response was, "Stop bleeding!" I stopped bleeding, and I never got out of step again.

After boot camp and some advanced training at Camp Pendleton, California, I was assigned to L Company, 3rd Battalion, 1st Marine Regiment, 1st Marine Division. We made the landing on Okinawa on 1 April 1945. Nothing in my short life had prepared me for the fear, devastation, and carnage that we encountered during that campaign. One time our platoon was designated to clear out some burial caves in which the Japanese frequently hid. My sergeant ordered me to run up to the cave entrance and give it a couple of bursts from a flamethrower. At this time I was about 5'8" and weighed about 145 pounds. The flamethrower weighed about 65 to 70 pounds. There was no way I was going to *run* anywhere. At any rate, I got to the cave entrance and gave it a couple of bursts from the flamethrower and waited. Nothing happened. No one was in the cave. It was then that I discovered that the entire entrance area around the cave was *mined*! I knew that my number was up, but I didn't even know what my number was. I yelled long and loud for help. The sergeant got some engineers with mine detectors to clear a path for me to get out of harm's way. It was scary, to say the least.

With Okinawa behind us and the war over, we were sent to China. Our presence there can be explained only by the politicians in Washington, D.C. However, China was an interesting tour of duty. I was assigned to H & S Company, 1st Marines, 1st Marine Division, at Tientsin. I was the bodyguard for the regimental commander, Colonel Arthur T. Mason, both at work and at his residence. I frequently sampled his supply of good Chinese beer.

After a year and a half in China, I returned to the States and was selected to do a tour of recruiting duty in Reno, Nevada. This, too, was an interesting tour, but it came to an abrupt end when they closed the recruiting office. From Reno, I was sent to the San Francisco Bay area and was assigned as brig warden at the naval prison on Treasure Island.

Next came the Korean conflict, and I was off to war again. I was with the 1st Shore Party Battalion, 1st Marine Division, at Inchon on 15 September 1950. A short time later, we landed at Wonsan and started the trek to the Chosin Reservoir. I didn't make it all the way to the reservoir, but I endured enough 38° below zero weather to last me a lifetime. Although I had been in combat on Okinawa and at times in China, I was unprepared for Korea. It was cold, deadly, and dreary. I had friends killed, friends wounded, and friends lost – and I remember them all.

I returned to the States in March 1951 and was stationed at Camp Lejeune, North Carolina. I was a master sergeant by this time. In 1953, I returned to Camp Pendleton, then left for duty in Japan with the 3rd Shore Party Battalion, 3rd Marine Division. I returned to the States in 1954 and was stationed at Camp Pendleton for four years.

In 1958, I was assigned recruiting duty in Redding, California. Four summers at 103°+ and three cold winters later, I was assigned to the Far East again. It was back to the familiar grounds of Okinawa, where I reported to Headquarters Company, 3rd Marine Division, and was assigned duties as division career-advisor NCO.

By 1962, I was back in the San Francisco Bay area as a first sergeant, overseeing military and administrative duties on Treasure Island. I retired from the Marine Corps as a first sergeant on 31 August 1964 at Treasure Island. I was married during my entire twenty-year Marine Corps career. Needless to say, my wife was the better part of our "military family."

Harry Belanger went to work for the Boeing Aircraft Company after he retired from the Marine Corps. After a few years with Boeing, he took a shot at real-estate sales. He then worked for the Bon Marche department stores for sixteen years, retiring in 1990. Harry and Allene, his wife of fifty-two years, live in Seattle, Washington. They have four children, seven grandchildren, and one great-grandchild.

John M. Cucka

Age 16 – United States Navy

I was living in Chicago, Illinois, at the time of the bombing of Pearl Harbor. I listened to the radio for the reports on the bombing and later the announcement by President Roosevelt that we were at war. My

> *Later, when it was publicized that seven ... pilots had been selected by NASA ... I knew I had made a mistake.*

cousins, most of whom had been in the CCC (Civilian Conservation Corps), enlisted in various branches of the armed forces and would stop by our house when they were on leave. I had a strong desire to participate in World War II, mainly because of their visits.

I thoroughly disliked high school and was anxious to enlist. Although I was born in Cleveland, Ohio, on 11 January 1929, I filed for a delayed birth certificate in the state of Illinois declaring that I was born in Chicago on 11 January 1928. A friend who looked much older than he was, signed the form as my older brother.

Right after my sixteenth birthday, I went to the Navy recruiting office and tried to enlist, but I was underweight. The doctor told me to buy a dozen bananas, eat all of them, drink all the water I could hold, not go to the bathroom, and then come back. I did all of the above and passed the physical.

The next hurdle was to get my father to sign my enlistment papers. I told him that I was determined to enlist, and if he didn't sign the papers, I would run away and find someone else to sign them. He signed them. I was sworn into the Navy on 29 January 1945.

While I was in boot camp at the Great Lakes Naval Training Center, Illinois, I was selected for the V-8 program, but I turned it down for fear that they would do a background check and find out my real age. My first duty assignment was on a minesweeper, the USS *Mainstay* (AM-261). While we were in the South Pacific, my commanding officer called me to his quarters and told me that he knew I was only 16 years old. He told me that since there was a war on and I was doing a good job, he would give me a choice of staying on board or returning to the States. I chose to stay on board.

When the war ended, I didn't have enough points to return to the United States, so I was transferred to another minesweeper. My old ship *Mainstay* returned to the States, but I stayed in the Far East. By the time I had enough points to get out of the service, the job market was quite grim, so I reenlisted.

While I was in the Navy, I took the GED tests and received my high school diploma two years before I would have received it had I stayed in school. While I was at the Naval Air Station, Corpus Christi, Texas, I took the 1½ year college-equivalency test and passed.

Passing these tests qualified me for flight training, so I immediately applied for flight school and was accepted. At that time, I informed the Navy of my correct age. The commanding officer of NAS, Corpus Christi, court-martialed me for fraudulent enlistment and found me guilty. But because of a good service record, I was not punished. In fact, the CO informed me that the reason he court-martialed me was that if I decided to make the military a career, I could not be denied my retirement benefits because of fraudulent enlistment, since I had already been tried for the charge. My service record was changed to show that I was born on 11 January 1929 in Cleveland, Ohio, but my medical records were not. To this day, my medical records show that I was born on 11 January 1928 in Chicago, Illinois. Unfortunately, the girl I was dating at the time didn't want me to be transferred to Pensacola, Florida, for flight training. What she did is not fit to print, so it will suffice to say that my orders to flight school were canceled.

Shortly thereafter, the Korean War broke out and I was assigned to the patrol frigate USS *Evansville* (PF-70). Immediately after the Inchon landing, I put in for flight school again and was accepted. While I was in flight training, I damaged two aircraft during carrier-landing qualifications. I decided that I didn't want to fly from "Bird Barges" (carriers), so I took a commission in the U. S. Marine Corps. Yes, you guessed it. My first duty assignment was with VMA-211 flying AD Skyraiders from the deck of the USS *Wright* (CVL-49). Ironically, I ended my military career with 304 carrier landings.

While I was home on leave in 1953 or 1954, I was sitting at the bar in a cocktail lounge in Chicago when an individual in a business suit sat down next to me and struck up a conversation. He told me that he worked for the Douglas Aircraft Corporation. He pulled a pencil from his pocket and told me that they had a top-secret mission that was going to build and fly an aircraft that looked like the pencil he held in his hand. He further informed me that I was one of a hundred pilots to be considered for the program. From that hundred, seven pilots would be selected for the mission. He gave me his address at McDonald/Douglas Aircraft Corporation and requested that I write him when I returned to my base. I thought he was full of BS and never wrote to him.

Later, when it was publicized that seven military pilots had been selected by NASA for the space program, I knew I had made a mistake. I also knew why I had been approached: I was a pilot; I had a background in electronics; I weighed only 145 pounds at the time, and weight was critical; and publicity-wise because I had served in both the Navy and the Marine Corps. Had I been approached at my duty station, Marine Corps Air Station, Edenton, North Carolina, I would have accepted the challenge. The question of why I was approached in a bar in my hometown often bothers me.

While I was in the Marine Corps, I flew every type of aircraft it had. I also acquired a commercial pilot's license for single- and multi-engine aircraft and helicopters. I am type-rated in the DC-3. The license shows that I am instrument-qualified in both fixed-wing and rotary-wing aircraft.

I was a captain when I retired from the Marine Corps at the Marine Corps Air Station, New River, North Carolina, in June 1967.

John Cucka went to work as a production controller for Page Aircraft, Lakehurst, New Jersey, after retiring from the Marine Corps. He left that job, returned to North Carolina, and enrolled in college. After earning a B.S. in business administration and an M.B.A., he did graduate work at Mississippi State University. In 1974, he took a position as professor of accounting at Northwestern State University of Louisiana at Natchitoches, Louisiana. He became a certified public accountant and operated a small CPA firm in addition to teaching. He fully retired after twenty years of teaching, bought two new vehicles, and spends most of his time attending military reunions. John lives in Natchitoches, Louisiana.

Harry R. Wallace

Age 16 – United States Navy

I left my hometown of White Plains, New York, a month after my sixteenth birthday to join the Merchant Marine at the Kings Point Merchant Marine Academy, Long Island, New York. After a few months there, I decided to join the Navy. I was born on 12 October

> *That fool will never know how close he came to heaven or hell that night.*

1928, so I had to do something to get older fast. My father was born in 1907, and since we both had the same name, I took his birth certificate, changed the "0" to a "2," and became 17 years old. With this certificate, I didn't have any problem joining the Navy. I was sworn in on 15 March 1945.

After boot camp at Sampson, New York, I was sent to Lido Beach, Long Island, New York, where I took combat training under the guidance of the U. S. Marines. This was a highly classified mission, and we found out later that it was in anticipation of the invasion of Japan. The war ended by the time I reached the West Coast, and I was assigned to the USS *LST-464*, which we took through the Panama Canal and on to Texas for decommissioning. I was at Treasure Island on 2 May 1946 waiting for transportation to Shanghai, China, when the "Alcatraz Revolt" took place. Prisoners on the nearby island of Alcatraz had taken guards hostage, and thirty-three Marines from Treasure Island were dispatched to help subdue the prisoners. I could hear all the shots being fired during the 30-hour siege.

After a 17-day trip by troopship to Shanghai, I boarded a cruiser, the USS *Duluth* (CL-87). We went to Manila in time to march in the parade on 4 July 1946 in celebration of Philippine independence. I was among the troops that General Douglas MacArthur reviewed that day. As I remember, it was a very hot day.

I remained on the *Duluth* for eighteen months. When we came back to Bremerton, Washington, for repairs in 1947, I was assigned to an escort carrier, the USS *Rendova* (CVE-114), and served aboard her for the remainder of my enlistment.

I was discharged from the Navy in November 1947. I stayed out just long enough to discover that I really did not belong in civilian life, so in 1948, I enlisted in the U. S. Army. After completing military police school, I was sent to Germany, where I would stay for five years.

I was assigned to the 709th MP Battalion in Frankfort during the time of the Berlin Airlift. I may have been the only MP to wear a parachute, a Thompson submachine gun, and a 45-caliber pistol at the same time. I escorted 50 million German marks from Frankfort to Berlin in a C-47 aircraft full of bags of coal.

I was assigned later to the 62nd Military Police Highway Patrol. We covered the German Autobahn, normally driving about 260 miles each day. We had jurisdiction over German nationals as well as our own troops. Our unit was first formed by a Colonel Schwarzkopf, father of General Norman Schwarzkopf of the 1991 Gulf War fame.

While I was on patrol one day, I stopped a large limousine that evidently was carrying a VIP. The driver readily got out of the limo, and I gave him a ticket for speeding. A beautiful blonde also got out of the car and started to give me all sorts of hell for delaying her. She asked me if I knew who she was. When I said no, she informed me that she was Maria Ekk, Germany's Marilyn Monroe. I then felt compelled to tell her who I was. Neither of us made much of an impression on the other, and they still got the ticket.

We were on patrol near the Austrian border one day when my partner and I were instructed to set up a roadblock and were given a description of the car in question. About an hour later, we intercepted the car and noted that before it stopped, someone had thrown a rather large object from the vehicle. We had been warned that this might happen and were instructed to guard the item but not to touch it — for safety reasons. We learned later that the item was a container of uranium.

One evening, I received a complaint from a local establishment that a drunken soldier was waving a gun around. Like any other hero of that era, I immediately went in and discovered to my dismay that indeed there was a drunken soldier with a pistol. As soon as he spotted me, he pointed the gun in my direction. I was about to go for my own weapon when the joker suddenly lit a cigarette with his pistol. It was only a cigarette lighter! That fool will never know how close he came to heaven or hell that night.

I was discharged from the Army in 1952 and discovered again that I was not cut out to be a civilian, so I enlisted in the U. S. Air Force. I was assigned to the security police and remained an Air Force policeman for the next twenty years.

I was assigned to Mitchell Air Force Base, New York, for a time, then was sent to Wheelus Field, Tripoli, Libya, where I was NCO in charge of the security police investigations section. My five years in the investigations section at Wheelus were filled with incidents that are as amusing now as they were then. Wheelus was a huge base surrounded by a wall twenty miles long.

One night about 2:00 a.m., as I was riding the perimeter of the base, I came to an area where a B-29 had crashed some years before. The fire department used the wreckage as a training area for firemen. We all knew that pieces of aircraft had appeared in various forms in downtown Tripoli and were being sold back to Americans as souvenirs. When I noticed that the tail of the B-29 had a 3-inch rope attached to it and that the rope was taut with the other end obviously attached to something over the wall, I figured an Arab was trying to make off with the entire tail section. I cut the rope with an axe and as I did, I heard the sound of a donkey sliding on his you know what. I returned to the station and made a report.

The next morning I discovered an Arab outside my door. This man was seeking damages resulting from his donkey being injured by unknown U. S. Air Force personnel. After I heard his story through an interpreter, I had him escorted off the base. I got a good laugh out of that, but perhaps he got the last laugh. Apparently, he persisted with his claim and was eventually paid a small sum.

I investigated a case involving the sexual assault on a USAF captain's son by an English lieutenant colonel. I turned over what I had found to the English security people who soon determined that the colonel had committed the same acts on other children. Four weeks later, I was requested to fly to the nearby island of Malta for his trial in an English court. I had to appear in full uniform and speak while standing before a group of lawyers who were wearing wigs. The court reporter took all of the testimony in long hand, in a rather large ledger, a rather tedious job, to say the least. The suspect was convicted, stripped of his rank, and flown back to England. I received a commendation from the Queen of England for my work on the case.

In 1966, I was NCO in charge of the security police investigations section at Danang Air Base, Vietnam. One day I received a report that the only USAF fire truck in the motor pool was missing. During questioning, the airman at the motor pool reported that a Marine second lieutenant and a Marine sergeant had been there that morning and had inquired about when the airman took his lunch break. With this information, I knew the culprits had to be Marines. I asked the Marine CID (Criminal Investigation Detachment) for assistance, and about a week later, the agent called me and asked if I would accompany him to the Marine side of the base. Inside a large hangar was the fire truck, now repainted, but under the hood it still had USAF markings. Needless to say, we confiscated the truck.

Ironically, during this time we had a shortage of jeeps, so we would go to the port where USMC jeeps were stored and "borrow" what we needed. Two weeks before I left Vietnam, I was approached by a Marine CID agent looking for the missing vehicles, which by then numbered in the high twenties. I admitted that I was driving one of them, but I asked him if I could keep it until I was to leave for the States. He agreed, but added that I was to deliver it to him personally before I departed.

I also served five years in Japan (1966-70) and 1-year tours in France, Morocco, Saudi Arabia, China, Vietnam, and Thailand. In all, I served twenty-three years overseas. I retired from the Air Force in 1972 as a chief master sergeant and security police superintendent.

Harry Wallace received two U. S. Air Force Meritorious Service Medals, citations from the Japanese government and the government of Thailand, and a letter of commendation from the Queen of England for his work with security investigations. After his retirement, he continued with police work, serving in Saudi Arabia and the Sudan as a security consultant. He has also worked as an auxiliary policeman in small towns around Durham, New Hampshire, where he lives. Harry has a daughter, a son, and four grandchildren. His daughter served in the Air Force.

Tommy J. Coleman

Age 16 – United States Navy

Living conditions at home were not the best for me in early 1945. I was born in Boyle, Mississippi, on 19 April 1929, and at age 15, I was ready for a change. In February 1945, I altered my birth

> ..., the Navy found out I was underage and threw me in the brig ...

certificate and proceeded to the Navy recruiting station. There were two questions that I had difficulty with on the exam, but the recruiter helped me with the answers. I was given papers for my mother to sign, but I knew she wouldn't, so I found a lady I didn't know and paid her to sign them. I was sworn into the Navy on 21 April 1945, two days after my sixteenth birthday.

At the Naval Training Center, San Diego, California, I was assigned to Boot Company 198. While I was in boot camp, the Navy found out that I was underage so they threw me in the brig for five days on bread and water. The charge was lying to an officer. However, I was allowed to remain in the Navy, and after boot camp I was assigned to the *APL-29* (amphibious personnel, living) at Oakland, California.

After the war, we were sent to Tsingtao, China, where we remained until June 1946. At that time, the ship was given to the Chinese navy.

I returned to the States and was sent to the Naval Training Center, Memphis, Tennessee, where I was discharged on 1 August 1946.

I returned home, and things were no better than when I left. I couldn't find a decent job. The one I did find paid 50¢ an hour. After Social Security taxes were taken out, my pay was $18.50 per week. After the second week on the job, I decided that this work was not for me. I wanted to return to the Navy, but at age 17, I still needed my mother's permission. This time she signed for me.

I was sent to Charleston, South Carolina, where I was assigned to the destroyer, USS *Borie* (DD-704). I was on the *Borie* for about a year, then in late 1947, I was transferred to the USS *Vesole* (DD-878). We cruised all over the Mediterranean Sea. We showed the flag when Yugoslavia went Communist. In 1948 we were involved when Israel became a country.

I was discharged from the Navy for the second time in January 1950, but I was not through with the military. I returned home and decided to join the Air Force Reserve. I served for over a year, then the unit was disbanded.

Tom Coleman became a finance company manager, a real-estate salesman, and a broker. He spent the last twenty and one-half years of his career as executive director of the East Arkansas Family Health Center in West Memphis, Arkansas. At his retirement in 1996, he was honored by having the building where he worked named after him. Tom and Helen, his wife of forty-five years, live in De Bary, Florida. They have three children, four grandchildren, and one great-grandson.

William S. Hanson

Age 15 – United States Navy

While attending high school in my hometown of Weymouth, Massachusetts, I developed an attitude that was not conducive to getting along with people. I was determined not to do anything that anyone told me to do. To put it bluntly,

> *... I went ... to Bremerhaven, Germany, to help bring our "prize of war" home.*

I was incorrigible. When I was 15, I was told to leave school and not to return. I was not a problem just at school, but also at home. My mother couldn't handle me. I was just plain bad!

After I was kicked out of school, I went to Tennessee to find work. I worked on an oil truck for a time, then was hired at the Hardwick Woolen Mills in Cleveland, Tennessee, as a card-machine stripper. My mother came to visit me there. During her visit, she said to me, "How

about going into the Navy?" I said, "Sure." Apparently, she had decided that it would be best for me to be in the service because she had already altered my birth certificate before coming to see me. She had changed my birth date from 12 July 1929 to 12 July 1927.

The altered birth certificate indicated that I was 17, so she still needed to sign my enlistment papers, which she did. I enlisted and was sworn into the U. S. Navy in Chattanooga, Tennessee, on 11 May 1945.

My enlistment period was from the time I was sworn in until my twenty-first (forged) birthday, a so-called "kiddie cruise," where I would be credited for four years of service although it would actually be three years and a few months. I was 15 years of age.

I was sent to boot camp at the Great Lakes Naval Training Center. When I was asked what type of work experience I had, I told them that I was a truck driver. After all, I had driven my father's pickup quite a bit. Several weeks after starting boot camp, an orderly came into the barracks and called out five names, one of which was mine. We were told to roll our gear in our mattresses, that we were going to Chicago. A strike had been called by truck drivers in Chicago, and since the five of us said that we were experienced truck drivers, we were going to help keep the war-related activities going. We were taken to Aurora, Illinois, where we picked up Navy trucks and drove them to Chicago. Here I was, a 15-year-old kid, driving a truck bigger than I had ever been in before, in a city where I had never been before. I drove every day for two weeks. When the strike was settled, I went back to Great Lakes and graduated from boot camp with my company.

After boot camp, I was sent to Manila, Philippine Islands, via Shoemaker and Yerba Buena Island in California, and to Samar, also in the Philippine Islands. I was assigned to the USS *Panda* (IX-125). The *Panda* and four other ships were Liberty ships converted into tankers, but they still looked like cargo ships. The designation "IX" meant unclassified.

I had been aboard the *Panda* just two or three days when we were fueling a good-sized Army boat. The fenders between the ships kept them about three feet apart, but the swells in the harbor would cause one ship to move up while the other would move down. The mascot on our ship was a male dog, and yes, the mascot on the Army boat was a female dog. When the male saw the female, he took off, intending to jump to the Army boat. The two ships moved just then and our dog ended up in the water between the two. I didn't even think. I kicked off my shoes and jumped in. I grabbed the dog and kept it afloat while the crew threw a line to me and pulled us aboard.

I was taken to sick bay where a pharmacist's mate made a drink for me using 190-proof alcohol. Wow! A few hours later the captain sent for me. He congratulated me on saving the dog, then gave me the job of running his small boat that took him around the harbor. One of the captain's friends happened to be a financial advisor to the President of the Philippines, so I would take the captain to the presidential palace at times. This was great duty until I took too many chances in dodging some of the sunken hulls in the harbor and the captain found other duties for me.

After V-J Day, we fueled some Japanese destroyers and destroyer-escorts that had surrendered. We sailed the *Panda* to Norfolk, Virginia, in the spring of 1946. I really don't think the Navy wanted her back, but I don't think our skipper would have left her in the

Pacific even if ordered to. The skipper went aboard the *Panda* when she was commissioned at New Orleans, Louisiana, in 1943. He was a machinist's mate third class at the time. By 1946, he was a full lieutenant and skipper of the ship.

From Norfolk, I boarded a destroyer bound for Gibraltar. From there I went through France to Bremerhaven, Germany, to help bring our "prize of war" home. The prize was the largest floating crane in the world. Hitler had four of these 500-ton cranes built for the purpose of launching submarines in areas with 20-foot tides. Two of the four were sunk by bombs during the war. The English had tried to tow one fully erected across the channel and lost it at sea. We took the boom and 500-tons of counterweights off, tied on with a fleet tug, and towed it out to sea. At one time, we found ourselves well within an uncleared mine-field. The fleet tugs towing us were changed every thirteen days. A tanker would come from Norfolk with fuel. Our destination was Long Beach, California, via the Panama Canal.

Getting the beast through the canal was another problem. Its hull width was the widest of any vessel to ever go through the canal. There was a genuine fear that it would get stuck and put the canal out of use for awhile, but we made it. It took us seven months to tow the crane from Bremerhaven to San Pedro in Long Beach harbor. The last I heard, the crane was still in use at the Long Beach Navy Yard and known by the name "Herman the German."

In late spring of 1947, I became a plank owner on the USS *Keppler* (DD-765) at the Bethlehem Steel Works, San Francisco. We conducted maneuvers with the USS *Boxer* (CV-21), which had the first carrier-based jet aircraft. Later, we formed Task Force 38 with the USS *Law* (DD-763), USS *Wood* (DD-764), USS *Thomas* (DD-721), and the carrier USS *Valley Forge* (CV-45). This task force made a goodwill tour to many ports: Sidney, Australia; Hong Kong; Shanghai, China; Tsingtao, China; and Yokosuka, Japan.

In addition to being a plank owner on the *Keppler*, I hold the distinction of being the first man aboard the ship to receive a captain's mast. I returned to the base one night after hoisting a few, and I couldn't find the right ID card to show the Marine guard at the gate. Most of us had several doctored ID cards and liberty cards so that we could drink in the bars. In fact, I had seven. During the proceedings the captain found out that I was carrying seven cards, so he decided that my punishment would be to serve seven hours of extra duty. He thought for a minute and decided that seven wasn't enough, so he turned to the executive officer and asked, "How fast are we going?" the exec replied, "Thirteen knots." The captain turned to me and said, "OK, twenty hours of extra duty. Do you have anything to say?" I replied, "I'm glad that were not on a speed run!"

While in Sidney harbor during our around-the-world cruise, the destroyers were all tied up side by side. I returned to the dock one night, again after hoisting a few, went aboard ship and went directly to my bunk. When I got there, I found a man asleep in it. I was furious! I grabbed the man and tried to pull him out of my bunk. It turned out that I was on the wrong ship. That was a bit embarrassing.

By the time we arrived in Shanghai, China, I was still on restriction. A friend, who was also on restriction, had grown up in China and spoke the language fluently. While we were in the harbor, sampans would tie up to the ship, and for a price, clean the sides. My friend spoke to the Chinese in their language and arranged that we would provide them some food from the galley, and after dark, they would take us into Shanghai and bring us back before dawn the next morning. They took us to the restricted part of Shanghai, and we had a ball. From then on I was known as "Sampan Bill."

We stopped at Pearl Harbor on our way back from Japan, then went on to San Diego, where I was discharged on 12 July 1948. I served three years and two months in the Navy. I was 19 years old.

Bill Hanson worked in the heavy construction industry from the time he was discharged from the Navy until he retired. He was involved with road building, subway construction, and essentially all types of heavy construction. He drove a dump truck, was a master mechanic for several large construction companies, and was a crane operator at the time he retired in 1992. Bill is now home-bound and under a nurse's care. He is hooked up to an oxygen bottle at all times. In his words, "I stopped smoking, but it was fifty-five years too late." Bill and Virginia, his wife of forty-seven years, live in Whitman, Massachusetts. They have three sons, three grandchildren, and two great-grandchildren. Their oldest son served in the Navy during the war in Vietnam.

Jack Michaelson

Age 15 – United States Army

In the summer of 1945, the war with Germany was over. Although I was only 15, I was very patriotic and wanted to serve my country. I was born in Philadelphia, Pennsylvania, on

> *We were the only units stationed in the Russian Zone of Germany.*

7 November 1929, but I didn't want to send to Philadelphia to get a birth certificate. We were living in Springfield, Massachusetts, at the time, and my brother had been born in Holyoke, just eight miles away. I went to Holyoke and obtained a copy of my brother's birth certificate, then went home and proceeded to alter it. I changed the birth year to read 1927, and since I wanted to use my own name, I changed his name to mine. With the altered certificate, I managed to enlist in the Army on 9 July 1945. My records indicated that I was born in Holyoke, Massachusetts, on 21 July 1927.

I was sent to Fort Devens, Massachusetts, for indoctrination. From there, I went to Camp Croft, South Carolina, for seventeen weeks of infantry training. The war with Japan ended after I had been in training one month. I believe that if the A-bomb had not been used on Japan, we would have participated in the invasion of that country.

We were sent to Europe in December 1945. I could not believe the devastation that war can bring. I was only 16 and saw survivors from the concentration camps and other refugees. I was assigned to the 3160th Signal Service Battalion, although I was trained as a rifleman. After a short period of training, I was assigned to a telephone repeater-station in the small town of Greding, Germany. There were only three American soldiers in the town of 3000 people. We were there for four months, and then we were assigned to a crew maintaining telephone lines. We were the only units stationed in the Russian Zone of Germany. Later, I was assigned to company headquarters at Nuremberg, Germany, where the Nuremberg trials were held. I was there when Herman Goering swallowed a poison capsule.

In July 1947, I was discharged from the Army at the age of 17, still too young to enlist legally. Less than a year later, on 10 May 1948, I reenlisted in the Army and volunteered for the Medical Corps. I was sent to Fort Sam Houston, Texas, for training, then returned to Germany and was stationed at Munich and at Weisbaden. We were involved in the Berlin Airlift. When the Korean War broke out in 1950, I volunteered to go there, but my request was turned down. I was told that I was needed in Germany, and my enlistment was extended for one year. I received my GED certificate while I was in the Army.

My last tour of duty was with a reserve artillery unit at Camp Edwards, Massachusetts, near Cape Cod. I was discharged from the Army on 9 May 1952 with the rank of staff sergeant. Sometimes I regret that I didn't make the military a career. When I was 62, I applied for early retirement and was told to bring my birth certificate and both military discharge papers in to the Social Security office. I was concerned that they would notice the difference in dates between the two. I was told not to worry about it. To this day, the Army does not know about my underage military service.

Jack Michaelson operated a wholesale-produce business for many years in partnership with his brother. He retired from the business in 1992. Jack and Frances, his wife of forty-three years, live in Suffield, Connecticut. They have two children and three grandchildren. Jack is the Connecticut State Commander of the Veterans of Underage Military Service.

Richard J. "Jim" Thomas

Age 16 – United States Navy

I had always wanted to join the Navy. My father had served in the Navy during World War I, and my older brother was in the Navy. I had lived all my life in Seattle, Washington, where I was born on 5 July 1929, and it was time to see the world.

> *There are not many chief enginemen who skippered a tug for the last three years of their Navy career.*

In May 1945, when I was 15 years old, I went to the Navy recruiting office to enlist. I took all the tests, including the physical, although I passed out when I was given a blood test. When the recruiter asked how old I was, I said, "Sixteen, but I'll be 17 in July." He said, "Come back then." I didn't say anything to my folks. I went back to the recruiting office in late July and said, "I'm back – I'm 17 now." They had kept all my records and everything was in order except that my dad had to sign the papers. My dad went with me and

told them that my birth certificate had been burned. He signed the papers verifying that I was 17. I was sworn into the regular Navy on 3 August 1945. I had signed up for a "mini-cruise," which meant that I was to be discharged on my twenty-first birthday.

We went to the train depot in Seattle and got on an old, old train, and when I say old, I mean *old*. It even had gas lights! It took us about five days to get to San Diego on that old train. Upon arrival at the Naval Training Station, I was assigned to boot

company 377. After graduation from boot camp, I got back on an old train – it wasn't the same train – but it was also an old, old train, and rode it back to Seattle. I told my dad that I was scheduled to go to hospital corpsman school. He said, "Ha, I don't know if you really want to be a hospital corpsman if you passed out during your blood test. Maybe you can get it changed."

When I returned to San Diego, I went to see the executive officer and told him that I didn't want to be a hospital corpsman. He asked, "What do you want to be?" I replied, "I want to go to sea and be a fireman." He said, "Great, you are on your way." A few days later, I was on a ship headed for Okinawa, but we were rerouted to Sasebo, Japan, because of a typhoon.

At Sasebo, I reported aboard an LCT (landing craft, tank), a boat with two officers and a crew of eight. I was assigned guard duty on the night of 7 December 1945. Everyone was somewhat nervous thinking that maybe the Japanese would cause some trouble on the anniversary of the attack on Pearl Harbor, but everything was quiet.

One day we took our LCT to an LST (landing ship, tank) anchored in the bay. The LST had brought Japanese soldiers from Manchuria back to Japan. The LST's bow doors were open, so we dropped our ramp on the ramp of the LST. The soldiers all wore hobnail boots, and as they transferred from the LST to our ship, they slipped and slid on the metal ramp. About every other one of the soldiers carried a little white box in which he was bringing back to his homeland the ashes of a friend who had died in the war.

In early 1946, we took supplies to a Marine garrison at Nagasaki, the city devastated by the A-bomb. There were globs of glass still lying around. Some things were simply liquified by the blast. What an experience!

When they started phasing out the LCTs and other small craft at Sasebo, I didn't know what was going to happen to me. I was 16 years old and the only regular Navy man on the ship. The reserves couldn't wait to get home. One day we were asked if anyone knew how to type and I said, "Yes, I do." Then I was asked the size of my uniform. I was issued Marine greens and sent to an MP office in Sasebo to serve as clerk. They wanted everyone there to be in the same uniform. I typed the MP reports and anything else that needed to be typed. I drove a jeep for the first time and survived my first experience of driving on the left hand side of the road.

The Marines treated me just like they treated Navy medical corpsmen. I have respected the Marines from that day on. About the middle of 1946, when my stay with the Marines was over, I was put on a train and sent to Yokosuka. My dad had told me that I should take the GED tests and get a high school diploma, so while I was in Yokosuka, I did. The test scores were sent to Madison, Wisconsin, and then forwarded to Broadway High School in North Seattle. When I returned to the States in the spring of 1947, I found that I had been awarded a high school diploma in the Seattle public schools before my own class had graduated. I was just 17 years old.

I was assigned to the USS *Ackinar* (AKA-53) in 1947. We were sent to the Pribilof Islands to bring back seal skins. The government treated the Pribilofs as an Indian reservation and brought seal skins back to the States for sale. I was an engineman on an LCVP. We would go to the boat landing, load pallets of seal skins on board, and take them to the ship. From Alaska, I went to Hawaii for duty with CINPAC (Commander in Chief, Pacific Fleet), where I was assigned to the boathouse. I operated barges reserved for high-ranking officers and VIPs.

My mini-cruise was up on 5 July 1949, and I was discharged at Treasure Island in San Francisco Bay. The records said that I was 21, but I was really only 20. This time I flew home instead of taking the train. After I had been home a few days, my dad told me,"You better go back in the Navy before you break a leg or something." So in September 1949, about sixty days after I was discharged, I reenlisted and was assigned to the Sand Point Naval Station, Sand Point, Washington.

Many of my close friends were members of the Marine Reserve. After the Korean War started, most were recalled to active duty and were soon in Korea. I stayed on shore duty until 1952, then I was sent to Kodiak, Alaska, where I boarded an ATF (auxiliary tug, fleet) and proceeded to Attu in the Aleutian Islands. We were there for six months as an air-sea rescue vessel. Just before we left Attu for our home port in Hawaii, our chief engineman had a stroke. I had just made first class petty officer, so I became the engineman in charge. It was a very responsible job.

We spent quite a few months in Hawaii, then went back to San Diego. By this time I was up for discharge again. I went back to Seattle, and after a few days, my dad repeated his advice of four years earlier. He told me, "You better hurry up and reenlist." I guess he didn't want me to be a bum like some of the people who were just hanging around, so I reenlisted. I received orders to report to Mobile Boat Pool #1. I thought, "Oh, my God, I'm going to Mobile, Alabama." But it was the Mobile Boat Pool #1 in Sasebo, Japan.

In the fall of 1953, at Treasure Island, I was assigned to an LST with an LCT piggy-backed on it. It took us more than forty-five days to make it to Yokosuka. My brother was stationed at Yokosuka at that time, so I was able to be with him quite a bit during the couple of weeks I was there. My orders were to go to Sasebo by train. I had gone from Sasebo to Yokosuka by train in 1946, and now it was 1953 and I was completing the circle by taking a train from Yokosuka to Sasebo. The train was in much better condition the second time.

At Sasebo, I was attached to Mobile Boat Pool #1. This was very good duty. We lived aboard an APL (auxiliary personnel, living). In the latter part of 1954, a close friend received orders to go to Subic Bay, Philippine Islands, so I volunteered to go with him. Big mistake! About seventy-five of us, comprising what was called Mobile Boat Pool #1, Detachment Able, were sent to Subic Bay. Detachment Able's job was to maintain and issue small craft to ships, mostly AKA's, that would go to North Vietnam and take people who wanted to leave that area to South Vietnam. This was 1954 and was the first stage of the war in Vietnam.

We had been at Subic Bay less than two weeks when my friend was transferred back to Japan. I spent over six months there and hated every minute of it. In early 1955, I was accepted for engineman school at the Great Lakes Naval Training Center, Illinois. After twenty weeks of school and a 30-day leave, I was assigned to a destroyer, the USS *Lofberg*, in San Diego. My brother's ship, the USS *Prairie*, was in the same division and was also based at San Diego. The Navy allowed brothers to serve in the same division, but not on the same ship. When our ships would pass alongside we would wave to each other.

I was aboard the destroyer for nearly six months when we received orders to deploy to WESPAC (Western Pacific Command). My wife was pregnant at the time, and I didn't want to leave her. I arranged a swap with a sailor on a destroyer-escort based at Pier 91 in Seattle. The entire arrangements for the swap were completed in one week, an unheard-of speed for the Navy bureaucracy to move.

I had to have another blood test, and once again, I passed out, but this time I hit my head when I fell. It required sixteen stitches to close a cut above my eyebrow.

In March 1956, I reported aboard a radar picket ship, the USS *Lowe*. Duty was good. We would be at sea for twenty-seven days and in port for twenty-four or vice versa, depending on the weather. We patrolled from the northern end of Vancouver Island, British Columbia, south to the Oregon border, usually about 300 miles offshore.

I was due for discharge in 1957, but I shipped over immediately without waiting for my dad to tell me to. By then I had a family and was scheduled for shore duty. I was sent to Whidbey Island. I had my records corrected to reflect my true age while I was there. Whidbey was a long drive from home, so when an opening came in the Puget Sound Naval brig, I asked to be transferred there. The brig was run by Marines at that time. I was the first sailor to be a brig warden at the Marine brig in Puget Sound. The Navy took complete charge of the brig operation later.

My shore-duty time was up in 1958, so I left the brig and went aboard the tug YTB-537 that was stationed at pier 91. Would you believe that this was considered sea duty? What choice duty that was, sea duty right out of pier 91! I stayed aboard her until I retired in 1965.

I made chief in 1961, about the time the Vietnam war was starting to escalate. They needed boatswain's mates to run the river-patrol boats over there, so we lost our chief boatswain's mate. I was asked if I could run the tug until they could get a chief boatswain's mate on board, and I said, "Of course!" This was the highlight of my naval career, becoming the chief in charge of the YTB-537. It was quite an honor! There are not many chief enginemen who skippered a tug for the last three years of their Navy career.

When the time came that I would be transferred overseas again, I decided that twenty years was enough. I retired from the Navy on 26 July 1965.

Jim Thomas, after retiring from the Navy, went to work for the Patrol Division of the Washington State Department of Fisheries as a "fish cop." After about twelve years with the department, he became an equipment supervisor. He retired in 1991. Jim and Darlene, his wife of forty-one years, live in Seattle, Washington. They have two children, two grandchildren, and a great-granddaughter. Jim is the Washington State Vice-Commander of the Veterans of Underage Military Service.

William G. Hood, Sr.

Age 15 – New Jersey State Guard
Age 16 – United States Marine Corps

I was born in a little town along the Delaware River called Burlington, New Jersey, on 25 January 1929. During World War II, I was too young to enlist in the regular military, so in 1944, at

> ... when the Communists started shooting at us ... we gave that up.

the age of 15, I joined the New Jersey State Guard. When I turned 16, I wanted to join the U. S. Marine Corps, so I asked for a discharge from the Guard. I knew the first sergeant very well, and I asked him to list my age as 17 on the discharge papers. The State Guard discharge was sufficient to prove my age to the Marines.

I enlisted in the Marines at Philadelphia, Pennsylvania, on 16 August 1945. From there I was sent to Parris Island, South Carolina, for boot camp. I was in Platoon 555. After boot camp, I was sent to Camp Lejeune, North Carolina, and was soon assigned to China duty. I was in the 96th Replacement Draft. We boarded the USS *Wakefield* in Portsmouth, Virginia, and went from there through the Panama Canal to Pearl Harbor, then to Taku, China. We arrived in Taku in January 1946, and in the

middle of the night, we boarded a train for Tientsin. The train would go forward about five miles, then back up for about two miles. We finally arrived in Tientsin in the morning.

I was told that I was to be an MP. I pulled guard duty at the general's house and at different stations in the city of Tientsin. After a time, I became friends with a Chinese policeman. He and I did duty on the same street corner for awhile.

I was transferred later to the 1st Assault Signal Company of the 1st Marine Division. I had all I wanted of being on guard duty outside in the cold, so when I arrived at the Assault Signal Company, I became a cook striker. I ended up cooking for the 1st Recon Company, the 1st Division Band, in addition to my own company. For a time, I was chief cook for the 1st Marine Air Wing at Tientsin.

Two Chinese brothers worked for me as cooks. We called them Big Jim and Little Jim. Big Jim was a heavy drinker and Little Jim wouldn't touch the stuff. They would argue all day long, so you can imagine the noise in the kitchen. They were good cooks, though.

The Hai Ho River ran through the city of Tientsin. Many times I would see bodies of babies that had washed up on the banks of the river. There were also many bodies of pigs and dogs along the banks.

I watched the Chinese Nationalist soldiers marching through the city as they were retreating from the Communists. They looked beat and demoralized because the Communists were taking control of all the countryside.

My buddy Harry Bramin was stationed at the French Arsenal about ten miles out of the city. I would visit him at times. We would drive there in a truck, but when the Communists started shooting at us both coming and going, we gave that up.

We had to leave after about two years in China. I returned to the States and was stationed at Camp Pendleton and at Barstow, California, for a little while, then I was transferred to Quantico, Virginia, where I was discharged in 19 October 1949.

Bill Hood went to work for the Rohm & Haas Company in May of 1950 and married the following month. He and his wife Evelyn had a son, William, Jr. Evelyn died in 1985. Bill retired from Rohm & Haas in 1989. He met his present wife Dolly soon after retiring. Bill and Dolly live in Little River, South Carolina. Bill is the South Carolina State Commander of the Veterans of Underage Military Service.

Billy E. Bruton

Age 15 – United States Navy

I grew up in a very abusive home with the feeling of not being wanted. My oldest brother had earned a battlefield commission in Normandy, and another brother was serving in the Navy. My dream was to remove myself from the

> *... I would give him five dollars and a jug of wine if he would ... sign my enlistment papers.*

abusive situation and to prove myself in the military as my brothers had done. Sometimes dreams that you create while young become so urgent that you bypass all fear of consequences in later years to make those dreams become reality. Such was my case.

I ran away from home on a Sunday night, 19 August 1945, after my parents had gone to bed. I walked several miles from the little town of Katy, Texas, before I caught a ride into Houston, Texas. The next day, I went to the Federal Building and tried to enlist in the U. S. Marine Corps. During a very short interview with a Marine recruiter, I was told that I would need one of my parents' signatures before I could be sworn into any branch of service.

I left the Marine recruiting office and walked down the street where I noticed a man, obviously a wino, sitting on the sidewalk near the main entrance to Walgreens. He asked me for some money. I told him that all I had was a $10.00 bill (which I had taken from my mother's purse, along with my birth certificate, just before I left home), but I would give him $5.00 and a jug of wine if he would agree to sign my enlistment papers. He agreed. We then went to the Greyhound Bus depot where he shaved with just a razor blade and peeled off three layers of clothing to reveal a fairly clean suit.

We then returned to the Federal Building. I didn't want to be seen by the Marine recruiter that I had talked to before, so we went into the

Navy recruiting office. My "father" signed the necessary papers and I filled out forms and took my physical. I was sworn into the Navy that same afternoon, and along with nineteen others, I was put on a Southern Pacific train at 6:00 p.m., headed for San Diego, California. Part of my dream had become a reality.

At the U. S. Naval Training Center, San Diego, where I would take twelve weeks of boot training, I was assigned to a barracks, then issued clothes. I received more new clothes than I had ever seen or owned in my life. I was in hog heaven. Then it was off to the sick bay for shots!

My boot camp training was great. I was the platoon leader of Company 396, shot expert with the M-1 rifle, and sharpshooter with the machine gun and pistol. As a welter-weight, I was champion boxer of the nine companies against which we competed. I auditioned for the Navy band and was scheduled to go to the Navy Band Training School in Anacostia, Maryland, after completion of boot camp.

After graduation from boot camp on 15 December 1945, I was given a 10-day leave. When I returned to the base, I found that I would not be going to the Navy Band but to sea on a destroyer. Six destroyers were in San Diego harbor, all needing personnel to fill out their crews. I was assigned to the USS *Mansfield* (DD-728) and reported aboard at about 8:30 p.m. on 29 December 1945. We left for Pearl Harbor, Hawaii, on 31 December 1945. At Pearl, the *Mansfield* was designated as the flagship of DesPac-9, a destroyer squadron destined for China and the China Coast Patrol.

We were the first American vessel to enter the Whangpoo River in mainland China after World War II. Our main station was Shanghai. On the China patrol, we would go from Shanghai to Tsingtao to Hong Kong, then to Jinsen, Korea, where couriers would go to Seoul and pick up the fleet mail and payroll. We would then return to Shanghai. While our ship was in port, I operated a LCVP liberty boat that would stop at all U. S. Navy ships in the harbor, then proceed to a dock known as "liberty landing."

This routine continued until October 1946, when I was summoned to the captain's quarters. The captain showed me a birthday card that somehow had fallen into his hands. It was from a friend congratulating me on my sixteenth birthday. The captain asked me if that was my age and I said yes. He told me that I would be court-martialed for fraudulent enlistment and that I would be returned to the States for discharge.

I received a summary court-martial and was found guilty of fraudulent enlistment. My sentence was six months at hard labor and a bad conduct discharge. The hard labor was waived, but the bad conduct discharge was upheld. I was sent to San Francisco aboard the USS *War Hawk* and from there to the Orange Naval Station, Orange, Texas, where my discharge would be carried out. My dream was shattered.

The saddest day of my life came on 5 November 1946 when I had to stand at rigid attention at the main gate of the Orange Naval Base, have the uniform that I loved stripped from my body, then be handed a bad conduct discharge.

However, I enlisted again, this time in the U. S. Air Force. That was on 16 March 1947, two months after my seventeenth birthday. I received a direct appointment to the Air Force Bandsmen Training School at Bolling Field, near Washington, D.C. I was honorably discharged on 23 December 1948.

Several years later, I decided to try to get the bad conduct discharge from the Navy changed. After a number of attempts and a number of years, I succeeded. In 1984, the Navy changed my discharge to honorable, and I received the back pay and all the veterans benefits that had been stripped from me.

Although nearly fifty years have passed, I still feel the humiliation of having my uniform cut off from me. I hope and pray that no one ever has to suffer the humiliating experience that I did, all because of a dream. Yet, if I had it to do over, I'd do it the same way!

Billy Bruton worked for many years as an operator and a mechanic in heavy equipment. Since 1973, he has been a professional bus operator and still works part-time driving busses. Billy and his wife Anne have lived in Richland Hills, Texas, for the past twenty-eight years. They have four children and eight grandchildren. He is the Texas State Vice-Commander of the Veterans of Underage Military Service.

Clarence J. Rockey

Age 16 – United States Navy

I was raised near Green Bay, Wisconsin, and had the pleasure of knowing players on the Green Bay Packers football team. They would play ball in the street with us kids. I was born in Green Bay on 2 March 1929.

> *... a beautiful young lady ... requested that I serve as her military escort ...*

The Depression years adversely affected my family, as it did millions of Americans. My father emphasized the importance of an education and prior to my entering the service, insisted that I promise to graduate from high school.

I enlisted in the Navy for several reasons: I was not satisfied with school, finding it boring; I was strongly influenced by the patriotism of the day; I wanted to travel; and remembering the era of the Great Depression, I was afraid of not having a job and being a burden on my family. My birth certificate had been filled in using a fine-line pen, so I went over the writing with a broad-point pen, changing the date. The recruiter, in my opinion, realized I was underage – but didn't discourage my efforts.

I was sworn into the Navy on 26 September 1945 and reported to the Great Lakes Naval Training Center for boot camp. After boot camp, six other seamen and I were assigned to the Navy Department on Constitution Avenue in Washington, D.C. Our duties involved participating in the development of an automated system to account for and control Navy and Army code machines and manuals in custody of the Navy.

The war was over, and most of the higher-ranking enlisted personnel were being demobilized. By April 1946, the staff of chief petty officers and WAVES serving during the war was almost completely replaced. For those of us whose memory of boot camp was very recent, the change in our personal environment was beyond belief.

We "lived ashore," that is, we received subsistence and quarters allowances and lived essentially as civilians.

In September 1946, I was promoted to petty officer third class. About this time, the unanticipated incidents and their consequences involved with unsupervised enlisted men living ashore caused a drastic change in our living conditions. None of these men would earn the Good Conduct Medal for that period of time. We were transferred to the Naval Communications Annex near American University and were required to live in a nearby naval barracks. This unexpected disciplinary move proved beneficial to me. I ordered and completed a series of naval correspondence courses, which led to the completion of my high school education.

May 1947 was a very significant month for me. First, my promotion to petty officer second class became effective. Second, a beautiful young lady I had never seen before requested that I serve as her military escort when she laid a wreath at the Tomb of the Unknown Soldier on Memorial Day. She became my wife a short time later. Third, I was transferred to Radio Central, located in the Navy Department, where I worked on a system involving world-wide communications. Finally, honoring the promise I had made to my father, I took my first leave and returned to Green Bay for my high school graduation.

In the fall of 1948, I was transferred to the Norfolk Naval Base, Virginia, where I assisted with the design and implementation of PAMI (personnel accounting machine installation). Midway through my tour of duty at Norfolk, I was issued orders transferring me to Treasure Island, California, to attend the first computer class offered by the Navy. The next year, prior to the outbreak of the Korean conflict, I was promoted to petty officer first class.

Early in 1951, I was transferred to the Naval Training Center at Great Lakes to continue working with naval data-processing. During this time, I also earned money for a down payment on a home by working for Abbott Laboratories as an evening-shift supervisor in the data-processing department.

I was discharged from the Navy on 1 March 1953.

Clarence Rockey, married and with three children, enrolled at St. Norbert College, where he earned a B.S. in biology in 1957. While he was in school, he contracted polio and was placed in an iron lung, but that did not deter him from graduating in 1957. He immediately enrolled at Alfred University and obtained an M.A. in education. After he taught high school for one year, he changed to industry where he designed and implemented management-information systems and taught computer-science classes in the evenings. He left industry in 1975 and taught computer science at a technical college and spent a year as associate professor at the University of Wisconsin. In 1982, Clarence joined Teledyne-Brown Engineering, a defense contractor. In addition to his work load there, he taught in the University of Alabama graduate school two evenings a week and attended classes at the Southeastern Institute of Technology, Huntsville, Alabama. He received an M.S. in business, and M.S. in computer science, and a Doctor of Science in software systems. When he called his mother to inform her of his Doctor of Science degree, she responded, "Big deal — it took you fifty years!" Clarence and Agnes, his wife of fifty-one years, live in Appleton, Wisconsin. At last count, they had ten children and seventeen grandchildren.

John T. Stamelos

Age 16 – United States Marine Corps

When I was 10 years old, I saw the movie "Devil Dogs of the Air." From that time on, I knew that the "eagle, globe and anchor" was for me, that I was going to be a Marine. When World War II started, I was 13 years old, 6-foot tall, and I couldn't wait to get in.

> *The Nationalists were on one side, the Communists on the other, and we were in the middle.*

By the time I was 14, I had gone through a dozen copies of my birth certificate trying to make one look like it hadn't been altered. I finally made one that convinced the recruiting officer that I was old enough to join, but I was turned down, not because of my age, but because of a weak right eye. The same thing happened when I was 15. By the time I reached 16, I had the eye chart memorized well enough that I passed the physical.

I was sworn into the U. S. Marine Corps on 18 September 1945 and was immediately sent to boot camp at Parris Island, South Carolina. The day after graduating from boot camp, we went by train to Norfolk, Virginia, where we boarded the USS *Wakefield*. We were told that we would be going to North China as replacements for Marines stationed there.

En route to China, we went through the Panama Canal and on to Pearl Harbor, where we were allowed a half day of liberty. We spent two hours of this precious time standing in line to buy a can of Iron City beer. From Pearl Harbor, we went on to Tsingtao, China, where the 96th Replacement Draft went ashore. The 94th and 95th Drafts went on to Taku-bar where we disembarked and were assigned to units. We thought that we would all freeze to death because the temperature was near zero and we didn't have any cold-weather gear.

I was assigned to Ordnance Company, 7th Service Regiment in Tientsin, and later to a guard company. That is where I found out that, although the war ended in August, a shooting war was still going on in China. The Nationalists were on one side, the Communists on the other, and we were in the middle. Marines became casualties because neither side was particular about whom they shot. We often wondered what the telegrams said that were sent to the next of kin back home. How can you be killed in action when there wasn't supposed to be any action? The war was over!

When the Guard Company was deactivated, I was assigned to B Company, 1st Marine Regiment, in the British concession in Tientsin. I remained in Tientsin except for an excursion to Peitaiho Beach where a group of Marines had been taken prisoner by Communist forces. While returning to our base, a storm had passed through, and as the sun broke through the clouds, it lit up our flag that was silhouetted against a background of black clouds. I had never seen such bright colors. My chest tightened and a lump came in my throat. I will never forget that beautiful sight!

I returned to the States and was discharged at Camp Robert Smalls, near the Great Lakes Naval Training Center, on 16 October 1946. I returned to Saint Louis, Missouri, and joined the 3rd Infantry Battalion, U. S. Marine Corps Reserve, in April 1947 and served with that unit for more than three years.

John Stamelos went to work for the Southwestern Bell Telephone Company in 1950 and retired in 1984 after thirty-four years of service. He is now a disaster volunteer with the American Red Cross, working in over forty disaster areas during the past ten years. John and Lorraine, his wife of forty-nine years, live in Springfield, Missouri. They have three sons. One son served with the U. S. Marines in Vietnam.

Richard L. Bowlby

Age 15 – United States Navy

I was born at Saint Francis Hospital, Wichita, Kansas, on 24 August 1930. In the fall of 1944, my mother enrolled me in a military school and then joined the Army. At the time school was over for me in the spring of 1945, my mother was

> *I took six highline rides in one day! My ass was soaked and I was a nervous wreck.*

stationed at Fort Des Moines, Iowa. She made arrangements for me to room with some people she knew, so I joined her there.

I already had experience as a busboy, dishwasher, and counterman, so I went job-hunting. I was hired as a busboy and counterman at Bishop's Cafeteria, but there was a problem: in Iowa, one had to be 16 to work. I went to the Social Security office to get a card and a work permit. I gave 24 August 1928 as my date of birth, dropped the middle initial from my name, changed the place of my birth, and went to work.

On my supposed seventeenth birthday, 24 August 1945, the cafeteria employees baked a cake for me, and we had a little party after the noon rush. Two Navy recruiters were having their lunch nearby. After they finished eating, they walked over to me and said, "Happy birthday! Now that you are 17, you can join the Navy." I had never thought about joining the military. Like everyone else in those days, I was patriotic, and I listened as the recruiters painted a pretty picture of life in the Navy. They said that they would send me to cooks and bakers school.

I had only a ninth-grade education, and the chances of getting more ranged from slim to none. I was looking for security. The Navy not only offered security, but the chance to learn a trade. I went to the recruiting office and filled out the papers. They gave me some papers to take home to have my parents sign, but there was a problem. My mother had been transferred and I knew not where, so I told the recruiters that I was homeless. They asked if I knew someone who would serve as my legal guardian. I had moved in with a friend and his mother, and I thought that his mother might be willing to become my guardian. Besides, her son (my friend) was going to join the Navy with me. I asked her if she would be my guardian and she said yes. We appeared before a judge and asked that my friend's mother be appointed my guardian. He agreed, and I paid $10.00 court costs. I have never heard of anyone else who had to pay to get into the Navy.

I was sworn into the Navy on 17 September 1945 and was sent to boot camp at the Naval Training Center, San Diego, California. My first assignment after boot camp was to the ammunition depot at Port Chicago, California. My next assignment was a unique one. I was sent to Alameda, California, to be part of the decommissioning crew for the yard houseboat, YHB1. This was an old stern-wheel sugar boat that had sailed up and down the Sacramento River. It was just like the ones that sailed the Mississippi. After World War II, the Navy started moth-balling ships, and they used the old stern wheeler as a berthing ship for crews that decommissioned LSTs. I found the YHB1 in dry dock at Todd Shipyard in Oakland, California. She was having her hull caulked before being towed to the Vallejo Reserve Fleet. Every time we floated her, she sprung leaks. After being in three different dry docks, it was thought that all the holes were caulked and she was towed off. I heard that she broke up and sank on the way to Vallejo.

My next assignment was to the Navy Communications Station in San Francisco. I wanted to be a cook, and I wanted to go to sea. I kept putting in for sea duty until they finally gave it to me. I went aboard the carrier USS *Shangri La* (CV-38) and became a cook. However, I soon found that shipboard cooking was not my cup of tea, so I put in for a transfer to the communications division.

We made a trip to Australia while I was on board the *Shangri La*. We were the first ship to send messages from Australia to Hawaii via radio teletype. This was on Mother's Day 1947. My next ship was the USS *Badoeing Straits* (CVE-116), then I was assigned to the USS *Boxer* (CV-21), where I served on the staff of Commander, Carrier Division Three. While on the *Boxer,* I watched as the first all-jet aircraft landed on an aircraft carrier. The last "bird farm" (aircraft carrier) that I served on was the USS *Valley Forge* (CV-45).

I was on shore duty at the Naval Communications Station, Washington, D.C., when the Korean "police action" broke out. I was assigned to the recommissioning crew of the USS *McKean* (DDR-784) at Long Beach, California. During our tour to Korea, I was transferred to the USS *Quincy* (CA-71). I took six highline rides in one day! My ass was soaked and I was a nervous wreck. I will never forget them.

For those who have never taken a highline ride, I'll explain. Whenever commodities and personnel needed to be transferred from one ship to another at sea, the receiving ship approached the transferring ship and shot a small line over to the other ship. The small line was attached to a larger line, and that to an even larger one. When the large line was in place, a cargo net or a special seat was attached. The series of lines were essentially a block and tackle. Twenty or so sailors on each ship would run down the deck pulling on a line to move the cargo net or the chair over to the other ship. Sometimes the lines between the two ships were not kept taut enough and they would dip in the middle, causing the passenger to drop close enough to the water to get wet from the spray. I never heard of anyone being lost on a highline ride, but it was a hair-raising experience as far as I was concerned.

After the Korean War ended, we brought the *Quincy* back to the U. S. where she was decommissioned. I was transferred to the Naval Communications Station at Adak, Alaska. While in Adak in 1955, I was selected for promotion to chief petty officer. I had not been required to have a security clearance up until that time. When my promotion came through, I knew that I had to do something to correct my records. Lying about your age was still considered fraudulent. I had ten years of service and a clean record, so I decided that all I could do was to write and confess what I had done and how I did it. The Bureau of Personnel answered with a letter telling all concerned to change my records to reflect the correct information and that I was forgiven. All it did was make a bunch of yeomen and hospitalmen mad because they had to go through ten years of records to make the changes.

After completing my tour at Adak, I attended the teletype-repair school at the Naval Training Center, San Diego. While attending the school, my promotion to chief petty officer came through, effective 16 November 1965. After completing the course at San Diego, I reported to the USS *Burton Island* (AGB-1) and made three trips to the Arctic on her. We sailed around Point Barrow, Alaska, to break ice and escort ships that were resupplying the DEW (distant early warning) line radar sites.

My next tour of duty was as an instructor at the Instructor Training School, U. S. Naval Training Center, San Diego, California. From there it was to the USS *Ashtabula* (AO-51), and later to the USS *Ajax* (AR-6) whose home port was Sasebo, Japan. I was promoted to senior chief petty officer while aboard the *Ajax*. My last assignment was at the Naval Communications Station, Rough and Ready Island, Stockton, California, where I served for a year before retiring.

I retired on 3 April 1967 as a senior chief radioman after twenty-two years and six months of service.

Dick Bowlby went to work for Western Union as a service technician after retiring from the Navy. Ten years later, he was promoted into management and was an operations supervisor at the time of his retirement in 1990, after twenty-two years with the company. He then went to work for Continental American Satellite which became Contel Federal Systems, later bought by GTE. In 1993, he injured his back while moving a large equipment cabinet. He was offered a "golden parachute," which allowed him to retire for good. Dick and Ellen, his wife of forty-five years, live in Moreno Valley, California. They have four children and five grandchildren.

Melford A. "Pete" King
Age 16 – United States Navy

I was raised on a farm near Payson, Utah, where I was born on 4 November 1929. As a young farm boy I was fascinated by the men who were wearing the different uniforms of our country's armed forces. I knew that I had to become one of them,

> *I became an LCU skipper and helped put the 1st Marine Division ashore at Inchon.*

but there was one small problem, I was short a year or two in age.

With the help of a friend, I made the necessary changes to my birth certificate. With some very delicate erasing and a trusty old – very old – Underwood typewriter, the "9" became an "8," and I proceeded to the Navy recruiting office. The recruiter either had very poor eyesight or was way behind in his quota for that month, because I was accepted.

There was one more problem to overcome: I had to get my parents' consent to join the Navy. They knew of my desires, but like all moms and dads, they didn't like the idea of their child undertaking such an adventure. My dear old dad was the one who finally made the decision that was to start me on my way. The trip to school each day was a waste of time. My grades were low, and I was firmly convinced that they couldn't teach me any more because I already knew it all. My performance around the farm wasn't much better. Dad informed me that since he was unable to put me on the right track, maybe a short time in the loving arms of Uncle Sam was what I needed. With his signature on my papers, I went back to the recruiting office, and on 10 December 1945, I was sworn into the Navy for a 4-year tour of duty.

A new life – I'll say! I was sent to the U. S. Naval Training Center, San Diego, California, where I was introduced to the biggest and meanest Texan that I ever saw, my company commander. A size-sixteen boot was too small for him, and for the first two weeks there, I thought that his shoe was part of the back of my uniform. In those days, a little corporal punishment was not unheard-of. I also learned that a toothbrush was not just for dental hygiene. I was the guy who kept our quarter-deck to the barracks spotless, all of it done with a toothbrush. It wasn't long before I composed a letter to my folks telling them that I would sure love to get my hands on that old Underwood typewriter! However, I was not about to tell anyone my secret. I had joined a man's world, and I was not about to go back down that road to being a boy again.

My first taste of sea duty was just what all sailors dream of, duty on a battleship. I was assigned to the USS *Arkansas* (BB-33). The *Arkansas* was the oldest battleship in the fleet, and before long would become a target for the atomic bomb tests at Bikini Atoll, so my life as a battleship sailor was short-lived.

Upon arriving back in the States, I was sent to the U. S. Naval Amphibious Base, San Diego, for assault-boat training. I couldn't understand why because soon I was assigned to a destroyer, the USS *Myles C. Fox* (DD-829). I went from a "Cadillac" of the fleet (battleship) to a "greyhound" (destroyer). We patrolled the China Sea for eight months, chasing smugglers that were trying to get through the blockades set up by the occupation forces.

Instead of returning to the States aboard the *Fox*, I was transferred to the U. S. Naval Port Facilities at Tsingtao, China. I had not yet reached my eighteenth birthday. I still had a lot of growing up to do, but this was not the place to do it. However, it was a very good place to learn just how nice it was to be an American. With the filth, the poverty, and always the stench of death, it was a place where growing up happened in a hurry. One of our final duties in China was to evacuate the American consul, his staff, and all their families before the Communist armies entered the city. It would be two more years before I returned to the States.

My duty stations alternated between destroyers and their repair ships until it came time for my discharge. I was a civilian for six months, then I did just what I had always wanted to do — walk into that recruiting office and to be accepted without fear of being laughed at and shoved back out on the street. This time there wasn't anything to hide. I reenlisted on 3 April 1950.

By June 1950, I became a full-fledged member of "Truman's Police Force," shelling the coast of Korea. On my return to the States, I was assigned to an amphibious boat unit. My assault-boat training would be of some use after all. I became an LCU skipper and helped put the 1st Marine Division ashore at Inchon. They must have liked the job I did, because from there, my unit was assigned to the support of Army troops up and down the coast of Korea. I spent a total of five years in Japan and Korea before returning to the States.

When I returned to the States, I was assigned as a recruit instructor at the Naval Training Center, San Diego, the same place where ten years before a young farm boy was introduced to the Navy by a Texan with a big foot. This was the most enjoyable assignment of my career. It was the most challenging and the most rewarding job of any that I ever had in the Navy.

After completing my tour at the Naval Training Center, I was assigned to the Atlantic Fleet. Up until this time, I had been on the western side of the world, now it was time to try the eastern side. I made it to the East Coast just in time to make a cruise that was a first. I was assigned to the destroyer USS *Lyman K. Swenson*, which was one of a 56-ship fleet that celebrated the opening of the Saint Lawrence Seaway. We were the first ships of the "salt-water Navy" to sail in the Great Lakes and visit all the major ports. It was the trip of a lifetime for a sailor, and to top it off, all the natives spoke English!

For the next few years, our ship was on antisubmarine patrol, playing games with the Communists who were trying their hand at snooping along our shores. We watched as our space program was born, and we were positioned downrange when there was an attempt to put one of our men in space. Then, just to keep from growing stale, we had the Cuban missile crisis to contend with.

I was in Norfolk, Virginia, when President Kennedy was assassinated. Here, along with many others, I learned another lesson on how our system of government works and just how wonderful it is to watch it work.

Next, it was a tour of duty in Vietnam, a place I hope I never have to see again. With all of that behind me, it was time to seek another pasture. This was another time in my life when I became truly scared. It was time that I separated from my Navy family and became an orphan. I retired at Norfolk, Virginia, on 20 August 1974 with thirty years of service to my credit.

Pete King received two Presidential Unit Citations during his service in Korea and was awarded the Purple Heart for wounds received while in Vietnam. After retiring from the Navy, he returned to Payson, Utah, where he lived for about ten years. But the pull of the sea was so strong that in 1984 he returned to Virginia. He is now a charter-fishing boat captain. When talk of retiring again comes up, Pete says, "Not me, hell, I'm not about to. I just got my engine running!" Pete and his wife Joy live in Newport News, Virginia. They have five children and six grandchildren.

✓ **VUMS Note** ⇒ **The Juneau and the I-26.** The USS *Juneau* was struck by a torpedo launched from the Japanese submarine *I-26* on 13 November 1942. Among the 700 man crew of the *Juneau* were the five Sullivan brothers and Allen Heyn, a 17-year-old who had joined the Navy at age 16. Only ten men are known to have survived the explosion and the subsequent days on rafts at sea. The Sullivan brothers perished, but Allen Heyn survived. It is interesting to note that a member of the VUMS (see page 323), was a crew member on the destroyer-escort USS *Lawrence C. Taylor* (DE-415) on 17 November 1944 when the *Taylor* teamed with the USS *Anzio* (CVE-57) to sink the *I-26*.

Jack L. Cannon

Age 16 – United States Army

I decided to join the U. S. Army shortly after my sixteenth birthday. I was born in Stoney Creek, Tennessee, on 6 October 1929, but my birth date was not

> **When they dug us out I was the only one alive.**

recorded. Since I didn't have a birth certificate, I altered my birth date in our family Bible and convinced the recruiters that I was 17. My parents reluctantly gave their permission for me to join.

I was sworn in at Richmond, Virginia, on 1 January 1946 and was sent to Camp Robinson, Arkansas, for basic training. After that, I was assigned to the 66th Tank Battalion, 2nd Armored Division (General George S. Patton's old "Hell on Wheels" division), at Camp Hood, Texas. Sometime in the fall, my true age was discovered, and I was discharged on 19 November 1946. I was told to come back when I was old enough.

I joined the Army again in January 1948. I requested and was assigned to the 82nd Airborne Division and went to jump school at Fort Benning, Georgia. While there, I packed my own parachute for five of the jumps. During this time, I was with Fox Company, 505th Parachute Infantry Regiment, and served under General "Slim" Jim Gavin. Later, I was transferred to Battery A, 376th Parachute Field Artillery. I made a total of twenty-eight jumps. I was discharged in the fall of 1949. I got married during this enlistment, but it didn't work out.

In early 1950, I sent for information about enlistment in the French Foreign Legion. I received orders on where to report, but before I was scheduled to leave the country, the North Koreans invaded South Korea. Instead of the French Foreign Legion, I joined the U. S. Marine Corps. Ironically, I would fight alongside the French Battalion at the Punchbowl in North Korea in August 1951.

I completed boot camp at Parris Island, South Carolina, in November 1950 and was shipped to Camp Pendleton, California, then sailed for "the land of the morning calm." In Korea, I was assigned to Fox Company, 2nd Battalion, 7th Marines, 1st Marine Division. I was a BARman, meaning I carried a Browning automatic rifle.

We came out of the Yanggu Valley on 1 July 1951 and had a few days of rest. During this time, I was assigned as a 1st Marine Division combat artist. When we went back into the meat grinder in the hills just northeast of the Punchbowl, I went with my outfit, the 7th Marines, as a combat artist and as a sniper. Being a sniper was of my own choosing. I carried a 1903 Springfield rifle with a 12-power Unertyl scope.

On the morning of 6 September 1951, just prior to the assault on Bunker Hill, I was providing cover fire for a patrol when I was caught in a crossfire by machine guns from Ridgeline 749 and Hill 856, and I was wounded in both legs. No bones were broken, so I refused evacuation and stayed with my outfit. On 1 November 1951, I was wounded a second time. A 122mm artillery round exploded in the side of our bunker about six feet away from us. It destroyed the bunker and buried everyone who was inside. When they dug us out I was the only one alive. I was hit by shrapnel in the head and chest, suffered a brain concussion and a broken vertebra, and was unconscious for four days. I was evacuated to the hospital ship *Repose*. Two weeks later, on 15 November 1951, I requested to be returned to duty, although this wound would be the one that would later retire me from the Corps.

On 19 December 1951, we came under attack on Hill 812. I was hit through the right arm by a 82mm mortar fragment. I was evacuated to the hospital ship *Consolation* and taken immediately to the neurosurgical ward. Later, I was moved to the naval hospital at Yokosuka, Japan. When I returned to the States, I was assigned to the 2nd Marine Division at Camp Lejeune, North Carolina. The medical officer there recommended that I be sent to the naval hospital at New River, North Carolina. After three or four months there, I was put on the temporarily-disabled retired list for five years. In 1957, after spending four months in the Bethesda Naval Hospital, I was put on the permanently-disabled retired list with sixty percent disability. I was retired from the Marine Corps as a private first class. I am currently on sixty percent disability with the Veterans Administration.

During the war, many of my buddies were killed near or alongside me. One buddy, Sergeant Fred Mausert, received the Medal of Honor posthumously for his actions at Hill 673, Bunker Hill. We were with Baker Company, 1st Battalion, 7th Marines at the time. During the attack on Bunker Hill and Kanmubong Ridge, the fighting was brutal. Within four days, four Marines (including Mausert) earned the Medal of Honor, all posthumously. This was the second time in Marine Corps history that four Marines had won the Medal of Honor in four days. The first time was on Tarawa, nine years before.

While at the Bethesda Naval Hospital in 1957, I was diagnosed as having what is now known as post-traumatic-stress disorder (PTSD). In 1990, two civilian doctors also diagnosed me as having delayed, moderate to severe PTSD. Although it was first diagnosed in 1957 and again in 1990, this condition has been with me since 1952.

Jack Cannon received three Purple Hearts for wounds received in action with the Marine Corps in Korea. Earlier, he had earned jump wings and glider wings while serving with the Army. He was a combat artist while he was in the Marines. He has paintings on exhibit at the Marine Corps Recruit Depot, Parris Island, South Carolina, the Leatherneck Gallery at Quantico, Virginia, and at Headquarters Marine Corps, Washington, D.C. He painted two covers for Leatherneck *magazine and two for the* Military Order of the Purple Heart *magazine. He has paintings in private collections as well as in many museums world-wide, including Moscow, Russia. His poem, "The Purple Heart," was the first poem to appear in the first issue of the* Military Order of the Purple Heart *magazine to include poetry (Nov-Dec 1995). Today Jack is a professional artist residing in Walsenburg, Colorado. He has five children and ten grandchildren.*

James R. White

Age 16 – United States Army

I was placed in an orphanage in Cadiz, Ohio, at age 7 because my mother was seriously ill and died a short time later. I lived in the orphanage until I was 13, then spent 2½ years in a foster home.

> *I was shot and captured while I was attempting to find friendly troops.*

At age 15, during my sophomore year in high school, I had one particular male teacher who blamed me for everything bad that happened in his class. One day, after taking numerous thumpings, I hit him back. I knew that I was in serious trouble and was facing reform school or worse, so I ran away and hid from the authorities.

Luckily, I found an older brother who had recently been discharged from the Army after serving five years during World War II. He was going to reenlist. He acted as my legal guardian and swore that I was born on 21 November 1928, a year before my true birth date.

I enlisted in the Army on 29 January 1946 at age 16. Not only was I underage, I was also a couple of pounds below the minimum weight requirement. I convinced a doctor that I really wanted to go into the Army, and he obliged me by adjusting my weight to meet the minimum requirement.

I was sent to Camp Plaushe, Louisiana, for basic training and was shipped overseas immediately after. I got seasick the first day at sea and remained that way for the ten days it took us to get to Le Havre, France. Three other soldiers and I were hospitalized there with various afflictions. The other troops aboard our ship were assigned to the 1st Infantry Division.

After my hospital stay, I was assigned to the 7749th Port Company, just as the company was moving to Bremerhaven, Germany. My first assignment there was to the dependents' hotel located on Haven Straus, which was downtown and away from the main post. I remained there for ten months before our group was replaced by WACs and War Department civilians. I had reached the rank of buck sergeant before my seventeenth birthday and still didn't have to shave.

I was sent to the Occupational Intelligence School at Oberammergau, Germany, for sixteen weeks. After graduation, I returned to the 7749 staging area, which was my permanent post. I was assigned to Class 6 Rations, which was helping to oversee the receiving and redistribution of all the beer and whiskey coming into the occupied zones. I had this assignment for about four months and again was replaced by War Department civilians. I was then assigned to port security at the dock area and later became an armor artificer of the 7749 Port Company until my return to the States. Shortly before leaving for the States, I shaved for the first time.

I was discharged in February 1949 and reenlisted on 25 June 1949. I was assigned to A Company, 23rd Infantry Regiment, 2nd Infantry Division, as an armor artificer, MOS-511 (military occupational specialty).

The 2nd Infantry Division was sent to Korea in August 1950. We landed at Pusan and soon moved on the line. I was in every engagement the division was in, from the Naktong River crossing in August until the Chinese entered the war on 24 November 1950 near the Yalu River.

On the night of 24 November, my company commander, Captain Melvin R. Stai, was ordered to a battalion headquarters meeting near Chinaman's Hat — so named by the GIs. I rode shotgun for Captain Stai on the way to the meeting. I manned a 50-caliber machine gun mounted in the back of the jeep. Near the designated meeting area, we had the driver back the vehicle into a cove, and Captain Stai and I proceeded on foot to the battalion headquarters.

At about 2000 hours (8 p.m.) the headquarters area was overrun by Chinese. They seemed to come out of nowhere, lots of them. A Chinese soldier was trying to shoot the battalion commander with a pistol. Corporal Tracy Young wrestled him to the ground, and I grabbed a nearby carbine. I shot and killed that Chinese soldier, as well as two others. We scrambled out of there with orders from Captain Stai to return to the vehicle and man the 50-caliber machine gun against the oncoming Chinese.

I returned to the vehicle and found the driver dead and the vehicle disabled. I manned the machine gun and fired every available round of ammunition at the oncoming Chinese. I then picked up a Browning automatic rifle and went searching for a safer position on higher ground. The Chinese were everywhere. I was shot and captured while I was attempting to find friendly troops. I was lying on the ground when the Chinese came up to me. They stood me up and could see that I was shot in the leg, so they put me on a stretcher. They carried me to what appeared to be a bivouac area. A Chinese doctor gave me a shot and treated my wounds. There were other wounded GIs nearby. I can't remember just what happened, but after a few days, the Chinese just seemed to disappear. Everything was very quiet. I don't know how long it was before a group of U. S. Marines appeared and took us to a field hospital. From there we were flown south by helicopter, then to Japan, then home.

The events at Chinaman's Hat were documented in two books: *Decisive Battles of the Korean War*, by Lieutenant Colonel Sherman Pratt, who was company commander of Baker Company and was at the meeting that fateful night; and *The River and the Gauntlet*, by Colonel S. L. A. Marshall. Colonel Marshall included my name in his book. Colonel Pratt told me forty-five years later that he would have used my name also, but he didn't know it at the time. When Colonel Pratt contacted me, we swapped stories about that night at Chinaman's Hat and events the next day.

I was discharged from the Army on 25 June 1952. After over six years of Army service, a kid who had started with the Army at age 16 came home feeling 50 years old. I would not trade my experience for anything, but I would not recommend it to anyone, either.

Jim White was awarded the Bronze Star for meritorious service at the Naktong River, an Oak Leaf Cluster in lieu of a second Bronze Star for his actions near Kunu-ri and a second Oak Leaf Cluster in lieu of a third Bronze Star for his meritorious service at Chinaman's Hat. He received two Purple Heart Medals for wounds received in action. After his discharge from the Army, he held various jobs — in sewer-pipe manufacturing, coal mining, railroading, selling door-to-door, and in foundry work. He was never fired, but was frequently laid off because of reductions-in-force. In April 1955, he trained under Public Law 16 as a disabled veteran, learning the silk-screen printing process at Tusco Manufacturing Company, Gnadenhutten, Ohio. After twenty-two years without missing a day of work, he became bored and accepted a position with a surface coal mining company as a land-acquisition agent for future mining projects. He also acquired land for drilling gas and oil wells. He retired at the age of 65 but still works on a limited basis. Jim and Johanne, his wife of forty-four years, live in Gnadenhutten, Ohio. They have two daughters and four grandchildren.

√ **VUMS Note** ⇒ *The Combat Infantryman Badge.* This award is unique to infantrymen of the U. S. Army. To be eligible for the Combat Infantryman Badge (CIB), an individual must be an enlisted man or infantry officer of the grade of colonel or below, who subsequent to 6 December 1941, has satisfactorily performed duty while assigned or attached as a member of an infantry unit during any period such unit was engaged in active ground combat. Battle participation credit alone is not sufficient; the unit must have been in active ground combat with the enemy during the period. Only one CIB can be awarded to an individual during a war, regardless of the number of tours of combat duty the individual served during that war.

Twenty-four men whose stories appear in this book earned the CIB. Three of them served in two wars and earned the badge twice. Two served in three wars and are among the few triple recipients of the award. A plaque at the National Infantry Museum at Fort Benning, Georgia, honors about 290 triple recipients of the CIB.

Eugene A. Gordon

Age 15 – United States Navy

I was born in Whitehall, New York, on 23 December 1930. My mother died in 1934, and I was farmed out to a number of state homes in New York. I joined the Navy mostly because I didn't

> *I did not tell my sister nor my seven brothers that I had joined the Navy.*

have a home to go to. I had a favorite aunt who knew of the family circumstances. I approached her about my going into the Navy. She assisted me in forging a birth certificate, and when I learned how it was done, I forged a church baptismal record and presented that to the Navy recruiters. It worked, and I was sworn into the Navy on 5 March 1946.

I did not tell my sister nor my seven brothers that I had joined the Navy. I was gone for almost a year before they knew where I was. Six of my brothers were in the military at the same time. My brother Max had joined the Marines when he was 16. I believe that the Gordon family holds the New York State record for having the most sons in the military.

Although I was the smallest of a group of enlistees leaving for the Bainbridge Naval Training Center, Maryland, I was put in charge of the group. I knew that I was underweight, so before our physicals at Bainbridge, I ate six bananas and drank tons of water. After boot camp, we were asked what type of assignment we would like. I asked for and was assigned to the USS *Saipan* (CVL-48) at the Philadelphia Navy Yard.

I remember an ensign aboard the *Saipan* to whom I was talking one night on the flight deck. He was a pilot, and I expressed to him my desire to be a pilot some day. He looked me in the eye and said, "You'll never make it because you're stupid, you don't have enough education to be a pilot." At first I thought about cleaning his clock, but then he said, "If you're interested, Gordon, there are education courses

that you can take, and if you work hard enough, you can make it."
That bastard helped me with my work and would talk straight to me.
He did not believe in throwing bull. It was either you can do it with
help, or you will be a perpetual failure. It was people like that who
inspired me to work, and I did become a pilot.

I had shore duty briefly at Lakehurst, New Jersey, where I was
training as a weather observer. One time I was twenty-four hours late
in returning from a pass, and was given a deck court-martial. I was
about twelfth in line to appear before a commander. By the time I was
standing before the commander's desk, I had heard all the stories the
other men told, and I had watched as all were sentenced for their
infractions. When the commander asked me what my excuse was I
said, "Sir, there is no excuse. I got drunk and my brothers put me on
the train for the city, but I got off at the next stop because there was
a bar right at the station. I took the next train back to my hometown,
but my brothers put me on the train again and threatened to kick my
butt if I didn't go back and report in. So it's all my fault." The
commander put his head down, and I could see that he was laughing.
He looked at me and said, "Gordon, you are the only SOB that told me
the truth." I received five days' restriction to base.

I served on the *Saipan* for about fifteen months, then was
transferred to the destroyer USS *Cory* (DD-817) operating out of
Pensacola, Florida. I am a plank owner of the *Saipan*, being one of
fifty men who put the carrier in commission.

I had left the eighth grade when I enlisted in the Navy, which didn't
qualify me for an admiral's position, but I was seriously working on my
education by the time I was discharged on 8 January 1948.

After a brief stint as a civilian, I enlisted in the Army on 16 April
1948 at Fort Bank, Massachusetts. Since I was a veteran, I didn't
have to go through basic. I was sent to Fort Dix, New Jersey, for some
training. I asked for and was assigned to the Far East and was sent
to Guam. I was eventually assigned to the office of the Chief of Staff,
Major General Bob Beitler. It turned out that General Beitler was one
hell of a general and one hell of a nice man to work for. He was
instrumental to my getting an education. He pushed all young people
to go as far as they could. When I talk about help from military
people, Captain John Crommelin, the commander of the *Saipan*, was
another officer who took great pains to assist young people to further

themselves. I finished high school and earned several college credits through the Armed Forces Institute while I was on Guam.

I served on Guam until 1950, then transferred to Eta Jima, Japan, for training as an instructor. I was there during the first year of the Korean War. My brother Max had been recalled by the Marines and was with the 1st Marine Division in Korea at the time. I returned to the States in 1952 and was discharged from the Army on 15 April 1952.

I served in two branches of the service, and when I watch the Army/Navy game, I cheer for one side for the first half and for the other side the second half, just to keep it even. I learned a lot during my six years, ten months, and thirteen days of service. Uncle Sam doesn't owe me a thing!

Gene Gordon used all the GI Bill educational benefits for which he was eligible. He attended college and obtained a commercial-pilot's license. After his discharge from the Army, he entered the Whitehall Police Force, and a short time later, he became a New York State Trooper and graduated from the state police academy in 1955. He became an investigator for the Delaware and Hudson Railroad Police in 1959 and was promoted to superintendent in 1976. He was also the corporation pilot. He retired from police work in 1986 and started his own real-estate firm. Gene and June, his wife of forty-six years, live in Latham, New York. They have three daughters and three grandchildren. Their son died of cancer in September 1996 at the age of 44.

E. E. "Gene" Wheeler

Age 14 – United States Army Air Forces

I was born near Drumright, Oklahoma, on 25 August 1931, but I was raised in the small town of Tonkawa, Oklahoma, population 3000. I had great parents and a good home life. However, when I was in the seventh grade I became bored with

> On my fourth day in uniform, I was assigned to guard a work detail of German prisoners ...

school, and since I was larger and, I thought, more mature than my classmates, I started to associate with 17- and 18-year-olds. When some of them got married and others enlisted in the military, I felt that I was losing all of my friends, so I decided that I would enlist the next time some of my friends enlisted.

There were five of us wanting to enlist, so we went to a Navy recruiting office. The recruiter asked us what we were doing at the time. It was February, and three of us were still in school; two were seniors, and I was in the ninth grade. He told us to stay in school and come back in June.

This wasn't what we wanted, so we started to plan our next move. About that time some Army recruiters came to town, so we went to see them. When a recruiter asked what we were doing, we all said that we were out of school and ready to go, so he started the paperwork. Of the five of us, two were 18, two were 17, and I was 14, but I said that I was 17. The recruiter told us that we would take our physicals on 25 March, and those of us who were 17 would have to get our parents' consent. I knew that my parents wouldn't sign for me, so I did some fast thinking and told the recruiter that I would be 18 on 21 March. He told me to go to the draft board and register, then take my draft card to Oklahoma City when we went for our physicals.

On 21 March 1946, I went to the Selective Service office to register. I puffed up my chest and went in. A lady asked if she could help me and I told her I needed to register. She asked, "When is your birthday?" I replied, "Today." She filled out the papers and gave me my draft card. The five of us went to Oklahoma City, and we all passed our physicals. We were sworn in at 5:00 p.m. on 26 March 1946. I was exactly 14 years and 7 months old.

We were put on buses and arrived at Camp Chaffee, Arkansas, at midnight. They processed us the next day, giving us uniforms, shots, tests, etc. Then the split-up started. Three of us had signed up for three years, and two for eighteen months. The three 3-year enlistees were assigned to the Air Forces, and the other two went to the artillery.

On my fourth day in uniform, I was assigned to guard a work detail of four German prisoners of war while they picked up trash on a portion of the base. I was given a carbine but no ammunition. The war was over, and the prisoners were only waiting to go home. But how was I to know what was going on?

Soon we were off to Sheppard Field, Texas, for basic training. During basic, there were six trainees in my flight who were underage. About three weeks into our training, our commander told us that he knew that some of us were underage, but if we didn't cause any problems, it would be all right. I was the youngest of the six and the only one to finish basic.

My parents found out where I was when the Army mailed my civilian clothes home. My mother went to the school superintendent for advice on how to get me out of the Army. He suggested that she consider leaving me where I was. He told her he couldn't keep me in school, and perhaps it was best that I stay in the Army. She agreed.

After basic, I went to Lowry Field, Colorado, for typing school and then to Shaw Field, South Carolina, for training to become a medic. When the Air Force became a separate branch in September 1947, I had to choose between the Army and the Air Force. I don't know why, but I decided to remain in the Army. Since I was on an Air Force base, they assigned me to SCARWAF (Special Category, Army with Air Force). There were several of us in this category. We kept the same job, except that we were Army attached to the Air Force for pay, duty, and rations.

While I was at Shaw Field in early 1947, I got a pass and went to town on a date with a girl that I had met. We went to the movies, and I was walking her home when a police car pulled up beside us. They put us in the car, took my friend home, and took me to jail. I was charged with contributing to the delinquency of a minor. The girl was 17 and we were out after curfew. The next morning, my commanding officer, who was also the hospital commander, came to the jail. When he was told what the charge was, I could hear him laughing. He told the police that they had the wrong one locked up. He knew that I was only 15. The charges were dropped, but every time the commander saw me going to town he told me to leave the young ones alone.

I attended surgical technician school at Fort Sam Houston, Texas, and extended my enlistment two years so that I could go overseas. I spent a year at Kadena Air Force Base, Okinawa, then returned to Lowry Air Force Base. I was still SCARWAF. When the Korean War started, I returned to the regular Army and was sent to Fort Hood, Texas, with the 2nd Armored Division. At this time, my enlistment was extended one year, the so-called "Truman year." I had nine months left on my enlistment when our division was sent to Germany. After eight months there, I returned to the States. I was discharged in March 1952 with six years' service and two overseas tours. I was 20 years old.

My parents had relocated to Enid, Oklahoma, so when I received my discharge at Fort Sill, I went 100 miles north to Enid. About the only jobs available there were as a service-station attendant or the post office. Both of those possibilities sounded very boring, so I went to Vance Air Force Base and talked to the base hospital commander with whom I had worked at Lowry Air Force Base. When I told him I was looking for work, he called the base recruiting office and told them he was sending me over to them and that he wanted me assigned to him. So after sixty-five days as a civilian, I enlisted in the U. S. Air Force.

When my tour of duty was up at Vance AFB, I was transferred to the 529th USAF Infirmary, Paine AFB, Washington. I didn't care for Washington, so I put in for overseas duty, and in February 1956, I was sent to the 918th AC&W Squadron, Baldy Hughes Air Force Station, Prince George, British Columbia, Canada. When I arrived, it was 40° below zero and the snow was seven feet deep. The road to the base looked like a toboggan run. It was the best assignment of my career. I was the senior medical technician, and with my assistant, we took care of the medical needs of 165 military and over 200 dependents.

In May 1958, I was transferred to the 325th USAF Hospital at Richard-Gebaur AFB, Missouri, where I worked in the emergency room. In December 1960, I was sent TDY to Gunter AFB, Alabama, to a medical school for independent duty. It was a very difficult course, one which I should have had before I went to Canada. After completing the course, I returned to Richards-Gebaur AFB.

In August 1960, I went to the 731st AC&W Squadron, Sundance AFS, Wyoming. This was another great assignment. Sundance was an experimental base whose sole purpose was to determine the feasibility of powering a radar base with nuclear energy. We had Army, Navy, and Air Force personnel on the base. In addition to providing medical service, we collected water, soil, and vegetation samples each month to test for radiation leaks, and monitored the film-badge program for all nuclear technicians. The experiment was a success; a 20-pound core provided power to the base for over two years.

In December 1962, I went overseas again, this time to a Greek air force base at Tanagra, Greece. We were assigned the duty of safeguarding, maintaining, and loading nuclear weapons on Greek aircraft in the event of a NATO emergency. In addition to operating the dispensary, I was the first sergeant, motor pool NCOIC, and I also ran the post exchange.

I went to my last duty station, Amarillo AFB, Texas, in January 1964. It was here that I finally had my records changed to my correct age. I worked at the 3320th USAF Hospital, handling student sick call and the emergency room. At the age of 34 years and 10 months, I retired on 30 June 1966 with the rank of technical sergeant.

Gene Wheeler, ten days after retiring from the Air Force, went to work for a large nonprofit group that operated hospitals. He worked as a hospital administrator in Worland and Sundance, Wyoming, then went to Soldotna, Alaska, where he was in charge of a hospital from its construction phase through its opening. He also worked as a hospital administrator in Crawford, Nebraska, and Hugoton, Kansas. He sold insurance in the state of Washington for a time, went to the beach in Florida, then returned to Alaska where he worked in real estate for six years. Gene and Anna, his wife of 42 years, bought a condo in St. Marie, Montana, which they use as a home port while touring the country in a motor home. Gene and Anna have maintained their Alaska residency and plan to retire to their cabin on the Kenai Peninsula in a few years.

Delmar J. Dyer

Age 16 – United States Army

I was born in Sioux City, Iowa, on 27 July 1929. When I was 12 years old, my father died, and from then on I was a real handful for my mother. I quit high school when I was 15 years old and started to get into trouble.

God must have been looking out for me ...

Two friends and I had a job unloading coal for the local coal company. We made a good wage and had plenty of pocket money. I was over six feet tall and didn't have any trouble hanging out in dance halls and bars. Another boy and I would bring booze from South Dakota to Sioux City for a bar owner. One day we were caught by the police, and I was given the choice of joining the Army or going to jail. I had told the police that I was older than I was.

I changed my birth certificate to show that I was born in 1927 instead of 1929, and feeling full of adventure, I enlisted in the Army for eighteen months. I was sworn in on 27 March 1946 in Sioux City, was sent to Des Moines, Iowa, and from there to Fort Snelling, Minnesota. I was assigned to an antiaircraft artillery unit and sent to Fort Bliss, Texas, for basic training.

After basic, I was assigned to the 284th AAA-AW Battalion, SP (self propelled). We trained troops on the operation and maintenance of 40mm, quad 50, and 90mm antiaircraft weapons. During this time, a group called "Task Force Frigid" was being formed to test equipment in Alaska. I think the boys in Washington were afraid of the Russians. I volunteered for this force. We were sent to Fort Ord, California, for winter training – twenty-five mile hikes, etc. – and to winterize our equipment.

We went to Camp Stoneman, California, then on to the Oakland Army Base where we boarded a Victory ship and sailed to Alaska, going through the Inner Passage after we were north of Seattle. The seas were a little rough. We arrived at Fort Richardson, Alaska, in September 1946 and found 10-foot high snowdrifts. I thought to myself, oh, oh, it's going to be cold! The coldest temperature we experienced during the eight months I spent in Alaska was 72.3° below zero. We were living in five-man tents on the tundra near the Arctic Circle.

The normal recoil for a 40mm cannon is between five to seven inches. It was so cold that when we tested our guns, it took about six rounds before they would recoil even one inch. After our tests, the Army developed different oils for the guns, vehicles, and power plants. There were other provisional companies testing various gear. What we learned later helped in the development of cold-weather gear for use in Korea.

After eight months in Alaska, I returned to Fort Bliss where I was assigned to a searchlight detachment to finish my enlistment. That was probably the best job I had while I was in the Army.

I was discharged in September 1947 and joined the enlisted reserves. Civilian life lasted for two months, and I reenlisted for three years. I was assigned to the military police at Fort Sheridan, Illinois. By this time I was 6-feet, 3-inches tall, but I weighed only 175 pounds. I became a prison guard for garrison prisoners. I really hated that job! I was supposed to be a guard for one year, but I hated it so much that I volunteered for an overseas assignment in any direction. I was sent to Japan in April 1948 and assigned to the MPs. Once you get an MP MOS (military occupational specialty) number, it almost takes an act of Congress to get transferred.

In Japan I began drinking seriously. Japanese beer was delicious, as was sake, Tommy's gin, Sochu, and anything with alcohol in it. I had a civilian friend who could get me American booze. One day I bought a 25-pound tin of coffee and a 200-package carton of gum from him. When I got off the train at the Tokyo station, I tripped, fell, cut my head, and bled profusely. I was not wearing my MP insignia. An MP arrived and told me he was taking me to the 361st Station Hospital, but we went right past the hospital and ended up at CID (Criminal Investigation Detachment) Headquarters. The MP who interviewed me asked me what I was going to do with the coffee and chewing gum. I told him that I was going to drink all the coffee and chew all the gum. Well, after a couple of months of doing odd jobs around the battalion, I asked the first sergeant for a transfer. Oddly enough, I got it and was assigned to Headquarters and Headquarters company, 8th Army Dependent Housing, Yokohama Command. I was with this unit from early 1949 until the Korean War started.

I drank too much and had been placed on report a number of times, so when the war started, I volunteered for Korea. I sailed from Sasebo, Japan, on a Japanese LST and arrived in Pusan, Korea, on 23 July 1950. I was assigned to the Hialeah Compound, a former KMAG (Korean Military Advisory Group) Headquarters on the northern edge of Pusan. After a week or so, I heard that the Army was forming an amphibious boat company for an upcoming invasion, which turned out to be Inchon, so I volunteered for this job.

We went to Yokosuka, Japan, on an LST and loaded eleven LCM boats, four LCVPs, one LCI, one LCT, and one Q-boat on two Navy LSDs (landing ship, dock), the *LSD-5*, and the *LSD-22*. We made a couple of dry runs on the beaches near Pusan and Pohang-Dong. At Pohang, we heard that the 1st Cavalry was cut off, but when we got there, the 24th Division had already helped them out.

Our unit landed part of the 7th Division on Blue Beach, the mud flats behind the seawall at Inchon, on 18 September 1950. I worked on an LCM that brought chow, ammunition, and vehicles from the ships to the beach. In mid-October, we filled two LCMs with chow and ammunition and went up the Imjin River for delivery to the 5th Cavalry, which had been cut off on the northeast side of the river by the North Korean army.

In December of 1950, I was tired of the 12- to 14-hour days, so I volunteered for the infantry, but was turned down. In January, I tried again for a transfer, unaware that the Chinese had intervened and were rapidly moving south. I didn't know what I was getting myself into.

On 19 February 1951, I was assigned to Company L, 38th Infantry Regiment, 2nd Infantry Division. Company L had taken part in the Hoensong-Wonju roadblock just a week before I joined. Out of 138 enlisted men, the company lost 87 men as prisoners, and 30 or so were killed in action. Two officers were killed and two were captured. The commanding officer died on the march north as a POW. The 3rd Battalion, with parts of the 15th and the 503rd Field Artillery, lost 1779 men missing in action, killed in action, or taken as prisoners of war.

When I arrived at Company L only twenty-five men were left. I was among fifty-three men that joined the company that day — ten of the fifty-three would later be killed. Another fifty arrived a few days later, and on 13 March, Company L went back on the line with a strength of about 130 enlisted men.

In December 1950, General Walton Walker was killed in an accident, and General Matthew Ridgeway took command of the Eighth Army. When our division was pushed back to the area around Wonju-Hoensong-Chipyong-ni, Ridgeway put "Operation Killer" into action, and we started north again. We patrolled a lot from mid-March through April, then the Chinese and North Koreans began their second offensive in our area.

We were positioned on No Name Line. Company L was assigned to Hill 800, K Company was to our left, Item Company was in reserve, and part of the 5th Republic of Korea Division was between us and the 1st Battalion of the 38th Regiment. The Chinese offensive started in our area on 16 May. By 19 May, the division stopped them, and on 20 May, we pushed north toward Enje along the Soyang river in a pincher movement to capture or kill 60,000 North Koreans and Chinese.

On 25 May, our company was on a ridge line when we were hit by 4.2 mortars. God must have been looking out for me because all of the men in my squad were hit. One was killed, but I was only blown down the hill about ten yards, my nose and ears bleeding.

We continued to push north toward Enje until we were relieved on 8 or 9 June 1951. Some men were rotated home, and we received a lot of new men. We went back on the line about 13 July. I was injured on 20 July, but I went back to the company on the 28 July. We were the lead company in the attack on Hill 1179 (also called Tauesan), the beginning of the battle for Bloody Ridge. On 29 July, I was again hospitalized. I stayed at the 121st Evacuation Hospital until 5 September 1951 and rotated back to the States on 24 September 1951.

I was discharged from the Army on 22 December 1951, but in August 1952, I reenlisted and was sent to Germany. While I was on maneuvers, I caught pneumonia and later came down with tuberculosis. I went on TDRL (temporary-duty retired list) from December 1953 until December 1958.

Delmar Dyer earned the Combat Infantryman Badge and was awarded the Silver Star for gallantry and the Purple Heart for wounds received in action. After his release from the Army in 1953, he continued to drink and get into trouble. He left California and on 25 July 1973 arrived in Omaha, Nebraska, where he was met by a cousin, a recovered alcoholic. From that day on, Delmar has not had a drink. He went back to school where he met Irene, his future wife. They were married in November 1981. He worked as a vocational supervisor for the Eastern Nebraska Office of Retardation until he was medically retired in 1991. Delmar and Irene live in Omaha, Nebraska.

√ *VUMS Note* ⇒ *Manipulating the draft.* While the draft was in force, all men were required to register upon reaching their eighteenth birthday. A number of underage veterans took advantage of the draft registration procedures to get into the military. Age was not always questioned, and often no proof was required, so youngsters would merely go to the draft board, register, and wait to be inducted. Some knew that the penalty for late registration was immediate induction, so they would register a few months after their "acquired" eighteenth birthday and would be inducted with the next group, which was their objective in the first place.

Those who joined National Guard or State Guard units seldom had to prove their age. Once accepted in a Guard unit, it was a simple matter to enlist in the regular military using documents from the Guard to verify their ages.

Hershel C. Burd

Age 16 – United States Army

My first twelve years were spent on a farm in Hart County, Kentucky, where I was born on 17 November 1929. I was the youngest of five sons. My mother died when I was 8 years old, but my father kept the family together, and we

> *The aftershock and the mushroom cloud that rose over the desert floor were awesome.*

continued to live on the farm until 1941. By that time, my oldest brother was in the Navy, two brothers were in the CCC (Civilian Conservation Corps), a brother just older than I went to live with an uncle, and I went to live with a second cousin in Louisville. When my cousin was drafted in 1942, I went to live with my grandparents in Hodgenville, Kentucky.

My oldest brother Aubrey was aboard the USS *West Virginia* at Pearl Harbor on 7 December 1941. His ship was hit, but he was not wounded. In August 1942, my brother Daymon joined the Marines and served on Guadalcanal and in the Marshall Islands. My brother Les joined the Navy and served in the Aleutians and later in the Philippines. My brother Bill was drafted into the Army in 1944 and was wounded on Okinawa in April 1945.

I was 14 years old by this time, and I wanted to follow my brothers into the service. I went to the Navy recruiting office and claimed that I was 17. During the physical examination, when the doctor checked out my teeth, he told me to go back to school and come back when I was 18. Not being one to take no for an answer, I tried again when I was 16. I changed my birth certificate to show that I was born in 1928, and with a lot of arm twisting and pleading, I was able to get my dad to let me join.

I was sworn into the Army on 4 April 1946 and went to Camp Polk, Louisiana, for basic training. I was sent to the Philippines after basic and was stationed in San Fernando, about eighty miles north of Manila. I worked in the post exchange and on the docks checking the loading of equipment for shipment back to the States.

A number of Japanese prisoners of war were there awaiting shipment back to Japan. We were allowed to have one of the prisoners as a houseboy to take care of our huts. My houseboy was a big Japanese marine, and he was very good with the work assigned to him. He thought it was rather funny that I was so young and in the service. He was 32 years old and had not seen his folks since 1934, when he left for China. The Japanese POWs were shipped home in May 1947.

I returned to the States in June 1947 and went to Fort Sam Houston, Texas, for discharge. I was one of the soldiers who helped prepare a retirement party for General Jonathan Wainwright[23] given in Freeport, Texas. I was discharged from the Army on 18 September 1947 and returned to Louisville, Kentucky.

On 15 November 1947, I enlisted in the Marines and was sent to Parris Island, South Carolina, for boot camp. Marine boot camp was much tougher than the Army basic training I had gone through the year before. After boot camp, I went to Camp Lejeune, North Carolina, for motor-transport school, followed by twelve weeks of automotive-mechanics school. From Lejeune, I went to the Marines' West Coast Repair Depot at Barstow, California. I arrived there in August 1948 and was one of only four PFCs on the base. This meant mess duty (KP) for eighty-four days, until a replacement came in.

When the Korean War started, all enlistments were extended one year by President Truman. There was a need for tank mechanics, so I was one of the Marines chosen to become a tank mechanic. I had volunteered to go to Korea, but I was informed that I would go to Korea when the Marine Corps wanted me to go. So, for the next two years I helped rebuild tanks and amphibious tractors. From the last

---

[23] General Jonathan M. Wainwright took over as commander of the U. S. forces in the Philippines in 1942 at the time that General Douglas MacArthur was ordered to Australia. After the fall of Bataan, and after the Japanese had landed on Corregidor, General Wainwright surrendered his forces. During his years as a Japanese POW, he was convinced he would be court-martialed when the war was over. Instead, he was released in time to be present on the USS *Missouri* to witness the Japanese surrender, and upon his return to the States, he was awarded the Medal of Honor by President Truman.

part of June 1950 until early September, we rebuilt enough Sherman tanks to meet the requirements of the 1st Marine Division before they sailed for the Inchon landing on 15 September 1950. We all worked around the clock to accomplish this feat.

In April 1952, I volunteered to take a Sherman tank and some other equipment to Camp Desert Rock, Nevada, for the atomic tests. The equipment was part of a simulated battalion arranged in battle formation on the desert floor. We Marines were placed in a trench about seven miles from ground zero and told to lie face down and to put our goggles over our eyes at a given signal. The bomb was detonated at an altitude of about 2000 feet. This was an experience that I will never forget. The aftershock and the mushroom cloud that rose over the desert floor were awesome. Some years later, I learned from the National Association of Atomic Veterans that this test was known as "Tumbler Snapper." My participation in this event does not appear in my service records. Although I don't seem to have suffered any adverse effects from the atomic tests, many military and civilian personnel have.

I was discharged from the Marines on 15 November 1952.

Hershel Burd started working for a commercial dishwashing equipment company a short time after his discharge from the Marines. He began as a route salesman in Atlanta, Georgia, transferred to Los Angeles for four years, then went to Saint Louis, Missouri, to take over as branch manager. He retired from that company in May 1992 after being with them for thirty-nine years. He has worked part-time since then, selling restaurant equipment and serving as an election judge on election days. Hershel and Charlotte, his wife of forty-six years, live in Florissant, Missouri. They have five children and seven grandchildren.

Raleigh G. Stinnett

Age 14 – United States Army

I was born in Knoxville, Tennessee, on 15 September 1931. It was in May 1946 during summer break from elementary school that I carried out my boyhood dream of becoming a real soldier. I was 14 years old and nearly six feet tall. I just lied

> *"Son, you are no more 18 years old than I can take wings and fly like a bird."*

through my teeth and convinced the recruiting sergeant that I wanted to join the Army. He bought the lie and I was off to Fort Oglethorpe, Georgia, for a physical examination and further processing to another Army installation.

During my physical, one of the doctors looked me right in the eye and said, "Son, you are no more 18 years old than I can take wings and fly like a bird." So I laid another pack of lies on this doctor. I told him I came from a family of eleven brothers and sisters (which was the truth) and that all I could look forward to in life was wearing hand-me-down clothes and going hungry a lot of times. The doctor just kept looking at me and said, "In one way, what I'm going to do is wrong, but if it will help you out, then my conscience is clear. I'm going to keep quiet about your being underage, and I'll pass the word to the other Army medical people to pass you on and not say anything." Before we left the induction center, I looked up this doctor who had helped me with the "big lie" and asked him

how he knew I was not 18 years old. He said, "Son, you are from the mountains, so how do you tell the age of your horses and mules?" I looked at him for a minute and said, "From their teeth, naturally." The doctor said, "Well?" Then I got the message.

It was at Fort Oglethorpe that I heard for the first time the strident melody of reveille and the haunting strains of evening taps. The memory of those bugle calls remains with me to this day. Fort

Oglethorpe was the home of the 6th Cavalry, and they still had horses for ceremonial purposes. It was a grand sight to behold those horses and cavalrymen in parades. I was thrilled beyond words. All of my boyhood dreams had become a living reality.

After physical examinations, we were shipped by Army bus to Fort McPherson, Georgia, where we stayed for ten to twelve days, and then we were sent to Fort Eustis, Virginia, for basic training. None of my buddies could quite understand my vigor and enthusiasm. I was enjoying each and every minute of basic training, and they literally hated it. We were housed in an old-time Army barracks with not one ounce of insulation in the walls. The hot Virginia sun would make an oven out of the barracks, so we tried to stay outside as much as possible to keep from being cooked alive. It was hard to sleep at night because of the heat, so many of the boys would grab their mattress and go outside.

During the last week of basic training, just before we were to ship out, I got quite a shock. Unknown to me, the commanding officer had submitted two names to be considered to attend OCS (officer candidate school). I happened to be one of the two. Headquarters followed through with their usual routine of having the FBI run background checks on the prospective candidates. The FBI check uncovered my real age and this ended my Army career. I will always believe that if I had not shown such vigor and energy during basic training that maybe my CO (commanding officer) would have picked some other future "general" instead of me.

When the FBI report came to my CO, he called me into his office. There he told me the facts of life in regard to telling lies about my age. All the time, he was nearly falling out of his chair from laughing so hard about "his" boy soldier being just 14 years old. He would say a few words, then break into loud laughter. The CO told me that I would be sent to Fort Bragg, North Carolina, for discharge.

At the discharge center, I was told to report to the pay office to pick up my money. I tried to argue with them that I didn't have any money at the pay office. They explained to me that I would receive between $150 and $175 as mustering-out pay. I tried to tell the paymaster that I didn't want any of that money since I was just 14 years old, and I didn't want any more trouble than I was in already by telling lies about my age. He just laughed and said I had to take the money whether I wanted to or not. I was still scared about the whole thing.

The officer explained that I was not going to jail for lying about my age. He said that all the Army wanted to do was see to it that I went home and that I got there all right. I was discharged on 1 August 1946.

I arrived home in time to play out the last days of summer and prepare to enter school as an eighth grader. Many of my chums would not believe that I had been in the Army, and I had to wear my Army fatigues with my name and serial number sewed on them to really convince the die-hards. The Army even issued me a World War II Victory Medal. They said I was entitled to it, but I didn't feel that way, so I gave it to my mother as a keepsake that she kept in an old cigar box.

I enlisted in the U. S. Navy in 1949 and was serving on the USS *Dixie* (AD-14) when the Korean war started. The day of the Inchon landings, 15 September 1950, was my nineteenth birthday. We had been firing high-explosive shells towards the assault area since midnight. I vividly recall thinking that I was having one heck of a birthday. One of my best buddies who had a journalist's bent leaned over close to me and yelled into my ear, "If I was writing your birthday story for the local newspaper, I'd just have to include that all those present at the birthday boy's party certainly enjoyed the fireworks." I didn't find his remarks funny, but I guess this type of graveyard humor kept some of us from going mad at times because of the death and destruction going on around us.

I wondered how our Marines were going to get over the sea wall and onto the mud and sand flats leading off the beach. I watched as they landed and carried wooden ladders to the sea wall, ladders that they had made aboard ship just days before. The Marines went up the ladders one at a time. Many were shot as they topped the sea wall, but enough got over to clear the enemy and secure the beachhead.

We watched as many civilians and enemy soldiers ran into a centuries-old Buddhist temple to escape our shells. I was looking directly at this temple through our most powerful binoculars when the temple took numerous direct hits. When the air cleared, all I could see was one vast hole where the temple had been just seconds before. The temple was not supposed to be fired upon. Someone didn't get the word. When I looked up from the binoculars, I saw men staring at the place where the temple had been, their mouths hanging open. We all knew that a huge mistake had just been made. We certainly did not grieve for the enemy soldiers taking shelter in the temple, but we did for all those innocent women and children.

The medals I acquired in Korea went into the same box with my World War II Victory Medal. Forty-three years after the Inchon assault, I received a Korean Presidential Unit Citation from the Navy Department. It, too, went in the cigar box.

Recently, my little grandson looked at my cigar box with the medals in it and said, "Wow, Papaw, you're a hero with all these medals!" I told him those medals and ribbons were souvenirs of a misspent youth who loved his country and flag very much and had gone off to a faraway country to do a job that his country had asked him to do, did the job and came home, nothing more and nothing less, that I was definitely not a hero in any sense of the word. My little 9-year-old grandson looked me right in the eye and said, "Papaw, you'll always be my hero!" At that instant I knew my military life finally had some meaning. It made it all worthwhile. I gave him the box of medals to keep. That was one happy grandson — all nine years of him.

As a 14-year-old, I just couldn't wait to get my own uniform and my own gun. My ardor dimmed after seeing the horror of battle in Korea. I would love to see a world without wars. After Korea, I had a strong feeling that I never wanted to fire another gun, nor wear another uniform, but I did.

Raleigh Stinnett enlisted in the Tennessee Army National Guard in October 1947 at age sixteen and attained the rank of sergeant by the time he was discharged in July 1949. He joined the U. S. Navy in 1949 and served until 1953. In 1954, he again joined the Guard and served until 1956, leaving after "verbally assaulting" an officer during field maneuvers. He reenlisted in the Navy in 1958 and served for five years. After being discharged, he was with the Tennessee Highway Patrol for a short time. He worked for Bowater-Southern Paper Corporation and later the Guided Missile Division of Pan American World Airways. He was a pipefitter at the Watts Bar Nuclear Power construction project in Spring City, Tennessee, at the time of his retirement in 1984. Raleigh and his wife Sarah live in Charleston, Tennessee. They have one child and two grandchildren.

Baker W. Herbert, III

Age 14 – United States Navy
Age 15 – United States Coast Guard

I was born in Washington, D.C., on 26 October 1931, the youngest of six children. Dr. Mudd, a grandson of the infamous Dr. Mudd who set John Wilkes Booth's leg, had been my mother's doctor

> ... "How old are you?" I simply answered, "How old do you have to be?"

for many years and was the attending physician at my birth. My mother died shortly after I was born. My father had been a machine gunner with the American Expeditionary Force in France during World War I. He became an alcoholic and was very despondent after the death of my mother and provided very little, if any, help for his children after she died. My siblings and I were sent to live with relatives. One of my brothers ended up in an orphanage, so in 1943 he enlisted in the Coast Guard at age 14.

I was living with an aunt and uncle in the tidewater area of Charles County, Maryland, at the time World War II was over. Financially, it was a bad time for us. My uncle had been shell-shocked and gassed in France during World War I, and it was hard to survive on his $17.00 per month veteran's pension.

My oldest brother Francis had served in the Navy during the war. When he returned home and saw my situation, he suggested that I join the Navy. With his help, I enlisted at the Anacostia Naval Air Station, District of Columbia, in July 1946. Things went well for me until the Navy received my school records. A chief petty officer told me, "You have an I.Q. of 140, but you are only 14 years old. Go back to school!" My Navy career ended after one month.

A few months later, I enlisted in the U. S. Coast Guard after completing some needed dental work. I didn't have to show a birth certificate, and when an older chief petty officer asked, "How old are you?" I simply answered, "How old do you have to be?" The chief replied, "Seventeen." So I told him I was seventeen. The chief then told me that if I had two years of high school, I could be enlisted as a seaman second class (E-2). So I told him that I had two years of high school.

I was sent to boot camp at Mayport, Florida, in January 1947, and upon completion, I was assigned to the USCGC *Bibb*, based in Boston, Massachusetts. While I was en route to a weather patrol, a message was received from the Commander, North Atlantic Patrol in Argentia, Newfoundland, asking if any of the seamen on board could type. I told the yeoman that I could type, so I was put ashore as a storekeeper striker in Argentia, NOB (Naval Operating Base) 103.

Later, I was assigned to the Ninth Coast Guard District, Cleveland, Ohio. I attended an evening high school and completed the tenth grade and passed the GED tests for a high school diploma and some college credit. When the Korean War broke out in 1950, I was a SK1 (E-6) and was transferred to the West Coast and assigned to the USCGC *Escanaba*, a weather ship that patrolled between Russia and Korea and vectored U. S. aircraft.

Upon completion of my shipboard tour, I was assigned to the Coast Guard supply center in Alameda, California. While I was ashore, I applied for and was admitted to the University of California at Berkeley, and I was finally able to complete my college degree at Baldwin-Wallace University in 1969.

In 1966, during the war in Vietnam, I was assigned as a contracting officer to construct Loran-C stations in Vietnam and Thailand for the U. S. Air Force. I was given $16,000,000 in funding and was also assigned the duties of funds-accountable officer.

When we reported in Thailand, we checked in with Major General Richard G. Stilwell, Commanding General, Military Advisory Group, Thailand. General Stilwell asked that one of our officers attend their staff meeting at 0900 on the following Saturday. As contracting officer, I was the logical one to attend the meeting. When I entered the room, General Stilwell asked me who I worked for, and I told him the President of the United States, as do all contracting officers. He was impressed.

As the conference proceeded and 1200 hours (noon) arrived, I raised my hand. General Stilwell asked if I had a question and I told him that it was 1200 hours. He asked what that meant to me, and I told him it meant lunch. The General then said that in the Army you ate when you were finished with your task. I told the General that was precisely why I had joined the Coast Guard, and that we even ate while at battle stations. The following Saturday, General Stilwell told me that I could give my report first and that I would be excused.

Our project was completed in the summer of 1966, and all hands received a Unit Commendation Medal. Three years later, in 1969, I retired from the Coast Guard as chief warrant officer-4.

Baker Herbert, after his retirement from the Coast Guard, worked as a field-claims representative for State Farm Insurance, retiring from that position in 1986. He became treasurer of Lafayette Township, Ohio, and retired for the third time in 1993. In 1985, he organized a reunion of the Southeast Asia Coast Guard Veterans in Chicago, Illinois. The present-day Coast Guard Combat Veterans Association developed from this reunion. Baker currently serves as treasurer of the association. Baker and Marylou, his wife of forty-five years, live in Westfield Center, Ohio. They have three daughters, one son, and six grandsons. Their son served a four-year tour with the U. S. Marine Corps.

Richard B. Peterson

Age 16 – United States Marine Corps

At the end of the 1945-46 school year, I was promoted to my junior year in the Long Beach, Mississippi, school system. I tried for three weeks to find a summer job, but World War II was over and returning veterans were

> *"Let him join, if he can get in without your signature."*

filling most vacancies. The previous two summers, at ages 14 and 15, I had worked for the government as a laborer, unloading box cars and LSTs. But in 1946, jobs were hard to come by.

On Saturday, 13 June 1946, I had a date with my girlfriend to attend a movie matinee at 1:00 p.m. The only problem was that I didn't have any money, and my mother wouldn't give me any. Early that Saturday morning, my mother, an aunt who was visiting us, and I boarded a bus to go to a larger town nearby where my mother was going to an interview for a job. I was unhappy. I didn't have a job, I didn't have any money, and I would not be able to go to the movie that afternoon. I asked my mother if I could join the military, but she said

no. I kept asking and kept getting the same response. Finally, my aunt said to my mother, "Let him join, if he can get in without your signature."

That's all that I needed. As soon as we arrived in Gulfport, I jumped off the bus and ran to the third floor of the post office building where the Selective Service offices were located. I walked in and the lady asked what I wanted. I stated that I wanted to register for the draft. She asked me how old I was and I told her 18. When she asked for a birth certificate, I told her that I was born at home in the country, and that my birth date was registered in the family Bible. She filled out all the forms and issued me a temporary draft card. I took the card and went down to the second floor where the Marine Corps recruiting office was located. I told the sergeant that I wanted to enlist in the Marines and asked him how long it would take to get in. He replied, "Two weeks." I informed him that I would go to the Army recruiter and get in sooner than that. He then told me that there was a bus leaving for Jackson, Mississippi, at 10:00 a.m. It was 8:45 a.m., but at 10:00 a.m. I was on that bus headed for Jackson. Just before boarding the bus, I used a nickel to call a neighbor to ask her to notify my mother that I had joined the Marine Corps. For the next two days, I prayed that the Marine Corps would not discover my real age. I was born on 11 May 1930, but I had used the birth date of 13 June 1928 when I registered for the draft.

I was sworn into the Marine Corps on 15 June 1946 for a 2-year hitch. I left immediately for Parris Island, South Carolina, for eight weeks of boot camp. The Marine Corps was short of money in 1947, so they instituted a program for early discharge of men who were on 2-year enlistments. I was discharged in April 1947 "for the convenience of the government."

In 1948, I joined the Marine Corps Reserves in Santa Ana, California. Our unit was recalled to active duty on 1 August 1950. I went to Korea in 1951 and served with the MTACS-2 (Marine Tactical Air Control Squadron-2), 1st Marine Air Wing. MTACS-2 was assigned to the 1st Marine Division and coordinated air support for the division. I was assigned as the operations staff NCO.

I was recommended for a battlefield commission while I was in Korea, but they waited until I returned to the States in October 1952 to act on it. I was to report to a Marine Corps Air Station, Opa Locka, Florida, with a 30-day leave en route from California. I purchased a house trailer and towed it across the country to Miami. I started checking into MCAS Opa Locka at 0800 one morning, and thirty minutes later, I was checking out with new orders to report to Quantico, Virginia, to attend OCS (officer candidate school). I drove to Quantico and all but completed officers training. Two days before I was to be commissioned, I was called to the school office and was requested to provide the Marine Corps with a copy of my birth certificate. I couldn't, and I explained why. I was advised to correct my records. I was also told that they would recommend that I go through officer candidate school again.

Two days later, my classmates were commissioned and went on to basic school (specialized training after being commissioned), but instead of starting OCS again, I was transferred to Camp Lejeune,

North Carolina. When my classmates graduated from basic school, they received orders to go to Korea. I also received orders to go to Korea, but they were going as second lieutenants and I was going as a staff sergeant. I returned to the same unit, Sub-Unit-1, 1st Marine Division, and replaced the sergeant who had replaced me the year before.

I was discharged from the Marines on 31 July 1957 with the rank of gunnery sergeant. I stayed in the inactive Marine Reserves until 2 February 1969. Oh, by the way, about the girlfriend that I was going to take to the movie eleven years before — she waited until 5:00 p.m., and I didn't show. I had started traveling then, and I have been traveling ever since!

Dick Peterson received a Navy Unit Citation and the Korean Presidential Unit Citation. After his discharge, he served as a police officer, sergeant, and lieutenant in Orange, California, for ten years, then went with the Department of State as a police advisor. He spent more than four years as a senior police-advisor in Vietnam. He received the Department of State Award for Valor, the highest award given by that department, for leading over 100 military and paramilitary operations in one of four area assignments in Vietnam. After leaving Vietnam, he worked with the Liberian police for a time, then became an instructor at the International Police Academy in Washington, D.C. Following that, he became a security officer in the Office of the Secretary of the Treasury, and in 1980, he went with the Department of Justice, retiring from there on 30 April 1995. Dick now lives in Bay Saint Louis, Mississippi. He has four sons. Dick is the Mississippi State Commander of the Veterans of Underage Military Service.

Richard L. Pelham

Age 16 – United States Army

I joined the U. S. Army at age 16 because of a very bad home situation. My parents were divorced, and I was living with my dad and stepmother. My mother never remarried and was

We rode past the Leaning Tower of Pisa on the way to being locked up.

having a hard time financially. She was a cook in a restaurant/supper club and lived in a rented sleeping room.

My stepmother hated me and would slap my face and ears at the least provocation. She would hit me with the palm of her hand on one side of my face, then with the back of her hand on the other. She would only do this when my dad was at work. I would tell him what she did, but he would never believe me. Through the years, I would just stand there and take the beating.

I weighed 200 pounds before I was 16. One day, just a week before my sixteenth birthday, my stepmother started the double slapping of my face, hitting me as fast as she could. I lost control and pushed her against the wall and was choking her with both hands. I told her I wasn't going to turn her loose until she promised to stop slapping me. I wondered why she didn't say anything, then I looked down and saw that her feet were four or five inches above the floor. I realized that I could kill her, so I let her go.

When my dad got home, she told him what I had done, but she didn't tell him that she had been hitting me like a punching bag. My dad took off his belt and chased me throughout the house until he caught me. That was the only time I remember him whipping me. My stepmother said to my dad, "Either that kid goes, or I do." He said, "You heard what she said, Dick." I replied, "Give me time to pack a suitcase."

I went to my mother, knowing that she didn't have room for me to stay for long. She showed me where the office was in the restaurant where she worked, and when the owner wasn't there, I took my birth certificate, erased the "30," and used the office typewriter to replace it with "29." I didn't especially want to go into the Army, but in 1946 there weren't many jobs for anyone, especially for a 16-year-old.

Using the altered birth certificate, I enlisted in the Army on 18 June 1946. My mother did not want to sign my papers, so my dad signed them. I went to Fort Eustis, Virginia, for basic training, then was sent to Leghorn, Italy, where I was assigned foot-patrol duty with the military police. One day we were informed that a motorcycle patrol was to be started. The next morning, an officer announced, "Anyone who ever rode a motorcycle take one step forward." At first no one did. Finally, I did because I wanted to get off foot patrol, but I had never ridden a motorcycle in my life.

I didn't know that they already had the motorcycle there. An MP sergeant pushed it out of a building, sat on the back fender and said to me, "Let's go down the road." I never would have gotten it moving if it hadn't been for the 1, N, 2, 3, and 4 marked on the tank by the shift lever. I started jerkily down the road, never got it out of first gear, and dumped us on the pavement two or three times. I said to the sergeant, "It's been a long time since I rode, and I'm a little rusty." He said, "This is Friday, practice over the weekend, and we'll start the road patrol on Monday," as he walked away limping and rubbing his back. I went on road patrol on Monday, learned to ride motorcycles, and have been riding them since that time.

After I could handle a motorcycle quite well, I bought a surplus Harley 45 from a man going back to the States. He said that the machine was in town being painted and gave me the address of where to find it. When I got there, I found that the motorcycle was torn apart and the separate pieces were placed on newspapers on the floor. I didn't know that a motorcycle had to be torn apart to be painted. The man who owned the shop didn't understand or speak English, and I didn't speak Italian. I went to the street in front of the store and asked everyone I saw if they understood English. I finally found a young Italian who translated for us. He told the shop owner to send a card to my address when he figured out how to get the motorcycle back together. He did, but it took two months.

I was riding up and down a road on my motorcycle one day, adjusting the carburetor, when I heard a siren. It was two MPs. They said I was out of bounds and asked for my pass. There weren't any signs, and I wasn't watching the miles on the cycle's odometer. You could see the base on both sides of the highway, less that one-half mile away. I told the MPs that I would like to ride back to the base, but they took my dogtags and told me to follow them. We rode past the Leaning Tower of Pisa on the way to being locked up. What a way to see the tower! I called a buddy to come get my motorcycle and take it back to the base because, if it was left there, the MPs would steal it and I would never see it again.

My friend told the sergeant of the guard what had happened. He didn't like it because I had guard duty from midnight to four in the morning. I don't know what happened, but a few days later I was informed that I would receive a general discharge under AR-615-369, meaning that I was judged as unable to adapt to military life. I had served a little over a year on a 3-year enlistment. They did not know that I had enlisted at 16.

In 1947, I went before five colonels at the Pentagon in an attempt to get back into the Army, but I wasn't successful. In 1948, I enlisted in the U. S. Marine Corps for four years. When we finished boot camp at Parris Island, South Carolina, we were asked if anyone wanted to go to the 2nd Marine Air Wing at Cherry Point, North Carolina. Two of us stepped forward, thinking that we would get a chance to fly. When I got to Cherry Point, I was assigned to the MPs and walked foot patrol.

I finally was taken off foot patrol and assigned to drive a truck and post the guards around the base. One rainy night while I was coming back in after posting the guards, the truck skidded on a slick spot as I was rounding a curve. The truck hit the cement end of a culvert, and the driver's side was smashed in. When I got out, I found that my left leg was broken. A couple in a Volkswagen stopped and took me to the dispensary. Three days later, they transferred me to the 2nd Marine Division hospital at Camp Lejeune, North Carolina. They put pins in my leg to straighten it out, but it took ten and one-half months for it to heal. I was later transferred to the hospital at the Great Lakes Naval Station where I could go to my hometown of Jackson, Michigan, on weekend passes.

When I was released from the hospital, I was assigned as a brig guard. I didn't like that duty at all. We had to *run* the prisoners, never just march them. This meant that I had to run, also. I finally put in for overseas duty. The only thing open was Guantanamo Bay, Cuba.

When I arrived in Cuba, I found the duty there was to guard the fence between the base and Cuba. After midnight one night, I was walking a post in the area where ammunition was stored and was ten minutes late in reporting in to the corporal of the guard. I was given a captain's mast before the colonel in charge of the Marine Barracks and was sentenced to ten days of hard labor.

I was discharged from the Marine Corps in 1952 and immediately joined the U. S. Air Force Reserves. I had never told the Marine Corps about being in the Army, and I did not tell the Air Force until 1954. In 1954, my 2-year Air Force Reserve enlistment was up, and I enlisted in the regular Air Force for six years. I was always afraid of being caught on a fraudulent-enlistment charge for never telling anyone about getting thrown out of the Army. I wanted to get the situation cleared up. The legal officer at Atterbury Air Force Base, Columbus, Indiana, looked through the Uniform Code of Military Justice and found an out for me. What saved me was that I had completed a full 4-year enlistment in the U. S. Marine Corps between my Army service and my service in the Air Force.

In the Air Force, I worked as a driver and dispatcher in the motor pool and in aircraft refueling later. I drove gasoline tanker-trailers and refueled aircraft through hydrants and underground tanks along the flight line. I was stationed in many places: Columbus, Indiana; France; Columbus, Ohio; South Dakota; Newfoundland; and finally, Blytheville, Arkansas where I retired 1 August 1967.

Dick Pelham went to work for the Cummins Engine Company, Inc., Columbus, Indiana, shortly after retiring from the Air force. He took early retirement from Cummins in October 1987 after working nineteen years and nine months for the company. Dick and his wife Marjorie live in Columbus, Indiana. They have one daughter and four grandchildren.

Richard A. Edgington

Age 13 – Ohio State Guard
Age 14 – United States Army Air Forces

In May 1945, at the age of 13, I joined the Ohio State Guard by telling them that I was 18. That summer I went to camp with the Guard and qualified with the 1917 Enfield 30-caliber rifle at the Camp Perry rifle range.

> *... at the age of 15, I made my first training flight as a gunner on a B-29.*

In the fall I began the ninth grade in school. The year was not a happy one for me as I was doing poorly in math, and my other grades were not so good either. A teacher caught me smoking a cigar on the school grounds and I had to go to juvenile court. One day in May 1946, a friend and I skipped school to attend a movie. Next door to the theater was an Army recruiting office. We were looking at the pictures in the window of the recruiting office when a sergeant stepped out and talked to us. My father signed papers attesting that I was 17, and consequently, on 26 June 1946, at the age of 14, I became a private in the Army Air Forces. I turned 15 while in basic training.

After basic training, I was sent to Lowry Field near Denver, Colorado, to attend turret-mechanics school. My poor math skills caused me problems and I washed out of the school. In December 1946, I volunteered to go to the Pacific area. I arrived on Okinawa in January 1947 and was assigned to the 22nd Bomb Group. My records indicated that I had some knowledge of the B-29 gunnery system, so I was sent to gunnery school. On 5 April 1947, at the age of 15, I made my first training flight as a gunner on a B-29. After completing gunnery school, I was assigned to a crew in the 33rd Bomb Squadron as a tail gunner. By June 1950, I was a 19-year-old sergeant and the central fire-control gunner. At that time our squadron had been transferred to March Field near Riverside, California.

In July 1950, we were sent back to Okinawa to fight in the Korean War. We flew our first combat mission on 11 July 1950 and completed twenty-eight missions by October 1950. On 19 October, at the start of our 29th mission, our plane caught fire on takeoff and we crashed into the sea. Sadly, nine out of twelve crew members were killed. This ended my flying career.

The remainder of my time in the Air Force was spent working on bombing systems and in munitions. In 1957, I advised my commander of my true age. By this time I was a technical sergeant with eleven years of service. After much paperwork, I received a waiver of fraudulent enlistment, and my records were changed. I retired from the Air Force as a master sergeant on 1 July 1966 at the age of 34.

I have no regrets about joining the Air Force at the age of 14. I would not trade anything for the memories of the people I met and the places I was able to see as a member of the Air Force. The only thing I would do differently would be to obtain a better formal education.

Richard Edgington was awarded the Air Medal with two Oak Leaf Clusters. He finished high school and received some college credits while in the Air Force. His post-retirement plan was to become a nurse, but his lack of math skills prevented this. Consequently, he joined the police department in his wife's hometown of Salina, Kansas, and retired as a lieutenant after twenty years. His first wife died in 1979 after a long illness. In December 1981, Richard finally solved his problem with mathematics by marrying his present wife Mary who has a Ph.D. in mathematics. Richard and Mary live in Wichita, Kansas. Richard has a son, a daughter, and five grandchildren.

Lewis E. Elliott

Age 15 – United States Army

My father died in 1937, leaving my mother to raise four small children. The youngest of the four was born one month after his death. This was during the worst of the Great Depression, and we were left with very little to survive

> *I spent the next eight months in no man's land and was ambushed and overrun several times.*

on. We lived in Pensacola, Florida, where I, one of the older ones, was born on 12 January 1931. The four of us were blessed with a strong, religious, and caring mother. Somehow, she managed to keep us clean, clothed, and fed. In 1939, we were fortunate to be allowed to move into a newly built federal housing complex in the city of Pensacola. Over one-half of the families were headed by single mothers, and the neighborhood was congested with young children.

When I entered the seventh grade and I had to switch schools, my mother wouldn't allow me to attend the same school that my neighborhood friends did. I had to walk an extra mile across town. Sometimes I just wouldn't make it to class. Often I would go to the old Corry Field facility north of the city and watch student pilots do their "touch-and-go" maneuvers in their yellow Stearman biplanes. I have always had a deep love for the military.

As a result of frequently not making it to class, I flunked the seventh grade. This convinced my mother to take drastic measures, and I found myself fifty miles in the country with my step-grandmother's family. This was my mother's alternative to reform school. I returned home the following year after failing the seventh grade for the second time. At age 15, the very idea of having to tolerate one more year of classroom boredom was unthinkable. I didn't have many choices. I tried to join the Merchant Marine, but they told me to come back in a year. I tried the Navy and they told me to come back in three years.

After the high school held its graduation exercises in 1946, I learned that a lot of the boys were going into the service. When I found out that some of them were going to join the paratroopers, I knew that I would be with them. The recruiting sergeant was a friend of the family. I told him that I didn't want to go to high school the coming year. I lied to him when I said that I was "only" 17, but I didn't lie when I said that I wanted to join the paratroopers. He gave me a copy of the consent forms for my mother to sign. It took a lot of talking to convince my mother how much better it would be for me. I told her that I wanted to join the Airborne. Not knowing about the newer military organizations, she thought it was some sort of an Army Air Force unit. She signed the forms, then turned around and looked up at the ceiling. I didn't hear what she said, but I'm sure it was, "THANK YOU, LORD!" A burden had just been lifted from her shoulders. I must have broken the record for the 4-minute mile getting back to the recruiting office. I was sworn into the Army on 12 July 1946.

One of the older boys had told me that the paratroopers would pay $50.00 for every jump I made. Being a fair student of mathematics, I quickly figured that I'd have bulging pockets in less than a year. I got the bad news later.

The eight weeks of basic training at Fort McClellan, Alabama, and the six weeks of Airborne training at Fort Benning, Georgia, were easy. I was in great physical shape and enjoyed every bit of it. For me, the only new things were the glider rides, the parachute rigging, and the jumping part. I'm sure I had to be kicked out of the plane a couple of times. I did get kicked off of a 34-foot tower – that, I well remember. I was "Airborne All The Way," a 130-pound gung ho trooper.

After a few days' leave at home in Pensacola, I returned to Fort Benning and boarded a train for Camp Stoneman, California. The boat trip across the Pacific was an experience in itself. I felt like I was on a roller coaster for seventeen days. We were packed into the ship *Pomona Victory* like sardines. The quarters were wet and cold, with an ever-lingering smell of vomit. I believe that our first meal was intentionally scheduled to cause sickness before we even got on the high seas. They served us boiled, greasy pork chops.

Upon arriving at the docks in Yokohama, and after a short stay at a replacement depot, I boarded a train to my final destination, Camp Haugen, in northern Japan. My assigned unit was Company I, 511th Parachute Infantry Regiment of the 11th Airborne Division. Of the 130 men in our company, only 10 of us were qualified parachutists. The company was scheduled for jump school in the early spring of 1947.

My CO summoned me to his office the morning following my sixteenth birthday. I told him the truth about my age and begged him to let me remain in the military. He contacted my mother, and she agreed to let me stay, but she didn't realize that I was jumping from planes while they were flying. My CO took me off jump status and transferred me to a noncombatant unit, the 172nd Station Hospital in Sendai.

I don't know if it was the different environment, or just my time to blossom, but the food-service section at the hospital captivated me. I was immediately enrolled in a food-service school in Yokohama, graduated in the upper ten percent of the class, and remained there for an advanced course. I returned to the hospital, was assigned to many different sections, and promoted to corporal. Thirteen days after my promotion to corporal, I received my third stripe (sergeant) with a letter of recognition from the mess officer.

Towards the end of my enlistment, I returned home and stayed out of the service for almost ninety days, then reenlisted. During my reenlistment processing at Fort Jackson, South Carolina, I took a battery of tests and was interviewed about attending OCS (officers candidate school). I declined the invitation.

I asked for assignment to the European theater when I reenlisted, but upon my arrival at the port of Seattle, I realized that I was on my way back to Japan. I was assigned to an artillery battalion of the Seventh Calvary Regiment. About three months after reporting to my new unit, I was promoted to staff sergeant and interviewed again about returning to the States and going to OCS. Again, I declined.

In July 1950, our battalion boarded LSTs in Yokohama and proceeded to land on a beach in southeastern Korea. We pushed north to Taejon, but we were stopped and repelled back to the Pusan Perimeter by the North Korean Army. When I learned that a third battalion of the Seventh Cavalry Regiment was being formed, I volunteered as the liaison sergeant to our artillery officer. I spent the next eight months in no man's land and was ambushed and overrun several times.

Because of my combat points, I was among the first group to return to the States from Korea. My new assignment was with the artillery at Fort Sill, Oklahoma. My previous training had been infantry, and I knew absolutely nothing about artillery, but I was determined to be the best at whatever assignment I received. The first atomic gun battery was being formed, and I was to be the fire-direction chief. I attended an 8-week course to learn the basics. Our first gun was named "Atomic Annie" and is on display at the museum at Fort Sill. A fire-direction center was involved with numbers, numbers, and more numbers. If ever the Army had placed a square peg in a square hole, they did an excellent job this time. Numbers were my cup of tea.

During off-time periods, while others were engaged in sport activities or bar-hopping, I was in the artillery library digging for more knowledge about the principles of field artillery. In early 1952, when the Army froze my promotion to sergeant first class, I decided to let the OCS further my knowledge in the science of artillery. I wasn't particularly interested in becoming an officer, but again, I didn't have much choice. I knew that the special training would be of great benefit to my military career, and I was definitely a career soldier. At that time, I wanted to spend at least fifty years in the military. I enjoyed OCS training even more than I had enjoyed basic training and jump school.

A week before graduating from OCS, I was told to report to the school personnel officer. Even though I didn't think that I would make it this far into the course, I was confident that I had already accomplished my goal. If I got booted out at the eleventh hour (only 47 out of 85 graduated), I was still content with my performance. However, the personnel officer just wanted to correct my records before sending me to my new unit. He wondered why my birth certificate indicated that I was 22 years old and my military records showed that I already had seven years of active duty. The next week I learned that I was one of the distinguished graduates from OCS.

I was assigned to the 82nd Airborne Division at Fort Bragg, North Carolina. In mid-1955, after two years with the Airborne, I elected to leave active duty temporarily to pursue an education. I was assigned to the Army Reserves in Pensacola and was recalled to active duty in September 1955 to serve as an umpire for the Army maneuvers

(Operation Sagebrush) in Louisiana. On my return to Pensacola, I joined the Florida National Guard and spent six months at Fort Bliss, Texas, attending the Basic Officers Training Course for antiaircraft artillery and guided missiles.

In the summer of 1957, I was the battalion convoy commander for a move to Fort Stewart, Georgia, and back to Pensacola.

I became a full-time student at Pensacola Junior College while working three part-time jobs. After I completed school, I never gave military life another thought.

Would I do it again? The answer is YES! But with my vast reserve of built-up wisdom, I would make a few minor changes. I would get all of my basic education after my first 3-year hitch. Or, I would have exchanged my OCS commission for a chance to enter West Point. The more your learn, the better your luck!

Lew Elliott earned the Combat Infantryman Badge and three battle stars during his service in Korea. While he was in the Army, he completed courses at Cameron Community College in Oklahoma and at the University of North Carolina. When he "temporarily" left the Army, he studied at Pensacola Junior College, Louisiana State University, the University of Missouri at Rolla, and Lamar University at Beaumont, Texas. He was a stockholder and an employee of Geotechnical Engineering of Houston, Texas. For twenty-three years he was an engineering, technical, and geotechnical laboratory supervisor. He supervised the soil-sample analysis and testing for a number of major construction projects such as office buildings, power plants, condominiums, and airport hangars. He retired at the age of fifty-five. He still enjoys adventurous travels to Alaska, Canada, and all of the lower forty-eight states. Lew lives in Conroe, Texas. He was the second Texas State Commander of the Veterans of Underage Military Service.

Scott L. Webb

Age 15 – United States Army

I was born in Toledo, Ohio, on 17 August 1930. When I was in the eighth grade, my parents divorced. My brothers were in the service, and I was living with my father in a cheap hotel on skid row in

> *... I was taken out of Seoul in an armored car for my own safety.*

downtown Toledo. I was a poor student at school and when eighth-grade graduation approached, I borrowed my dad's good shoes to wear for the class picture. However, I didn't graduate. I was tall for my age, so I had a tattoo put on my lower arm where everyone could see it, put on a sailor hat, and visited the local recruiting office. They must have been hard up for recruits because, although I was 15, I looked like I was 12. I was told to bring in my dad to sign the papers and if I was really 17, I could enlist. My dad went with me to the recruiting office, signed the papers, and I was sworn in on 12 August 1946.

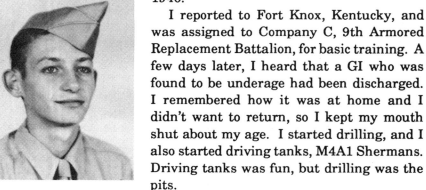

I reported to Fort Knox, Kentucky, and was assigned to Company C, 9th Armored Replacement Battalion, for basic training. A few days later, I heard that a GI who was found to be underage had been discharged. I remembered how it was at home and I didn't want to return, so I kept my mouth shut about my age. I started drilling, and I also started driving tanks, M4A1 Shermans. Driving tanks was fun, but drilling was the pits.

After graduating from basic training, I was assigned as a personal aide to the commanding general. One day I fell asleep at lunch, so I was promptly replaced. I was sent to Fort Holabird in downtown Baltimore, Maryland, and assigned to the MP company. I walked a beat on East Baltimore Street, checking IDs of the military personnel to see if they were of legal age to be in a drinking establishment. The drinking age at that time was 21. Here I was, a 15-year-old kid with an MP arm band, going around checking to see if others were old enough to drink. If they only knew!

Early in 1947, I was sent to Germany and was assigned to the 381st Railroad MP Company. We traveled all over Europe by train and had a ball. I had often heard that a milk train was always slow — not so in Germany. Every day, railroad MPs would pick up a train at Bremerhaven with several boxcars of fresh milk. They would take the train directly south to Munich for further distribution. This "milk train" was of highest priority, and everything in its way was sidetracked until it passed, including the Berlin Express and the International Express, if they were on the tracks. The priority for the milk train was because of its highly perishable cargo.

I had enlisted for eighteen months, so I was sent home in late 1947. A couple of months after I was discharged, I reenlisted, again using 1928 as my birth year. Almost immediately, I was sent to Vienna, Austria, where I served as an MP again. We were with the international patrol working the Russian, French, English, and American zones. Vienna was a dream — very beautiful — and it had everything. I was able to get some schooling there, and I still speak German fluently.

Well, all good things come to an end, and I was sent home in 1952. After a brief leave, I was on my way to Korea for the "police action" there. On the first day at sea, I was sent to the galley for KP duty. Since I was the first one to arrive, the Navy cook said, "You must be the cook," and I said yes. So, from that day on I supervised the kitchen and all of the Army cooks for the ten days it took us to get to Japan. We cooked for about 1800 troops. Many of the Army cooks were sergeants. My secret was that I was only a corporal, and I had never cooked a day in my life. Some of the higher-ranking cooks could have died if they had seen me in uniform with only two stripes. Oh, well, it was a good trip for me. I ate what I wanted — when I wanted.

At Camp Drake, Japan, I did the usual thing — nothing. It was New Year's Eve, 1952, and we were given passes. I was told Japan celebrated New Year's for three days, so I came back three days later. To my surprise, my processing company was gone! I found out that my gear was in the supply room and that I was on special orders to go to the chemical, radiological, and biological warfare school in southern Japan. So, with my luck, I was taken to the train depot, got on the train, and reported on time to the school. After school, I was put on a fishing boat and taken to southern Korea, then I caught a train from there to Seoul.

I was assigned to the 55th MP Company and became the Seoul patrol supervisor and desk sergeant. While I was in Seoul, I lived on the second floor of a schoolhouse. During my first night there, "Bed Check Charlie," a North Korean light aircraft that flew at treetop level to avoid radar, flew over as usual. We all ran down to the bunker until the all-clear was sounded. When the alarm sounded I got scared, and in my rush to put my boots on, I got them on the wrong feet. I had a hell of a time running to the bunker! That night, "Charlie" got the fuel dump.

In mid-1953, I was reassigned to the 51st CID (Criminal Investigation Detachment) and worked homicides, counterfeiting, black market, theft, and the sex detail. I did my job so well that, after receiving several citations, when it was time to return to the U. S., I was taken out of Seoul in an armored car for my own safety. It seems that a few bad guys wanted to talk to me.

I was also involved with Operation Big Switch, the returning of Communist prisoners of war back to North Korea. The North Korean prisoners wrote in blood on small pieces of paper that they didn't want to return to the North, but part of the peace agreement was that they had to. Our job was to make sure that they didn't escape from the train that took them to North Korea. We felt pity for them because we knew some of them would be shot, but there was nothing we could do.

I arrived in the States in early 1954 and was put in charge of motorcycle police at Fort Lewis, Washington. During the summer of '54 we helped with the production of the movie, "To Hell and Back," the life story of Audie Murphy, the most decorated soldier in World War II. In the parade scene at the end of the movie, I was next to Audie as his MP escort.

I was discharged at Fort Lewis on 10 January 1955. I did OK, and I am proud of my service.

I write this in the aftermath of the untimely death of Admiral J. M. Boorda, also an underage veteran who started as an enlisted man and worked his way up to the rank of four-star admiral. He gave it everything he had and was a truly great human being. I consider him a hero.

Scott Webb was awarded the Army Commendation Medal for his work in the police field while in Korea. After his discharge from the Army, he attended the City College of San Francisco, San Francisco State University, and the University of California at Berkeley under the GI Bill. He received a degree in criminology. During his eleven-year tour with the San Francisco Police Department, he was promoted to the famous "S" squad, a night detail working felonious crimes headed, by Chief Al Nelder. Later, he joined the Sheriff's Department of Santa Cruz County, California, and retired in 1988. Scott and Maxine, his wife of forty-two years, live in Prescott Valley, Arizona. They have four children and five grandchildren. Scott is the Arizona State Vice-Commander of the Veterans of Underage Military Service.

√ **VUMS Note** ⇒ *Famous entertainers.* "What a thrill!" was the comment of an underage WAC who was chosen to dance with Bob Hope. Bob was entertaining the troops in the base theater, and she was the lucky one to be picked to dance with him. Another well-known entertainer, Dinah Shore, is remembered gratefully by another vet. On his return to the States after nearly four years overseas, he watched from the deck of the troopship as Dinah Shore welcomed the troops from a blimp flying over the harbor at San Pedro, California, where his ship was anchored.

Ray D. Jackson

Age 16 – United States Marine Corps

I was born on a farm north of Shoshone, Idaho, on 28 September 1929. My mother died when I was five years old, leaving my father with the task of raising six children in the midst of the Depression. Two of my

> *I was underage, underweight, and under height.*

brothers served in the Army during World War II. One was killed in action at Fédala, near Casablanca, on the first day of the Allied landings in North Africa. Another served on Okinawa. I followed the war very closely and at one time could name most of the generals commanding Army divisions in the European theater.

My first year in high school was cut short when my father became incapacitated and I quit school to attend to him. The following year I went back to school, a year behind my classmates. After I completed two years of high school, I decided that it was time to enlist.

During the war, the Navy had converted a famous ski resort at Sun Valley, Idaho, into a convalescent center. Many Marines who had been wounded in the Pacific were sent there to recuperate. On leave, they would visit the small towns in southern Idaho. One day I noticed a Marine captain sitting in a local cafe, resplendent in his green uniform adorned with ribbons. I couldn't see his wounds, only his uniform, ribbons, and military bearing. The sight of him was better than any recruiting poster. I knew then that I had to be a Marine.

However, I had to overcome three problems before I could become a Marine. I was *under*age, *under*weight, and *under* height. The recruiting sergeant helped me overcome all three. He furnished me papers which my father signed stating that I was seventeen; he told me to eat a lot of bananas just before the physical; and he showed me how to shift my weight to my toes unobtrusively and lift my heels when they were measuring me for height. It worked. I enlisted just after school ended in 1946. However, the Marines had decided to form a platoon recruited entirely from Idaho. This meant a delay of two or three months before I was actually sworn in. The "All Idaho" platoon took the oath on the steps of the state capitol building in Boise, Idaho, on 31 August 1946. In boot camp, we were known as "spudheads," in addition to other choice descriptions the drill instructors used.

During boot camp, two of the three "under" problems caused me some difficulty. It wasn't being underage – it was being so small. I was the smallest man (boy) in the platoon, a true "feather merchant." Keeping up with the long-legged guys up front was difficult for me with my short legs. But when the DI shouted, "To the rear, march," I became the platoon guidon, although for a very short time.

One day while I was in boot camp, I was assigned special duty. I still don't know why they chose me, the smallest and youngest in the platoon, to be the one to report to the brig. I was to escort a prisoner to sick bay for a medical examination, then bring him back to the brig. I reported in, and a grizzled old gunnery sergeant grabbed my rifle and put a full clip of ammunition in it. "If he gets out of line, shoot the son of a bitch!" the sergeant admonished as I was going out the door with the prisoner. As if I weren't scared enough already! My arms were shaking so much that my rifle was bouncing up and down. I think the prisoner knew better than to get out of line because he knew I was so scared that I probably would shoot him, or at least shoot *at* him.

My 3-year hitch was rather uneventful. I trained as a radio operator and was assigned to Marine Tactical Air Control Squadron-2 at the Marine Corps Air Station, El Toro, California. We were the link between the infantry and the air wing that provided close air support.

I was discharged in August 1949, returned to Idaho, and went to the local high school to enroll. The principal convinced me that I should go to college and arranged for me to take the GED tests. Two weeks after leaving the Marines, I was enrolled at Idaho State College (now Idaho State University) on probation. I completed one year at ISC and was working on my brother-in-law's farm when the Korean War started. I knew that all my friends who were still in the Corps would soon be in Korea, and I wanted to be with them. I joined the Marine Reserves on 4 August 1950 and requested active duty. I reported to the Naval Ordnance Depot, Pocatello, Idaho, for a physical examination on 10 September 1950, and arrived at Camp Pendleton,

California, on 15 September 1950, the day the 1st Marine Division landed at Inchon, Korea.

I was sent to Tent Camp Two for six weeks of combat infantry training. When the training was completed, we were destined for Korea as 1st Marine Division replacements. While we were loading on trucks to go to San Diego to catch a ship for Korea, the company commander called me from the truck and told me I was staying. I was to be a platoon sergeant to help train another company.

I finally got to Korea in March 1951. Instead of being a replacement in the infantry, as I had expected, I was assigned to Marine Aircraft Group-33, 1st Marine Aircraft Wing. I worked in communications and led a plush life compared to my buddies in the line companies. In one sense I was lucky, but in another sense, I felt cheated. I was in a combat unit, but did not experience the pure hell of front-line combat.

I returned to the U. S. and was released from active duty on 15 November 1951 at the Marine Corps Base, San Diego. I was a staff sergeant at the time. I received an honorable discharge from the Marine Corps Reserve on 7 August 1953.

Ray Jackson worked as an electrician's helper and as a plumber's helper for about two years, then returned to school. He used the educational benefits of the GI Bill to the fullest extent and graduated from Colorado State University with a Ph.D. in June 1960. He was a research physicist with the Agricultural Research Service, U. S. Department of Agriculture for more than thirty-five years. He received a Distinguished Service Award from the Secretary of Agriculture in 1986, and was an Agricultural Research Service Outstanding Scientist of the Year in 1992. In 1993, the National Aeronautics and Space Administration and the U. S. Department of Interior presented Ray with the William T. Pecora Award for his leadership in the advancement of remote sensing for the management of natural resources and environmental monitoring. He retired in 1993 and spends his time tinkering with computers and writing. Ray and his wife Susan live in Tempe, Arizona. They were married in 1968, raised a combined family of seven children, and now have fourteen grandchildren. Ray is National Vice-Commander of the Veterans of Underage Military Service.

Charles L. Miller

Age 16 – United States Army Air Forces

I was born in a logging camp near Sulphur Springs, Oregon, on 15 June 1930. My father was a logger and my mother cooked for the men at the camp. When I was only 4 years old, my father became a single parent with six children ranging in ages

> *... as the "cool, calm, commander," I had forgotten to put in my upper plate!*

from 2 to 18 years. We moved to Salem, Oregon, then to Hillsboro, Oregon, where my father worked in the Kaiser Shipyard. My sisters were married by 1944, and my older brother was in the Navy, so my younger brother and I were the only children still at home. My father died that year, and my younger brother and I went to live with our oldest sister. I was 14 and my brother was 12 years old. When my brother got out of the Navy, we went to live with him and his bride in Sweethome, Oregon.

I worked in a sawmill during the summer of 1946. In September of that year, my brother George, age 14, and a close friend, Ed Brunell, age 15, visited an Army Air Forces recruiter and told him that they were 17 years old. The recruiter convinced them that they should enlist and told them that all they needed was a letter stating they were 18 years old. Ed and George talked me into enlisting with them, so we went to our older brother's mother-in-law who gladly signed a letter stating that we were 18 years old. We were accepted into the Air Forces and were sworn in on 25 September 1946.

We were sent to Fort Lewis, Washington, for initial processing and then by troop train to San Antonio, Texas, for basic training. I wanted to be an aircraft mechanic, so I was sent to Geiger Air Force Base in Spokane, Washington, to learn how to operate heavy equipment, specifically, cranes, and shovels. In March 1947, I graduated from the school and was sent to Guam in the Mariana Islands where I was assigned to the 1952nd Engineering Utilities Company at Harmon Field.

We were shipping old, heavy, World War II equipment to China for scrap metal. I was operating a truck-mounted crane one day when Brigadier General Farthing stopped and spoke to me. I'm not sure what I said, but he must have liked it because two days later orders came promoting me to buck sergeant! This was thirteen days after my seventeenth birthday and nine months of service in the military.

I returned to the States in December 1948 and was honorably discharged at McChord Air Force Base, Washington. I went back to Salem, Oregon, enrolled in high school, and obtained my diploma. After I completed high school, a former Army buddy and I hitchhiked around the country for nine months. We would stop at a town, work until we had a sufficient bankroll, then move on to the next town.

I went back to Atlanta, Georgia, in January 1951 to see a girl I had met on my travels around the country. The Korean War was going strong by then, and I decided to reenlist. Faced with a choice between the Marine Corps and the Army Airborne, I chose the Airborne because I thought that they paid more. I was sent to Fort Jackson, South Carolina, for qualifying and leadership school, then was assigned to the 503rd Infantry of the 11th Airborne Division at Fort Campbell, Kentucky. About a month later, while I was visiting some members of the Headquarters Company, 127 Airborne Engineers, a sergeant found out that I was a school-trained crane and shovel operator. The result of this visit was that I applied for a transfer, and the brass instructed the first sergeant to hand-carry my request through the division hierarchy.

I went through jump school at Fort Benning, Georgia, in July 1951 and returned to the 127th Engineers. Eighteen months after I had reenlisted, I had been promoted from private to sergeant first class and was platoon sergeant of the heavy-equipment platoon. I spent the remainder of my tour with the 127th and was discharged in January 1954.

I returned to the West Coast and went to work for Weyerhauser Timber Company in Longview, Washington. I was out of the service for eighty-seven days and decided that the Army really was my "family" as well as my home. I knew that if I waited more than ninety days to reenlist I would lose my rank, so I immediately went to the recruiting office and reenlisted. I was sent to Fort Ord, California, for qualification, then I went back to the 127th Engineers at Fort Campbell to take over my former platoon as heavy-equipment platoon sergeant.

I applied for OCS (officer candidate school) and the infantry school. The Army, in their great wisdom, sent me to artillery officer school at Fort Sill, Oklahoma. Upon graduation, the two top-rated candidates were allowed to apply for their choice of branch, so I chose the Corps of Engineers. I was sent to Fort Belvoir, Virginia, for the engineer officers basic course, then was assigned to the 100th Float Bridge Company in Camp Prince, West Virginia. I applied for pilot training in 1956 and was transferred to Gary Air Force Base, San Marcos, Texas.

I finished pilot training at Fort Rucker, Alabama, in March 1957. At that time, the Army was forming an aviation unit for the 82nd Airborne, and anyone who was jump-qualified was assigned to the unit. I was assigned to the 307th Engineer battalion and was TDY to the 82nd Aviation Company, Provisional. I spent three years with the 82nd, primarily as aviation maintenance officer and platoon leader of the H-13 Helicopter Platoon at Fort Bragg, North Carolina.

I received orders to go to the 30th Engineering Topographical Survey Battalion at Fort Belvoir, Virginia, in 1959. I was immediately sent TDY to Iran for a year to map the country. During this period, I flew H-13 choppers all over Iran with an Iranian classifier/interpreter as a passenger. The Shah was in power during this time.

During a mission one day, I was struck with a bad case of diarrhea. I needed to find a spot to land to take care of my urgent needs, so I sat the chopper down on what appeared to be a deserted sand bar in the middle of a river. I was preparing to drop my drawers when two Iranians came swimming across to the river to see what great steel and plastic bird had landed! Needless to say, my objective was completed with great haste! Many villages in Iran were remote from each other at that time, and there was little, if any, communication between them. Many villagers had never seen an automobile, let alone a plane or a helicopter.

I completed my Iranian tour and went back the States for a ground duty (non-flying) tour as an engineer company commander. I went to

Panama for jungle-warfare school and then back to Fort Belvoir, Virginia, where I became a battalion commander while still a captain.

In 1963, I was sent to Livorno, Italy, as a pilot in the Mediterranean Engineer Division. Our division was responsible for all construction for the Agency for International Development in Africa, the Middle East as far as Burma, and southern Europe. I flew a twin-engine Beechcraft Queenaire over sixty countries.

From Livorno, I went to Vietnam, where I was assigned to A Troop, 1st of the 9th Cavalry Squadron, 1st Air Cavalry Division. I commanded a scout platoon and a cavalry troop at An Khe. I served with the USARV (US Army, Republic of Vietnam) flight detachment in Saigon for a short time in January 1967, then joined the 214th Assault Helicopter Battalion in Bearcat, Vietnam. Just prior to my departure from Bearcat, our headquarters building was named "Miller Manor."

I returned to the States and went to Fort Rucker, Alabama, as a branch chief in the helicopter school, teaching aviation cadets to fly helicopters in combat situations. In December 1968, I was assigned as a regular Army advisor to the California National Guard at the Presidio, San Francisco, California.

It was back to Vietnam in 1970, this time with the 12th Aviation Group as an airfield commander at Dong Tam, in the delta region of Vietnam. On the second night at Dong Tam, we came under a heavy mortar attack. Being a seasoned combat veteran, I jumped from my bunk, donned my flak vest, grabbed my weapon, leaped into my waiting jeep, went to the flight line, and took command of the airfield evacuation of aircraft. After things were under control, I went into base operations and discovered, much to my chagrin, that as the "cool, calm, commander," I had forgotten to put in my upper plate!

Early in 1971, I was given the job of forming up a new airfield command at Marble Mountain, Da Nang, Vietnam. We relieved the last Marine air unit that had been based there. I returned to the States in mid-1971. The California National Guard requested my return, so I was assigned as engineer advisor to a Guard unit in Santa Rosa, California. After twenty-four years of service, I retired from the Army at the Presidio, San Francisco, in May 1972 with the rank of lieutenant colonel.

Chuck Miller was awarded the Distinguished Flying Cross, a Bronze Star with two Oak Leaf Clusters, the Meritorious Service Medal with Oak Leaf Cluster, the Air Medal with "V" device and ten Oak Leaf Clusters, the Army Commendation Medal, the Vietnamese Cross of Gallantry with Palm, and the Vietnamese Civil Action Honor Medal First Class. He holds Master Aviator Wings and Senior Parachute Wings. After retiring from the Army, he worked as superintendent of construction for American Building Systems at Bear Valley Springs, Tehachapi, California, then worked briefly as a pilot for a California commuter airline before being hired by the city of Paso Robles as an airport manager in 1973. He also started an industrial park at the airport. He retired from his job with the city of Paso Robles in 1985, built custom homes in Camarillo, California, for a time, then traveled extensively around the country in a motor home. Chuck and his wife Betty spend part of the year in Atascadero, California, and part in Bend, Oregon. Chuck has two children and two grandchildren.

Curtis H. Marzolf

Age 14 – United States Army Air Forces

I was born in the little town of Radium, Minnesota, on 10 March 1932. Our family moved to Harvey, North Dakota, when I was 2 or 3 years old. By the time I completed the eighth grade, I was quite tall and ran with a

> *I directed fire from the USS Missouri on two occasions.*

group of boys who were older than I was. In 1946, a number of us decided to join the Army. I "acquired" a couple of signatures on my enlistment papers and joined the Army on 1 October 1946. I was only 14 years old but I was hot to become a fighter pilot. Of the number of us who had decided to join the Army, I was the only one who did.

I was sent to Fort Snelling, Minnesota, the last cavalry outpost in the U. S. Army, then to Fort Sheridan, Illinois, and on to San Antonio, Texas, for basic training. After completing basic, I went to Keesler Field, Mississippi, for airframe and powerplant school, then to P-51 specialist school at Chanute Field, Illinois. While waiting for a school slot, my job was to fire hot-water heaters and furnaces. When a slot became available, it was for P-80 specialist, not P-51.

After completing the P-80 school, I was sent to Dow Field, Maine, to work on P-47s. I became the crew chief on an adjutant's aircraft. I was a proud lad – 15 years old and a private first class! While I was with the 37th Fighter Squadron at Dow Field, we transitioned to P-84s. Lieutenant Colonel Samway, who became an ace while flying a P-47 in Europe during World War II, was one of many admirable people in the squadron.

I had always wanted to be a fighter pilot. My buddy McGrew and I applied for flight school, but I couldn't produce a birth certificate. McGrew was accepted for flight school, and I was told to list my three top choices overseas for assignment. I was sent to Japan, which was not among my three choices. Sound familiar?

I went to Misawa, Japan, with the 49th Fighter Wing of Richard Bong fame. I was assigned to the engine shop, where I acquired an engine specialist MOS (military occupational specialty) and corporal stripes. I soon became an engine inspector, which came with sergeants stripes.

At about that time, the Berlin Airlift was being instituted. I was a flight mechanic (engines) on a C-46 transport plane called the *Oklahoma Kid*. We were the 49th Group Courier and were alerted to go to Berlin, but the 314th Troop Carrier Group out of Tachikawa got the assignment, and we stayed in Japan until I rotated Stateside and was discharged from the Air Force.

I spent about a year in Iowa as an airport service-man and implement dealer and ended that year by riding in a rodeo. I went back to North Dakota and went to work as a fireman on the Soo Line Railroad, with the job of hand-firing steam locomotives. It was the best job I've had in my life to this date. I have been drawing railroad retirement benefits since I became 62.

With the war starting in Korea, the year 1950 brought quite a change in the world. By 1 January 1951, I was a first sergeant in the North Dakota National Guard and on my way to Camp Rucker, Alabama, with a May departure date for Korea. After a stop at Camp Drake, Japan, I boarded the troopship *Sergeant Joe Martinez* and proceeded to Inchon, Korea. I was scheduled to go to the 1st Cavalry Division, but I ended up as first sergeant of the 19th Tank Company, 7th Infantry Division. Our division headed east and relieved the 7th Marine Regiment at the Punchbowl.

My next stop was at the 8209th MASH hospital to get patched up from a wound received in the Punchbowl. Upon leaving the 8209th and arriving at the regimental rear, I was greeted by the sergeant major who said, "Boy, are you lucky!" When I asked why, he told me that I was to go back to the 6149th Tactical Control Squadron as an observer in AT-6 *Texans*, light observation-aircraft that were called "mosquitos."

The squadron had one man from each infantry regiment and each artillery battalion directing artillery fire, fighter strikes (Air Force, Navy and Marine), and naval gunfire. I directed fire from the USS

Missouri on two occasions. That was quite an experience for a "man" 19 years old!

I was discharged from the Army at Camp McCoy, Wisconsin, on 8 August 1952. I was out of the military for twenty years, then in September 1972, I enlisted in the Air Force Reserves, hoping to become a flight engineer and complete twenty years of military service to qualify for a pension. This was not to be, as I was more of a loner and not a "sheep-type" follower.

By this time I had acquired a commercial license as a pilot with instrument and multi-engine rating, a ground-instructors license, and I still had adventurous blood flowing in me. I signed on with Bell Helicopter and went on three maneuvers with the Iranian Air Force, which was quite impressive. I left Iran just prior to the fall of the Shah, drove to Switzerland, then flew to Angola to work with the Ministry of Agriculture. This was an interesting assignment because of the presence of Russians, Bulgarians, East Germans, Italians, Cubans — you name it!

During my travels, I was told by an official at one of our American embassies that I was not an "official" American because I was not a U. S. military or a government employee, nor was I retired from either. It made me feel good to know how my youthful patriotism was appreciated!

Curt Marzolf received the Purple Heart for wounds received while in Korea. In addition to his excursions to Iran and Angola, he has circled the globe four times. He returned to Africa on a two-year assignment, came back to the U. S. and worked in several states. He operated a couple of aircraft businesses, flew the Caribbean, and took an aerobatics course in Jamaica. He spent some time at an aeronautical complex in the state of Tamil Nadir, India, and returned there in the fall of 1996. Curt married Pei Lin, a native of Guonjon, China, while he was in Argentina. They now live in Bulverde, Texas, when Curt is in this country.

Joseph J. Champagne

Age 16 – United States Army

As a boy in the Kennewick-Pasco-Richland area in the state of Washington, I enjoyed going to the Naval Air Station at Pasco with my Boy Scout troop to swim in the base pool. As often as I could, I would sneak out to the flight line and climb into an airplane.

> *So we pulled a Jesse James trick ... We commandeered the train.*

Pretending that I was a pilot fighting the enemy, I would operate the stick and rudders until someone would notice me and chase me out of the plane with a stern warning never to do that again.

A friend of mine showed up one day in an Army uniform. I was very impressed. I believe he was the one who told me how to circumvent the age requirements. I went to the Army recruiting office and obtained the necessary papers for my parents to sign. It took a lot of arguing and threatening them with the idea that I might end up in jail, but I finally convinced my mother to sign that I was 17. I think my dad was glad; it meant one less mouth to feed.

I joined the U. S. Army on 5 October 1946, a little over two months past my sixteenth birthday. My enlistment was for eighteen months, and looking back, I find it hard to believe that the Army would have such a short enlistment. After basic training, I was sent to Japan for occupation duty as a light machine-gunner with Fox Troop, 12th Cavalry Regiment, 1st Cavalry Division.

Those were exciting times for a 16-year-old. One day, six of us from the troop were on a pass in a small Japanese town. We had to catch a train back to a station where we would meet a truck to take us back to the base. We were having a great time and were somewhat tipsy when we caught a train. We didn't realize that we were going in the wrong direction until we came to the end of the line and the engineer shut the train down for the night. In sign language and broken English, the engineer informed us that the train would not be leaving for three or four hours. So we pulled a Jesse James trick, but without weapons. We commandeered the train. We yelled, "Train leaving, all aboard!" One of our group took over as engineer and started the train moving. Seeing what was happening, the Japanese engineer jumped on and took over. Many Japanese also got on board. We forced the engineer to take the train at high speed to our destination, bypassing many stops along the way. We caught the last truck back to the base. Had we been a few minutes later, we would have been AWOL. Needless to say, I was very nervous and uneasy for several days after that.

After serving in Japan for about a year, I returned to the States and was discharged at Camp Stoneman, California, on 14 February 1948.

After I had been a civilian for about a year, I reenlisted in the Army on the same day that my younger brother joined for the first time. He was sent to Fort Ord, California, for basic training and I was sent to Vienna, Austria, where I joined the 796th Military Police Battalion of "four men in a jeep" fame. Four men — a U. S. soldier, a French soldier, a British Soldier, and a Russian soldier — would patrol parts of Vienna in a jeep. I was on occupation duty both in Japan and in Austria, but for some reason, there is no mention of occupation duty in Austria on my second set of discharge papers.

After I had been with the U. S. Forces in Austria (USFA) for about six months, I joined the USFA boxing team. I traveled all over Europe with the boxing team.

In March 1950, I applied for a hardship discharge which was granted on 4 April 1950. I went home to help provide for my mother, a sister, and a younger brother. After my family became financially stable, I joined the U. S. Marine Corps. I was sworn in on 19 November 1952, went through boot camp at San Diego, California, then to Camp Pendleton for combat training.

When our training was completed, we boarded trucks for transportation to a ship bound for Korea. Before the trucks could pull out, my name was called, and I was told to get off the truck. I was told later that I was to be a coach at the Marine rifle range at Camp Matthews. This assignment may have saved my life because most of the others on the truck ended up in heavy fighting with the 1st Marine Division in Korea.

At Camp Matthews, I taught recruits from the Marine Corps Recruit Depot how to shoot and qualify with pistols, carbines, rifles, and how to throw hand grenades properly. After some months as a coach, I was assigned to the newly reactivated 3rd Marine Division and went through additional combat training at Camp Pendleton. Our division was sent to Japan to prepare for immediate insertion into Korea if the truce were broken. We were constantly training. We conducted cold-weather exercises near Mount Fujiyama and made amphibious landings on many small islands. Once, we landed on Okinawa and fought the U. S. Army in mock war games. The games had to be held up for awhile because someone didn't get the word and was firing live ammunition.

Perhaps the most memorable training exercise for us was when we "invaded" Iwo Jima. It looked like a remake of John Wayne's movie "Sands of Iwo Jima." I can really appreciate what the Marines had to contend with during the real invasion in 1945. We could still see sunken landing-craft and equipment. We found helmets with large holes in them that had been dropped and had lain there for years. After the exercise was completed, the Marines held a ceremony in honor of the men who had fought and died there almost ten years before.

I returned to San Diego, California, in late 1954 and spent the last twelve months of my enlistment at the Marine Corps Recruit Depot, where I was assistant brig warden. I also pulled shore patrol duty in San Diego, working with the San Diego Police Department. I was honorably discharged from the Marine Corps on 18 November 1955.

I was a civilian for two years during which time I studied radio, television and electronics. I enlisted in the U. S. Air Force in November 1957 and was sent to the Air Force Electronics School at Keesler Air Force Base, Biloxi, Mississippi. After graduation, I was sent to another Air Force technical school at Scott Air Force Base in Illinois. I was then sent to France and assigned to the 2nd Mobile Communications Squadron (2nd MOB) at Toul-Rosieres Air Force Base near Nancy, France.

We (the MOB) supplied all the electronics equipment and men to different countries when they had a need or when they shut down bases for overhaul of their equipment. We supplied electronics for all the big war games. We also taught the Dutch military how to use our equipment. We operated remote sites with beacons to keep allied aircraft from flying into East Berlin. We received an outstanding unit award for the support of the United Nations in the Congo.

My enlistment was extended for six months while I was in France. Afterward, I was sent to a Strategic Air Command base at Albany, Georgia, where I was honorably discharged from the Air Force on 31 May 1962.

I entertained the idea of joining the U. S. Navy to complete my service to the United States of America, but my wife said, "No way!" So my time in the U. S. military ended.

Joe Champagne worked as an electronics technician at the Seattle-Tacoma International Airport for a time, then went back to truck driving, a skill he had learned previously. He owned and operated an 18-wheel tractor-trailer rig, making runs mostly up and down the West Coast. Later, he sold his rig and drove for other companies, spending about twenty-eight years behind the wheel. He retired in 1992 and lives in Auburn, Washington, with his wife, Leona. Joe and Leona have two children.

John D. Tosh

Age 14 – United States Army Air Forces

I was raised in the small town of Moody, Texas, where I was born on 17 April 1932. As a young boy in school, I lacked the enthusiasm to concentrate on my education. My mind was always wandering. I would think about airplanes and dream of somehow serving my country in the armed forces.

> *The only regret I have is not knowing that the military services had forgiven those who had lied about their age ...*

In 1946, my parents divorced (but later remarried), and this presented me an ideal opportunity to enlist. I told each of my parents that I would be staying with the other one. I proceeded to the recruiting office, told them that I was 18 years old, filled out my enlistment papers, and on 4 November 1946, I was sworn into the Army Air Forces.

I went to Camp Hood (now Fort Hood) in Texas for my induction physical. After that, I was sent to Dodd Field at Fort Sam Houston, Texas, for further assignment. From Dodd field I went to Headquarters, Indoctrination Training Center at San Antonio, Texas, which is now Lackland AFB. I was assigned to the 3543rd AAFBU (Army Air Forces Base Unit), Squadron BM-4, Flight 1401, for basic training. After thirteen weeks of basic training, I was sent to Lowry Field, Colorado, where I was assigned to the 3705th AAFBU and attended automobile mechanics school. Upon completing mechanics school, I was transferred to the 146th AAFBU at Selfridge Field, Michigan, with further assignment to the 745th Air Material Squadron, 503rd Air Service Group. I worked in the preventive line-maintenance section of the motor pool.

Unfortunately for me, there was a shortage of cooks at Selfridge, and after serving in the motor pool for about one year, several of us were "volunteered" to transfer to Squadron D, 56th Airdrome Group, to be trained as cooks. I hated the transfer, but in my situation, I did not feel that I could afford to object because I did not want to bring attention to myself and risk being discovered to be underage. I made the best of the situation and learned very quickly. On 31 July 1948, at the age of 16, I was promoted to corporal and became 1st Cook. As 1st Cook, I was in charge of the shift and was responsible for preparing the menu, insuring that adequate supplies were available, and that the food was properly prepared and served on time.

The aerial gunnery and bombing range for Selfridge Field was at Oscoda, Michigan. The range was operated only during the summer months, and I had the opportunity to spend the summer of 1948 there. It was at Oscoda that I met the girl who would become my wife. Fortunately for me, the Air Force decided to keep the base at Oscoda open year-round, so I was able to remain there. On 14 February 1949, at age 16, I attained the rank of sergeant.

My enlistment was up on 3 November 1949. After my discharge, I returned to my home in Texas. The Korean War started the following year, and I thought that I would probably be called back to duty, so on 12 October 1950, I enlisted in the Air Force Reserve and requested immediate recall to active duty. I was told that I would be recalled as soon as my Air Force records were assembled, but for some reason, I was not recalled during the Korean War period. While waiting for the recall that never came, I began my civilian career as a technician at the Southwest Research Institute in San Antonio, Texas. I also learned to fly and later became an independent flight instructor.

After getting into the Air Force Reserve, it didn't take long for me to change career fields. I definitely knew that I did not want to remain a cook, so I became an aircraft loadmaster with the 433rd Troop Carrier Wing. In January 1968, during the Vietnam conflict, my unit, the 921st Military Airlift Group, was called to active duty. We were flying C-124 aircraft and I was group standardization loadmaster as well as a loadmaster instructor and flight examiner. During 1968, I flew numerous missions in and out of Vietnam and other Southeast Asia locations.

I was released from active duty in November 1968 and returned to my civilian job, and to my Air Force Reserve assignment as well. In 1972, I became squadron operations superintendent for the 74th APS (Aerial Port Squadron). I was promoted to chief master sergeant on 27

February 1974. During Desert Shield/Desert Storm, I was recalled for short tours of active duty, but remained in my position as superintendent of the 74th APS.

I retired from the U. S. Air Force on 31 March 1992 after serving a total of forty-four years of active and reserve duty.

The only regret I have is not knowing that the military services had forgiven those who had lied about their age when they enlisted. In the early 1960s, I had the opportunity to be commissioned, but I declined because I feared it would be discovered that I had lied in order to join the service in 1946. Several friends accepted commissions at that time and later retired as full colonels. I would like to think that I, too, would have accepted a commission had I known that no action would be taken against me. But I really have no regrets about my decision. I had a great military career and would certainly do it over again. I'm not sure that I would recommend that young people join the military underage today because education is much too important. I feel strongly that all young people should pursue their education *before* embarking on any other endeavor.

John Tosh was awarded the Air Force Meritorious Service Medal with Oak Leaf Cluster, the Air Force Commendation Medal, the Air Force Achievement Medal, and a number of service medals. After his discharge from the regular Air Force, he attended college at night while he was working as a technician at the Southwest Research Institute. Later, he became a research engineer and conducted research on engines, fuels, and lubricants. Some of the fuels-research work he did in the 1970s became the basis for the removal of tetra-ethyl lead from gasoline, which resulted in the production of unleaded gasoline as we know it today. Later, he became a principal investigator for alternative-fuels research, particularly alcohol fuels. John's thirty-eight years of engineering research produced more than sixty publications on fuels and lubricants. He retired from his civilian career in 1990, but he continues to be active in alternative-fuels research by serving as a consultant to the U. S. Department of Energy. He also continues to teach flying. John and Evelyn, his wife of forty-six years, live in San Antonio, Texas.

Donald L. Price

Age 16 – United States Army

I was born at Napa, California, on 29 November 1930. My father was a career Navy man, so we didn't stay in one place very long. We moved so frequently that I didn't really put down roots anywhere, and

... and for the first time, the reality of war came home to me.

there was little chance to develop long-term friendships. When my father was recalled to active duty by the Navy in 1939, he was stationed on Goat Island in San Francisco Bay. I attended a small, one-room school there. We were still living on the island on 7 December 1941, and I can tell you, things were hectic during that time. My father was assigned to sea duty in 1943, so my mother and I moved to the "mainland" and life went on.

At the age of 15, along with a couple of other boys my age, I attempted to join the Merchant Marine, but our efforts weren't successful. We were ready for a life of adventure, and the war wasn't

that much of a reality to us at that age, so we gave the Navy a try, but with the same result. Finally, during the summer of 1946, one of my best friends enlisted in the Army's 25th Infantry Division. After he left, things got kind of lonely, school was a drag, and I felt my life was going to waste.

I attempted to enlist into the 25th Infantry on my sixteenth birthday. When I told the recruiting sergeant that it was my birthday, he told me that I would first have to register for the draft. I almost gave up at

this point, but instead, I walked down to the draft board office in Oakland, California. They were extremely busy at the time, so when I told the girl that I wanted to register for the draft, she didn't bother asking for proof of my date of birth. After filling out the forms, she advised me that I would be notified of my draft classification. I told her it was my intent to enlist, so she prepared a registration card for me. When I presented the card to the recruiter, he was more than happy to get down to the business of enlisting me. However, he started making a pitch for me to go Airborne instead of going to the 25th Infantry Division. He made it sound so appealing that I made the switch and enlisted directly into the 11th Airborne Infantry Division, which was engaged in the occupation of Japan at that time.

I was sworn into the Army on 3 December 1946 at San Francisco and was sent to Camp Beal, California, a short distance from Sacramento. I was there for nine days during which we were issued equipment, received our shots, and underwent other processing in preparation for basic training. It was at Camp Beal where I attended my first "GI Party." Of course, it wasn't anything like I expected.

I was sent to North Fort Lewis, Washington, for basic training. This was not only my first experience on a train, but my first on a troop train, and also the first time I was away from home longer than two weeks. Needless to say, basic training was a unique experience, and it was here that I was introduced to another unique military procedure referred to as "short-arm" inspection. After completing basic, I was sent to Camp Stoneman, California, and on to Japan for occupation duty with the 11th Airborne.

The voyage across the Pacific was very interesting. We made stops at Guam and Okinawa, and for the first time, the reality of war came home to me. I could see first-hand the devastation caused by war, and the far-flung islands that I had only heard about were now a reality.

Upon arrival in Japan, I was assigned to the 81mm Mortar Platoon, Headquarters Company, 3rd Battalion, 511th Parachute Infantry Regiment, at Camp Haugen, Hachinohe, Honshu, Japan. It was here that I learned what it meant to be Airborne. On my first morning there, my platoon, with M-1 rifles at port arms, double-timed to the airfield, a distance of about two miles. We then engaged in a series of rifle exercises, after which we took a run around the airfield, then double-timed back to the barracks. When it was time to fall out for breakfast, I opted to flop on my bed for a much-needed rest. After a brief respite, the platoon, with me in tow, embarked on a day of field exercises. I became well acquainted with the 44-pound weight of a mortar tube.

Several weeks later, I was transferred to Service Company and was assigned to the Transportation Platoon. Finally, in June 1947, my time came to attend parachute training at the 11th Airborne Division

Jump School in Yamato, Japan. Of great help to me during training was the fact that the platoon ahead of us was comprised of officers. Competition swiftly developed between our platoons, especially on the runs. After a couple of miles of running, the officers would start heading for the ditches to deposit their last meal. We would just bear down, all the more determined not to drop out.

Normally, students would make one jump a day for five days. Our schedule was changed because the troop-carrier aircraft were to be grounded for service prior to the Fourth of July celebration in Tokyo for General MacArthur. We completed ground training on Friday, made two jumps on Saturday, two on Sunday, and one on Monday. We received our certificates and were on our way back to the regiment on Monday afternoon.

In November 1947, prior to my seventeenth birthday, I had the opportunity to complete glider, or "silent wings" training, a unique experience in itself. This consisted of learning to load and lash equipment in a glider and then taking a ride with your load. What I learned about tying loads then has proved most useful to me today. I can't say much for glider rides, though.

I was transferred to the Defense Platoon, Division Headquarters and Headquarters Company, 11th Airborne Division, at Camp Crawford, Sapporo, Hokkaido, Japan, in the spring of 1948. This was a return to line company duty, which I enjoyed more than the Transportation Platoon, but it didn't provide much experience for a future civilian. I returned to the States with this unit in March 1949. After a scenic trip back across the Pacific, we stopped in Hawaii for our first Stateside visit, then went on through the Panama Canal, where we stopped for a visit to Camp Clayton. We proceeded to New Orleans, where we boarded a troop train for Fort Campbell, Kentucky. Fort Campbell had been in mothballs, and it was up to us to reopen the base and make it habitable.

While at Fort Campbell, I had the opportunity to spend time in southern Illinois with some friends from the area. I was discharged at Fort Campbell on 8 December 1951.

Don Price decided to settle in Mount Carmel, Illinois, after his discharge from the Army. He joined the Mount Carmel police force in December 1955. During his tenure with the force he served as a patrolman, detective, and chief of police. He retired from the force in April 1981. He continued his education while he was a policeman and received a B.S. in general psychology from the University of Evansville, Indiana, in 1974 and earned an M.S. in child psychology from the same institution in 1977. At the present time, Don is the city inspector for the City of Mount Carmel and holds a position on the faculty of Southeastern Illinois Community Colleges. He has lived in the same location for thirty-three years, a major change from his childhood days. Don and Jean, his wife of forty-two years, live in Mount Carmel. They have four children and six grandchildren.

√ **VUMS Note ⇒ *Well-known military figures.***
Instances in which underage veterans had contact (to varying degrees) with well-known military figures include:

- serving in the same Navy Air Group as Joe Kennedy, Jr.
- meeting Colonel Robert L. Scott, the famous Flying Tiger of World War II.
- having Lieutenant John Glenn as a commanding officer.
- attending staff meetings with Major General Richard G. Stilwell.
- receiving the Bronze Star and Purple Heart from Admiral C. W. Nimitz.
- serving in the same fighter group as Captain Chuck Yeager.
- marching in review before General Douglas MacArthur during the celebration of Philippine independence.
- marching with Audie Murphy in the movie "To Hell and Back."

David M. Jordan

Age 14 – United States Army

I turned 15 years old while I was aboard a troopship bound for Guam. I had joined the U. S. Army on 9 January 1947 at age 14 by convincing my parents to sign papers attesting that I was 17. I used 13

After eight weeks of basic training ... I was on my way overseas.

December 1929 as my birth date, but I was born on 13 April 1932 in Tillman, Mississippi. After eight weeks of basic training at Fort Ord, California, I was on my way overseas.

After serving twenty months on Guam, I was transferred to Fort Bliss, Texas, in 1949, and assigned to the 502nd Antiaircraft Artillery Battalion. I was sent to Alaska in April 1950 and returned to Fort Bliss in 1952, where I was assigned to the radar school and trained for one year on the Nike/Ajax missile. From 1954 to 1956, I served at a missile site near Los Angeles, California.

I went to the Redstone Arsenal, Alabama, for training as a Nike maintenance supervisor and graduated from that course in December 1956. I wanted to apply for warrant officer, but I knew that it would be necessary to correct my age first because of the required background checks. I wrote to the Adjutant General and requested that my records be changed. I became three years younger in one day and made warrant officer in February 1957.

I left Redstone in September 1957 and was stationed in Europe until August 1961. I served at the Fifth Army Headquarters in Chicago, Illinois, and at Thule, Greenland. I returned to Redstone in 1965 and was assigned to Burlington, North Carolina, where the prime contractor for the Nike missile system, Western Electric, had its plant.

In 1967-68, I served with the Korean military assistance advisory group, then returned to Redstone in 1968 to work at the project office for the Hercules missile. After a year, I was assigned to Taiwan with the Republic of China military-advisory group.

While I was in Taiwan, I suffered a heart attack and was evacuated to the hospital at Fort Ord, California, and had a second attack in the hospital. I was medically retired from the Army on 25 May 1971 as a

CWO-4 after serving twenty-four years, four months, and seventeen days.

David Jordan returned to Burlington, North Carolina, determined to go back to school since his formal education had ended at the eighth grade. He completed high school and received three associate degrees from a community college. From 1982 until 1994, David and Patricia, his wife of forty-five years, owned and operated an alarm company. They installed and maintained burglary, fire, closed-circuit TV, and access-control systems. David and Patricia live in Burlington, North Carolina. They have three children and two grandchildren.

✓ **VUMS Note** ⇒ *Lessons learned.* Many veterans credited their success later in life to valuable lessons learned during their underage military service. The lessons mentioned most often have to do with discipline, teamwork, respect, order, and responsibility.

"It was a great education for a country kid," commented a former WAC about what she had learned. A Marine found out that "... you don't get something for nothing ... you have to work for it," a lesson which served him well all his life. One veteran described how he learned self-confidence when he wrote, "The Army taught me that I could hack it; that age, size, and to some extent, lack of education, couldn't stop me."

490

Billy J. Scott

Age 15 – United States Army

I was born on 3 April 1931 in Turnersville, Texas, a small farming community about forty miles west of Waco. Most of the boys I ran around with in high school were older than I, and some were in, or had been in the

> *After six trips across the Pacific Ocean, working seven days a week, I was about fed up with it.*

military. I became disillusioned with high school in the eleventh grade, and there were very few ways that a 15-year-old boy could make spending money at that time.

In January 1947, a buddy (who was also 15) and I decided to join the armed forces. We went to the U. S. Army recruiting office in Gatesville, the county seat, and asked them if we could join. We were told that we had to be 17 and have our parents' written consent. I took the paperwork home and talked my dad into signing that I was two years older than I actually was. At age 15, I was 5'11" and weighed 165 pounds, so I had no problem, once my dad signed the papers. We were shipped to Fort Ord, California, for basic training. We were issued more clothes than I had ever owned, plus a rifle, which I had always wanted but never owned. I loved it!

After basic, I was sent to Brooke Army Medical Services at Fort Sam Houston, Texas, to attend their hospital technician course. I enjoyed being at Fort Sam because it was near enough that I could sometimes hitchhike home while on pass. After I became a medical corpsman, I was sent to Fort Mason, California, where I was told to report to the U. S. Army Hospital Ship *Mercy*. The ship was a 700-bed floating hospital. About twelve doctors, twenty nurses, and forty or fifty enlisted medics were assigned to the ship.

We loaded the ship with Army troops at Fort Mason and transported them to Hawaii, Japan, Okinawa, Korea, and the

Philippines. At each port, we would load patients who were being evacuated from the different countries. At that time, there were no medical evacuation aircraft, and all infirm troops were brought back to the U. S. by hospital ships. When we arrived at Fort Mason in San Francisco, ambulances would transport the patients to Letterman Hospital. We also brought back a few Philippine war brides from Manila.

After six trips across the Pacific Ocean, working seven days a week, I was about fed up with it. I went to see the chaplain and asked him what would happen to me if I admitted my true age. He looked up the Army regulation concerning minority discharges and told me that as long as my service was honorable, they would give me an honorable discharge when we returned to the U. S. I had a clean record and had been promoted to private first class. I also had a copy of my birth certificate, which showed that I was 16.

After we docked in San Francisco, I was sent to Camp Stoneman, Near Pittsburg, California, for processing. I was discharged on 9 December 1947 after serving eleven months. I received mustering-out pay, travel pay back to my home of record, and leave pay, since I had not taken any leave.

I arrived home just before Christmas. Although it was mid-year, I enrolled as a junior in high school, a year behind my classmates with whom I had started the first grade. I went to the Veterans Administration and signed up for the GI Bill. I received $75.00 per month for going to high school. When school was out that summer, I applied for a job as a hospital technician. I was told that I wouldn't be able to get a hospital job without relocating, which I didn't want to do. I was 17 by that time, so I drew the 52-20 unemployment pay for the summer months. Twenty dollars per week was quite good for a country boy!

After graduating from high school in May 1949, I went to a vocational school for a few months under the GI Bill. Using my correct age, and with my Army discharge, I joined the U. S. Navy Reserve. A short time later, November 1949, I was talked into joining the U. S. Air Force. When I enlisted, the Air Force gave me one stripe for my prior service. I was assigned to a prior enlistee squadron at Lackland Air Force Base, Texas, for ten days of orientation, a clothing issue, and assignment to a technical school. Later, I attended a cryptographic technicians school and entered the communications career field, in which I remained for the next twenty-five years.

I served in Alaska, twice in Japan, Okinawa, Germany, Hawaii, Vietnam, and on extended TDY tours to Taiwan, Johnston Island, and Vietnam. In 1968-69, I served a full tour in Vietnam. I was assigned to a C-47 Aircraft Electronic Countermeasures Squadron.

I retired from the U. S. Air Force Security Service Command as a master sergeant on 1 May 1976 at Kelly Air Force Base, San Antonio, Texas, with over twenty-six years of service.

In retrospect, I don't believe that I would have accomplished what I did, had I not joined the Army when I was 15 years of age. That eleven months in the Army gave me a view of life that I would have never seen if I had stayed in the little town of Turnersville, Texas, population 78. I have never regretted my service to my country and flag.

Billy Scott was awarded the Bronze Star during his tour in Vietnam. Later, he earned two Air Force Commendation Medals. After retiring, he attended college for three years, earning two A.A. degrees. He worked in the logistics field at Kelly Air Force Base for eleven years, retiring in 1993. He has been active in several veterans organizations. Billy and his wife Virginia live in San Antonio, Texas. They have two daughters and four grandchildren.

Dennis G. Mounts

Age 15 – United States Army

As a young boy, I wanted to be in the military. I was living with my grandparents because my parents were divorced. My grandparents would not allow me to continue in school, so I decided to join the Army.

> "I still think you are underage, but I'm tired of messing with you ..."

In 1946, at the age of 14, I registered for the draft, stating that my age was 18. I tried to enlist in the Army a few months after receiving my 1-A classification. I was sent to Fort Hayes, Ohio, for a physical. The sergeant in charge asked me how old I was and I replied, "Eighteen!" He said BS, and that was it for the time being.

The next year (1947), I tried again to enlist in the Army and was sent again to Fort Hayes for a physical. Believe it or not, the same sergeant was still there. He asked me if I had been turned down for

military service in the past. I told him I was turned down the year before. He asked why and I said I didn't know. He looked up the record of my previous try and found that I was rejected because I was a minor. He then said, "I still think you are underage, but I'm tired of messing with you, so I'm going to let you go."

I was sent to Fort Bragg, North Carolina, in January 1947 for eight weeks of basic training, just one month before my sixteenth birthday. It didn't end there. When I had completed about six weeks of basic, my mother wrote to the commander of my company and told him I was only 16 years old. The captain called me in and informed me of the letter he had received, and asked how I felt about getting out of the Army. After he explained to me that the worst of basic was over, and if I got out then, I would be drafted in two years and would have to complete basic all over again. I told him that I would rather stay where I was. He said, "OK,

I am tearing up this letter from your mother, and as far as I am concerned, I never received it!" I stayed in the Army, completed my enlistment, and received an honorable discharge in September 1949 at 18½ years of age.

Two and one-half years after my discharge from the Army, I enlisted in the U. S. Air Force and was sent to Langley Air Force Base, Virginia, where I was assigned to the base commissary. I received my GED diploma while at Langley. In 1956, I was one of the first group of U. S. military personnel to be sent to Spain. I helped set up all the offices for the support forces assigned to the Madrid area. I was transferred from Spain to Beale Air Force Base, California, in 1959.

During my assignment at Beale, I completed nine Extension Course Institute courses and noncommissioned officer preparatory school, finishing in the top three of my class. From Beale AFB, I was sent to Goose Air Base in Labrador, and I was promoted to master sergeant while there. I returned to the States in 1967 and was stationed at Barksdale Air Force Base, Louisiana. A short time later, I was assigned to Headquarters, Second Air Force, as part of the staff-assistance team. My duties included monitoring all commissaries and exchanges in the Second Air Force. In August 1969, I was transferred to Anderson Air Force Base, Guam.

After nine months on Guam, I had completed twenty-one years of active duty, so I retired in 1970. I had my records corrected to show my true age after the regulation was changed to allowed time served as a minor to count toward military service.

Dennis Mounts received the Air Force Commendation Medal for meritorious service. After leaving the Air Force, he went to work for a military food broker, selling various major-brand groceries to commissaries and exchanges. During his fourteen years with one company, he was "Salesman of the Year" five times and "National Salesman of the Year" three times. He was inducted into the "Master's Club" or "Salesman's Hall of Fame." He worked in the same business for two years with another company. Then, in 1986, he decided to retire again and move from Texas to Tennessee. Dennis and Helen, his wife of forty-five years, live in Speedwell, Tennessee. They have four sons and eight grandchildren. Two sons served in Southeast Asia during the Vietnam war.

Merle E. Hyatt

Age 15 – United States Army

When I was 3 years old, my mother abandoned me. From then until I was 15 years old, I lived either in a foster home or a children's home. Of the seven foster homes that I lived in, all were good except

> *Within minutes after being sworn into the Army, I was on KP.*

the last one, which was not a happy place to be. I decided to run away.

I had lived on a farm most of my life and was experienced in general farm work and in milking, feeding, and caring for animals. When I left, I knew that I had to go someplace where I could find work. I had heard of two ranches, the PK Ranch in Wyoming and the King Ranch in south Texas. I knew that Wyoming was quite cold in the winter, so I picked Texas as my destination. I hoped to find work riding fence or herding and feeding cattle, but first I had to get there.

I had never been farther than fifty miles from Kansas City, Missouri, so I obtained some maps and started planning. My plan was to go to Salina, Kansas, then south to Fort Worth, Texas, and on to the King ranch. It didn't work out that way.

I left my foster home, a farm near Liberty, Missouri, on 10 January 1947 with a pack of Lucky Strike cigarettes and a $5.00 bill in my pocket. I was dressed in a suit and tie and wore an overcoat with a felt hat. The next morning, I was picked up by police at the Greyhound bus station in Salina, Kansas, and jailed for vagrancy. I was released thirty-six hours later and walked out of town on Highway 81. Meeting people along the way was an adventure in itself.

I arrived in Abilene, Texas, after dark. It was cold and I had to find a warm place to stay. I asked a fellow on the street if he could tell me where I could find a flop house. He told me not to go to a place like that, but to go to the police and they would take care of me. The police station was just down the block, and they took care of me in a way I didn't expect. An officer took me out to eat. They didn't put me in a cell, but they let me sleep on a bench that night. The next morning they took me to breakfast, gave me $3.00, and sent me on my way.

That evening, Friday, 17 January 1947, I was in Sonora, Texas. It was not yet dark, and since things had worked out so well at Abilene, I figured they would work out just as well in Sonora. I walked to the county courthouse looking for the police station. As I walked up the courthouse steps, an Army sergeant with a limp and a cane came out of the door. I asked him for directions to the police station. He told me the constable ran a gas station and he would take me there. It was cold, and the steps had ice on them, so I helped the sergeant down the steps. He asked me if I'd like to join the Army. I told him I wasn't old enough. He asked my age, and since I was going to be 16 in February, I told him 16. He asked me when my birthday was, and I told him February 20th. "Well," he said, "You'll be 17. I'll talk to you later."

We arrived at the constable's filling station, and I went in and told him that I needed a place to sleep that night. He jailed me for vagrancy and put me in a cell on the third floor of the courthouse. The cell had a window but no glass to keep out the cold, just three bars. There was a thin pad on a slab to sleep on and a single Army blanket for cover. The bathroom in the corner was a 2½-gallon galvanized bucket. The jailer, whose Mexican wife cooked for the prisoners, brought me my supper. I had never eaten Mexican food in my life. That night I kept warm by traveling between the bunk and the bucket.

On Saturday morning after breakfast, the jailer and the man I got to know as Sergeant Walker came to my cell. The sergeant again asked me if I'd like to join the Army. When I told him, again, that I wasn't old enough, he said that he thought he could get me in anyway. My cell was left unlocked for the rest of the weekend, and I was able to come and go as I pleased.

Monday morning, Sergeant Walker came for me, took me downstairs to his office, and told me I was to register for the draft. He left me in his office looking over some Army brochures while he went across the hall to the draft office. There he discussed the possibility of registering me. When he returned, he told me what to say and sent me over to register. From then on, my draft card served as my birth certificate.

I returned to Sergeant Walker's office, and he asked me what outfit I wanted to join. I told him the First Cavalry because I wanted to go to Tokyo, Japan. While he was filling out the papers, he told me that the last eleven people he had sent to Fort Sam Houston had failed either their physical or written exam. He said he liked his job and was counting on me to pass my examination.

At Fort Sam, those of us who had passed our exams sat in a room waiting. A lieutenant came in and said, "Gentlemen, you have passed your examinations. After lunch, return to this room and I'll swear you in." Just then a cook came in and whispered in the lieutenant's ear. The lieutenant turned to us and said, "Gentlemen, raise your right hands and repeat after me ..." I was now in the Army. The lieutenant then picked up the roster and said, "Hyatt." Within minutes after being sworn into the Army, I was on KP. This occurred on 22 January 1947, twelve days after I had run away.

After basic training at Fort Lewis, Washington, I was sent to Japan, arriving there in June 1947. I was a member of Fox Troop, 8th Regiment, 1st Cavalry Division. We were quartered in Tokyo where we guarded the Meiji Shrine, the main Shinto shrine. Our job was to keep dogs, GIs, and vehicles out of the shrine grounds.

In October 1948, I applied for a morale leave to go home to meet my mother. At that time, I didn't know that she had abandoned me, and I had spent years looking for her. When I found her, I learned that I had a sister. I had to furnish a copy of my birth certificate and some letters from my aunts to get leave. In going through the paperwork, someone at headquarters with sharp eyes noticed that I was still underage, which put an end to my Army service.

I sailed for home in late November and received a general discharge under honorable conditions on 9 December 1948, after one year, ten months and twenty-three days in the Army. The reason for discharge was given as "minority."

My eighteenth birthday was 20 February 1949, and on 5 May 1949, I enlisted in the Air Force. I was an air-traffic controller for eleven years. After a year in electronics school, I was assigned to maintain and repair aviation navigation facilities. I retired from the Air Force on 1 August 1967, after twenty years of service.

Merle Hyatt worked for the Federal Aviation Administration for thirteen and one-half years after retiring from the Air Force. His main job was to brief pilots on weather conditions and to assist them in flight planning. He also became a pilot and a HAM radio operator. He is listed in the HAM Radio Operator's Directory as KDODK. Merle and his wife Clara LaVon live in Springfield, Missouri. They have five daughters, nine grandchildren, and three great-grandchildren.

Jack H. Brown

Age 15 – United States Army

I was born in the mining town of Galena, Kansas, on 21 July 1931, the youngest of five children. My father, who worked in the lead and zinc mines, died of miner's tuberculosis when I was 7 years old. This

> ... *after a few more beers, I found myself reenlisting in the Army.*

was during the Depression era, and times were bad. My mother worked at any job she could find to provide for us kids. We were also on relief, as were most people.

When I was 13 years old, I was the last child at home. My sister and her family lived in Bremerton, Washington. She urged my mother and me to move to Bremerton where Mom could work in the Navy Yard. So off we went, and Mom did go to work at the Navy Yard.

I went to high school for a year and a half in Bremerton but quit when I was in the tenth grade. I didn't care much for school, and I certainly wasn't the best student. A friend of mine and I decided to lie about our ages and join the Army. This was a patriotic decision on my part. Two of my brothers had served in the Army during World War II, one in Italy and the other in the South Pacific. Also, I didn't want to be a burden on my mother. I went to the recruiting office and got the necessary papers. Mom had to sign that I was 17. It nearly broke her heart to do it, but she did. The recruiters didn't even question my age. They had a quota to fill.

I was sworn into the Army on 25 February 1947 at the age of 15. I was sent to Fort Lawton in Seattle for processing. At this time, I made out an allotment for my mother. I was sent to Fort Lewis, Washington, for basic training. In spite of my age, I handled basic without any problems. I was a pretty good-sized young man and in good physical shape. I had boxed some in high school and also at Fort

Lewis. One of my instructors was impressed and told me that he might be able to get me stationed there in special services. I didn't go for it, so after basic training, I was sent to Camp Kilmer, New Jersey, for processing before being sent overseas to Germany. Boy, what a long trip – 13 days – and I was seasick nearly all the way across the Atlantic.

I was assigned to several different units in the U. S. Zone in Germany for four months and then was transferred to Berlin. I was with the 759th Military Police Battalion before, during, and after the Berlin Airlift. There were times when I didn't think we had much of a future if the Russians really got serious because there were not many U. S. troops there. We had one battalion of the 1st Infantry Division, some Air Force, and a few constabulary and engineering personnel.

During my service in Berlin, my rank went up and down, but there were no court-martials. I left there in December 1949 for the States and was discharged at Fort Dix, New Jersey, on 16 December 1949.

I went back to Seattle to see my mom. I think she may have been a little proud of me. I couldn't find work in the Seattle area, so I went to Eugene, Oregon, where my brother was. I couldn't find work there either, but I was able to draw 52-20 ($20.00 per week for fifty-two weeks). While at the employment office, I was asked if I was registered for the draft. I wasn't, so I went down and registered.

I became acquainted with a gentleman in a bar, and he bought me several beers on different occasions, although I was still too young to be legally in a bar. This gentleman turned out to be an Army recruiter, so after a few more beers, I found myself reenlisting in the Army. I was sworn in again on 22 May 1950, and that same day, I was on a bus going to Fort Ord, California, for two weeks' refresher training. I was then assigned to the 701st Military Police Battalion at the Presidio in San Francisco.

At the time, I didn't have any idea there was trouble brewing in Korea. Shortly after the war broke out, I found that the "Truman year" had been added to my three-year enlistment. However, I did not go to Korea. I volunteered to go several different times and was told that my previous overseas duty would keep me from going over. I found that hard to believe. Anyway, I was stationed in the Sixth Army area for the duration. During this time, I completed my GED and also received a notice from my draft board.

I was discharged at Fort MacArthur, San Pedro, California, on 22 May 1953. Somebody goofed; I didn't have to do "Harry's year," but it's on my discharge that I did. I was a staff sergeant when I was discharged. No ups and downs this time. I even got the Good Conduct Medal. Later, I joined the Army Reserves.

I am proud of my military service and am not sorry that I lied about my age to get in the Army. I lied to get in, not to stay out. There were times when I was afraid that my age would be discovered, but no one ever questioned me. I served a total of twelve years in the regular Army and the Reserves.

Jack Brown stayed in California after his second discharge from the Army, served an apprenticeship as a machinist, and later had his own machine shop. He left California in 1970 and moved to Joplin, Missouri, seven miles from his hometown of Galena, Kansas. He was a supervisor of tooling for Sperry Vickers Hydraulic Pump Manufacturing Company until they closed the plant in 1987. He took early retirement at that time. Jack and his wife Nancy live in Grove, Oklahoma. They have a combined family of nine children (Jack's daughter, his three adopted daughters, and Nancy's five sons) and a total of nine grandchildren. Jack is the Oklahoma State Commander of the Veterans of Underage Military Service.

Winston L. "Mac" McGinnis

Age 16 – United States Army Air Forces

I was born in Olive Hill, Kentucky, on 15 July 1930, one of twelve children. When I was very young, my parents moved from Kentucky to Michigan to improve their living conditions. Four of my older brothers joined the military

> *I was given an invitation to her coronation.*

during World War II, and I was envious of their sharp uniforms. I "borrowed" a coat from one brother so I could go to town and impress the girls. I really thought I was hot stuff. Wearing that coat got me to thinking that although I was only 16, I could wear a uniform legally, so I went to the recruiting station and enlisted. I told them that I was 18 years old, and they never asked me to show proof. I was sworn in on 17 April 1947, just five months before the U. S. Army Air Forces became the U. S. Air Force.

After basic training at Lackland Air Force Base, Texas, I was sent to Langley Field, Virginia, for communications training. From there I went to Scullthorpe Air Force Base in England. While I was at Scullthorpe, a tidal wave hit the beach area without advance warning. The town of Hunstation, which was right on the beach, suffered a great deal of damage and loss of life. Several hundred people died, including some U. S. Air Force families. I was assigned to a detail to help locate survivors and clean up the area. It was a real tragedy. Three days after the tidal wave, Princess Elizabeth, the future Queen of England, came to look over the destruction and to talk to the people. She shook hands

with all of us and thanked us. I was given an invitation to her coronation, and it was a thrill to see history being made.

After returning to the States, I served at Air Force bases in Texas, Virginia, Georgia, and Oklahoma. In 1962, I was sent to Guam where I worked primarily as a mechanic on aircraft going to Vietnam. It was hard work, and the frequent rains made life miserable. On 9 January 1965, while responding to an alert, I was in a jeep accident that left me a paraplegic. I was air-evacuated back to the air base where I had started my career, Lackland Air Force Base, Texas. I spent six months there, and then I was sent to the Veterans Hospital in Memphis, Tennessee. While there, Air Force officials came to the hospital and presented me with my twenty-year retirement papers.

Since my retirement, I have found that a lot of adjustments had to be made to living in a wheelchair. I spent a lot of time in VA hospitals for the first year or two. I tried living in Mexico for a time, then returned to the Long Beach, California, VA Hospital. There I met an "angel of mercy," a volunteer who eventually married me and has helped me live a very normal life.

The Veterans Administration provided me with training in jewelry-making and repair. I have continued with that vocation for years, primarily making bolos and belt buckles for various veteran and fraternal organizations. I also make women's jewelry.

Mac McGinnis has received many awards for volunteer work in Veterans Administration hospitals, as well as work with the Disabled American Veterans and the Paralyzed Veterans of America. He has been very active in "Accessibility for the Handicapped" projects and spends a lot of time trying to make places accessible to the wheelchair-bound and anyone with a mobility problem. One of his most treasured awards was from a grade-school class in California. After he spoke to them about veterans and about living in a wheelchair, they presented him with a certificate that reads, "A century from now it won't matter how large your bank account was, the type of house you lived in, or what kind of car you drove. But the world may be different because you were important in the life of a boy or girl at Park View School." Mac and his wife Lelia lived in Anaheim, California, for ten years and Apple Valley, California, for thirteen years. In 1990, they moved to Melbourne, Arkansas, where they now reside. Mac and Lelia have a combined family of twelve children (including three who were adopted), twenty-five grandchildren, and twelve great-grandchildren. Mac is the Arkansas State Commander of the Veterans of Underage Military service, and Lelia is the National President of the VUMS Auxiliary.

Joseph W. "Bill" Snodgrass

Age 15 – Indiana State Guard
Age 16 – United States Army Air Forces

My early years were spent on a farm in Tennessee. My father died when I was eight years old and we moved to Arkansas to be near my mother's people. We lived in a small house with my grandparents for two years

> **We were literally "up Ship Creek without a paddle."**

before my mother could afford to rent a house where she could raise my brother Dick and me. The rent was $6.00 per month, but in 1940 my mother was making only $9.00 per week repairing clothes in a dry-cleaning establishment. By 1944, she was making $25.00 per week. During those times, we wore cardboard shoes and ate cereal-filled bologna. In spite of hard times, my mother kept us together.

In the spring of 1944, Mother thought she could make more money for us, and at the same time, help with the war effort by working in a defense plant. We sold our furniture and household goods and moved to Evansville, Indiana. I was born in Evansville, but we had moved to the South when I was eighteen months old.

We arrived in Evansville about the first of June 1944 and didn't have a place to stay. While the troops were landing in Normandy on D-Day, we were living and sleeping on park benches on the West Side Library lawn. We bought a homemade trailer, parked it on squatter land near Pigeon Creek, and lived there for some time. In winter, we would gather coal from alongside the Illinois Central Railroad tracks and burn it in a little stove.

Due to health problems, Mother didn't get into defense work right away, so she was back to sewing in a dry-cleaning shop and cooking in greasy-spoon restaurants. Just before V-J Day, she was hired by Koch Steel Company. Times were tough, but never once did we want to live in another country, never once did we feel unpatriotic, and we would always get a lump in our throats when we saw the American flag go by.

I was a street kid in those days. My mother didn't have time to ride herd on me and my little brother. She had her hands full just putting food on the table and keeping us in school. I liked a good, clean fight and enjoyed putting bullies in their place.

I wanted to be in the service, but I couldn't figure out how to get in at my age. Two months after my fifteenth birthday, I talked my mother into signing that I was 17 years old so that I could join the Indiana State Guard. Early in 1947, the State Guard was to be taken over by the National Guard. We were given honorable discharges with the option of joining the National Guard, but I had another idea. I used my State Guard records to prove that I was 18, although I was only 16, and joined the U. S. Army Air Forces. By joining, I could serve my country, send my mother an allotment, help pay my brother's school expenses, and impress my girl by being in uniform. Later, she told me she would have been more impressed if I had stayed home and courted her.

I was sworn into the Army Air Forces on 3 June 1947 and sent to the indoctrination training center near San Antonio, Texas. Within a month, the facility was renamed Lackland Air Force Base, and on 18 September 1947, the U. S. Army Air Forces became the U. S. Air Force.

My street-kid attitude and my penchant for putting bullies in their place did not serve me well during basic training. It was only natural that I considered the drill instructors bullies. I didn't like it when they shouted in my face, so I would mouth off to them. As a result, I became well acquainted with the "Burma Road," an area out near the perimeter of the base that was full of rocks and prickly-pear cactus. After a hard full day of basic training, and after evening chow, the other miscreants and I would be forced to run the "Burma Road" with full packs. I ran the course several times before I learned to keep my mouth shut.

While in basic training, I made the cover of *Life* magazine — well, I and about a thousand other guys. This was just after the Air Force became a separate service, and *Life* did a story on the new organization. Several basic training squadrons were assembled on a physical training field. We formed a large round Air Force patch. Dark green areas were made by some of us in fatigues and helmet liners. The white area was made by bareheaded guys in white T-shirts. I was only a minute speck somewhere, but at least I can say that I was on the cover of *Life* magazine.

After completing basic training, I attended airplane and engine mechanics school and B-29 specialist training at Keesler Air Force Base, Biloxi, Mississippi, and aircraft electrical technical training at Chanute Field, Rantoul, Illinois. I was transferred to Hamilton Air Force Base, San Rafael, California, then in late September 1948, I was assigned to Elmendorf Air Force Base, Anchorage, Alaska, where I was assigned to the 57th Air Group Maintenance Squadron, and later, the 57th Headquarters and Headquarters Squadron.

In basic training, I had not qualified with the pistol, nor the 45-caliber "grease gun," nor the M-1 carbine. But I did well in Alaska when I shot the M-1 rifle for qualification. My first shot was a "Maggie's drawers." I missed the target completely and got the red flag. I then adjusted my sights and put all the remaining shots in the bulls-eye at 200 yards.

On a long weekend, a friend and I decided to go out towards the beautiful Alaska mountains and camp in the woods. We checked out a rifle, some C-rations and our tent halves, and set out. After our legs would carry us no further, we pitched camp, built a fire, and had our supper. We had drinking water in our canteens, but not enough to wash our mess kits. We had not camped near a stream, so we followed the sound of running water and in this way we found Ship Creek. We washed our mess kits, filled our canteens, and just enjoyed our surroundings. It was close to dusk when we started back to our tent, but our tent didn't make noise like the stream, and we hadn't used a compass when we set out looking for water. There were bears in the woods and we were lost — at least we had lost our camp. We were literally "up Ship Creek without a paddle." We decided to spend the night in an old prospector's cabin. We gathered some wood and started a fire on the dirt floor of the cabin. During the night, we ran out of firewood but we were afraid to go outside because a herd of moose had bedded down around the cabin. We ended up tearing the door off its hinges and burning it.

I returned to the "Lower Forty-Eight" and was discharged at Fort Lawton, Seattle, Washington, on 24 May 1950.

Bill Snodgrass received his GED from the state of Illinois in the 1960s. He took some college classes and also earned a private pilot's license. He enjoyed flying until he could no longer pass a medical exam. Bill worked for Chrysler Corporation for six years, then moved to Peoria, Illinois, and worked as a diesel-engine inspector for Caterpillar Tractor Company for over thirty years, retiring in 1989 just before reaching the age of 58. Bill and Betty, his wife of nearly forty-six years, live in Chillicothe, Illinois. Bill claims that he and Betty had a selector switch because they alternated their five children, boy-girl-boy-girl-boy. They also have nine grandchildren and two great-grandchildren. One son served ten years in the Navy, and a grandson served four years in the Army. As yet, none of the great-grandchildren have "stepped-off on the left foot" and joined the military.

√ **VUMS Note** ⇒ *The Battle of the Bulge.* The mid-December 1944 attack by three German field armies against the Allied forces in Belgium was officially named the Battle of Ardennes, but to the GIs who fought there, it was the Battle of the Bulge. This battle was second only to the Meuse-Argonne of World War I in terms of duration, ferocity, and cost in lives. Five underage veterans tell about participating in the Battle of the Bulge in their stories. One who was with the 101st Airborne Division at Bastogne observed, "We thought Normandy and Holland were bad, but it was here in Bastogne and in nearby towns that we were not only fighting the Germans but also the elements."

Arthur W. Buckley

Age 13 – United States Army

I was 13 years old, weighed 112 pounds, and was 5-feet 9-inches tall when I completed the seventh grade at San Fernando Junior High School in San Fernando, California. Soon after

> *The first two or three days were a "piece of cake," ... then all hell broke loose.*

school was out, a 17-year-old friend suggested that we join the Army. My friend and I went to the recruiting office in San Fernando to enlist. While we were planning this escapade, he had told me that the courthouse in Renton, Washington, had no records prior to 1939. So, when I filled out the enlistment papers I put Renton, Washington, as my place of birth. I used a sister's birthday (18 April) and a brother's birth year (1929). Therefore my records showed, "Born Renton Wash 18 April 1929." Actually, I was born in North Hollywood, California, on 22 July 1933. When we took the enlistment examination, I passed, but my 17-year-old friend failed.

I asked my mother to sign my enlistment papers. I told her that I would run away and join the Army if she didn't sign. I think that when she signed, she was sure they wouldn't take me. After I was in, I think she was afraid she would go to jail if it were discovered that she had lied for me.

I was sworn into the Army on 17 June 1947 and sent to Fort MacArthur in San Pedro, California, for my physical, and then I was put on a train for Fort Ord, California. I remember quite well how impressed I was when I was issued all of my clothing and equipment. In all of my life, I had had only one new pair of shoes, and I don't remember ever having any new clothing. Now, here in Uncle Sam's Army, I was rich beyond belief. I had two pairs of combat boots, a pair of dress shoes, two winter uniforms, seven pairs of khaki summer uniforms, underwear, socks, hats, a belt, etc. I was overwhelmed, to say the least. In addition, I had my own M-1 rifle and a set of field gear. For a kid who had just turned 14, I was in heaven! On top of all these riches, they were going to pay me $75.00 per month, good grief! I made out a Q allowance for my mother. They took about $30.00 per month out of my pay, and the government added some to that, so she received between $90.00 and $100.00 per month for her and the four or five of her eight children still at home.

I took basic training with Company H, 12th Infantry Regiment, 4th Infantry Division. I don't remember that it was particularly difficult, except for the long days. I put in for parachute training while I was in basic. My weight was now up to 128 pounds, but I had to get a medical waiver because the minimum weight was 132 pounds at that time. I went to Fort Benning, Georgia, for jump school, and other than the physical training being quite hard, I found it very exciting. I did my five jumps and graduated. I expected to be sent to either the 82nd Airborne Division or the 11th Airborne Division, which was in Japan at that time. To my dismay, there were no openings in either unit. I was sent to the 501st Engineer Construction Group on Guam.

We went from San Francisco to Guam by troopship. I was lucky to be assigned guard duty on the way over, so I could sleep on deck most of the time. I think that is what helped me avoid becoming seasick. I was taught to drive (not really operate) a bulldozer while in the 501st Engineers. I was on Guam for six or seven months before I could finally get a transfer to the 11th Airborne in Japan.

I flew from Guam to Japan in early 1948. After a short stint at the 4th Replacement Depot near Yokohama, I was assigned to B Battery of the 674th Parachute Field Artillery Battalion stationed on northern Honshu, near Sendai. I loved being in the Airborne in Japan, and being an occupation soldier was great duty. We jumped twice a month and got a lot of practice with the 75mm pack-howitzers and 105s.

When the Airborne was reposted back to Fort Campbell, Kentucky, at the end of 1948, I transferred to the 1st Cavalry Division at Camp Drake, near Tokyo. I was assigned to B Troop, 5th Cavalry Regiment, at Camp McGill, near Yokuska. Again, I loved the Army life. I trained as an infantryman and obtained a light weapon infantry MOS. The duty was good, and the off-duty was fantastic! We trained a lot at Camp McNair, near Mt. Fujiyama, and did a lot of ceremonial stuff, including a Fourth of July parade for General MacArthur on the grounds of the Imperial Palace in Tokyo.

I returned to the States at the end of 1949 and was assigned to the post signal unit at Camp Stoneman, California, for a time. I decided to take a short discharge, then reenlist to go back to Japan. I was discharged on 8 February 1950, reenlisted on 9 February 1950, and was sent to Fort Ord for a few weeks of refresher training. My next assignment was to Company D, 76th Engineer Construction Battalion, at Naha, Okinawa. We built housing at Kadena Air Force Base.

When the Korean War started in June, our unit was alerted for shipment to Pusan, Korea, and arrived there towards the end of July 1950. We built a lot of roads and depots around Pusan. However, I wanted to get back to the infantry. My request for transfer was not approved, so I went AWOL with a couple of buddies and hitchhiked to the front, which at that time was not far away, just up near Masan. We were warmly received by what was left of the 29th Infantry Regiment, which had came from Okinawa a few weeks earlier. The unit was not at all bothered by our AWOL status. They were down to about sixty men to a company. We were integrated into B Company, 1st Battalion, 29th Infantry. By some Army magic, B Company became Company K of the 35th Infantry Regiment of the 25th (Tropic Lightning) Division a week later.

My first fight was very traumatic! Until then, I and many others had what I call the "Audie Murphy Syndrome." We wanted to be heros, but had no real idea what combat was all about. I found out at about 2:00 one morning when our unit was attacked. In a very short time, the thought of being a rear-echelon trooper looked quite attractive. In any case, our unit fought many actions throughout the length of Korea. We thought that the war was about over in November 1950 when we started the final push toward the Yalu River after Thanksgiving. The first two or three days were a piece of cake, with little or no resistance, then all hell broke loose. We were savagely attacked by the Chinese in the early morning (about 2:00 a.m.) of 1 December. We cleaned their plow! We had only two or three casualties, but we killed a couple of hundred Chinese in front of our company position. I was platoon sergeant of the 2nd platoon, a sergeant first class, and an "old man" at age 17.

We were told that our entire regiment had a similar experience that night. We were also told that our regiment was pulling back to consolidate the line. The 2nd Division was getting the crap kicked out of them at Kunu-ri, and the Chinese People's Army was raising hell all over Korea. Both the 8th Army and the X Corps were pulling back.

I got hit by shrapnel for the second time on 3 December and was evacuated to the 8th Station Hospital in Kobe, Japan. By the time I got back to the unit in January, the Division was back near Seoul. General Walker had been killed, and General Ridgeway had taken command of the 8th Army. Only twenty-five of my company were still present and accounted for. My platoon received about twenty replacements and a new platoon leader. He was our fourth in four months. Around April, there was a lot of talk about a rotation system that would allow us folks with lots of combat time a chance to go back to Pusan, or even back to the States. I was one of those selected. When I left King Company, only three men, other than myself, were left from the time I joined them in August.

In June 1951, I was rotated back to the States and assigned to Company D, Shore Battalion of the 369 Engineer Amphibious Support Regiment, at Fort Flagler, Washington. While we were with that unit, we joined with the U. S. Marines on some landing exercises near Camp Pendleton, California. I went to Ranger school and helped build Camp Desert Rock, near Las Vegas, Nevada. We participated in three atomic bomb tests during the six months we were in Nevada.

By this time, I was tired of duty in the States, so I asked for a transfer to an infantry unit in Germany. I was initially assigned to Headquarters and Headquarters Company, 118th Combat Engineer Battalion, 43rd Infantry Division, in Munich. We were constantly on maneuvers somewhere. Building various types of bridges across rivers and streams in the German winter was a real pain in the ass.

I was also getting tired of engineering. I considered myself an infantryman. I was able to transfer to the Division Honor Guard Platoon at Flak Kaserne in Augsberg, but after one year there, I had to transfer back to the engineer battalion. The engineer MOS that I obtained way back on Guam kept coming back to haunt me. They wouldn't let me get back to the infantry, so I decided to get out of the Army.

I was discharged from the Army on 14 May 1954, about two months prior to my twenty-first birthday. I had served six years, ten months, and twenty-one days.

I don't begrudge being raised during the Depression, nor being poor. I would not change for anything having joined the Army when I did.

I have great memories of my life in the service. If I were king, I would mandate military service for all high school boys prior to their entering college or a career.

Art Buckley earned the Combat Infantryman Badge and was awarded the Silver Star, the Bronze Star, and three Purple Hearts. He wore parachute wings and attended Ranger school. After leaving the Army, he used the GI Bill to complete his high school diploma at a junior college, then earned a B.S. in engineering. Later, he earned an L.L.B. Although he enjoyed the law more than engineering, he never practiced law. Art has worked for an American company in Australia for the past seventeen years. He plans to work there for two more years, then retire to Nevada or Wyoming. Art and his wife Elizabeth live in Alice Springs, Australia. He has three children.

√ **VUMS Note** ⇒ *The Purple Heart.* The Purple Heart is the oldest military decoration awarded to personnel of the armed forces of the United States. The medal, stemming directly from General George Washington's Badge of Military Merit, is in the shape of a heart with a profile of Washington on it. The only way the medal is earned is by being wounded as a direct result of enemy action. Thirty-six of the contributors to this book earned the Purple Heart: twenty-five received it once; five received it twice; three were wounded three times and received three medals; one received five medals for his five wounds; and one received six medals, three for wounds sustained during World War II, and three that were sustained during the Korean War.

Ben L. Huddleston

Age 15 – United States Army

I was born in West Plains, Missouri, on 29 October 1931. My mother passed away when I was quite young, and that was the end of a real home life for me. I went to Kansas City, Missouri, to live with my sister, and what a change of life style that was!

> *Going into the Army seemed the wise thing to do.*

Shortly after I arrived in Kansas City, I went to a self-service supermarket near where my sister and I lived. When I entered the store, the first thing that caught my eye was the turnstile. I had never seen one before. Not knowing what to do and not wanting to make a mistake, I paused, then *crawled* under the chain instead of going through the "thing" with all kind of prongs on it.

Before leaving West Plains at the age of 12, I went to a recruiting office intending to enlist in the Army. The recruiting sergeant turned out to be my aunt's boyfriend, so that didn't work out.

I worked on farms for my room and board in the Kansas City area, but I wasn't satisfied. Going into the Army seemed the wise thing to do. I would get free food, clothes, and shelter. My sister and I went to an Army recruiting office in Lexington, Missouri. I told the recruiter that I was 17 years old, and my sister signed my enlistment papers as my legal guardian. I was 15 years old and weighed 112 pounds. I was sworn into the Army on 21 July 1947 at Fort Riley, Kansas, and from there I went to Fort Knox, Kentucky, for basic training.

Life was getting more exciting all the time, and during basic training, I thought that it would be even more exciting if I went Airborne although I had never seen an airplane on the ground. When I showed interest in joining the Airborne, the recruiters laughed at me because I was so small. However, they sent me to Fort Benning,

Georgia, with a group of young men that they thought were much more suitable for the Airborne than I was. I think they thought it was a joke to send me.

At Fort Benning, I became friends with a combat veteran by the name of James Howe. Jim took me under his wing and protected me until I won my first fight, then he decided that I could take care of myself. The morning that we were to take physical examinations for jump training, the cooks fed me all the milk and bananas that I could handle. During the physical, I weighed in at 119 pounds. My friend Jim looked at the papers and said, "Huddleston, you have got to weigh 132 pounds to pass — let's fix it." Jim changed a "1" to a "3" on the papers, and I instantly weighed 139 pounds.

Jump school was rough, and many men were dropping out. Jim counseled me to consider dropping out because he thought I might get hurt. He convinced me to go see a first lieutenant and tell him that I was underage. I considered it for awhile and decided he was right. I went to the lieutenant, told him I had just turned 16, and asked him if my sister would get in trouble for signing my papers. He replied, "Boy, she would be in a heap of trouble!" So I went back to my company. I saw the lieutenant about a year later, and he said that he wasn't about to let me quit because I was showing up the bigger, stronger men who were dropping out. Over 300 men started jump training with the company, but only about 130 of us finished.

After I completed parachute and glider training in 1948, I was sent to Japan and was assigned to the 11th Airborne Division. I came back to the States in 1949 when the 11th Airborne was brought back to Fort Campbell, Kentucky. It was there that I met the girl who would become my wife.

I was discharged from the Army at Fort Campbell in June 1950.

Ben Huddleston began driving trucks soon after his discharge from the Army. A career truck driver, he was active in the Teamsters Union. He retired from the trucking business in 1992. Ben and Mildred, his wife of forty-six years, have been active in the ministry, serving in several posts, including that of pastor. They live in Marionville, Missouri, and have two children, four grandchildren, and three great-grandchildren.

Leo E. Kibble

Age 16 – United States Navy

I was born in a small farming community in northwest Pennsylvania on 5 March 1931. I was one of five siblings, two sisters and two brothers. We were a very close family, blessed with wonderful parents.

Would I do it all over again? You bet I would!

When I was a teenager, and when my chores were done, I could often be found on warm summer days lying in a lush, green meadow or along a babbling brook looking at the beautiful blue sky and an occasional white fluffy cumulus cloud passing by. My thoughts always centered on faraway countries that I had either read or heard about. Thus my quest began, and in 1947 at age 16, I ran away from home and enlisted in the Navy, looking forward to sailing the high seas.

My dream was short-lived, however, and after two months, I was called to headquarters, questioned as to my exact age, given an honorable discharge, and encouraged to reenlist when I became of age. Sadly, my dreams were put on hold, and I returned home.

In 1950, when I was 19, the Korean War had started, and I enlisted in the Army. After basic training, I was sent to Korea, arriving there in March 1951. I was assigned to the 3rd Infantry Division. In July of that year, much to our surprise, my eldest brother and I met in Chorwon Valley. He was assigned to the 5th Regimental Combat Team, 24th Infantry Division.

After I returned from Korea and spent some time at home, I reported to my new assignment at Fort Banks, Massachusetts. There I immediately signed a waiver requesting to return to Korea. This request was denied, as were two more. The fourth request was granted, and once again, I was off to the "The Land of the Morning Calm." I arrived on Christmas Eve 1952 and was assigned to Company B, 461st Infantry Battalion, 8th U. S. Army, where I served as a platoon sergeant until September 1953.

In April of 1953, lo and behold, I met my youngest brother in the Kumwha Valley. He was in the 2nd Infantry Division. All three of us brothers were awarded the coveted Combat Infantryman Badge, and we will always give credit to our dear mother's prayers for our safe return home.

Following my discharge from the Army, I enlisted in the Air Force and spent a year in Long Island, New York, where I met my "pot of gold" and married her. After three years in Japan and four and a half years in North Dakota, I was discharged in 1963 because of a disability, thus ending the dreams of my childhood days.

Now, in my senior years, I can still see that beautiful blue sky and an occasional cumulus cloud and relive those memories of years long ago, as my precious "pot of gold" sits by my side.

Would I do it all over again? You bet I would!

Leo Kibble served in the U. S. Navy, the U. S. Army, and the U. S. Air Force. He earned the Combat Infantryman Badge and five bronze battle stars during his two tours of duty with the Army in Korea. After leaving the Air Force because of a service-connected disability, he worked in the plumbing and heating supply business until retiring in 1986. He and Anna, his wife of 40 years, live in Smethport, Pennsylvania. They have four children and five grandchildren (with the potential for more).

Billie R. "Bill" Burns

Age 16 – United States Army

I was born at the beginning of the Depression, on 28 April 1931, the youngest of ten children. My parents were subsistence farmers in White County, Arkansas. Long hours of chopping cotton, hauling hay, and performing a myriad of

> *"You here for a discharge too? You a quitter?"*

other chores on the farm during the Depression of the 1930s convinced me that I should seek another occupation. This, and observing the soldiers of World War II, were probably the determining factors that influenced my entering the Army.

On 12 August 1947, at age 16, I dropped out of high school and joined the Army. I do not recall the exact details, but I do remember obtaining a false birth certificate. I knew my parents would not lie to

help me join the Army, so I requested a birth certificate using a birthday of 28 April *1929* and the name *Billy Ray* Burns, instead of *1931* and *Billie Rex* Burns. The Arkansas Health Department informed me I had no birth certificate and gave me a form to request one. It was necessary to complete the form and have it notarized. If I recall correctly, I forged my mother's name and asked a neighbor lady, a Justice of the Peace, to notarize the document, and she obliged. In hindsight, I think she knew the

document was a forgery and simply conspired to help me. In any event, I obtained a false birth certificate that became my ticket to the Army at age 16.

I had wanted to join the infantry and become a first sergeant, but somehow the recruiting personnel talked me into entering the Army Air Corps. I was shipped by troop train from Little Rock to Lackland Air Force Base in San Antonio, Texas, for basic training. While I was in training, an older brother who had served in the Coast Guard during World War II wrote my commander and informed him that I was a minor. He told them to discharge me so I could finish high school.

I first learned about the letter when I was required to report to the orderly room. Having never done so, I had to undergo instruction on how to report to an officer. When the sergeant was satisfied that I was prepared, he had me report to a lieutenant who promptly gave me a dressing down and told me to report to the separation center. At this point, I was depressed and trying to determine how I would explain this escapade to all my buddies and avoid embarrassment. As subsequent events would show, luck was with me.

Eligibility for the World War II GI Bill ended the last day of July 1947. Individuals entering the Army during a short period after 1 July 1947 were afforded an opportunity to be discharged if they signed a statement indicating they *thought* they would be entitled to benefits under the GI Bill. Many dissatisfied trainees took advantage of this provision. When I reported to the separation center, there was a line of trainees being processed for discharge because they *thought* they would be eligible for the GI Bill. They were being called quitters and other unprintable names by the cadre processing them. I was directed to a line and my interrogation began: "You here for a discharge, too? You a quitter?" When I stated that I did not want a discharge, a sergeant had me repeat it. I explained that a lieutenant had instructed me to report to the center, and that I had not requested a discharge. After chewing me out, probably thinking I was goofing off, he told me to return to my training platoon. I happily complied.

I don't know what happened to the letter or how it was overlooked during the remainder of basic training. After completing training, I was shipped to Castle Field, California, by troop train. The trip required three or four days from Texas to California and was an adventure for me, a 16-year-old. We stole enough watermelons for the entire trip by forming a daisy chain while we were sidetracked in a loading yard someplace in Texas. In Bakersfield, California, we stopped and attended a high school football game. Before the train pulled out, there were some long good-bys with the girls at the station.

The letter regarding my minority status eventually caught up with me again at Castle Field. I was called into the orderly room and informed by the adjutant that they would have to discharge me for fraudulent enlistment. By this time, I had a little more confidence and asked the officer to help me remain in the service. He called me to his office later and asked if I wanted to go to Germany. He had to fill a quota. He told me to take a 30-day delay en route and that he would hold the letter for awhile. By the time I arrived in Germany, I would be 17. I jumped at the suggestion and was issued a bus ticket to New Jersey. After a visit with my family, I reported to Camp Kilmer, New Jersey. My 17th birthday was on a ship somewhere in the Atlantic.

In Germany, I was assigned to the 1196th Military Police Company at Erding. From there, I was assigned to a remote site with a Polish Guard Company, later to become a German Industrial Police Company. I was in charge of the guard dog unit. In late 1948, there was a request for volunteers for the Airborne. I still thought about the infantry, so I volunteered. After acceptance, I was assigned to Fort Benning, Georgia, and completed Airborne training on 4 March 1949.

After jump school, I was assigned to the 325th Airborne Infantry at Fort Bragg, North Carolina. In 1950, I talked with a personnel officer about my fraudulent enlistment. He informed me that Congress had passed a law, and service as a minor was no longer considered bad time. I obtained a true birth certificate and submitted a request for a correction of my records. Subsequently, I was promoted to NCO rank, attended officer candidate school, and received a commission.

After serving in the Korean War, Vietnam, two tours in Germany, and several posts in the U. S., I retired with the rank of lieutenant colonel on 1 March 1974.

Bill Burns was awarded the Legion of Merit, the Meritorious Service Medal with Oak Leaf Cluster, and the Commendation Medal with Oak Leaf Cluster. While in the Army, Bill completed a B.A. in business from the University of Omaha. After retiring, he worked for Merrill-Lynch for two years, then returned to school and earned a B.A. in accounting from the University of Arkansas, Little Rock. He was an accountant with the Arkansas Public Service Commission for three years, then ran the business office for First Electric Corporation of Jacksonville, Arkansas, for ten years. He recently retired from First Electric. Bill and his wife Marie live in Cabot, Arkansas. They have two daughters, two sons, and ten grandchildren. Both sons and a son-in-law are currently serving in the military. One grandson is a graduate of West Point and is now serving in the Army. A granddaughter is a West Point Cadet, class of 1997.

Robert G. Thorpe

Age 16 – Wisconsin National Guard
Age 16 – United States Air Force

On 7 December 1941, I decided that I wanted to make the military my career, and specifically, I wanted to be a fighter pilot. I was just 10 years old at the time. I followed the war very closely during the

> ... *I flew 575 combat missions and had 600 hours of combat time.*

next four years. As a sophomore in high school, I entered the Junior ROTC Program. In September 1947, as a 16-year-old senior, I joined Company L, 128th Infantry Regiment, 32nd Infantry Division, Wisconsin National Guard. I couldn't get enough of the military. In April 1948, a friend came home on leave after completing Air Force basic training. He and two other friends and I illegally obtained four quarts of Schlitz beer and sat around talking. The three of us, still in high school, decided that the following day we would quit school and

enlist in the Air Force with the understanding that if one couldn't go for whatever reason, then none of us would go.

I had a problem. I was only 16, and the other two were 17 and 18. The Guard had not asked for proof of age, but I knew that the Air Force would. I got my baptismal certificate, and using a needle, scratched out the "1" and replaced it with a "0" to make me a year older. It was my luck that when I wrote in the "0," the ink blotted in the area that I had scratched with the needle. The

blotched baptismal certificate was all that I had, so I had to go with it. At the recruiting office the recruiter looked at the blotched certificate and asked me, "Are you sure you are 17?" I replied, "Yes, and unless all of us go, none of us go." He thought for a moment and replied, "You sure look like 17 to me." Actually, I looked more like I was 12. My nickname was "Baby Face."

After basic training at Lackland Air Force Base, near San Antonio, Texas, I was assigned to the occupation forces in Germany. I was assigned to a barracks in which all the regular rooms were full, so I was given a cot and told to sleep in a small space in the attic. I was only an airman with no skills and no training. Initially, I was told to go to work in the mess hall. That wasn't part of my plan, so I hid in my attic space and never went to the mess hall except to eat.

After several weeks, the first sergeant spotted me and asked why I was still in his squadron. I told him that the mess sergeant said he didn't need me. The first sergeant told me to report to work in the finance office. That wasn't part of my plan either, but I went. I told the finance officer that I wasn't interested in finance, that I wanted to fly. He told me to get to work or I would be on a plane to England the next day where I would be filling coal sacks for the Berlin Airlift. I took the finance job. The next day, the plane going to England crashed on landing, killing all on board. I got the message! I was offered the position of cashier in finance. This position called for a staff sergeant, and I was a private first class. I could hear opportunity knocking. I was promoted to staff sergeant in less than three years.

All along, I was worried about being caught for being underage when I joined. Once I had an honorable discharge, I knew that I'd be safe. While in Germany in 1951, I reenlisted and extended my overseas tour to four years. Now I had that discharge.

In 1952, the Air Force opened up aviation cadet training to enlisted personnel with high school diplomas. I had obtained my diploma through a GED on my way to Germany, but my age was still wrong, and I knew that I wouldn't pass an FBI background check for top-secret clearance unless my records were correct. I went to the legal office and signed a sworn statement that I had lied about my age in order to enlist. My records were corrected, and I have been legal ever since. As soon as my age was squared away, I applied for aviation cadet training.

After serving forty-five months in Germany, I was assigned to Lowry Air Force Base, Denver, Colorado, which just happened to be the testing site for all aviation cadet applicants. I was accepted for flight training in 1952. I had to wait a year for a class opening, but I could see some light at the end of the tunnel. In 1953, I was assigned to Pilot Training Class 54-K. My dream of being a fighter pilot was within reach if I could hack the sixteen months of intensive training. To give myself an edge, I spent three months' pay taking civilian flying lessons while awaiting the start of my class. I was desperate to get my pilot wings. I was sent to Lackland Air Force Base for preflight training, to Malden Air Force Base, Missouri, for six months of primary flight training, and to Greenville Air Force Base, Mississippi, for basic flight training.

I completed all phases of training with above-average grades. Finally, graduation day arrived on 10 June 1954. I will always remember that day as the happiest in my life. To make it even better, I graduated eighth in my class, which guaranteed that I would get a fighter assignment. My thirteen-year-old dream had come true!

After primary gunnery training at Laughlin Air Force Base, Texas, and advanced gunnery training at Luke Air Force Base, Arizona, I was assigned to the 434th Fighter Day Squadron, 479th Fighter Wing, George Air Force Base, California. Our squadron received the new F-100 Super Sabre, and we became the first combat-ready, supersonic fighter squadron in the world.

In 1959, I was assigned to the 345th Bomb Squadron, 98th Bomb Wing, Strategic Air Command, Lincoln, Nebraska as an aircraft commander on a B-47 bomber. This duty involved a lot of alert duty at home base, and 30-day rotational trips to the Royal Air Force Base at Upper Heyford, England, for more alert duty. Our work week averaged 103 hours of duty time.

In 1963, I was selected for a 1-year tour in Vietnam where I was aircraft commander in C-123 assault transports. I was assigned to the 309th Troop Carrier Squadron, 315th Troop Carrier Wing, Ton Son Nhut Air Base, Saigon. Technically, we were advisors, and in theory, we never saw combat. I never advised anyone, but I flew 575 combat missions and had 600 hours of combat time. At the end of the tour, all of us in the unit who were rotating home had to sign a statement that we would not discuss our activities in Vietnam. If we refused to sign the statement, we would not be rotated home. If we signed, then violated the agreement, we would be subject to court-martial.

I have some bitter memories about how things were handled in Vietnam.   Dwight Eisenhower was the first president to send "advisors" there, and John Kennedy not only greatly increased their number, but also their role in the war. I believe that Lyndon Johnson and Robert McNamara perpetrated a fraud on the American people with the Gulf of Tonkin resolution. A lot of good people died because of political shenanigans over nearly three decades.

I was the first Vietnam veteran to return to my hometown of Beloit, Wisconsin. Few people there even knew that a war was going on. A friend who ran a local radio station asked me to appear on a breakfast talk show and tell people about the war. I had to decline because of the restrictions and the threat of a court-martial.

After returning from Vietnam in 1965, I was assigned to Truax Field, Madison, Wisconsin, as base-operations and training officer. After one year, it was back to flying F-101 fighter-interceptor aircraft in the Air Defense Command with the 445th Fighter-Interceptor Squadron, Wurtsmith Air Force Base, Michigan. In 1967, I went to Selfridge Air Force Base, Michigan, where I was base-operations and training officer.

As I approached twenty years of service, my record indicated that I had flown over 4000 hours in eleven different aircraft. I had been around the world and had moved twenty-one times, not counting the times I was TDY. I had fulfilled my childhood dream. Now it was time to give it up.

I applied for retirement at the age of 36. After considerable difficulty, my request was approved. I retired at the rank of major on 1 May 1968 at Selfridge Air Force Base, Michigan. I later attended a reunion of my high school class. Although I was in the Air Force on graduation day, at 16 I was the youngest in my class to receive a diploma. Also, out of the class of 400, I was the youngest to retire.

Bob Thorpe was awarded ten Air Medals for completing 575 combat missions and an Air Force Outstanding Unit Award for his service in Vietnam. He also received a Combat Readiness Medal for being a combat-ready crew member for five or more years. After his retirement, he returned to his hometown of Beloit, Wisconsin, where he owns and manages rental real estate. He enjoys hunting, fishing, gardening, and traveling. His goal is to visit all fifty states, and he has twelve more to go. Bob lives in Clinton, Wisconsin, and has four children. He is the Wisconsin State Commander of the Veterans of Underage Military Service.

Doughty J. Dominique

Age 15 – United States Marine Corps Reserve
Age 15 – United States Air Force

During the summer of 1947, when I was 15 years old, I talked my father into signing papers attesting that I was 17 so that I could join the U. S. Marine Corps Reserve. I went to Camp Lejeune, North Carolina, for two weeks of training that

> *... each time that I was about to be promoted to corporal, I would get into just enough trouble ...*

summer. In September, I wanted to go into the regular Army, so I talked my dad into signing papers again.

I enlisted on 11 September 1947 and was assigned to the Air Force. This was just one week before the Army Air Forces officially became the U. S. Air Force. I was sent to Lackland Air Force Base, San Antonio, Texas, for thirteen weeks of basic training. From there I went to Smokey Hill Air Force Base, Salina, Kansas, and was assigned

to the 301st Heavy Bombardment Group. I worked in the hospital mess as a cooks helper and later worked up to become a cook.

I was transferred to March Air Force Base, Riverside, California, and assigned to the 22nd Heavy Bombardment Group. After a few weeks, I was sent to Fort Ord, California, where I attended cooks and bakers school for three months. Then I returned to the 22nd and worked as a cook and bread baker.

I was scheduled for discharge on 11 September 1950, but the Korean War started in June, and all enlistments were extended for one year by presidential order. We called it the "Truman year."

On 28 June 1950, our group was transferred to Kadena Air Force Base, Okinawa. From there our B-29 bombers flew twenty-nine missions over both North and South Korea. By fall, the United Nations forces had driven the North Koreans to the Yalu river. We were sent back to California with everyone thinking that the war was nearly over. Boy, were we wrong!

I never held a rank higher than PFC. It seemed like each time that I was about to be promoted to corporal, I would get into just enough trouble to shoot down the promotion. But I was never in any major trouble.

While I was a PFC at March Air Force Base, I started dating Sergeant Marilyn Sowerby. I was discharged on 15 September 1951, and Marilyn and I were married at her parents' home in Keene, New Hampshire, on 11 October 1951.

Doughty Dominique began working in the oil and gas industry in New Orleans after leaving the Air Force. The several companies he worked for include Kerr McGee (15 years) and McMoran Oil and Gas (10 years). He retired from McMoran in 1992 and worked as an independent oil and gas consultant. He spent the summers of 1992 and 1993 in Montana drilling natural-gas wells. In August 1995, he returned to work full-time supervising oil and gas production from thirteen platforms in the Gulf of Mexico. Doughty and Marilyn live in Houma, Louisiana. They have two children. Doughty is the Louisiana State Commander of the Veterans of Underage Military Service.

Herbert R. "Lefty" Luster

Age 16 – Arkansas Air National Guard

I was born in Hearne, Texas, on 21 June 1931. My father died when I was 9 years old. Several years later, my mother remarried, and we moved to Little Rock,

> *I was alive, but part of me was gone.*

Arkansas. I was 13 years old at the time and rather tall for my age.

In 1943, the 66th Division, which was stationed near Little Rock, was preparing for overseas duty. Apparently, there were some desertions, and the authorities were on the lookout for men who may have gone AWOL. You could tell that this was going on because, even while waiting in line to buy movie tickets, you could hear soldiers talking about how to avoid going overseas. I was walking along the street one day when a second lieutenant stopped me and asked, "Why aren't you in the Army?" I replied, "Because I'm only 13 years old."

He asked if I had identification, so I pulled out my wallet and got out the card that came with wallets in those days, the kind that you filled in with your name and address, and I showed it to him. He said, "This is not good enough, don't you have a library card from school?" I said no. He said, "Let me see that wallet." He took it, and when he looked inside and didn't find even a penny, he said, "OK, you must be a teenager."

The encounter with the lieutenant started me thinking that I looked old enough and big enough to be in the military. I approached my mother about letting me join, but she refused. After the war, there was a plea for men to join the National Guard. This time, I was successful in getting my mother to sign that I was 17 so that I could join. On 30 September 1947, I was sworn into the Arkansas Air National Guard at Little Rock, Arkansas, and was assigned as a medic to the 154th Fighter Squadron. I was 16 years old.

At summer camp in 1948, my age was changed again. Apparently, none of the medics wanted to drive the ancient old Army ambulances. An NCO approached me and said, "Give me 50¢ and I'll get you a driver's license." I gave him 50¢ and a short time later, he returned with a driver's license that showed my age to be 21, and I was assigned to drive an ambulance! This was the high point of my duties with the Air National Guard. I had a ball driving the ambulance around and getting it serviced. I had to drive an officer around one day, and he obviously disapproved of a kid being the driver. It all came to an end later when a P-51 pilot who had just made an emergency landing saw me, a punk kid, carrying a first-aid bag up to his oil-covered cockpit. After that, I was quietly assigned other duties such as giving physical exams and shots. When a pilot failed a depth-perception test that I had administered, my commanding officer came to his rescue and helped him pass. It was an interesting summer.

On 19 August 1948, I went to the post office in Little Rock, Arkansas, and joined the Marine Corps. I was sent to the Marine Corps Recruit Depot, San Diego, California, where I became a member of Boot Platoon 83. I received my National Guard discharge while I was in boot camp, but I never admitted to anyone that I had been in the Guard because I knew they would harass me about it, especially the DI (drill instructor). The best compliment I received at San Diego was when my DI said, "You *might* make a Marine, lad." It must have been a weak moment for him.

I was sent to Midway Island after boot camp, then to Marine Barracks, Pearl Harbor, where I was a member of the Hawaiian Area Rifle Team. When I returned to the States, I went to Camp Pendleton, California, and was assigned to Company A, 1st Battalion, 5th Marine Regiment, or, in Marine parlance, A-1-5.

On 7 July 1950, less than two weeks after the war had broken out in Korea, orders were received at Camp Pendleton to form the 1st Provisional Marine Brigade and to prepare for immediate departure to Korea. The Brigade was formed largely from the 5th Marines. We arrived in Pusan, Korea, on 2 August 1950, and we were on our way to Ch'angwon the next day.

The road was crowded with people who were loaded down with children and belongings, most going in the direction opposite us. The road wasn't wide enough for two-way traffic, so the whole scene was a dusty mess. On 5 August, we were taken by truck to Chindong-ni to prepare for an offensive action.

That morning, some mail had caught up with us, and I received a letter from my girl Patty. I was very fond of Patty and had named my BAR (Browning automatic rifle) after her. The letter took only a few moments to read. It said, "Dear Richard, I have a boy friend now, and feel I must ask you not to write me again. You will be pleased to know that he is a Marine, too." In spite of the "Dear John" letter, I decided not to change the name of my BAR. Anyway, I still liked her.

On 7 August, we started moving west with the objective of capturing Sach'on. By 12 August we were nearing the objective when the brigade was ordered to pull back and move to the Naktong area where two Communist divisions had broken through. On 17 August, we were attacking Obong-ni Ridge. I spotted an enemy position and emptied my BAR on it. I pulled out the empty magazine, loaded another, and raised the BAR to my shoulder. Before I got it all the way up, red dirt was kicked up in my face, a big jerk on my right arm told me that I had been hit. I looked down and saw blood squirting onto the broken BAR stock.

Someone from my team called for a corpsman, and somehow they got me back from the ridge. A doctor checked me at the aid station, and I was quickly loaded into a field ambulance and taken to a train aptly dubbed the "Purple Heart Special." All the way to Pusan, the other casualties and I took turns asking for water. One of the nurses scolded me. She said, "You should be ashamed of yourself. Some of these boys are hurt bad, and you only have a broken arm." I apologized, "Sorry, ma'am, I didn't know I was causing so much trouble."

The train stopped near the docks, and I was carried from the train in a stretcher. Cables were attached to the stretcher handles, and I was suspended in air until I was lowered on the deck of a hospital ship. The stretcher was soaked by my blood, and as it dried, my clothes got stuck to the canvas. I was pried loose from the stretcher and rushed to an operating room. A man standing beside me asked, "Can you move your fingers?" I tried to open and close both hands. "The other hand," the man said. "Are you trying?" I replied, "Yes, sir." After a brief moment of decision, the man said, "OK, son."

Some one placed a mask over my face. "Breathe deeply, please," came the matter-of-fact command. The next sound that I was aware of was of someone moaning and groaning. When I recognized my own voice, I quieted down. I slowly moved my body — all except my right arm which seemed to be anchored to the bed. I strained to look to see what was the matter. All I could see were clean white sheets. My right shoulder was anchored to the hospital bed and a pulley with about five pounds of weight was where my arm used to be. I was alive, but part of me was gone.

After recovering on the hospital ship for a time, I was sent to the U. S. Naval Hospital at Oakland, California. I was the first Korean War veteran to graduate from the Amputee Center at USNH, Oakland. While still a patient at the hospital, I went on leave to Hollywood. I got off the bus at Hollywood and Vine and was soon offered some tickets to the Campbell Soup "Double or Nothing" quiz show. A lady explained what I should do, and I was given the answers to some of the questions. On my way back to Oakland I was $40.00 richer — I actually had $45.00! Also, a case of Campbell soup was sent to my family back in Little Rock, but my siblings did not save a single can of my favorite, chicken noodle. It was all gone by the time I got home.

I received a medical discharge from the U. S. Marine Corps on 8 May 1951 at Treasure Island, California.

Lefty Luster received the Purple Heart for wounds received in action. He went to Hawaii immediately after receiving a medical discharge and enrolled at the University of Hawaii in anticipation of the Korean GI Bill being passed. The bill was not passed until the fall of 1951, and Lefty was forced to return to Little Rock because of a lack of funds. When the bill passed, he enrolled at Ouachita College in Arkadelphia, Arkansas. His first two years of college were very difficult, because he had been right-hand dominant before losing his arm. Learning to do everything with his left hand was so difficult that he started stuttering. He dropped out of school for a short time, then enrolled at the University of Arkansas at Little Rock where, in 1961, he received a B.A. in education and social studies. He taught school and coached for thirteen years, including two years in Queensland, Australia. During the 1980s, Lefty made several trips to Korea in search of information about the war. Currently, he is the pastor of the Believers Bible Church in Nucla, Colorado. Lefty and Romaine, his wife of forty-five years, live in Naturita, Colorado. They have seven children and sixteen grandchildren.

Theodore P. Jakaboski

Age 16 – United States Naval Reserve

I was a small-town Connecticut boy of 100% Polish ancestry, but more of a Connecticut Yankee than anything else. I became acquainted with a former chief gunner's mate who

> *Few other experiences teach a half-baked kid as much about responsibility ...*

worked as a security guard at a factory where my father worked. He talked constantly about his service in the Pacific. After "amending" my birth certificate with ink eradicator and a portable typewriter, and after convincing my dad to sign a permission paper, I enlisted in the Naval Reserve on 22 October 1947.

I was assigned to Reserve Medium Division 3-84. We drilled in the National Guard Armory on Main Street, Middletown, Connecticut, near the Middlesex Hospital where I was born on St. Patrick's Day, 1931. At the armory, I had my first taste of standing in formation, attending lectures, and receiving shots. I could not help but admire the beribboned veterans of World War II, and I could not wait to go on a "cruise" about which they spoke so enthusiastically.

Originally, I was assigned to the USS *Little Rock* for my first cruise. This was my first time away from home except for automobile trips with my parents. Upon arriving at the fleet landing at Newport, Rhode Island, after dark, my two companions (both World War II veterans) and I were taken to the *Little Rock* in a motor whaleboat with our seabags piled up in the bow. After boarding the *Little Rock*, we were told to go to the USS *Portsmouth* instead. Another boat ride in the dark and we were where we belonged, at last. We were shown to our living space that was eerily lit by red light, compartment C-204-1L. It held perhaps fifty seamen and had a scuttle leading to another berthing area directly below. As a reservist, I was assigned a "buddy," one Seaman Throop from Florence, Alabama. Our destination was Kingston, Jamaica. Since this was my first time at sea, I suffered from *mal de mer*. At first I was afraid that I was going to die, then I was afraid I wouldn't.

We went on liberty in Kingston, and I made the obligatory rounds of the bars and dives. I went to a dance at the Myrtle Bank Hotel where I met some British sailors and was introduced to Players cigarettes. I also took a left-hand-drive taxi up into the hills to see the botanical gardens.

My next period of training duty was from July to November 1948 on the submarine chaser, USS *PC-1182*, which was used by the reserves and was tied up on the river in Middletown, Connecticut. Our function was to take groups of reservists to sea for 2-week training periods. We went to many ports: Nantucket Island; Provincetown, Massachusetts; Charleston, South Carolina; New London, Connecticut; Bar Harbor, Maine; and Halifax, Nova Scotia.

In 1950 when the Korean War broke out, I asked for active duty, but the Navy said it would call me when it got around to it. I had anxieties about my underage enlistment and wanted to get that matter straightened out. I had heard a variety of rumors about what happened if you were caught with a fraudulent enlistment. With these anxieties, combined with the fact that the Navy did not appear anxious to call me to active duty, I enlisted in the U. S. Air Force on 25 July 1950, using my correct age.

The Air Force seemed rather slack compared to the taut discipline I experienced during my 6-months training duty with the Navy. I was sent to Lackland Air Force Base, San Antonio, Texas, for basic training, then to Brooks Air Force Base for three months of cryptanalysis school. I spent half of my 3-year overseas tour in Darmstadt and half in Landsberg/Lech, where Polish guards in black uniforms guarded high-ranking Nazi generals who were in the same prison where Adolph Hitler had written his book, *Mein Kampf*.

In our offices, we wallowed in tons of paper that was classified super-top-secret, the raw material of communications intelligence. Every fall, we were on edge as we watched the Russians race toward our border with thirty-two divisions of troops. Fortunately, they stopped at the border every time. There was nothing between them and us except the 26th Regiment (Blue Spaders) of the 1st Army Division (Big Red One).

The commander of the Russian forces that faced us across the border was Marshal Ivan I. Jakubowski. Forty years after leaving Germany, I learned that Marshal Jakubowski was a distant relative of mine. His ancestors were among the several hundred thousand Polish nobility left stranded when the Russian Empire swallowed up the eastern half of Poland in 1772, 1793, and 1795.

I was discharged from the Air Force in June 1954 after forty-seven months of service. Although I was a high school dropout, I had taken my college-entrance exams at Nuremburg, and in the fall of 1954, I enrolled at Yale University. I hung my Air Force fatigues in a closet, and each time I would become discouraged as a student, I would take one look at them and get right back to the books.

In 1965, I received a reserve JAG (Judge Advocate General) commission in the Navy. As a reserve officer, I performed a variety of legal duties for the Navy both aboard ships and on land. I retired as a captain on 17 March 1991 upon reaching the mandatory retirement age.

My early experiences as an underage reservist ingrained in me a great deal of nautical lore, which gave me a lifelong respect for the Navy as well as for the life and life style of the selfless patriots who dedicate their careers to our national defense. Few other experiences teach a half-baked kid as much about responsibility, teamwork, personal health and safety, and patriotism.

Ted Jakaboski was a Phi Beta Kappa at Yale University, where he graduated Magna Cum Laude in 1958. He continued at Yale and received a law degree. His specialty was immigration and nationality law, which he practiced for a number of years while maintaining his reserve-officer status in the Navy. Ted is now semiretired. A chance meeting with a professor from Vilnius, Lithuania, who had access to genealogical sources hidden since the 18th century, led Ted to engage the professor to research his family history. The research confirmed that Ted is a descendant of a Polish noble family and has the inherited title of Count. In March 1996, Ted and his sons, age 10 and 11, went to Warsaw for interviews with officers of the Polish military and officials in the Ministry of Defense. He is currently involved with a group that is trying to revive the famous Polish Cadet Corps. Ted lives in Houston, Texas, with his two sons.

John A. Kotan, Jr.

Age 16 – United States Marine Corps Reserve

During World War II, I read about all of the major landings the Marine Corps made in the Pacific. I felt a strong sense of duty to my country and wanted to enlist. I was not successful in getting my birth certificate altered before the war ended, but I was still imbued with the idea of joining the Marine Corps.

We were attacking a mountain called Bloody Ridge when I was hit.

In 1947, at the age of 16, I joined the Marine Corps Reserve in my hometown of Chicago, Illinois. I was a "weekend warrior" while going to high school. After I graduated from high school, I planned to enroll at Iowa State University, Ames, Iowa, on a swimming scholarship.

However, my plans were abruptly changed by the outbreak of the Korean War. My unit was activated in July 1950, and I was sent to Parris Island, South Carolina, for training. Following advanced infantry training at Camp Pendleton, California, I was shipped to Korea. I arrived in April 1951 and was assigned to Weapons Company, 1st Battalion, 1st Marine Regiment, 1st Marine Division, as an 81mm mortar man.

In the fighting for the Hwachon Reservoir in April 1951, half of the men in our battalion were combat casualties. During the summer and fall, the fighting was very intense. We lost about half of our battalion again during battles in the Iron Triangle and the Punchbowl. However, the North Koreans and Chinese suffered much higher casualties than we did.

I was wounded in October 1951 while we were under heavy mortar fire. We were attacking a mountain called Bloody Ridge when I was hit. I was air-evacuated to the Yokuska Naval Hospital in Japan. After surgery and therapy, I was sent to the VA hospital in Chicago. I was honorably discharged as a sergeant on 18 November 1952.

John Kotan was awarded the Purple Heart for wounds received in action. With help from his parents and the GI Bill, he attended Woodrow Wilson City College in Chicago, then enrolled at the University of Illinois at Urbana where he received a B.S. in electrical engineering. He worked for Illinois Bell Telephone for many years and is currently employed by the city of Chicago as a cable and telephone engineer. In 1989, John and his wife Eva received an invitation to return to Korea for a ceremony. He and other Korean War Veterans were decorated with the South Korean Peace Medal by the commander in chief of the Korean military forces. John and his wife Eva have three children and four grandchildren. They live in Chicago, Illinois.

√ ***VUMS Note*** ⇒ ***The Silver Star.*** "For Gallantry in Action" — These are the words inscribed on the back of the Silver Star Medal. Simple in design — a raised silver star mounted on a gold-colored star — the Silver Star Medal is awarded for heroism of a high degree involving the risk of life. It is the third highest award for combat action. The medal may be awarded to any person — military, civilian, or foreign — who, while serving in any capacity with the U. S. Armed forces, distinguishes herself or himself by gallantry in action against an enemy of the United States. Eight underage veterans whose stories are included here received the Silver Star, and one of them received it twice.

James W. Geygan

Age 15 – United States Air Force

By the time I was a teenager living in Columbus, Ohio, where I was born on 8 January 1932, there wasn't anything to do around the neighborhood. Many of the older boys were getting into trouble,

> **After dark, he picked me up and carried me piggy-back all night long.**

usually just minor scrapes with the law. One day, one of my friends was picked up by the police for some minor infraction. He had a picture of several of us boys in his pocket. The police brought us all in for questioning. I thought that it was time I got out of there, and the best place to go would be the military.

I tried changing my birth certificate, but I didn't do a very good job, and it was easy to see that the date had been changed. My brother Jack had been discharged from the Army a short time before, and I knew that he was not going to reenlist, so I just borrowed his name and his birth certificate, and on 23 December 1947, I enlisted in the U. S. Air Force. I did not tell my mother what I was going to do, but my dad and my older sister knew.

I was sent to Lackland Air Force Base, San Antonio, Texas, for basic training. Early on, the commander announced that if anyone's records needed correcting, it would be best to do it now rather than later. He said there would be no penalties, that he just wanted the records corrected. I went in and had my real name and birth date entered on the records.

Everything went well until the tenth week of training. By this time, my mother had found out where I was and had called the squadron commander. She told him she wanted me home, that I was only 15 and was too young to be in the military. The commander called me in and asked me if I wanted to stay. I told him that I did, but that wasn't the last of it. My mother called our congressman and got him involved. The

Air Force bent to congressional pressure, and I was discharged on 14 April 1948 after serving three months and twenty-one days.

After I was discharged, I never went back to school. I worked at odd jobs until 19 July 1949 when I enlisted in the U. S. Army. I joined with a friend, and we were sent to Fort Knox, Kentucky, for basic training. I probably could have gotten out of going through basic again, but I wanted to stay with my friend.

After basic training, I was sent to leadership school at Fort Knox. Following that, I received orders to report to the Far East Command. In the spring of 1950, I was assigned to Company H, 19th Infantry Regiment, 24th Infantry Division, in Beppu, Japan.

The Korean "police action" started on 25 June 1950, and by 4 July 1950, our division was in Korea. I saw my first North Korean soldier at the Kum River near the town of Taepyong-ne, eight miles from Taejon. Our company dug in, but there was no sleep that night. The North Koreans blew bugles most of the night and set off flares when the loudspeaker was shut off. I had turned 18 by then, but I was still young.

Two days later, the regiment was told to stage a counterattack. In doing so, we lost half of our regiment. When that happened, we started to pull back, but we got caught in a lot of roadblocks. North Korean machine gunners fired at every tunnel that we had to go through.

On the 6th or 7th of July we got a lot of "incoming mail" (artillery fire). I was knocked unconscious for over two hours and was left for dead. When I woke up and joined my outfit, I asked why they had left me there. Their response was that since I did not move, I was dead!

Taejon was the worst fight we had. T-34 (Russian) tanks were in the town. We were trying to get our people together and decide what to do when I saw General Dean,[24] the division commander. I thought

---

[24] Major General William F. Dean was in command of the 24th Infantry Division in Japan at the outbreak of the Korean War. His troops were the first to see ground combat in Korea. At Taejon, General Dean was credited with personally leading an attack that knocked out a T-34 tank. The withdrawal from Taejon was chaotic, and on 25 July 1950, Dean was captured and was held as a prisoner of war until September 1953. He was awarded the Medal of Honor for "intrepid leadership and outstanding valor." (See Edward F. Murphy, *Korean War Heroes*, Presidio Press, Novato, CA.)

to myself, "Well, we'll be all right now because the division commander is here, and he will have a lot of troops with him." I went up to the general and asked him what we should do. He said, "You regroup and head south." The general looked very tired, and I could tell that the responsibility of the battle and the safety of his troops were weighing heavily on him.

The General went on down the road, and about a week later he was captured. Before I saw him, General Dean and his crew had destroyed a T-34 tank. He was assisted by an underage soldier, Tommy E. Gilbert. Gilbert was wounded three times and was discharged before he was 18 years old.

I watched Taejon burn! After we left there and went south, we ran into roadblocks at every tunnel we came to. Just south of the city, I was wounded by a North Korean machine gun that was set up at a tunnel entrance. I was hit in both legs, and the right leg was broken. I couldn't walk, and nobody would help me. Finally, a friend, Corporal Jim Kenchen, came back for me. He bandaged me up the best he could and stayed with me. After dark, he picked me up and carried me piggy-back all night long. In the late afternoon of the next day, after slipping and sliding through seemingly endless miles of rice paddies, we finally found a 21st Regiment aid station. They wouldn't believe that we were from the 19th Regiment until Corporal Kenchen found an old class-A pass in his pocket to show them. Kenchen left me at the aid station and returned to our unit. He was later awarded the Silver Star for saving me from capture and probable death.

The medics patched me up and moved me to a field hospital. While I was there, some North Koreans infiltrated the hospital area and shot some of the patients in the hospital tents. It wasn't safe even in the field hospital! I was taken to a small airstrip nearby, loaded into a C-47 transport plane, and flown to Japan. From there it was back to the States and a hospital in Hot Springs, Arkansas. After I was released from the hospital, I was assigned light duty because of my bad legs. I was discharged with the rank of sergeant first class on 2 July 1953 at Fort Sheridan, Illinois.

Jim Geygan earned the Combat Infantryman Badge and was awarded the Bronze Star for meritorious service. He received two Purple Hearts for wounds received in action. After his discharge from the Army, he returned to Columbus, Ohio, and was a traffic-

control supervisor for the state of Ohio for four years. He worked for the city of Columbus as a permit supervisor for twenty years, then was the communications officer for the base fire department at Rickenbacker Air National Guard Base for the next sixteen years, retiring in 1992. Jim married, raised eight children, and has fourteen grandchildren. Now divorced, he lives in Hebron, Ohio.

✓ ***VUMS Note*** ⇒ *Poverty.* Since most underage veterans grew up during the era of the Great Depression (roughly 1929-1940), poverty is a common denominator in their stories. For some families, poverty was a burden even during World War II and after. Conditions required that youngsters work to help out, if they could find jobs. One underage veteran states in quite a matter-of-fact manner, "My boyhood was unpleasantly poor." He worked very hard for 12- to 15- hours a day on Saturdays for 50¢ — plus a chicken. The chicken was the family's Sunday meal. Another veteran remembers wearing cardboard shoes and eating cereal-filled bologna. Some families had no choice but to move in with relatives when they could no longer pay their rent or mortgage. Thus, experiencing the hardships of poverty, many youngsters decided that enlisting in the military offered a way to provide greatly needed help to their families.

One story vividly illustrates an effect of deprivation. This veteran remembered very well how impressed he was when he was issued his clothing and gear upon his induction into the Army. He had never owned any new clothing, and he had owned only one new pair of shoes in his entire life. "Now, here in Uncle Sam's Army, I was rich beyond belief," he wrote, going on to list all the items of clothing and gear issued to him, summing it up with, "For a kid who had just turned 14, I was in heaven!"

Thomas V. Huntsberry

Age 15 – United States Army

I was born at Reisterstown Road, Baltimore County, Maryland, on 13 March 1932, the youngest of thirteen children. In early 1941, we moved to a 100-acre farm east of Timber Ridge, Virginia, near the West Virginia line.

> *"You are underage, and I know it, and you know it!"*

Three of my brothers served during World War II, one in the Army, one in the Marines, and one in the Navy. I tried to enlist when I was 14 years old, but I was 15 before I finally succeeded.

I convinced my parents to go with me to a notary public where they signed an affidavit stating that I was 17 years old. In 1948, the Army was taking anybody that was breathing, so with the affidavit, I didn't have any problem enlisting.

I was sworn into the Army on 1 January 1948 and sent to Fort Jackson, South Carolina, for basic training. I was assigned to Company H, 3rd Battalion, 11th Infantry Regiment, 5th Infantry Division. I applied for paratroop training during basic. The sergeant looked at me and said, "No way are you going to be a paratrooper. You are underage, and I know it, and you know it!" Then he asked, "Do you want to stay in the service?" I replied, "I certainly do!"

After basic, I was sent to the Caribbean Command, Panama Canal Zone, where I served with Battery D of the 903rd AAA (antiaircraft) Battalion. I must have been a pretty good soldier because I made colonel's orderly five times in a row. I was asked if I wanted to be transferred to General Ridgeway's headquarters and become his orderly, but I decided to stay with my outfit.

At the time I was in Panama, that country was having an election, and there was some unrest. A friend and I were on guard duty way out in the boondocks near the back gate of Fort Davis. It was a dark

night, and the light was out in the guard shack. My friend lit a
cigarette, then sat down immediately. Just as he sat down, a 30-
caliber round struck the door frame where he had been standing. We
were so scared that we never bothered to shoot back. It was a good
thing the lights were out because they would have shot us for sure. An
old gray-haired captain came out to see what happened. He gave us
an extra round of ammunition and said to us, "Shoot anything you see,
and I mean shoot to kill!"

After I had been in Panama for about a year, my mother became
very ill, and I returned home on emergency leave. After my leave, I
reported to Fort Campbell, Kentucky, where I was assigned to the
185th Combat Engineer Battalion. I remained at Fort Campbell until
I was discharged on 1 January 1950.

I returned to Baltimore and joined the 445th Combat Engineer
Battalion, U. S. Army Reserves. In October 1952, we were activated
into the Army. Two other reserves and I were sent to Fort Lewis,
Washington, as guards for a plane load of forty-four prisoners who
were being sent to Korea. These men had been in the stockade for
desertion and for being chronically AWOL. Our orders were to deliver
them to front-line units in Korea.

After delivering the prisoners to Korea, I was attached to the 139th
Signal Detachment, 5th Regiment, 1st Cavalry Division, for 30-days
duty in Koje-do, Korea, where prisoners of war were held.

I returned to Japan, and in 1953, I was put in charge of 800
replacements for the 1st Cavalry Division who were being transferred
from Camp Drake to Camp Crawford, Hokkaido, Japan. It was a
4-day trip by train. At Camp Crawford, I was assigned to the 1st
Cavalry Division's 13th Signal Company and later to the 16th Corps.
Another invasion of North Korea was planned, and we were all
prepared to move to the debarkation port to board landing craft when
we heard that an armistice had been signed.

Later that year, my wife joined me in Japan. We lived in private
quarters in a village just outside the camp. I returned to the States in
1954, and on 12 October 1955, was honorably discharged from the
Reserves with the rank of staff sergeant. Being in the Army helped
me a lot in my life. The Army was like a second family to me.

*Tom Huntsberry worked as a technician for the Giddon-Durkee
company until December 1974 when he retired with a disability*

after suffering a heart attack in 1971. After quadruple-bypass surgery in 1981 and more heart surgery in 1996, he is still doing quite well. To release his pent-up energies, Tom began to research his family history. When he found that some of his ancestors had served in the Civil War and in the War of 1812, Tom decided to expand his research. He began the task of listing the names of soldiers who fought in those two wars, along with the units to which they belonged. Tom observes that, "We know who the generals were, but we never hear about the privates." With the help of Joanne, his wife of forty-five years, Tom published six books of such lists, along with stories of the times. These books, invaluable to genealogists and historians, are available in schools and libraries across the country. Tom and Joanne live in Martinsburg, West Virginia. They have six children and ten grandchildren. Five of their six children have served in the military.

√ **VUMS Note** ⇒ *The "Truman year."* When underage veterans referred to the "Truman year" or "Harry's year," they meant the 1-year extension of their enlistment by executive order of President Harry S. Truman one month after the start of hostilities in Korea. Executive order 10145 reads in part: "By virtue of the authority vested in me ... and as President of the United States and Commander in Chief of the armed forces of the United States, I hereby extend for a period of twelve months all enlistments in the Army, the United States Navy, and the United States Marine Corps, including the Naval Reserve and the Marine Corps Reserve, and in any component of the Air Force of the United States, which shall expire at any time after the date of this order and prior to July 9, 1951."   Harry S. Truman

The White House   July 27 1950.

Gary R. Walcott

Age 16 – United States Army

I was born in Whitney, Nebraska, on 11 July 1931 and raised on a farm near there. I was lucky and had a good home situation, but money was scarce. I could see that there was no future in the rural area where I lived, so I quit high school

> ... *I met one who was only 13 years old and had already been through jump school ...*

and joined the Army. I was only 16, but the recruiter never questioned my age.

I was sworn into the U. S. Army on 20 January 1948 and was sent to Fort Ord, California, for basic training. I met several other underage soldiers during basic. The youngest was 15, but later I met one who was only 13 years old and had already been through jump school at Fort Benning, Georgia.

After completing basic, I was assigned to the 11th Airborne Division in northern Japan. I went to jump school at Sendai, Japan, graduating on 1 September 1948. After jump school, I was assigned to the 511th Parachute Infantry Regiment at Camp Haugen, Hachinohe, Japan. After I had been overseas for nine months, the 11th Airborne was sent back to Fort Campbell, Kentucky.

In 1951, I was sent back to Japan, then on to Korea as a replacement in the 187th Regimental Combat Team. My enlistment was up after six months, and I was returned to the States.

My fondest and most humorous memories are of the four years I spent in the Army. For example, while I was stationed at Fort Campbell, Kentucky, I went to Nashville, Tennessee, on a weekend pass. I had hoisted a few and was feeling no pain as I walked down a street. I noticed a long line of people waiting to enter an old brick building, so I walked up to the door, ignored the ticket counter, and went right on in as if I owned the place. It was then that I learned that I was at the Grand Ole Opry, or "Grand Old Uproar," as we used to call it. To top it all, I didn't like that kind of music. The building was the Ryan Auditorium in downtown Nashville, which since has been moved to a new location.

I was discharged on 20 January 1952 at Camp Carson, Colorado. I have never regretted my time in the service.

Gary Walcott joined the Merchant Marine after his Army discharge. He worked hard and acquired the education necessary to advance in the maritime industry. He earned his Masters license and accumulated thirty-one retirement years before retiring in July 1996. Gary still enjoys jumping out of perfectly good airplanes. He has earned jump wings by participating in parachute jumps with military forces in Israel, Thailand, Russia, and Slovakia. Gary lives in Monroe, Washington.

Carl R. "Rod" Rodriguez

Age 16 – Virginia National Guard
Age 16 – United States Air Force

When I enlisted in the Virginia National Guard on 16 September 1947 at the age of 16, I said that I was 17, and I was not asked to prove it. I was discharged six months later, on 5 March 1948, in order to

> *The lieutenant looked at me, smiled, and said, "Move along."*

enlist in the U. S. Air Force. I enlisted in the Air Force because three of my buddies who were older than I was talked me into it. They didn't have to talk very hard because I liked aircraft and thought that I would like a career in aviation. The Air Force recruiting sergeant requested proof of age. He said that if I didn't have a birth certificate, a signed document from my high school principal was all right. So I got a document from the principal, erased the birth date, and typed in a date indicating that I was 17 years old. I was sworn into the Air Force on 6 March 1948.

At the processing center at Camp Lee, Virginia, a lieutenant placed my proof of age document on a magnifying screen. A big, round spot was evident where I had erased my true birth date. The lieutenant looked at me, smiled, and said, "Move along." It was obvious what I had done, but he didn't pursue it.

We went by train to Lackland Air Force Base, San Antonio, Texas, for thirteen weeks of basic training. Our flight won first place in a base-wide, close order drill contest. Our reward was an airplane ride at Randolph Air Force Base. We had to march from Lackland to Randolph because recruits just didn't ride in a bus or truck.

Three C-47s were used to give us a 1-hour flight around San Antonio. Everyone had to fly. Some of the group had never been in an aircraft before and didn't want to go. It was my first flight, also. I was scared and had a fear of high places, but I was looking forward to the flight. I found that height while flying didn't bother me. The private sitting next to me stared at the floor the entire flight — he never looked up.

After basic training, I completed twenty weeks of jet-aircraft maintenance school at Chanute Air Force Base, Illinois. After graduation, I was assigned to the Fourth Air Force at Hamilton Field, California. Although I had no training or experience with reciprocating engines, I was assigned as an assistant crew chief on a B-26. I was put on flying status and authorized flight pay. This was a big thrill for a 17-year-old corporal.

One day, an F-84 crashed while landing. The crew chief and mechanics ran to the burning aircraft, but they could not get the pilot out because of the flames. Another F-84 pilot who was awaiting takeoff taxied to the burning plane and turned his aircraft around so that the tail was aimed at the cockpit of the burning aircraft. The exhaust from his aircraft blew the flames away from the cockpit, allowing the pilot to be rescued. He was given a medal for his quick thinking that saved a fellow pilot.

Three years later, while I was stationed at Itazuki Air Base, Japan, I was shooting the breeze with my OIC (officer-in-charge), and I told him about the incident. He told me that he was that pilot. He said that before he realized what he was doing, he was taxiing toward the burning aircraft. He never planned it; it just happened.

I was with the 6160th Field Maintenance Squadron, Itazuke, from 1952 to 1954, then I was transferred to the 22nd Bomb Wing, March Air Force Base, California, where I served from 1954 to 1962. From 1962 to 1965, I was assigned to the 49th Tactical Fighter Wing, Spangdahlem, Germany. We had F-105 fighter bombers. I returned to the States in 1966 and was assigned to the 835th Combat Support Group, McConnell Air Force Base, Kansas. The following year, 1967, I went to Thailand, where I joined the 355 Tactical Fighter Wing at Tahkli Air Base. We serviced F-105s, KC-135 refuelers, and B-66 radar-jamming aircraft. Our F-105s bombed and strafed North Vietnam targets.

On 1 April 1968, I retired from the Air Force as a chief master sergeant, a rank that I had attained in 1961 at age 29. At that time I was one of the youngest chiefs in the Air Force.

Rod Rodriguez was awarded the Bronze Star for meritorious service during the war in Vietnam. While he was in the Air Force, he earned a B.A. in general education from the University of Omaha. After retiring from the Air Force, he used the GI Bill to earn a commercial pilots license and an instrument rating and was certified as a flight instructor. He was an active pilot from 1970 to 1989. During that period, he owned a fixed-base operation for three years and was an airport manager for ten years. He held the position of certified airport executive. In August 1986, at age 55, he played Fantasy Camp baseball against the former Chicago Cubs greats: Ernie Banks, Andy Pafko, Ron Santo, Randy Hundley, and others. In his words, "Playing left field in Wrigley Field was the most fun I had in years." Rod and his wife Beverly live in Weatherford, Texas. They have four daughters and ten grandchildren. Their son Scott died of cancer on 28 October 1996.

√ **VUMS Note** ⇒ *Law and law enforcement.*
Although they may have circumvented the law to enlist in the military underage, law and law enforcement were the career choices of a number of underage veterans after they left the service. Four contributors to this book became lawyers, one of whom served as Deputy State Attorney General of California during his career. Fourteen served as police officers or highway patrolmen, with several of them becoming chiefs of police. Two worked as fish and game wardens, combining their enjoyment of the sea with their careers.

Leon D. Underdown

Age 15 – United States Army

I was the youngest boy in a family of eight children. In 1945, two of my brothers were in the Navy, and I wanted to do my part. So at age 12, I went to

> *"Son, does your mother know where you are?"*

the Army recruiting office in Amarillo, Texas, told them that I was 18 years old and that I wanted to join the U. S. Army. I filled out all the papers, took my physical, and was sent to a base in New Mexico where I was to be sworn in. When I got off the bus, a lieutenant looked at me and said, "Son, does your mother know where you are?" He called my mother and told her he was sending me home the next day. In the morning, the lieutenant told a sergeant to take me to the bus station and make sure that I was on the bus when it left.

At home, I went to school but I didn't like it. When I was 15 years old, I decided it was time to try to join the Army again. I went back to the recruiting office in Amarillo, and as I had done when I was 12, I told them I was 18. They did not ask for a birth certificate. I was sworn in on 21 March 1948 and was sent to Fort Ord, California, for basic training. After basic, I was selected to go to the Pentagon in Washington, D.C., to be a runner. This sounded like a real exciting job to me. I didn't realize that it was just carrying papers back and forth among the buildings. To get the job, I had to be cleared by the FBI. Of course, they found out my true age and reported it to my captain. The captain said that he would never have recommended me for that job if he had known that I was only 15 years old. He had to let me go, so I was discharged after serving for four months and fifteen days.

On 21 March 1951, with the Korean War in full swing, I enlisted in the Army for a 3-year hitch. Because of the war, all enlistments were automatically extended for one year, the so-called "Truman year," so

I served four years. I was stationed with the 4th Infantry Division's 46th Antiaircraft Artillery Battalion in Germany for two and one-half years.

Leon Underdown served with the Army in Germany, and after being discharged, returned to Texas where he met a German girl named Irma. She had come to the United States as a student, intending to return to Germany when her studies were completed. Leon changed her plans. They were married in Lubbock, Texas, and later moved to Oklahoma where Leon owned and operated a forklift sales and service company. He retired in 1993. Leon and Irma live in Bristow, Oklahoma. They have two children and two grandchildren.

√ ***VUMS Note*** ⇒ ***Royal encounters.*** An Air Force veteran who had enlisted underage had the opportunity to shake hands with the future Queen of England. He had participated in the clean-up and rescue efforts after a tidal wave struck a beach area near Scullthorpe Air Force Base, England, where he was stationed in 1947. The tidal wave hit without warning and several hundred people died. Three days later, Princess Elizabeth, soon to be crowned Queen of England, came to view the destruction. She shook hands with the rescuers, thanked them, and invited them all to her coronation.

A WAC who had enlisted at age 16 experienced the thrill of having tea with the King and Queen of England. While she was visiting London for a few days, she was one of a lucky few who were selected by the USO to have tea in a garden at Buckingham Palace with the royal couple present. She said in her story, "I thought nothing could top that for a farm girl from North Carolina!"

William V. Brand

Age 15 – Florida National Guard
Age 16 – United States Army

While attending high school in Jacksonville, Florida, I would frequently accompany my friends to the monthly meetings of the Florida National Guard. I was allowed to attend classes and to observe close

My nickname immediately became "Hot Water," and it stuck throughout my Army career.

order drill and riot-control formations. I became friends with many of the officers and NCOs (noncommissioned officers). During the meeting in April 1947, the subject for discussion was summer camp at Camp Blanding, Florida. One of the NCOs asked me if I would go with them to summer camp. I told him that I wasn't a member and couldn't go. When he asked if I wanted to become a member, I replied that I did, but that I was underage. He took me to meet with an officer and an NCO, and in May 1947, I enlisted in the Florida National Guard.

During our two weeks of summer camp, I was on KP every day but two. I spent those two days on the beach. Summer camp was fun. I was the youngest man in the unit. Most of the guardsmen were aware that I was underage, but this caused no problems.

In 1948, I was in the tenth grade at Andrew Jackson High School in Jacksonville. I was making passing grades and had a good home life. My Uncle Elmo had served in the Army during World War II, and I would listen to him tell stories of his Army life. He is the one that put the bug in my ear to enlist.

A few days later, I visited the Marine Corps and Navy recruiters in my hometown. They both told me to return when I was a bit older. Then I strolled over to the Army recruiter who really seemed interested in my well-being. I filled out the necessary paperwork and was to leave for duty at a later time. The recruiter visited my parents a few times and talked with my friends. Meanwhile, I was talking about the U. S. Army to my friends.

On 25 March 1948, five of my friends and I joined the Army together. We went to Fort Jackson, South Carolina, for basic training. All six of us were in the same company. During the second week of basic, my CO discovered that I was underage. He wrote to my parents informing them that I was underage, and requested their advice on how to proceed. My parents' response was that I knew what I was doing, that they did not want me discharged just because of my age. Meanwhile, the CO took me under his wing. During the week that the company went to the firing range to learn to fire the M-1 rifle, the BAR, and machine guns, I was baby-sitting at the CO's quarters. When the qualification scores were posted, I was listed as expert on the rifle, carbine, and machine gun. The company spent a few days in the field playing Army games, sleeping in pup tents, eating C-rations, doing map reading, etc. You guessed it – I didn't go. I was at the CO's quarters.

After basic training, the six of us were sent to the Panama Canal Zone. Two of my friends and I were assigned to the 20th Military Police Company at Fort Davis, Canal Zone. We attended MP school at Fort Amador, Canal Zone. On my seventeenth birthday, 4 August 1948, we qualified with the 45-caliber pistol. Now I was legal.

There were about one hundred troops in our company. The hot-water boiler for our barracks was very small. Unless you were among the first in the showers, there was never any hot water. One winter night, I went to take a shower and the water was cold. I was very tired of cold showers, and since I was 17 years old and didn't know any better, I put my clothes on and went to the CQ (charge of quarters) office. I requested to borrow the phone book and to use the phone. I called the post commander. When he answered the phone, I identified myself and then asked him, "Do you have hot water to take a shower in your house tonight?" He replied, "Of course. What's your problem?" I explained to him that we ran out of hot water every night while taking a shower. He wanted to know in what building my company was located, so I gave him the building number.

I made the call on a Friday evening. Within an hour, my CO was in the barracks demanding to see me – immediately! When I told him what I had done, he became very upset. However, on Monday morning the post engineers were at the barracks installing another hot-water boiler. We had plenty of hot water after that. My nickname immediately became "Hot Water," and it stuck throughout my Army career.

I did not obtain a release from the Florida National Guard when I joined the Army. While I was in Panama, I received a letter asking why I was not attending the meetings. I had the personnel office respond to the letter, and a few weeks later, I received a discharge from the Guard dated 20 April 1948, almost a month after I went into the Army. The reason for termination was listed as "business interference."

I completed my GED while I was in Panama and remained there for nearly four years. In 1952, I transferred to Fort Benning, Georgia, and a year later to Okinawa where I served with the 550th MP Company. In 1957, I returned to the U. S. and was a bookkeeper and bartender at the NCO club at Fort Monroe, Virginia, for a year. I was assigned to the 7th MP Company, 7th Infantry Division, Ton du Chon, Korea, for a year, then I returned to Okinawa. From 1960 to 1965, I was stationed in Kentucky, at Fort Knox and at the Kentucky Military Institute at Lyndon. I was sent to Stuttgart, Germany, in 1965 and stayed there for about nine months. While I was at Stuttgart, I received a notice from the Selective Service System in Jacksonville, Florida, stating that I was not registered for the draft and that I should supply the information requested *at once*. I had more than fifteen years' service by that time.

I returned to Okinawa from Germany. This tour included six months' TDY duty in Vietnam. In 1967, I returned to the States for a year, then it was back to Yong-san, Korea, for another year.

I retired from the U. S. Army as a sergeant first class on 1 October 1969, after serving for more than twenty-one years.

Bill Brand was employed by Florida's Marion County in animal control at six different times after retiring from the Army. He would work at another job for a time, then return to his old job with the county. He worked for Prestige Courier delivering packages all over the Southeast for five years, then returned to Marion County again. He retired for the last time in May 1994, but he keeps busy with his hobby of digging up and collecting old bottles. He has displayed his collection at bottle shows throughout the southeastern U. S. Bill lives in Ocala, Florida.

Ronald E. Evenson

Age 15 – United States Air Force

In March 1948, two of my high school pals and I decided to play hooky from our school in Arcadia, Wisconsin, and go to Winona, Minnesota, to talk to the Navy recruiter about enlisting. Winona was just across the Mississippi River from Arcadia.

> *Just as we were about to raise our hands and be sworn in, the principal arrived ...*

We couldn't try to enlist in Arcadia because the recruiter there was well aware of our ages. All three of us were underage; Melvin Abts was 16, I was 15, and Vilas Hanson was 14.

When we arrived at the Navy recruiting office in Winona, it was closed for lunch. However, the Army recruiter asked us into his office. He told us that he couldn't get us into the Navy, but he could get us into the Air Force. He explained that the Air Force had become a separate service only six months before, and the Army was still recruiting for the Air Force. His story was convincing, so we signed up. Somehow, we all convinced our parents that this was the thing to do. We obtained their permission, and they signed statements to the effect that we were 17 years old.

After getting our parents' permission, we again had to make the trip to Winona to be sworn in. We had told our friends at school that we had joined the Air Force, and naturally, word got to the principal. Just as we were about to raise our hands and be sworn in, the principal arrived and informed the recruiter that we were underage. We thought that this was the end of our Air Force careers. However, recruits were hard to come by in 1948. After the principal left the office, sure that he had squelched our enlistment, the recruiter told us about all the terrible things that would happen to us if we enlisted fraudulently. Not wanting to let the other two buddies down, we all swore that we would never tell anyone we were underage. So we raised our hands and were sworn into the U. S. Air Force on April Fools' day 1948.

After eleven weeks of basic training, I was hospitalized with pneumonia. I had just received orders to report to Cheyenne, Wyoming, to attend diesel-mechanics school after completion of basic training. After recuperating from the pneumonia, I had to complete the last two weeks of basic. This meant that diesel-mechanics school was out. I was sent to Kelly Air Force Base, Texas, where I received on-the-job training in the air transportation field, and I ended up spending my entire career in this field.

In 1949, I was reassigned to Malmstrom Air Force Base, Montana. This, according to my wife, was my lucky day. I met her in Great Falls, Montana, and we were married in 1950, just after we both turned 18. My father-in-law felt that our marriage was the worst thing that could possibly have happened to his daughter. Looking back, I probably would have felt the same way if our daughter had married a young airman at age 18. However, we celebrated our 46th wedding anniversary in the summer of 1996.

Just one month after we were married and a short time after the Korean War started, I was reassigned to Elmendorf Air Force Base, Alaska. During this period, I, as well as all enlistees, received the "Harry Truman" 1-year extension to our enlistments. From Alaska, I was transferred to West Palm Beach, Florida, then to Westover Air Force Base, Massachusetts.

During the ensuing years, I was again assigned to Elmendorf and subsequently to McChord Air Force Base, Washington, Tachikawa Air Force Base, Japan, and Glasgow Air Force Base, Montana. Glasgow was remote, but my next assignment was to an even more isolated area just east of the Afghanistan border called Peshawar, Pakistan. Peshawar is best remembered as the place where Gary Powers took off in a U-2 for his ill-fated flight over Russia.

On my return to the States, I was assigned to Travis Air Force Base, California, with two years to go before I could retire. In 1967, after just fourteen months at Travis, I was sent to Udorn Air Base, Thailand. I returned to the States in 1968 and retired as a master sergeant, exactly twenty years to the day after my enlistment. I was thirty-five years old.

Ron Evenson went to work for the Air Force a few months after his retirement. He worked at Travis Air Force Base as a civilian in the same career field he pursued while in uniform. His pay was much better as a civilian, and there were no reassignments. He retired again in 1989. In 1993, Ron and Donna, his wife of forty-six years, purchased a home on a five-acre lot ten miles from Roseburg, Oregon, and are thoroughly enjoying the retired life style. Ron and Donna have a son, a daughter, and three grandchildren.

√ **VUMS Note** ⇒ *Career military.* Over one fourth of the contributors to this book, 59 out of 199, retired from military service. Fifty served for 20 years or more on active duty, 7 served in a combination of active duty and reserve status, and 2 received medical retirements. Six attained the rank of colonel or Navy captain at the time of their retirement, 3 were lieutenant colonels or Navy commanders, 3 were majors or Navy lieutenant commanders, and 5 were captains or Navy lieutenants. Seven of the 59 were warrant officers and 29 were in the top three enlisted ranks at the time of their retirement. One was medically retired as a private first class. Four did not include their rank at the time of their retirement. Admiral Boorda was in his fortieth year of naval service at the time of his death.

Vilas L. Hanson

Age 14 – United States Air Force

I was the seventh of eight children, money was scarce, and I didn't like school. The thought of military service intrigued me. Two of my buddies, Ron Evenson, age 15, and Melvin Abts, age 16, told me they were going to enlist in the Air Force. I thought that if they could enlist, I could, even though I was just 14.

> *My parents just laughed and said that I couldn't pass the physical.*

On a Friday afternoon, we went to the Air Force recruiting office in Winona, Minnesota, about twenty-five miles from our hometown of Arcadia, Wisconsin, and filled out all the paperwork. We were told to have our parents sign the papers and return with them on Monday. Over the weekend, we told our parents our plans and asked them to sign the papers. My parents just laughed and said that I couldn't pass the physical. On Monday morning, my dad told me that if I really wanted the papers signed, he would sign them. I thought for a few minutes and then told him that I had changed my mind. Later, while getting ready for school, I changed my mind again. This time, my mother said that she would sign because my father had said that it was okay. My oldest brother looked at the papers and said that they had to be notarized. He took my mother and me to a local insurance agency where her signature was notarized.

I went to the house of my friend with papers in hand. His father, who owned a beer distributorship, was to take us to Winona. We loaded his truck, and the four of us delivered beer all the way to Winona. The recruiter checked our papers and told us that we would be sworn in the next morning if we passed our physical. We passed, and we were sworn into the Air Force on 1 April 1948, exactly six months before my fifteenth birthday. Just before boarding the train, I called my mother and told her we were on our way to Texas.

At Lackland Air Force Base near San Antonio, Texas, we took and passed another physical. After thirteen weeks of basic training and a 15-day home leave, I took a 5-day trip by ship to Hawaii, where I was assigned to Hickam Field. I went to military police school and became an MP. After four months of MP duty, I asked for a transfer to air installation as a driver. That job lasted about two months, and then I was transferred to Johnston Island, a three-quarter by one-half mile island in the Pacific west of Hawaii. Johnston was an aircraft refueling base serviced by three hundred personnel.

After sixteen months overseas, I returned home, enjoyed a 30-day leave, then reported to Chanute Field, Illinois, to await orders. I was assigned to Scott Field, Illinois, where I remained for twenty-seven months. I worked in base housing while there. We took care of officers' quarters and enlisted men's barracks for housing transient personnel. Many aircraft came in loaded with wounded from the Korean War. Some would be sent to hospitals, others home, and some to other installations throughout the country.

I was discharged on 31 March 1952. My 3-year enlistment had been lengthened by a year, the so-called "Truman year," because of the Korean War.

Vilas Hanson worked on the loading dock for a trucking firm for about two years, then worked for a woodworking firm for three years. He began working for Golden Plump Poultry as a truck driver, then moved to feed-mill operations, where he operated a computerized pellet-mill. He was diagnosed with Parkinson's disease in 1990 and received a medical retirement from his company in 1994. He is active in veterans affairs, and for the past eight years, has served on the Arcadia City Council. He has been president of the council for the past five years and served as parks and recreation chairman. He was instrumental in getting the city to purchase fifty-two acres of land for a park. A highlight of the park is what has become known as "the soldiers walk," where veterans of all wars are recognized. Vilas and Joan, his wife of forty-one years, live in Arcadia, Wisconsin. They have four children and three grandchildren. Vilas is the Wisconsin State Vice-Commander of the Veterans of Underage Military Service.

Johnny Camp

Age 14 – United States Coast Guard

I was born on a little ranch back in the hills near Medina, Texas, on 25 May 1933. I lived with my grandparents from the time I was born. We were very poor and times were hard. By the time I was 14 years old, I could see that my grandmother

> *Being a few feet from a jungle-covered bank on a dark night is no place for sailors.*

was getting too old to care for me. My mother was living in San Antonio, Texas, about seventy miles from our little ranch. During a visit to my mother, I met a young man who lived across the street from her. He told me he had joined the Navy at age 16, but he didn't like it and got out. He told me where I could go to join the military.

I went to the building where the recruiting offices were and went into the first door that I came to. This was the U. S. Coast Guard. I wasn't asked for a birth certificate or to prove my age in any way. I was sworn into the Coast Guard on 4 April 1948, and a few days later, I was sent to Mayport, Florida, for boot camp.

It was after dark when I arrived. I was taken to a big barracks and told to find a bunk. I settled into a bottom bunk, and as I lay there, I never heard so many strange snoring sounds, nor smelled such strange smells in all of my life. As I lay on my bunk, I felt something dripping on me. I finally figured out that it was the man on the top bunk. He had wet the bed. I was so scared that I just lay there all night and let it drip on me.

Boot camp was very rough for this 14-year-old, and Coast Guard life would remain rough for the next couple of years. At first, I couldn't call home because I had grown up with the old crank-type telephones, and I was too embarrassed to ask anyone to show me how to use a dial phone.

I drew mostly sea duty during my twenty years in the Coast Guard. I served on all types of the old Coast Guard ships, only the last one being air-conditioned. I served on the beach about forty miles west of Pusan, Korea, during the war in a non-combat role, but we made our own combat when we could.

I served thirteen months in Vietnam from 1965 to 1966 as an engineer in charge of a gun boat. During a patrol, I manned the two 50-caliber machine guns in the stern of the boat. We worked the Mekong River, its tributaries, and the coastline, mostly at night because that is when the Viet Cong would move ammunition and supplies. Many times, the rivers were so restricted that we barely had room to maneuver the boat. Needless to say, that situation was bad for the nerves. Being a few feet from a jungle-covered bank on a dark night is no place for sailors.

One night, while on a two-boat patrol along the coast, we captured an enemy ship containing 100 tons of guns and ammunition. This was the largest amount of Viet Cong armaments captured at one time during the entire war.

I retired in August 1968 after twenty years and four months of service. I was three months into my thirty-fifth year. Most of the twenty years were great. I saw a lot of the world, and I learned a lot.

Johnny Camp was awarded the Bronze Star with a combat "V," the Vietnamese Cross of Gallantry with Gold Star, and a unit citation for his actions in the Mekong Delta. After retiring from the Coast Guard, he returned to Bandera, Texas, and worked off and on at a number of jobs to supplement his retirement pay. He was a heavy-equipment operator, painter, and tree trimmer, and he worked at a natural-gas plant for a time. Johnny and his wife Kay live in Bandera, Texas. In Johnny's words, "I have a wonderful wife, a daughter, three grandchildren, two dogs, good health, and a nice home. What more could a man ask for?"

Don H. Burton

Age 16 – United States Marine Corps

I was born at home on Hondo Street in Devine, Texas, on 6 November 1931, the fifth of six children, five boys and one girl. One boy died before his second birthday, but all four surviving boys served in the military. Shortly

> *Thank God the safety was on the rifle, or an old man ... would have dumped his last load of trash.*

after the start of World War II, my oldest brother joined the Army Air Forces. In 1946, the brother just older than I joined the Marines. In 1948, I joined the Marines, and in 1950 my youngest brother joined the Army. Of the four of us, three enlisted underage, and three made the military a career. But I'm getting ahead of my story.

By the time I was 14 years old, I had developed a strong urge to travel and was searching for adventure. My friend and I would hitchhike to San Antonio, about thirty miles away, hang around for awhile, then hitchhike home. Later, I hitchhiked to Houston, about 200 miles away, to visit relatives. My mother didn't like it, and my dad was in bed with TB, so we took advantage of her love for us and did essentially as we pleased.

In 1947, a school friend, Victor Pierce, and I decided to join the Marines. I was only 15 years old, but we headed for the recruiting office in San Antonio. The recruiting officer asked me for my birth certificate, and I told him that there wasn't one. He questioned me further and then called the Medina County Courthouse and found that I was underage. My friend Victor was sworn in and sent to San Diego. I was told to go home and come back in a few years.

My encounter with the recruiter was a setback, but that's all it was. I still had my sense of adventure. My cousin and two acquaintances were looking for a fourth to accompany them to California. It took me about twenty minutes to figure out what argument I could use with my mom. I told her I would be going to Phoenix with my cousin to see my Aunt Ella. She gave in pretty easily, but little did she know that we wouldn't be stopping at Aunt Ella's, but instead would be going directly to California. We each had $20.00 in our pockets, which seemed like a lot of money to us, but when we arrived in Riverside, California, we had only 50¢ among the four of us. We decided to split up in twos and look for work. I worked as a dishwasher in a restaurant and did a little ditch digging. After two months, we returned home just in time to start school in September 1947.

I still had a great desire to be a Marine. One day I was talking about the military with a friend, James Oppelt. I told him about my experience in trying to enlist with Victor Pierce and about how disappointed I was in being turned down when the recruiter called my bluff and checked with the courthouse about my birth certificate. We decided to try another way. I got a copy of my birth certificate, and we went to a lady in San Antonio who altered my birth date to read 6 November 1929. From there we proceeded to the Marine Corps recruiting office in the post office building. We filled out all the necessary forms, and I submitted my altered birth certificate. I was questioned about the obvious alteration. I told them the county clerk had made a mistake and corrected it. The recruiter looked at me, shrugged his shoulders, smiled, and said something to the effect, "Well, if you want it that bad, you got it." I was sworn into the Marine Corps on 28 April 1948.

After boot camp at the Marine Corps Recruit Depot, San Diego, California, I was assigned to VMP-254, a photographic squadron of Marine Air Group-33 (MAG-33), located at the Marine Corps Air Station, El Toro, California. VMP-254 was disbanded in early 1950, and I was assigned to Headquarters and Maintenance Squadron, MAG-33 (H&MS-33).

The Korean War began in June 1950, and the following month, the 1st Provisional Marine Brigade was formed and shipped to Korea. We loaded on ships at Long Beach and met the ships with the grunts (infantrymen) at sea. Just prior to landing in Japan, the infantry units broke convoy and proceeded to Pusan, Korea. I was sent to Itami Airbase, Japan, and worked at the docks at Kobe for awhile.

In September 1950, we boarded a cargo ship and sailed for Korea. We off-loaded at Wambido Island and proceeded to a Seabee base in preparation for going on to the airfield at Kimpo. I was assigned as a driver for a captain and a corporal from a radar unit.

We saw the evidence of war all the way to Kimpo, including a group of about five enemy tanks that were destroyed. Later, my brother told me that it was quite a battle. The North Koreans lost those tanks and about 200 men in that engagement.

After we made the delivery to Kimpo, another driver, whose name was Jerry, and I returned to Inchon to guard equipment. The terrain overlooking the beach area at Inchon appeared to be well-landscaped, and there appeared to be a very nice church on a hill, except for a hole in the roof. We checked it out and found that it was completely gutted. While looking around, we could see that the entire hill was entrenched for battle. We commented that this would be a good place for a sniper. We were carefully going through an earth-covered building, checking for booby traps and land mines as we went. When we came out the other side, Jerry started to look around when we heard a sudden crashing sound. Jerry's eyes became very large, and he kept trying to pull the trigger on his rifle. Thank God the safety was on the rifle, or an old man who caused the noise would have dumped his last load of trash.

I learned later that my brother Johnny was in the Seoul area, about thirty miles north of Kimpo. I had just spent a week on guard duty at Inchon and was allowed a couple of days off. I confirmed my brother's location and went to visit him. I had to hitchhike as there was no transportation available. My brother's outfit had just come off the line but would be going back soon. We had a very nice visit.

I caught a ride back to Kimpo in a helicopter. While waiting for the chopper, I wandered through a small village and noticed a girl about 7 years old with a wound in her left calf. Maggots were in the wound, and nits were in her eyes. I located a medic and a hospital jeep and they took her to a large civilian hospital in downtown Seoul.

When the Chinese entered the war and surrounded the 1st Marine Division at the Chosin Reservoir, I joined a support group and flew into Hagaru-ri to help. I located my brother again while there, but I was ordered to leave by his lieutenant. By then, I was ready to go because it wasn't like the visit near Seoul. The weather and the situation were entirely different.

I served two tours of duty in Korea and a total of eight years in the Marine Corps. I decided to leave the military and was discharged on 23 July 1956.

Don Burton pursued a career in law enforcement after leaving the Marine Corps. He retired in 1987 after twenty-eight years with the Orange County Sheriff's Office and the Orange County District Attorney's Office. Don and Eunice, his wife of forty-one years, live in Santa Ana, California. They have two daughters and nine grandchildren.

√ **VUMS Note** ⇒ *Chesty Puller.* A legendary Marine, Lewis B. "Chesty" Puller, won the Navy Cross five times during nearly forty years of military service. When he retired as a lieutenant general, he held more combat decorations than any other Marine in history. Two underage veterans served under Chesty during the battle for Peleliu. Another was the guidon and reported front and center with Chesty at the ceremony where he was awarded his fifth Navy Cross.

James A. Pressley

Age 11 – United States Army Air Forces
Age 13 – United States Navy
Age 16 – United States Navy

I was always big for my age, and I even played high school football for two years *before* I was in high school. I didn't play football in high school, but that's another story. From the time I was 11 years old

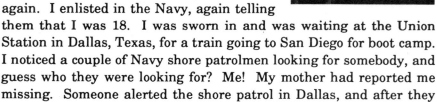

... we were ... having a ball, but ... we knew that men were dying ...

until I was past 30, I wore pants with a 32-inch waist and a 32-inch length.

I was born in Denison, Texas, on 1 January 1932. Like everyone in Denison during World War II, I was very patriotic and anxious to get into the war. So at age 11, since I was physically big enough to enlist, I did. In 1943, I went to Sherman, Texas, a town not far from Denison, and enlisted in the Army Air Forces, telling the recruiter that I was 18 years old. They sent our group by train to Camp Kelly, near San Antonio, where we spent the night and were given physical examinations the next day. The doctor determined that I was tone-deaf in one ear, so I was put back on the train and sent home to Denison. In 1992, I tried to obtain the official records of my Air Forces enlistment, but I was told that they were destroyed in the fire at the National Records Center in Saint Louis in the early seventies.

In 1945, at 13 years of age, I tried it again. I enlisted in the Navy, again telling them that I was 18. I was sworn in and was waiting at the Union Station in Dallas, Texas, for a train going to San Diego for boot camp. I noticed a couple of Navy shore patrolmen looking for somebody, and guess who they were looking for? Me! My mother had reported me missing. Someone alerted the shore patrol in Dallas, and after they picked me up, they put me on the interurban electric train and told the conductor to watch me and make sure that I didn't get off until I was back home in Denison.

By early May 1948, when I was 16, my dad had had enough, so he gave me his permission to join the Navy and signed the papers verifying that I was 17 years old. I was sworn in on 17 May 1948 and sent to the Naval Training Station, San Diego, California. While I was in boot camp, my true age was discovered. I can't remember the details, but my mother had to come to San Diego and was with me when I was taken before a captain. The captain asked me if I wanted to stay in the Navy, and I said yes. He asked my mother if she would give her permission, and she told him that she would sign for me if that was what I wanted and if I could handle the situation.

After boot camp, I was sent across the bay to the North Island Naval Air Station. They flew a group of us to the Alameda Naval Air Station near San Francisco where we boarded a seaplane. It was late at night, and there was just a dim, red light illuminating the cabin. There were probably a hundred men fresh out of boot camp in the plane. We taxied out into the bay, and as we started to take off, the pilot cut in the jet-assisted take-off units. When those jets kicked in, all hell broke loose in the cabin. Men were screaming, hollering, and praying, all at the same time. Not one of the passengers had ever heard of a jet engine before. They were certain that the horrible noise meant that the plane was going to crash. It's funny to look back on it now, but it wasn't funny then.

The pilot shut the jets off as soon as we were airborne, and the next morning we arrived in Hawaii. When we touched down on the water at Pearl Harbor, the pilot made as smooth a landing as anybody ever did on land. We didn't feel anything until the plane was settled in the water.

We were put aboard a troopship at Pearl Harbor and set sail for Guam. Although we were passengers, Navy personnel stood watches and could move about the ship, but the 200 or so Air Force personnel aboard were limited to certain areas. When we hit the outer edge of a typhoon, seasickness was rampant among the Air Force people. We had to pass through their compartment to get to ours, but it was so rank in there that we just stayed away and found other places on the ship to sleep.

I spent eighteen months on Guam. It was there that I started studying for my GED tests. I had to go to Anderson Air Force Base to get the study materials.

After my tour on Guam, I returned to the States on a 30-day leave, then reported to the naval base at Long Beach, California, where I was assigned to the USS *Ashtabula* (AO-51). From Long Beach, we went to Seattle, where we would be for a short time, then we were to go to Point Barrow, Alaska.

In Seattle, I met Larry Shwall, a very good friend from boot camp who was stationed on another ship. Larry had fallen in love with a girl from San Francisco, and he wanted to marry her. He asked me to go to San Francisco with him. That was a mistake, but I did. By the time we hitchhiked to San Francisco, the girl had found somebody else and was already married.

It was obvious that we were not going to make it back to Seattle before our passes were up, so we turned ourselves in at the Alameda Naval Air Station, hoping that we could catch a flight to Seattle. We made it back in time for Larry to catch his ship, but the *Ashtabula* had gone and I was AWOL. I was put aboard the USS *Hector*, where I was immediately court-martialed for being AWOL. My sentence was thirty days of solitary confinement on bread and water. Fortunately, a friend from Denison saw me come aboard. When he found out that I was in the brig, he would come by and slip me food. If it hadn't been for him, I don't know what I would have done. During my sentence on bread and water, I was given a meal every third day, which was not enough food for me. The brig was directly over the ship's screws. During a storm, the screws would come out of the water and the vibration was terrible. After we were underway to Korea, I was released from the brig but was assigned extra police duty.

The USS *Hector* delivered me to Inchon, Korea, just a few days after the invasion. I was transferred immediately to the USS *Comstock* (LSD-19), where I was assigned to Mobile Boat Pool #1, given an LCVP, and told that I was a coxswain. That was the day I met Ted Fleming from the Bronx, New York. You talk about a New Yorker! He was one, accent and all. Ted and I were to be together for the next twenty-one months and would become the best of friends.

After hauling supplies and ammunition to the troops for days, the *Comstock* crew had a recreation party on the beach. We had beer, played softball, and just had a ball. But when we looked up into the mountains some distance away, we could see little puffs of smoke from exploding artillery shells that were so far away that we couldn't hear them. It seemed strange to me that here we were on the beach playing softball, drinking beer, and having a ball, but when we looked up towards the mountains, we knew that men were dying there. It didn't seem right, but we had done our job. We had put the troops on shore and brought them tons of supplies and ammunition.

Shortly after the beach party, the *Comstock* sailed for Sasebo, Japan, arriving there on Christmas Day 1950. We were transferred from the *Comstock* and assigned to the *APL-30*, which was to be my home until I was discharged. It was at Sasebo that I completed my GED exams.

The APL-30 was essentially an oversized apartment house. It had accommodations for many men to sleep and eat. It didn't have a motor, so when it was moved, it had to be towed. Its sole purpose was to provide living space and services for a large number of men.

Personnel of the Mobile Boat Pool were known as "Orphans of the Pacific." This was the best duty that a Navy man could ever hope for. My friend Ted Fleming and I were assigned to the *LCM-15*. We worked for various ships in the harbor, but every other night we were released for shore patrol. We would go to the liberty dock, pick up stragglers, and take them back to their ships. The big aircraft carriers and battleships would sometimes anchor outside of the harbor, so we would have a long run whenever we picked up men from those ships. Most of the time, we just delivered the stragglers to the ships tied up in the buoy area. Being young and foolish, we would deliver all the stragglers, then head for the dry dock, tie up and go ashore to see our girlfriends. At daylight, we would find our way back to the boat and go back to our ship just in time for muster, then hit the sack. We would sleep until noon, get up and work on the dock for awhile, then do the same thing all over again that night.

Just before I left Sasebo, my friend Ted married a Japanese girl and transferred to the ship's company aboard the APL-30. I was never to see Ted again, but I was to hear from him one more time. I returned to the States and was discharged at Treasure Island, California, on 20 April 1952.

For years after the war, I had hoped that someone would organize a reunion of the Mobile Boat Pool personnel. Finally, in 1987, I decided that I would try to organize one to be held in 1988. I placed notices in several veterans magazines, and Ted Fleming was the first to respond. He called and we talked for a long time. I didn't know at that time, but Ted knew that he had cancer, and though he told me he couldn't wait for the reunion, he knew he wouldn't make it. I sent him a picture of the two of us taken at Sasebo. Ted died shortly after that. His son told me later that receiving the picture was one of the happiest, but also one of the saddest, days of his dad's life. We had our reunion, and it was great, but it would have been much better if Ted could have been there.

Jim Pressley worked for a railroad for some time after his discharge from the Navy. Later, he became a lineman with the Radiant Electric Company in Fredonia, Kansas. Jim organized the Orphans of the Pacific Association, a group originally comprised of men who had served with the Mobile Boat Pool in Sasebo, Japan. The group has enlarged to include men from the APL-30 and other units stationed at Sasebo. Jim, currently the association president, reports that four of the "Orphans" are underage veterans, including the secretary, Harrison Roberts. All four are members of the VUMS. Jim retired in 1993 and returned to Denison, Texas, where he and his wife Lorene now reside. They have a combined family of six children and eleven grandchildren.

Jerome M. "Jerry" O'Sullivan

Age 16 – United States Marine Corps

My grandfather, Timothy O'Sullivan, immigrated to the United States in 1865 during a time of intense discrimination against the Irish. He dropped the "O" from O'Sullivan,

> *President Truman got out of the pool and came over to where I was sitting.*

thinking that he would be less likely to be taken as Irish with the name Sullivan.

I was born in Worthington, Minnesota, on 1 August 1931 and given the name Jerome Dale Sullivan. Before entering high school, I decided that I wanted my name to sound a bit more Irish, so I enrolled as Jerome Michael O'Sullivan, using my confirmation name Michael as my middle name because it was more Irish than Dale.

My brother-in-law, Wayne Keep, a Marine veteran of Iwo Jima, portrayed life in the Marine Corps as such an adventure that I couldn't wait to enlist. At the Marine recruiting office in Minneapolis, I told the recruiter that I was 18 years old. A birth certificate with my acquired name could not be found, so I was given a waiver on that requirement. I was sworn into the Corps on 4 June 1948 at the age of 16.

I was assigned to Platoon 44 at' the Marine Corps Recruit Depot in San Diego. Our senior drill instructor, Staff Sergeant Richard Tyner, a Guadalcanal veteran, trained us so well that 100% of the platoon qualified at the rifle range, the first time that had happened since 1942. Major General Hermlee, the commanding general of the recruit depot, was so pleased that he issued an order stating that every man in Platoon 44 could choose his military specialty and his duty station. I chose the post band, thinking that with the band I might have time to complete high school. The band leader, CWO Rupe, asked me what musical instrument I could play. I replied, "The violin," and he ordered, "Get this Marine a violin." After I played it, he said, "You should make a good field music (bugler)." I learned over 100 bugle calls at field music school and then was assigned to the post guard detachment. I was on duty for twenty-four hours, then off for twenty-four hours. This allowed me ample time to complete high school through the Marine Corps Institute.

In April 1949, I was assigned to the 1st Marine Division, Fleet Marine Force, at Camp Pendleton, California, as a field music with the additional duty of stretcher-bearer. We lived in tents, but we had an Olympic-size swimming pool nearby. Beer sold for 10¢ a bottle at the local slop chute, and a ticket to the movies was also 10¢. The nearest city, Oceanside, was thirty miles away. A stray dog that we named "Dog" made his home with us. Dog would bark at anyone wearing civilian clothes. Having neither a wife nor a car, it was easy for me to save half of my paycheck and devote full-time to being a Marine.

In June 1949, I received orders to report to the Marine Barracks, 8th and Eye, Washington, D.C. The Marine barracks was the home of the Commandant of the Marine Corps, the Marine Corps Band, the Marine Corps Institute, and the Presidential Guard. I reported to First Sergeant Newsome who looked me over with a jaundiced eye and marched me in to meet my commanding officer, First Lieutenant John Glenn. Lieutenant Glenn ordered me to stand at ease, asked me a few questions, then informed me that I would be an economics instructor. I was given additional duty as a presidential guard at Camp Shangri-la, now Camp David.

Sergeant Robert Fleishauer appointed himself as my mentor. In one of his counseling sessions, he told me that he was wounded in South America. I knew that Bob was only 25 and that the "Banana Wars" were fought chiefly in the 1920s, so I was skeptical. To prove his veracity he rolled up his left sleeve. On his arm was a large tattoo of a Marine Corps emblem — the eagle, globe, and anchor. He pointed to a scar on the globe where a Japanese bullet had pierced South America.

One afternoon at Camp Shangri-la, I was sitting at the edge of the pool holding my M-1 rifle. President Truman got out of the pool and came over to where I was sitting. He asked me what I did when I was not guarding him. I said, "Nothing, Mr. President." He said, "We have a pretty good movie we are going to show tonight. Come up, if you can, and bring a couple of your buddies with you." That evening, three

Marines, in the company of Harry Truman, his wife Bess, his daughter Margaret, Admiral Denfield and his wife, and a chief petty officer who ran the projector, watched "Broken Arrow," starring Jimmy Stewart. In addition to the full-length movie, there was a short one titled "Fifty Years Before Your Eyes," which covered highlights of events that shaped our country from 1900 to 1950. Near the end, a scene showed Harry Truman holding the *Chicago Tribune* with the headline "Dewey Wins." A few choice comments were made by our host and his daughter. President Truman was the most democratic man that I have ever met.

In the summer of 1950, after the outbreak of the Korean War, I was sent TDY to Quantico, Virginia, as a rifle-range coach, training members of the Marine Corps Reserve who were on their way to Korea. I was promoted to sergeant and reenlisted for a six-year tour. The Corps needed platoon leaders. I was advised to apply for a commission. I sent for a copy of my birth certificate and turned it in with my application. The major handling my paperwork noted that the name on the certificate was different from the name under which I had enlisted. I explained to him what I had done. The major said, "You could be court-martialed." Instead, I received orders to the Naval Academy Prep School and chose the NROTC program which required that I be transferred from the Marine Corps to the Naval Reserve.

On 4 June 1954, I was commissioned a second lieutenant in the Marine Corps and was assigned to Alpha Company, 5th Marine Regiment, as a machine-gun platoon leader and later as company executive officer. In June 1956, I was assigned as aide-de-camp to the commanding general of Camp Pendleton.

In June 1957, I received orders to report to the Marine Barracks, 8th and Eye, Washington, D.C., for duty with the Marine Corps Institute and as a congressional escort officer. In June 1958, I resigned my regular commission and accepted an appointment as a captain in the Marine Corps Reserve.

The following year, I lived in Latina, Italy, where I was a language-school supervisor in the United States Escapee Program. I returned to Minneapolis, Minnesota, in June of 1959, worked at the post office, and joined the Minnesota National Guard. With the Vietnam conflict heating up in 1963, the Army was looking for volunteers, so I volunteered. In September 1963, I was assigned to Fort Leonard Wood, where I served as a company commander and battalion executive officer with the 3rd Training Regiment. I attended the Nuclear Weapons Employment Officers Course at Fort Benning, Georgia, in August 1964. I was assigned to the 7th Infantry Division in Korea in January 1966. I was a company commander until I was promoted to major and was then assigned as deputy post commander at Camp Kaiser, Korea. In January 1967, I reported to Hunter Army Airfield, Savannah, Georgia, where I served as brigade S-3 for the school.

One year later, in January 1968, I was sent to Vietnam, where I was assigned as the headquarters commandant of the 25th Infantry Division. When I returned to the States, I received orders to Fort Hood, Texas, as executive officer of the 110th Replacement Battalion. I graduated from the Command and General Staff College at Fort Leavenworth, Kansas, in July of 1971. My last Army assignment was at Fort Carson, Colorado, where I served in the G-3 Section of the 4th Infantry Division. I retired from the Army on 31 July 1976 with the rank of major.

Jerry O'Sullivan earned the Combat Infantryman Badge and was awarded the Bronze Star, the Purple Heart, and the Republic of Vietnam Cross of Gallantry with Palm. While in the NROTC program, he earned a B.A. at the University of Minnesota in 1954 and after his retirement from the Army, completed an M.A. at the University of Colorado. He worked as a supervisory accounting technician at the Army Commissary at Fort Carson from 1980 until his retirement from the civil service on 1 August 1993. He is now a self-employed tax consultant and an avid big-game hunter. In 1959, Jerry married Maria Szabo of Kormend, Hungary, at St. Peter's Basilica in Rome, Italy. They live in Manitou Springs, Colorado. Jerry and Maria have two sons.

Robert L. Smith

Age 14 – United States Army

As a boy during World War II, my dream was to be a soldier. I read every book or paper I could find that had war stories and war pictures. I was especially interested in the paratroopers and Darby's Rangers. Even at that young

age, I had a real sense of patriotism. I knew the military was the life for me, and I was right.

I was born in Bristol, Tennessee, on 7 March 1934. In June 1948, three months after my fourteenth birthday, I decided it was time to start living my dream. I went to the recruiting office in Bristol and enlisted in the U. S. Army, giving my age as 17. Parental consent was required, so the recruiter was going to drive me home to get my mother's signature. When we arrived at the end of the road, and my

house was still a mile up the mountainside, he said, "You go get your mother to sign here." I was counting on him not to want to climb the mountain for a signature, and it worked. I took the paper and had a cousin sign my mother's name.

I was sent to Camp Pickett, Virginia, for basic training with the 513th Airborne Infantry Regiment. During basic training, after I had committed some small infraction of the rules, my platoon sergeant walked up to me and said, "You little SOB, I know that you are not old enough to be in the Army, and if I thought you could make a living on the outside, I would have your ass kicked out." I have never forgotten those words.

After basic training, I remained at Camp Pickett and went to driving school. I had never driven anything before I went into the Army. (I hadn't tied a necktie before I went into the Army, either.) I was the commanding officer's driver for a time and later went to radio school.

I volunteered for the Airborne and completed jump school on 8 March 1949, one day after my fifteenth birthday. The 11th Airborne Division was coming home from Japan, and the 82nd Airborne was at full strength, so I was assigned to the 1st Infantry Division in Germany. I flew as security on aircraft involved in the Berlin Airlift.

I joined the 511th Airborne Infantry Regiment of the 11th Airborne Division at Fort Campbell, Kentucky, in April 1950. In June 1950, when the Korean War started, I volunteered for duty in Korea. I arrived there on 3 September 1950 and was assigned to the intelligence and reconnaissance platoon of the 7th Infantry Division. Most of the time, we just went up the mountains and down the valleys of Korea. I was wounded for the first time while on patrol near Souwan.

Toward the end of December 1950, the 2nd Ranger Company (Airborne) was assigned to the 7th Division. Being Airborne-qualified, I volunteered and was assigned to the Ranger company. A short time later, I was wounded again and sent to a hospital in Japan. After recovering, I returned to Korea for a time, then was rotated back to the States.

I returned to Fort Campbell in August 1951. By coincidence, I ran into my old basic-training platoon sergeant who, in the meantime, had apparently committed a *big* infraction of the rules and had been reduced in rank from master sergeant to private, and I was a sergeant first class. Ah — sweet revenge!

In November 1952, I volunteered again for duty in Korea and returned to my old division, the 7th, and was assigned to the 32nd Infantry Regiment. We were in and around Old Baldy, Pork Chop Hill, White Horse, and Jane Russell, places familiar to many Korean War veterans. For a time during this period, I was assigned as a forward observer with the Ethiopian Battalion. I was wounded for the third time during the last battle for Pork Chop Hill.

After the Korean War was over, I adjusted to the peacetime Army and had some interesting assignments. In either 1956 or 1957, the Army decided to change the dress uniform to green, and it needed a few men to model the new uniform. The requirements were that a soldier had to be 6-feet tall or over and be a combat veteran. Of the 258 men from the 3rd Army who were screened for the job, only four were selected, and I was one of the four. Essentially, all I had to do was wear the new uniform and display it on Army bases throughout the world. In three and one-half years, I traveled throughout the United States, Europe, and Japan, modeling the new uniform. Great duty! When this gravy train ran out, I patrolled the border between East and West Germany for about five years.

One Monday morning in 1964, I walked into the Pentagon looking for the enlisted branch records department. When I found it, I signed in, filled in the space for stating the reason I was there, and sat down. I was the only person in the room, but that soon changed. In about thirty minutes the room was full. A sergeant picked up the sign-in sheet, left the room, then returned in a few minutes. He said, "There are twenty-eight noncommissioned officers trying to get out of going to Vietnam. There is only one trying to go there. Sergeant Smith, come with me." I had an assignment within thirty minutes and served a short tour in Vietnam as an advisor. I was wounded for the fourth time during that tour. My second tour (1966-67) was with the 11th Airborne Cavalry's Long Range Patrol. We were involved in typical Vietnam operations – patrol, and search and destroy. I was wounded for the fifth time during that tour.

I retired from the Army on 30 December 1969. There was a big ceremony for about twenty of us who were retiring, with a major general in charge. I was also to be awarded my fifth Purple Heart (actually my fourth, as I had already received the fifth, and this one finally caught up with me) and the Army Commendation Medal for Valor. When the general looked at me he said, "Sergeant, how old are you?" Before I could answer he continued, "You look like you should be coming in, not going out. You have more medals than I do." Instead of pinning them on me, he handed me the medals and said, "Put them on wherever you can!"

I always considered myself a professional soldier. I still can't believe that I was able to do everything I had dreamed of as a boy and get paid for it! And I still remember the first time I saw my mother after I enlisted underage. She said, "Son, when you get enough of the Army and want to come home, don't ask me to get you out!" She and I have had many good laughs about that throughout the years.

Robert "Smitty" Smith earned the Combat Infantryman Badge and was awarded a Bronze Star for Valor and a Purple Heart at age 16, the Silver Star, a second Bronze Star for heroism and two Purple Hearts at age 17, all while serving in Korea. He also received the Navy Commendation Medal for leading a squad that assisted the return of a U. S. Marine patrol that had been surrounded by an enemy force. During his two tours in Vietnam, he received two Purple Hearts, another Combat Infantryman Badge, the Army Commendation Medal for Valor, his third Bronze Star for Valor, the Air Medal, and the Vietnamese Cross of Gallantry with Palm. He proudly wore a Master Parachutists Badge. After retiring from the Army, he went to Florida and worked for the Highlands County Property Appraiser's Office until retiring from that position in November 1995. Smitty and his wife Ann live in Gilbert, South Carolina. They have three sons, a daughter, and five grandchildren. All three sons served in the Airborne infantry. One son, an underage veteran who joined the Army at age 15, was killed in an automobile accident in 1993.

√ **VUMS Note** ⇒ *Three wars.* Five of the contributors to this book participated in combat operations in three wars: World War II, Korea, and Vietnam. Two Army infantrymen earned a Combat Infantryman Badge for each war, and three Navy men earned a combined total of thirty-four battle stars on their campaign ribbons for the three wars. One earned nine stars during World War II, three in Korea, two in Vietnam, and participated in a secret operation in Cuba during the Bay of Pigs.

Robert D. Dodson

Age 16 – United States Army

I first attempted to enlist in the Army at Salt Lake City, Utah, when I was 14 years old. I was unsuccessful because I didn't have documentation of my birth date. I was born in Best, Nebraska, on 4 July

> *We arrived in Pusan on 2 July 1950 at 1400 hours in a C-47, ...*

1932, but my birth was never recorded. Getting a notarized statement from my parents would mean returning home, and I had just run away from our home in Colorado, where we were living at the time. Besides, I'm sure my parents would not have signed such a statement.

I hitchhiked to Los Angeles, California, for the sole purpose of mailing a post card postmarked "LA" to my parents, advising them not to worry about me. I then hitchhiked to eastern Utah, where my

cousin was employed in a coal mine. I was hired by the mining company, based on my cousin's verification that I was 18 years old. I became a member of the local union of the United Mine Workers of America while I was still 14 years of age. Three weeks after I started working in the mines, we had a national strike that lasted for two weeks. After returning to work for two months, our local voted for a strike against our mine. During this extended strike, a job opening occurred at the company store. I applied for

the job, was hired, and I remained there until my parents found me. Once the smoke cleared away, it was agreed that my parents would sign the required statement adding one year to my age, provided that I would finish high school in the Army. I was sworn into the Army on 8 July 1948 at Salt Lake City, four days after my sixteenth birthday.

I was sent to Fort Ord, California, for basic training. I passed the GED tests while in basic, but I had to wait two years until my original class graduated to receive a high-school equivalency certificate from the state of Colorado.

I was one of perhaps twenty trainees who were 16 years old. There were also about ten who were 15 and three who were 14. These were the ones that I knew about; there may have been more. The company commander interviewed us "doubtfuls" and asked that we tell him whether we were underage. He promised not to initiate elimination action as long as we toed the mark but that he needed to know. As I understood it, release for minority reasons could be initiated only by the parent or guardian of the underage soldier. Basic training had a certain attrition rate, and some of those that I knew to be underage drifted away. All three of the 14-year-olds completed training and went on to other assignments. I still wonder how long they stayed in the Army.

My first assignment following basic training was to the signal school at Fort Monmouth, New Jersey. While in basic, I had selected cryptographic technician school, and I was given what I had been promised. We were taught touch-typing and teletypewriter operation while our required security clearances were being processed. One day, I was called into the office of the course chief. His first words after I reported to him were, "You are sixteen?" The FBI had done me in! I still think that one of my five personal references blabbed. After showing me the papers that I signed, "... if any of the foregoing information is incorrect, rights to receive subject training are voided." He stated his solution, "I'm recommending you for radio-repair school." My appeal, "But, sir, I don't want to go to radio-repair school," was overridden by his rejoinder, "Maybe you didn't hear me, soldier." The following Monday morning I started the 26-week radio repair course.

Television was in its infancy in 1948. Our company day room had a TV set, and four of us were designated as "television operators." We were the only ones who could touch the controls, even to change channels. This was rostered duty, so we were exempt from KP and guard duty.

After finishing radio-repair school, I received orders to serve in the occupation forces in Japan. I observed my seventeenth birthday at Fort Lawton, Washington, awaiting departure of our troopship. A few days later, I crossed the international date line for the first of many times. I reported to an 8th Army signal company in Kyoto. Once, I overheard my company commander talking to the first sergeant. He said, "Ninety percent of my men are teenagers, and they'll all be alcoholics by the time they are 21." The age composition of our unit remained very young until we received replacement personnel during the Korean War.

On Wednesday, 28 June 1950, we had a company picnic on the shores of Lake Biwa. A courier arrived instructing our company commander to return to his headquarters. Within an hour, we were on our way back to the company area to prepare for departure to Korea. Initially, one communications terminal team of fifteen men and one radio-relay team of eight men were dispatched to Kokura, where we were placed on detached service with the Signal Battalion of the 24th Infantry Division. The radio-relay team was sent to Tsushima Island, and the terminal team of which I was a member was sent to Pusan, Korea.

We arrived in Pusan on 2 July 1950 at 1400 hours in a C-47, one of the few aircraft to get through because of inclement weather. The first contingent of the 24th Division arrived later that night. We set up on the rooftop of a Korean army hospital, but we could not establish communications from there because of line-of-sight restrictions. We moved our equipment to Songdo, about three miles south of Pusan, which was the entry site to Korea of the Tokyo-Mukden, Manchuria, cable that was completed in 1936.

We spent our first night in Korea in sleeping bags on the floor of the American Consulate. Breakfast was served at the Seamen's Overseas Service. The second night, we were assigned a house near the Songdo site, and it was C-rations for quite a while thereafter. Communications were established on 3 July with our team on Tsushima Island, which in turn, tied in with existing facilities at Fukuoka, which terminated at Kokura. This provided four radio-telephone channels between Pusan and Kokura to augment the two lines leased by the American Consulate via the Mukden cable. It was a very hectic five days getting from Kyoto to Songdo and establishing communications. I had survived on catnaps for a week and finally got a night's sleep. Our second day in Korea was my eighteenth birthday. I could now join the Army without parental consent! I was to remain in Korea for seventeen months.

The remaining elements of my company arrived in Pusan in mid-July. Our mission was to link 8th Army Headquarters by radio-telephone to all major subordinate elements. To accomplish this, we had teams at each corps headquarters, all division headquarters, the Marine element, and headquarters of all allied contingents. Because of the constant movement of the various headquarters, jump teams were required to establish communications at each new location while maintaining communications at the old location until they could be shut down. In this way, the members of our unit were exposed to much more of Korea than those assigned to more traditional units.

A sore point still exists because of that distinction. Monthly rotation points were given according to where your unit was based, not where you were physically located. Our unit headquarters was always with Eighth Army Headquarters where fewer points were given, but ninety percent of our people were physically located with corps and divisions whose members received higher rotation points. Many of us became eligible for rotation even though we accumulated fewer points per month. But forget it! Our MOS (military occupational specialty) was designated "critical," and no end was in sight. Compounding the inequity of the points structure was the fact that many of us were now in the "Truman year," a 1-year involuntary extension of our enlistments.

Morale was very low; bitterness was prevalent. Our company had now been absorbed into a signal-service battalion. The battalion was tasked to provide a twelve-man composite team to become jump-qualified to augment the 187th Regimental Combat Team on future operations. Each company was allocated three volunteers. Those selected would receive two weeks' training in Japan. My company had 150 volunteers who wanted a chance to get out of Korea — even for two weeks. This was indicative of our total frustration with still being in Korea. I was one of three chosen from my company. All of us completed the training, but before the next operation of the 187th RCT, I had acquired fifty-three of the required thirty-six points and was finally rotated home.

Given my attitude when discharged, I'm still amazed that I chose to reenlist after seventy-eight days of civilian life. In retrospect, it was one of my better decisions.

My entire career was in the Signal Corps. I completed eight service schools during this time. I served four years with Headquarters, Allied Land Forces, Central Europe, from 1952 until 1956, then returned to Korea for a second tour in 1959-60. I was assigned to the 8th Army Signal Long Lines Battalion. Many of the forty-five sites operated by that unit were locations we had used during the Korean War. It was ironic to see concrete block buildings where we once had pitched tents and to have diesel power-units instead of the portable power-units we had lugged around.

I was promoted to the rank of warrant officer on 15 September 1961. Subsequent duty assignments encompassed all levels of signal maintenance both in the States and overseas, including general support (avionics) of all Army aircraft in Vietnam.

I retired from the Army as a CWO-4 on 30 June 1977, after twenty-nine years of service. I am glad that my service career was completed during the time I served rather than under present-day conditions.

Bob Dodson was awarded the Bronze Star with Oak Leaf Cluster, the Meritorious Service Medal, the Joint Service Commendation Medal, The Army Commendation Medal with two Oak Leaf Clusters, the Parachutists Badge, and a number of campaign and service medals. He graduated from California State University, Sacramento, in 1980 with a B.A. in history. He was a realtor in California for three years, then managed a pipe, cigar, and tobacco shop in California until 1994. He moved to Colorado, where he is currently assistant manager of a tobacco shop. He works limited hours due to Social Security earnings restrictions. While stationed in France, Bob married Catharina Mulder of Rotterdam, Holland, in 1954. Bob and Cathi live in Colorado Springs, Colorado. They have two children, four grandchildren, and one great-grandson.

Billy L. Booth[25]

Age 16 – United States Army

Billy Booth was born in Huntington, West Virginia, on 4 September 1932. He tried to enlist in the U. S. Marine Corps at age 13, but Bill said, "They just kinda laughed at me." He was

> "... I was too young and too stupid to be frightened... til I started getting shot at."

sworn into the U. S. Army on 4 September 1948 at age 16 after convincing his grandmother to sign enlistment papers indicating that he was 18.

Bill related to a *Winona Daily News* reporter, "All my teenage years, I saw war movies. You know, John Wayne and all this stuff. They had so much propaganda for the war (World War II), all these war movies. I was gung ho since I was 10 years old. I just thought that would be the best thing for me, to go into the service. I didn't want to hang around street gangs."

In 1949, Bill was assigned to an Army unit in Japan. When the Korean War started, his unit was sent to Korea and was in combat soon after. When asked how scary it was, Bill said, "Any war is frightening. I've seen men with combat experience who were scared to death. To me, I was too young and too stupid to be frightened when I first got in there, 'til I started getting shot at. Then I realized it was a different war, that I'm being shot at.

It's not cowboys and Indians. We're fighting for our lives."

While using a minesweeper to clear a road for American tanks, Bill was shot in the right leg. He was put on a tank to be taken back to the rear area, but the tank was hit by an artillery shell and he was

---

[25] This account was compiled from the following sources: correspondence with Sue Booth; *Winona Daily News*, Winona, Minnesota, 31 May 1991 and 5 October 1992.

blown off. His right arm and leg were badly injured by shrapnel. He spent one and one-half years recuperating in hospitals.

Bill earned the Combat Infantryman Badge and was awarded the Bronze Star for heroism and the Purple Heart for wounds received in action. Although they were awarded on paper, it would be 1991 before he actually received his medals.

He stayed in the Army after he had recovered from his wounds. In 1960, he was with a group that was sent to Vietnam to provide training for the Vietnamese Army. In 1963, he left the U. S. Army after serving for fifteen years.

Bill went into law enforcement after leaving the Army. He was a police officer in Texas and in Indiana. He served as police chief in Rushford, Minnesota, from 1967 to 1971. After retiring, Bill and his wife Sue made their home in Winona, Minnesota. They had two children and four grandchildren. Billy Booth died on 30 December 1992. He was the first Minnesota State Commander of the Veterans of Underage Military Service.

Robert R. Crepeau

Age 16 – United States Army

I was born in Montreal, Canada, on 27 February 1932, the third of four boys. We were raised by wonderful parents who were married sixty-nine years before my father passed away a few years ago. During my youth, we lived

> *I will never forget Korea, the cold weather ... the human-wave attacks, and the Chinese artillery.*

in Canada, Massachusetts, and Southern California.

In the summer of 1948, my cousin, his friend, and I were unloading banana boats on the docks at San Pedro, Wilmington, and Long Beach, California. Our pay was $1.67 per hour, not bad for kids. That September, the longshoremen went on strike, so we quit our jobs. My cousin and his friend suggested that we join the Army, serve our country, and see the world. This sounded like a good idea to me, so I quit school and went to Fort MacArthur, California, to join the Army. I presented a false affidavit verifying that I was 18 years old, which was accepted without question. I was sworn into the Army that day, 8 September 1948, then I was told to go home and pack my bag because I would leave for Fort Lewis, Washington, the next morning.

On the way home, I couldn't believe that I had made it. Here I was, 16 years old, couldn't read, and didn't know that I wasn't a U. S. citizen, but was a citizen of Canada. When I got home, I went into my room to pack my bag. My mother came in and asked me what I was doing. I told her that I had joined the Army and had to leave for basic training in the morning. My mother thought I was just kidding her. After I convinced her that I had joined, she told me that she wouldn't let me go, that I was too young. I told her that if she tried to stop me, the Army would put me in jail. Hearing that, she and my dad told me I could go and that they were very proud of me. I told them that I would never let them down.

That was the first and the last time that I ever lied to my mom and dad.

I went to Fort Lewis, Washington, for eight weeks of basic training with Baker Company, 53rd Infantry Regiment. After basic, I was assigned to Able Company, 1st Battalion, 4th Infantry Regiment. Our regiment was sent to Alaska, and the 1st Battalion was assigned to guard Ladd Air Force Base near Fairbanks.

My enlistment was up in 1951, but it was extended for a year, the "Truman year." In August 1951, I volunteered for duty in Korea, the only one in my company to do so. In Korea, I was assigned to Fox Company, 2nd Battalion, 7th Infantry Regiment, 3rd Infantry Division, and served as a rifleman. In November 1951, we participated in the battle for "Dagmar," or Hill 355. I will never forget Korea, the cold weather, the poor resupply, the human-wave attacks, and the Chinese artillery.

In February 1952, I was rotated back to the States and was discharged at Camp Roberts, California, on 9 May 1952. I married, worked at several jobs, and fifteen years later, I joined the Army again.

I reenlisted on 15 September 1967 and was sent to Fort Ord, California, for basic training, again. After basic, I completed eight weeks of advanced infantry training, then volunteered for duty in Vietnam. I arrived in Vietnam in 1968, just in time for the Tet offensive. I was assigned to the 1st Infantry Division, and I participated in four campaigns during 1968. I returned to the States in late fall, and was discharged on 1 December 1968.

As a civilian, I made my home in Missouri and worked for a construction company. On 22 July 1971, I enlisted in the Army for the third time, but this time I didn't have to go through basic training. I joined the 1st Battalion, 12th Cavalry, 1st Cavalry Division, at Fort Hood, Texas. In May 1972, I volunteered for Airborne school. I was 40 years old and the age limit was 36, so I had to get an age waiver. At age 40, I was the oldest one in the class. I successfully completed the course on 2 June 1972 and became Airborne-qualified.

When I returned to Fort Hood, I asked my company commander if I could join the 75th Ranger Company. He said, "Go see if they will take you." I was accepted by the Rangers and went on to participate in five major parachute operations. One of the operations was in Germany on 16 October 1973. I made one jump with the German

Airborne and another with the French Airborne, and was awarded parachutist badges from both units.

After I had been two years with the Rangers, the three Ranger Companies were deactivated. I was sent to Berlin and assigned to Able Company, 2nd Battalion, 6th Infantry Division. I was a squad leader and performed honor-guard ceremony duty. I trained in both Germany and Italy, and in 1975, I went to a French commando school for three weeks.

I returned to the States, was stationed at Fort Bliss, Texas, for two years, then returned to Germany and was assigned to the 3rd Armored Division. My next post was Fort Benning Georgia, where I was assigned to the Airborne school and charged with maintenance of the 250-foot jump tower. I was required to make one jump per month. In December 1980, I was one of a three-man team that participated in the Lamar A. Welch Memorial Leapfest. Our team won second place. I was almost 49 years old and was very proud of our second-place trophy for technical proficiency.

After two years at the Airborne school, I went to Vicenza, Italy, where I joined Charlie Company, 1st Battalion, 509th Airborne Infantry Regiment, and the USMCAV (United States Military Community Activity, Vicenza). After one and a half years, I was sent to Germany, where I stayed for another year and a half. I returned to the States in 1985 and spent my last year in the Army with the 9th Infantry Division at Fort Lewis, Washington, where it had all begun thirty-eight years before.

I retired from the Army at Fort Lewis on 1 October 1986. Over a thirty-eight year period, I had served twenty years on active duty and two years in the reserve.

Bob Crepeau earned the Combat Infantryman Badge during the Korean War and another Badge in Vietnam. He received four Army Commendation Medals. After his retirement from the Army, he settled in Columbus, Georgia, and returned to school. He was forced to leave school after six months to have a triple-bypass operation. He is now retired with a 100% service-connected disability pension. Bob and Mary, his wife of twenty years, live in Phenix City, Alabama. They brought eight children into their marriage and now have thirteen grandchildren.

Buddie C. Kiser

Age 16 – United States Army

I was born in Clinchco, Virginia, on 17 May 1932. I registered for the draft listing my birth date as 29 December 1930, which would make me 18 years old. I then used my draft card to prove my age to the Army recruiters and enlisted in the Army on 5 January 1949.

> ... *the Chinese attacked at night north of the town of Honsun.*

I was sent to Camp Breckenridge, Kentucky, for basic training with the 101st Airborne Division. After basic, I was transferred to Fort Lewis, Washington, and assigned to the 1st Battalion, 38th Infantry Regiment, 2nd Infantry Division, for advanced infantry training. I became friends with Omega Gene Hibbert, a World War II veteran who was in my platoon. Gene later transferred to the Division Headquarters.

Shortly after the war broke out in Korea, our division was alerted that we would soon be shipping out. We left for Korea on 1 August 1950, arrived in Pusan on 19 August, and were on the front lines on 21 August. I was in the message center, and my main job was to deliver mail to the companies on the front lines and bring morning reports back to battalion headquarters.

About three weeks after we arrived in Korea, my friend Gene Hibbert rejoined our regiment. His request for combat duty with a rifle platoon had been granted, and he was assigned to Charlie Company. He was on the line only a few days before he was wounded. Forty-five years later I learned that he too was an underage veteran, having joined the Army at age 14. (Gene's story appears on page 92).

We crossed the Naktong River on 15 September 1950, the same day that the landing was made at Inchon. It wasn't long before we had driven the North Koreans across the 38th Parallel. We kept moving north until we reached the Yalu River. The Chinese entered the war at that time, and we retreated to the south. Getting through the six-mile roadblock at Kunu-ri on 28 November was rough. The regiment that preceded us was mauled. We made it through but suffered many casualties.

One of the most controversial and hard-fought battles of the Korean War, at least for the 38th Infantry Regiment, took place on 11 and 12 February 1951. We were supporting the 8th ROK (Republic of Korea) Division when the Chinese attacked at night north of the town of Honsun. After a day of fighting, we made it to the Han River, then withdrew to the south to reorganize our unit. We had suffered about 80% casualties and had lost a considerable amount of equipment. I have heard this battle referred to as the "Honsun Ambush" and the "Honsun Massacre." I was lucky — God was with me.

I was rotated back to the States in June 1951 and was discharged at Fort Benning, Georgia, in 1952. I reenlisted in 1954 and was assigned to the 5th Infantry Division in Munich, Germany. The entire division returned to the States in 1956 and was sent to Fort Ord, California. We were assigned the job of training new recruits. I was discharged from the Army on 6 October 1956.

Twenty years later, in 1976, I enlisted in the Virginia National Guard and served for two years. I serve with the Honor Guard of VFW Post 8979 in Clintwood, Virginia, at the present time. I am proud to have had the opportunity to serve my country.

Buddie Kiser earned the Combat Infantryman Badge during his service in Korea. He worked for the Occidental Petroleum Company, Coal Division, for fifteen years and retired in 1991. Buddie and Ollie, his wife of thirty-two years, live in Clinchco, Virginia. They have three children, four grandchildren, and one great-grandchild.

Thomas A. Lyke

Age 16 – United States Army

I was born in Hollidays Cove, West Virginia, on 5 October 1932. As a teenager, I was actually disappointed that World War II had ended because I had looked forward to serving my country. I spent the night of my sixteenth birthday, 5 October 1948,

> *I was at several different camps on the Yalu River during my twenty-eight months as a prisoner of war ...*

working on my birth certificate, altering it to read 1931 instead of 1932. The next morning, I showed it to my mother and said, "Look, I'm 17 years old. If you sign for me I can join the Air Force." She laughed and said, "If they believe it, I'll sign." My dad wouldn't sign.

I went to the recruiting office and passed the written test, then came the physical. I weighed only 105 pounds, and according to the guidelines, I had to weigh 115. The recruiting sergeant sent me home and told me to come back in three weeks. Three weeks later, we went back to Wheeling, West Virginia, for another physical. On the way to Wheeling the recruiting sergeant bought five pounds of bananas and a gallon of milk. I ate all of the bananas and drank the gallon of milk before we got to the doctor. The doctor weighed me, then looked at me and said, "Put your clothes on." Then he said, "Put your boots on." He weighed me again and asked, "Didn't you have a leather jacket when you came in?" I said yes. The doctor said, "Put it on – get back on the scale – ah, just right, 115 pounds!"

After I had met all the requirements, the recruiting sergeant informed me that the Air Force quota was full, and it would be the next month before I could be sent to basic. I said, "No way." I didn't want to go back home again; I had already said goodby to everyone twice in the past month. So I asked him what else I could do. He said

I could change my enlistment to the regular Army and they would transfer me to the Air Force in six months. I believed him! I was sworn into the Army on 17 January 1949.

I was sent to Fort Knox, Kentucky, for basic training. One day while in basic, I was in a group undergoing PRI (primary rifle introduction) when a jeep pulled up. A sergeant in the jeep called my name and said I was wanted at battalion headquarters. We went to headquarters where I was told to report to Colonel Crombez. When I reported to the colonel he asked me, "How old are you, soldier?" I replied, "Seventeen, sir." He said, "If there is one thing I can't stand, it's a liar. Now let's pretend that you have just walked in the door and reported, and I asked you, 'How old are you soldier?' " I replied, "Sixteen, sir." He told me that if I wanted out of the Army between that time and my seventeenth birthday to come and see him. But if I screwed up, he would have both me and my mother put in adjoining stockade cells for fraudulent enlistment. I believed him. This little 16-year-old kid was scared! Ironically, a little over two years later in Korea, Colonel Crombez would pin a Bronze Star on my tunic.

I was sent to Camp Hood (now Fort Hood), Texas, for advanced armored training with the 6th Medium Tank Battalion. I vividly remember my first dinner at Camp Hood, a steak. It looked like a piece of whole sirloin that covered half of the mess tray. I looked at my food tray and thought to myself, "That is more food than my parents, my brother, and my three sisters have in one meal!"

Our battalion was shipped to Korea in July 1950, where we were essentially a "bastard battalion" because we were used in support of many different units. On 26 October 1950, I was wounded while serving with the 1st ROK (Republic of Korea) Division near Sinanju, and I was evacuated to the Tokyo General Hospital in Japan.

There were about five of us tankers that wanted to get back with old outfits rather than be assigned to different units when we left the hospital, so in December 1950, we volunteered to go back to Korea. We believed our own propaganda that the war would be over by January. I went back to my unit, which was on the front lines.

On 14 and 15 February, elements of the 23rd Infantry Division had been cut off near Chip-Yong-ni. Colonel Crombez, who then commanded the 5th Cavalry Regiment of the 1st Cavalry Division, initiated a plan to rescue the 23rd. Infantrymen from L Company boarded our tanks, and we started towards the trapped men. The

Chinese raised heck with our column by shooting the infantry off our tanks to the point that we had to abandon the idea of taking the infantry in. On one occasion, I left the tank and picked up a couple of the wounded and placed them on my tank. Colonel Crombez watched me from the tank directly in back of mine. My platoon leader was going to court-martial me for leaving my tank, but instead, Colonel Crombez recommended me for the Bronze Star. My company commander and two of my friends in a tank behind the colonel's were killed. The Air Force was grounded that day because of weather. There was a lot of second-guessing about this action, but it worked, and we were able to break the Chinese plan to wipe out the 23rd Regiment of the 2nd Division and their supporting units.

We were working an area with our tanks on 25 April 1951. We had heard that there were sixty-five wounded rangers left behind after a particularly hard battle, so we took a platoon of tanks and went to get them. We found them, loaded them on jeeps and trucks and sent them out of there. We stayed behind as a rear guard. Later that night, all hell broke loose and we lost the entire unit. Many of us ended up wounded or missing, and several were killed. I managed to avoid capture for four days by hiding in a cave before I was finally captured on 29 April 1951. For some reason, my captors thought that I was an officer, or they would have killed me. They couldn't speak English and I couldn't speak Korean or Chinese.

I had been hit in the head and chest during a bombardment by our own artillery and was having a hard time. I didn't see another GI for about nine days. Finally, I was placed in a staging area with 200 other prisoners, where we were interrogated, then marched to a mining camp. I escaped one time and was gone for two days before they caught me. I was beaten quite badly. I told my friends that I would not try to escape again unless I had two other people with me, one who knew the language and customs of the Korean people, and the other a full-blooded American Indian who knew how to survive in the countryside. Within a week, new POWs were brought to our camp. Among them were Kazumi Airkiki, a Japanese-American who spoke Korean and Chinese, and William Deer, whose Indian name was "Deer With Two Horns." About a month later, Kazumi, Deer, Larry Bridgewater, and I made our escape while our group was being moved from one camp to another. Within forty-five minutes the bugles sounded for the prisoners to assemble, and the Chinese knew we were missing. We were soon caught by Chinese soldiers and severely beaten. William Deer was probably the biggest and strongest of the four of us, but they beat him on the head so hard that he bled to death two days later.

I was placed in solitary confinement at several different locations in North Korea because I was part of a group that tried to disrupt indoctrination programs. We also tried to steal food for the sick. The enemy's policy was to split up the reactionaries and ship them to various locations, hoping to reduce the amount of trouble they caused. I was at several different camps on the Yalu River during my twenty-eight months as a prisoner of war of the North Koreans and Chinese.

When I was captured, I weighed about 155 pounds. After three months in the camps, my weight was at its lowest, 87 pounds, mostly due to disease. When I was released from the POW camp on 28 August 1953, I weighed 120 pounds. I had survived quite a few of the diseases that were common among the POWs, but they had taken their toll on me.

Shortly after I was captured, my mother received a telegram stating that I was killed in action. The next day, she got a letter from our company cook who told her that some of our friends had seen me alive. Shortly after that, she received a telegram saying that I was missing in action, and a year later she received word that I was a prisoner of war.

I returned home and was discharged from the military on 24 October 1953. I considered reenlisting several times, but it just never worked out. I always tell people that I was born in West Virginia and grew up in the U. S. Army. The friends that I made during the time of my Army service are just as close as my family.

Tom Lyke was awarded the Bronze Star for valor and three Purple Hearts for wounds received in action. After his release from the POW camps and his return home, he received the POW Medal. Tom worked at the post office in Weirton, West Virginia, for seven years, then started his own construction business. He moved to the Dallas/Arlington area of Texas in 1983 and continued in the construction business. He built homes and small strip-centers until 1986 when his health failed. Since his retirement on a 100% service-connected disability, he has had cancer and a stroke, but he reports that he is currently doing great. Tom served as National President of the Korean Ex-POW Association for three years. During the 1992 ground-breaking ceremonies for the Korean War Memorial in Washington, D.C., he had a photo session with President Bush. Tom and Charlotte, his wife of forty-two years, live in Sugar Land, Texas. They have two children and one grandchild. Tom is currently Texas State Commander of the Veterans of Underage Military Service.

✓ **VUMS Note** ⇒ **Audie Murphy, underage veteran?** The widely held view that America's most decorated soldier was an underage veteran is apparently a myth. People who knew Audie thought he was underage because he looked so young. The movie, "To Hell and Back," in which Audie plays himself, contributed to the confusion. In the final scene in which Audie is to receive the Medal of Honor, the narrator states that he received the award on 9 August 1945, "shortly after his nineteenth birthday." This is Hollywood manipulating the facts.

Audie was born in a tenant farmer's house located in a cotton field near Celeste, Texas, on 20 June 1924. He joined the Army on 30 June 1942, ten days after his eighteenth birthday. He received the Medal of Honor on 2 June 1945, eighteen days before his twenty-first birthday.

Although a birth certificate for Audie is not on file with the Texas State Department of Vital Statistics, the numerous books that have been written about him, including his own autobiography, *To Hell and Back*, confirm that he was born on 20 June 1924. Had Audie been underage, his birth year would have had to be 1925 or later. It is doubtful that it could have been later, because a brother was born in 1926 and another in 1928. The evidence is strong that Audie Murphy was 18 years old when he enlisted in the Army.

Reference: Don Graham, *No Name on the Bullet*, Penguin Books, 1989.

Walter L. "Bud" Murray

Age 15 – United States Army

In the years just after World War II, jobs were hard to find for young men, especially around Enid, Oklahoma, where I was raised. I was the oldest of six children, my father had died, and my mother was struggling to keep food on the table. I decided to join the

> ... my CO found me on the battlefield and demanded to know my true age.

Army. In order to do this, I had a statement notarized signifying that I was born on 29 December 1931 instead of my true birth year of 1933. With this statement, I enlisted in the Army on 17 January 1949, nineteen days after my fifteenth birthday.

I was sent to Fort Chaffee, Arkansas, for basic training and from there to Fort Bliss, Texas, for training with antiaircraft weapons. The training at Fort Bliss was interrupted while I attended artillery mechanics school at Fort Sill, Oklahoma. After completing the training at Fort Bliss, I was sent to Fort Lewis, Washington, and assigned to Battery A, 82nd Antiaircraft Battalion, 2nd Infantry Division. In early June 1950, I received orders to go to Japan. I was given a leave before going overseas, but during my leave, the Korean War began, and I was ordered to report back to my unit for duty. My orders to go to Japan were changed; I would be going to Korea with the 2nd Infantry Division.

We left the port of debarkation in Seattle on 3 August 1950 and arrived at Pusan, Korea, on 16 August. At this time, the North Koreans were on the offensive, and the Pusan Perimeter was shrinking. We didn't have far to go to be in combat. In mid-September, after the landings at Inchon, we headed north and by November reached the Yalu River. When the Chinese intervened, we were forced to pull back. The trip from Kunu-ri to Sunchon on a narrow road through mountains was, to put it mildly, rough. The

Chinese, positioned on both sides of the road, were determined to stop us from reaching Sunchon. We had to run what soon became known as "The Gauntlet," with wrecked vehicles everywhere and the Chinese all around shooting at us. My section made it through, but many didn't.

During this time, I was chief of a gun section, and I was only 16 years old. The section consisted of eleven men who operated a half-track with quad-mounted 50-caliber antiaircraft machine guns and an M-19 light tank with twin-mounted, 40mm cannons. We were an antiaircraft outfit, but since there weren't many enemy aircraft to shoot at, we provided close support for the infantry.

Meanwhile, my Aunt Terry in Fairplay, Missouri, found out where I was and contacted my commanding officer. Soon after that, my CO found me on the battlefield and demanded to know my true age. I admitted my age and was immediately pulled out of combat and sent back to the States. I was given an honorable discharge on 7 July 1951. I had served two years and five months, and I was not yet 18 years old.

Soon after my eighteenth birthday, still feeling the need to serve my country, I joined the National Guard. I served four years as a drill sergeant with the 45th Division of the National Guard in Enid, Oklahoma.

Bud Murray went into the construction industry after being discharged from the Army. He owned and operated Murray Construction at Great Salt Plains near Jet, Oklahoma, for thirty-five years. During this period, he built many homes in the Jet area, helped build the Vining Church and the fire department building. After retiring from construction, he spent several years as a hunting guide and was a volunteer fireman. Currently, he is employed as a building and maintenance technician with the Oklahoma State Park and Tourism Department. Bud is the father of three children from previous marriages. He and his wife June live in Jet, Oklahoma.

Tony "Doc" Zdanavage[26]

Age 15 – United States Army

Tony Zdanavage was born in Dorrance Township, near Wilkes-Barre, Pennsylvania, on 29 May 1933. From the time he was 7 years old, Tony worked on neighboring farms during the summer months and attended school in a one-room school-

> *"I was in the last war, your brother will be in this one, and you will be in the next!"*

house. He was 5'11" and weighed 178 pounds when he graduated from the eighth grade. At age 14, tired of farm work, he got a job working on a highway being constructed seventeen miles from his home. That winter, when the highway job came to an end, he returned to farm work. He had been thinking of joining the military for some time. He wanted to wear a uniform like his dad wore in World War I and his older brother and uncles wore during World War II. He often remembered an incident on 7 December 1941 when his dad said to him, "I was in the last war, your brother will be in this one and you will be in the next!" At that time, Tony didn't realize how prophetic that statement was.

At age 15, Tony tried registering for the draft, but he was told that he would need a birth certificate. He tried the Navy, but it too wanted proof of age. His cousin, a veteran of World War II, had stayed in the Army and was now a recruiting sergeant in a nearby town. Tony approached his cousin about joining the Army. His cousin, thinking that Tony was 17, said that he could join if he could get his parents' written consent. Tony walked the seven miles home and told his parents that he needed them to sign papers so that he could join the Army.

Tony's cousin, the recruiting sergeant, came to the house the following day, and his parents signed the papers. Tony took the entrance tests, a physical examination, and was sworn into the Army

---

[26] This account was compiled from the following sources: correspondence with Esther Zdanavage; Tony Zdanavage and Esther Zdanavage, *Korea, the War America Forgot to Remember*, published by Tony and Esther Zdanavage, 1991.

on 18 January 1949. He was sent to Fort Jackson, South Carolina, for basic training, then to Fort Lewis, Washington. Tony wanted to be a truck driver, but three days after arriving at Fort Lewis, he was assigned to the First Mobile Army Surgical Hospital (MASH) for training as a medical and surgical technician. He worked in all departments of the hospital. After his training period was over, he was assigned to the Madigan General Hospital at Fort Lewis. Tony often pondered on how lucky he was that the Army trained him in a job he truly loved.

In early 1950, Tony received news that his mother was gravely ill and not expected to live. He obtained a 30-day emergency leave and returned to Pennsylvania, but it was too late to see his mother alive. When he returned to duty in Washington, he applied for a hardship discharge, intending to return home to help care for two younger brothers and his father, who suffered from being gassed in World War I and from black lung disease as well, the result of working in coal mines.

While he was waiting for discharge, he received orders to go to Japan. His commanding officer removed him from the orders because of the pending discharge. Two weeks later, he was ordered to Tripler Army Hospital in Hawaii. Again, his commander intervened. On 25 June 1950, the war began in Korea and Tony was transferred to the 2nd Infantry Division, which was preparing to go to Korea. In November 1950, while under heavy enemy fire, an officer informed him that his hardship discharge request was denied.

After arriving in Pusan, Tony was sent to a staging area where he was assigned to the 37th Field Artillery Battalion as a combat medic. That very same day, his unit moved to the front lines. The artillery guns were positioned, and everyone was told to dig a foxhole. Tony was sitting in a truck writing a letter home when he heard explosions. A soldier called to him and asked him where his hole was. Tony pointed to the hole and started to get out of the truck. The soldier and an enemy shell landed in the hole at the same time. Tony's first job in combat was to gather up the pieces of that soldier, a duty that would be repeated many times in the coming months.

Tony's unit broke out of the Pusan Perimeter and moved north with the rest of the Eighth Army. In November 1950, the Chinese intervened and forced the Eighth Army to withdraw. Caught in a roadblock, Tony was wounded in the head and later captured by the

Chinese. He was forced to treat wounded Chinese and was constantly harassed. He was released later and found his way back to friendly lines where he was picked up by an American truck and given medical attention. During an 83-day period, from the time he was picked up by the truck until he was back in Pennsylvania and discharged from the Army, he remembered nothing. Eighty-three days were gone from his life.

Adjustment to being home was not easy for Tony. He was discharged on 17 February 1951 and returned to find that most people were unconcerned about the war going on in Korea. Medically retired from the Army at 17, he would go looking for a job, only to be told to come back when he was old enough. Living with relatives put such a strain on both him and his relatives that at times he resorted to sleeping in his car.

He finally found a job with a bakery contractor to run a bread route for $15.00 per week, plus commissions. During that time, he started to date a local girl. Her parents accepted him into their home, gave him a roof over his head, and treated him like a member of the family. Within a few months, Tony and Esther were married. Esther's father took him into his school-bus business as a partner. He drove a school bus until someone complained to the authorities that he was only 18 years old, not 21, as the law required. A wounded combat veteran who could drive any vehicle in the United States Army was too young to drive a school bus!

Tony went to work in the coal mines after his wife made out a card that claimed he was 21 years old. He and Esther were then able to afford a place of their own. During those years, Tony worked at a number of jobs and completed a college degree in business administration. He was a patrolman, a deputy sheriff, a criminal investigator for a local police department, a top insurance salesman, and later, a manager for one of the largest insurance companies in America. Tony and Esther had two sons and four grandchildren.

Health conditions stemming from the Korean war caught up with Tony in 1977. He was forced to retire from his job as district manager for the Prudential Life Insurance Company. In 1986, his right leg was amputated because of poor circulation and gangrene brought on by his feet having been frozen while he was a prisoner in North Korea.

Fed up with the treatment received by Korean War veterans and with the fact that the war was essentially forgotten by the American people, Tony and Esther Zdanavage formed the Korean War Awareness Project. From 1985 until 1991, they received over 35,000 letters from veterans who had the experience of coming home to a country that was not only unaware of the war, but didn't care. They held an annual memorial service in commemoration of Korean War veterans and were instrumental in getting memorials in several states. They received letters commending their efforts from General R. G. Stilwell, who headed the Korean War Memorial Advisory Board until his death, and from General A. M. Gray, Commandant of the Marine Corps.

Tony and Esther were co-authors of the book, *Korea, The War America Forgot to Remember*. The book relates Tony's life story and contains letters from a number of war veterans who had problems adjusting when they returned home. Tony died in July 1993.

√ **VUMS Note** ⇒ *Witnesses to surrender.* Three underage veterans told about witnessing the surrender of the Japanese on 2 September 1945, marking the end of World War II. It is not very well known that there were actually several ceremonies of surrender going on at the same time. The main one, and the best known, was the ceremony aboard the USS *Missouri* in Tokyo Bay. A sailor who had just turned 17 watched the ceremony from his ship a short distance away. It was a great thrill to him to be a part of such a historic event. Another underage veteran, watching the ceremony from his ship anchored close by, had sailed into Tokyo Bay the day before as part of a naval force escorting Army occupation forces to Japan. A third sailor was the youngest crew member aboard the USS *Portland* anchored in the harbor at Truk Island, the site of the surrender of Japanese forces in the Central Pacific. He had a front row view of that historic ceremony.

Richard A. Noland

Age 15 – United States Army

I grew up in the small town of St. Marys, West Virginia. My friends were all older than I was, and most of them enlisted in the military when they were 17. After my friends left, there was nothing for me in St. Marys, so I went to see the Army recruiter. He told me that my parents would have to sign some papers, and I would have to bring a birth certificate. I told him that I was born at home and didn't have a birth certificate. I said that my birth was recorded in the family Bible. The recruiter gave me the papers for my parents to sign and told me to meet him at the post office in two days, at eight o'clock in the morning.

> *I landed at Inchon a day or two after the assault.*

My parents would not sign my papers, although they reluctantly gave me their permission to enlist. I signed the papers myself, using a pencil. I met the recruiter at the post office on the appointed day, and we went to his office in Sistersville, West Virginia. When I gave him my papers, he said that they should be signed in ink. I told him that we didn't have a pen. He gave me a pen and I traced the names in ink.

I took a couple of tests in Sistersville, then was sent to the recruiting office at Wheeling, West Virginia, for a physical. The doctor listened to my heart, I peed in a tube, went down the hall, was given a meal ticket and a train ticket, and at 11:30 that night, I was on a train to Fort Knox, Kentucky. This was on 27 January 1949.

I completed basic training at Fort Knox, then was sent to Fort Benning, Georgia. I was assigned to the 537th Quartermaster Laundry Company, but we didn't have a laundry, so I walked a lot of guard duty. I went to Little Creek, Virginia, for amphibious-assault training, and in December 1949, participated in war games in Puerto Rico and Haiti.

Early in 1950, we were sent to Camp Stewart, Georgia, to reactivate the post. It had been closed since the end of World War II. The men all came from Fort Benning, mostly from the 3rd Infantry Division. I was at Camp Stewart for a short time only. When the Korean War broke out, I returned to Fort Benning, was issued some new clothes, and put on a train for the West Coast, destination Korea. I landed at Inchon a day or two after the assault. I was still with the 537th Quartermaster Laundry Company, still without a laundry, so I took care of a small P.O.L. (petroleum, oil and lubricants) dump and did whatever duty that came up, nothing fancy.

By November 1950, we were set up near Wonsan, this time with a laundry. When the front-line troops could leave their positions, they could come to our unit, have a shower and get clean clothes. When the Chinese intervened, we withdrew to Pusan, regrouped, then started moving north again.

On 31 December 1951, we were at Inchon ready to go aboard a ship. It was dark and the tide was out. We had to climb down over a bank and slosh through mud to a landing craft that would take us to the ship. We pulled out of Inchon harbor on New Year's Day 1952 and returned to the States. I was sent to Fort Lee, Virginia, for discharge, but came down with yellow jaundice and spent some time in the hospital. I was discharged on 9 June 1952.

Dick Noland worked at a number of jobs all over the eastern part of the United States as a jack-of-all-trades and master-of-none. However, he did master the art of bricklaying and worked for seventeen years on units four, five, and six of the coal-fired power plant at Conesville, Ohio. Dick helped lay the high-temperature clay and bricks in the boilers. His crew built two of the stacks at the plant. He vividly recalls laying the final bricks on the stacks, 812 feet in the air. He retired after thirty years. Dick and his wife Rachel live in Newcomerstown, Ohio. They have three children and one grandchild.

Edward I. Arthur

Age 13 – Ohio National Guard
Age 15 – United States Army

I was born in Columbus, Ohio, on 15 June 1935. During the 1940s, everyone in our household would listen to the evening radio broadcasts, and I soon became a student of world affairs. While attending

> *I knew that the chopper could go up in flames at any minute.*

the Starling Middle School, I changed the date on my birth certificate, and on 1 March 1949, at the age of 13, I joined the 174th Field Artillery, Ohio National Guard. I served for two years in the Guard and was honorably discharged.

On 15 February 1951, at age 15, I enlisted in the U. S. Army, again using my altered birth certificate to prove that I was old enough. After basic training, I was assigned to the 508th Airborne Infantry Regimental Combat Team. Shortly after I completed jump school at Fort Benning, Georgia, I volunteered for assignment to Korea. At this

time, the Army was scrutinizing all personnel whom they suspected of being underage. Consequently, my real age was discovered, and I was honorably discharged on 31 July 1951.

I bided my time, and in 1961, I joined the Anti-Castro Freedom Fighters, Commandos "L," who were supported by the CIA, and was with that unit until 15 June 1965. I served as a gun runner, organizer, and guerilla fighter, with the rank of captain. Most of my time was spent in surveillance in

Cuba, Costa Rica, and Nicaragua. However, I participated in surveillance activities in some iron-curtain countries of Eastern Europe. Had any of us been captured during these undercover operations, we would have been exploited and then eliminated.

I reenlisted in the Army in 1966, and on 22 June 1966, at the age of 31, I graduated from basic training as outstanding trainee. After basic training, I went to Vietnam and was assigned to B Troop, 1st Squadron, 9th Cavalry, 1st Air Cavalry Division. I was a door gunner in a Huey gunship on the Red Team and later a recon-scout gunner in an OH-13 helicopter with the White Team. We were known as "The Headhunters." We would fly just over the treetops to draw enemy fire. When they spotted us, they would shoot everything they had at us. We would radio their location to gunships that would come in and work over the area. My job was to lean out of the chopper and shoot it out with the Viet Cong. We were quite successful for about eight months, but while on a mission on 13 May 1967, my helicopter was shot down near Duc Pho.

After the crash, I could see fuel leaking from the chopper's tank. I knew that it could go up in flames at any minute. I shouted to the pilot to get out, and I managed to pull myself a short distance away. Looking back, I could see that the pilot was still in the cockpit. I realized that he was knocked out, maybe even dead. I had to find out for sure, so I crawled back under the rotor blade, which was still turning, and made it to the cockpit. Somehow, I unbuckled the pilot and pulled him to safety. He was semiconscious and kept brandishing his pistol saying, "Where are they?" I coaxed and pulled him into a bombshell crater where we could survive if the chopper blew up. It would also provide a little protection if the Viet Cong were nearby, which they were.

We heard the sound of a helicopter close by. It was the other OH-13 that had started the patrol with us. Soon, four gunships were circling overhead and firing rockets and machine guns at some hedgerows nearby. The return fire indicated that there were a lot of VC in the area. One chopper went down. By this time the pilot's mind had cleared, and he pointed to a chopper that had landed to pick us up. Because of severe injuries to my spine, pelvis, and left foot, I was hurting so badly that I didn't think I could make it, so I told him to make a run for it. He said, "We're in this together," and proceeded to drag me to the rescue chopper.

I returned to the States for hospitalization and was discharged later that year. I underwent several years of medical treatment after that, but I always felt that I needed to return and finish my assignment. I enlisted in the Army for the third time in December 1969. I had to fake a physical exam to get in this time. Upon returning to Vietnam, I was a reconnaissance scout in the "Rat Patrol." I was injured again, evacuated from Vietnam, and I completed my military service as an instructor at the Reconnaissance Commando School (Recondo) at Fort Carson, Colorado, training Army Airborne Rangers. I was discharged on 3 July 1971 and began an equally interesting and exciting career in law enforcement and undercover narcotic investigations.

Ed Arthur earned the Combat Infantryman Badge and was awarded the Bronze Star, five Air Medals with combat "V," and the Purple Heart with Oak Leaf Cluster during two tours in Vietnam. He held a number of jobs in law enforcement after his release from the Army. As an undersheriff in Teller County, Colorado, he made a heroic arrest during a hostage situation for which he received the Silver Star for Bravery from the American Police Hall of Fame. In addition to being inducted into the American Police Hall of Fame, he received its Lifetime Achievement Award, Certificate of Achievement in Criminal Investigation, and its Merit Award for Excellent Arrest, as well as the Silver Star. He has worked with the FBI, the ATF, and a number of state organizations and agencies in both overt and covert operations. His Vietnam exploits are described in the book Sgt. Ed Arthur's Nam, *by Ulf Goebel, in Matthew Brennan's* Headhunters, *and in Turner Publishing Company's* The Legacy of the Purple Heart, Vol. II. *His many years as an undercover agent are described in Mike Wales' book,* Ed Arthur's Glory No More. *Ed lives in Lancaster, Ohio. He has three daughters and a son. One daughter served in the U. S. Air Force and is now with the Army Reserve and another is currently serving in the U. S. Navy. Ed is the Ohio State Commander of the Veterans of Underage Military Service.*

Robert O. Buyanovits

Age 16 — United States Army

I was born in Passaic, New Jersey, on 23 December 1932. My brother John and I were raised in an orphan's home in Passaic. During World War II, my father was in the Seabees. When he came home

I got in trouble with my sergeant, and a few weeks later ... overseas.

from overseas after the war, he remarried and took us out of the orphan's home. The marriage lasted about six months, and afterward, we moved into a one-room apartment. I was 15 years old at the time.

I was not going to school at age 16, so I got a job washing dishes during the day and delivering hot dogs and rolls to push carts in New York City at night. I soon tired of that life, so I decided to join the service. Since my dad was in the Navy, I tried to join the Navy, but I failed the I.Q. test. Undaunted, I went next door to the Marines. The sergeant took one look at me and kicked me in the butt and said, "Come back when you grow up." So, I went next door to the Army. I

had changed the date on my birth certificate so that I would appear to be old enough. I passed, was accepted, and was sworn into the Army on 5 May 1949.

I was sent to Fort Dix, New Jersey, for basic training. After basic, I was assigned a cooks helper MOS. I got in trouble with my sergeant, and a few weeks later I received orders for shipment overseas. I was sent to Trieste, Italy, became a "Trust Trooper," and had my MOS changed to infantryman. I spent two years, six months and eleven days

in the 4th Platoon of Company A, 351st Infantry Regiment. We were a very well-trained outfit. I was first gunner in a 57mm recoilless rifle section.

We were told we were ambassadors, and that our main objective was to keep the Yugoslav Army from crossing into the Free Territory of Trieste. At that time, the Yugoslavs had one of the largest armies in Europe. We patrolled borders on foot and in jeeps during my tour. We also spent a lot of time on outposts.

I was discharged from the Army on 18 November 1952 after serving more than three and a half years, of which nearly three years were overseas. My brother served with the Air Force in Korea, and my father was aboard the aircraft carrier USS *Leyte* off the coast of Korea.

Bob Buyanovits became an auto mechanic and went to work for Vey Cadillac in Rockaway, New Jersey. He worked for that company for thirty years, the last twenty as service manager. In 1983-84, he was given an award as "Service Manager of the Year" for Cadillac. After leaving the automobile business, he became head of maintenance at two schools in Blairstown, New Jersey. Bob and Doris, his wife of forty-three years, live in Stillwater, New Jersey. They have five children, fourteen grandchildren, and two great-grandchildren.

√ **VUMS Note** ⇒ *Growing up fast.* Serving underage in the military triggered the feeling of "growing up fast" for some veterans. After two years overseas and fighting in several battles, one veteran said he felt like a 40-year old man in an 18-year old body — although he admitted that he was a *proud* old man. Another veteran who enlisted in the Army at age 16 came home after six years feeling 50 years old. He added that although he wouldn't trade that experience for anything, he wouldn't recommend it, either. Mike Boorda summed it up very well. While reminiscing about his late teens when he had begun to settle down, he commented, "You don't have to be very old to grow up fast."

Edward E. Gilley

Age 16 – United States Air Force

By the time I was 11 years old, I was on my way to growing up fast. We lived in Middletown, Ohio, where I was born on 28 August 1932. In 1944, my father died as a result of an industrial accident, and my mother was hospitalized in another state, recovering from an automobile accident. I tried to take care of myself and to help out at home. I had a paper route, cut grass around town, and caddied at the golf course. I was working on a vegetable farm at age 14. It was a good job. It paid $40.00 a month, with room and board in the bunkhouse. We worked from sunup until dark, seven days a week, with one week off each month.

"Dammit, Gilley, do it again, and this time don't let me see you sweat!"

At age 15, I got a job working the second shift at a defense plant in Trenton, Ohio, grinding valves for the Navy. When I applied at the plant, I gave 19 as my age. I was in the tenth grade at the time. I would go to school during the day then hurry to the plant to start the 3:30 shift. When the management found out I was only 15, I was quietly paid off and asked not to tell anyone. If the school or the juvenile authorities had found out that the plant had hired me, the management would have been in trouble.

I didn't know what else to do, so I decided to join the military. I changed the date on my birth certificate to read "10 February 1931" instead of "28 August 1932," and took the altered certificate to a photographer to have a "poor" copy made so that the changes wouldn't be too obvious. The closest recruiting office happened to be the U. S. Air Force. I was filling out my application when I looked up and saw my high school basketball coach, a Reserve Air Force captain, enter the room. I hurried into the restroom before he had a chance to recognize me. Other than that, I had no problem enlisting.

On 20 June 1949, I was off to Lackland Air Force Base, San Antonio, Texas, for basic training. Basic was rough, but for the first time that I could remember, I had more than one pair of shoes and a lot of new clothes. The chow was plentiful, and I gained twenty pounds in a short time. I was squad leader of the first squad and on my way to great things in the Air Force. Unfortunately, the Air Force checked my school records, found that I was underage, and decided that I was to be discharged. My mother wrote a letter giving her approval for me to stay in the Air Force, and my drill sergeant gave me a favorable recommendation, but to no avail. I was given an honorable discharge from the Air Force on 16 September 1949.

Eighteen days later, now 17 and with my mother's permission, I returned to the recruiting office to reenlist. On 4 October 1949, I was again sworn into the U. S. Air Force and sent to Lackland Air Force Base. When I reported in at the base, a lieutenant said that there were only two lines: one for those reenlisting with over ninety days of previous service, and one for those who were to go to basic training. He told me to get in the basic-training line.

I didn't have to take the shots or the blood test, but they shaved my head again. After we were issued clothing, we were standing outside when we heard this drill sergeant coming toward us shouting that he didn't deserve this miserable, stupid-looking bunch. After he took about three steps past me he suddenly stopped, turned and said, "Gilley, is that you?" "YES, SIR!" I shouted. "Do you want some more?" "YES, SIR!" "Do you like it?" "YES, SIR!" "Give me twenty-five!" While all the other guys were laughing I dropped to the ground and started doing pushups, loudly counting, "One, two, three, ..., etc." Sergeant Goetz stood there amazed, and after I had finished and recovered, he looked at me and said, "Dammit, Gilley, what are you doing back here? Give me another twenty-five and this time sound off, and don't you dare sweat. Dammit, Gilley, I told you not to sweat. Now do it again, and this time do it right – no sweating!" Ah, good old basic training, and Sarge hadn't changed a bit.

Throughout basic training, Sarge would say, "Gilley, show 'em how to double time around the grinder. Dammit, Gilley, that looks too easy – now run backward." After graduation, Sergeant Goetz said to me, "Gilley, you are a tough SOB, but don't let me catch you back here again!" We parted with a smile and a handshake.

While waiting for assignment, I was told, "Gilley, we need a drill instructor, and after six months of basic training you should be able to get it right." So they kept me for a few weeks as an assistant drill instructor, mostly for laughs. Then it was off to Chanute Air Force Base, Illinois, to attend parachute riggers school, and then off to Europe. During a 30-day delay en route to Europe, I went home and married the girl I had known since childhood. We were married just a few days after the Korean War started.

I went to Marburg, Germany, then was assigned to Erding Air Depot, near Munich, Germany, where I remained for two and one-half years. While I was there, I flew as a crew member to many different countries in Europe, Africa, the Near East, and the Middle East. I met Colonel Robert L. Scott, the famous former Flying Tiger fighter pilot during World War II and author of the book, *God is My Co-Pilot*, which was made into a movie with the same name.

My enlistment was up in 1952, but all enlistments were extended one year because of the Korean War. My wife wanted me to come home, but I tried to talk her into returning with me to Erding where I would reenlist, get my old job back, and start another 3-year tour. That didn't work out. I returned home and was discharged at Lockbourne Air Force Base, Columbus, Ohio, on 3 February 1953.

I will never forget Sergeant Goetz shouting at me, "Dammit, Gilley, do it again, and this time don't let me see you sweat!" Oh yes, I would do it again – and again.

Ed Gilley learned the sheet-metal trade after leaving the Air Force. He advanced in the trade until he was in an accident requiring several operations and about two years of convalescence. While still on crutches, he started engineering studies at Miller-Draughton College in Cincinnati, Ohio. After college, he worked as a design engineer for Tibbetts Mechanical Contractors in Dayton, Ohio, eventually becoming head of their Ohio engineering branch. He started his own construction firm in 1970 and operated it for several years while working as a project superintendent. He retired in 1993. Ed and Bessie, his wife of more than forty-six years, now live in Gulf Breeze, Florida, where they built a home near a golf course. Ed and Bessie have two sons and two daughters. Both daughters are in the Air Force. Their oldest is a lieutenant colonel, and their youngest is a captain.

Robert E. Joseph

Age 15 – United States Army

In June 1949, I got the idea to try joining the Army. My home life was leading me down a path to potentially major problems, and I thought the Army could straighten me out. I was living in Chelsea, Michigan, where I was born on 27 June 1934.

> *I was lucky to have been able to serve my beautiful country ...*

A cousin who was a year older than I also wanted to enlist. We had one thing in our favor. Our next-door neighbor was an Army recruiter with an office in nearby Ann Arbor, Michigan. We talked to him every day. He thought we were both too young and not really serious, but we were serious. Getting our parents' consent was a difficult task. We begged, pleaded, and even threatened to run away to California if they didn't sign our papers. They finally relented, and with their consent and a few amended documents, we were on our way.

I took a physical exam and a battery of tests three days before being sworn in. I became a soldier at the Fort Wayne, Michigan, induction center on 27 June 1949, my fifteenth birthday. Three days later, a troop train loaded with volunteers left for basic training at Fort Riley, Kansas. I was assigned to the 2nd Platoon, Fox Company, 85th Infantry Regiment. My cousin was assigned to the 87th Regiment.

Basic training was not difficult for me, although it was summer and very hot. After completing basic training, we were given a battery of skills tests to determine for which field we were best suited. I was very pleased to find that I had scored high enough on all the tests to be considered for OCS (officer candidate school). I didn't pursue OCS because I was concerned that a background check would reveal my true age.

I accepted an offer to attend the engineer school at Fort Belvoir, Virginia. I enjoyed working with 'dozers and graders, and I really did quite well in school. After graduation and a short furlough, I shipped out of New York for Germany. I was assigned to an aviation engineer battalion at Kelsterbach, near Frankfort, Germany.

Kelsterbach was a former Russian POW camp, so the accommodations were nothing to write home about. After a few months, we moved into new barracks at Rhine/Main Air Force Base. Our battalion did the maintenance work on the runways and other facilities on the base. I operated an earthmover named *Tournapull* and really enjoyed it. When work was over and weekend passes were available, I spent time in Frankfort, Garmish, Munich, and Oberammergau. I really loved Germany.

In September of 1950, I was called into the orderly room and advised that my true age was now known to the Army. I was told that I would be returned to the States and would be given an honorable discharge. I returned by ship to New York and reported to Fort Dix, New Jersey, for separation. In mid-October, at the age of 16, I became a civilian, returned to my hometown of Chelsea, Michigan, and rejoined my former classmates in the tenth grade.

The following summer, I turned 17 and became legally eligible to rejoin the military. I enlisted in the Air Force on 10 July 1951, and because of my prior service, I did not take Air Force basic training. I was assigned to the 63rd Fighter Squadron at Oscoda Air Force Base, Michigan. Six months later, I volunteered for overseas duty.

I was assigned to the 6332nd Air Installation Squadron at Kadena, AFB, Okinawa. We were a support group for the bomb wings that flew bombing missions to Korea. Our unit was blessed by the presence of Master Sergeant George "Pop" Hunt, age 72, from Adrian, Michigan. Pop Hunt had served under Captain Harry S. Truman during World War I, and he was a personal friend of President Truman. At that time (1952), Sergeant Hunt was the oldest enlisted man on active duty in the armed forces of the United States. During a routine Saturday inspection, the inspecting officer, a major who was a graduate of West Point, asked Pop if he had ever been "gigged" for an infraction of the rules. Keeping a very straight face, Pop replied, "Yes, sir. Once — for having buffalo shit on my rifle butt." After the stunned major finally regained his composure, he told the old sergeant, "At ease," and hurriedly left the barracks without completing his inspection. I'm sure he felt the need to laugh without being seen.

After eighteen months on Okinawa, I returned to the States and was assigned to Fairchild AFB, Spokane, Washington, in support of the 92nd Bombardment Wing (B-36s), Strategic Air Command. I was an airman first class when I was discharged in July 1955.

In October 1956, I reenlisted in the Army and was sent to Fort Campbell, Kentucky, and assigned to the 101st Airborne Division. Later I was transferred to the 169th Combat Engineer Battalion at Fort Stewart, Georgia. After being back in the Army for about a year, I was discharged because of service-related injuries.

During the years I spent as a GI, I was fortunate to have crossed both oceans and to have seen a lot of memorable sights. I enjoyed every day that I was in the service. It doesn't seem like that long ago, but forty-seven years have slipped by since that day at Fort Wayne when I was sworn in at age 15 — and I would gladly do it all over again! I was lucky to have been able to serve my beautiful country, and I am thankful for the privilege of serving with a multitude of patriotic young men and women. I feel that as long as there are young patriots, our country will always be free, and I say, "God bless America and all of our veterans."

Bob Joseph worked as a conductor for the New York Central Railroad for four years after leaving the Army. A reduction in the work force caused him to find another occupation. He went into the trucking business where he spent thirty years, retiring in July 1996. Bob and his wife Rose moved from Eaton Rapids, Michigan, to Ocala, Florida in the fall of 1996.

Lennart D. Wedeen

Age 16 – United States Air Force

I was born in Chicago, Illinois, on 2 December 1932, the youngest of three children. My parents separated when I was quite young, and it was hard for my

> "... if you can pass the test, I'll lie for you."

mother to provide for us. My brother and I would set pins in bowling alleys and do almost any job we could find to help out. We would go to the movies every chance we got. I needed a hero, and I found mine in the war movies of World War II. The shows, "Back to Bataan" and "Sands of Iwo Jima," thrilled me. I graduated from high school in Chicago in June 1949. I was only 16, but I wanted to enlist in the military. After seeing another war movie, I asked my mom if I could enlist in the Air Force. She said, "You can't go to college because we don't have the money, so if you can pass the test, I'll lie for you."

I passed the test, changed my birth year to 1931, my mother signed for me, and I was sworn into the Air Force on 19 August 1949. I was sent to Lackland Air Force Base, San Antonio, Texas, for basic training.

I completed several schools, including aircraft engine and mechanics school at Sheppard Field, Wichita Falls, Texas , and C-54 specialty school, Anchorage, Alaska, where I received my crew-member wings. I was assigned to the 64th Fighter Squadron at Elmendorf Air Force Base, Anchorage.

Our squadron was sent to Korea in August 1951. In November 1951, we went to an area known as the Gook's Castle, which was near the town of Kosong. Three C-54 transport planes from the 1701st Air Transport Wing brought about one hundred of us in. We were to service the F-86 Sabre Jets of our 64th Fighter Squadron. We were quite near the front lines, so we would take the door off the C-54s, mount a machine gun in the doorway, and make low-level runs over enemy lines.

Just before Thanksgiving, Chinese troops attacked our revetments. It was a blitzkrieg! Of the hundred men in the revetment areas, about seventy were killed, but we held. Later we moved to an airbase at Osan, Korea, about forty miles south of Seoul, where I stayed until I returned to the States.

I left Korea in March 1952, went to Hawaii for a few weeks, then flew to McChord Field, Tacoma, Washington. I went to Great Falls Air Force Base, Montana, for a time, then back to McChord AFB, where I was discharged on 8 November 1952 at the rank of staff sergeant.

Len Wedeen was awarded the Bronze Star, the Air Medal, and the Purple Heart. After his discharge from the Air Force, he worked for the General Motors Company as a body-shop estimator and as a manager. In 1987, he graduated from Triton College, River Forest, Illinois, with a B.S. in engineering. He worked as a boiler engineer in Skokie, Illinois, for eight years, then retired in 1995. Len and his wife Thordis live in Chicago. They plan to move to Norway next year.

Gerald Garcia

Age 16 – California National Guard

On the day that I was born in Dos Palos, California, 23 May 1934, the Texas Rangers ambushed and executed Clyde Barrow and Bonnie Parker. I was not aware of the events in Louisiana at the time, of course, but by 1950, I was aware that Communism

> *I sat by myself on the dirty, cold, hard floor, like a fool, reading a little book.*

was spreading towards America, and I was concerned. On my sixteenth birthday, my two closest boyhood friends and I decided to join the Army. Our plan was simply to say that we were 17. Our goal was to stop the spread of Communism.

On 23 May 1950, we met a California Army National Guard officer at his office and took several tests. After grading the tests, the officer told my two friends to come back after thirty days to be retested. He told me, "You are scheduled for a medical exam tomorrow." I was ecstatic, and I ran home to tell my brother, who had served in the Navy during World War II. My brother's non-supportive remark was, "Gerald, stay in school and let someone else fight." Nevertheless, I was

elated and looked forward to joining. My mother, bless her, said to me with tears in her eyes, "I know God will protect you; He protected your three brothers. We will continue to love you."

I enlisted in Battery A, 951st Antiaircraft Artillery Battalion (mobile), in Richmond, California, on 24 May 1950 for a 3-year tour. I requested immediate assignment to Korea, but Master Sergeant Holimitos ordered me to draw my uniform first. I had faced Sergeant Dodge in supply for no longer than

a minute and he said, "Size-8 boot, 28-inch waist, 31-inch legs, size-10 sock, size-7 cap, and a 33-inch belt." He continued, "Remember the 34-regular overcoat and the duffel bag." After I had gathered everything up, he said, "Now, Recruit Garcia, put everything in that duffle bag."

I pushed, packed, and prayed, but everything did not fit. Another sergeant dumped everything out and simply said, "Again." Once more I prayed for a minute, then packed, pushed, and pushed some more. Still, I had things left over. For the second time, the sergeant dumped everything from the bag and said, "Read the book." I sat by myself on the dirty, cold, hard floor, like a fool, reading a little book. I read it three times. I now realized that everything in the Army has a book written about it somewhere. I packed my duffel bag in eleven short minutes and had three or four inches of space to spare.

I was assigned as a cannoneer on a 40mm antiaircraft gun. Later, I trained on the quad 50mm machine gun and completed the atomic indoctrination course. In August 1950, I requested transfer to Korea again, but I was told that I had to be trained first. I was promoted to private first class, effective 1 January 1951, and was told that my name had been forwarded for assignment to the 8th Army in Korea. I was not sent to Korea, but I was assigned to the medical detachment of the 951st AAA and sent to Camp Irwin, California, for medical aid man training. After assignment to several units, it became obvious that I was not going to be sent to Korea, so on 12 August 1952, I left the National Guard, joined the Air Force, and asked for assignment to Korea.

I completed basic training at Camp Parks, California, in October 1952 and was selected as a potential drill sergeant. After completion of the Air Force Drill School, I was assigned to receiving Air Force recruits. One day my older brother came in as a trainee!

In September 1953, I was assigned to the 86th Fighter-Bomber Wing, 12th Air Force, Sembach Air Force Base, Germany. I requested a transfer to Etain Air Force Base in France later because my brother was stationed there. Months later, I went on TDY to Wheelus Air Force Base near Tripoli, Libya, North Africa, working with F-86 aircraft in air-to-ground machine-gun firing. I returned to Landstuhl Air Force Base in Germany, then returned to the States and was discharged at Manhattan Air Force Base, New York, in August 1956.

I returned to California and reenlisted in Battery B, 951st AAA Battalion, California National Guard, on 12 April 1957. I was promoted to sergeant in 1958 and worked as a supply sergeant and as a full-time training technician, preparing mock 20-foot radar-controlled aircraft to be towed for ground-based missile targets. I held a number of positions in several units during the next several years.

My infantry unit was called to active duty by the state in 1965 to take part in controlling the Watts riots. Two books were published about the riots in which my involvement is discussed: *Rivers of Blood, Years of Darkness* by Robert Conot (in 1967) and *Fire This Time* by Gerald Horne (in 1995).

I was appointed artillery senior first sergeant in 1968, was promoted to warrant officer (WO-1) on 4 November 1971, and to chief warrant officer (CWO-4) in November 1986. During this period, I served as both administrative and supply officer for the 347th General Hospital (1000B), Hamilton Air Force Base, near Novato, California, and as recruiting officer for the 124th Army Reserve Command at Fort Lawton, Washington. My last two active-duty posts were property book officer for the 5th Battalion, 28th Field Artillery, Cincinnati, Ohio, and supply technician for the 364th Civil Affairs Brigade, Portland, Oregon.

At the time I reached the mandatory retirement age (60), I could still do maximum push-ups and sit-ups, and I scored 287 out of 300 on my PT. My request to remain on active duty until age 62 was denied, and I was forced to retire on my sixtieth birthday, 23 May 1994, after serving forty-three years, eleven months, and thirty days. Communism had died, and my goal was accomplished.

Jerry Garcia's numerous awards include the Legion of Merit, three Army Commendation Medals, and many letters of appreciation, including one from President Clinton and another from General John M. Shalikashvili, Chairman of the Joint Chiefs of Staff. After retiring, he enrolled as a full-time student at Portland College and has completed 112 units towards his B.S. degree. He mastered the twelve-meter diving board and recently received a 1000-mile jogging award from the college athletic department. He continues to upgrade a historical Army showroom at Fort Vancouver, Washington. Jerry and Marlys, his wife of thirty-nine years, live in Tualatin, Oregon. They have four children and five grandchildren.

William C. Morgan

Age 16 – United States Marine Corps

I was born into a large farm family in Madison County, about thirteen miles west of Columbus, Ohio, on 29 May 1934. This was during the Great Depression, and my father was recuperating from a serious accident.

> *... we were told that we would be the first troops to be used in the A-bomb tests at Yucca Flats ...*

With medical bills piling up, things were getting financially bad for us. Without the help of insurance, my parents knew that we had to sell, or practically give away, everything in order to survive. We moved from the farm into a small house without running water or electricity. As Dad's condition continued to fail, my brothers and sister knew we were faced with going to a children's home. As a child, I lived with a fear about survival, something that no child needs.

In 1940, my neighbor and many others went into the CCC camps, the National Guard, the Army, the Navy, and the Marines. They ate well in the service and were paid for doing a job. As little as the pay was, it seemed big to me. I would pray that someday I could go into the military and be a sergeant.

My sister was killed in a horrible accident in 1945, and my dad passed away four months later. We were now living in the small town of West Jefferson, Ohio. I may have been young, but I delivered newspapers to nearly everyone in West Jefferson at one time or another. Not only did I deliver newspapers, but I also read them. At a very young age, I knew that the United States was facing war on at least three fronts at the same time. We were involved in a cold war with Russia, French paratroopers had just landed in Indo-China (Vietnam), and there was great turmoil in Korea. All this had my attention at a time when football, baseball, and school should have been occupying my thoughts.

The military reserve forces were busy recruiting, and a number of kids from West Jefferson joined up. Three seniors from my high school joined the Marine Corps Reserve. Our football coach, a combat veteran of World War II, entered the reserves as a second lieutenant. This got my attention in a big way. I asked the seniors many questions, all of which they were eager to answer. I went with them to the recruiters to make my interests known. The recruiters thought that I was the same age as the seniors. I told them that I did not have a birth certificate but that I would be able to bring a notarized document stating my age. By this time I had a stepfather, and I knew that he would sign the document. My stepfather also knew a notary who was willing to notarize it.

With the notarized document, I enlisted in the Marine Reserves for an indefinite period of time. I was sworn in on 8 June 1950 and became a member of Charlie Company, 7th Marine Infantry Battalion, United States Marine Corps Reserve. I attended one drill before the North Koreans crossed the 38th parallel on 25 June 1950.

That fall, school was scheduled to start on 5 September. But on the day before it was to start, our battalion received orders to report to Camp Pendleton, California. That meant I had to turn in my football shoes for boondockers (combat boots). We left by train for Camp Pendleton and arrived there four days later. We left the train at midnight, and as we formed up, we were asked if any of us had a critical MOS (military occupational specialty). Four medical corpsmen raised their hands. They were promptly fed at the mess hall and put on a plane destined for Korea. Within ninety days, one of the four was killed. We knew then that this was serious business.

The remainder of our company was sorted into groups according to training needs. I was assigned to a recruit-training group along with three other men from my high school. The coach was assigned to advanced training at Tent Camp Two. Four of us from West Jefferson High School and twelve others headed for boot camp in San Diego. We started training with 100 men in our platoon. Only sixty-eight finished. My football coach could have blown the whistle on me at any time, but he didn't. He stayed in the Marine Corps and retired as a colonel.

One month before I graduated from boot camp, a 17-year-old Marine was killed in Korea. The Commandant of the Marine Corps put out an order that no Marine under the age of 18 would be assigned to a combat zone. Most of the graduates of my boot platoon were sent to Camp Pendleton for advanced training, then sent on to Korea. Since my records indicated that I was 17, I reported to the 1st Automatic Weapons Battalion, FMFPac (Fleet Marine Force, Pacific). We were assigned cold-weather training and got to sleep on the snow at 39° below zero. Some of us were involved with making military movies. I was in one called "Close Air Support." We were dressed as Chinese soldiers and manned our 40mm and quad-50 guns.

In the fall of 1951, Brigadier General Lewis B. "Chesty" Puller came to Camp Pendleton to form the 3rd Marine Brigade. I had the honor of carrying the guidon and to report front and center with the general at the ceremony where he was awarded his 5th Navy Cross. The spirit on that parade ground was greater than at the Ohio State/Michigan football game.

I did quite well as a Marine and was promoted to corporal after six months. Six months later, I was a sergeant, the rank I had aspired to as a boy. Several of us were selected to attend the new atomic school. This sounded very exciting to us. We received numerous lectures about the atomic bomb. We learned about neutrons, protons, plutonium, uranium, and gamma rays until we would dream about them in our sleep. We never questioned what this stuff was all about. Finally, we were told that we would be the first troops to be used in the A-bomb test at Yucca Flats, Nevada, during the summer of 1952.

Six weeks before we were to go to Yucca Flats, my time on active duty was up. It was my choice to stay or return home to the reserve unit. I chose to go home. I was released from active duty on 9 April 1952. I returned to high school, played football, kissed the homecoming queen, and later married her. I stayed in the Marine Reserves for fifteen years, then switched to the Air Force Reserves and retired as a master sergeant in 1986.

Early on, I had met a young man in my platoon who was from Minnesota. His name was Frank H. Dowden. Forty-five years later, I learned that he too was an underage veteran and a member of the Veterans of Underage Military Service. Tom Planinc, a buddy from boot camp, has remained my friend for life. I could write a book about the interesting people I met during my time in the military.

Bill Morgan attended California Coast University and received a B.S. in 1981 and an M.B.A. in 1982. He led a dual life as a reservist with a civilian career in the industrial field. He was involved with the start-up of industrial plants ranging in cost from one million to two billion dollars. He held positions from the first level of production scheduling to general manager. For several years, his work included heavy-machinery rigging throughout the United States and overseas. While working in South America, he was the Foreign Guest of Honor in the City of São Paulo, Brazil. Bill and Ann, his wife of forty-three years, live in Galloway, Ohio. They have three children and five grandchildren.

√ **VUMS Note** ⇒ *Recruited by a poster.*
Recruiting posters seemed to have influenced at least a few youngsters into enlisting. One underage veteran tells about the Marine poster he saw every day in his father's barber ship that said, "Uncle Sam Needs You!" Since a recruiting office was just down the street, the 13-year-old went in and joined. The suggestion in Navy posters to "Join the Navy and See the World," appealed to the sense of adventure and the desire to travel of some, especially to one who wanted to go to China. Another put it this way: "When I saw a Navy recruiting poster, bells went off in my head." Still another felt that a sailor on a Navy poster was beckoning him into the post office where the recruiting office was located, so he went and got the necessary papers to enlist at age 14.

Ronald M. Smith

Age 15 – United States Marine Corps

I did not join the Marines at age 15 because of patriotic zeal to defend my country. My reason was more personal – I was looking for a challenge. I went through some kind of "mid-life crisis" between the ages of 14 and 15 (ninth and tenth grade). I was on the academic honor roll in the ninth grade, but was skipping school and failing in the tenth grade. I had lost interest and had a bad attitude toward authority.

> *Marine boot camp certainly fulfilled any desire I had for a challenge ...*

I am proud of the fact that I chose to cure my problem rather than let it get worse. With my limited knowledge, I do not know how I sensed that the Marine Corps was what I needed. Marine boot camp is a great place for teenagers with bad attitudes and inability to concentrate on goals.

I went to the Marine recruiting station, filled out an application, and took a written test on the first day. I was told to return the next day with my birth certificate and that I would be taking a physical then. That night, I used ink eradicator on my birth certificate and wrote in a new year, adding two years to my age. It was obviously altered and undoubtedly the worst example of forgery in history. The next day, I returned to the recruiting station with my birth certificate and found that a different sergeant was on duty. The sergeant checked my name on a list and told me that all I needed was a physical. He assigned me to a group leaving right away, so I took the physical without ever taking the phony birth certificate from my pocket. I was told to come back on the third day, 5 July 1950, to get sworn in and pick up my train ticket to San Diego.

Marine boot camp certainly fulfilled any desire I had for a challenge, and my attitude toward authority and my ability to concentrate on goals improved tremendously. I highly recommend it to teenagers with problems.

After boot camp I went to Camp Lejeune, North Carolina, to auto-mechanics school, then back to Camp Pendleton, California. I left for Korea in February 1951. Except for a very brief tour on the line with Item Company, 3rd Battalion, 7th Marines, 1st Marine Division, I spent my time in Korea "in the rear with the gear," serving in the Maintenance Company, 1st Combat Service Group, at Masan, Korea.

During my tour in Korea, I met a girl named Chung Pang Ja. We dated for a year, then in August 1952, I was rotated back to the States, over my objections. I was stationed at Camp Pendleton and carried on a romance by mail with Pang Ja. In 1953, I went to Nara, Japan, with the 3rd Battalion, 4th Marines, still writing to Pang Ja and constantly filling out requests to transfer to Korea.

While stationed in Japan, my unit, the 3rd Battalion, was selected to escort a number of Chinese prisoners of war to Taiwan. The Korean War was unique because, for the first time after an armistice was signed, many POWs did not want to return to their native countries. About 14,000 Chinese did not want to return to China, twenty-one American soldiers did not want to return to the U. S., and one British soldier did not want to return to England. The South Korean president, Syngman Rhee, had already released the North Korean POWS to his custody, nearly starting the war over again. Indian soldiers took control of all POWs for a 90-day period, during which all countries were given an opportunity to talk to their troops about returning to their homeland.

When the ninety days were up, about 14,000 Chinese were loaded in fifteen LSTs (landing ship, tank), and my battalion had the responsibility for feeding and providing medical care for them during the voyage. We were also charged with maintaining order. We knew that there were Communist agitators who stayed behind and were among the prisoners because we found two bodies deposited on the deck with knives in their backs and notes tied to them identifying them as Communists.

Our job was also to insure that the POWs did not change their minds and try to take over the ship while we were sailing along the China coast. Also, we were on guard against mainland Chinese intercepting us on the high seas in an attempt to force their wayward sons home.

When we arrived in Taiwan, they set up a huge banquet for all Marines. The Nationalist Chinese government gave us medals and presents and put on a spectacular show for us. We stayed in Taiwan for two days, then returned to Japan.

I finally made it back to Korea in January 1954. I was assigned to the 1st Combat Service Group at Masan and could now resume my romance with Pang Ja in person. After filling out an unbelievable amount of paperwork, Pang Ja and I were married. I returned to the States in June 1954 and was discharged on 5 July, but it was another year filled with paperwork before my wife could join me in Texas.

So, from the time I proposed until we were together in Texas, three and one-half years had elapsed. Three and one-half years of paperwork, letters, applications, and frustration. Finally, through the efforts of my congressman, a special bill was passed by Congress that allowed her to join me in the United States.

Ron Smith returned to Texas to work in the oil-field equipment industry in Houston after his discharge from the Marine Corps. He earned a B.S. from the University of Houston and an M.B.A. from Laredo State University. His wife Pang Ja died in 1989 after a long bout with Lou Gehrig's disease. The beginning of their thirty-five-year marriage was long and hard because of paperwork, and the end was long and hard because of illness. Ron credits his Marine Corps training for helping him concentrate on goals and doing what was necessary during trying times. Ron and Pang Ja's family includes a son, a daughter, and three grandchildren. Ron worked for a company in Brownsville, Texas, for a number of years. After retiring, he returned to Houston, Texas, where he now lives.

Lawrence E. Hamlet

Age 15 – Washington D.C. National Guard
Age 15 – United States Army

I joined Company B, 163rd Combat Military Police Battalion, Washington D.C. National Guard, on 1 August 1950 at the age of 15. We were federalized on 3 August 1950, and

The Army taught me that I could hack it ...

one month later, on 3 September, we were sent to Fort Custer, Michigan. Most of us had joined the guard as a lark, but when we were called, there were few complaints. It was our duty as U. S. citizens.

I wasn't the only one in my battalion who was underage. There was at least one other in my company and six or eight in the battalion. We were suspected of being underage, but in the confusion of being activated and shipped to Michigan in thirty days, no one had the time to investigate. Anyway, most of us had papers signed by our mothers.

Most of my outfit was sent to Korea, and many did not return. I had volunteered to go to Korea, but instead, in early 1951, I was sent to Germany. I have no idea whether my company commander just didn't want to send an underage kid into harm's way, or whether it was just the Army way. My platoon leader also ended up in Germany. We served together for a short time. I served with the 110th Infantry Regiment, 28th Infantry Division.

One thing that surprised me in the Army was that the bigger and older troops really resented the fact that we smaller youngsters were able to keep up with them. If we surpassed them, they went crazy.

The Army never found out that I was underage. I returned to the U. S. in the spring of 1952, was released from active duty in June, and returned to my Guard unit in Washington, D.C. I was discharged from the Guard in August 1953.

One of my concerns when I was discharged was that I was really only 17 and could get into trouble if I didn't register for the draft when I became 18. The general opinion was that since I had joined the Army illegally, my service time was invalid and I could be drafted. I didn't register for the draft, but I was never comfortable about that.

I wondered if would I be sent to jail for not registering or if I would be drafted.

The Army was not for me, but it did have a profound effect on my life. The Army taught me that I could hack it — that age, size, and to some extent, lack of education, couldn't stop me.

Larry Hamlet studied at the Spartan School of Aeronautics in Tulsa, Oklahoma, under the GI Bill. After graduating, he worked in the aircraft industry all over the United States and in many parts of Mexico and South America, finally settling in San Antonio, Texas. He was vice-president of S&H Jet Services, vice-president of Fiesta Aviation, and president of Air World. Currently, he spends about ten hours a week running a one-man steel brokerage company. His early enlistment caused a recent problem with the Social Security Administration. Their records showed that he soon would be eligible for retirement. He had to go to the Social Security office with his original birth certificate and photo ID and sign a statement that their information was incorrect and that he had lied to enter the Army. Larry credits the Army for teaching him responsibility, the GI Bill for educating him, and his excellent choice of a wife for his successful and rewarding life. Larry and Rosie, his wife of thirty-three years, live in Bulverde, Texas. They have four children and one granddaughter. Their granddaughter joined the Army in April 1996.

William E. Cranston, Sr.

Age 16 – United States Marine Corps

I was raised in Minneapolis, Minnesota, where I was born on 23 July 1934. During my teenage years, I had no direction, and I was always getting into trouble. I came home quite late one night

> *It seems rather strange that I finished high school in North Korea.*

and found my mother waiting up for me. She told me about the war that had just started in Korea.

Since I was a patriotic, gung ho, American boy, I told her I was going to join the Marines. She said, "You are only 16 years old, how are you going to do that?" I said, "I'll find a way." I asked my older brother to change the date on my birth certificate to 1933 from 1934. He did, and I had a photostatic copy made of it. I went to the Marine recruiting office and handed my phony birth certificate to a sergeant. He looked at it, smiled, and said, "You're OK, young man." I was sworn into the Marines on 2 August 1950.

This was a big, big change in my life. The next day, I was on a train headed for San Diego, California, and boot camp. From boot camp, I went to Camp Pendleton for infantry training, after which I joined the 14th Replacement Draft and went to Korea.

Upon my arrival in Korea, I was assigned to Charlie Company, 1st Battalion, 1st Marine Regiment, 1st Marine Division. This was my home for thirteen months. During this time, I was involved in quite a few skirmishes with the North Korean army and the Chinese army as well. The battle that sticks in my mind is Bunker Hill in August 1952. We had many casualties, but this young rebel didn't get hit at all, just got plenty, plenty scared. Have you ever been so scared that you urinated in your pants? This happened to me more than once.

One day when we came off the line, just as we reached the rest area, an Army officer drove up in a jeep. The officer asked, "Any of you jarheads (Marines) want to take the GED test and get your high school diploma?" I said, "I'll take it." I passed the test and sent the results to my mother, who took them to my old high school, where they issued me a diploma. It seems rather strange that I finished high school in North Korea.

I was rotated back to the States in October 1952, and I have thanked the Lord many times for bringing me back safely from Korea. I returned to Camp Pendleton and was assigned to a weapons company in the 3rd Marine Division. Less than a year later, I volunteered for duty with an amphibious reconnaissance company, the first one formed after World War II. We went to Hawaii for thirteen great months. We worked from the USS *Perch*, a troop-carrying submarine. We also learned how to jump out of helicopters and get picked up out of the ocean. I returned to the mainland in the spring of 1954 and was discharged on 2 August 1954.

I am thankful for the privilege of having served this great country of ours. I will always be grateful to the United States Marine Corps, the best outfit in the world, for taking me in as an underage, rebellious teenager, teaching me so much, and making a man out of me.

Bill Cranston returned to Minneapolis and worked for a defense plant that manufactured guided missiles for the Navy. In 1964, he started driving an 18-wheel truck for a Minneapolis grocery chain. After an injury in 1990, he retired on a disability pension. In 1991, Bill and Donna, his wife of forty-two years, moved to Peoria, Arizona, where they now live. They have three children and eight grandchildren.

Jesus "Dick" Mendoza

Age 15 – California National Guard
Age 16 – United States Army

I joined the California National Guard in September 1950 when I was 15 years old, but I told them that I was 17. When my father signed my enlistment papers, he said that he didn't think I

> *"You were infantry while in the Guard, and that is sufficient, period!"*

would be in any harm by going in for training one weekend each month. My training with the Guard consisted of normal drills and two weeks of summer camp at Camp Cook, California. Summer camp consisted of setting up a demonstration for the governor.

I didn't like school, although I could get good grades. I was 16 years old and in the tenth grade when I decided to join the regular Army in December 1951. The recruiting officer said that I should register for the draft because my Guard papers indicated I was past 18. I went to the draft board and told them I thought the National Guard would inform them that I was enrolled, and that I would not have to register on my eighteenth birthday. They believed me, so I registered and was issued a draft card.

The day I was leaving for basic training, my brother told my father that I had enlisted in the Army. He came to get me at the bus depot where I was waiting, but after we talked, he decided it would be okay.

I was sent to Fort Ord, supposedly for basic training. While I was at the replacement center waiting for an assignment to a training company, I was issued orders to go to the Philippines. I boarded the USS *Fred C. Ainsworth*, and

three weeks later, we anchored in Manila Bay. This was the early part of March 1952. As I was preparing to debark, I was informed by an officer that my orders were changed and that I was to going to Korea. I explained to the officer that I didn't go through basic training and that my entire military experience at that time was weekend drills with the National Guard. He said, "You were infantry while in the Guard, and that is sufficient, period!"

I left the ship and spent about two weeks in the Philippines before flying to Japan. From there I caught a ship to Pusan, Korea, where I joined the 224th Infantry Regiment of the 40th Infantry Division. Shortly after I joined the unit, someone informed the commanding officer that I was only 16. When I reported to him, he asked me how old I was and I told him. He decided to let me stay. I became a squad leader after we were on line for several months. At one time, my unit was pulled from the line to guard prisoners at Koje-do, an island off the coast of Korea, near Pusan, for a couple of months. After the brief tour at Koje-do, we went back on line. I finished my tour as a forward observer for 4.2 inch mortars.

I returned to the States in February 1953 and applied for the Airborne. I went to the 11th Airborne Division at Fort Campbell, Kentucky, for jump school in July 1956 and stayed with that unit until March 1958. I was with the 504 Airborne Battle Group from July 1959 until July 1962. I served two tours of duty in Europe and another tour in Korea from 1963 until 1964.

I was discharged from the regular Army in April 1965 after twelve and one-half years of active duty. I rejoined the California National Guard in 1967 and served until 1978. I'm retired military now.

Dick Mendoza earned the Combat Infantryman Badge before his seventeenth birthday. At age 16, while in Pusan, Korea, he earned a high school diploma by passing the GED exams. After leaving the military, he worked for Pacific Telephone for a number of years and is now employed by an independent telephone contractor. Although many years have passed since he served with the Airborne, Dick still enjoys jumping from aircraft. He has earned jump wings by participating in parachute jumps with military forces in eight foreign countries. Dick and his wife Cheryl live in Daly City, California. They have two children. Dick has three children from previous marriages and five grandchildren.

Roger D. Lessin

Age 16 – Minnesota National Guard
Age 16 – United States Army

During World War II, I was totally consumed by the war and the home effort. I participated in every scrap drive that was held in my hometown of Pipestone, Minnesota, where I was born

> *The itch to roam came back, and I eloped with the undertaker's daughter.*

on 9 June 1934. I grew a victory garden, memorized Morse code, and trained myself to be an aircraft observer for the wonderful day that I would be called on. It was pretty devastating for this 11-year-old to see the war end without my help!

When the shooting started in Korea, I was still underage. Once again, heart-broken and driven by the Audie Murphy/John Wayne syndrome, I prayed for a way that this underage kid could get into the action. The gods were with me. I heard a rumor that the Minnesota National Guard would be activated. I ran to the Guard office and got an application. That night, I presented it to my parents and asked

them to sign it. They answered with an emphatic *NO* and reminded me that I was underage. I continuously pestered, ranted, and threatened to run away until they relented. I joined the Guard on 1 October 1950. In February 1951, we were activated for duty. My parents were shocked when we were activated, and they felt bad about letting me fib about my age. They talked to the first sergeant about getting me out, but he suggested that they let me go. He said he would look after me.

They sent us to Camp Rucker, Alabama, and made me a gunner on a 75mm recoilless rifle. I spent most of my time on detail, cleaning grease pits, scraping paint, and doing other fun jobs. Our newly arrived draftees taught me the ropes about "off-post activities." In the meantime, I wanted out of Camp Rucker and out of the Guard. I volunteered for the Airborne, the Rangers, or Korea, whichever came first. They obliged and sent me to Korea. In August 1951, I was dropped off at a rifle company of the 5th Regimental Combat Team and handed a BAR (Browning automatic rifle). That was good because I had never fired a live round from a 75mm recoilless. My specialty was more along the lines of KP, cleaning grease pits, and stoking coal stoves.

I was put into the kids' squad. We were all 16 and up, with an old-timer being 18 years old. I had turned 17 on my way to Korea. I became buddies with a guy named Ed Searcy, who was also underage. Ed saw to it that we volunteered for every patrol or activity that exposed us to the action. At one point, our CO called four of us whom he suspected of being underage, in to see him. He offered to rotate us back to the States if we would admit our age. We all stayed.

I was used as the platoon point-man when it was decided that I was the most qualified. I was offered a battlefield commission, but when they saw I was just 17, it didn't come through. I was wounded and sent to a MASH unit in the rear for two weeks, then it was back on the line. Most of us underage kids managed to get our Purple Hearts and other medals.

I returned to the States in 1952 and was released from active duty in September of that year. I returned to high school and was placed with the same class I had left two years before. I had a new car, money, and a bag full of war stories. I was the idol of my class but a pretty bad example. The year in Korea had imprinted on my mind that it was most important to have a hellava good time twenty-four hours a day. This was a given, since I had seen so many in my outfit killed or wounded. I didn't let school interfere with my good times, so the principal decided that I should leave and offered me a GED if I left.

The itch to roam came back, and I eloped with the undertaker's daughter. Since my goose was cooked, I, along with a traffic judge, decided that I should get back in the service. I took the Air Force route and ended up in aircraft maintenance. I was assigned to the Army for six months during my 1-year tour in Vietnam. We were taking possession of the fixed-wing Caribou aircraft used in the field. Later, I served a tour in Guam in maintenance support of the B-52 bombers flying missions over Vietnam.

I retired from the Air Force in 1972 at the rank of chief master sergeant. I still get the old itch to climb the last hill, but when I get the big head, my 89-year-old mom knocks me down a notch when she reminds me of how embarrassing it was to have her snot-nosed kid standing by that troop train with a long cigarette in his mouth back in 1951.

Roger Lessin earned the Combat Infantryman Badge and was awarded the Bronze Star with "V" device and the Purple Heart for wounds received in action. After his retirement from the Air Force, he worked for the U. S. Postal Service for twenty-one years. He retired in 1995. Roger and his wife Wilma (Lee) live in Austin, Texas. They have three children and five grandchildren.

√ **VUMS Note** ⇒ *Reality of war.* Many underage veterans told in their stories about coming face to face with the reality of war. "Nothing in my short life had prepared me for the fear, devastation, and carnage that we encountered during that campaign," wrote a veteran about the invasion of Okinawa. Almost exactly the same words were used about the same campaign by another: "... for the first time, the reality of war came home to me. I could see first-hand the devastation caused by war...." One veteran explained how he learned about war at 2:00 one morning when his unit was suddenly attacked. "Until then," he wrote, "I and many others had what I call the 'Audie Murphy Syndrome.' We wanted to be heroes but had no real idea what combat was all about." He found out in his first fight, which he described as being "very traumatic."

Edmund R. Ciriello

Age 16 – United States Army

As a young boy growing up in Boston, Massachusetts, where I was born on 10 December 1934, curiosity was my predominant trait. All things mysterious were of great interest to me. Solving

> *It seemed like the perfect beginning for life as a "private eye."*

riddles and puzzles, finding the solution to problems, and unearthing secrets were my passions. At age 14, I sent away for a private-detective course because it seemed to me to be the embodiment of my career dreams. I still remember some of the things I learned from that course. The theory of personnel surveillance, undercover investigations, and other esoteric arts made a strong impression on me and set me in a direction on which I was to remain all my life.

After forging a birth certificate and convincing my parents that I wanted to join the military, I tried to join the Marines, but they rejected me because of my small size (5'10" and 125 pounds). A Navy recruiter would not accept my dubious birth certificate, so I tried the Army. The Army recruiter actually came to my house to talk with me. During our conversation, he decided to telephone city hall to verify my age as he didn't quite trust the birth certificate I had offered. I was too embarrassed to sit and wait for the impending death knell of my enlistment, so I left the house to pace in the front yard. Moments later, the recruiter walked out of the house and approached me, a smile on his face. "Couldn't get through to anyone, so to hell with it," he said. Shaking my hand, he welcomed me into the Army and drove off.

I was sworn into the Army on 15 June 1951, six months after my sixteenth birthday, and I was off to Fort Dix as a member of the Army

Security Agency. It seemed like the perfect beginning for a life as a "private eye."

Army life for a 16-year-old was an exciting time. In the shadow of the greatest hero of World War II, Audie Murphy, I trudged through miles of New Jersey countryside with all the equipment known and loved by a "dogface." I pulled targets, dug foxholes, threw hand grenades, and even managed to win a couple of I.D. bracelets for night- and day-firing. It was a dream come true for any kid who grew up during the World War II era. I was a proud recruit carrying my share of pride and anxious to get into the war that was Korea.

Listening to the war stories of our platoon instructors recently returned from the battlefield was better than any John Wayne movie. One DI wore a ripped leather jacket, a souvenir of combat, and I vowed to wear such a jacket when I left for Korea. I couldn't wait, but others were making plans for me that did not include conventional warfare.

During my eight weeks of training, I was recruited by Army Intelligence to become an investigator. My first assignment for them was simply to go to the PX and purchase a pair of dress trousers. I was instructed to pay the exact amount and not wait for a receipt. Later, I found out that the clerk had pocketed the cash without ringing it up. I was then reassigned to an infantry basic-training company for an additional eight weeks while my background was more thoroughly investigated. My true age was discovered, so after four months in the Army, I received an honorable discharge, and I returned to my home in Boston, a disappointed veteran.

Three months later, I turned 17 and enlisted in the U. S. Navy. As a trained veteran, I was appointed acting chief petty officer of my recruit-training company in Bainbridge, Maryland. By the time I completed boot camp, I had been recruited by the Office of Naval Intelligence on the basis of my previous recruitment by Army Intelligence. Upon completing basic training, my first assignment was to participate in various surveillance situations in Washington, D.C. To build my cover, I was assigned to the U. S. Naval Mine Warfare School in Yorktown, Virginia. I was sent to Korea in the fall of 1952 to participate in prisoner interrogations and to get my feet wet in a combat zone. Thirty days later, I returned to the States for some further training on undercover investigations.

My first real assignment was to a cargo-handling battalion at the Guantanamo Bay Naval Base, Cuba. I was to investigate thefts of material from the base, so I worked undercover unloading ships. My investigations led to the apprehension of several Cuban nationals. They belonged to a theft ring headed by a recently imprisoned Cuban who had led an attack on a military outpost in southeast Cuba in 1953. His name was Fidel Castro.

After completing my 4-year enlistment, I was discharged from the Navy at the Brooklyn Navy Yard on 25 July 1955.

Ed Ciriello continued his work as an investigator after leaving the Navy. As a civilian agent, his work took him to Korea, Vietnam, Iran, and other hot spots, including a stint in Saudi Arabia during Desert Storm. He made a long-term dream a reality in 1973. He founded the Global School of Investigation, a home-study training program for private detectives. Over the years, Global has become the world's largest private-investigator correspondence school. Ed and his wife Bobbe live in Stoneham, Massachusetts. He has three children and two grandchildren.

Gil Coronado

Age 16 – United States Air Force

I was born in Corpus Christi, Texas, on 21 February 1936. By 1952, I was a 15-year-old Mexican-American orphan, a street kid, a juvenile delinquent, and a high-school dropout with no future,

> The foundation of my military career was built as an enlisted man ...

roaming the streets of San Antonio, Texas, where I was raised. At that point, I took a hard look at my life. I asked myself whether I was going to be part of the problem or part of the solution. As an American, was I going to make a contribution to this great country, or was I going to end up in a correctional institution? The military was an alternative. However, at age 15, I was too young to enlist in the armed forces. After some deliberation, I came up with what I thought was a way to beat the age limitation for enlisting.

I was told that I needed a birth certificate confirming that I was old enough to join the Air Force. I sent away for a copy of my birth certificate, and I studied it to determine a way to alter it to my advantage. After some quick thinking, I intentionally typed over, or double-struck, some of the letters on it to make it seem sloppy. The only outright tampering was changing the birth year from 1936 to 1934.

Taking the altered birth certificate with me, I went to the local Armed Forces Recruiting Station in San Antonio to enlist. Although I was only 15 years old, I looked older because of my 5'10" height, and I hoped that would help with my ruse. The Korean War was in full swing, which I thought would also help to get me into the service. I presented the altered birth certificate to the Air Force recruiter. He gave me the proper forms to fill out, and I took the aptitude tests and the physical examination. Everything was going well until a recruiter started to ask questions about the birth certificate. I quickly took the initiative and pointed out the numerous other typos and overstrikes on the document. This diversionary con worked, or so I thought.

I was wrong about the Air Force needing volunteers for the Korean War; they had more than enough. I was placed on a waiting list for active duty. Eight weeks later, near my sixteenth birthday, a telephone call came asking me if I was still interested in early enlistment, and I replied that I was. Five days after my sixteenth birthday, on 26 February 1952, I was sworn into the Air Force. I was sent to Lackland Air Force Base for basic training, then went on to become a clerk-typist and a distinguished graduate of my cryptographic specialist class.

Everything went just fine for two and a half years, then it was time to pay the price for my underage enlistment. Special agents of the Air Force Office of Special Investigations called on me and asked me questions about my entry into the military. They had caught me, but because of my performance during those two and a half years, I was allowed to stay in the Air Force. However, I left the service at that time because I had to return to San Antonio to take care of a family member who was dying. I was discharged on 4 September 1954 and left the military for good, or so I thought.

A short time later, I joined the federal civil service as a civilian aide with an Army Reserve battalion at Fort Sam Houston, Texas. Since I was a GS-5, I was obligated to join the Army Reserves and become a member of the Reserve battalion. I took advantage of every opportunity. I had obtained my high school diploma by taking the GED tests while on active duty. I became a sergeant within eighteen months from the time I joined the Reserves. After becoming a sergeant, I set my sights higher and thought that I would give OCS a try. A year later, in 1958, I was a candidate in Infantry Officers Candidate School at Fort Benning, Georgia. Fort Benning was affectionately known by officer candidates as the "Benning School for Boys." We had 350 candidates, all noncommissioned officers, in our class. At the end of the course, only 149 remained. Candidates were being scrubbed regularly from the intense course, even up to thirty minutes before graduation. I made it and I was commissioned, but it was by the skin of my teeth! My class ranking was 147, only two from the bottom.

I returned to Fort Sam Houston, and while serving as a Reserve Army officer, I obtained a GS-7 civilian position at nearby Kelly Air

Force Base. This new full-time job placed me in a position where I could not continue to serve in the Army Reserve and attend drill every week. I could, however, join the Air Force Reserve, since they drilled only one weekend a month. I was married with three children, working a full-time job and attending college full-time, so I transferred to the Air Force Reserve.

A year and a half later, I received a letter from the Air Force Reserve telling me that I was being called to active duty because I hadn't served on active duty as a commissioned officer. Five categories of exceptions were available, and I qualified for three, but I volunteered for active duty anyway.

I started my active-duty career as a first lieutenant at Fort Lee Air Force Station, Virginia. I remained there for three years as a weapons control officer, then I was transferred to Germany. Eventually, I ended up in Thailand, where I was an operations officer for a radar site supporting air operations over North Vietnam. I left the tropics of Southeast Asia in 1969 for the tropics of Central America, where I was assigned to the Inter-American Air Force Academy, Albrook Air Force Base, Canal Zone. This was followed by a number of squadron command assignments. I served a year in Alaska and was Deputy Commander, then Commander, of Torrejon Air Force Base in Spain from 1980 until 1983.

After thirty years of service to my country, I retired in 1989 as a full colonel. The foundation of my military career was built as an enlisted man, with a number of noncommissioned officers contributing directly to my success. I am very proud of that. I came a long way from the semi-slums of South San Antonio, Texas, where I was a high school dropout without a future.

Gil Coronado was awarded the Legion of Merit and the Bronze Star during his service in the Air Force. He was named "Commander of the Year" by the Latin American Clubs in Europe and was inducted into the Army OCS Hall of Fame in 1984. Gil was the initiating force in the creation of National Hispanic Heritage Month that was designated by Congress in 1988. This effort earned him a Presidential commendation for which he was honored at a Rose Garden ceremony. He is the chairman and founder of Heroes and Heritage and a member of the National Consortium for Educational Access. Gil served on the Clinton presidential transition team in 1992, and in 1994, he was appointed as the ninth Director of the Selective Service after being nominated for the position by President Clinton and confirmed by the U. S. Senate. He holds a degree from Our Lady of the Lake University, San Antonio, and is a graduate of four U. S. Government service schools. Gil and Helen, his wife of thirty-eight years, live in Washington, D.C. They have four children and two grandchildren.

√ **VUMS Note** ⇒ *Taking charge.* Being underage didn't prevent several veterans from taking charge of men and women much older than themselves, some as old as their parents. This includes instances in which a 16-year-old served as the coxswain in command of a 3-man boat crew, another as the chief of a gun section in combat, and a third who became a squad leader after being on the line for several months. A number of VUMS became sergeants at 16, one a second lieutenant at 17 and another, after completing 50 combat missions, became a gunnery instructor at age 18. All had older men in their charge. A veteran of the WAC who was assigned as a training sergeant remarked, "It was quite an experience for me to be telling people twice my age what to do and when!"

After he had been assigned to an MP company, one underage soldier's duty was to check IDs of military personnel to see if they were of legal drinking age, which was 21 at the time. In his story he observed, "Here I was, a 15-year-old kid with an MP arm band, going around checking to see if they were old enough to drink. If they only knew!"

Allan C. Stover

Age 14 – United States Coast Guard

During the winter of 1952, I played hookey from my eighth-grade classes at Addison Junior High School in Cleveland, Ohio, and went downtown to enlist in the U. S. Marine Corps. I

"My goodness, I thought you were here to see a big brother take the oath."

knew the Korean War would soon end, and I wanted to see some action. As most teenagers do, I felt invincible. I was too young to realize I could be killed. I had prepared for this day by convincing my sister Irene to alter my birth certificate and add three years to my age. Irene worked in a state office where they used the same typewriters that were used in the birth records office.

Armed with my altered birth certificate, I arrived at the Marine recruiting office and found it closed. It would be open the next day, but I didn't want to play hookey again, so I walked to the U. S. Coast Guard recruiting office. A family friend had enlisted underage in the

Coast Guard, so I figured I would have a good chance there. When I walked in, the recruiting officer, a first class petty officer, looked at me and frowned. "I want to enlist!" I blurted out. "Do you have a birth certificate?" he asked. I handed it to him, he looked it over, and he gave me a pile of forms to fill out. Another petty officer in the room grinned at me. They knew that I was too young, but I had presented them with an official birth certificate, so they had to go through the motions.

As I filled out the forms, the two recruiters talked. "Got another letter from headquarters. They say we're below their quota, especially in Reserve recruiting," one mumbled to the other. He turned to me and asked, "Would you like to go into the Reserve?" I stuttered, "Uh – I – uh." I wanted active duty, but he seemed to be offering me a compromise, which was to choose the Reserve and go in without question. I considered it, but I would have to dress in a uniform every month and sneak downtown for Reserve meetings without anyone in the neighborhood seeing me. Anyway, I wanted out of the neighborhood, and only active duty would give me that. "Uh, no, I want active duty," I replied.

When I took the test, the recruiter stood over me and prompted me. "Are you sure you want to answer that question with a 'c' ?" he would ask. "Uh, should it be 'a' ?" I would answer. He'd roll his eyes to indicate that I had picked the worst possible answer. "I guess it must be a 'd' then." And so forth. I know I could have passed that test without his help, since it tested just basic skills, but he wanted to make sure I qualified so that he could meet his quota.

I knew the Coast Guard would send a permission form to my mother, so I checked the mail every day after school. I usually checked the mail only when I had ordered a Captain Midnight ring or something like that. When the permission slip arrived, I forged my mother's name on it and sent it back. I also received a notice to report for my physical. I had to play hookey again. I barely made the 120-pound weight requirement and was a little shy on the height. The doctor said, "Pull back your shoulders and take a deep breath." I did, and he mumbled, "Just enough, five feet, two inches." I would grow six inches by the end of my enlistment.

I received a notice to report to the recruiting office and take the oath on 6 January 1953. An officer had to administer the oath, so I settled into a chair and waited. Finally, an officer walked into the room, smiled at me, then looked around with a confused look on his face. I cleared my throat and said, "Uh, are you supposed to swear me in?" He said, "My goodness, I thought you were here to see a big brother take the oath."

They gave me some meal tickets and a train ticket to boot camp at Cape May, New Jersey. I was scared to death at the time. I was leaving home with only an eighth-grade education and I had joined the military illegally. I knew that I had made a decision that would change my life, but I never hesitated.

At Cape May, a chief petty officer with a weather-beaten face made us line up. He walked back and forth and told us — in the tradition of drill instructors everywhere — how worthless we were and how much we would suffer before we could graduate in twelve weeks. He scowled as he passed by me, then shoved his face into mine and shouted, "How the hell old are you?" I almost lost my cool and blurted out my real age. Instead, I squeaked out, "Seventeen, sir." He shook his head and said, "Yeah, and I'm the Queen of Sheba."

He was the first of many doubters who questioned my age. I gave them all the same answer: "Seventeen, sir." Even the guys in my boot camp company, with whom I grew very close during the rigors of training, got the same answer. "I guess I just look young for my age," I would say.

During the last few weeks of boot camp, we listed our choices for assignment after graduation. I put the 14th Coast Guard District on top of the list. The war in Korea was still on, and I wanted to get into it. The 14th District covered all of the Pacific, including Korea. I had also applied for radioman school. We were told our assignments in the last week. I got the 14th District. I thought, "Korea, here I come." Just then, the chief took me aside and told me that I had been accepted for radioman school. He said that it was a good school, it would guarantee me a good job aboard ship, and that I would be a third class petty officer when I graduated. I knew that it was a great opportunity, but I wanted to go overseas.

I reported to the Coast Guard base at Alameda, California. That is where I got my first tattoo, a ship on my forearm. I felt like a real sailor, but most of the guys just shook their heads. We boarded a troopship for Hawaii with a group of soldiers and Marines who knew they would end up in Korea. "That's where I'm going, too," I told them.

At the Coast Guard base on Sand Island in Honolulu harbor, I was assigned to the Coast Guard cutter *Basswood*. I didn't like the name *Basswood*. I'd hoped to get a ship with a name like *Intrepid* or *Valiant*, but that wasn't to be. I could taste my disappointment in my throat. This ship would never get to Korea. In fact, the closest I got to Korea aboard the *Basswood* was Wake Island, about halfway between Hawaii and Korea, a few thousand miles short of my goal.

When I reported aboard the *Basswood*, the chief boatswain's mate took one look at me and said, "You're too young to handle the deck work. How would you like to be a captain?" Surprised, I asked, "A captain? You mean captain of this ship?" He laughed, and a few of the guys standing around laughed too. "No," he said, "I mean Captain of the Head." And so I began my first job aboard ship: cleaning the crew's bathroom, or head. With a hundred men using it, keeping it clean was a full-time job.

After a year on the *Basswood*, I requested a transfer and was sent to Guam. I was on the island less than a day when I went to the personnel office and said, "I want a transfer." The clerk asked, "Where to?" I replied, "Anywhere but here. How about the Philippines?" The clerk said, "That's a different command, and you can't request a transfer for six months." I was desperate, so I asked, "Isn't there anyplace I can transfer to?" He replied, "Well, you could ask for isolated duty on one of the outlying islands, but no one in his right mind would want that." I told him to put me in for isolated duty.

I spent a boring two months on Guam painting buoys and working in the motor pool. When my transfer came through, I was flown to the island of Anguar in the Palau group of the Caroline Islands. The Coast Guard had a LORAN station there that sent out radio navigation signals for ships. It was a tropical island with about 600 natives of Malay and Japanese descent with a bit of American blood thrown in. We were a few miles from the island of Peleliu, where the Marines had fought a bloody battle during World War II. When it was time to rotate back to the States, I was lucky, and instead of flying directly to Guam, I caught a ride in an admiral's plane that went on to the Philippines, Hong Kong, China, and Japan.

At age 16, I reported aboard the U. S. Coast Guard Cutter *Androscoggin*, the flagship of the 7th Coast Guard District. It was the custom in those days to stencil the names of all the significant places you had visited on your ditty bag, a small bag that contained personal effects. Mine had the names Hawaii, Guam, Anguar, Palau, Manila, Hong Kong, and Tokyo. There I was, 16 years old, and the other young men looked at me with awe as I passed by on my way to the crew's quarters. One whispered, "That guy's really been around!" I was a real "salt," the term for a well-traveled sailor.

I completed my 4-year enlistment, and at age 18, walked down the gangway with an honorable discharge in my hand and returned to Cleveland. A few months later, my best friend from the sixth through eighth grades was stabbed during a fight and died within a few hours. I am convinced that if I had stayed around Hough Avenue in Cleveland, I would have died an early death also. Fortunately, something motivated me to escape that environment by joining the military. My underage enlistment gave me another chance, as it did to so many others.

Al Stover dropped out of school in the eighth grade. After his discharge from the Coast Guard, he worked at several jobs, including as a seaman on an ore ship in the Great Lakes. He enrolled in the Pacific States University, Los Angeles, California, and received a B.S. in electronic engineering, summa cum laude. Later, he received an M.S. from Vanderbilt University, Nashville, Tennessee. Allan worked at the missile range at Cape Canaveral, Florida, and was a technical advisor to the Philippine Air Force, the Venezuelan Air Force, and Greek aerospace industries. While in the Philippines, he established a depot for maintenance of ground and airborne radar and communications equipment for the Philippine Air Force. For more than ten years, he was a lead systems-engineer for Westinghouse Corporation and is now working in Saudi Arabia for that company. He is the author of a number of technical articles and several technical books, including You and the Metric System, *which was named* Outstanding Science Book *by the National Science Teachers Association. In 1991, Allan organized the Veterans of Underage Military Service (VUMS) and was its first National Commander. He built the association into a nationwide group of nearly 600 members by 1994 when he became Past National Commander. Allan and his wife Elizabeth presently reside in Saudi Arabia. They have two daughters. Their oldest daughter graduated from the U. S. Naval Academy and is currently a Navy lieutenant. For a time, their youngest daughter Natalie edited the VUMS newsletter,* The Underage Veteran.

Lars O. Ohrn

Age 16 – United States Marine Corps

I was born in Stockholm, Sweden, on 8 December 1936. Ten years later, I emigrated from Sweden with my parents, a brother, and a sister. None of us spoke English at the time. We settled in Grand Rapids, Michigan,

> *It was one of the proudest moments of my life when I was sworn in as a U. S. CITIZEN!*

where my maternal grandparents had lived since immigrating to the U. S. after World War I.

I was enrolled in high school ROTC during the Korean "police action." News from the war was very exciting for me, and I could envision myself being part of the action, but I was only 16. My ROTC instructor had served in the Pacific during World War II and also in the Korean conflict. He related to me what it was like, both good and bad, and convinced me that it was our duty to do what we could to defend our country. He was a very patriotic person.

I managed to get jobs in the city by falsely adding a couple of years to my age. One day, my age was discovered, and I was out of a job. A friend and I decided that we would enlist in one of the services as soon as we could. He was 17 and would have no problem, but I was only 16. There was a page in my mother's passport that had my birth date written in it. My siblings' birth dates were in my father's visa. I removed the page with my real date of birth and wrote in a new date with an official-looking

signature, taking care to fade it and make it look the same as the other writing, all in Swedish, of course. It was really a good forgery.

My friend Dennis Leech and I then went to the recruiting station in Grand Rapids and took and passed the basic test for enlistees. We were told by the Navy recruiter that new companies would be formed in a couple of weeks, and we would have to wait. This did not suit us, so we went to the Marine recruiter. He told us that we could be on our way the next day for our physical in Detroit. All that we needed was a birth certificate or proof of age, and we would be on our way. I told the Marine sergeant that I had a passport visa, but no birth certificate. He looked the visa over, and after a telephone call to his superiors in Detroit, I was on my way to get my physical the next morning.

I passed the physical and was told that I would get sworn in as soon as the passport visa was verified by the State Department and the Immigration Service in Washington, D.C. I was sent home to await the certain doom that I thought would ensue when the falsification was discovered. Four days later, I received a call from the Marine recruiters. They told me that everything was OK, that I would be sworn in the next day. I could hardly believe that I had succeeded.

I was sworn into the U. S. Marine Corps on 23 September 1953. Now I had to convince my parents that everything was just fine. They spoke and read English poorly, so I had to "translate" my own version of enlisting in the service to them, and they believed me.

After boot camp, I was assigned to the 1st Battalion, 5th Marine Regiment, 1st Marine Division, in Korea. The war had been over for about six months by the time I got there. I had served about half of my tour when I was discovered to be underage. I don't know how they found out that my enlistment was fraudulent. I was told that I could not serve in Korea, even though I was 17 by that time. I told them that I wanted to stay in the Corps and did not want to be sent back to the States. They dropped the fraudulent enlistment charges and transferred me to Headquarters Company, FMFPac (Fleet Marine Force, Pacific), at Pearl Harbor. It was while I was stationed at Pearl Harbor that I applied for U. S. citizenship. It was one of the proudest moments of my life when I was sworn in as a *U. S. CITIZEN*!

In 1954, I was detached from FMFPac at Pearl Harbor and sent to Tokyo, Japan, where I was a part of a small group of Marines representing FMFPac. After my third year in the Corps, I was reassigned to the Marine Barracks, Great Lakes Naval Training Center, Illinois. By then I was a sergeant. I was a troop handler, and as collateral duty, I was an orderly to Admiral Forrestal.

I completed my enlistment and was discharged in September 1957. By November 1957, I found myself in Sweden with little money, so by using my language skills, I worked on a cruise ship for the Swedish Merchant Marine for five months. I returned to the States and enlisted in the U. S. Air Force in April 1958. I was assigned to the Strategic Air Command and detailed to "isolated duty" at Sonderstrom, Greenland, in a support group for the DEW (distant early warning) sites. After one year, I was assigned to Plattsburgh Air Force Base, New York. My enlistment in the Air Force was extended during the Cuban crisis, so I ended up serving more than four years.

I was discharged in July 1962, but I stayed in the Air Force Reserve for about three years, then transferred to a reserve unit of Navy Seabees when I returned to Michigan. I was recalled to active duty by the Navy in 1968 and served in the recruiting office at Grand Rapids, Michigan, until released to inactive duty in 1969. I retired from the military in 1977.

Lars Ohrn attended the Tool and Die Institute in Chicago, Illinois, for three years after his discharge from the Air Force. He returned to Grand Rapids, Michigan, where he worked as a precision machinist for the Oliver Machinery Company for about three years. He worked for the U. S. Postal Service from January 1969 until his retirement on 2 January 1992. Lars and Barbara, his wife of thirty-seven years, live in Grand Rapids, Michigan. They have three children and two grandchildren. Lars is the Michigan State Commander of the Veterans of Underage Military Service.

Jack L. Frasier

Age 15 – Oklahoma National Guard

I was born in Everton, Missouri, on 31 May 1939. My family moved to Commerce, Oklahoma, when I was 6 years old. In 1954, a buddy, Chuck Buckmaster, and I decided that we would join the Oklahoma National Guard

> "... I just run over a pickup truck with that tank!"

although we were only 15 years old. The 45th Infantry Division, Oklahoma National Guard, had returned from Korea a short time before and was returned to state control. Chuck and I were going to school at Commerce, so we went to Miami, Oklahoma, and enlisted on 13 December 1954. Our parents had to give their consent and sign that we were 17 years old, which they did.

We were assigned to the 45th Infantry Division's AAA Battalion, Battery D. The battalion had just been issued an M-19 tank. Our unit was scheduled to go to summer camp, and drivers were needed for the tank and for a half-track. Although Buckmaster and I had been with the unit only a short time, Chuck was issued a military driver's license for the tank, and I was issued a military driver's license for the half-track. Neither of us could operate an ordinary vehicle on the highway because we were only 15 and couldn't get a regular driver's license.

When we got to summer camp, I was told to drive the half-track. Thank goodness it had the same shift arrangement that our old farm truck had, or I would never have been able to drive it. The tank that Buckmaster was to drive had an automatic transmission.

I was in the barracks one evening, and Buckmaster came in to see me, all shook up. When I asked him what was the matter, he said, "I never will get out of the military – I just run over a pickup truck with that tank!" He told me that they were forming a convoy, getting ready to go out on the firing line. A pickup truck left the convoy, pulled up behind his tank, and parked. When he went to put the tank in gear, he slapped the gear shift, and it went into reverse and backed up over the hood of the pickup. Buckmaster was more afraid of being discovered to be underage than of being the driver of the tank that backed over the pickup. Luckily, the investigating officers decided that it was the fault of the pickup driver for parking behind the tank. No one ever found out that Buckmaster and I were only 15.

The only time that we could drive any kind of vehicle was when we went to National Guard meetings, then it was either a tank or a half-track. We would go to school during the week and act like the kids we were, but on weekends and at other Guard meetings, we had to behave like adults. I spent six years in the National Guard and enjoyed it very much.

Jack Frasier became a master electrician and operated his own electrical company in Springfield, Missouri, for sixteen years. He is semiretired now but still works part-time as a security guard. Jack and his wife Wanda live in Fairland, Oklahoma. They have three children and six grandchildren.

√ **VUMS Note** ⇒ *Troubled youth.* In navigating the teenage years, some underage veterans ran into some very rough waters, but somehow found a safe port in the military service. One describes himself when he was a teenager as "... a juvenile misfit of World War II." The turmoil and rebellion of his teenage years are aptly described by another who observes, "I went through some kind of 'mid-life crisis' between the ages of 14 and 15." Most simply say that they were regularly getting in trouble, both at home and at school.

Getting in trouble sometimes included becoming involved with the wrong crowd and getting into minor scrapes with the law. Returning home years later, a number of veterans found that some of their former friends from the wrong crowd had gotten into serious trouble with the law and had served, or were serving prison terms, or had even been killed committing crimes. Enlisting in the military underage may have been the way that some underage veterans avoided a similar fate.

Jeremy M. "Mike" Boorda[27]

Age 16 – United States Navy

Mike Boorda was born in South Bend, Indiana, on 26 November 1939 and grew up in north-central Illinois. At the time he joined the Navy, Mike was living in Momence, Illinois, where his family ran a

> "I am, modestly, the best ship handler in the Navy," ...

clothing store. His parents' marriage was breaking up, and he decided to quit high school and strike out alone. Using a phony birth certificate, he joined the Navy at age 16 on 10 February 1956. Remembering that time he said, "I was cool. I was tough. I was scared to death. Hell, I was 16 years old and had nobody to help me."

He was sent to the Great Lakes Naval Training Center for boot camp. Boot camp was tough and Mike wanted out, but his company commander ignored his claim that he was only 16 when he enlisted. Soon he began enjoying the camaraderie. He scored high on his skill exam, and a counselor suggested he become a personnelman and learn about regulations for feeding, housing, and paying sailors.

After completing boot camp, Mike was assigned to personnelman school at San Diego, California. On one of his first liberties in San Diego, he went AWOL for a few hours. A first class petty officer took him aside and advised him how to get along in the Navy, how to get through the training courses, and how to obtain his high school diploma.

---

[27] This account was compiled from the following sources: Admiral Boorda's official biography, Office of the Chief of Naval Operations; The *Baltimore Sun*, 12 November 1991; The *Youngstown Vindicator*, 20 February 1994; Tom Philpott, "Can Mike Boorda Salvage the Navy?," *The Washingtonian*, February 1995; Tom Philpott, "The Sailor's Admiral," *The Readers Digest*, August 1995; Peter J. Boyer, "Admiral Boorda's War," *The New Yorker*, 16 September 1996.

Mike learned his lessons well. He graduated first in his class at personnelman school, which gave him first choice on his next duty assignment. He chose a destroyer whose home port was San Diego. Before Mike was assigned to the ship, he talked with a classmate who was scheduled to go to the Naval Air Technical Training Center in Norman, Oklahoma. The man's wife was sick and was going to have a baby, and he wanted to stay with her in San Diego. Mike traded assignments with him.

While he was at Norman, Mike met Bettie Moran, a student at the University of Oklahoma. They married in April 1957. Their first child David was born with Goltz syndrome, a rare congenital condition. Advised to institutionalize their son, Mike and Bettie took him home instead, vowing to do the best they could for him. At age 18, Mike Boorda began to settle down. In reminiscing about those times, he commented, "You don't have to be very old to grow up fast."

He was promoted to the rank of petty officer first class within six years after joining the Navy, serving primarily in naval aviation. His last two enlisted assignments were with Attack Squadron 144 and Carrier Airborne Early Warning Squadron 11. In 1962, he was selected for a "seaman to admiral" program, attended officer candidate school, and was commissioned an ensign. He admitted that he had no ambition to attain high rank. He said, "When Bettie and I got our first apartment, I wanted to buy her some nicer furniture. I don't know if I ever had a grander plan than that."

After being commissioned, he served aboard the USS *Porterfield* (DD-682) as the combat information center officer. After attending the Naval Destroyer School in Newport, Rhode Island, in 1964 he was assigned as weapons officer aboard the USS *John R. Craig* (DD-885). The captains of the two destroyers, in Mike's words, "Let me drive a lot." He became adept at bringing a ship to a pier without the use of tugs. He often bragged about his skill in driving a ship. "I am, modestly, the best ship handler in the Navy," he would say.

As a lieutenant in 1966, he got his first command, the USS *Parrot*, a coastal minesweeper with a crew of forty-three. This was his favorite command. Later, he commanded the guided-missile destroyer USS *Farragut*, and after a stint in the Pentagon, he took command of Destroyer Squadron-22.

In 1984, he assumed his first flag-officer assignment as executive assistant to the Chief of Naval Operations, remaining in that position until July 1986 when he became commander, Cruiser-Destroyer Group 8, in Norfolk, Virginia. He also served as commander, Battle Force Sixth Fleet, embarked on the USS *Saratoga* (CV-60).

In August 1988, Mike Boorda became Chief of Naval Personnel. Under his policies, the Navy achieved its highest retention rate in history. Mike received his fourth star in November 1991, and a month later, was assigned command of all NATO forces in Southern Europe, including all operations in the Balkans. He also became Commander in Chief, U. S. Naval Forces, Europe. On 23 April 1994, he was appointed the 25th CNO (Chief of Naval Operations), the first chief to rise from the lowest enlisted grade to the Navy's highest rank.

During his 40-year Naval career, Boorda received the Defense Distinguished Service Award, three awards of the Distinguished Service Medal, three awards of the Legion of Merit, two awards of the Meritorious Service Medal, and a number of other personal and campaign awards, including the Navy Commendation Medal and the Navy Achievement Medal, the two that would become the center of controversy later.

Admiral Boorda died on 16 May 1996 of a self-inflicted gunshot wound to the chest. Questions had arisen in the press about whether he was authorized to wear "V" devices on the Navy Commendation and the Navy Achievement Medals he had earned while serving aboard ships off the coast of Vietnam. A common speculation was that this relatively minor controversy was the "last straw" added to the weight of many serious issues with which he was dealing as CNO at the time. The nation honored him at a memorial ceremony at the National Cathedral in Washington, D.C., on 21 May 1996 in which the President and other high-ranking civilian and military leaders eulogized him. He is buried at Arlington National Cemetery.

Mike and Bettie had four children and eleven grandchildren. Two of their sons and a daughter-in-law are Navy officers. Their daughter is a mother and a teacher.

George W. English

Age 14 – United States Navy

I was born in Seattle, Washington, on 7 July 1944. My father, grandfather, and great-grandfather had all gone to sea, and although I was only 14 years old, I wanted to become a sailor and carry on the family

> ... my "loose lips" almost sank my underage enlistment.

tradition. My older brother, who was not physically able to serve in the armed forces because of an injury, let me use his birth certificate. With his certificate and a form signed by my mother, I enlisted in the Navy and was sworn in on 28 May 1959. To this day, I still use my brother's name. (It confuses the hell out of the Social Security Administration.)

I was sent to the Naval Training Station, San Diego, for boot camp. I contracted pneumonia and spent my fifteenth birthday in the Balboa Naval Hospital. A month later, I was back in boot camp.

While home on boot leave, I received a tentative appointment to the U. S. Naval Academy Preparatory School in Newport, Rhode Island. However, after an encounter with the shore patrol, the appointment was withdrawn, and I was sent to sonar school in San Diego. I didn't complete sonar school because of too many liberties in Tijuana, Mexico, which caused me to nod off during class, and I was booted out.

In November 1959, I was assigned to the USS *Wedderburn* (DD-684), a World War II, *Fletcher* Class destroyer. On 7 July 1960, my sixteenth birthday, we steamed for the Western Pacific and a 6-month tour of the Orient. I was assigned to the deck force and learned how to use a paint scraper, wire brush, and chipping hammer. I learned all about red lead, deck gray, and haze gray. After I had applied many gallons of these Navy colors to hull and superstructure, I decided that that wasn't the life for me.

In junior high school, I had belonged to the chess club, and I enjoyed the game immensely. The best chess players on board the *Wedderburn* were all fire controlmen. I asked for a transfer to the Fire Control Gang, but was turned down. However, the unbeatable FT3/c Jim Buonocore told me that if I could beat FT1/c Sam Butler at chess, the picture might change. So one day during noon mess, Sam and I commenced a game in the starboard radar room. The game lasted for hours. I was supposed to have turned to on the fantail right after lunch, but it was 1700 hours before I checkmated Sam. When I went to my rack in an after-berthing compartment, I was cussed out by BM3/c Elmer "Red" Coward, and told to never pull another disappearing act, or he would have me sent to a captain's mast. A week later, I was in the FT Gang.

While I was in the Orient, my "loose lips" almost sank my underage enlistment. However, Navy regulations at the time stated that a 16-year-old could not be discharged unless forms were filled out and supporting documents provided to prove actual age and identity. In other words, you had to make an application for discharge, but I didn't.

I served on the *Wedderburn* for three years and on the USS *Hoel* (DDG-13) for a short time. I was released from active duty at San Diego on 22 October 1962 and was transferred to the reserve ship USS *McGinty* (DE-365) based in Seattle, Washington. I was discharged from the Navy on 28 May 1965.

I have fond memories of my three years on the *Wedderburn*. I was a disciplinary headache for my petty officers, but I owe a great debt of gratitude to many of my shipmates, both officers and enlisted men, for lessons learned that became useful later in life. I regard my *Wedderburn* shipmates as family. In 1990, I co-founded the USS *Wedderburn* Association and served as its president for several years. I still love the Navy and support it in as many ways as I can.

George English traveled extensively after leaving the Navy. He lived and worked in Alaska, British Columbia, Oregon, California, New Zealand, Hawaii, Wake Island, Bolivia, Argentina, Kentucky, and Brazil, holding jobs too numerous to list. He was in Bolivia when the Argentine-Cuban guerilla, Ernesto "Che" Guevara, was captured, and he was near the Falkland Islands when an Argentine general surrendered his forces to the British. In 1983, George started an international business in Houston, Texas, dealing with centrifugal air compressors. The business continues to occupy his time. George and his wife, Pham Thi Kim Hoang, formerly of Ho Chi Minh City, Vietnam, live in Missouri City, Texas. He has a daughter from a previous marriage.

654

Index of
Contributors

658

Index of VUMS Notes

√ *VUMS Note* ⇒ *INDEX (cont.)*